Temple Israel

Library

Minneapolis, Minn.

RULES

1. Not more than one book may be drawn at one time on this card (unless special permission is given for more.)

2. Books may be kept two weeks unless otherwise indicated.

3. A fine of three cents a day will be charged on each book which is not returned according to the above rules.

4. Fines will be charged for damage to books or loss of same.

The Philosophy of Judaism

THE MACMILLAN COMPANY
NEW YORK · CHICAGO
DALLAS · ATLANTA · SAN FRANCISCO
LONDON · MANILA
IN CANADA
BRETT-MACMILLAN LTD.
GALT, ONTARIO

The Philosophy of Judaism

The development of Jewish thought throughout the ages, the Bible, the Talmud, the Jewish philosophers, and the Cabala, until the present time

by Zvi Cahn, Ph.D.

New York ❦ The Macmillan Company ❦ 1962

First Printing

The Macmillan Company, New York
Brett-Macmillan Ltd., Galt, Ontario

Printed in the United States of America

Library of Congress catalog card number: 61-14705

To

Helen Liebson and Isaac A. Liebson
of Detroit, Michigan, and Hollywood, Florida

generous supporters of Jewish culture and
scholarship, who gave invaluable aid and
advice in the publication of this work

this book is gratefully dedicated

Preface

One evening, some ten years ago, I addressed the members of a Jewish center in a small town near New York on "What Is Judaism." My audience was composed of businessmen, professional people, and college students. At the conclusion of my formal address, the chairman declared a question period. I was amazed at the lack of knowledge of even the basic elements of Judaism that the questions from my listeners revealed. This was particularly disconcerting to me because I knew that my audience consisted largely of men and women who played an active part in the affairs of the Jewish community.

A short time later, I had a parallel experience with a non-Jewish audience. On that occasion, too, I found that even the most well-informed in the group knew surprisingly little about one of mankind's most ancient religions.

These two experiences gave me something akin to a "mission complex," and I set out to produce a work which, I hoped, would provide answers for some of the layman's basic questions on the origin and development of the ideas and ideals that make up Judaism.

I was particularly eager to fulfill this self-set task because, while I discovered the lack of precise knowledge among the people I addressed, I found that the degree of genuine interest in, and curiosity about, the underlying concepts of Judaism was greater still.

I should feel more than rewarded for my labors if this work, in part, satisfies that interest and that curiosity.

Acknowledgments

It is with profound gratitude that I acknowledge the assistance generously rendered by Miss Gertrude Hirschler, who took charge of the sifting and assembling of the material included in this volume, saw the manuscript through every stage of its production, critically reviewed and revised the final product and, in general, gave invaluable suggestions and counsel. I am also indebted to Messrs. Hillel Rogoff, Editor-in-Chief, and Alex Kahn, Managing Editor of the *Jewish Daily Forward,* whose steadfast aid and encouragement proved a tower of strength.

Finally, I wish to pay tribute to the memory of my wife, Mildred Cahn. Herself a writer and educator, she gave me generously of her inspiration and support through all the years of labor, study, research, and writing. It was ordained in God's decree that she did not live to see the final result of the undertaking to which she gave so much of herself.

Z. C.

Contents

Introduction

1. Universalism and Nationalism in the Course of Jewish History

For many decades the scholarly world could not agree as to whether the *Weltanschauung* of Judaism as reflected in the Bible and in subsequent Jewish literature was essentially nationalist or universalist. George Foot Moore, the eminent scholar, was the first to point out the incorrectness of the entire line of reasoning upon which this discussion was premised. In his book entitled *Judaism in the First Centuries of the Christian Era* (published in two volumes, 1927), Moore states that it should be obvious to anyone familiar with the original texts of the Bible and the Talmud that nationalism and universalism go hand in hand in Judaism. This is the principal characteristic of Jewish history and ideology. In some eras in the history of Judaism we find the spirit of nationalism dominant, with the ideals of universalism taking second place. At other times, we see universalism in the ascendancy and nationalism only in the background.

This phenomenon we see prevalent during the era beginning with Moses and ending with the latter prophets, and again in the writings of the Tannaim and Amoraim which are found in the Talmud. The place occupied by either viewpoint at any given period in Jewish history was determined by the times, the environment of those who happened to be in the forefront of Jewish life at the moment, and the personalities and inclinations of the individual leaders.

If we consider the writings of the prophets, we find that some of them addressed themselves to the Jewish people in particular, exhorting the children of Israel to mend their ways, or comforting them with promises of better days to come, and said only little that might be construed as being applicable to the rest of mankind as well. Others directed their prophetic messages to the entire world, reprimanding or comforting all the nations of the globe, while paying only a little attention to the people of Israel as a separate entity. Most of the prophets, however, managed to combine nationalism with universalism in their writings. They viewed the Jewish people as part and parcel of the rest of the world, and could visualize a flourishing and prosperous Israel only in a world of justice and moral integrity.

This too was the ideal which we find predominant in the thoughts of Moses, the prime architect of Judaism. This great teacher had no desire to create one more "nation among nations." It was his aim to bring into being a nation that would be unique among the others, a "holy nation," one that would serve as a leader for all the peoples of the world. The function of this new nation, which was to be neither master nor slave, would be to teach all other nations and to serve to uplift them. It was to be a "kingdom of priests." Contrary to the interpretation that some would give to this term, a "kingdom of priests" does not mean a theocratic state. What Moses envisioned was a nation of spiritual aristocracy, for the "priests" of those days were nothing more and nothing less than spiritual leaders in the truest sense of the word. That this is so is most clearly evident from the Biblical account of the incident when Moses was told that Eldad and Medad were uttering prophecy in the camp of Israel. The person who reported this to Moses demanded that he silence them. Moses replied, however: "Would that all the Lord's people were prophets, that the Lord would put His spirit upon them" (Num. 11:29).

This is the reason why Moses wanted the Jews to regard God as their king, and therefore they did not need a ruler of flesh and blood. The people of Israel were to be guided by one ideal, to promulgate the concept of One God throughout the world. In practice, this meant that, above all, Israel was to abolish idolatry and introduce monotheism everywhere. At that time, the substitution of the worship of One God for the worship of many idols was the first step taken by this group of primitive tribes on the road to civilization. Moses did not want the Jewish people to have a king. But Moses also knew that men were only men and not angels, and he foresaw a day when the children of Israel would want to be "like the other nations" and would elect a king for themselves. He therefore made provisions for this eventuality by setting down laws limiting the powers of the kings so that no Jewish ruler would be able to establish an absolute dictatorship over his people.

Moses was not mistaken. During the time of the judges, the children of Israel did come to Samuel to demand that they be given a king who would reign over them. The prophets argued that such action would not be in accordance with the will of the Lord. He pictured for them the difficulties they would encounter once they had a king, and he predicted that "ye shall be his servants. And ye shall cry out in that day because of your king whom ye shall have chosen you, and the Lord will not answer you in that day" (I Sam. 8:17, 18). But the people persisted in their demand and in the end Samuel himself anointed Saul king of Israel. When the prophet cried to God that the Jews had rejected him, the Lord replied, ". . . they have not rejected thee, but they have rejected Me, that I should not be king over them." (I Sam. 8:7).

Thus the Jewish people got their king. This was the beginning of the kingdom which, after the death of Solomon, divided Israel into two separate nations; the Kingdom of Judah and the Kingdom of Israel. The Jewish people became two separate states, Judah *and* Israel, with Jerusalem as the capital of the former and Samaria capital of the latter, with two royal courts pervaded with all the pernicious intrigue that was the custom in palace circles. But throughout this period there were Jewish prophets in both kingdoms who rebuked the kings for the evil they had perpetrated. These same prophets also turned to the other nations of the world and pleaded with them to come to their senses and abandon the path of evil. They directed their appeals to Ammon, Moab, Edom, Zur, and all the other nations then in existence, but their words were also intended for all the other generations that were to come after them. They spoke of a new world which would rise up someday in the future, a world dedicated to the principle of "absolute justice."

Among these prophets we find some who tended to a nationalist outlook, while the prophecies of others were more universalist in nature. But almost all the prophets have in common a broad outlook that embraces both Jews and non-Jews, both their own country and the rest of the world. All of them, without exception, do not ignore the rest of mankind in their prophecies. None of them is so singularly nationalist as to be unable to see beyond the destinies of his own people. We find in the writings of every prophet at least a few words addressed to the other nations. Thus Amos, for example, calls out in his wrath: "Thus saith the Lord: For three transgressions of Moab, yea, for four, I will not reverse it: Because he burned the bones of the king of Edom into lime" (Amos 2:1). Amos, a citizen of the Kingdom of Judah, was concerned about the manner in which the king of Moab had settled his grievances with the ruler of Edom who, as a matter of fact, had been a bitter foe of the people of Israel. The people of Moab, too, had been guilty of countless atrocities against the Jews, but yet the Jewish prophet says, "My heart will cry out for Moab." Isaiah addresses Cyrus, the king of Persia, as "[God's] anointed." And the Book of Jonah gives us an inspiring account of the mission given by the God of the Jews to Jonah, to punish the City of Nineveh for its sins.

Perhaps the most outspoken exponent of universalism was the Prophet Amos. He viewed the God Yahwe not solely as the God of the Jews, but as the God of all nations, a God before whom all the nations of the world would be equal. He gives preference to his own people only to the extent that his first words are addressed to the Jews, to remonstrate with them because of their sins. He does not feel that God has chosen the Jewish people from among the nations in order to give them special privileges. On the contrary, Amos says that God chose Israel only to entrust it with the important task of teaching God's ways to the rest of the world. He fearlessly speaks out against all those, Jews and non-Jews alike, who robbed others, who abandoned the poor in their midst, and he proclaims that both Jews and non-Jews are equal in the sight of the Lord. "Are ye not as the children of the Ethiopians unto Me, O children of Israel? saith the Lord" (Amos 9:7). The Book of Amos also contains prophecies concerning other nations such as Edom, Ammon, and Damascus.

The universalist spirit in prophetic literature finds its most beautiful expression in the glorious description given in the Book of Isaiah of the Utopian state that will prevail throughout the world one day, when justice will reign supreme. "And they shall beat their swords into plowshares, and their spears into pruning-hooks, nation shall not lift up sword against nation, neither shall they learn war any more" (Isa. 2:4) and "the wolf shall dwell with the lamb . . ." (Isa. 11:6), and other similar statements. A new world based upon righteousness was the ideal of all the prophets who felt that the welfare of their own people was inextricably bound up with that of the rest of mankind. Therefore they all had a broad, cosmopolitan point of view which reached far beyond the narrow confines of their own nation.

Dr. Joseph Klausner was quite right when he said in his book *The Prophets* (Jerusalem, 1954), "the prophets had no parallel in any of the other civilizations of the world. Can the Greeks claim such giants as Isaiah or Jeremiah, Amos or Zechariah? Socrates, Plato, Aristotle, and all the others cannot lay claim to such world renown. And we certainly cannot find among the rulers and philosophers of ancient Rome the equals of such prophets, even though it is true indeed that some dabbled in philosophy and made pretty speeches . . ."

We also find this combination of nationalism and universalism in later Jewish literature, particularly among the compilers of the Talmud. Here, too, we can see the same broad, cosmopolitan spirit linked with the great aspirations for the Jewish ideology. It has even been incorporated into the Jewish liturgy. When the Jew enters his synagogue on Rosh Hashonah, the Jewish New Year, to pray for a year of happiness and prosperity, he asks God to inscribe his name in "the Book of Life" for good health and success, and to return to Zion in compassion; but during that same service the Jew also prays that "all the nations may form one united group to serve Thee" and that "all evil may vanish from the earth." The prayers for his own personal well-being and that of his people go hand in hand with supplication in behalf of the rest of the world, and these two parts of Jewish liturgy form one inseparable whole. We cannot conceive of one without the other.

Let us now make a brief study of the Apocryphal writings, the Talmud and Midrashic literature, as well as of the works of the Cabalists in order to see which of these points of view predominates in each. We find that universalism is predominant in the Apocrypha, particularly in those parts which we call the Apocalypse, as, for instance, the "Sybillia" and in other such "visions." Here the universalist idea has taken on definite form, and there is advanced a modus by which it is hoped that the cosmopolitan ideal will eventually gain ascendancy throughout the world. It may all be in the realm of legend and fantasy, but these visions are not mere speeches such as can be found in earlier Biblical writings. The "seers" of the Apocalypse envision a day when God will reign supreme over all the earth and when all men, regardless of race or nationality, will serve Him. The present "evil time" in which Satan holds sway will pass away, to be followed by the days of the Messiah. At that time the world will be enmeshed in a bloody struggle between Satan on one hand, and those who seek to perpetuate justice in the world, on the other. Those will be "days of much suffering," much blood will be shed, and even those who survive the slaughter will go through untold pain and anguish. Those days will be the "birth pangs" of the Messiah. But once the struggle is over, there will follow the dawn of a new morning, a day when justice will triumph. There will be a Day of Judgment when all those who suffered at the hands of evil will receive their just reward, and all the evildoers will be amply repaid for their crimes. Then the "kingdom of heaven" will begin. The writers of the apocryphal literature describe these glorious days in a most beautiful manner, and most of them stress the significance of the Messianic era not merely for the Jewish nation, but for the entire world. Only a very small part of these writings is devoted to a discussion of the effect which the beginning of the "kingdom of heaven" will have upon the people of Israel in particular.

We find this balance of universalism and nationalism also in the Mishna and later on in the Gemorah, in both the Babylonian and the Jerusalem Talmud, as well as in later Midrashic literature. Of course it varies from work to work, because these literary gems were conceived at different times and in different countries. Thus, of necessity, they were subject to the influence of the spirit prevailing at the time of their creation, and to that of the environment in which they were written, not to speak of the individual personalities and views of the authors.

Let me give some examples of what I mean. There is the beautiful declaration of love of man set down by Rabbi Akiba. This sage, who was one of the great spirits of Judaism during the days of the Second Temple, was not only a splendid teacher and spiritual leader but also fought valiantly in the rebellion led by Bar Kochba. Rabbi Akiba set down this fundamental tenet of love for all mankind, regardless of race, creed, or station. He said, "man is beloved because he was created in a definite form" (meaning that man is different from all other creatures in that he stands erect upon his own feet and does not crawl on the ground). "But he is more beloved still because he was created in the image of God" [this means that man was endowed with the capacity to reason and to feel emotion] (Ethics of the Fathers III:17). This open avowal of humanitarianism is classed among the great sayings of the sages who have left their mark on world history.

Nor was Rabbi Akiba the only Jewish scholar to advocate such liberal views. A student of his, Ben Azai, said in similar vein, "Despise not all men . . . for there is no man who has not his hour . . ." (Ethics of the Fathers IV:3).

The wise men of Yavneh said: "I am a creature of God and my neighbor was also created by Him. My work is in the city and his is in the fields. I rise up early to do my work and he, too, rises up early to do his. Even as he would not be very adept at my work, so I could not be adept at his. You may say, 'I can achieve great things and he cannot do much.' But we have learned that it matters not whether one achieves much or little. The important thing is that he should have God in his heart."

Rabbi Mattathias the son of Charash said: "Be forward to greet all men" [before they greet thee] (Ethics of the Fathers IV:20).

Rabbi Meir, another great mind of those splendid days, and a student of Rabbi Akiba, expresses it quite simply: "Thou shalt love mankind." He also said: "How do we know that even a Gentile who studies the Torah is equal to the High Priest of Israel? It is written 'that man should fulfill them and live thereby.' Not 'priests, Levites and Israelites' but simply 'man' " (Baba Kamah 38, et seq.).

There is the profound statement in the Talmud where we are told that when Moses sang his song of praise after Israel had crossed the Red Sea and the Egyptian hordes were drowned, the Lord was wroth with him and asked: "My creatures are drowning in the sea and you sing songs of praise?" (Megillah 7).

Similar quotations can be found in the Talmud by the hundreds, and it is not possible to cite them all here. But even the few examples we have chosen are sufficient evidence of the broad universalist outlook that characterized Judaism during the time of the prophets and during the Biblical era. Even later in Jewish history the literature contains references to people outside Israel. Jewish literature is permeated throughout with the spirit of universalism.

Everything we have quoted thus far falls within the realm of theory. How, then, did all the theory hold up in its practical application to everyday life? In other words, how were these two trends applied in daily life in the course of Jewish history? We shall soon see.

The spirit of universalism which, from the very beginning, shared with nationalism the dominion over Judaism, could not remain confined to the written word, and therefore it sought an outlet in practical life. We know of segments of the Jewish people who applied these views much to the detriment of Jewish nationalist aspirations, for the ideal of universalism, if followed without deviation, must of necessity lead to assimilation. Whether we like it or not, universalism begets the absorption of smaller groups into a larger whole. It cannot be otherwise. Cosmopolitanism denotes the creation of one great unit into which all the smaller entities are then absorbed—in other words, assimilation. Therefore it is not without reason that the trend toward assimilation has been a continuous threat throughout the long history of the Jewish people.

During the days of the judges and the kings of the Biblical era the tendency was to assimilate to the pagan civilization of the neighboring nations of Israel, and the loyal servants of the Lord had to struggle mightily to prevent the Jews from falling prey to idolatry and the influence of idolators. In the Book of Judges there is a description of how "the Jews took the daughters [of the idolators] to be their wives . . . and served their gods" (3:6). Even as loyal a servant of the Lord as King Solomon, the son of David, married the daughter of a Pharoah and "his wives turned away his heart after other gods" (I Kings 11:4).

During the days of the First Temple assimilation was rampant in Palestine. It was fashionable to worship idols and it was only at rare intervals that there would arise a king in Judah or in Israel who would destroy the idols and return to the worship of God, to the belief in One God who created heaven and earth. How strong the temptation was to assimilate to the cult of idolatry is best illustrated by the story of the dream of Rabbi Ashni. King Manasseh appeared to him in a dream and Rabbi Ashni asked the king, "How did it happen that a man as wise as thou art should have worshiped idols?" Thereupon King Manasseh replied, "Hadst thou lived in my day, thou wouldst have lifted up the hems of thy garments in order to run after them faster still" (Sanhedrin 102:72). So compelling was the urge to assimilate to the fashionable practices of those days.

It can be safely said that, until after the destruction of the First Temple, most of the Jewish people strove to assimilate to the dominant cultures that surrounded the land of the Jews. Whole tribes intermingled with the pagan nations and were thus lost to their own people. Of these tribes, Ephraim was the first to separate itself almost entirely from the Jewish God, as the prophet Hosea put it, "Ephraim, he mixeth himself with the peoples" (Hosea 7:8). The other nine tribes of the kingdom of Israel went the same way after the fall of the First Temple. Therefore these nationals of the kingdom of Israel did not think it too great a tragedy that they should be driven out of their own land to live among idolators, for they were themselves but idol-worshipers who had now been exiled from their former country to dwell among other pagans. Moreover they had not been too fond of their fatherland. In view of all the bloodshed, dishonesty, and corruption that prevailed at the courts of the kings of Israel in the days prior to the destruction of the First Temple, it is quite possible that the ten tribes of Israel went abroad of their own accord because they felt more akin to an alien nation than to their own country. This explains Rabbi Akiba's contention that the ten tribes of Israel were lost to the Jewish people forever, and that they had assimilated completely and intermingled with the idolators. He said, "The ten tribes shall never return and we must think about them no more."

Let us follow the problem of assimilation further still in the history of the Jewish people.

Ezra and Nehemiah, who strove to bring about the national renaissance of the Jewish people at the time of the building of the Second Temple, were faced with a gigantic task, even as it is told in the Book of Ezra, "The people of Israel and the priests and the Levites have not separated themselves from the peoples of the lands . . . For they have taken of their daughters for themselves and for their sons; so that the holy seed have mingled themselves with the peoples of the lands . . ." (9:1-2). Only the tribes of Judah and Benjamin were somewhat better than the rest in this respect. The Prophet Ezekiel who lived at that time left us a picture of the period in his prophecy concerning the dried bones which rise again to a new life. Ezekiel says in the name of the Lord: ". . . and that which cometh into your mind shall not be all; in that which ye say: We will be as the nations, as the families of the countries, to serve wood and stone. As I live, saith the Lord God, surely with a mighty hand and with an outstretched arm, and with fury poured out, will I be king over you" (Ezek. 20:32-33). And the Talmud states that "When the Torah had been forgotten among the Jews, Ezra renewed it" (Succah 20).

The period of the Second Temple, on the other hand, was exceptional. It is characterized by one of those great miracles which we see throughout the history of the Jewish people. After many generations of idolator-domination, after centuries of idol worship, there arose the great generation of the Tannaim and the Amoraim, the creators and founders of Judaism as we know it today. It was an era without parallel in all the generations that followed. Those were the days when intellectual giants such as Hillel and Shammai, Rabbi Yohanan ben Zakkai, Rabbi Meir, Rabbi Judah the Prince, and a host of others were the spiritual leaders of the Jewish people. It it truly not easy to explain how it happened that the children and the grandchildren of those who, only a few short years before, had bowed before idols of stone and wood, were able to create such great ethical values. We must not forget the brevity of the span that bridged the destruction of the First Temple and the building of the Second. According to Jewish tradition, the Babylonian exile lasted seventy years; modern historical researchers say that it was only fifty-two years.

After the building of the Second Temple, assimilation again became rampant, this time in a slightly different guise. Now it took on the form of Hellenism which had a telling effect on the course of Jewish history. In the days of the First Temple, the tendency had been, in the words of King Manasseh, to "lift up the hems of their garments in order to run all the faster" after the idols of the other nations. In the era of the Second Temple, we once again find in Israel the urge to imitate the culture then dominant in the ancient world. This time the model nation was Greece and the culture that of the ancient Greeks.

It all began in the city of Alexandria where Simon (also known as Jason) and his followers showed by example how Jews could ape the ways and sports of the Greeks, and adopt their cult of physical beauty and also their philosophy of divinity, all of which was entirely alien to the spirit of Judaism.

There was also Philo, the Jewish philosopher who was raised abroad and was far removed from all things Jewish. These admirers of Greek culture, who were known as Hellenists, also managed to disseminate their ideas in

Israel itself, and soon there was a group of Hellenists in Palestine who advocated assimilation of the dominant culture of Greece. This group exerted great influence in the land because it sought first to impose its views upon the ruling class before attempting to influence the masses. Here we see a type of assimilation not entirely similar to that which prevailed before the destruction of the First Temple. The Hellenists claimed that they did not seek to impose a culture of inferior value, such as ancient paganism represented, but on the contrary, to raise the culture to a higher intellectual plane. The Jews were admonished not to be influenced by the worshipers of primitive idols and imitate their ways, but rather to enrich and beautify their own lives by accepting what was good in the culture of Greece.

Of course this was nothing but rationalization, because once the gates of assimilation are opened, there is no stopping the tide. Then, too, it was impossible to say, 'set limits, this far and no further,' and assimilation did grievous damage to the Jewish people even in those days. It precipitated the conflict between the Pharisees and the Sadducees, in the course of which both sides lost much of the influence they had formerly exerted, not to speak of a great many precious lives.

But despite all the efforts of the Hellenists, and despite their influence on the ruling classes of the people, Hellenism was never able to gain a solid foothold in the land during the era of the Second Temple. It was a movement that gained the support of only a small group of the people, and toward which the majority had a negative attitude. The greatness of the Tannaim, the teachers of the Law, lay in the fact that they, the spiritual leaders of Jewry in those days, did not exclude the Hellenists from the fold of Judaism or put them outside the pale of the Jewish people. They did not hinder the Hellenists in their attempts to introduce Greek customs into Israel. In general, however, it can be said that the efforts of the Hellenists did not bear much fruit.

And so, for centuries, assimilation has been a thorn in the side of the Jewish people wherever its scattered members happened to dwell.

During the Middle Ages the Jews were confined to ghettos and were thus isolated from the non-Jewish world. The high walls around the Jewish sections of the cities cut off the inhabitants not only from the lives and ways of the Gentiles, but also from Gentile ways of thinking. For centuries a heavy curtain separated the Jews from their non-Jewish neighbors. There could be hardly any assimilation because the Jew was almost never permitted to leave the narrow confines in which he was completely isolated and cut off from the world about him.

Only at the end of the eighteenth century, when the ghettos were abolished and the Jews given equal civil rights, did the threat of assimilation rise again. It began first in Berlin and then spread throughout Germany. There arose groups which advocated assimilation openly. Then came the Reform movement which lent powerful impetus to the assimilationist trend. Those were the days when certain exponents of radical Reform attempted to abrogate those customs which were the very identification marks of the Jewish people, such as circumcision, Sabbath observance, and the ban against marriage to a non-Jew. In 1844 these first Reformers, among them men like Samuel Holdheim and Abraham Geiger, openly stated that it was permissible for Jews to marry unconverted non-Jews. These were followed by others who, at a conference in the city of Augsburg in 1871, adopted a resolution to the effect that even a Jewish male who had not been circumcised could be regarded as a full-fledged member of the Jewish people. Thereafter came the more radical reformers who sought to change the Jewish Sabbath services from Saturday to Sunday. The reform movements differed from country to country, but the basic idea behind Reform Judaism has always been the same, that is, assimilation to the cultural patterns of the majority.

This tendency to assimilate, which is basically nothing but an outgrowth of the cosmopolitan ideals found within Judaism itself, is very often synonymous with the urge to strive for cultural or spiritual advancement. It is not as it was in the days of idol-worship, a descent to a lower form of civilization, but a movement toward a united world in which all men would be brothers and, together, create a harmony of noble spirits. That is universalism at its best.

It is strange that the Jewish religion as such never feared assimilationist tendencies, even when assimilation caused many a withered leaf to fall away from the main trunk of the tree of Judaism. It was viewed, rather, as a natural phenomenon, something that could not be helped, even as it is sad but natural for a tree to lose its withered leaves even while the tree itself is in full bloom. One of the Amoraim states that "Israel shall never be destroyed" (Minchoth 53). True, from time to time, the branches may lose withered leaves or entire branches that have lost their sap and vigor may fall, but the tree itself will not be the poorer for it, and will remain standing upright in its original position. "The eternity of Israel shall not be taken away from it."

2. Faith and Reason

In the course of generations the Jewish religion has evolved into a purely rationalistic teaching. This was a natural development and the tendency in this direction was evident quite early. Judaism, then, is not a "faith" or a "belief"—as a matter of fact, the whole concept of "belief" is alien to the spirit in Judaism. Our religion is a doctrine ("For a doctrine hath Moses given unto us"). It is a doctrine and not a faith.

In this one word "Torah" (doctrine) lies the essence of the difference between the Jewish religion and other religions. As a matter of fact, even the word "religion" does not rightfully belong in our philosophy, because "religion" denotes a form of worship through belief and pure emotion. But Judaism has nothing in common with these two concepts. The teachings of Judaism contain no dogmas; those are the result of "belief." Our scriptures are called, "Mikra," "Mishna," "Talmud," all of which are words for "learning"; our spiritual leaders, too, are called "Tannaim," "Amoraim," all corresponding to "teachers."

It cannot be denied, of course, that at the very beginning there were certain dogmas in our Torah. There were some commandments which were not based on logic or reason; instead, their observance was enjoined simply because they were divine commandments which were to be accepted without question. Yes, even despite the efforts of Moses, the great teacher of the Jewish people, to set up for us a "doctrine of life" based purely on reason and intellect, some dogmas still managed to find their way into the Torah, for instance, such laws as those concerning the sacrifice of the red cow, of which Rashi said: "It is a divine commandment and thou art not permitted to question it." This statement is the true definition of "dogma." But with the passing of time the dogmas have disappeared. In the course of generations our great sages have cleansed Judaism of all such extraneous "beliefs," of superstition, of dogmas, and laws appealing only to the emotions, until finally there has emerged a refined, polished, and purified doctrine.

The Torah requires of us first of all to "understand"; and only then to "do." "Thou shalt *know* the Lord thy God," we are told.

Let us make a brief study of these two ideologies and see how they stand in relation to each other.

Belief in a God is naturally the basic tenet of all religion. But must a Jew believe in God?

Of course, without a God there is basis neither for a Torah, nor for a

13

Jewish people, and anyone who does not acknowledge the existence of God is a heretic. But the question before us is: *Must* a Jew have faith in God? Does a commandment to believe exist in Judaism?

If we understand it correctly, faith is the opposite of reason. Faith is based on emotion. You can make a person understand something, but you can never make him have faith in anything. No one can command the heart of another; no human being can do that. One can usually understand that which one seeks to understand, but one cannot have faith just because one desires to believe. Therefore there can be no commandment saying, "Thou shalt have faith" for emotions are not subject to commandments.

And, indeed, there is nowhere in the Torah a commandment demanding faith. It is nowhere stated that we must believe in God. There are 613 commandments. Does any of these enjoin us specifically to believe in God?

Maimonides, who in his great work *Yad Hachazakah* enumerates the 613 commandments of the Torah, does count belief in God as a positive commandment expressed in the words, "I am thy God" (Maimonides: *Foundations of the Law,* 81-86). He also advances the same view in his *Book of Commandments.* Maimonides bases his opinion on a place in the Gemorah where it is stated that "I am the Lord thy God" as well as "Thou shalt have no other gods beside Me." Both are part of the 613 commandments (Succah, 23). The same view is also expounded by Ibn Ezra in his commentary to the Torah (Portion of Yithro) and in a similar commentary—also in the part dealing with the Portion of Yithro—by Nachmanides.

But this view has been opposed by great scholars and commentators, who firmly contend that "I am the Lord thy God" is not a positive command to believe in God. The first to voice this dissent was the author of the work entitled *Great Laws,* who declares that "I am the Lord thy God" is not a separate commandment, but merely an introduction to the laws that follow immediately. This scholar bases his position on a place in the Gemorah which states that the first commandment was the prohibition of idolatry (Chorioth: 8); "I am the Lord thy God" is considered only an introduction to the commandment "Thou shalt have no other gods beside Me."

This can also be seen in the Mekilta (Portion of Yithro) where we find the following commentary to the statement, "I am the Lord thy God." "It may be compared to the parable of a king who takes possession of a new kingdom and is asked by the people to proclaim laws for them. He replies, 'No, I shall not proclaim any laws for you until you shall acknowledge that I am indeed the king for if I am not your king, what good would my laws be?'" From this it can be seen that "I am the Lord thy God" is not considered to be the first commandment.

Many scholars and commentators adhere to this school of thought. The Rashbatz in his commentary entitled *Zohar Harakiah* also does not include "I am the Lord thy God" in the commandments because, he explained, had it been meant to be understood as a separate commandment, it would have been prefaced with "Hear" or with "Know that I am the Lord thy God." In his book *The Light of the Lord,* Rabbi Abraham Crescas is greatly opposed to those who want to make faith in God a principle of Judaism. He declares, in effect, that we have no "faith," only a "Torah" which simply means a doctrine, reason. Moses said: "Make known to me Thy ways, for I desire to know them." The prophet says: "He who desires to glory in something may glory in understanding Me and in knowing who I am." All these quotations speak of knowledge and not of faith.

The aforesaid would bring us to the conclusion that in Judaism the principal factor is intellect and not faith. This has been its basis almost from the very beginning. Moses said, "And thou shalt . . . search after Him with all thy heart and with all thy soul" (Deut. 4:29) but not "And thou shalt believe." The concept of belief does not occur in any form in any of our holy writings and it is contrary to the spirit of Judaism.

Let us go one step further.

At the very end of the Ten Commandments there is the commandment, "Thou shalt not covet." One must not covet his neighbors' material possessions or his wife. But the matter of coveting is a matter of the emotions, which cannot be controlled. How, then, can there be such a commandment? And what can even the most righteous man, who wants to be completely good and pious do if suddenly he finds that he is envious? It is said: "Thou shalt not covet"—and what if one *does* covet? Can he control it?

Much space is devoted in the Talmud to this problem, and the Talmud concludes that one has transgressed the law only if one has actually perpetrated an act violating that law. Mere coveting itself means nothing, because one cannot be punished for one's emotions. This is expressly stated in the Mekilta (Portion of Yithro), as follows: "Thou shalt not covet; can one covet even in speech? This could lead one to understand that even by the mere putting into words of feelings of envy one has already transgressed the law 'Thou shalt not covet.' " Here is the answer to the question. It is said, 'Thou wilt desire it and take it unto thyself.' Just as it said there that one sins only when actually committing an act in violation of the law, so it means here too that no sin has been committed unless an actual act has been perpetrated.

The same applies to the law, "Thou shalt not covet thy neighbor's wife." Here again the interpretation is that the commandment is violated only through the perpetration of an act: that is, if a man causes a woman's husband by bribery or blackmail to divorce her so that he can then marry her. This would be a violation of the law.

The foregoing demonstrates once more that there is no power in Jewish law to punish a person for his emotions. True, there are such statements in Jewish literature as "The thoughts of sin lead to sin," or "As the thought, so the deed," but this is homiletic in nature. According to actual law it is quite different. According to the law, everything must be in accordance with reason and on such a level that man may be able to exercise self-control, and this is possible only in matters involving the intellect, not in those involving feelings or emotions.

The lengths to which the Torah goes in its concern with the inner life of man is evidenced by the fact that although throughout the entire Torah striving toward truth is stressed, yet we have no expressly stated commandment to speak the truth. Commandments to speak the strict truth are found only in the form of "negative commandments"; one in Exodus (23:7): "Keep thee far from a false matter" and in Leviticus (19:11): "Ye shall not . . . lie to one another." Why were these commandments so formulated? Simply because a commandment to speak only the truth is impossible of fulfillment. You cannot command a human being to speak the truth, and the truth only, all his life. On the contrary, we can find some places in the Talmud where it is stated that under certain circumstances it is even a *mitzvah* to utter an untruth. In the famous debate between the school of Shammai and the school of Hillel concerning dancing before a bride, the school of Hillel is of the opinion that one must compliment the bride even if these compliments are not truthful. The school of Shammai, however, takes the position that one must speak only the truth, regardless of the circumstances. The law in its final form, however, was laid down in accordance with the opinion of the school of Hillel. If someone buys a garment and it turns out that he has been cheated as to its quality, the school of Hillel declares that he must not be told about it even if he asks whether he has been cheated. It was found proper in certain cases not to tell the truth even to a scholar. As a matter of fact, the Talmud points out that even the Lord Himself once told a falsehood for the sake of peace. When Sarah said: "My husband [Abraham] is old," God told Abraham that she had said of herself, "And I am old," in order not to kindle Abraham's wrath (Yebamoth 25). Moses understood that for the sake of preserving peace one may speak other than the strict truth, something which would be impossible. He therefore phrased his commandment in a negative form; that is, do not tell a lie.

All this demonstrates that the trend in our Torah has from the very beginning been guided by reason, and that all commandments and prohibitions must be within the scope of reasonableness. The Tannaim and Amoraim, the Jewish philosophers and commentators, and all the leaders in Judaism in general have continued to interpret the law along those lines. And because of this our Torah has been refined in each generation, culminating in the period of the great master of Hassidism, Rabbi Shneur Zalman Schneirson, who built up a lofty edifice of "wisdom, understanding, and knowledge" and authored the saying, "understanding is greater than emotion."

3. What Are the Basic Principles of Judaism?

Judaism, at the time of its inception, had no basic principles. Neither the Pentateuch nor the works of the prophets have set down any tenets that could be construed as "basic" to Judaism. The Bible contains only one principal declaration, that is: "Hear, O Israel, the Lord, our God, is one God."

Even the Ten Commandments do not constitute a set of "basic principles" or "articles of faith." They are simply a group of ten commandments, and, as far as the Jewish people are concerned, they do not even have the distinction of being the first commandments received by Israel, for the precept concerning circumcision and the ban against the sinew which shrank are mentioned in earlier parts of the Pentateuch, long before the account of the giving of the Ten Commandments. The Bible also speaks of a commandment concerning Sabbath observance prior to the story of the revelation on Mount Sinai.

The Law of Moses, which deals with man's relationship to God and to his fellow men, contains a statement to the effect that no one commandment or prohibition is more important than another. There is no indication that any of the laws are cardinal precepts which must be observed in order to be considered a Jew.

Nor do the writings of the prophets contain any declarations as regards fundamental principles for Judaism. The prophets are concerned mainly with man's conduct toward his fellow men. They speak of justice, honesty, righteousness, but these are not basic principles; they are simply moral and ethical teachings. Nowhere does any prophet state that any one law is more "important" than any other and therefore constitutes a "basic principle" of Judaism. We search in vain throughout the Bible for indications to that effect.

This absence of basic principles in Jewish ideology created no problems so long as the Jewish people did not seek recruits for Judaism and the belief in One God from among the heathen nations around about. Those were the days when the Jews themselves still had to resolve serious differences within their own ranks in order to rid themselves completely of the shackles of idolatry. Surrounded by pagan nations, many Jews naturally tended to ape the example set by the dominant majority. True, the Jews had already been in possession of the Law of Moses for many centuries, but they had still not as yet fully absorbed it and made it an integral part of their lives. These internal ideological conflicts flared up throughout the days of the First Temple, with spells of quiet only at those times when the Jews regained their sobriety and returned to their own God.

It was only much later, when the Jewish people had shaken off idolatry completely and become proud bearers of the banner of Judaism, that the other nations took notice of Judaism. There arose movements among the various heathen nations to adopt the Jewish way of life for themselves. This important step was actually taken by the Samaritans and others. It was only then that the question arose as to what the basic principles of Judaism really were.

And yet, to this very day, Jews who never thought in terms of "principles of faith" and "proselytes," still do not have a basic statement establishing the essential tenets of Judaism. It is not easy to formulate a "declaration of basic tenets" since Judaism is intrinsically hostile to the very idea of rigid articles of faith. The Torah, the Law of Moses, was intended to serve as a guide for daily living, and not as a set of dogmas. Basic principles are, after all, nothing but dogmas. However, at the time of the Second Temple, some efforts were made to determine certain premises which should serve as cardinal commandments of Judaism. But even those premises never came to play the important role that they occupy in other religions.

The first scholar to formulate a general premise concerning Judaism was Hillel. When a Gentile came to him to be converted and requested him to teach him the entire Torah while he, the prospective convert, stood on one foot, Hillel replied: "That which thou wouldst not have others do to thee, do not thou do to others; this is the entire Torah. All the rest is commentary. Now go thou and study" (Sabbath 31). As we see, Hillel made no attempt to teach the man any principles or tenets concerning the belief in One God. All that Hillel imparted to the would-be convert was a general moral code, and this not even in the positive, precise terms of "Love thy neighbor as thyself," but rather in the negative terms which are much easier for the simple mind to understand. It is easier to "refrain" from sin than to "do" good.

Rabbi Akiba, who also searched for some general principles by which to characterize Judaism, finally stated it in these terms: "And thou shalt love thy neighbor as thyself, that is the general premise on which the Torah is based" (Bereshith Rabbah, Chapter 24). This is the same thought, expressed in positive terms.

Similarly there is the premise set down by Ben Azai: "This is the record in which is written the history of the origins of man—is the great premise on which the Torah is based" (Bereshith Rabbah, Chapter 22). This is a broad and generalized statement, because the sentence speaks of "man" in general, and does not mention race, religion, social status, or other such groupings into which mankind is divided. This means that all men are equal in the sight of the Lord.

We are told, further, in the Talmud (Makkoth 24) that "Rabbi Somluy said that Moses had given us 613 Laws. Then came King David and summarized them in terms of eleven precepts" (in Psalm 15). "Thereafter the Prophet Isaiah stated them in terms of six" ("He that walketh righteously and speaketh uprightly . . ." (Isa. 33:15). "Then Micah rephrased them in terms of only three" ("It hath been told thee, O man, what is good . . ." Micah 6). "Finally, Habbakuk summarized them all in one sentence in the verse 'the righteous shall live by his faith' " (Hab. 2:4).

The great spiritual leaders of Judaism have done nothing more than indicate general premises along broad lines. They have never attempted to formulate definite, rigid principles of faith. They have never said: "This is the general premise upon which the Torah is based." There is a great deal of difference between a "general premise" and a fundamental principle of universal binding force.

The general statements which all of the later great minds have left to the Jewish people are all along the same lines. They are ethical teachings concerning the relationships of man to man. They do not deal with such academic questions as "the beginnings of God" or "the unity of the Creator." It would have been quite natural to expect at least one of the expounders of Judaism to say, for example, "Hear, O Israel, the Lord, our God, is One; that is the general principle upon which the Torah is based." But the Jewish sages attached much more importance to ethical and humanitarian precepts than to abstract teachings concerning the nature of God, or even the acknowledgment that there is only One God.

There is a statement in the Talmud which reads much like a basic principle or combination of principles. It is said that if a Gentile should request conversion to Judaism, he must first be taught about the unity of the Creator and be advised of the prohibition against idolatry. The teacher is instructed to devote a great deal of time to a discussion of these aspects of Judaism. The prospective convert must also be told about a few of the commandments, both major and minor, but the instructor need not go too deeply into them (Yebamoth 46).

Yet these statements in the Talmud were not intended to indicate any "fundamental principles." Had they been so intended, the text would have read "and they [the instructors] are to tell him [the convert] the basic principles of the Torah," or "they are to teach him the basic principles of the Torah." But the Gemorah meant to point out only that, in order to give the prospective convert some idea of Judaism, the rabbi or teacher should tell him that Jews are firmly opposed to idolatry. These two ideas should be explained in great detail. The student of Judaism ought to learn how Father Abraham came to discover that there is One God and how the unity of God became one of the prime teachings of Judaism. He should be told, too, that the Jewish people was the first to advance the ideal of monotheism and to pioneer in the struggle to eliminate idolatry from the world. Thereafter the teacher is to give the inquirer some examples of Jewish laws, of various commandments and prohibitions. But the Gemorah recommends that not too much time be devoted to these. In other words, the Gemorah has made no attempt to formulate any basic principles, but rather to set forth the things a prospective convert should be told about Judaism. Nothing more.

None of the men who participated in the compilation of the Talmud, neither the sages of the Mishna nor the Amoraim, have ever presumed to set down tenets to be revered as the fundamental principles of Judaism.

It was only centuries later that the Jewish philosophers felt a need for the formulation of at least some specific principles which might be regarded as basic to Judaism. Circumstances made such action imperative. There were new sects within Judaism which revolted against the authority of the Talmud. Some of these groups advocated the abolition of many of the laws of the Talmud in order to make religious observance easier. Others, like the Karaites, felt that the interpretation of Jewish law as given in the Talmud was far too liberal, and they prohibited many things the Talmud had permitted. At that time, too, Mohammed precipitated a religious upheaval in the Middle East which had previously been dominated by paganism. With the formation of so many new sects and religions, it became necessary for Judaism to set forth at least a few basic principles to determine by the standards thus set who was, and who was not, a Jew. This brings us to the philosophical conception of these so-called "principles" which were then incorporated into Jewish ideology.

The first thinker actually to attempt to formulate such basic principles, Philo of Alexandria, was born long before the historical period we have just discussed. He lived from about the year 20 B.C. until 40 A.D. Philo set down these points as basic principles of Judaism: (1) Belief in God; (2) Belief in the unity of God; (3) God is the creator of the world; (4) He made the world without any aid; (5) He governs the world. All this has nothing to do with ethical or moral principles; Philo said nothing about man's relationship to man, and that is the reason why his basic points were never accepted as being fundamental to Judaism.

During the Era of the Philosophers, which began in the tenth century, Jewish scholars made serious efforts to promulgate those points which, in their opinion, constitute the cardinal tenets of Judaism. But even these were not basic *principles;* they were merely fundamental *thoughts* on the subjects of Judaism. The first to formulate some of these was Saadia Gaon. In his book entitled *Beliefs and Opinions* he summarized the main concepts of Judaism in these terms: (1) That there is a God; (2) That there is only one God; (3) That God gave the Law of Moses to the Jewish people; (4) That man is endowed with free will and has the choice of doing either right or wrong; (5) That there are reward and punishment in this world; (6) That the human soul lives on after the body has died; (7) That the dead will be resurrected; (8)

That the Jewish people will be redeemed from exile; and (9) That there are also reward and punishment in the "afterlife."

Rabbi Hananel, another Jewish scholar of that period, formulated his concept of Judaism in terms of four points in his commentary on Exodus 14:31: (1) There is a God; (2) Belief in the sacred nature of the words of the prophets; (3) There is an "afterlife"; (4) There are reward and punishment. But Hananel himself is quick to point out that these statements are not meant to be cardinal tenets of Juadism, but merely represent his own views of it. He says: "There is no such thing as principles which would be accepted as such by all Jews. There are only general premises. I have enumerated some of them, but there may be others [scholars] who might set forth new, additional premises."

Thus, as late as the tenth century A.D. there was no one formulation of basic principles which all of Jewry and its spiritual leaders would have agreed to adopt as standards by which to determine whether or not a person is a Jew.

Those familiar with Jewish liturgy will ask: "And what of the Thirteen Articles of Faith?" These are the thirteen statements in the Jewish prayer book which begin with the words "I believe" and which are, in fact, called the "Thirteen Articles of Faith." Let us determine now whether these Articles have indeed been recognized as basic tenets of Judaism at all times in the history of its religion.

In some Jewish prayer books (though not in those of the Hassidic sect and many others) are contained the so-called "Thirteen Articles of Faith" which are to be recited each day. In brief, they are as follows:

(1) The belief that there is a God;
(2) There is only One God;
(3) God has no physical shape or form;
(4) There has been no other god before Him;
(5) Man must serve Him alone and not worship "representatives" of Him;
(6) The prophets have been sent by God;
(7) Moses was the prophet above all other prophets;
(8) The Law of Moses was given to the Jewish people by God himself;
(9) Nothing may be added to, or subtracted from the Law;
(10) God is the Supreme Ruler of the world;
(11) There is a reward for good and punishment for evil;
(12) There will be a Messiah and, even though he may delay his advent, one must never cease to believe in his eventual coming;
(13) The coming of the Messiah will bring with it the resurrection of the dead.

In addition to these thirteen "beliefs" which some Jews recite after their daily prayers, the Hebrew prayer book also contains, at the very beginning of the morning service, two liturgical poems that summarize the Thirteen Articles of Faith. One, entitled "Lord of the Universe," was written by an unknown author. The other, "Extolled and Praised Be the Living God," is ascribed to Daniel ben Yehuda, judge of the rabbinical court of Rome, who lived at the end of the thirteenth century.

But who was the author of the "Thirteen Articles of Faith"? And why is it that he dared write them even though there never had been such a thing in Judaism before? Or how, in the first place, did he come to use the words "I believe" to preface each "article" when the vocabulary of the Jewish ideology had never before contained such terms of "faith" or "belief"? True, the Pentateuch does employ the forms of the verb "to believe," but not in the sense of a law. We read in the Bible ". . . and they *believed* in the Lord and in Moses His servant," and ". . . he *believed* in the Lord," and so forth. But nowhere in the Scriptures do we find it stated in the imperative form that you *must* believe in the Lord. Whenever the Bible discusses man's attitude toward God, it uses some form of the verb "to know," as for example, "And you shall *know* this day that the Lord is God indeed." How, then, did the author of the Thirteen Articles of Faith come to make use of the words "I believe" in his summarization of what he thought to be the basic tenets of Judaism? And furthermore, when were these Articles first set down? Where is the original source in which they first appeared? As a matter of fact, such principles are not mentioned in either the Pentateuch or in the prophetic writings, and are not found in this form either in the Mishna, the Gemorah, or elsewhere.

We have, therefore, four specific questions which come to mind in connection with the Thirteen Articles of Faith. First of all, who was actually the author? Secondly, how did he come to formulate such explicit Articles when no one before him had dared take such action? Thirdly, why did he preface each of these Articles with the words "I believe"? And, fourth and finally, from where did he derive the number thirteen?

The answer to the first question is that the original author of these thirteen statements is anonymous, but it is known that they were formulated in accordance with ideas set down by Moses Maimonides. When Maimonides was thirty-three years of age, after ten years of diligent work, he had completed a commentary to the Mishna written in the Arabic language. In his commentary to the Tractate Sanhedrin, Chapter Helek, he sets down quite a number of his thoughts concerning Judaism. He states that there are basically three different types of Jews. The first are the fanatically religious and the pious, who believe that everything written in the Gemorah about the coming of the Messiah, the subject of reward and punishment, and the resurrection of the dead, is literally true. They accept completely the concept of paradise and hell, and the resurrection of the dead on the day of the coming of the Messiah. The second group of Jews gives a more spiritual interpretation to these statements. The third group, which could hardly be called a group because it is so small in number, believes that these pronouncements are only allegories or figures of speech, and that it is man's duty to serve the Lord of the World without hope of reward or fear of punishment. Maimonides compares the "promises" of "reward and punishment" to the bribes employed to get a child to study his lessons. When he is still very young, he is promised candy if he will apply himself to his studies. As he gets older, the candy may lose its charm for him, and the best way to get him to do his schoolwork is to tell him that he will get a new suit if he does what is expected of him. Many adults will study only for the sake of receiving honor. But those who are truly mature will seek no reward. They will understand that study is important for its own sake. Maimonides stated that he would set forth certain fundamentals (note: he said "fundamentals" and not "Articles of Faith") for the simple masses who, he felt, were in need of such guidance. He said: "I have done it for those who have no education concerning the important issue which not all people can comprehend." Only after these prefatory remarks does Maimonides set down the thirteen *fundamentals* of Judaism. They could also be called the "thirteen concepts" or "premises," for that matter—and then he proceeds to discuss each of them in detail.

It was from those thirteen "fundamentals" of Maimonides that an unknown author devised the Thirteen Articles of Faith, adding to each "fundamental" the words, "I believe"—something which Maimonides had never implied or intended. True, Maimonides does use the phrase, ". . . which we *believe*," but he does not use it as an imperative. At any rate, the thirteen "beliefs" were actually modeled upon the thirteen "fundamentals" laid down by Maimonides, but the idea of the Thirteen Articles of Faith is not his. A "declaration of faith" as such is actually contrary to the spirit of Maimonides. This is clearly evident from his other works in which he gives quite a different explanation of his "fundamentals." In his *Yad Hachazakah* (code of Jewish laws) he states that certain things which he mentioned in his own thirteen fundamentals are not by any means basic articles in which a Jew must believe if he is to be considered a Jew.

In his monumental *Guide to the Perplexed,* Maimonides goes further still. He discusses the question of the Messiah and the resurrection of the dead, and the interpretation he gives to these ideas is by no means literal. He says that the "coming of the Messiah" is actually an allegory for the advent of an era when the world will have attained a high level of wisdom and moral perfection, when men will be delivered from darkness and come to understand what they had not been able to grasp before.

Again in the *Yad Hachazakah* there is further proof that Maimonides had never intended his thirteen fundamentals to be regarded as articles of faith. We read that, if a non-Jew should seek to be converted to Judaism, he should be told about the unity of God and about the prohibition against idolatry. He should also be told about some of the precepts of Judaism, both the stringent ones and the more liberal ones, even as they are set forth in the

Talmud (Yebamoth 56). But nowhere does Maimonides say that a candidate for conversion should be taught a set of Thirteen Articles of Faith.

The Thirteen Fundamentals as set down in the Thirteen Articles of Faith met with vehement protests both from the rabbinical world and from the so-called "enlightened" elements within Jewry.

Among the great number of Jewish scholars who criticized these fundamentals were two who were emphatic in their opposition, Rabbi Chasdai Crescas and Rabbi Joseph Albo. In his book *The Light of the Lord,* Crescas demonstrates that the Thirteen Fundamentals have absolutely no connection at all with Judaism; at the most, only five out of these thirteen can be regarded as fundamental to Judaism. Joseph Albo, in his book entitled *Articles of Faith,* which deals solely with this issue, states simply: "To this day, we Jews have never known of 'Articles of Faith' in Judaism. It is therefore dangerous to attempt to fix such principles because, according to these 'Articles,' anyone who does not believe in such things as reward and punishment, the coming of the Messiah or the resurrection of the dead, is not a Jew. Such a concept of Judaism is entirely false. True, there is a statement in the Gemorah to the effect that 'he who denies the resurrection of the dead will not have a portion in the world-to-come,' but this only means he will never enjoy the bliss of afterlife simply because he does not believe in a world-to-come. One Amora named Hillel states in the Gemorah, 'The Jews no longer have a Messiah,' and no one said of him that he could not be considered a Jew because of this statement."

In general, Rabbi Albo felt it was quite clear that Maimonides himself did not attach undue significance to the thirteen fundamentals. Maimonides actually had two different formulations of his ideas of Judaism. One was intended for the simple masses, for whom he had devised the fundamentals. The other was for the more educated and sophisticated classes. For the latter, he did not feel it was necessary to enumerate any set of fundamentals at all; it was sufficient for them to read his liberal thoughts in his various works.

Hence there is no basis at all for the idea that Maimonides' thirteen "fundamentals" were truly meant to be Articles of Faith in which a Jew had to believe in order to be considered a Jew. They are actually neither Articles of Faith nor are they binding upon all of Jewry.

With regard to "premises" or "concepts" (*not* Articles of Faith) of Judaism, each one of the great scholars of the Sephardic era held a different view. Joseph Albo set forth three concepts, and others have postulated other fundamentals. We find them in *Duties of the Heart* by Rabbi Bahya ibn Pekudah, in *The Kuzari* by Judah Ha-Levi, and in the works of Solomon ibn Gabirol, Abraham ibn Ezra, and many others. According to Don Isaac Abrabanel, all the commandments set down in the Bible are essentials of Judaism which a Jew must observe if he is to be included as a member of the Jewish people.

The *Poskim* who interpreted the law at a later date went one step further and said that not only the commandments of the Bible, but also all the restrictions imposed by the expounders of the Law were such essentials. Other scholars again added to this definition the regulations, and also the various customs that became traditional in the countries where Jews have lived.

From all the foregoing evidence it is apparent that, basically, Judaism does not have any definite writing which can properly be called "Articles of Faith." Those scholars who sought to formulate such basic tenets were greatly at variance with one another, their views ranging from extreme rigidity to extreme latitude. Some were ready to summarize all of Judaism in one single basic principle, adherence to which would be sufficient to identify one with Judaism. Those who were at the other extreme, however, said that every minor religious law and custom was an indispensable essential of Judaism which every Jew was bound to observe punctiliously.

4. Light and Shadows in Jewish History

When we read the Five Books of Moses from beginning to end, we will be amazed to see the simplicity and frankness of the accounts given there of the transgressions of the very first men in God's world. We find the same unadorned record of the weaknesses of the Patriarchs, including such personalities as Moses and Aaron and other great figures in Jewish history. Many things which are not flattering at all are recorded here openly and without a trace of squeamishness. True, the outstanding men and women of Jewish history have become immortal because of their virtues and abilities, but the Bible does not deny that they were all human and therefore not immune to sin and error.

The same frankness is shown in all of the prophetic literature and, in fact, throughout all the Scriptures. We are told the plain truth even about the failings of Israel's great rulers such as David and Solomon.

A similar spirit of truthfulness also pervades the Talmud and its accounts of the personalities of the Tannaim and the Amoraim, and it is present, too, in every work that the genius of Judaism has ever brought forth. Good and bad go hand in hand. Nothing is ever all sweetness and light. Even leaders, kings, and expounders of the Law of the Lord are no angels. Judaism knows no demigods. The men and women of Israel, no matter how important the role they played in its history, are only human and possessed of all the virtues as well as failings to which mortal men fall heir. Those who have set down the historical records of the Jewish people have always felt that if posterity is to get a true picture of the great figures of the past, it must be told in detail not only of the virtues and of the mighty acts wrought by these personalities, but also of their shortcomings and failings.

There is mention of sin at the very outset of man's history. The Bible tells us that Adam and Eve disobeyed the command of the Lord not to eat of the fruit of the Tree of Knowledge. Eve ate of the apple and gave Adam a part of the forbidden fruit, and God was wroth with them, rebuked them, and drove them out of Paradise.

The generations that followed Adam were no better. The first instance of murder in the world was when Cain slew Abel. Evil increased and multiplied until, as the Bible tells us, "the world was filled with violence." Then God no longer restrained His wrath and caused the world to be inundated by the Great Flood.

Or take the story of the Patriarchs. We are told that God made a covenant with Father Abraham, a saintly man. And yet the Bible does not remain silent about his shortcomings. Without any apologies or attempts at justification, the Bible records the incident when Abraham told a falsehood to the Pharaoh of Egypt, pretending that Sarah was not his wife but only his sister. Nor does the Bible omit the account of Abraham's banishment of his own son, Ishmael, together with Hagar his mother, both of whom almost starved to death in the wilderness.

And certainly the Bible does not gloss over the story of the deceit of Jacob, when he went before his blind father disguised as his brother Esau so that he, Jacob, might obtain Isaac's paternal blessing which was intended for his first-born brother. Then we have the incident of the speckled sheep, an attempt on the part of Jacob to outwit Laban, his father-in-law. Jacob's sons were also not angels, for they sold their young brother Joseph to a band of Ishmaelites and told their father that the boy had been devoured by wild beasts. And then we read of the illicit relationship of Jacob's son Judah with Tamar, his own daughter-in-law.

In the account of the early career of Moses, we are told that he slew an Egyptian who had beaten a Hebrew slave. Nor does the Bible hide the fact that Moses had married a Negress and that his brother and sister had disapproved of the match. The Bible also speaks of the rebellions of the children of Israel against Moses, particularly the revolt of Korah and his band, which included about two hundred and fifty of the most prominent leaders among the people. These men, who represented the ruling class of each tribe, had argued that Moses had ruled over them long enough. "Ye take too much upon you, seeing all the congregation are holy. . . . Wherefore then lift ye up yourselves above the assembly of the lord?" (Num. 16:3).

In the account of the Golden Calf, we are told that Moses commanded the innocent to kill the guilty even if this would entail the slaying of one's own brother. We also have mention of some of the other punishments that Moses had decreed for the Jews when they rebelled against his leadership. But all this does not nullify the basic greatness of Moses. He has remained immortal as the leader of the Jewish people, even as the Bible has it, "There hath not arisen a prophet since in Israel like unto Moses" (Deut. 34:10).

All the great works that Judaism has produced have emulated the great example given by the Pentateuch. They all tell the simple truth about every man or woman of whom they speak. They withhold nothing and enumerate, impartially, both the sins and the virtues of them all. For good and bad alike are parts of human nature; they are present in every man both great and small, simple and righteous, sinful and just, for we are all no more than human.

We meet with the same frankness in the accounts of Joshua, of the judges, of Samuel, and particularly of the kings of the Jewish people and especially of David. Here we have a detailed account of David's love affair with the beautiful Abigail, the wife of Nebal. The King, who passionately desired her, married her after the sudden death of her husband. And we are also told of David's lust for Bathsheba, who was the wife of Uriah the Hittite. David, the great singer of the glorious Book of Psalms, married Bathsheba after he had sent her husband to the battle front to make sure that he would never return.

We are also told how, thereafter, Nathan the Prophet came to David, and reported to him a case of flagrant injustice which had supposedly occurred in David's kingdom. There was a wealthy man, said Nathan, who owned many sheep and much cattle. In the same town there lived a man who owned nothing at all except one little lamb. The wealthy man, who possessed hundreds of sheep, desired that one little lamb and therefore took it by force from its rightful owner. King David was outraged at this wrong, and he cried out, "The man that hath done this deserveth to die." But the prophet pointed his finger at David and fearlessly declared: "Thou art the man."

As for King Solomon, the Book of Kings, which refers to him as "the wisest of all men" is also quite candid about his weaknesses. Solomon, when he first ascended the throne, prayed to God not for wealth or for strength to defeat his foes, but only for wisdom so that he might be able to lead his country with justice and righteousness, and to be an upright judge and honest ruler of his people. But there is also a less saintly side to his character. He loved to have many wives about him and he married women from nations which the Lord had explicitly listed as groups from which men in Israel were not to take wives. "When Solomon was old, . . . his wives turned away his heart after other gods, and his heart was not whole with the Lord his God, as was the heart of David his father" (I Kings 11:4).

And yet, despite all their faults, both Solomon and his father David have been glorified throughout the ages as heroes in Jewish history. King David became immortal as the "sweet singer in Israel," the author of the most beautiful prayers in existence, and as the greatest king the Jewish people have ever had. Solomon has come to be regarded as the symbolic figure of the heyday of Israel's splendor and prosperity, and it is for this reason that Jews expect the Messianic era to be inaugurated by a direct descendant of the house of Jesse, who was the grandfather of King Solomon and the father of King David.

This is the way of the Bible's frankness and candor about both good and bad in its heroes. But the less bright aspects of Israel's annals never obscure those things which are right, even as the spots that appear on the sun cannot possibly keep the sunlight from shining on and lending warmth and radiance to all that is in God's world.

The great masters of the Talmud followed along the same lines as in the Bible. No one would have been the wiser and there would never have been any objections if the shortcomings of certain expounders of the Law had remained unmentioned. But such a hush-hush attitude would not have been in keeping with the spirit of Judaism, for Judaism does not believe in the concealment of the uglier aspects of human nature, but regards it as important to render a full account of them, along with the brighter facets of human personality.

Take the example of Rabban Gamaliel, who was president of the great Talmudic Academy of Yavneh. He is given full credit for all his great achievements, but the accounts in Talmudic lore make no attempt to conceal the less attractive aspects of his personality. We are told that he was extremely stubborn; he demanded blind obedience and dealt sternly with those who refused to accept his word without question. As a result, his disciples revolted against him. One day he insulted Rabbi Joshua who happened to differ with him regarding the interpretation of a point in Jewish law and, as a consequence, Rabban Gamaliel was relieved of his high office. Later on, however, he was restored to favor once again.

The most splendid figure of the Talmudic era, save for Hillel and Rabbi Akiba, is the great leader who arranged the Mishna in its final form, Rabbi Judah the Prince, known as "Rabbi." Judah had been given authority even broader than that of the ancient Sanhedrin. He was empowered to appoint judges and to give rabbinic ordination to deserving disciples. And yet, without thereby detracting from Judah's greatness, the Talmud describes him as a man who was easily moved to anger and who lacked a sense of humor. If one of his students did not pay him the respectful homage he felt was due him, he refused to confer ordination upon the unfortunate scholar. Certainly this is not a fine trait. Still, Rabbi Judah the Prince has remained immortal in Jewish history as "Rabbi," the eminent leader who was an important bulwark in the fortress of Judaism.

The Amoraim, too, freely discussed both the virtues and faults of their colleagues.

Take the example of Rabbi Nachman, who was recognized as an outstanding legal mind so that the Law was always interpreted in accordance with his views and opinions. Yet we are told quite candidly that a woman claimed he had used her wood to erect a Succah for himself. She said that one of his servants had taken it away for this purpose and that all her pleas and tears were of no avail and Rabbi Nachman curtly dismissed her with a meager compensation. It is also said of him that he gloried in the fact that he was the son-in-law of the Exilarch.

All these facts about the lives of the masters of the Law can be found within the Talmud itself. They were all written down by the very scholars who had compiled the Talmud. Had they omitted these side lights, no one would have known otherwise. And yet they felt that they had no right to conceal the truth from posterity. They wished to show Rabbi Nachman, for instance, not as an angel, but as an ordinary man. They extolled his merits and praised his virtues, but they took care also not to gloss over his faults, for such is human nature, and Rabbi Nachman was a man with all the traits associated with mortal humans.

Frankness and candor are the rule in all Jewish history, not only through the days of the Bible and the Talmud, but also through the Era of the Gaonim, through the halcyon days of the Jewish community of Spain, down to modern times. Judaism does not seek to canonize human beings. Judaism glories in its great teachers and leaders, but it knows of no demigods or saints.

No less a man than Moses himself showed Israel the way to view the lives of great men. The Bible says of him, "No man knoweth of his sepulchre unto this day" (Deut. 34:6). This is quite in accordance with the wishes of this immortal Master. Moses did not want the site of his grave to become a shrine, lest, as a result, posterity would come to worship there and deify him.

In the Talmud, too, we find that many scholars oppose the erection of imposing monuments to the memory of the departed ones. Therefore the Jewish people has never dedicated monuments or shrines to the memory of Moses, of prophets, or of any of its great teachers and philosophers. What remains important to posterity is their works, their teachings, and the things they achieved during their lives. Judaism attaches importance only to what its departed masters have done for others, namely for Israel and mankind. These are the important and permanent values which remain after such a man has died. The rest means little.

This has been the Jewish view throughout the history of Judaism.

5. The Fight for Ideals in Jewish History

From the very beginning, the Jewish people has always been anything but meek and submissive. On the contrary, Israel has been a nation of fighters at all times. Even Moses had cause to call Israel "a stiff-necked people," thus characterizing it as a nation that would not take abuse quietly and good-naturedly, but would show its dissatisfaction if there were cause for discontent.

Throughout Jewish history we see evidence of revolutions, some bloodless and others involving loss of life. Of course, Israel had time for internal struggles only when the surrounding nations left it at peace and when it therefore had no need to fear attack or destruction from without. In times of danger or oppression from the outside world, the Jews forgot their own conflicts; their hearts were united as one in the concerted effort to rid themselves of the danger that threatened them all.

The conflicts that took place within Israel itself were always those involving the fight of a minority against a majority. However, one thing is important to remember: these conflicts were never solely struggles for power, or, at least, they were not waged for the sake of power alone. They were fought not to overthrow established dynasties and replace them with revolutionary governments, but simply for the sake of truth and justice. If attempts were indeed made to depose those who happened to hold the reins in their hands, this was not done simply so that the rebels would come to power, but to remove from authority those who did not lead the people in accordance with the requirements of truth, justice, and righteousness. Such revolutions were protests, alliances against the strong. The Jewish people, which began its independent existence with a revolution against Egyptian slavery, has never ceased to offer resistance to any man or nation that threatened to enslave it. Whenever the plague of tyranny cropped up within the camp of Israel, whenever groups of individuals sought to enslave part of or all of the people, revolution would soon break out. The history of the rest of the world is full of accounts of wars waged by one group in order to gain the ascendancy over another. But such is not the case in Jewish history. The struggles of which Jewish history has to tell cannot be explained away as having been motivated solely by a lust for power. There has always been another motive much greater and more significant. It was the desire for justice and equality, freedom and democracy, but never for the replacement of one form of tyranny with another.

The factors that motivated Israel in its wars against outside enemies will be discussed elsewhere. Now, let us outline briefly the major upheavals that went on within the camp of Israel itself through the course of its history.

1. When Israel wandered through the wilderness, there were a number of mutinies, such as the incident of the Golden Calf, the rebellion of Korah against Moses, and other revolutions described in the Pentateuch.

2. During the so-called Biblical era, there was the upheaval that led to the division of the Jewish nation into two separate kingdoms, Judah and Israel, the result of the controversy between the idol-worshipers and the servants of the One God.

3. In the Talmudic Epoch there was the conflict between the Pharisees and the Sadducees, and the fight against the Samaritans and other such sects.

4. The struggles of such sects as the Karaites against the majority viewpoint.

5. The opposition to Jewish thinkers such as Maimonides, Rabbi Levi ben Gershon, Spinoza, and others.

6. The fight against the leaders of the cabalist movements in different times and against the movements of false Messiahs such as Sabbatai Zvi, Jacob Frank, and others.

7. The intra-Jewish conflicts of modern times, such as those involving Hassidism, "Haskalah," Zionism, socialism, and other more recent trends within Judaism.

Now let us examine the character of all these mutinies and rebellions.

If we turn back to the very beginning of Israel's existence as a nation, we will see that the generation that traveled through the wilderness was constantly embroiled in internal conflicts. The motives that lay behind these rebellions are not clear; still we know some of them.

Take the revolt of Korah and his band. We are told explicitly in the Bible that Korah had said to Moses and Aaron, "Ye take too much upon you" (Num. 16:3), meaning, "Why should you believe yourselves to be better than the rest and be the leaders of the Congregation of the Lord?" Korah himself was the instigator of that revolt. He gathered about him two hundred and fifty of the most respected men in the tribes of Israel, "princes of the congregation" and "men of renown" who supported his stand. The demands of Korah and his followers were quite frank—they wanted power. But even in this instance, when the lust for power would be the most obvious explanation, the sages of Jewish lore give an entirely different interpretation. They explain this mutiny as a revolt for the sake of justice. This we see in the Midrash. There we are told that Korah came to consult Moses with reference to a question that involved a fine point in Jewish ritual. This is to say that the mutiny of Korah had an ideological basis. Korah felt that if the laws had truly been divine they would have been more just, equitable, and logical than they actually were.

So we can find ideological motivations also for all the other struggles that went on within the camp of Israel.

The warfare between the Kingdom of Judah and that of Israel was actually a fight against idolatry and an effort to bring back the nation of Israel to the One God. The Kingdom of Judah waged war against the Kingdom of Israel whose king, Jeroboam, had erected two statues of calves and commanded his subjects to worship them. In the end, the great prophets had reason to rebuke both of the Jewish nations because by that time Judah, too, had become tainted by sin.

It is obvious that the dispute between the Pharisees and the Sadducees was a conflict of ideologies. The same was true of the revolt against the Hasmonean and the Herodian dynasties.

It was the same, too, in the case of all the other internal conflicts of the Jews such as the revolt of the Karaites, the rise of the false Messiahs, the fight against Hassidism, and all the others. All were ideological fights, as we can see.

All through Jewish history we find evidence of disputes and warfare constantly going on within the camp of Israel. The motives were almost all ideological in nature. The principles at stake were justice and righteousness, and the subject of the great debates was the proper interpretation of the word of God.

6. *Hebrew and Aramaic, the Languages of the Jews*

The first language spoken by the Jewish people was Hebrew. It was the tongue employed by the ancient Hebrews long before their scattered tribes became one people, and they retained it when they became known as "the children of Israel" through the days of the First and Second Temples. However, the Hebrews, soon after their birth as a nation, acquired a sister tongue to Hebrew, namely Aramaic, which had been the dominant medium of communication in Mesopotamia and throughout Asia Minor. Hebrew and Aramaic go through Jewish history like a pair of twins, with each performing vital functions in its own sphere of influence. Of course there were instances of intermixture when the Hebrews would speak Aramaic, and the Aramaic group would employ Hebrew.

The word "Aramaic" is derived from the name "Aram" (signifying "Aram Naharaim," the land between the Tigris and the Euphrates) and refers to the language spoken by the inhabitants of that region. The language was also called "Chaldean" after the national group that dwelt there. Aramaic is very close to Hebrew with regard to actual vocabulary, syntax, and grammar.

We see from the Pentateuch (Gen. 31:47) that Laban, the Aramean, spoke the Aramaic language. For when Jacob made his peace with Laban, and the two men erected a monument in memory of their reconciliation, they called that monument a "testimonial stone." And Laban referred to it in Aramaic as "Jegar-sahadutha" while Jacob, who spoke Hebrew, designated it as "Galeed."

We know also from the Second Book of Kings (18:26) that, during the reign of Hezekiah (eighth century before the Christian era), Aramaic was understood by all the intelligentsia of Palestine, who were familiar with both Aramaic and Hebrew. In the days of Ezra the Scribe, Aramaic was the language used for all official documents. Later, the popularity of Aramaic grew greater still, so that it became the vernacular of the Jewish people, with Hebrew relegated to the background. The Jews who were exiled to Babylonia spoke Aramaic, and by the time they returned to Palestine they spoke no other language. Hebrew was the language of the Torah and the prophets, and was employed only for the recitation of certain prayers. Entire passages of the Bible, especially parts of the Book of Ezra and of the Book of Daniel, were written in Aramaic. Aramaic, too, was the language of the Jerusalem and the Babylonian Talmud. It was employed for many prayers in Jewish

34

liturgy, in the Jewish marriage contract form which is still in use today, and in the writings of the Gaonim, of Midrashic literature, and also in a great many cabalistic books such as the *Zohar*.

But Aramaic, even though it was so closely related to the Hebrew language, did not exert an influence on Jewish life and thought and probably no other language might have done so, for basically the sages of the Jewish people did not put too much stress on the concept of language. They considered that language served only as a means of expressing thought. The thought was the important thing. What was said counted more than the language in which it was set forth. For this reason the wise men of Israel decided that Jews might say their prayer of "Shema" in whatever language they employed as their vernacular, and not solely in Hebrew. This ruling applied also to the Grace after Meals, and the taking of official testimony from a witness who could not speak Hebrew. Language was only the garment in which the thought was clothed, and the important thing was not the garment but its wearer, even as it is said: "Do not look at the bottle but only at that which is within it." Thus it came about that there was not too much concern about whether or not Hebrew only should be spoken by the Jewish people. Eventually Hebrew gradually disappeared from the roster of the so-called living languages to be replaced by other tongues. While the Jews dwelt in Babylonia, the other language was Aramaic. Later, when they migrated to Asia and parts of Europe, the dominant language was Arabic, particularly in communities within the territories ruled by Arabs. As the Jews migrated to other European countries, they adopted the vernaculars of the nations among whom they lived.

As a result, Hebrew became a so-called dead language, a language used primarily in literature. Sad as this was, some good did come out of it. For Jewish scholars the world over have expressed their ideas in the languages of the peoples in whose midst they resided, and thus they were able to broadcast the ideas and ideals of Judaism to all the nations of the earth. Because they thus became a cosmopolitan people, the Jews now had the opportunity to impart to the rest of the world their own great spiritual treasures, their profound teachings of social justice and of Jewish ethics for society, the individual, and the family. Thus the Jew managed to reach the goal after which he had striven for generations; that is, to disseminate throughout the world the great ideals proclaimed by the prophets and the spiritual values set forth by Jewish sages and their successors.

However, with the return of the Jewish people to Israel as a Jewish state in 1948, the Jews there proclaimed Hebrew as their official language and it is again a living tongue, spoken by all inhabitants of the land.

7. Bible Criticism

The aim of Bible criticism is twofold, first to establish who were the actual authors of each of the books that comprise the Holy Scriptures, and, secondly, to determine the exact dates when these works were composed.

These two questions had long occupied many brilliant minds, both Jewish and non-Jewish. But before we go into greater detail about Bible criticism, let us first examine the opinions of those scholars who were concerned with the dates and authorship of the various books of the Bible in ancient times.

We will begin with the era of the Talmud, which was closest to that of the Bible. The Tannaim, and the Amoraim, their followers, had raised a number of questions about certain parts of the Pentateuch, the Prophets, and the other parts of the Holy Scriptures. They all based their conclusions upon the belief that the Pentateuch, the Five Books of Moses, had been written by Moses himself, except the last eight lines which were added by Joshua. The Jewish sages have left us also their ideas concerning the authorship of the other books of the Bible. So, according to them, Joshua was the author of the book which is know by his name. Samuel was held responsible for the book named after him, as well as for the Book of Judges and the Book of Ruth. King David produced the Book of Psalms with the assistance of ten elders. Jeremiah was thought to be the author not only of the Book of Jeremiah, but also of the First and Second Books of Kings and the Book of Lamentations. King Hezekiah and his group of disciples had fathered the Book of Isaiah, Proverbs, Song of Songs, and Ecclesiastes. The prophets Haggai, Zechariah, and Malachi had written the Book of Ezekiel, the messages of the twelve minor prophets, the books of Daniel and Esther. Ezra was deemed the author of the book known by his name and also of the Book of Chronicles up to Chapter 36; the rest was attributed to Nehemiah (Talmud, Baba Bathra 15). We are also told that the last verses of the Book of Joshua which dealt with his death were appended by Eleazar and Pinhas, and that Gad the Seer and Nathan the Prophet performed a similar task for the Book of Samuel.

The Amoraim disagreed among themselves concerning the authorship of the Book of Job. One of them went so far as to say that there had actually never been such a person as Job and that the entire book was simply an allegory. With regard to the time of the prophets, some of the Amoraim felt that Hosea had lived before Isaiah, Amos, and Micah. Haggai, Zechariah, and Malachi, they said, were the last of the prophets. Isaiah preceded Jeremiah and Ezekiel. As to the Sacred Writings (Ketubim), the sages of the Talmud aligned them in chronological order as follows: Ruth, Psalms, Job, Proverbs, Ecclesiastes, Song of Songs, Lamentations, Daniel, Esther, Ezra, Nehemiah, and Chronicles.

We see now that Bible criticism existed in some form even at the time the Talmud came into being. But it was not a Bible criticism that sought to detract from the sacred nature of the Holy Scriptures.

In many places in the Talmud and in Midrashic literature we find quotations of verses from the Bible reading quite differently from our own standard text. Sometimes the difference is minor; at other times, however, the discrepancy is so great that the entire meaning of the verse is changed. All this is quite readily understandable when we consider that the Bible is thousands of years old. It would be impossible to expect that after the lapse of so many years, every word of the text would be handed down exactly as the authors had originally written it. For this reason we must accept the assumption put forth by modern Bible criticism that, in the course of the generations, some changes, though minor in nature, have crept into the original Bible text.

In the ninth century there arose among the Jews a new form of Bible criticism. It was first proposed by a heretic, Hiwi Albalki, who wrote a book about the Bible in which he raised two hundred questions. This book itself has been lost, but some Jewish authors have quoted portions of it in which he challenges the divine origin of the Bible. In the eleventh century, Isaac ibn Yashush and Moshe ibn Gikatilla, two Bible commentators, had other questions to ask. Their writings, too, have been lost, but some of their questions and interpretations are quoted by Abraham ibn Ezra, who vehemently opposed their theory that parts of the Pentateuch had been written down only at the time of King Jehoshaphat (ninth century B.C.), declaring that his book deserved to be burned. However, he himself regarded the Bible from a critical point of view, for his works contain remarks about additions which he thought were made to the Pentateuch and to the Prophets at some date much later than their original writing.

Another early Bible critic was Baruch Spinoza (1632-1677). He believed that the first eleven books of the Bible, up to the Second Book of Kings, had been written by one person, presumably Ezra the Scribe. In the year 1712 another Jewish scholar, Richard Simon, came to the conclusion that Ezra the Scribe, rather than Moses, had been the author of the Pentateuch.

Bible criticism, however, took a new turn when certain scholars, Jewish and non-Jewish, in the next three centuries made their own investigations and came to radical conclusions. Jacques Astruque, in a book published in Paris in 1753, stated his theory that the Pentateuch had been compiled from two separate ancient sources. In one of these works the appellation used for God was "Yahveh" (read Adonai), while the second employed the term "Elohim." In some instances in the Bible we find both names for God used simultaneously as "Adonai Elohim" (the Lord God), but in most cases the two titles are employed independently of each other. Astruque designated one of these sources as the "Yahvist Code" (Y) and the other as the "Elohist" (E).

On the basis of this theory, other scholars divided the "Y" group into two parts, each of which was presumably written at a different time. The second part, they said, dated to the time when the priests ruled in Israel, and therefore they designated the second half of the "Y" group by the initial "P," (meaning Priestly Code). Now the field was thrown wide open for every one who desired to add his own "critical" views on the Bible. One such scholar made still another classification, "D," denoting Deuteronomy, which was considered by him as an entirely separate work, written at a period of time quite different from that of the other Biblical works. Still another scientist discovered a new source which he labeled as "C." To this was added another source called "H," and so on ad infinitum.

The new science of Bible criticism was now taken over by many German scholars such as Wellhausen, Franz Delitsch, Dillman, Neldecke, Covach, Kittel, Haupt, and others. The aim of these men was to prove that, actually, the Jewish people had not been the original authors of the Bible, so that the ideals of monotheism, Sabbath observance, and many of the beautiful prayers and psalms found in the Scriptures had not been originally Jewish at all. These scholars claimed that monotheism originated not with Abraham, of whom the Bible says that he "called in the Name of the Lord," but with an Egyptian king, the Pharaoh Achenaton, who had promulgated the cult of only one God, namely Ammon-Ra, the Sun God, and none other beside him. How these scholars could reconcile the idolatrous worship of the Sun God with the monotheistic belief in the God of Israel, of whom we are explicitly told that He is the creator of the sun, is difficult to understand. Those Bible critics also did not take into account the fact that the whole cult of the Sun God had so little meaning even for the Egyptians that it disappeared entirely after the death of Achenaton and the new creed lasted only some sixteen or seventeen years. Is it not a more plausible theory that this Pharaoh, whom history describes as an intelligent person, might have acquired some of his own ideas on religion from the Hebrews who dwelt in Goshen; that those Hebrews might have taught him something about a chief God who is supreme over all things, and on this basis, the Pharaoh might have decided that this chief God should be Ammon-Ra? At any rate, the Bible critics do not seem to realize that the worship of a Sun God was widespread at that time, not only in Egypt, but also in many other lands, and that this was precisely what the Torah meant when it voiced the explicit prohibition against the worship of heavenly bodies.

The other great idea for which some Bible critics were against giving credit to the Jews was that the day of rest, the day of Sabbath, was of Jewish origin. They found in the ancient chronicles of the Babylonians that this culture had dedicated a specific day to their rulers, and that this day was called Shabbattu. But this was not a day of rest at all, for the rulers of Babylonia never worked. It was solely a day set aside for the worship of certain gods, particularly Baal.

The Bible critics have also attempted to demonstrate that the beautiful prayers and psalms which the genius of Judaism had created actually stem from heathen ritual. They have sought to find some similarity between the prayers of the pagans to the Sun God, and Psalm 104, that sublime song of David, which begins with the words, "Bless the Lord, O my soul." Actually, the similarity between these two is no greater than between a man and a monkey.

All these spurious theories have been disproved to a great extent by the findings of Biblical archaeology. Students of this science have made important discoveries which have served to confirm the accuracy of the many facts set forth in the Bible.

On the whole, Bible criticism has not shaken the Jew's own attitude of profound respect for the Scriptures. To the people of Israel the Bible still remains, and has ever been, the great work that influenced the entire life of the nation. Even if a thousand Bible critics should attempt to dissect the Bible in order to discredit it, the Jews will never cease to treasure it as "the Law of Moses." To the Jewish people, the words of the prophets will always be as fresh and as new as they were long ago when they were first uttered, and the moving prayers of King David and the wise sayings of Solomon will forever be Israel's source of wisdom and sanctity.

The Bible is the greatest work ever to have been created by the Jewish people. It has determined not only the fate of the people of Israel itself, but also the course of history of many other nations. It is in this light, the light shed by the Holy Scriptures, that Judaism shall always view the events of history, present, past, and future.

8. Biblical Archaeology

Biblical archaeology is still a very young science. It began only at the start of the nineteenth century. In former days, those who desired to delve into the Bible had no other proof of the truth of the Biblical accounts than the words of the Bible itself. But early in the nineteenth century, when excavations were first made at those sites mentioned in the Scriptures, there was discovered a veritable treasure trove of historical objects, inscriptions, writings, potsherds, and other relics which verified that what is told in the Bible is true and accurate. Other excavations helped explain and interpret correctly many statements in the Bible which had not been understood before.

Of course it was not so easy to evaluate properly the findings of archaeologists. Before that could be done, the scientists first had to be able to interpret the ancient writings such as, for example, the hieroglyphics and cuneiform inscriptions left by the ancient Persians, Assyrians, and Babylonians. Only after these were properly understood could we find a wealth of historical materials, the existence of which we had never even suspected before. The archaeological work which is now done at many universities and other institutions of higher learning took great strides forward, particularly in 1930 when the key was discovered to the script of the Hittites, the nation so often mentioned in the Bible. This excavation work still goes on today in the countries around Palestine and, above all, in Palestine itself. It is only now that we are beginning to get some knowledge of the life of the ancient Philistines and Canaanites. The paintings on the earthenware fragments which are being excavated help us to determine when they were made, and various seals and inscriptions aid us in reconstructing the epochs in which the various kings of the Bible reigned. For instance, the discovery of a coin which was called a *pim* helped clarify the meaning of Verse 21 of Chapter 13 in I Samuel, which reads, ". . . and the price of the filing was a *pim* for the mattocks. . . ." It was found that the value of this coin had been about two-thirds of a shekel. In the same manner, excavations helped determine the exact date of the accession of King Jehu, namely, the year 842 before the Christian era. This also made it possible to establish all the dates mentioned in the First and Second Books of Kings regarding the kings of Israel and Judah, even down to one hundred years prior to the year 842 B.C.

The findings of archaeology shed much light on the time when the land of Canaan was first occupied by the children of Israel. Excavations dating back to the fourteenth century before the birth of Jesus include writings telling of the "Habiru" who had come from the wilderness and occupied large stretches of the land. This happened during the days of Joshua. The Habiru are none other than the ancient Hebrews, as the Jews were called in those days. Inscriptions originating from one hundred years subsequent to that date no longer speak of the "Habiru" but only of the "Israelites." This appellation for the Jewish people was found for the first time on a monument of the Pharaoh Mernephta. In the inscription it is told that this Pharaoh had annihilated the "invader Israel of Canaan." This shows that Egypt at that time had aided Canaan in its fight against the children of Israel. The excavations also indicate that the original ancient name for Jerusalem had been "Urushalaim," that the Philistines had originally come to Canaan only after the downfall of the Cretan civilization, and that the children of Israel had regarded them as strangers and therefore fought them much more actively than they had fought against any of the other nations that had dwelt in Canaan much longer.

As we have already stated, the findings of archaeology have special significance in determining the times of the kings of Judah and Israel. It is worth mentioning here, too, that the excavations proved conclusively that the "Wailing Wall" was indeed a part of the ancient Temple and had been built at the time specified in the Scriptural account. In the same manner, archaeology confirmed the accuracy of the description given in the First Book of Kings, 10: 26-29, of the stables where King Solomon kept his horses. Archaeology also gave evidence concerning the actual existence of the "Shishak King of Egypt," who, as we are told in the First Book of Kings, 14:25-28, attacked the kingdom of Judah during the days of Rehoboam and carried off the treasures of both king and temple. In like manner, much material was found with reference to kings Omri and Ahab (I Kings, 16:23-28). Other excavations confirmed the truth of the story of Hezekiah as given in Chapters 36, 37, and 38 of the Book of Isaiah. Much historical material was also found concerning King Manasseh and his fight against Egypt.

Archaeology has helped make certain laws of the Torah more understandable. It was found that many other nations had similar laws, which, however, had much more stringent and cruel provisions against transgressors than the Law of Moses. Such legislation was found in the records of the Hittites, Babylonians (the Code of Hammurabi), and many others. Archaeologists have uncovered Egyptian statues of those days, and others such as Baal and the goddess Astarte whom the Bible calls Ashtaroth.

In general, archaeology has done much to confirm and explain a great many things in the Bible. The simple grandeur of the Bible becomes truly obvious only when we are in a position to compare it with the boastful writings left by some of the kings of other nations. Particularly when we examine other ancient codes, we can see how liberal Jewish law has been with regard to theft, robbery, and even murder, as opposed to the cruel punishments provided for such crimes by the laws of the other nations that populated Asia Minor at the time.

The greatest achievement of Biblical archaeology, however, is that it has been largely able to refute the arguments of the Bible critics and to demonstrate the truth and accuracy of the dates and facts given in the twenty-four holy books of the Bible.

9. The Jewish Chronology

The establishment of a chronology, a system of reckoning time according to a definite calendar, differs in Judaism from systems employed by non-Jews, because the Jews reckon time from the beginning of Creation. Jewish chronology, however, has its difficulties too. There are a great many questions concerning its accuracy. The fact of the matter is that the historians of the ancient world did not concern themselves overmuch with recording the exact dates of events. This is common to all the historians and chroniclers of those days. They attached importance only to events and the persons who figured in them. Dates as such meant little to them. Jewish chroniclers suffered from the same weakness and therefore the annals of Jewish history contain many dates which are not entirely accurate. Even the sages of the Talmudic era raised questions concerning the accuracy of certain dates. For instance, in one place in the Bible, we are told that the Jews had spent four hundred years as slaves in Egypt and in another place it is said to be four hundred thirty years. In like manner, there are discrepancies with regard to the days given for the eras of the judges, of the kings of Judah and Israel, and others. According to some sources, the Babylonian exile lasted seventy years, but some others maintain it was only fifty-two. Despite all these problems and uncertainties, Jewish chronology as such is still recognized among the Jews. True, we may have our doubts as to whether the present Jewish chronology as we know it today really does go back to Creation, but, at any rate, it is a continuous calendar.

Hence, according to Jewish chronology, Adam, the first man, was born immediately after Creation. Seth was born in the year 130, Enos in 235, Cainon in 325, Mahalaleel in 395, Jared in 460, Enoch in 622, Methuselah in 687, Lamech in 874, Noah in 1056, Shem in 1558. The Great Deluge took place in the year 1656 after Creation. Abraham was born in the year 1948 after Creation, Isaac in 2048, and Jacob in 2108. Jacob and his children went to Egypt in the year 2238. Moses was born in 2268. The Exodus from Egypt occurred in 2448, and the Law was given to the children of Israel on Mount Sinai in the same year. Joshua led the Jewish people into the Holy Land in 2489. The era of the judges extended from 2503 to the days of Eli the Priest (2831), and the Prophet Samuel was born in 2871.

The period of the kings began with the accession of Saul in 2882 and continued to the year 3338 through the reign of King Zedekiah. In between these dates, King David was proclaimed ruler in Jerusalem in the year 2892. Rehoboam, the first of the following kings of Judah, and Jeroboam, the first king of Israel, both ascended their thrones in 2964. The ten tribes of Israel were driven out of the land by Shelmaneser in the year 3205. The kingdom of Judah survived until the days of Nebuzaradan, who destroyed the First Temple in 3338.

The Second Temple was completed in the year 3408. Ezra the Scribe returned to Jerusalem in 3413. The era of the Tannaim begins with Simon the Just in the year 3442, Rabbi Johanan ben Zakkai was born in 3713, and Hillel and Shammai were both born in 3728. The Second Temple was destroyed in the year 3829 (according to the Christian calendar, on Sunday, August 5, of the year 69 after the birth of Christ).

The uprising of Bar Kochba against the Romans took place in the year 3893 (or 133 A.D.). Rabbi Judah the Prince finished the compilation of the Mishna in 3895 (or 135 A.D.), and the Talmud was completed in 4260 (or 500 A.D.).

We know, too, that the era of the Gaonim ended in the year 4798 (1038 A.D.). Rashi, the great commentator of the Bible, died in 4865 (or 1105 A.D.). Maimonides died in 4967 (1204) and the Spanish Inquisition expelled the Jews from Spain in the year 5252 after Creation which is 1492 A.D.

This, in brief, is a summary of Jewish chronology according to a calendar reckoned in terms of "years after the Creation of the World."

There were certain periods when the Jews employed another method of reckoning time, but this never lasted long. At any rate, no chronology ever permanently replaced the one based upon the creation of the world. At one time the Jews, in imitation of the custom of neighboring nations, based their calendar upon the date when Seleucus of Syria had won a decisive victory in the Orient. This happened in the year 4348 after Creation, forty years after the erection of the Second Temple and six years after the reign of Alexander the Great who had defeated Darius (312 B.C.). But the method of figuring dates in terms of years since the victory of Seleucus was employed by the Jews only in the drawing up of contracts and promissory notes.

The first effort at establishing an orderly chronology dating back to Creation is found in the treatise *Seder Olam Rabbah* (*The Great Order of the World*) by Rabbi Josi ben Chalaphtah. There we are told that a period of three hundred years elapsed between the days of Joshua and the era of Jephthah; that the First Temple stood for 410 years and the Second for 420. Palestine was under Persian domination for thirty-four years, under Greek rule for 180 and under the Hasmonean dynasty for 103. The dynasty of Herod and his family endured for another 103 years. Later there was created a second work on Jewish chronology, entitled *Seder Olam Zuta,* which was of minor value. Subsequently, similar treatises came into being, each continuing the listing of dates for important historical events down to the date of the writing of that particular work.

In accordance with Jewish chronology we shall divide our entire study of the development of Jewish thought into three main eras as follows:

1. *The Biblical Era*—from Abraham to the days of Ezra the Scribe (a period of almost 1500 years).

2. *The Talmudic Era*—from Simon the Just to the end of the Gaonic period (almost 1400 years).

3. *The Era of the Philosophers*—from the time of Saadia Gaon (about 950 A.D.) down to the present day (circa 1000 years). This era we shall divide into two parts; namely, the epoch preceding the expulsion of the Jews from Spain, and that period which extends from 1492 until the present.

The Biblical Era

1. The Patriarchs: Abraham, Isaac, and Jacob

The Forefathers of the Jewish People: Abraham, Fighter for Truth and Right—Isaac, Who Allowed Himself to Be Led to Slaughter Because He Believed It to Be God's Will—Jacob's Twelve Sons from Whom the Tribes of Israel Are Descended—The Matriarchs of the Jewish People.

Let us examine first the role of Abraham in Jewish history. He was called "Father Abraham," for he was truly the father of the Jewish people, and, to some extent, the father of much of civilized mankind as well. Abraham was the first to fight idolatry, and to proclaim the truth concerning the existence of One God, the Creator of Heaven and Earth.

Jewish legend has it that Abraham came to know in his very early youth that the idols had none of the divine qualities his contemporaries ascribed to them. At a very early age, Abraham began the fight against all those who continued to worship figures of clay, stone, and wood.

According to a legend, Terah, the father of Abraham, had a shop in which he sold idols. One day Terah left his young son alone in the store. A customer came in and desired to buy an idol. Abraham asked him, "How old art thou?" Upon being told that the customer was sixty years of age, the boy burst into laughter and asked, "How can it be that a man sixty years old should bow down to an idol which was carved only today and hence is not yet one day old?" The customer, unable to answer the boy's question satisfactorily, left the store in embarrassment without making a purchase.

The next person to enter the store was a woman with a bowl of flour which she wanted to offer up as a sacrifice to the idols. Abraham accepted the flour from her, saying that he would perform the rite in her stead, and sent her on her way. After she left, Abraham took a hammer and shattered all the idols with the exception of the largest of the group, into whose hands he then placed the tool of destruction. When Terah returned and saw all his merchandise in ruins he asked Abraham what happened. Abraham explained to him that a woman had brought in an offering of flour over which all the idols had promptly proceeded to fight. Finally the largest idol in the group attacked and destroyed all the others and took the offering for himself. Terah, furious, replied, "Why dost thou make sport of me? The large idol is only a figure of clay. How, then, could he have destroyed the others?"

Abraham quietly asked, "Father, if this be so, why dost thou bow to him?"

However the same source tells also that it took Abraham a good many years before he understood the true nature of the God of Heaven. At first he thought that the sun was God, since it gave life to every living thing on earth. But when the sun set and he beheld the soft light of the moon and the stars, he asked himself whether those heavenly bodies, too, could possibly be endowed with divine qualities. Gradually he came to the conclusion that there must be some power greater than either the sun or the moon, a power who created both, a God, One God. And it was this concept of *One God* which Abraham handed down to his children who, in turn, passed it on to their descendants.

Hence Abraham was the person who laid the foundations for the Jewish concept of God, of "the God Most High, the Creator of Heaven and Earth." Abraham did not conceal his views. He made them known to all, so that all men, including the kings with whom he was engaged in warfare, knew that Abraham believed in only one God. And when these kings finally made peace with him, they did so in the Name of his God.

Abraham was also endowed with the gift of prophecy. We are told in the Bible that God had told Abimelech, "Now therefore restore the man's wife, for he is a prophet, and he shall pray for thee." The Bible tells us further that Abraham had many of the unique qualities that distinguish a real prophet from ordinary men. He was a fighter for truth, who was not afraid at any time to preach the truth about God as he saw it, and therefore he regarded it as his principal task to proclaim the Name of the One God, and he courageously fought against every form of idolatry.

Let it be remembered that in those days the entire world was pagan. And it was in the face of the entire heathen world that Abraham, inspired by the truth, took it upon himself to travel from place to place to declare the Name of the Lord, and erect altars to His honor and offer sacrifices to Him.

Abraham shared with other prophets a strong sense of justice. The Bible records that God told Abraham of His intention to destroy the city of Sodom because of the sinful ways of its inhabitants. Abraham, like a true prophet, begged God not to do this. Abraham prayed for the lives of men who were total strangers to him, because God could not "slay the righteous with the wicked . . . shall not the Judge of all the earth do justly?" Thereupon the Lord promised Abraham that, even if there would be only fifty righteous men in all of Sodom, He would spare the entire city because of them. Then Abraham prayerfully asked, "Peradventure there shall lack five of the fifty righteous; wilt Thou destroy all the city for lack of five?" And God promised that He would not destroy Sodom even if only forty-five righteous men would be found there. But Abraham, still not satisfied, asked the Lord whether He would not spare the city even if there were only forty righteous men in all of Sodom, or only thirty, or even only twenty. Finally, he asked God whether

He would also relent even if Sodom could produce only ten righteous men, and the Lord gave His word that He "would not destroy it for the ten's sake." Abraham would probably have gone on pleading with God, but at that point, we are told, the Lord terminated His meeting with Abraham.

According to the Pentateuch, Abraham dwelt in the Negev, the southern part of Palestine, which was then a very fertile territory. Abraham had settled there when he left Ur of the Chaldees, the land of his birth, to go to the Promised Land. Later on, after he had sojourned in Egypt for some time because of the famine of Canaan, he returned to the Negev once more and remained there.

And it was in the Negev that Abraham saw his visions. It was there, according to the Bible, that the Lord revealed Himself to him and told him of the future of his descendants. There, the Bible tells us, the Lord reassured Abraham several times that He would give all the land "from the river of Egypt unto the great river, the river Euphrates" to his children as their possession and drive away all the other nations from that land which would become the inheritance, forever, of the seed of Abraham.

These Divine promises came to be the "Magna Charta" that guaranteed to the people of Israel the possession of the land of Canaan. According to Jewish tradition, God Himself had promised the land to the Jews and it was on the basis of this promise that Moses led the people of Israel out of Egypt through the wilderness so that they might come to the land of Canaan and occupy it. Finally, after the death of Moses, Joshua, the son of Nun, Moses' disciple and spiritual heir, led the Jewish people into the land, occupied it, and divided it among the tribes in accordance with a prearranged plan.

When the Bible discusses Abraham's encounters with God, it always says, "And the Lord said unto Abram," or "God revealed Himself to Abram and said. . . ." It is only in one instance that the phrase "in a vision" is added and we are told that "the word of the Lord came unto Abram *in a vision.*" (Gen. 15:1) In another instance we are told that the Lord revealed himself to Abram *in a dream at night.* According to Maimonides and other Jewish Bible commentators all these visions which Abraham experienced took one or two forms. Some of them came to him in the nature of dreams as he slept, while others occurred during the day, with Abraham transposed into a dream-like trance for their duration. Such visions were rare phenomena which only a few mortals were privileged to experience.

Abraham's discovery that there is only One God, who reigns supreme over all the world and who created both heaven and earth would have remained unknown if he had not communicated it at least to the members of his own clan. It is possible that a man such as Abraham of Ur of the Chaldees could have held views far in advance of his time and yet it might well have been that his own children might not have walked in his footsteps. It could quite conceivably have come to pass that his children would have been so deeply immersed in idolatry that Abraham's ideas of a higher type of God might have been entirely forgotten.

It is for this reason, apparently, that, at the very outset of the history of the Jewish people, it had been predetermined that Abraham, the first Jew, should have a son of the caliber of Isaac, who would walk in his father's footsteps and be known to future generations as "Father Isaac." And Isaac, in turn, was to bring forth a son such as Jacob, who, also known as "Father Jacob," would sire twelve sons whose descendants would be the prime ancestors of the twelve tribes of Israel.

Once Abraham had seen the revelation of the Lord, he did not hesitate to proclaim it, and wherever he went, "he called the Name of the Lord." Hence even Melchizedek, the king of Salem, knew that he had to salute Abraham in a manner different from that he would use to greet others, and that he would have to bless him in the Name of the Lord, the God of Abraham, the Creator of Heaven and Earth. And so Melchizedek said to Abraham when they met, "Blessed be Abraham of God Most High, Maker of heaven and earth." Abraham had also proclaimed his discovery of the One God to all the other kings of his generation.

Jacob was a fitting spiritual heir of his grandfather Abraham. When Jacob came to understand his own great mission in the world, his name was changed to "Israel" from which the Jewish people, in turn, derived the name of "the children of Israel," who were to occupy the land promised to Abraham to be called the Land of Israel.

There is a wealth of drama in the story of Jacob's life. First we are told of his struggle with his brother Esau for the paternal blessing of Isaac. Then we read of the desperate battle of wits with Laban. After Jacob had served Laban for seven years with the understanding that, at the end of this term, he would be given Laban's daughter Rachel as a wife in payment for his services, Laban deceived him and married him to Leah, Rachel's elder sister. Thus Laban obtained the free services of Jacob for another seven years, because Jacob loved Rachel and wanted to marry her no matter what the cost to him would be.

The third dramatic episode in the life of Jacob began when his sons sold Joseph, his favorite, into slavery. Jacob suffered years of anguish which ended only when Jacob discovered that Joseph was still alive and had become the governor over all of Egypt. The climax came when the aged father was reunited with the son whom he had given up hope of seeing among the living.

This story is indicative of the fate of the generations which were to follow Jacob, generations that had to wage an eternal struggle through which they have passed undefeated. Therefore the name of the people descended from Jacob has been "Israel" since that time ("because he had struggled with both God and men"). Herein lies the secret of Israel's eternity.

No less important were the matriarchs of the Jewish people, Sarah, Rebecca, Rachel, and Leah. They were the faithful companions of Israel's patriarchs and, together with their masters, they built and shaped the destinies of the people which was to be descended from them.

Thus the chain of Israel's founders extends through the early history of Judaism. The most important link of that chain, perhaps, is Moses, the great leader who brought the tribes of Israel out of Egypt, and who gave them the Ten Commandments, which came to be the basic Law of the world, and the Torah, which became the foundation of Western civilization as we know it today. Standing loyally at the side of Moses was his brother Aaron, the first priest in Israel. Thereafter came Joshua, the son of Nun and the disciple of Moses, who completed the task of leading the Jewish people into Canaan and divided the land among the twelve tribes. The final link in the chain of the founders of Judaism is Samuel, who united the twelve tribes into one nation, and, much against his own will, gave them a king so that the unity of Israel might be achieved and preserved.

After the patriarchs we come now to Moses, the first leader of the Jewish people.

2. Moses and Aaron

The Significance of Moses—Moses Proclaims the Name of the God of Israel Throughout the World and Turns the Slave Tribes into One Nation—The Ten Commandments and the Torah Which Moses Gave to Israel—Aaron, the Symbol of Spiritual Leadership.

"Who was Moses?" This is a question which has concerned the great minds in the world for centuries, and which has never ceased to be of profound interest to teachers and students of history and religion.

The Talmud and Midrashic literature contain much material about Moses, the circumstances of his birth, his life and his death, but all this is legendary in nature and not sufficiently documented to be of much help in reconstructing his personality. Nor can we place much more reliance on the scholars who have set forth a variety of their own thoughts and theories on the subject. There are a great many books which make claims about Moses that have no foundation at all. Even the Egyptologists who employ somewhat more scientific methods are groping in the dark with regard to the personality of Moses. All they know is that, in addition to the legendary ten dynasties that ruled Egypt until the year 2500 B.C., there were another seven ruling houses which reigned until the year 1578 B.C. and that epoch in the history of Egypt is referred to as the Middle Kingdom of Egypt. According to the Egyptologists, it was at that time that alien tribes from Asiatic countries came into Egypt and conquered the land. These invaders were called the "Hyksos." In those days there arose a king during whose reign Joseph came into Egypt. After the death of Joseph the Egyptians revolted against the invaders, and the rebellion ended in the defeat of the foreigners. It was then that there came a new king "who had not known Joseph," Ramses II, the founder of Egypt's nineteenth dynasty, who lived at about 1200 B.C. and it was during his reign that the cities of Pithom and Ramses were built and Moses was born and grew up.

However, all this is of little importance to our own study of Moses as a leader of the children of Israel. Therefore we shall concern ourselves solely with Moses' personality and the influence he exerted upon the Jewish people.

Moses was one of those few great personalities in the history of mankind who was born not only to lead a nation, but actually to create the nation he was to lead. Moses did not want merely to create an ordinary nation: it was his desire to bring into being a "chosen nation," a "holy people" to fight for the dissemination of the concept of the belief in One God.

It is true that Abraham was the first man to declare that there was only

One God who rules over all things, but he had not been able to spread his beliefs all over the world. He had to content himself with communicating his ideas to his own children, grandchildren, and, later, to the twelve sons of Jacob. Therefore it took other generations (546 years according to Jewish chronology) until the advent of a man of action upon the scene. This man was Moses.

Moses knew that if he really was to disseminate the ideal of monotheism among mankind as a whole, he first had to have a people which would fight for this ideal. Hence he began laying the groundwork to this end while he was still in Egypt. When he first came before the Jews, he spoke to them of the One God, the God of their fathers. The Bible tells us that, at first, the people paid him little heed because "of lack of breath and hard work," but Moses ultimately managed to convey to them the message that God had sent: "I shall take you as a people, to be a God unto you." Soon it became obvious to him that he would make little headway while in Egypt and he therefore asked Pharoah to allow the children of Israel to go out into the wilderness to worship their God there. He knew full well that only in the wilderness would he be able to take these twelve loosely knit tribes and shape them into one people and communicate to them the concept of the One God.

Never in the history of the Jews or in the entire history of mankind has there been a leader such as Moses. In his leadership lies his greatness. History knows of no other leader of whom it can be said that he liberated so great a mass of men, women, and children from bondage and led them out into freedom, as we are told in the Bible and as has been confirmed also by other sources, particularly by recent archaeological findings. Nor can history tell of another teacher like Moses who bequeathed to the world a code of laws like the Ten Commandments (which became the basis of our entire civilization), the precepts concerning the worship of One God, a weekly day of rest, the respect due one's parents, and prohibitions against theft, murder, perjury, and adultery. History has no parallel to Moses the lawgiver, who gave to his own people (and also to the rest of the world) a code of laws with safeguards to protect the poor and defend the rights of labor. Nor has there ever been in history another fighter like Moses who labored without rest to extirpate idolatry and who, at the end of his life, could claim he succeeded in his efforts at least among his own people.

It would seem, therefore, that the traditional theory that Moses was responsible for compiling the Pentateuch from beginning to end is borne out by the fact that only a man so thoroughly imbued with the spirit of God as Moses was could have written a work like the Torah, which still lives today, and which will endure throughout the generations to come, remaining ever new and fresh through the millennia. One can see also the greatness of Moses in the remarkably unvarnished simplicity of style in which the Pentateuch was set down, a style characteristic of those who write for eternity.

Therefore the arguments of the critics of the Bible who separate the Pentateuch into various parts and claim that these parts were written at various times by different authors are not acceptable to the traditional Jew. He believes that anyone with an ear sensitive to the monumental music of the Five Books of Moses cannot doubt that they were composed by a unique mind unmatched either before or after his time, a personality who incorporated into his work the enormous strength of his soul, ensuring his spiritual outpouring of eternal life. In other words, a book such as the Pentateuch is eternal and could only have been set down by a man of divine inspiration such as Moses was.

The Bible also gives us an account of the role of Aaron, the brother of Moses, which began soon after God's revelation to Moses from amidst the burning bush. When God commanded Moses to go to Pharaoh and ask him to let his people go, the Lord told him that, since he was "heavy of speech," a stammerer, he would send with him Aaron, his elder brother, to plead Israel's cause with Pharaoh. It seems that Aaron was not exactly pleased with the subordinate role given him, the elder of the pair, but the fact of the matter was that Aaron was eminently qualified for the task. He was a brilliant orator of distinguished appearance, with his beautiful long beard cascading down over his garments ("Aaron's beard that cometh down upon the collar of his garments"—Ps. 133:2). But Moses said to Aaron that God had intended Aaron to be "thy spokesman unto the people . . . and thou shalt be to him in God's stead" (Exod. 4:16). Thus Aaron complied with the request of Moses and went with him into the presence of the king of Egypt.

In the beginning of the Biblical account of the two brothers, we are told that the Lord spoke to both Moses and Aaron. The Lord said, "I . . . will teach you what ye shall do" (Exod. 4:15). And for every time (or every second instance) that we are told that "the Lord spoke unto Moses," we are also told "and the Lord spoke unto Moses and unto Aaron." Later on, however, we read only that "the Lord spoke unto Moses." At that time Moses already felt within his soul the strength which was to make him a leader of men. (It is quite possible that the very fact that he was indeed "heavy of speech," a stammerer, was an important contributing factor to the remarkable status which he achieved in history, for he rose above his physical handicap to develop his capacities to the fullest possible extent. It has often been demonstrated throughout the history of mankind how men afflicted with serious physical impairment have risen above their handicaps to greatness and glory.)

The drive for achievement, which is often characteristic of the physically handicapped, appears to parallel the phenomenon of compensation which we find in nature, whereby one organ of the body will assume the function of another afflicted part. Thus Moses' stammering may well have helped provide the motivation that helped spur him to his monumental achievements.

In Greek history we find a similar example. One of the greatest orators in the history of Greece was Demosthenes, a stammerer. By unrelenting devotion to the correction of this speech defect, Demosthenes overcame his handicap and rose to great fame as a spellbinding orator.

As we read on in the story of Exodus, we find Aaron involved in the incident of the Golden Calf. When Moses returned from Mount Sinai, he could not restrain his anger, and demanded of Aaron: "What did this people do unto thee, that thou hadst brought a great sin upon them?" Aaron meekly replied: "Let not the anger of my lord wax hot; thou knowest the people, that they are set on evil; so they said unto me: Make us a god which shall go before us; for as for this Moses, the man that brought us up out of the land of Egypt, we know not what is become of him" (Exod. 32:21-23).

From then on, we no longer read of God speaking "to Moses and to Aaron" (Lev. 11:1). In fact, the name of Aaron is mentioned with ever decreasing frequency, and in the end Moses takes unto himself a disciple, young Joshua the son of Nun, who "departed not out of the tent" (Exod. 33:11).

During Israel's wanderings in the wilderness there occurred quite a number of revolts against Moses. According to the Biblical account there was a total of twelve instances of mutiny. The motives in each case were fright or hunger and thirst, and, to some extent, the lust for power. The first four revolts, which occurred at the banks of the Red Sea, in Marah, in the wilderness of Sin, and in Rephidim, were all resolved by peaceful means. The other eight, among them the sin of the Golden Calf, the incident involving the spies, the revolt of Korah and the rest, were much more serious in nature, and severe penalties were imposed upon those who were implicated in each of these revolts.

However, there is some disagreement among the various Bible commentators as to whether the punishments described in the Biblical account were actually imposed upon the people. Some say that these punishments were actually meted out because those involved in the mutinies had indeed deserved them, since they had in fact sinned against the Lord. More liberal minds, however, claim that these punishments were never carried out and that they are mentioned in the Bible to show the grievous penalties the sinners deserved.

At any rate, by the time Moses died the whole strain of idolatry had been stamped out in the camp of Israel, and "they [the people] believed in the Lord, and in His servant Moses" (Exod. 14:31).

Unfortunately, however, as we shall see later, this happy state of affairs did not continue for long after the passing of Moses, whose role as leader of the people of Israel was assumed by Joshua.

3. Joshua, the Son of Nun

Joshua Leads the People of Israel into the Holy Land—His Fight Against the Neighboring Nations—His Struggle Within the Jewish People to Eradicate Idolatry—The Era of the Judges Continues for Several Centuries After His Death.

After the death of Moses, leadership passed into the hands of Joshua, the son of Nun. It was he who actually led the Jewish people into the Promised Land and divided the land among the twelve tribes of Israel.

The generation that wandered through the wilderness knew that "Moses would die and Joshua would lead the Israelites into the land." This was all quite in accordance with the will of Moses himself. Moses deliberately took a child from among the people as his servant, as the Bible has it, ". . . his servant, Joshua, the son of Nun, a boy" (Midrash), and he carefully groomed him to take his place. Moses did not choose a son of the ruling class of his people; he deliberately sought out a child of the masses who would deem it an honor to wait upon Moses. Such a person, Moses was sure, would not depart even one hair's breadth from whatever he, Moses, would command him to do.

In the beginning Joshua lacked confidence in his own ability. He knew that the mere fact that he had been the servant of Moses was not sufficient to qualify him to lead the twelve tribes into the Holy Land, to occupy the country, and to apportion it among them. At that time, the Bible records, the Lord revealed Himself to Joshua and told him that He would be with him even as He had been with Moses. Three times the Lord told Joshua to "be strong and of good courage," and when Joshua thereafter came before the assembled people of Israel, they, too, addressed those same words of encouragement to him.

As Joshua grew in courage and self-confidence, he also won new stature in the eyes of the people of Israel who regarded him as a true heir of Moses. They knew, of course, that Joshua was not Moses, but then they also knew that he would be true to the teachings of Moses, and this assurance was sufficient.

Now, the twelve tribes of Israel came to occupy the Holy Land. To accomplish this they had to engage in almost constant warfare against thirty-one kings. Actually these "kings" were nothing more than the rulers of small city-states, but they had trained armies. The children of Israel now devoted all their energies to the fight against the inhabitants of the land of Canaan. Joshua was a splendid commander of an army of forty thousand men, generals, captains, and lieutenants; war raged everywhere, and the Israelites were Joshua's loyal followers. The people of Israel stood thus united behind Joshua and they said to him: "According as we hearkened unto Moses . . . so will we hearken unto thee" (Josh. 1:17). However, later on when the tribes had to consolidate their position in the land, they fell back gradually into their old habits of idolatry. This was so because, despite all the victories of Joshua and his troops, it had not been possible for them to eliminate from the Promised Land its ancient inhabitants, and thus the people of Israel were exposed to the influence of heathens and idolators.

Even after decades of struggle with the surrounding nations, Israel still dwelt in the midst of enemy tribes. The Book of Judges relates that Israel dwelt among Canaanites, Hittites, Amorites, Perizzites, and Jebusites. Ephraim dwelt among the Canaanites; Manasseh among the Jebusites of Jerusalem; the tribe of Zebulon had not been able to drive out the inhabitants of Nahalel and other places within its territory, nor could the tribe of Asher banish the inhabitants of Acco and of Zidon; the Tribe of Naphtali could not expel the inhabitants of Beth Shemesh; Dan still had to contend with the Amorites, and the tribe of Manasseh still had not succeeded in occupying in their entirety Beth Shean and other cities. The ancient Amalekites were still ensconced in Gaza, Gath, and Ashdod. The territories of the Philistines and Geshur remained intact. The Jewish people suffered much at the hands of the Philistines who constantly waged war against Israel. Thus it came to pass that the tribes of Israel which had dwelt among idolatrous neighbors themselves fell back into their old habit of idolatry and aped the pagan customs of their neighbors. "They took their daughters to be their wives, and they gave their own daughters to their sons, and served their gods" (Judg. 3:6).

Joshua, however, persisted in his struggle against the idolators. He continued to remonstrate with the people of Israel and urged them to return to the God of their fathers. Indeed, while Joshua spoke to them, the Israelites agreed to everything. They faithfully promised that they would serve one God alone, that they would worship only the God of their fathers and would never depart from the precepts of Moses. But as soon as they were out of his presence, they were tempted to idolatry and to the wanton excesses of those in whose midst they dwelt.

Joshua was one of the founders of the Jewish nation. Even as Moses had taken the Jewish people out of the land of Egypt, so it was Joshua who had brought Israel into the country which was to be its new homeland. Joshua took over where Moses had left off, and completed the mission of his master.

Joshua was a true leader. Moses "laid his hands upon him" (Num. 27:23) and thus recognized him as such. This was the manner in which leaders were appointed among the people of Israel in those days. The incumbent leader laid his hands upon his successor-to-be and thus conferred upon him the authority and power of leadership. (The Hebrew word *Smichah,* employed today to denote the ordination of a rabbi, is derived from the term "the laying on of hands." As in the days of the Bible, the power of leadership could be conferred only by another leader, so, today, the authority to be a rabbi in Israel can be vested in a rabbinical student only by an elder who himself has been a practicing member of the rabbinate.)

In addition to this official authorization, Joshua possessed authority as a result of his courageous and tireless efforts to uproot idolatry from among the Jewish people. He was constantly on the alert to quell the wild passions that drove the masses to imitate the orgies and the pagan way of life of their heathen neighbors. He constantly reminded the people of Israel that, if they should come to walk in the ways of their neighbors, the Lord would drive them out of the land and their fate would be tragic.

According to the account given us in the Book of Joshua, throughout his life (he died at the age of one hundred and ten) Joshua managed to keep the people of Israel on the right path, so that the majority of the twelve tribes served the Lord, observed the Passover festival, circumcised their sons and, in general, remained faithful to the God of Moses and of their fathers.

After the death of Joshua we come to the beginnings of the Era of the Prophets.

4. The Era of the Prophets

What Is Prophecy?—What Goes on in the Soul of a Prophet While He is Inspired? —How Many Prophets Were in Israel?—Were There Prophets also in Other Nations?

The exact beginning of prophecy in the history of the Jewish people is shrouded in mystery. Much has been written on the subject, so that the literature is now considerable. Yet there are quite a few questions which have as yet been unanswered. For example, what actually constitutes prophecy and who is a prophet? What goes on in the mind or soul of a person while he is inspired with the ability to prophesy? And how many prophets have there actually been among the Jewish people? Another question that also comes to mind is whether other nations have also had prophets, and, if so, were they of the same spiritual caliber as those of the people of Israel?

The truth is that the Jewish people, over a long period of time, produced quite a number of prophets whose messages helped form the Jewish ideology. As regards the other questions we shall deal with them one by one. Of the four questions mentioned we will try to answer the third one first. How many prophets have there been in Jewish history? For the answer to this question, let us consult our oldest historical source, the Talmud. The Tannaim, who produced the Mishna, the first part of the Talmud, flourished in Israel soon after the Era of the Prophets, so that the first of the Tannaim may very well have personally known one of the latter prophets. The Tannaim were succeeded by the Amoraim who compiled the Gemorah and who came to take over some of the traditions which the prophets had passed on to the Tannaim.

We shall now try to determine how many prophets there have been in Jewish history. The Tannaim left us very definite information on this subject and once we have some idea of the actual number of prophets, we shall more readily be able to see how they attained the gift of prophecy and how they distinguished themselves from their coreligionists.

According to Talmudic tradition, the Jewish people produced forty-eight prophets and seven prophetesses—a total of fifty-five men and women endowed with the ability to prophesy. The prophets were: Abraham, Isaac, Jacob, Moses, Aaron, Joshua, Pinchas, Elkanah (the man of God who appeared to Eli in I Samuel), Eli, Samuel, Gad, Nathan, King David, King Solomon, Iddo, Micaiah the son of Imlah, Obadiah, Achiah the Shilonite, Jehu the son of Chanani, Azariah the son of Oded, Uziel the Levite of the sons of Moniah, Eliezer the son of Dodavahu of Mareshah (Second Chronicles 20:37), Hosea, Amos, Micah the Morashtite, Amos, Elijah, Elisha, Jonah son of Amitai, Isaiah, Joel, Nahum, Habakkuk, Zephaniah, Uriah, Jeremiah, Ezekiel, Daniel (there are some authorities who say that Daniel was not a prophet and put a man named "Shemaiah" in his place on the list), Baruch the son of Naria, Shaziah, Mechasia, Hilkia, Hananel, Shalem, Haggai, Zechariah, Malachi, and Mordecai (of the Book of Esther).

The seven prophetesses were Sarah, Miriam, Deborah, Hannah, Abigail, Huldah, and Queen Esther.

This same roster of prophets is found in the Book of Seder Ha-Olam which is a product of the period of the Tannaim. As to the question why Ezra and Nehemiah do not appear in this list, it is stated that Ezra and Nehemiah, as well as Malachi are simply not regarded as prophets. It is stated also that the Jewish people actually had well over two hundred prophets, but that the only ones recorded as such are those whose messages have had a definite bearing upon subsequent generations.

Of course not all the prophets were of the same mental and spiritual caliber, so that their messages varied in content and significance.

If we go through the books of the Bible we shall see ten different terms employed to designate those men and women who had the divine inspiration of prophecy. The prophets are called "Tzir" (ambassador), "Ne-eman" (faithful), "Eved" (servant), "Shaliach" (messenger), "Chozeh" (visionary), "Roeh" (seer), "Tzofeh" (explorer or scout), "Malach" (angel), "Navi" (prophet) and "Ish Elohim" (man of God). All these words are meant to be employed interchangeably as synonyms for one and the same type of prophet, but denote various stages and degrees in the development of prophecy in the history of Israel.

If we go back to the very beginning of Jewish history, we find that our patriarch Abraham is called "Navi" (prophet). When Abimelech, the King of Gerar, attempted to kidnap Sarah, we are told that the Lord spoke to Abimelech in a dream, "Now therefore restore the man's wife; for he is a prophet, and he shall pray for thee, and thou shalt live" (Gen. 20:7). However, although Abraham is called a prophet, when the Jews speak of Abraham today, they do not refer to him as "Abraham the prophet" but as "Abraham our father"; Moses, too, is called a "prophet" in the Bible ("And there has not arisen a prophet since in Israel like unto Moses" is one of the concluding sentences of the Pentateuch), yet Moses has gone down in Jewish history not as "Moses the prophet," but as "Moses the teacher." This is so because Abraham and Moses were more than prophets. They were the founders of the Jewish faith.

Let us now consider how prophecy evolved in the history of Israel. A brief explanation in the Bible may help shed some light on the subject.

It is told in the First Book of Samuel, 9:3 that Saul, when he was still the humble son of Kish the farmer, went to look for his father's asses. "Before-time in Israel, when a man went to inquire of God, thus he said, 'Come and let us go to the *seer'*; for he that is now called a *prophet* was beforetime called a *seer"* (I Sam. 9:9). And then we are told that Saul and his young servant asked of the maidens who had come to the well to draw water, "Is the seer here?" (I Sam. 9:11).

This change of designation from "seer" to "prophet" was not a matter of mere substitution of words. It marked the beginning of a new stage in the evolution of prophecy. A "seer" was simply a man who "beholds," one who can forsee events before they actually occur, but a "prophet" is one who was sent by the Lord to speak words of rebuke to the rest of the nation. In the same manner, every other stage in the development of prophecy is signified to us by the fact that the designation appended *the name of that particular prophet* is different from the ones given to all the others.

We also have in the First Book of Samuel a detailed description of how a prophet (navi) would speak to his people and how such a prophet would behave.

First of all we see that the prophets were divided into groups. Such groups were called "Lehakat Neviim" or "Hevel Neviim" (group of proph-ets), or "B'nai Neviim" (sons of prophets). The class of prophets referred to as "Lehakat Niviim" was comprised of prophets *all of equal rank* while the "Hevel Neviim" were a group of fledgling prophets rallying round an older prophet whose disciples they were. The "B'nai Niviim" (sons of prophets, were those who were still apprentices, who had to go through a period of training before they could aspire to any title of "prophet" at all.

The Bible also tells us of the methods the prophets employed in impart-ing their messages to the people. They played musical instruments such as harps, drums, pipes, and flutes in order to bring themselves to the proper emotional pitch necessary for receiving and communicating words of inspira-tion before actually proceeding to the task at hand. We read in I Samuel 10:5-6: "After that thou shalt come to the hill of God, where is the garrison of the Philistines; and it shall come to pass, when thou art come thither to the city, that thou shalt meet a *band of prophets* coming down from the high place with a psaltery, and a timbrel, and a pipe, and a harp, before them; and they will be prophesying. And the spirit of the Lord will come mightily upon thee, and thou shalt prophesy with them, and *shalt be turned into an-other man."* The account is continued in verses 9-12 of the same chapter: "And it was so, that when he had turned his back to go from Samuel, God gave him another heart; and all those signs came to pass that day; And when they came thither to the hill, behold, a band of prophets [Hevel Neviim] met him; and the spirit of God came mightily upon him, and he prophesied among them. And it came to pass, when all that knew him beforetime saw that, behold, he prophesied with the prophets, then the people said one to another: 'What is this that is come unto the son of Kish? Is Saul also among the prophets?' "

We also find reference to the use of musical instruments by prophets in II Kings, 3:15, where Elisha says, " 'But now bring me a minstrel.' And it came to pass, when the minstrel played, that the hand of the Lord came upon him."

Hence we are told that when a prophet began to speak in the name of the Lord, he was indeed "turned into another man," as Samuel put it to King Saul. It was as if the man so inspired became part of another world as he spoke. It is said of King Saul that even later on in his life, when he already knew that his people vastly preferred David to him, *the spirit of the Lord came upon him* when he went to Naioth and there came upon a "Lehakat Neviim" (a company of prophets) who prophesied, with Samuel standing at their head. Then Saul stripped off his clothes, and "he also prophesied before Samuel, and lay down naked all day and all that night. Wherefore they say, 'Is Saul also among the prophets?' " (I Sam. 19:20-24).

Thus we know that men who were inspired "by the spirit of the Lord" were seized by such exaltation and ecstasy that they would throw off their clothes as if they were restraints on their spirits, and prophesy aloud all through the day or night, without being disturbed by any physical needs. In such a state, the human mind is freed entirely from the shackles of all things physical and the body becomes subject to the spirit.

Now the question arises whether such a state of physical abandonment is indeed the basic prerequisite for prophesy. Further, was the spiritual makeup of all prophets granted only to those who had attained a particularly high level of inspiration? It would also be important for us to know whether it was common to all prophets at all times, or only at specific periods, and also whether there were varying degrees of such states of ecstasy. This question will be answered later on.

5. The Four Periods of Prophecy

How the Prophets Conveyed Their Messages—The Strange Method Employed by Isaiah, Jeremiah, Ezekiel, and Hosea—Maimonides—The Various Categories of Prophecy.

When we study the manner in which the prophets of Judaism presented their message to the Jewish people, we find that they were enveloped in a mood of great ecstasy and exaltation, in a kind of trance. The man upon whom the spirit of God would come to rest or the person whom God chose to convey His word to Israel (and to mankind) actually was transfigured into a different being while he proclaimed the message of the Lord. Such were the personages whom God would send among men with His message. These were Israel's great prophets.

The prophets employed symbols and signs to convey their lessons. Thus we read that Isaiah went about "naked and barefoot" for a period of three years after Ashdod had been taken by order of Sargon, the King of Assyria. Isaiah adopted this unusual procedure to show the people of Israel that the King of Assyria would also conquer Egypt and Ethiopia and would lead his captives into exile naked and barefoot, as we are told in the twentieth chapter of the Book of Isaiah:

And in the year that Tartan came to Ashdod, when Sargon the king of Assyria sent him, and he fought against Ashdod and took it; at that time the Lord spoke by Isaiah, the son of Amoz, saying, "Go and loose the sackcloth from off thy loins, and put thy shoe from off thy foot." And he did so, walking naked and barefoot.

And the Lord said, "Like as My servant Isaiah hath walked barefoot and naked to be for three years a sign and a wonder upon Egypt and upon Ethiopia, so shall the king of Assyria lead away the captives of Egypt, and the exiles of Ethiopia, young and old, naked and barefoot. . . ."

The prophet Jeremiah also made use of special symbols, as we read at the beginning of the thirteenth chapter of the Book of Jeremiah:

Thus said the Lord unto me: "Go, and get thee a linen girdle, and put it upon thy loins, and put it not in water." So I got a girdle according to the word of the Lord, and put it upon my loins. And the word of the Lord came unto me a second time, saying, "Take the girdle that thou hast gotten, which is upon thy loins, and arise, go to Perath, and hide it there in the cleft of the rock." So I went, and hid it in Perath, as the Lord commanded me. And it came to pass after many days that the Lord said unto me: "Arise, go to Perath, and take the girdle from thence, which I commanded thee to hide there." Then I went to Perath, and digged, and took the girdle from the place where I had hid it; and behold, the girdle was marred, it was profitable for nothing.

Then the word of the Lord came unto me, saying:

"Thus saith the Lord: After this manner will I mar the pride of Judah, and the great pride of Jerusalem, even this evil people that refuse to hear My words. . . ."

In Chapter 18 of the Book of Jeremiah we read that the Lord told Jeremiah to:

"Arise and go down to the potter's house and there I will cause thee to hear My words." Then I went down to the potter's house, and, behold, he was at his work on the wheels. And whensoever the vessel that he made of the clay was marred in the hand of the potter, he made it again another vessel, as seemed good to the potter to make it.

Then the word of the Lord came to me, saying: "O house of Israel, cannot I do with you as this potter? . . . Behold, as the clay in the potter's hand, so are ye in My hand, O House of Israel."

In Chapter 19, Jeremiah employs yet another symbol:

Thus said the Lord, "Go, and get a potter's earthen bottle, and take of the elders of the people, and of the elders of the priests; and go forth unto the valley of the son of Hinnom, which is by the entry of the gate Harsith, and proclaim there the words that I shall tell thee. . . . Hear ye the word of the Lord. . . .

Behold, I will bring evil upon this place. . . . Then shalt thou break the bottle in the sight of the men that go with thee, and shalt say unto them: Thus saith the Lord of hosts: Even so will I break the people. . . ."

Jeremiah goes on to tell that "thus saith the Lord to me: 'Make thee bands and bars, and put them upon thy neck . . .' " (Jer. 27:2). This visible sign was to make it plain to the kingdom of Judah that all the nations, the neighboring states of Judah as well as Judah itself, would be enslaved under the yoke of the king of Babylonia.

We find symbolism also in the Book of Ezekiel. There the prophet relates that the Lord commanded him to eat up a scroll on which were recorded all the troubles which would befall the Jewish people, and that he, Ezekiel, did as he was commanded. (Ezek., Chapters 2 and 3). Thereafter, he was confined to his home throughout the period during which Jerusalem was besieged. He bound his body with cords, his tongue adhered to his palate and he was stricken dumb (Ezek. 3:25-26). Then God commanded him to take a tile and draw upon it a picture of Jerusalem, showing how it would be besieged. Ezekiel himself was commanded to lie upon his left side for three hundred ninety days and then on his right side for forty days. During all that time he was to be tied down with heavy cords, so that he should not be able to turn from one side to the other. During all that time he was to eat only "unclean bread" and only a restricted amount of even that—all this as a visible demonstration to the kingdom of Judah of how that kingdom would be destroyed and its children driven into exile to Babylonia.

Finally, Ezekiel was commanded to shave his head and to cut off his beard. He was to burn one-third of his hair in fire, cut the other third to pieces with his sword, and scatter the remaining third to the winds to symbolize the fate which would befall the kingdom of Judah after the destruction of Jerusalem.

The Prophet Hosea was commanded by the Lord to take unto himself a harlot and to beget children with her, giving the offspring symbolic names, to symbolize the sins of the Jewish people. In accordance with God's command, Hosea went and took Gomer, the daughter of Diblaim. She conceived and bore a son whom God bade Hosea to name Jezreel to indicate that He would "visit the blood of Jezreel upon the house of Jehu, and . . . cause to cease the kingdom of the house of Israel." Thereafter Gomer gave birth to a daughter, and the Lord said to Hosea, "Call her name Lo-ruhamah; for I will no more have compassion upon the House of Israel." When the third child, another son, was born, the Lord commanded Hosea to "Call his name Lo-ammi; for ye are not My people" (Hosea, Chapter 1).

Thus the prophets not only uttered words of vision, but also conveyed the message of the Lord through symbolic acts. Some of these acts involved much personal suffering for the prophet himself. It was their purpose to stress and underscore the truth of these prophecies and to warn the people of the consequences they would have to face if they should still refuse to heed the words of the prophet.

This is the nature of prophecy as Judaism understands it. God takes one man and favors him with one or more moments of divine inspiration and exaltation because He has chosen him to bring His message to the people of Israel only, and to all of mankind.

But even though we now know what prophecy can be like, we ought not to conclude that any person whom the Lord favors with such rare instants of ecstasy is therefore a prophet. In addition to inspiration, a prophet must have other qualities which are not all found in the same degree in every prophet. There are varying degrees in which the gift of prophecy has been found in mortals.

In his *Guide to the Perplexed,* Part 2, Chapter 48, Maimonides tells of eleven degrees or categories of prophecy, which are as follows, in order of importance:

1. A prophet must help men and protect the righteous against injustice.

2. He must have a special faculty enabling him to speak words of wisdom on things divine, or to remonstrate with those who do evil. This he must do during his waking hours and the Holy Spirit must rest upon him.

3. Prophetic vision which is revealed in a symbolic dream and its interpretation.

4. A kind of prophecy in which a human being speaks to the prophet in a dream, as occurred in part of the Book of Ezekiel, where it is written, "and the man said to me."

5. The prophet may hear words of prophecy explained and interpreted in a dream, but not see the one who is speaking to him. This happened to Samuel in the early days of his prophecy.

6. An angel speaks to the prophet in a dream. This happened to most of the prophets at some time, as it is said, "And the angel of God said unto me in a dream" (Gen. 31:11).

7. The prophet, in a dream, sees some indication of the Lord Himself speaking to him, as is recorded in the Book of Isaiah, "And I heard the voice of the Lord saying . . ." (Isa. 6:8).

8. The word of the Lord may come to the prophet in the form of a vision which his eye can discern, as, for instance, in the case of the covenant which the Lord made with Abraham (Gen. 15:18-21).

9. The prophet may hear words through a vision, as we are told in the case of Abraham, "And, behold, the word of the Lord came unto him . . ." (Gen. 15:4).

10. The prophet may see someone speaking to him in a vision, for example, in the story of Abraham at Mamre and Joshua at Jericho.

11. An angel speaks to the prophet, not in a dream—for example, an angel spoke to Abraham at the time of the sacrifice of Isaac. This is the highest degree of prophecy, save for that attained by Moses, of whom it is said that the Lord spoke to him face to face.

Prophets may also be classed in terms of the times in which they lived and worked. In accordance with this point of view, the period from the days of Abraham down to Samuel was the first period, that of "active prophecy," the era of the founders of Judaism. Those were the prophets who conveyed God's message through deeds that have had a lasting impact. Their exact words have not all been recorded for future generations, but their deeds still speak to us today. The second period was that of the "passive" prophets, those who communicated their messages by word of mouth and whose speeches were either not recorded at all or recorded only partially. These would include such prophets as Gad, Nathan, and others of whom very little is known today. The third period was that of the "fighting prophets" the fiery preachers, men of eternal truth and righteousness such as Isaiah, Jeremiah,

Ezekiel, Hosea, Amos, and others. The fourth period is that of the "minor prophets" who had visions of lesser importance, which had significance only for the times in which they lived.

Before we go on to study these in detail, we must first establish the difference between the true messengers of the Lord and so-called "false prophets."

6. Prophets, True and False

Who Is a True Prophet and Who Is Not—The Inspiration of a True Prophet and His Constant, Fearless Fight for Justice—Illustrations from the Lives of Elijah, Nathan, and Micaiah the Son of Imlah—The Prophets as Fighters, Both Nationalist and Universalist.

We now know that there are various categories of prophets and they are classified in accordance with their spiritual gifts, their acts in behalf of Israel or the world, and the extent to which they fought for truth and justice.

This last criterion, the ability and eagerness to fight for truth and justice, was the main qualification of a prophet. He had to possess, at least to some degree, a spark of that holy inspiration which would leave him no peace until truth had been vindicated and justice restored. He had to be prepared to endure great suffering, or even death, for the principles he represented. This was the touchstone by which to test whether or not a man had been sent by God to convey His message to mankind.

According to Jewish tradition, there were forty-eight prophets and seven prophetesses. As we have said in a previous chapter, this does not mean that all these men and women were of equal stature or even that all of them could be classified as genuine prophets. It does mean, however, that each of them possessed the gift of prophecy to some extent, and that all of them, to a greater or lesser degree, were imbued with the fiery spirit which inspired them to fight valiantly for truth and justice. If a man or woman was known to have performed an act, or made a gesture, or made a statement, or spoken out for a point of view representing a profound truth for which he or she was ready to fight, if necessary, he or she is included among the prophets of Israel. Hence all the men and women who achieved distinction in this respect were listed among the prophets while the others were forgotten. There were prophets whose messages have been recorded for posterity, and others whose words were never written down. But they all had within them a spark of that spirit which makes for a true prophet. This was true even in the case of the so-called "passive prophets," and there have been "passive prophets" throughout all the four periods of prophecy in the history of the people of Israel. Whenever a major prophet appeared on the scene, he would be surrounded by such "passive prophets" who would rally round him. However, one who did not have within himself some spark of prophecy could not remain in the prophetic circle. In addition, each one of these followers had to be a fighter for truth in his own right and to be ready to sacrifice everything, if necessary.

However, all through Jewish history we have had, aside from the true prophets, also "false prophets." There were two types of false prophets. First, the prophets of idolatry, such as, for instance, the prophets of the god Baal or of the goddess Astarte. These false prophets called upon the masses to worship these idols. Secondly, there were those who, while they did not attempt to convert the people to actual idolatry, still lacked within themselves that fire of divine inspiration that distinguishes the real prophet.

Both categories of prophets were legion at the courts of the kings of Judah and Israel. They numbered well into the hundreds. Most of them spoke only that which they felt would find grace in the eyes of the king.

Let us now examine several accounts in the Bible to understand better the difference between true prophets and false ones.

First, we read in the Book of Deuteronomy (18:15-22) that Israel was told to be on guard against a false prophet who might call upon it to stray from the path of God's Law.

A prophet will the Lord thy God raise up unto thee, from the midst of thee, of thy brethren, like unto me; unto him ye shall hearken; according to all that thou didst desire of the Lord thy God in Horeb in the day of the assembly, saying: "Let me not hear again the voice of the Lord my God, neither let me see this great fire any more, that I die not." And the Lord said unto me: "They have well said that which they have spoken. I will raise them up a prophet from among their brethren, like unto thee; and I will put My words in his mouth, and he shall speak unto them all that I shall command him. And it shall come to pass, that whosoever will not hearken unto My words which he shall speak in My name, I will require it of him. But the prophet, that shall speak a word presumptuously in My name, which I have not commanded him to speak, or that shall speak in the name of other gods, that same prophet shall die." And if thou say in thy heart: "How shall we know the word which the Lord hath not spoken?" When a prophet speaketh in the name of the Lord, if the thing follow not, nor come to pass, that is the thing which the Lord hath not spoken; the prophet hath spoken it presumptuously, thou shalt not be afraid of him.

So much for false prophets in the Pentateuch.

Now, in the eighteenth chapter of the First Book of Kings there is recorded the struggle which Elijah carried on against the four hundred fifty false prophets who called upon the people of Israel to worship Baal. Elijah fought single-handed against these false prophets and defeated them. Here is the account as given in the Book of Kings (Chapters 16-18).

It came to pass in the days of Ahab, king of Israel, who had married Jezebel, the daughter of Ethbaal, the king of the Zidonians, "and went and served Baal and worshipped him . . ." and it was after Jezebel cut off the prophets of the Lord that Obadiah (who had been appointed over the king's house) "took a hundred prophets, and hid them fifty in a cave, and fed them with bread and water. . . ." At that time, Elijah the Tishbite came to Obadiah and told him to tell King Ahab that he, Elijah, desired to see him.

Obadiah was afraid so to inform Ahab. He told Elijah that Ahab sought to kill him. And not only did Ahab search through his own country for Elijah, but he asked the rulers of many other lands to deliver Elijah to him should they find him in their territory. Obadiah explained that if Elijah would command him to go to the king and to inform him that Elijah was there, "It will come to pass . . . that the spirit of the Lord will carry thee whither I know not; and so when I come and tell Ahab, and he cannot find thee, he will slay me." Then Elijah swore to Obadiah in the name of the Lord that he, Elijah, would wait at that place until Obadiah would return with the message from the king. And Obadiah complied with Elijah's wish. Ahab told Obadiah that he desired to see the prophet. When Ahab and Elijah met, Ahab said to Elijah, "Is it thou, thou troubler of Israel?" Thereupon Elijah fearlessly replied, impelled by the fire that burned within his heart, "I have not troubled Israel; but thou, and thy father's house, in that ye have forsaken the commandments of the Lord, and thou hast followed the Baalim." And Elijah commanded Ahab to gather all the people of Israel at Mount Carmel, and also to bring there the four hundred and fifty "prophets" of the idol Baal, and there it would be revealed who was the true God, the idol Baal, or the God of Israel.

Ahab soon sent out messengers to gather all the prophets of Baal at Mount Carmel, and when they were all assembled there, Elijah said to the throng, "How long halt ye between two opinions? if the Lord be God, follow Him; but if Baal, follow him." Thereupon the people fell silent and answered not a word.

Now we are told of the miracle which Elijah brought to pass. He commanded the false prophets to bring an offering to the altar of Baal, but to light no fire beneath the sacrifice. The sacrifice remained upon the altar intact. Elijah himself placed a similar offering upon an altar erected to the God of Israel, also without lighting a fire beneath it. Then a fire came down from heaven and consumed the offering intended for the God of Israel.

Of course the important part of this story is not the fact that a miracle happened. What is of great significance is that Elijah, whom Ahab had sought to kill, was not afraid to come before the king who had called him a "troubler," and that Elijah, single-handed, fought the four hundred and fifty false prophets and was able to discredit them before all the people of Israel.

Here, then, we have the battle of Elijah against the first category of false prophets, namely, the prophets of idoltry. He fought them without fear for his own life, for he was inspired by that divine spark which led him upon the paths of truth and righteousness.

The Bible also tells of another instance in which a prophet, similarly inspired, single-handedly fought and defeated hundreds of false prophets. The false prophets in this case (I Kings, 22) are of the second category, namely, they were afraid to speak the truth candidly before the king. It is told as follows:

Jehoshaphat, the king of Judah, came to take counsel at Samaria with Ahab, because Aram had annexed Ramoth-gilead, a city in the kingdom of Israel, and he was desirous of having Jehoshaphat, the king of Judah, as his ally in that war. Jehoshaphat agreed to aid Ahab, but stipulated that they should first inquire of the Lord whether they would be able to win such a war. Ahab gathered some four hundred prophets and asked them whether he and the king of Judah should go to war against Aram. All the prophets unanimously replied that Ahab should go to war and could be confident of victory. Jehoshaphat, however, was not yet satisfied; he realized that all these prophets would not dare say anything that might displease Ahab. Therefore he asked Ahab whether there was not another prophet of the Lord of whom they could inquire and find out the real truth. The king of Israel replied that there was indeed another prophet, Micaiah, the son of Imlah, but that he disliked him because he never prophesied anything good but only evil. However, when Jehoshaphat insisted, Ahab sent for Micaiah. On the way to the place where the two sovereigns were waiting, the royal messenger attempted to persuade Micaiah to tell the kings the same thing that the other prophets had told him; that is, that Aram would lose the war. But Micaiah replied that he would utter only such statements as the Lord Himself would put into his mouth.

When Micaiah came into the presence of the kings, Ahab immediately asked him whether he and Jehoshaphat should go to war because of Ramath-gilead. At first Micaiah, like all the false prophets before him, told Ahab that he would win the war against Aram. Ahab, however knew that Micaiah was a true prophet who had never before hidden the truth from him, and suspected that this time Micaiah was deliberately lying to him in order to mock him. Therefore Ahab adjured Micah to tell him the truth. Then Micaiah came out with the whole truth. He told Ahab that all his prophets were not prophets at all, since God had never spoken to them. He advised Ahab not to go to war against Aram, because he, Ahab, would be the loser. Thereupon Zedekiah, the son of Chenaanah, one of the false prophets, angrily rushed up to Micaiah and slapped his face; whereupon Ahab commanded that Micaiah be arrested and kept on a diet of bread and water until such time as he, Ahab, would safely return from the war. Micaiah, however, was not intimidated, and refused to retract his statement, and said to Ahab, "If thou return at all in peace, the Lord that not spoken by me." And he said, "Hear, ye peoples, all of you."

Here, then, we have another instance of a prophet of God who defied four hundred false prophets. Of course, this time the four hundred were not prophets of a false god; they were false prophets only by virtue of the fact that they pretended to be prophets when in truth they were not. Their sole desire was to please the king and to tell him only what he liked to hear. The Lord had never sent them, nor had He ever inspired them. And there is, in II Samuel, 12 the story of a prophet, Nathan, who was not afraid to tell the truth even to his king, as in the instance of King David and Bathsheba.

The first essential qualification of a prophet is that he tell the truth always without fear of the consequences to himself. This is what all the prophets in Jewish history have done and all such fighters for truth have earned their place among the prophets of Israel.

There are no separate books containing the prophecies of Nathan, Elijah, and Micaiah the son of Imlah. They are not credited with statements of eternal significance, but they were prophets nevertheless, because they had borne within themselves the spark of divine inspiration that impelled them to be fighters for truth and justice.

Those who are imbued with such ideas are prophets not only to Jews, but to all the nations, wherever men suffer at the hands of falsehood and injustice. Therefore the visions of the Jewish prophets did not concern only the people of Israel, but also the other nations. The prophets of Israel were not strict nationalists. In varying degrees they all subscribed to ideals of universalism. All of them shared an equal passion for truth and justice, and therefore they were the prophets not only of Israel but of all of mankind.

Such are the personal characteristics that distinguish the true prophet from ordinary men.

Once we accept this, we have a vantage point from which to study the various categories of prophets. There can be no doubt that even the least significant of the prophets had within him at least a touch of that divine inspiration which leads men to fight against evil wherever it may appear. It was for this reason that even the lesser prophets were counted among the prophets.

7. Samuel and His Ideals

Samuel Welds All the Tribes of Israel into One United Nation—He Is the First Jewish Prophet to Establish a School for Prophets—His Teachings of What a Prophet Should Be—Fighter for Truth—The Prophets

At the end of the era of the Judges there arose among the Jewish people a great prophet who was also the last of the judges.

Samuel, the son of Elkanah, came upon the scene at a time when the Jewish people were suffering at the hands of judges who were dishonest and thoroughly corrupt. Even Samuel's own two sons, Joel and Abijah, who had also ruled as judges, had not behaved in accordance with the dignity of their high office. Samuel advanced a new goal for himself. He desired to fight not only for the acknowledgment of the Unity of God, but also for the union of the twelve Jewish tribes into one nation. He felt this to be desirable so that, if any one of the tribes should be attacked by an alien enemy, the other Israelite tribes would rally to its aid. In addition, Samuel was a valiant fighter for justice and righteousness among the Jews.

The Jewish people had grown dissatisfied with their judges and wanted to have a king instead. Deep in his heart, Samuel opposed the institution of kings for his people. For this reason he explained to them the meaning of a king for Israel, and he warned that a king would only rob the people to indulge his own love for pleasure and luxury.

Samuel knew, however, that even though the people of Israel had not yet been welded into one nation and each tribe was a separate national entity, injustice would not long be tolerated. Proof of this can be found in the account of the incident of Gibeah, which is recorded in the Book of Judges. A man took unto himself as his wife a woman from another tribe and took her to his home. On the way, at night, he came to Gibeah, in the province of the tribe of Benjamin, where they took lodging for the night. When the men of the city heard of the presence of the couple, they broke into the house of the host, took out the woman, assaulted her, and then killed her. They had based their act on an ancient Sodomite law. The dead woman's husband then cut up her body into twelve parts and sent a part of the body to each tribe as a sign that each one of them shared in the guilt for the terrible crime that had been perpetrated. In this particular incident, all the tribes of Israel gathered together and openly rebuked the tribe of Benjamin in whose territory the crime had been committed. There was fighting, and all the tribes of Israel forbade their young people to contract marriage with a member of the clan of Benjamin, until, finally, peace was restored.

But such spontaneous demonstrations, Samuel thought, could occur only as long as there was no king and public opinion was allowed free expression; on the other hand it would be very easy for a king to rule as a tyrant and to suppress every free expression of public opinion. Samuel therefore found himself on the horns of a dilemma. He wanted the unity of Israel but was afraid of a kingdom.

However, the people of Israel wanted a king. In the end, Samuel gave in and anointed Saul king. At the same time, however, he set up checks and safety devices as preventive measures against any attempt on the part of a king to assume dictatorial powers. He assembled the prophets and increased their number. Of course he carefully chose his recruits, requiring that the youthful fledgling prophets be imbued with the fire of truth, so that they might be trained to become prophets who would not be afraid to come before the king himself, if need be, to tell him that he had done wrong.

For this purpose Samuel set up what might be termed a "school for prophets," and it is then that we hear for the first time of a "gathering of prophets" and of "a band of prophets" who, with the aid of music, worked themselves up to a state of mind where they could utter prophecy. Even Saul, who came among them by accident one day, was so affected by them that he began to speak words of prophetic vision.

It was from these groups of young men, who called themselves "gatherings of prophets," "bands of prophets," and "sons of prophets," that there evolved those so-called "passive prophets" who were to play so important a role in the history of the Jewish people.

Samuel was the first man to give the Jewish people the true concept of what God really requires of men. He told them that the Lord desired no sacrifices; He needed no offerings of sheep or cattle, but demanded solely that men obey Him and deal justly with their brothers. Samuel anointed Saul, the son of Kish, as king, but when Saul did not obey his word, he relieved him of his position and anointed David, the son of Jesse, in his stead.

Samuel was recognized by the entire nation as a prophet, as we are told in the First Book of Samuel, Chapter 3, Verse 20: "And all of Israel from Dan even to Beer-sheba knew that Samuel was established to be a prophet of the Lord."

Samuel also broadened the concept of what a prophet should be. A prophet, in his opinion, was not only one who fought for the ideal of monotheism, but also a man who would side with his people, if necessary, against the king and his advisors. Those men who met with his standards he gathered unto himself and recognized them as prophets. He also changed the titles by which they had been known before. Formerly called "seers," they were now to be known as "Neviim," "prophets," from the Hebrew word "niv," meaning "to speak." A prophet was to be one who would have no fear of uttering the truth, one who would speak his mind even to kings and princes. He was not to consider the risks involved in such frankness, and any personal considerations such as his own well-being were not to enter into his thinking when justice and truth were at stake.

This new concept and mission of prophecy gained many adherents among the young prophets. And thus we see at the beginning of the era of monarchy among the Jews quite a number of so-called "silent prophets." The actual speeches of these men were never recorded for posterity, but it is known that they were outstanding fighters for truth and right.

From that time on, the prophet was no longer only a fighter for the ideal of One God, but also a protagonist of justice among men, an active advocate of truth. He was a preacher who called upon men to repent of their sins—two kinds of sins—those committed in one's relationship to God, and those committed against one's fellow men.

8. The "Silent" Prophets

The Prophets Who Lived at the Time of David and Solomon—The "Silent Prophets," Gad, Nathan, Ahijah the Shilonite, and Others—As the Sins of the Kings Increased, the Prophets Became More Outspoken.

Soon thereafter we see the advent of the first prophets of this new era. The first two of these were Gad and Nathan.

The Bible makes mention of Gad in several instances in the First and Second Books of Samuel and also in Chronicles. Gad was the one who came before King David to tell him that he had sinned. He told David that God gave him a choice of three punishments to atone for what he had done; seven years of famine in the land, or three months of constant flight from the pursuing foe, or else three days of plague. David chose the third of these penalties (II Sam., 24).

Nathan the Prophet presented an even more striking example of candor. He was not afraid to come before King David and to tell him that he was unfit to build the Sanctuary of the Lord which he had planned to erect, for his hands were stained with the blood that he had shed. The Sanctuary was meant to be a house of peace, and therefore could not be built by a man who had engaged in war. The second time Nathan came before David was to remonstrate with him quite openly and frankly for sending Uriah the Hittite to battle so that he might die and that he, David, might take Uriah's wife Bathsheba as his own. Nathan fearlessly told David that he was deserving of the death penalty for this grave transgression.

Of the same caliber, too, were the other "silent prophets" who lived during the period of the Kings, such as Elijah, who was not afraid to fight Ahab, and Elisha, the disciple of Elijah, who did not shrink from telling Jehoram, king of Israel, to his face: ". . . were it not that I regard the presence of Jehoshaphat the King of Judah, I would not look toward thee, nor see thee" (II Kings 3:14). The same qualities of frankness and fearlessness were displayed later on by other prophets too, such as Jeremiah and Hosea, who told the unadorned truth to the kings of both Judah and Israel.

With the establishment of a monarchy in the land of Israel there began a new era of struggle and intrigue at the courts of the kings. The first of these crises was the fight between Saul and David. After the death of David there were contention and discord among his children. Then came the contests for the dynasty in the days of Solomon, and finally, after the death of Solomon, the great struggle between his son Rehoboam, and Jeroboam the son of

Nebat, as a result of which the Jewish people was divided into two separate kingdoms, Judah and Israel.

The period of the kings lasted from the time of the anointing of Saul until the reign of King Zedekiah who, in the eleventh year of his rule, was driven into exile by Nebuzaradan at the time of the destruction of the First Temple. During this period, which lasted 456 years, discord, idolatry, and regicide were rife in both Judah and Israel. From time to time, it is true, there would be a king who would urge his people to return to the One God, or one who would call upon the spiritual leaders of his people to reinstitute the observance of Passover and Sukkoth. But the people were hopelessly chained by paganism. According to the Talmud, the worst of all the kings of the Jewish people was Manasseh, the son of Hezekiah, the King of Judah who placed an idol in the temple, instituted the most wanton excesses, and violated the Torah. (Sanhedrin 100:2).

And yet, despite the sins of the kings, the period saw the flourishing of the prophets. The Era of the Judges, which extended over a span of 336 years, produced no more than three prophets, Joshua, Deborah, and Samuel. The Era of the Kings, on the other hand which lasted only ninety years longer than that of the judges, could boast of sixteen prophets; namely, Nathan, Gad, Ahijah the Shilonite, Hosea, Amos, Micah, Elijah, Elisha, Jonah, Isaiah, Joel, Nahum, Habakkuk, Zephaniah, Ezekiel, and Jeremiah—in other words, the majority of the prophets in all of Jewish history. And yet, despite these great prophets and preachers, the Jewish people still continued to sin and to bow before pagan gods.

A great black cloud covers all of the period of 822 years preceding the destruction of the First Temple during which the people of Israel dwelt in its land. It was one long era of depravity and idolatry, when parents sacrificed their own children upon the altar of Moloch and wild orgies were committed in the name of the cult of Baal, Astarte, and other idols.

And yet it was precisely this sad era in Jewish history from which posterity has inherited the greatest treasures produced by Judaism, namely the works of the prophets. Some of these prophets had to suffer greatly for their idealism, but the sufferings they had to endure for the sake of their fight for truth were as nothing compared to the great heritage they left to all of mankind. It was these prophets who fought against despotic kings, against corruption in the ruling classes, against falsehood in the high places, and against injustice wherever and whenever it occurred.

As we have said before, prophecy began with the so-called "silent prophets" in the days of David and Solomon. But there were also "silent prophets" in the days of the subsequent kings of Judah and Israel. They worked simultaneously with the "fiery prophets" such as Isaiah, Jeremiah, Hosea, and Amos. But not all of them have been mentioned in the Bible. The only ones of whom such mention has been made are those of particular distinction. The others have been forgotten.

The reason why the first prophets were "passive" or "silent" rather than fiery was that, during the reign of David and Solomon, there was no need for drastic speech or action. Prophets did not then feel compelled to lash out against David and Solomon as was the case later against other rulers of the Jews. If either David or Solomon chanced to err, a prophet's reprimand would remind them that they had sinned, and they would repent. The people in those days were also ready and willing at all times to return to the God of their fathers and thus there was no need for the prophets to deliver fiery sermons or threaten dire punishments.

The situation was quite different, however, in later years, because many of the kings of the Jewish people, particularly those of the kingdom of Israel, actually worshiped idols. Then it did become necessary for the prophets to raise their voices in reprimand.

As we know, the Jewish state, soon after the death of Solomon, was divided into two independent nations. The tribes of Judah and Benjamin, with territories located in the southern part of Palestine, joined to form the Kingdom of Judah with Jerusalem as the capital. The other ten tribes created the Kingdom of Israel, also known as the Kingdom of Ephraim, with Samaria as the capital.

The Kingdom of Judah seems to have been more loyal to the One God than the Kingdom of Israel. During the 382 years that passed from the death of Solomon until the destruction of the First Temple, Judah had nineteen kings. Most of them did not practice paganism, and Asa, Jehoshaphat, Hezekiah, and Josiah even attempted to extirpate idolatry from among their subjects. The kingdom of Judah was ruled in a fairly orderly fashion, with the throne passing from father to son. At the court of the kings of Israel, on the other hand, intrigue was rife and many of the rulers of that nation came to power by means of murder and revolt.

The Kingdom of Israel endured for more than 233 years. Israel, too, had a total of nineteen kings, but their reigns were shorter than those of the rulers of Judah, for many of them met an untimely end at the hand of some assassin. Four kings, Nadab, Elah, Ahaziah, and Pekahiah, each reigned for a period of only two years, and Zimri ruled for seven days in all.

The silent prophets, and the fiery prophets after them, however, were not confined to one or the other of these kingdoms. Their words were addressed to both the Kingdom of Judah and that of Israel, and, at times, even to other nations.

According to Jewish chronology, Gad and Nathan lived at the time of David and Solomon. Ahijah the Shilonite, Ada the Seer, and Jehu the son of Chananiah lived during the period when Rehoboam, Abijah, and Asa were kings of Judah, and Jeroboam, Nadab, Bashah, Elah, Zimri, and Omri reigned in Israel. The prophets Elijah and Elisha preached and taught when Jehoram and Ahaziah and Queen Athaliah ruled in Judah, and Ahab, Ahaziah, Jehoram, Jehu, Jehoahaz, and Joash reigned in Israel. Two other silent prophets, Azariah and Chaninah, also lived about that time.

According to Jewish chronology, the fiery prophets, Amos and Hosea, preceded Isaiah and Jeremiah. Amos and Hosea lived during the reign of Uziah and Jothan in Judah and Jeroboam II, Zehariah, Shalom, Menahem, Pekahiah, Pekah, and Hoshea in Israel. In the Bible, however, the prophecies of Isaiah precede those of Amos and Hosea.

For our purposes we shall adhere to the chronological order and discuss the activities and prophecies of the fiery prophets. The first of these was Amos, who lived during the reign of King Uziah in Judah. The silent prophets, Uriah and Oded, were his contemporaries.

9. The Fiery Prophets: Amos, Hosea, and Micah

Amos, Shepherd and Day Worker—Amos as Universalist Prophet—Hosea and His Strange Vision—The Three Basic Principles of Judaism, According to Micah —A Comparative Study of the Prophecies of Micah and Jeremiah

Jeroboam II was king in Israel when the first of the fiery prophets to come after the era of the silent prophets sent forth his message. This was Amos, the first prophet to elevate prophecy to the highest plane which it was ever to reach, and Hosea, Isaiah, and Micah followed in his footsteps, as did all the other subsequent prophets in Jewish history.

Amos came from the town of Tekoa in the Kingdom of Judah, five miles south of Bethlehem. He was a shepherd and also a day worker in the fields. He said of himself that he was "Boles Shekomim," a "picker of mowings." But even though Amos actually came from the land of Judah, his prophecies were addressed primarily to the kingdom of Israel, from Beth El. Amos said of himself, "I am neither a prophet nor the son of a prophet." But the fact was that he did have within him the divine inspiration which makes for true prophecy. At the risk of his own life he went to Samaria to speak out against the sinful kings of Israel who worshiped idols. The danger to Amos was so great that, when Jeroboam II was told that Amos had incited his subjects against him, even Amaziah, the priest of idolatry, advised Amos to flee to Judah and not to turn to Beth El. (Amos 7:12-13). Amos, however, did not heed the advice of Amaziah and continued to prophesy that Jeroboam would die by the sword, and his land would be destroyed and that the Jewish people would eventually be driven into exile. Amos knew well that, by so doing, he was placing his life in jeopardy, but this did not deter him from continuing to utter his prophecies in the kingdom of Israel.

The Book of Amos has nine chapters. In the first two chapters, and also in three lines of the third, Amos utters prophecies concerning the nations that dwell near Judah and Israel. Beginning with 3:4, Amos discusses the transgressions of Israel and those of Judah. In Chapters 7 and 8 he gives an account of his visions. Chapter 9 contains a message of comfort and consolation to the entire Jewish people.

During the lifetime of Amos, King Jeroboam II defeated the Kingdom of

Aram (Syria), which had originally been far mightier than the Kingdom of Israel. Jeroboam, drunk with victory, ascribed his success to the aid of the heathen gods and put even greater emphasis on worshiping them. What Jeroboam failed to take into account, however, was that Assyria was ready and waiting to swallow up both Syria and Israel. For this reason it was quite in accordance with the plans of Assyria that Israel go to war against Syria, for, regardless of the outcome of the conflict, both Israel and Syria would be so greatly weakened by the war that it would be an easy conquest for Assyria to vanquish both.

Amos, realizing this, gave due warning to Jeroboam. Jeroboam, however, heady with victory, did not listen. But Amos did not cease to declare that Assyria would come and would take from Israel all that Israel had taken from Aram [Syria], and it would also destroy the kingdom of Israel and take its people into captivity.

Amos was also the first among the fiery prophets to speak out against the offering of sacrifices and against the many holy days at which such sacrifices were offered to God. At a later date, Isaiah was to paraphrase many of the statements of Amos in his own prophecies. Amos said, in the name of the Lord, "I hate, I despise your feasts. . . . Take thou away from Me the noise of thy songs; And let Me not hear the melody of thy psalteries. But let justice well up as waters, and righteousness as a mighty stream" (Amos 5: 21, 23-24).

Amos made it clear to the Jewish people that God would not exempt them from punishment for their sins because He had chosen them from among the other nations. In fact, Amos said, the Jews were much more liable to punishment for their errors for the very reason that they had thus been chosen. Moreover, they had no reason to deem themselves in any way superior to the other nations, for, actually, all men were equal in the sight of the Lord; all men were God's children. " 'Are ye not as the children of the Ethiopians unto Me, O children of Israel?' says the Lord" (Amos 9:7). The God of Israel, said Amos, was not only a Jewish God, but the God of all the world, of all mankind. For this reason Amos also uttered prophecies applicable to Edom, Moab, Ammon, Syria, and all the other non-Jewish nations.

Amos also castigated those who lived in luxury and exploited others, who "lie upon beds of ivory . . . And eat the lambs out of the flock" even while they "trample upon the poor," and women who anoint themselves, live in luxury, and exploit the needy. But, even as all the other prophets, so Amos, too, ends the book of his prophecies with words of consolation, reassuring the Jewish people that in the end God will be merciful.

Some ten or fifteen years later there arose the Prophet Hosea who prophesied toward the end of the reign of Uzziah until the beginning of the rule of Hezekiah. Hosea added a new element to prophecy—that of love and mercy. While Amos was the prophet of stern justice and righteousness, Hosea introduced the concept that the Jewish people should love the Lord, because the

Lord loved them also. In this manner he reaffirmed the commandment of Moses, saying "and thou shalt love the Lord thy God."

At the time of Hosea the situation in the kingdom of Israel was none too hopeful. The country was in a state of anarchy. After the death of Jeroboam II, his son Zehariah reigned only six months because Shallum the son of Jabesh entered into conspiracy against him and finally murdered him. But Shallum himself reigned only one month because he was assassinated in turn by Menahem the son of Gadi of Tirzah. Menahem managed to remain on the throne for twelve years, but these were years of unrest because Assyria had grown in strength and was preparing to attack Israel. When Menahem heard that Pul, the king of Assyria, was ready to march against his country, he went to him with a tribute of one thousand "kikar of silver" (one kikar of silver was worth three thousand shekels), and so redeemed himself and his kingdom. He had raised the funds from some of the wealthy among his subjects. Menahem was succeeded by his son Pekahiah, who had reigned for only two years when he was murdered by Pekah the son of Remaliah. Pekah ruled for twenty years, but he, too, did not die of natural causes. He was murdered by Hoshea the son of Elah who then usurped his throne. Hoshea's reign was terminated by the destruction of the kingdom of Israel by Assyria.

Like Amos, Hosea also fought against the corruption which was rampant at the courts of the kings in those days and which the kings had openly tolerated. He assailed the king and his people, telling them that, by their own vile conduct, they were weakening their country to such a degree that it would be an easy thing for any enemy to conquer it.

He also reprimanded the people who, though they had not cast off the God of Israel entirely, zealously served alien gods such as Baal as well. He spoke out sharply against the two calves which Jeroboam had put up for worship and before which the people still bowed down. He called to the people, "Thy calf, O Samaria, is cast off; Mine anger is kindled against them" and asked them when they would come to understand that their idols were not gods at all but only the works of human hands. Then he railed at those who did evil and then came to the calves which they worshiped to beg them for forgiveness, "They that sacrifice men kiss calves" (Hosea 13:2). He also castigated the priests who were anxious to have the people sin more so that they, the priests, might feed off the people's sin-offerings, "They feed on the sin of My people, And set their heart on their iniquity" (Hosea 4:8).

Hosea poured out his wrath not only in fiery sermons, but also through dire prophecies. He warned that even nature suffers because of the evil that men do. "Therefore doth the land mourn, And every one that dwelleth therein doth languish, With the beasts of the field and the fowls of heaven; Yea, the fishes of the sea are also taken away" (Hosea 4:3).

At the end, however, Hosea comforted his people and the rest of the world with the assurance that better days were certain to come.

Hosea had a vision which it is difficult to establish as a reality or as a product of his imagination. He tells how the Lord commanded him to take unto himself a harlot and to beget children of sin with her, as a sign to show the Jewish people that it had sinned against God.

It is hard to establish whether this entire vision was merely a flight of fancy which Hosea retold in order to impress upon Israel the gravity of its sins, or whether it had actually been a true experience. We have a similar vision in the Book of Isaiah, where we are told that Isaiah had been commanded by God to marry a prophetess who bore him a son whom God commanded him to call "Maher-shalal-hash-baz" (The spoil speeds, the prey hastes). At any rate, it is clear that, by telling this story, Hosea meant to stress the fact that Israel had strayed from the right path and that it would therefore be destroyed and laid waste.

But Hosea also spoke words of comfort, particularly of the love of Israel for God and of that of God for Israel. "And I will betroth thee [the Jewish people] unto Me forever; yea, I will betroth thee to Me in righteousness, and justice, And in lovingkindness, and in compassion. And I will betroth thee unto Me in faithfulness; And thou shalt know the Lord" (Hosea 2:21-22). With these words, spoken in the name of the Lord, Hosea introduced the element of love and mercy in the relationship between God and Israel.

At approximately that time, perhaps a few years later, in the days of Isaiah, there lived another prophet named Micah of Morashah (wherefore he was called Micah the Morashtite). He prophesied during the reign of Jotham, Ahaz, and Hezekiah, and emulated his predecessors Amos and Hosea.

The Book of Micah consists of seven chapters. The first two deal with the sins of Samaria. The third, fourth, and fifth chapters speak of the absence of righteousness in the land of Israel. In Chapter 6 he castigates the Jewish people for their ingratitude for all the good things which the Lord has given them. In the final chapter Micah reassures Israel with words of comfort. Micah liked to employ the word "hear" and began practically all his prophecies with it.

He turns to the Jewish people, to the other nations, and also to the world as a whole with the words "hearken unto me," or "hear, O ye peoples," or even "hear this, I pray you, ye heads of the house of Jacob."

Micah attacked the false prophets in whom the people took delight since they spoke only what the people wanted to hear. In the end, says Micah, truth will prevail and the false prophets will stand discredited and disgraced before the eyes of all. He also speaks out against the sacrificial practices, duplicating the words of the prophet Isaiah, The last part of Verse 3 of Chapter 4 reads exactly like Isaiah. Micah says, concerning the "end of days," that ". . . Nation shall not lift up sword against nation, neither shall they learn war any more."

There is one point upon which Micah lays stress and which none of the other prophets have set forth in the same forceful manner, namely, his statement concerning what God really requires of man, what man must do if he is to walk in the ways of the Lord. The Talmud tells us that the prophet summarized the entire Law of Moses in three main points, which he expressed in these words, "It has been told thee, O man, what is good, and what the Lord doth require of thee: Only to do justly, and to love mercy, and to walk humbly with thy God" (Micah 6:8).

These three points are a recapitulation of everything that God demands of man, and how man must live with his brothers. It is the most beautiful summary ever made of the teachings of Judaism.

As long as one hundred fifty years before the destruction of the First Temple, Micah prophesied: "Therefore shall Zion . . . be plowed as a field, and Jerusalem shall become heaps, and the mountain of the house as the high places of a forest" (Micah 3:12). These are the same words that were employed at a much later date by Jeremiah when he bewailed the destruction of the Temple which he witnessed with his own eyes.

10. The Great Prophecies of Isaiah

When Did Isaiah Live?—The Rise of Assyria as a World Power—Isaiah's Sharp Words to the Kings of His Day—His High Ideals Concerning the Future of Mankind—Were There Two Isaiahs?—The Truth About the Last Twenty-seven Chapters of Isaiah

The age of Isaiah the Prophet coincided with the reigns of Uzziah, Jotham, Ahaz, and Hezekiah in the kingdom of Judah. As we have said before, the throne of Judah had passed from father to son in due order. Jotham had been the son of Uzziah, Ahaz the son of Jotham, and Hezekiah a son of Ahaz. During the same period of time, the throne of Israel had been occupied by Menahem the son of Gadi, Pekahiah, Pekah, and Hosea. But it would not be correct to say that Isaiah prophesied *throughout* the reign of all these kings. For Uzziah alone reigned fifty-two years, his son Jotham for sixteen, Ahaz for another sixteen years, and finally Hezekiah, the son of Ahaz, for twenty-nine years. Hence to state that Isaiah prophesied through those years would be to credit him with prophesying for 113 years.

Thus it would appear that Isaiah had begun to voice his message only at the very end of the reign of Uzziah, perhaps only two or three years prior to the latter's death. In that case Isaiah would have prophesied for only sixty-one years, or for sixty-three at the very most. It may also be that his period of prophecy did not extend through the entire reign of Hezekiah, but only until about fifteen years prior to the date of the death of that king as is established in the Second Book of Kings. If this is so, then Isaiah's period of prophecy actually spanned only forty-six years, or forty-eight at the most.

At this point we might make mention of some of the other prophets who lived at the time when Isaiah preached his messages. According to the Talmud, Hosea, Isaiah, Amos, and Micah all prophesied at the same time (Pesachim 87). But this could not have been exactly so, since Amos and Hosea prophesied at the beginning of the reign of King Uzziah, while Micah and Isaiah did so only toward the end of Uzziah's rule. Accordingly, it seems that Amos and Hosea must have proclaimed their words of prophecy around the year 3134 after Creation (or 626 B.C.). Micah came twenty years later and Isaiah another thirty to forty years after Micah; that is, about the year 3200 after Creation, or about 558 B.C. Thus all these four prophets, though not all living and working at the same time, did live within a span of about seventy years of each other.

Some scholars, however, claim that Isaiah lived about one hundred years earlier. This will be discussed later.

If we take the story told in the eighth chapter of the Book of Isaiah as the recital of a true experience rather than as a parable (see the chapter on Hosea), then Isaiah was married to a woman whom he calls "the prophetess" with whom he had a son whom he called "Maher-shalal-hash-baz" to symbolize those days when the kings hastened to go to battle to gather spoils. The English meaning of the name is "The spoil speeds, the prey hastes," indicating that the kings "hurried to gather spoils, and pursued the property of others."

We can see from the narrative in the Second Book of Kings that Isaiah was not afraid of the kings before whom he came to prophesy. When Ahaz asked him to give him a sign of the Lord God, Isaiah retorted angrily, "Hear ye now, O house of David: Is it a small thing for you to weary men, that you will weary my God also?" (Isa. 7:13). Nor was he afraid to tell the ailing King Hezekiah, "Make a will, for thou wilt die." Isaiah knew of no fear or cowardice. When King Hezekiah asked him whether he should go to war against Assyria which was at that time a world power before whom the smaller nations trembled, he replied that Hezekiah should go to war, for the Lord would be at his side and help him defeat the foe.

Legend has it that Isaiah was killed by King Manasseh, the son of Hezekiah, when he spoke ill of him. This legend is found in the Talmud (Yebamoth 49) as well as in the New Testament and the Apocrypha. Another legendary source holds that Isaiah lived 120 years.

The rise of the kingdom of Assyria to the position of a first-rate power made a great impression upon the ancient world. Prior to that time, that part of the world was peopled by a great number of small kingdoms such as those of the Hittites, the Canaanites, the Amorites, and the Jebusites. Later on, there were some larger kingdoms such as Moab, Edom, and Ammon. Then, suddenly, the kingdom of Syria (Aram) came upon the horizon as a power to be reckoned with. Thereafter, and also quite rapidly, the kingdom of Assyria became an aggressive world power which annexed many countries and made ready to conquer a large pair of Asia. Assyria also intended to incorporate into its territory the two Jewish kingdoms of Judah and Israel, and the kings of both these countries lived in fear of this formidable new foe. Ahaz, the king of Judah, turned to the prophet Isaiah who was already playing an important role in the land, and asked him for advice as to what course he should take. Isaiah told him not to fear Assyria, because that power did not now intend to invade Judah. Assyria would first attack Egypt and several other nations before it would become a real threat to the Kingdom of Judah. Ahaz, however, was afraid and sought to appease Assyria by sending a huge gift to the king of Assyria, with the assurance that he, Ahaz, was "his servant" (II Kings, 16:7-8). When Isaiah found out about this, he bitterly assailed Ahaz and told him that he could not depend upon the protection of the king of Assyria, because, in return for such protection, Ahaz would have to subjugate himself to the king of Assyria and obey his every command.

Assyria gradually grew stronger and finally attacked the kingdoms of Israel and Judah. This took place during the reign of King Hezekiah. The first step Hezekiah took in defense was to contract alliances with the neighboring kingdoms of Moab, Ziddon, Ammon, and Philistia, who also had reason to fear Assyria. Sennacherib marched against Judah with a huge army and laid seige to Jerusalem. Thereupon Hezekiah once more sent costly gifts to the king of Assyria and begged him to relent. As a result, Sennacherib withdrew.

Hezekiah, however, was filled with resentment against Assyria, and a few years later he rebelled. Consequently Sennacherib once more went to battle and with his army besieged Jerusalem. At this point Isaiah encouraged the king to go to war against Assyria. The prophet knew that Assyria was thoroughly hated by all the surrounding nations, and that Sennacherib's army itself, consisting of mercenaries from the nations which Assyria had conquered, only waited for the moment when it could revolt against Sennacherib. Isaiah's prediction came true.

We see, then, that the prophet Isaiah feared neither the kings of Judah and Israel, nor even mightier rulers such as the king of Assyria. He was a fighter, a revolutionary, and imbued with high ideals and a deep faith in justice for all mankind. He therefore is considered one of the great leaders of the Jewish people.

As for the ideals of Isaiah, we may find them in the sublime, poetic chapters of the book that bears his name.

At first he berates the leaders of the kingdom who were corrupt, and those in positions of high trust who would indulge in drunken orgies for days, and who, in return for bribes, would let criminals go free and punish the innocent. He cries out: "Woe unto them that are mighty to drink wine, and men of strength to mingle strong drink; that justify the wicked for a reward, and take away the righteousness of the righteous from him!" (Isa. 5:22-23).

Then he proceeds to assail the judges who do not dispense justice: "The Lord will enter into judgment with the elders of His people, and the princes thereof: 'It is ye that have eaten up the vineyard; the spoil of the poor is in your houses; what mean ye that ye crush My people and grind the face of the poor?' " (Isa. 3:14-15).

In another part of the Book of Isaiah, we read his attack against those who dare offer up sacrifices to the Lord even though their hands are stained with sin. We read that the Lord says: "Bring no more vain oblations; It is an offering of abomination unto Me; New moon and sabbath, the holding of convocations—I cannot endure iniquity along with the solemn assembly. Your new moons and your appointed seasons My soul hateth; they are a burden unto Me; I am weary to bear them" (Isa. 1:13-14).

But the prophet also has a message of hope for better days to come for both the Jewish people and the rest of the world. He speaks of a time when absolute righteousness and eternal peace will reign supreme both in nature and in human society; a time when justice and honesty will prevail throughout the world:

And there shall come forth a shoot out of the stock of Jesse, and a twig shall grow forth out of his roots. And the spirit of the Lord shall rest upon him, the spirit of wisdom and understanding, the spirit of counsel and might, the spirit of knowledge and of the fear of the Lord. And his delight shall be in the fear of the Lord; and he shall not judge after the sight of his eyes, neither decide after the hearing of his ears; but with righteousness shall he judge the poor, and decide with equity for the meek of the land; and he shall smite the land with the rod of his mouth, and with the breath of his lips shall he slay the wicked. And righteousness shall be the girdle of his loins, and faithfulness the girdle of his reins. And the wolf shall dwell with the lamb, and the leopard shall lie down with the kid; and the calf and the young lion and the fatling together; and a little child shall lead them (Isa. 11:1-7).

And elsewhere: "And He shall judge between the nations, and shall decide for many peoples; and they shall beat their swords into plowshares, and their spears into pruning-hooks; nation shall not lift up sword against nation, neither shall they learn war any more" (Isa. 2:4).

Here we have the highest ideals ever preached by a leader among men, which even now, after thousands of years, inspires man to await the day when they will become a reality in life.

The message of Isaiah was universalist and nationalist at the same time. We could say that about half of his words were addressed to the Jewish people alone, and the other half to all the nations of the world.

Together with reprimands and words of comfort addressed to the Jewish people in particular, we can find entire chapters in the Book of Isaiah addressed to the nations of his day. Thus the entire tenth chapter deals with the Assyrian empire; so does Chapter 20. The thirteenth chapter speaks of Babylonia, the fifteenth and sixteenth of Moab; the seventeenth deals with Syria, the nineteenth with Egypt and the twenty-third with the Kingdom of Tyre, and so forth.

His message to the other nations, even as his words to his own people, contains both reprimand and reassurance. Sometimes he would interpolate passages specifically intended for the Jews into prophecies which applied to the other nations, and vice versa. For he considered the Jewish people inextricably linked with the rest of the world to form one inseparable whole. He knew that there could be no peace in the world as long as the people of Israel suffered, and, conversely, that there could be no peace for Israel as long as any part of the world endured suffering.

He felt that the common man had been misled by false leaders and he expressed a fervent hope for the coming of that day when there would be a new order in the world and justice would be supreme among all men.

The last twenty-seven chapters of the Book of Isaiah are messages of comfort addressed to the Jewish people as a nation in exile. These chapters are difficult to explain because Isaiah lived before the destruction of the First Temple, and therefore could hardly have spoken of the Babylonian exile. Therefore some Bible scholars, both Jewish and non-Jewish, are of the opinion that these last chapters were written by another prophet who lived at a later date than Isaiah, in other words, a so-called "Deutero-Isaiah." Jewish tradition, however, disregards this question. The Talmud regards the entire Book of Isaiah as having been written, as the title indicates, by one man named Isaiah. But let us examine the whole matter very carefully.

The Book of Isaiah, containing the prophecies of Isaiah, has a total of sixty-six chapters, and may be divided into six parts, as follows:

1. The prophecies to the King of Judah concerning wars with neighboring nations. Here the prophet tells the kings what nations to engage in warfare and with what nations they should remain at peace.

2. Reprimands to the leaders of the Jewish nations as well as to the people themselves, urging them to cast off idolatry and to return to the God of Israel. Isaiah bitterly berates them.

3. Censuring the nations neighboring on Judah and Israel such as Moab, Edom, Ammon, Egypt, Assyria, and others for their sins.

4. A declaration that God desires not sacrifices and burnt offerings, but solely that man do good and practice justice.

5. The prediction that Judah and Israel, because of their sins, would be driven out of their homeland and, at a later date, brought back by God to the land of their fathers.

6. Prophecies concerning the upward striving of man and the eventual eternal peace and harmony among men and in nature.

Before we go further, let us clarify what Isaiah means when he speaks of "sin." According to Jewish ideology, there are two kinds of sin, namely, transgressions committed by man against God, and wrongs perpetrated by man against his fellow humans. It is a sin against God, for instance, to worship graven images or animals, for a man who endows beasts or the works of his own hands with divine qualities, shows by so doing that he himself is something less than human. But the prophet speaks out with even more anger against the crimes men commit against other men, and against the injustice that prevails in human society. He states plainly that no corrupt society can long endure. A kingdom where theft and deceit are practiced in the open, a state where human life is cheap, lacks that inner moral force which unites men. Hence, if they should be attacked by a mighty foe from without, such nations would be unable to offer resistance since they are not one united whole, each man looking out solely for his own selfish interests. This is what Isaiah had to say to all the nations of those days, but particularly to Judah and Israel, since they were not much better than their neighbors. But in the end he tells Judah and Israel that, though they will be exiled to a strange land, the Lord will yet have mercy upon them and bring them back to their own country. This message of comfort is contained in the final twenty-seven chapters of the Book of Isaiah (Chapters 40-66).

As we have said before, some Bible critics maintain that these final chapters were not written by the same man who was the author of the first part of the Book of Isaiah. They claim that the writer of Chapters 40-66 of the Book of Isaiah was another man named Isaiah (or perhaps a man with a different name), who lived long after the original Isaiah, and whose words were incorporated into the prophetic book which originally had only thirty-nine chapters.

To support their case, the Bible critics point out that since Isaiah lived long before the exiling of the Jews by Nebuchadnezzar, he could hardly have made prophecies concerning the return of the Jews from Babylonia during the reign of Cyrus of Persia some two hundred years later. The second argument they advance is the fact that the Book mentions the name of Cyrus, who, of course, reigned long after the death of Isaiah. Finally, they point out that the style of those twenty-seven disputed chapters is quite different from that of the prophecies contained in Chapters 1-39. In view of the above, these Bible critics came to the conclusion that there must have been a so-called "Deutero-Isaiah" who lived at a time considerably later than the original prophet.

The opinion found some support in Jewish circles and was advanced by Abraham ibn Ezra in his commentary to the Bible. Subsequently such views were propounded by Christian scholars and finally by authorities on Biblical research, Jewish and non-Jewish. According to this point of view, the "first" Isaiah lived during the days of King Hezekiah, while the "second" Isaiah did his work in the early days of the Second Temple, in other words some 200 to 220 years subsequent to the "first" prophet.

This theory is not in accordance with Jewish tradition. The Talmud and other works speak of only one Isaiah. And even Josephus, the ancient historian, treats all the sixty-six chapters of Isaiah as one unit, all stemming from the same author. The same approach is followed also in the apocryphal work of Ben Sirah.

It is significant that there are now scholars who go even further and claim that Chapters 56 to 66 of the Book of Isaiah were written by still another man, a sort of "Trito-Isaiah." And there are some who go so far as to presume the existence of a "fourth" and "fifth" Isaiah, and so on and on.

If we examine the words of the prophets we find that, in general, they begin with reproof and end with a message of consolation. The message of consolation is usually left for the end so that the final aspect of the prophetic book will leave the reader or listener with a feeling of hope and confidence of better days to come. We see this pattern in the Book of Amos where the prophet, after castigating the Jewish people for its sins, concludes with the promise of a bright and better future, and also in the Book of Hosea, where, after a fiery sermon, there follows, "I will be as the dew unto Israel." And Micah, after first sharply reprimanding the sinners, employs much the same words as Isaiah to describe the "end of days" when peace eternal will reign supreme. Jeremiah, Ezekiel, and all the other prophets also follow this trend.

The Book of Isaiah contains more words of comfort and solace than any of the other prophetic writings, because Isaiah skillfully intersperses words of consolation into his stormy attacks on the sins of his people. Much like a good father, he chastises with affection. Thus we see that, after he has called the Jewish people "depraved children" he soon consoles them (Chapter 11) with the promise that they will yet rule over their enemies. This alternating of chastisement and consolation runs throughout the book, and therefore the sages have said that the entire Book of Isaiah is a "Book of Consolation."

Isaiah chastised the kings of the Jewish people in the harshest terms because even the kings of Judah, who did believe in the One God and worshiped Him, were unwilling to abandon idolatry entirely, so that they worshiped the Lord God and idols such as Baal simultaneously. They sacrificed their first-born sons to the Moloch, a practice which was carried on even by such kings as Ahaz (II Kings, 16) and Manasseh (II Kings, 21).

It can be said that, in general, the standard practice in the kingdom of Judah in those days was to worship both the Lord God and the idol Baal. The people did not wish to forsake the God of Israel altogether, but they found the worship of Baal more enticing since its ceremonials involved sensual excesses and orgies which were attractive to the masses. Much the same was true in the kingdom of Israel, so that the prophet Elijah was moved to cry out to the people to cease straddling the fence and to make a final choice between the Lord and Baal. "If the Lord be God, follow Him; but if Baal, follow him."

This "straddling of the fence" was prevalent to a greater extent in Judah than in Israel, for Judah had strayed much further from the Lord God than had Israel. Isaiah sharply rebukes them, and lectures the people concerning the greatness and holiness of the God of Israel in contrast to the shabbiness of the pagan idols. The man who casts himself down before idols lowers only himself, because he bows to the works of his own hands. But the man who worships the One God elevates himself to a higher plane because the object of his worship is the One who made heaven and earth.

Concerning Judah the prophet says, "Their land also is full of idols; every one worshippeth the work of his own hands, that which his own fingers have made. And man boweth down, and man lowereth himself" (Isa. 2:8-9). And he exclaims, "Enter into the rock, and hide thee in the dust, from before the terror of the Lord, and from the glory of His majesty" (2:10).

Isaiah was the first among the prophets to declare that the Lord was "holy." "Holy, holy, holy is the Lord of hosts," he proclaims, and sets up the sanctity of God as a model for man to follow, for a man who is "holy" will not do evil. In this manner he harks back to Moses who said, "Ye shall be holy . . . for the Lord your God is holy."

Now as we have said before, the last twenty-seven chapters (40-66) of the Book of Isaiah contain words of comfort to the Jewish people. After all the troubles Israel will endure, it will yet see better days, and God will forgive all its sins if only it will return to Him. These chapters begin with the words, "Comfort ye, comfort ye My people." Isaiah tells his people not to fear the nations around them. "Fear not, O Jacob My servant." Isaiah ridicules those who serve idols. "He burneth the half thereof in the fire." He speaks of the eventual building of a new Temple which would be a holy place for all nations. This Temple will not be a place where sacrifices will be offered, but will serve only as a house of prayer for all the nations. "For My house shall be called a house of prayer for all peoples" (Isa. 56:7). He also is scornful of those who think they serve the Lord merely by fasting: "Behold, ye fast for strife and contention, and to smite with the fist of wickedness. . . . Is such the fast that I have chosen? . . . Is it not to deal thy bread to the hungry, and that thou bring the poor that are cast out to thy house?" (Isa. 58:4-7).

And so the prophet goes on to describe the "end of days," the time when "The wolf and the lamb shall feed together, And the lion shall eat straw like the ox" (Isa. 65:25). Harmony will prevail in nature, and man, too, will change his ways. The lion will no longer rage, because he will eat straw like the ox instead of flesh. In like manner, man will no more be bloodthirsty and no longer shed the blood of his brothers. Peace and harmony will reign in nature and also among men—nature and man will be one. It is with these words that Isaiah begins his message, and it is in the same vein that he concludes it.

Isaiah alternates reproof with consolation, down to the end of Chapter

66. All this, according to Jewish tradition, is the work of one and the same man.

It is also quite possible, as some scholars maintain, that the word "Cyrus" in the verse reading "Thus saith the Lord to His anointed, to Cyrus" (Isa. 45:1) was not included in the original text at all, and that, during the reign of Cyrus, some person inserted it in order to explain that when the prophet spoke of "His anointed," he had actually *meant* King Cyrus of Persia. Thereafter all scribes who copied the ancient text over and over again retained the word "Cyrus," thinking that it was a part of the original version.

11. The Sufferings of Jeremiah

Jeremiah, Who Suffered for the Sake of Truth—The Persecution He Endured—He Bewails the Destruction of the Temple in the Book of Lamentations—His Words of Consolation to the Jewish People

The history of mankind cannot claim a more tragic figure than Jeremiah, who endured indescribable suffering for the sake of truth. From his earliest youth to the day of his death his troubles and sorrows knew no bounds.

It fell to Jeremiah to be the prophet for the Jewish people during the last days of the kingdom of Judah, and to witness the destruction of the land by the mighty armies of Nebuchadnezzar.

Jeremiah had come from the city of Anathoth, in the territory of Benjamin. He was a son of Hilkiah the Priest and began to prophesy when he was still very young indeed. As we are told in the Book of Jeremiah, God had sent him as a prophet to the Jewish people when he was still a boy. He had not wanted this burden and told the Lord, "Ah, Lord God! behold, I cannot speak; for I am a child." But the Lord bade him be of good courage and said to him, "Say not: I am a child. . . . Be not afraid of them; for I am with thee to deliver thee" (Jer. 1:6-8). He first began his prophetic activities in Anathoth, his own native town. But the inhabitants of his city were hostile toward him because he had already uttered dire predictions concerning the future of the kingdom of Judah. It went so far that his own brothers and sisters and other close relatives persecuted him (Jer. 12:6). Later on he went to Jerusalem and prophesied there. He stood in the gates of the Temple (Jer. 7:1), in the courts of the Temple (26:2), in the palace of the king of Judah (22:1) and in many other places and talked to the Jews and the rulers of his people.

At that time the kingdom of Judah was in a deplorable state. Corruption and depravity were widespread. The king and his advisors imposed heavy taxes upon the people and took the money to pay for their wanton pleasures. In addition, the land was plagued by false prophets who constantly praised the king and his minions and told them that all they had done was right and good.

Jeremiah could not tolerate this state of affairs and he spoke out loudly against the corrupt and false leaders of his people. The word of God was in his heart "as it were a burning fire shut up in my bones" (Jer. 20:9). He was afraid of none, neither of the king and his court, nor of the false prophets and the priests of idolatry. He told them the plain, unadorned truth about themselves. Small wonder then, that the men he attacked persecuted him at every opportunity. Jeremiah was beaten and imprisoned. Thus, for example, Pashhur the son of Immer the priest, beat him in the presence of many people and then threw him into prison (Jer., Chapter 20). Another time, after one of his fiery prophetic orations, Irijah, the son of Shelemiah the priest, beat him severely and there after brought him before the ministers who put him into prison (Jer., Chapter 37).

But Jeremiah still walked fearlessly about in the Temple, the holiest place of the Jewish people, to look about and see who was there. He beheld a band of swindlers, thieves, murderers, and hypocrites, who prated of holiness but were actually guilty of every crime conceivable. And he cried out:

> Thus saith the Lord of hosts, the God of Israel:
> Amend your ways and your doings, and I will cause you to dwell in this place. Trust not in lying words, saying "The Temple of the Lord, the Temple of the Lord, the Temple of the Lord, are these." Nay, but if ye thoroughly mend your ways and your doings; if ye thoroughly execute justice between a man and his neighbor; if ye oppress not the stranger, the fatherless, and the widow, and shed not innocent blood in this place, neither walk after other gods to your hurt; then will I cause you to dwell in this place. . . . Will ye steal, murder, and commit adultery, and swear falsely and offer unto Baal . . . and come and stand before Me in this house, whereupon My name is called, and say: "We are delivered?" . . . Is this house, whereupon My name is called, become a den of robbers in your eyes?" (Jer. 7:3-11).

Jeremiah went on to declare that if his people persisted in their evil ways their country would be laid waste, the Temple destroyed, and they would be driven into exile.

Of course the priests and the false prophets went to the king and told him that Jeremiah deserved the death penalty (Jer., Chapter 26).

But Jeremiah was not afraid. He wrote down his prophecies and read them before the people, who were profoundly stirred by them since they had also suffered much at the hands of their despotic rulers. When the princes of the land heard of this, they, too, desired to hear the prophecy which had been written down for Jeremiah by his devoted disciple, Baruch the son of Neriah. Baruch complied with their request and read them the words of his master. Jeremiah's message had a profound impact upon them, because, deep in their hearts, they knew that his words were true. They thereupon told the king that they wanted him to hear this message also. King Jehoiakim, the son of Josiah, was staying in his winter residence at the time. He commanded his secretary to read to him the prophecies of Jeremiah which had been set down on a parchment scroll, and, as the servant finished reading one part, the king would cut off with a penknife the length of the manuscript and burn it. At the end, the king angrily demanded that Jeremiah be brought before him. But Jeremiah remained hidden. Infuriated, the king swore that he would murder him, and Jeremiah had good cause to take this threat seriously because the same king had already disposed of another prophet, Uriah the son of Shemaiah. Uriah, too, had dared utter unfavorable prophecies to the king. When the king ordered Uriah's arrest, Uriah fled to Egypt, but the king's men followed him, kidnaped him, and decapitated him, much as dictators do even today with those who challenge them. Jeremiah, however, was more fortunate. He managed to remain in hiding for several years until the death of Jehoiakim. Zedekiah, the new king, regarded Jeremiah in much the same manner as his predecessor, but Jeremiah remained unafraid, and spoke openly and frankly. Zedekiah commanded that he be thrown into a pit of mire. This command was promptly carried out, but one of the king's servants, Ebed-melech, a Negro, pleaded with the king to let Jeremiah live. The king acceded to this request and sent thirty men with Ebed-melech to extricate Jeremiah from the pit and to bring him back to the surface.

Nevertheless Jeremiah remained unafraid and continued to proclaim his doleful predictions concerning the future of Judah.

So much for Jeremiah's zeal and courage. Now for the main characteristics of the book that bears his name. In what manner is he different from the other prophets? He suffered much, but then all the prophets had seen trouble, and even Isaiah had been beaten and pulled by the hair. Wherein, then, is he distinguished from the rest?

The answer is that Jeremiah was the most ardent fighter for truth in the history of mankind. He was the advocate of absolute truth, regardless of whether it be "good" or "bad" for either the individual or for the community. To Jeremiah, the truth was a thing that could not be changed, even at the risk of one's life. To him the preservation of absolute truth was even more important than human life itself.

Like all the other prophets, Jeremiah urges all men to deal justly and righteously and to treat all other men as equals. But, unlike the other prophets, Jeremiah rates these things only as second in importance, since they are the natural outgrowths of truth. To Jeremiah, truth comes first, and the requirements of justice and decency are only natural consequences thereof. We see therefore that all of Jeremiah's prophecies are directed against "untruths" because, to him, falsehood is the gravest sin in the world. It is for this reason that he fought so vehemently against the false prophets. His motto was, "The Lord God is truth; He is the living God and the King of the world."

One incident, recorded in the thirty-seventh chapter, clearly illustrates his unswerving adherence to truth, no matter whom it would hurt. Jeremiah had been imprisoned once again. Zedekiah, the king, was in great fear of Nebuchadnezzar, the king of Babylonia, the great power which had risen on the horizon. Zedekiah secretly sent an emissary to Jeremiah to fetch the prophet from prison and bring him into his presence. The messenger told Jeremiah of the king's fear of the threat of war. He reminded him of the sufferings which he had already been forced to endure because of his out-spoken adherence to the whole truth. If Jeremiah would thus modify his stand, the servant felt, the king might even free him. If, however, Jeremiah would be as blunt and outspoken as he had been on previous occasions, the king would surely return him to prison or even turn him over to the hangmen for execution. When Jeremiah finally came before Zedekiah, the latter asked him fearfully, "Is there any word from the Lord?" and Jeremiah replied, "There is" (Jer. 37:17). In response to the king's question, he continued, "Thou shalt be delivered into the hand of the king of Babylon." Thereupon the king had him arrested once more, but commanded that he be transferred to a different prison. Jeremiah could have easily spared himself such trouble by clothing the truth in kinder words. But he felt that this would have been tantamount to a shrouding of the facts and he would rather have died than not speak the whole truth as he saw it.

Jeremiah prophesied in this manner for forty-two years and lived until the destruction of the Temple, about which he had prophesied so much. He deplored and lamented the destruction of his people, the land, and the House of the Lord, devoting a separate work, the Book of Lamentations to that purpose.

Jeremiah was not troubled so much by his personal sufferings as he was by the falseness of other men. There were times when man's dishonesty plunged him into such utter despair that he cursed the day when he was born and cried out,

"Cursed be the day wherein I was born; the day wherein my mother bore me, let it not be blessed. . . . Because He slew me not from the womb; and so my mother would have been my grave, and her womb always great" (Jer. 20:14, 17).

Jeremiah, unlike the other prophets, could claim a devoted disciple who wrote down all his orations, Baruch the son of Neriah. It is for this reason that most of the Book of Jeremiah was written in the third person singular, while the words of most of the other prophets were set down in the first person.

Like all the other prophets, Jeremiah ends his book with words of con-solation, saying that God would yet redeem the Jewish people from exile and return them to the land of Israel. He even predicted that God would make a "new covenant" with Israel, saying that the Lord said he would "put My law in their inward parts, and in their heart will I write it; and I will be their God, and they shall be My people" (Jer. 31:30-33).

12. The Visions of Ezekiel

How Ezekiel Saw the Deity—His New Approach to Judaism—His Views on Sin and Punishment—The Famous Verse in the Book of Ezekiel Which Gave Rise to So Much Controversy

Ezekiel, one of the greatest prophets of Jewish history, occupies a specific place among all the other prophets, both because of the strange visions he experienced and because of the sharp tone of his exhortations to the sinners, and no less because of the words of consolation to his people which he couched in strange, allegorical terms.

Ezekiel, the son of Buzi the priest of the family of Zaddok, was one of those who, together with King Jehoiachin, had been driven into exile in Babylonia by Nebuchadnezzar (II Kings 24:14). Thus Ezekiel was the prophet of Exile. As he himself says, he began to prophesy in the fifth year of the captivity of King Jehoiachin in Babylonia. His first prophecies were uttered near the river Chebar in the land of the Chaldeans (Ezek. 1:3). He also gives the date for his last prophecy as the first day of Nisan, twenty-seven years after the Jews had been exiled to Babylonia. This means that his career as a prophet extended over a period of twenty-two years.

As we shall see from a study of the Book of Ezekiel, its author was endowed with extraordinary imagination and was able to immerse himself in a state of mind that would transcend the limits of reality. He also formulated some opinions of his own concerning Judaism, opinions in which he differed radically from the other prophets. Thus he built up his own philosophy of Judaism.

Ezekiel knew no restraint when he talked to his people. He employed the harshest invectives when he chastised the sinners among them. He spared none. Bitter, acrimonious, and filled with wrath against sin, Ezekiel exercised no control over anger.

But he was just as emphatic in his words of comfort which were frequently clothed in allegoric pictures. Here, too, he gave free rein to his imagination in his portrayal of the future of his people in the most glowing colors. In short, the Prophet Ezekiel can be described as great in every respect. He is vehement when it comes to cursing his people, but he can be sublime and tender when he blesses them. His words of reprimand are cutting, but his messages of comfort are healing. Every facet of his personality is intense, quite in keeping with his fiery nature and lack of restraint. But at the same time he was realistic enough to be able to see the new face of

Judaism that emerged at the end of the Babylonian exile, and envisioned the new day which would dawn with the rebuilding of the Temple.

Let us then first consider some of his strange visions. The first is one of Deity itself. Nearly all the prophets have left us a picture of the Deity as they saw it. Moses had said that one could view the Deity only from the back, but that it was impossible to behold its face. Isaiah portrayed God as sitting upon a throne surrounded by fiery angels, each one with six wings, and exclaiming, "Holy, holy, holy is the Lord of Hosts." But Ezekiel's concept of the Deity was quite different. He speaks of a chariot with four sacred creatures which run hither and yon upon wheels of Tarshish, a wheel within a wheel filled with eyes; and above them, an awe-inspiring firmament, and, above that, the Lord of Hosts. A very strange vision indeed.

Ezekiel goes on to say that he did not want to utter words of prophecy. But he does this not in a few words as the other prophets did. He expounds upon this thought in a detailed allegory, describing how God commanded him to swallow a scroll until his stomach was filled with it.

Ezekiel shows the same vivid imagination when it comes to symbols to illustrate his message. All the other prophets set themselves up as symbols and performed acts which at times entailed great personal suffering. But, again in keeping with the personality of Ezekiel, this aspect of his prophecy is also much more intense than it was in the other prophets. Thus he says that God commanded him to sleep lying on his left side for 390 days and then on his right for forty days; to eat a cake baked over dung and to shave off part of his hair and his beard. His imagination is inexhaustible, culminating in his description of "a form of a hand [that] was put forth, and I was taken by a lock of my head; and a spirit lifted me up between the earth and the heaven . . ." (8:3).

His most striking visions, however, are those that deal with the return of Israel to its own land. He beholds a valley filled with dried human bones, and the Lord asks him whether these bones could live again. He replies, "O Lord God, Thou knowest." And the Lord tells him that He will put flesh and sinews upon these bones, that He will instill a living spirit into the bodies thus rebuilt, so that these bones would live again. This is an allegory describing the return of the Jewish people to its own land in order to become a great, living nation once again.

The second vision alludes to the reunion of Judah and Israel into one single, mighty, Jewish nation. This he portrays by means of an allegory of a number of separate trees united to form one single, great forest.

The Prophet Ezekiel was outstanding not only in the realm of imagination, but in the field of logic as well. He presents to us a new approach to Judaism, and adds a new set of fundamentals to the doctrines cherished by the Jewish people.

The first such new concept put forth by Ezekiel deals with the question of responsibility for sin. When the Jewish people were still a united nation, dwelling upon their own soil, it was assumed that the Lord would visit "the iniquity of the fathers upon the children, and upon the third and upon the fourth generation. . . ." The community was held responsible for the actions of any one among them. It was assumed, therefore, that not only the individual sinner himself would be punished, but that his entire community would also suffer on his account. However, the dissolution of national unity which came with exile changed this. Hence Ezekiel advocated a new principle, which he formulates in these words, "The soul that sinneth, it shall die." It is only the sinner himself that will be punished for his wrongdoing, and no one else besides him. Ezekiel states it more plainly still: "The son shall not bear the iniquity of the father with him, neither shall the father bear the iniquity of the son with him; the righteousness of the righteous shall be upon him, and the wickedness of the wicked shall be upon him." (Ezek. 18:20). He also sheds more light upon the concept of penitence. According to Ezekiel, if a wicked man should become righteous, all his sins would be blotted out. Conversely, if a righteous man should turn to evil, all his past righteousness will be forgotten.

Unlike some of the other prophets, Ezekiel does not oppose the offering of sacrifices to the Lord. But it is readily apparent that he sees their prime value in the use to which they can be put to draw the Jewish people away from idolatry and to bring them back to the true God. He feels that it would be of little avail to tell the average Jew to cease bringing sacrifices, for the ordinary simple person would not be able to conceive of worship without the offering of sacrifices. However, the sacrifices must be offered not to an idol, but only to the God of Israel. Ezekiel felt it better that the Jews should serve God through the medium of sacrifices than not at all.

He promises his people that the Lord will redeem them from exile and return them to the land of Israel, not because Israel is indeed deserving of redemption but that the name of the Lord shall not vanish from among the nations. For, if the Lord were to destroy the Jewish people entirely, there would be none henceforth that would proclaim His name among men. Therefore, Ezekiel says, the Lord will redeem Israel from exile, not for the sake of its merits, but solely for the sake of His name. "I do not this for your sake, O house of Israel, but for My holy name" (Ezek. 36:22).

Against those among his people who had forsaken God and served idols, Ezekiel naturally struck out with the harshest possible invectives. Thus, in a moment of anger, Ezekiel said to them in the name of the Lord, "Wherefore I gave them also statutes that were not good, and ordinances whereby they should not live" (20:25). This verse caused great perplexity among the sages of the Talmud, and some of these teachers even felt it would be wise to conceal the Book of Ezekiel from the public because these words seemed blasphemy against God's Law. This verse was also cited by the philosopher Baruch Spinoza in support of his own negative attitude toward Jewish Law. However, it ought to be clear to anyone who reads the Book of Ezekiel with intelligence that this rash statement was intended only to make the Jewish people realize the enormity of their transgressions. It was an outburst much like that of an angry parent who does not literally mean all the things he says in a moment of rage. Thus the verse here is not to be interpreted literally as a statement of the prophet's opinion, but only as a scolding, administered in an instant of intense anger in order to reach the sinful in the most effective manner.

That this is true is best proved by the fact that, in a subsequent chapter, he describes the revival of the Jewish nation in its own land, a sort of Utopian state ruled by the Law of Moses. He speaks of a time when the Jews will not have a king, but only a prince, a kind of hereditary president (46:18). The land of the Jewish people will be governed by the Torah. If Ezekiel had indeed meant that the Law of Moses was wanting, he would certainly never have intended the new Jewish state to be governed by it. The new republic envisioned by Ezekiel was to be truly democratic, but founded entirely on Jewish law—a theocratic democracy.

In Chapters 38 and 39 the prophet speaks of the war of "Gog and Magog." The meaning of these two chapters is not entirely clear and we cannot quite understand their intent and purpose. They do indicate, however, that Ezekiel must have been afraid of a great world power other than Babylonia or Assyria, which would eventually destroy the new Jewish state and the Second Temple. These fears were not unfounded, for a third great power, Rome, arose and did destroy the land of Israel.

The Book of Ezekiel contains forty-eight chapters and can be divided into five parts: (1) Chapters 1-24, reprimand concerning the sins of the Jews; (2) Chapters 25-36, deal with vengeance to be taken upon the nations that cause the destruction of the Jewish state; (3) Chapters 37-39, describe the renaissance of the Jewish people and the wars of Gog and Magog; (4) Chapters 40-47, deal with the rebuilding of the Temple and the restoration of sacrifices; and (5) Chapter 48, outlines the new apportionment of the land of Israel among the tribes.

It is significant that, unlike the other prophets, Ezekiel does not end his book with a message of consolation. As we have already indicated, he put his words of comfort in allegorical terms in the middle of the book (37-39). The final chapters describe the renaissance of the Jewish people, but there are no words of comfort. It may be that the prophet had seen too much destruction and suffered too much in Babylonia to be able to speak words of comfort to his people. He was so embittered that, while he could picture to himself Israel reborn, he could not find it within himself to utter words of love and consolation to his brethren. There is also very little prophecy in the Book of Ezekiel which is directed toward the non-Jewish nations.

13. Five Prophets Who Prophesied Only to Non-Jewish Nations

Nahum, Habakkuk, Zephaniah, Obadiah, and Jonah—The Similarities Among Them—Their Prophecies Concerning Assyria, Babylonia, and Edom

Among the prophetic writings of the Bible, there is one book called "Trei Asar," which is the Aramaic term for "twelve." This book represents a collection, compiled by the men of the Great Synod, of twelve prophecies of the "minor prophets" who experienced only a few visions. Their brief writings were all collected in one volume so that they might be preserved for posterity. In arranging the collection, the compilers were not dictated by considerations of chronology or by the size of each book. It is possible that they followed some system in their work, but its nature remains unknown.

In the Bible, the minor prophets are arranged in the following order: Hosea, Joel, Amos, Obadiah, Jonah, Micah, Nahum, Habakkuk, Zephaniah, Haggai, Zechariah, and Malachi. In some of the previous chapters we have discussed three of these, namely, Amos, Hosea, and Micah, who were among the first prophets in Jewish history. They were practically contemporary with several other prophets. Of the nine that remain, then, five share the characteristic of prophesying not to Israel or Judah, but only to the non-Jewish nations of their times. Of course, many other prophets also devoted some discussion to the other nations, but the feature that distinguishes these five prophets is that they speak of the other nations more than to the Jewish people. They were Nahum, Habakkuk, Zephaniah, Obadiah, and Jonah, the great universalists among all the prophets. Let us study each of them separately.

Nahum the Elkoshite begins his book with these words: "The burden of Nineveh [prophecies concerning Nineveh, the capital of Assyria], The book of the vision of Nahum the Elkoshite." The entire book contains no more than three such visions, all dealing with the empire of Assyria. Nahum says little about the Jews. The main part of the prophecy concerns the catastrophe with which Assyria will be stricken. According to Jewish tradition, Nahum lived at the time of King Menassah, not long before the destruction of the First Temple. Some authorities, among them the historian Josephus, believe that Nahum lived at an earlier date, perhaps during the reign of Jotham, king of Judah. Others say that he lived at a later period and that he was among the Jewish exiles who dwelt in Assyria and lived in the City of Elkosh near the river Tigris.

In the first chapter of his book, Nahum declares that God will exact vengeance from those who destroyed the land of the Jews. The second chapter informs the cities of Judah that Nineveh has already been destroyed and that the Lord has taken vengeance on Assyria. In the third chapter he describes the extent of the corruption and depravity which prevailed in Nineveh, a city plagued by theft, rapine, and every other type of crime.

We find in the writings of Nahum a note not found elsewhere in prophetic literature, that is, revelling in the misfortune of foes. The prophets we have studied thus far spoke of compassion for the weak and the suffering, but none of them sought vengeance. Nahum, however, seems to have taken to heart the words of Moses about God, that God would take vengeance on all those who transgressed His will. Nahum elaborates still further upon this concept of a "God of vengeance." He says:

> The Lord is a jealous and avenging God,
> The Lord avengeth and is full of wrath;
> The Lord taketh vengeance on His adversaries,
> And He reserveth wrath for His enemies.

The Law of Moses contains the commandment which reads, "Thou shalt not take vengeance, nor bear any grudge against the children of thy people. . . ." It seems that Nahum interprets this law to apply only to relationships between individuals, but not to the relation of God against a power like Assyria which sought to conquer the whole world and subject all smaller nations to its despotic rule. He feels it is actually an act of virtue to harass a would-be tyrant nation. To take vengeance on a robber empire does not constitute vengeance at all but a favor to the rest of mankind. For this reason Nahum makes it plain that Assyria is not simply another kingdom but a "lion [which] did tear in pieces" and that the city of Nineveh is not just another metropolis but "a bloody city . . . full of lies and rapine." The prophet recounts all the atrocities perpetrated in Nineveh, the capital of Assyria, and explains that his joy at the calamity that befell Assyria is not vengeance but only rejoicing at the just punishment of a criminal nation. Therefore, "Keep thy feasts, O Judah, perform thy vows; for the wicked one shall no more pass through thee; he is utterly cut off" (2:1). The prophecies of Nahum were actually fulfilled. Assyria really fell and Judah was spared for the time being. But in the end there arose another great power, Babylonia, which took the place of Assyria and finally destroyed the kingdom of Judah.

Habakkuk, the second of the "universalist" prophets, also had only three visions, all pertaining to the Assyrian empire. It appears that Habakkuk came from the tribe of Levi, for he ends his book with the phrase, "For the Leader. With my string-music." Some authorities hold that he was a member of the choir in the Temple. The Book of Habakkuk has only three chapters. The first and second take the form of questions concerning God's guidance of the world. The third chapter is in the form of a prayer to God concerning the mistakes that men are wont to make. Habakkuk is the first prophet to question divine providence, asking why Judah should have cause to fear such nations as Assyria and Babylonia who are on a much lower spiritual level than the Jewish people. He attacks Assyria and Babylonia, saying that, even if Judah had indeed sinned, nations of such a low moral level should not be the ones chosen to punish the Jewish people for its sins. He asks a similar question concerning individuals, and, for the first time in prophetic literature, we find the question raised as to why a righteous man must suffer while the evil man is let off. Habakkuk asks God quite explicitly, "Wherefore lookest Thou when they deal treacherously, and holdest Thy peace, when the wicked swalloweth up the man that is more righteous than he. . . ?" (1:13).

This is unique in prophetic literature. Habakkuk has no complaints against his people, but he does feel called upon to remonstrate with God. The Lord must be the symbol of justice. He asks the Lord, "Wherefore . . . makest [Thou] men as fishes of the sea [that devour one another], as the creeping things that have no ruler over them?" (1:14). Nor is he content to wait for an answer indefinitely. He cries out, "I will stand upon my watch, and set me upon the tower, and will look out to see what He will speak by me" (2:1).

And then the Lord sends His reply. The Lord says to Habakkuk that whatever was ordained would come to pass, and "Though it tarry, wait for it; because it will surely come, it will not delay" (2:3). Man must not think that wickedness will be punished on the spot. But though it may take long until the evil man receives his just desserts, the day of reckoning is sure to come. The same will apply to Assyria and Babylonia. True, these countries were temporarily used by the Lord as instruments for the chastisement of the Jewish people, but in the end they must perish.

This is the manner in which the prophet views the advent of Nebuchadnezzar, the king of Babylonia. Nebuchadnezzar had been able to destroy the Assyrian empire, but the days of Babylonia too were numbered. Babylonia was doomed because it was no better than Assyria.

The third "universalist" prophet, Zephaniah, tells at the very outset of his book that he is the son of Cushi, the son of Gedaliah, the son of Amariah, the son of Hezekiah. This means that he was a fourth-generation descendant of King Hezekiah. He also says that he experienced his visions during the reign of Josiah, the son of Amon, king of Judah.

Zephaniah devotes his entire book to Assyria, but not to the nation as such. He is concerned solely with the idolatry that prevailed there, exerting its influence on the kingdom of Judah. He particularly assails those who worship the God of Israel and the idol Baal at the same time. He declares in the name of the Lord, "And I will stretch out My hand upon Judah, and upon all the inhabitants of Jerusalem; and I will cut off remnant of Baal from this place, and the name of the idolatrous priests with the priests; and them that worship the host of heaven upon the housetops; and them that worship, that swear to the Lord and swear by Malcam. . . ." (1:4-5). To Zephaniah the sinful priests of the Lord God are no better than the priests of the idol Baal.

Zephaniah paints a terrible picture of the "day of the Lord's wrath" which is sure to come, and he calls upon mankind to repent of its sins. This is another new feature in prophetic literature: repentance before it is too late. He says, "Gather yourselves together . . . Seek ye the Lord . . . Seek righteousness, seek humility. It may be ye shall be hid in the day of the Lord's anger" (2:1-3).

At the end, Zephaniah says that one day all of mankind will know the Lord and serve Him. He envisions not only a "day of wrath" but also a day when God will give of His spirit to all men, "For then will I turn to the people a pure language, that they may all call upon the name of the Lord, to serve Him with one consent" (3:9).

The Book of Obadiah has only one chapter, dealing entirely with prophecies concerning the land of Edom.

Little is known of Obadiah, because there is no record of his name, his father, or his birthplace. Some authorities hold that he is identical with the Obadiah who was mentioned in the Book of Kings and who lived in the days of King Ahab, serving as an employee in the royal household. Other scholars are inclined to believe that the author of the book of Obadiah lived at a period much later than the reign of Ahab.

The entire vision described in the book stemmed from the fact that Edom rejoiced because Assyria had attacked and conquered the kingdom of Judah. He announces to Edom the coming of a day of judgment when God will take vengeance on them both for their own sins and for their wicked rejoicing at Judah's downfall. At the end there are a few short words of comfort. Obadiah predicts the coming of a day when the Lord will reign supreme upon the mountain of Zion and pass sentence upon the "mount of Esau." He also predicts that the Jewish people will inherit and annex the cites of the Negev, meaning the land of Edom which was located to the south of ancient Palestine.

We can find prophecies concerning Edom also in the writings of Isaiah, Jeremiah, and Ezekiel, but unlike Obadiah, none of these prophets devoted his entire message to Edom alone, to the exclusion of all other men and nations. Obadiah also makes mention of Ammon and Moab, but the principal theme of his vision is Edom, which he views as the most sinful and corrupt of all the non-Jewish nations.

Jonah was another prophet who devoted most of his message to other nations.

The book that bears his name is different from all the other prophetic writings because it does not actually contain any prophecy as such. It is simply a narrative of a personal experience of the author. We are told that the Lord sent Jonah to the city of Nineveh, the capital of Assyria, to chastise its inhabitants for their sins. Jonah, however, was reluctant to go, and fled from the presence of the Lord, boarding a ship en route to Tarshish. We are not given any explicit reason why Jonah should not have wanted to carry out the Lord's command. It can be assumed, however, that his motive in opposing the will of the Lord was his fear of the kingdom of Assyria. Assyria posed a serious threat to Samaria, the capital of the kingdom of Israel. Jonah feared that if he were to go to Assyria and call upon its people to sin no more, they might actually repent, whereupon the Lord would have mercy and spare them from destruction. In that case, of course, Jonah might have assumed, Assyria would be free to attack Samaria at some later date. Therefore it may very well be that Jonah would be destroyed and thus rendered harmless.

The Book of Jonah goes on to relate that the ship on which the prophet sailed was battered by a storm, and the passengers and crew put the blame on Jonah. They threw him into the sea, where he was swallowed by a whale. In answer to his prayers from within the giant fish, the Lord caused the whale to eject Jonah and commanded him once more to go to Nineveh. This time Jonah felt it wise to obey. He walked through the streets of the city, crying out that Nineveh would be destroyed in forty days. The inhabitants of Nineveh thereupon repented of their sins and the city was spared. But Jonah regretted that he had saved Nineveh, a city of more than "sixscore thousand" from destruction.

Some scholars hold that the Book of Jonah was written at a much later date, but they have no concrete proof in support of their theory. At any rate, it is a beautiful narrative dealing with the Lord's desire to have sinners repent so that He could spare them from destruction. Assyria, the "sinner" in this story, actually repented and was spared from annihilation, but at a later date it fell back into its evil habits and was destroyed.

14. The Last Prophets

Joel, Haggai, Zechariah, and Malachi—Joel's Use of the Allegory of the Locust to Symbolize the Other Nations—Haggai Urges the Jewish People to Rebuild Their Temple—The Strange Visions of Zechariah—Malachi's Stand Against Intermarriage—Was Malachi the Last of the Prophets?

The last prophets of the Jewish people, Joel, Haggai, Zechariah, and Malachi lived during the period following the return of the Jews from Babylonia, at the time of the rebuilding of the Second Temple.

These men were not as fiery as their predecessors, nor did they advance any profound new thoughts. In part they repeated what had already been said by other prophets before them. Yet they all had within them some of the inspiration that characterizes prophecy, and therefore the sages of Israel included them in the group of the twelve minor prophets. In fact, Joel was given precedence over Amos, even though Amos should have preceded Joel by virtue of both chronology and forcefulness of speech.

All we know about Joel is that he was the son of Pethuel. We have no record concerning his birthplace or his later residence. In the Talmud it is said that whenever a prophet's name is coupled with that of his father, it indicates that the father was also a prophet, and that the prophet's place of origin is Jerusalem (Megillah 15). If we are guided by this, then we must assume that Joel's father was also a prophet and that Joel came from Jerusalem.

It seems probable that Joel prophesied only after the return of the Jewish people from exile, for he makes mention neither of a "kingdom of Israel" nor of a "kingdom of Judah." Moreover, he mentions that the service at the altar had been interrupted, which shows that the Greeks came upon the scene of world history only long after the destruction of the First Temple. And he says that "Then shall Jerusalem be holy, and there shall no strangers pass through her any more" (4:17). This indicates that at the time of his prophecy, Jerusalem had probably already been subjected to a period of foreign domination. In view of all the above, it is highly probable that Joel lived at about the time of Nehemiah.

The Book of Joel contains four chapters. The first two deal with the locust plague which had at one time devastated the land of Judah. The prophet describes the locusts in forceful, poetic language, as, for instance, "For a people is come up upon my land, mighty and without number; his teeth are the teeth of a lion, . . . he hath laid my vine waste, . . . he hath made it clean bare, and cast it down."

It seems odd for a prophet to devote so much space to a locust plague which struck his country more than a century before his own day. Therefore many scholars assume that the locusts symbolize the neighboring nations which attacked the Jewish kingdom very much like a swarm of locusts.

The other two chapters deal with "the day of the Lord" when God will come to judge the world. This account is strongly reminiscent of a similar vision by Zephaniah, who also spoke of a "day of the Lord" when God would pass sentence upon the earth. Joel sees all the nations coming into the valley of Jehoshaphat where the Lord would mete out judgment. Many of his words also suggest earlier prophets such as Isaiah, Amos, and Ezekiel. But he gives a beautiful and original description of the glorious era which will follow the "day of the Lord" when righteousness will win. It was probably for this reason that the wise men of Israel gave Joel a position of eminence immediately following Hosea in the Book of the Twelve Prophets.

The writings of the prophet Haggai are presented with those of two other prophets, Zechariah and Malachi, who were his contemporaries. We are told neither the name of Haggai's father nor the place from which he came. Haggai is introduced only by the statement that "Then came the word of the Lord by Haggai the prophet. . . ." We know from the Talmud that Haggai lived at the time when the Men of the Great Assembly first appeared in Jewish history. (This was a great academy of scholars which had been set up to deal with all the issues of Jewish interest and which began to hand down those interpretations of Jewish legislation known as the "Oral Law" that was later codified in the Talmud.)

The Book of Haggai consists of a total of two chapters which tell of the erection of the Second Temple. In those days the ancient world was dominated by a newcomer among the great powers, the empire of Persia which had fought and defeated Babylonia even as the latter had vanquished Assyria. The attitude of Persia toward the Jews was much more indulgent than that of either of the two earlier world powers. In the very first year of his reign, King Cyrus gave the Jews permission to rebuild the Temple in Jerusalem. The Jews soon began to work at this great undertaking. But the Samaritans and other enemies of the Jewish people deluged the kingdom of Persia with protests and false accusations against the Jews, and pressed Cyrus to command the cessation of building operations. For this reason work on the Second Temple was actually stopped. In the meantime Cyrus died and was succeeded on the throne by Darius. It was in the second year of the reign of King Darius that Haggai urged the people to resume the rebuilding of the Sanctuary, regardless of whether they had permission from Darius or not. Zerubbabel the son of Shealtiel had already been appointed governor of Jerusalem, and

Joshua the son of Jehozadak had been installed as High Priest, even though there was as yet no actual Temple edifice in which that function could be fulfilled. In those days Persia had under its dominion all the nations surrounding it, including, of course, the land of Judah. Judah was the only one of Persia's vassal states not to rebel against its dependence, and it was for this reason that the Persian kings entertained friendly feelings toward the Jews.

Haggai cries out to his people, "Thus speaketh the Lord of hosts, saying: This people say: The time is not come, the time that the Lord's house should be built!" Then came the word of the Lord by Haggai the prophet, saying: "Is it a time for you yourselves to dwell in your ceiled houses, while this house lieth waste?" (1:2-4). He goes on to say that "Because of My house that lieth waste . . . there is no dew, and the earth hath kept back her produce." His orations had a profound effect upon the people and they soon set to work, so that the new Temple was ready within a month. Of course the Jews no longer had as much gold as when they built the first Sanctuary in the days of Solomon and therefore the new Temple seemed poor in comparison. When the old people who could still recall the First Temple saw the new building, they wept. But Haggai said to them in the name of the Lord, "Mine is the silver, and Mine the gold, saith the Lord of hosts. The glory of the latter house shall be greater than that of the former . . ." (2:9).

The two chapters that comprise the Book of Haggai contain four main points. First, God's command to His people to rebuild His Sanctuary without waiting for permission from other authorities. Second, the promise that even though the Jews no longer had as much gold as at the height of their prosperity, the Second Temple would yet surpass the first one in splendor. Third, the call to all the people to cleanse their hearts first before entering into the new Temple. The final point which Haggai stressed out was that the Lord would eventually overthrow all the world powers and destroy their power to make war upon one another.

The Book of Zechariah follows that of Haggai. We are told that Zechariah was the son of Berechiah, son of Iddo the prophet. This means that Zechariah was not only a prophet in his own right but also the son and grandson of prophets. He began to prophesy in the eighth month of the reign of Darius, that is, six months after Haggai first began to utter words of prophetic import.

The Book of Zechariah has fourteen chapters. The first eight are written in a style very similar to that of Haggai, but the style of Chapters 9 to 14 is completely different.

The book begins with a reprimand to the Jewish people, with Zechariah urging them to rebuild the Temple. This is similar to the exhortations of Haggai. But then Zechariah digresses to speak of visions and he gives an account of a whole series of strange apparitions. This indicates that he no longer had within himself the spiritual strength of the ancient prophets, but that he was able to conceive of things in terms of certain allegories. Those were the last days of the Era of the Prophets and Zechariah himself poses the question, ". . . and the prophets, do they live for ever?" Zechariah gives vent to his wrath at the neighboring nations which had not permitted Judah and Israel to live in peace. He predicts that the Second Temple will be built and that God will dwell in Jerusalem. He also advocates the election of Zerubbabel as the chief of state and Joshua as the High Priest. He expresses the hope that Zerubbabel will lead the Jews and guide them in the rebuilding of their nation. He expresses the hope, too, that Zerubbabel and Joshua will live in peace and harmony. He dictates that it is no longer necessary to fast in commemoration of the destruction of the First Temple; it is much more important to help the poor. His final hope is that all the nations will one day come to Jerusalem to seek God there and to pray to Him.

So much for the first eight chapters. But, beginning with Chapter 9, the whole tenor changes, and even seems in contradiction with the first eight chapters. In the latter part of the book, Zechariah actually speaks out in favor of sacrifices and assails the prophets. He has the Lord say, "And also I will cause the prophets and the unclean spirit to pass out of the land" (13:2). He also makes mention of the Greeks who, of course, figured in world history many years later. For this reason many scholars hold that the final six chapters of the Book of Zechariah were written by another prophet who, though also called Zechariah, lived at a later date than the author of the first eight chapters.

Jewish tradition, however, does not acknowledge a "second Zechariah" and Jewish Bible critics ascribe the Book of Zechariah to only one author. It is generally believed that the prophet wrote the final six chapters of his book many years after he had completed Chapters 1 to 8. When Zechariah wrote these last chapters he was an old man and circumstances had changed a good deal since his youth. In those later days there were many false prophets to whom Zechariah referred when he spoke of the "unclean spirit" among the prophets.

At any rate, Zechariah was one of the last prophets and one who inspired the people to rebuild their country.

It is generally agreed that there was no such person as the Prophet Malachi. According to the Talmud the real name of the author of the Book of Malachi is Ezra, who took his "pen name" from Verse 1 of Chapter 3: "Behold, I send *My messenger*," "Malachi" being the Hebrew for "My messenger."

According to generally accepted tradition, Malachi was the last of the prophets (if we do not include Daniel among the prophets). The author of the book lived at the time of Nehemiah and actively helped in the rebuilding of the new Temple.

There are three chapters and they constitute one single sermon. The book is written in the form of questions and answers, for instance, "I have loved you, said the Lord. Yet ye say, 'Wherein hast Thou loved us?' " (1:2). "Was not Esau Jacob's brother? Saith the Lord; Yet I loved Jacob; but Esau I hated. . . . ' " (1:3). He then proceeds to reprove the priests who offer up unworthy sacrifices to the Lord, thus desecrating His name. He sharply assails those Jews who marry non-Jewish women instead of daughters of their own people, and those who are dishonest in their business dealings and cheat the widow and the orphan. He reassures the Jews that in the end the wicked will be punished and the righteous rewarded, and that, before the coming of the "day of the Lord," the prophet Elijah will descend to earth and will "turn the heart of the fathers to the children, and the heart of the children to their fathers" (3:24).

The strong terms in which Malachi condemns intermarriage support the theory that the book was written by Ezra or by one of his friends, as Ezra was the most outspoken opponent of mixed marriage at the time.

With Malachi the Era of the Prophets came to an end. The question remains whether the visions experienced by Daniel, who lived at a later date, entitled him to be included among the prophets.

15. Was Daniel a Prophet?

Daniel, Seer and Interpreter of Dreams—The Difference Between a Seer and a Prophet—Six of the Seven Prophetesses Were Seers Only—A Prophet's Attire— The Decision on the Authorization of Prophets—The End of the Era of Prophecy

Let us now look into the personality of Daniel in order to learn who he was and whether he was actually one of the prophets.

We know that Daniel was one of the exiles whom Nebuchadnezzar drove out of Palestine with King Jehoiakim. At that time the Babylonian king sought to take into his palace some beautiful and intelligent children, and his choice fell upon Daniel, Hananiah, Mishael, and Azariah. These boys strictly adhered to Jewish dietary laws and refused to eat the food served at court, subsisting solely on legumes. From his earliest youth Daniel distinguished himself from his contemporaries by his ability to see visions and to interpret dreams. Later in his life he was to interpret to Belshazzar the strange writing that appeared on his wall during one of the gala banquets held in his palace. This famed "handwriting on the wall" consisted of four words, "mene, mene, tekel upharsin" which Daniel interpreted as follows: "Mene" (it was counted") meant that the days of the king's rule were numbered; "Tekel" indicated that the king had been weighed in the balance and found wanting, and "Upharsin" that his kingdom would be divided and given to the Medes and the Persians (5:27). We are told that Daniel gained fame and that the king had appointed him to high office. The other officials, jealous of him, passed a law to the effect that, for a period of thirty days, prayers and petitions were to be offered only to the king. This law was directed at Daniel, because it was common knowledge that he daily recited his prayers to God. His enemies intended to put him in the awkward position of breaking the law of the land. Daniel was duly found out, charged with the crime of praying to Someone other than the king, and cast into a den of lions. However, a miracle came to pass: Daniel remained unhurt and the king, impressed by this evidence of God's protection of Daniel, released him and threw his accusers into the den instead, where they were promptly devoured.

According to the Jewish sages, Daniel was not a prophet but a visionary capable of interpreting dreams. His book is included not among the prophets, but with the "Writings" instead, taking precedence over the books of Ezra and Nehemiah. In the "Septuaginta" (the Greek translation of the Bible), the Book of Daniel was grouped with that of Ezekiel as prophetic literature. The New Testament also refers to him as "Daniel the prophet."

The Book of Daniel consists of two parts, with Chapters 1-6 being pure historical narrative, and Chapters 7-12 containing a recital of visions. Some portions of the book were written in Hebrew, others in Aramaic. Here, for the first time, angels are called by names such as "the man Gabriel." "Michael the great prince" or "Michael the prince of Israel," who together with Gabriel, fought against the angels who were the "princes" of other nations. This concept was taken from Babylonian mythology. The Bible always spoke of angels as messengers of the Lord, but never as princes of nations or as individuals bearing specific names. In fact, the Talmud explicitly states that the Jews took from the Babylonians the procedure of naming angels.

Here we find for the first time reference to the concept of the resurrection of the dead. Daniel says, "Many of them that sleep in the dust of the earth shall awake" (12:2). This was new in Jewish ideology. Prior to Daniel we find no evidence in Jewish literature of the existence of such beliefs in Judaic thought.

We said before that according to Jewish tradition Daniel was considered not a prophet but only a seer, a visionary. In Latin the ability to forsee the future is known as "Apocalypse" and those endowed with this talent "apocalyptics." An apocalyptic or a seer is not the same as a prophet. The difference between the two is very great. A seer may indeed see visions, either in a dream or while awake, but he lacks the compelling urge to fight for the ideal revealed to him in a vision, nor is he willing to sacrifice his life in his fight. A prophet, on the other hand, not only sees much further than a seer but also actually struggles for ideals, if necessary at the cost of his own life. His zeal "becomes as fire in his bones." A prophet knows that what he has seen in a vision is the "word of the Lord addressed to him" and he will never rest until he has brought the message of the Lord to those for whom it was intended.

Prior to the Era of the Prophets, the Jews could claim only wise men who could be classed as "seers." Men of this caliber were called "Roeh," (seer as in I Sam. 9:9) or "Hozeh" (visionary) or "Tzofeh" (beholder) and many other appellations which indicated the concept of "seeing" or "beholding." It was only later that some of the seers came to attain the spiritual level of prophecy.

After Malachi of the last group of prophets the gift of prophecy disappeared entirely from among the Jewish people. There came a group of seers of whom Daniel was the first. He in turn was succeeded by a number of other seers whose works became known by the collective title of "Apocalypse." The great teachers of the Jewish people however, did not attach great importance to them. An exception is the Book of Daniel, which the sages incorporated into the "Holy Scriptures."

Thus we see that the various prophets whom the Jewish people produced had all attained the spiritual level of true prophecy. There were also a number of women known as prophetesses but, with the exception of Deborah, none of them was outstanding. We may safely say that, while they can be called seers, they were not really prophetesses in the true sense of the word.

In the days when the spirit of prophecy was on the wane, there were many who posed as prophets even though they had none of the qualifications requisite to true prophecy. They created the impression of being prophets by dressing in the manner customary for prophets in those days. The prophets in Israel could be distinguished by the wearing of a hairy mantle girded around the waist with a leather belt. We are told, for example, of "the mantle of Elijah" in the second and thirteenth chapters of the Second Book of Kings. Toward the end of the Era of Prophecy, Zechariah, referring to the false prophets, says, ". . . neither shall they wear a hairy mantle to deceive" (13:4). From this statement we may infer that, in those days, the false prophets garbed themselves in such hairy mantles to pass themselves off for true prophets.

Now we come to the last days of the great era of prophecy among the Jewish people. There were now a great many men who posed as prophets, but who, in fact, were not prophets at all. Some of them were seers, but, as we have said before, vision is not synonymous with prophecy. In fact, many of the sages of Judaism regarded the seers as swindlers or, at best, crackpots.

For this reason the men of the Great Synod, the most eminent Jewish scholars who had joined to form the great academy for Jewish studies, ordained that they alone should have the authority to determine who was a true prophet and who was not. This meant that no man could claim that he was a prophet unless he had been so certified by the Great Synod.

Concerning this, the Talmud says, "The Great House of Jerusalem (the Sanhredrin) examined each prophet in order to establish whether or not he was a true prophet." In those days prophets could utter words of prophecy only if the Sanhedrin authorized them to do so. The sages base this procedure upon the original Biblical text as follows, It is said, "And I heard the voice of the Lord saying, Whom shall I send?" This means that the prophet must first have heard the voice of the Lord. The other half of the verse reads, "And who will go to the people in order to tell them this?" This means that the prophet must have the authorization to proclaim his message. Therefore we are told in the Talmud that Haggai, Zechariah, and Malachi sat in a corner of the Temple and uttered their words of prophecy in that place. At that time it was established as a definite ruling that "there is no prophet except such as were accepted by the Sanhedrin" (Sanhedrin 82).

And when the scholars of the Sanhedrin could no longer find anyone who could be classified as a true prophet, they issued a declaration to the effect that "the spirit of prophecy has ceased to be in Israel." Thus the Era of the Prophets came to an end.

16. Were There Prophets Among Other Nations?

Balaam the Son of Beor and His "Prophecies"—The "Mantes" of the Ancient Greeks and the Roman "Vates"—The Spiritual Vacuum in Ancient Greece—Why Other Nations Had No Prophets

Were the Jews the only people to produce prophets, or did other nations also number such men in their history?

On careful study, we find that the non-Jewish nations never produced prophets as we have defined the term in the preceding chapters.

We read in the Book of Numbers that Balak the son of Zippor, the King of Moab, called upon Balaam the son of Beor to curse the people of Israel. Now Balaam was a seer, for the Bible tells us "the Lord opened the eyes of Balaam." All this indicates is the capacity of "seeing," but not at all that of prophecy. Balaam was never a prophet nor has he ever been described as such.

The ancient Greeks too, had "seers" called "Mantes." These were men who foretold the future and therefore enjoyed the great respect of the masses. The "Vates" fulfilled the same function among the ancient Romans. But neither the Mantes nor the Vates could compare to the true prophets who had the fire of God burning within their souls and who continually fought for the divine ideals without fear for their own lives.

But why is it, really, that the non-Jewish nations can claim no prophets, while Jewish history can point to many such inspired and inspiring men and women?

We can find the answer to this question if we contrast the spiritual content of the Jewish faith with the spiritual level of the other ancient nations.

The Jewish people was born, as it were, with a basic concept of one God, while the other nations worshiped many gods. While Israel adored an invisible God, the pagan peoples prayed to birds, animals, and figures of stone and wood.

Let us state it in clearer terms:

The Jewish people actually came into being with a cosmography, with a basic thesis that "in the beginning, God created heaven and earth," a definite answer to the question of how the universe began. The Pentateuch tells the Jewish people that God, the Unseen One, who leads the world, who is the embodiment of absolute justice, is also the Creator of heaven and earth. Israel also had in its Sacred Scriptures an exact account and description of the process of Creation. Therefore the Jewish intellects of even the early days, the thinkers and students, did not have to concern themselves with searching for an answer to problems concerning God and Creation. As a result, they could devote more time and thought to the concepts of justice and righteousness, and they concentrated all their energies on the fight for righteousness, justice and peace. These were the prophets of the Jewish people.

It was quite different with the other nations such as, for example, the ancient Greeks. The early Greeks were so thoroughly steeped in idolatry that they endowed their gods with all the failings and vices of ordinary men. The gods of ancient mythology were the most wicked creatures imaginable; they lied and cheated and they indulged in sexual orgies (Cronus and Rhea, Zeus and Hero). Some showed cannibalistic tendencies (Cronus) and others were notorious cowards. Under such circumstances it is obvious that there could have been no real religion in ancient Greece. Greek mythology knew of no holy books or spiritual leaders; it had neither priestly authority nor even a definite ritual of prayers and ceremonies. Everyone was free to believe in the god or gods of his choice, or in no gods at all; he could offer up sacrifices to them all, to some, or to none.

At about the same time, the better elements among the people of Greece began to devote serious thought to life and the world and to speculate upon how all things came into being. It was in this spiritual vacuum that there arose the famous Greek philosophers who posed for themselves the eternal questions and sought to find the answers to them. The first problem with which they wrestled concerned itself with God, and they sought to establish what God really was and how heaven and earth first came to be. The Jews had already found their God.

In all fairness we must admit that the Jewish people also lapsed into paganism; there were periods in Jewish history, such as during the reign of the kings in Israel and Judah in the days of the First Temple, when the Jewish people worshiped the god Baal and the goddess Astarte, and participated in sexual orgies and other excesses. In those days the more serious elements among the Jewish people also felt a spiritual vacuum, but in the case of the Jews, this feeling of deficiency led not to philosophizing in abstract terms, but to the rise of the prophets, champions of righteousness and justice. In other words, unlike the ancient Greeks, the Jews did not need philosophers to determine who had created the world. The Jewish people could find the answers to these questions in the Holy Book, which begins with these words, "In the beginning, God created the heaven and the earth." Hence, whenever the Jewish people was able to cast off the yoke of idolatry, as during the days of Isaiah and Hezekiah, it would return immediately to the Torah, the Law of Moses. The Jews then acknowledged that their Bible had told them long ago that God had created heaven and earth, that there was only One God who was supreme over all things, a higher spiritual power which created and guided all things in the universe. Therefore the Jews had no need to ask questions or to search for a philosophy concerning the nature of the Deity and had a distinct advantage over the ancient Greeks who had no cosmography of their own. And so we have here the answer to why the non-Jewish nations had no prophets. It is because they were at that time still wrestling with the problem of the character of divine power while the Jewish thinkers had more time to devote themselves to the dissemination of truth and justice among men because they already had their answer from the Bible.

17. The Sacred Writings (Hagiographia)

The Old Testament is divided into three parts. First, of course, there are the Five Books of Moses, or the Pentateuch; then come the books of the Prophets, and thereafter the volumes which comprise the "Ketubim," the Hebrew term for "Writings." The works grouped in this category are not on the same high plane as is the Law of Moses, nor even as the messages of the prophets who spoke to the Jewish people in the name of the Lord. They are simply writings, created by some of the great minds among the Jewish people and were judged worthy of being incorporated into the Holy Scriptures. The entire Bible as such is a collection of the fundamental classics of the Jewish people, consisting of a total of twenty-four holy books. Therefore the Bible is known in Hebrew by the designation of "Tenach" (a combination of the initials of *Torah, Neviim,* and *Ketubim*—Pentateuch, Prophets, and Sacred Writings).

The Sacred Writings include the books of Psalms, Job, Proverbs, Song of Songs, Ruth, Lamentations, Ecclesiastes, Esther, Daniel, Ezra, Nehemiah, and Chronicles I and II. This would make a total of twelve books, but, according to the order in which the Bible is arranged, the books of Ezra and Nehemiah are viewed as one unit.

At every Sabbath service one portion of the Five Books of Moses is read aloud in the synagogue. Parts of the prophetic books are also read to the congregation immediately after the reading of the weekly portion of the Law. Of all the writings, however, only the so-called "Five Scrolls" are read in public on certain occasions. The Psalms are recited both in private and in public, by the congregation worshiping in the synagogue and by individuals at various times. The other books which comprise the Writings are never read as part of the synagogue service.

We shall now attempt to study the significance of these sacred books and try to determine when and by whom they were written and why they have been accepted as part of the Biblical classics of the Jewish people and canonized as Holy Writ. We shall examine them in the order in which they appear in the Jewish Bible.

❧ THE BOOK OF PSALMS

The Book of Psalms is the first of the Sacred Writings, and is presumed to contain the songs and prayers which King David created during his lifetime. Altogether the Book of Psalms has 150 chapters. Even as indicated in the psalms, some were written not by David himself but by other authors.

If we examine the headings with which each psalm begins, we find that only seventy-two of the 150 psalms were, in fact, written by David. Two (72 and 127) are attributed to King Solomon; one (90) to Moses; twelve (50 and 73-83) to Asaph; eleven to the "Sons of Korah"; one (89) to Ethan, and one (88) to Heman. There are 50 psalms in whose titles there is no mention of an author, but the Talmud states that King David was the author of all the psalms with the exception of those twenty-eight chapters which are explicitly ascribed to other sources. Rabbi Meir thinks that all the 150 prayers or psalms were written by David the son of Jesse (Pesachim 117).

The Book of Psalms is divided into five sections, namely, Chapters 1-41; 42-72; 73-89; 90-106, and 107-150. The final verse of Psalm 72 at the end of the second section, reads "The prayers of David the son of Jesse are ended." However this does not mean that only the chapters preceding were written by David, for the subsequent three sections of the Book of Psalms also contain quite a few prayers ascribed to David. According to some scholars, the prayers which actually bore the name of David were originally 72 in number and had all been grouped together in one unit, so that the seventy-second chapter of the Book of Psalms really was the final "prayer of David." At a later date, however, the order of the chapters in the Book of Psalms was altered, but the final verse "The prayers of David the son of Jesse are ended" remained in its old place.

Many of the psalms were sung by the Levites at the Temple during the ceremonies accompanying the offering of sacrifices. The singing was accompanied by various musical instruments.

The Book of Psalms covers the entire range of emotions which fill a man when he pours out his heart before the Lord or to another man because of some joy or sorrow in his own life. There are ten different kinds of Psalms: (1) hymns to God; (2) elegies; (3) songs to instruct men how to conduct themselves; (4) songs of victory; (5) the outpouring of feelings to a friend; (6) epic songs dealing with historic events; (7) lyrical songs; (8) hymns of thanksgiving; (9) ethical sermons; and (10) philosophical songs in which the purpose of men on earth is discussed and the correctness and justice of the world order is questioned.

Many of the psalms have been incorporated by the sages into Jewish liturgy—Psalm 95 on Friday evening to usher in the Sabbath; the Psalms comprising the so-called "Hallel" services on the New Moon and Festivals, Psalm 92 at Sabbath morning services, and many others at other specific occasions and seasons.

The Jews attached great importance to what was called "reciting *Tehillim*

(Psalms)." Psalms were read at time of crisis or serious illness. In olden times almost every Jewish community had an organization called "Chevra Tehillim" (a society to recite psalms).

Opinions differ as to the exact time at which the psalms were written. It is clear that, if they were not all set down by the same writer, they could not all have been written at the same time. Some seem to be very old indeed, for they still contain Hebraic word endings which date back to dim antiquity. Other chapters were written in later times. Apparently they were assembled later in one basic operation, which Jewish authorities assume was undertaken by the Great Synod. It may also very well be that each of the five sections comprising the Book of Psalms was compiled at a different time, and that parts of them were set down during the days of the Temple for use as a text-book for the Levites during the services in the Sanctuary.

The Book of Psalms is one of the most popular works in world literature today. The psalms or similar hymns have been sung and recited for thousands of years in the houses of worship of Judaism, Christianity, and Islam, the three great religions of the civilized world.

There are several words which occur repeatedly in the Book of Psalms and require explanation. First, we frequently find the words "For the Leader" at the beginning of a chapter. This indicates a direction to the choirmaster or orchestra conductor as to how the chapter was originally intended to be played or sung. The phrases "upon the Gittith," "upon Shoshannim," "for Jeduthun," and "upon Shiggaion" all refer to ancient musical instruments which were commonly in use at the time of the writing of the psalms but which are no longer known today. The word "Selah" which is found at the end of many psalms has approximately the same meaning as "amen," or "so be it." Some other Jewish scholars, however, believe that "Selah" is a sign indicating the end of the melody or of the music. The word "Michtam" indicates an important song; "Maschil," meaning "instruction" or "an explanation" signifies that the chapter contains an ethical lesson. The word "Hallelujah" at the end of a psalm is a direction to the choir, meaning that the song should be ended in unison fortissimo.

Let us quote here two chapters from the Book of Psalms which are of particular lyrical beauty:

Psalm 13
For the Leader. A Psalm of David.

How long, O Lord, wilt Thou forget me for ever?
How long wilt Thou hide Thy face from me?
How long shall I take counsel in my soul,
Having sorrow in my heart by day?

How long shall mine enemy be exalted over me?
Behold Thou, and answer me, O Lord my God;
Lighten mine eyes, lest I sleep the sleep of death;
Lest mine enemy say: "I have prevailed against him";
Lest my adversaries rejoice when I am moved.

But as for me, in Thy mercy do I trust;
My heart shall rejoice in Thy salvation.
I will sing unto the Lord,
Because He hath dealt bountifully with me.

Psalm 23

A Psalm of David.

The Lord is my shepherd; I shall not want.
He maketh me to lie down in green pastures;
He leadeth me beside the still waters.
He restoreth my soul;
He guideth me in straight paths for His name's sake.
Yea, though I walk through the valley of the shadow of death,
I will fear no evil,
For Thou art with me;
Thy rod and Thy staff, they comfort me.
Thou preparest a table before me in the presence of mine enemies;
Thou hast anointed my head with oil; my cup runneth over.
Surely goodness and mercy shall follow me all the days of my life;
And I shall dwell in the house of the Lord for ever.

The firm faith and optimism, the deep-rooted belief in the justice of God, and the lyricism contained in these two psalms clearly show the profound significance of these hymns. We can readily see how troubled spirits can read these words and find in them comfort and healing for their souls.

❦ THE BOOK OF PROVERBS

This book, second in the order in the "Sacred Writings," follows the Book of Psalms. It begins with the words, "The proverbs of Solomon the son of David, King of Israel." The first seven verses are a sort of introduction to explain the nature and purpose of the entire work. The basic theme is that "the fear of the Lord is the beginning of knowledge." The book proper begins with the tenth verse of Chapter One.

The first portion, comprising the first nine chapters, speaks of the duty of the child to heed the teachings of his parents and to strive for wisdom and knowledge. This is followed by a series of general ethical principles concerning personal conduct and our relationships with others.

The second portion (10-24) is prefaced by the words, "The proverbs of Solomon." Here we find a whole series of aphorisms dealing with such matters as careful deliberation before taking action, contentment with one's possessions, moderation in pleasures, gratification at the thought of having earned one's daily bread by honest toil, the keeping of promises, humility, truthfulness, hatred of lies and hypocrisy, conduct in the home, and many other moral and ethical teachings.

The third portion, which begins with the words, "These also are proverbs of Solomon," is an appendix, as it were, containing those sayings of Solomon which were compiled at a later date. These five chapters (25-29) are similar to the preceding ones. The Book of Proverbs ends with two chapters (30 and 31) which are explicitly attributed to authors other than Solomon; Chapter 30 is entitled "The words of Agur the son of Jakeh" and Chapter 31 "The words of king Lemuel." Chapter 31 ends with the classic description of a "woman of valour" which is a hymn of praise to the ideal of womanly virtue.

The author is fond of addressing the reader as "my son." This form of address is found at the beginning of practically every chapter.

At the very outset of the book, we read, "Hear, my son, the instruction of thy father, and forsake not the teaching of thy mother" (1:8).

The second chapter begins with the appeal, "My son, if thou wilt receive my words, and lay up my commandments with thee . . ." and the third, "My son, forget not my teaching; but let thy heart keep my commandments." In Chapter Four the form of address is in the plural, "Hear, ye children, the instruction of a father, and attend to know understanding." The fifth chapter opens with the admonition, "My son, attend unto my wisdom; incline thine ear to my understanding," and so forth, throughout the first portion.

Some of the aphorisms are quite apt and to the point:

"A wise son maketh a glad father; but a foolish son is the grief of his mother" (10:1).

"As vinegar to the teeth, and as smoke to the eyes, so is the sluggard to them that send him" (10:26).

"As a ring of gold in a swine's snout, so is a fair woman that turns aside from discretion" (11:22).

These are but a few of the wise sayings with which the book is replete.

As for the authorship of the Book of Proverbs, it is obvious that it is the work of King Solomon, since his name is mentioned as that of the author in three different places; namely, at the beginning of Chapters 1, 10, and 25. Chapter 25 is introduced by the statement that the proverbs of Solomon contained therein were "copied out" by "the men of Hezekiah king of Judah." The Talmud explains that the men of King Hezekiah copied the Book of Proverbs (Baba Bathra 15), and that "Agur the son of Jakeh" and "King Lemuel," were pen names employed by King Solomon himself, rather than individuals who were responsible for the two last chapters.

Some Bible critics claim that a great part of the Book of Proverbs is based upon the Egyptian Amen-en-opes (Book of Wisdom). This assumption, however, is erroneous. It is clear to any intelligent reader that the style of the book, the sentence structure, and especially the Hebrew stamp it as a product of the Biblical era.

The Great Synod which canonized the books of the Bible placed the Book of Proverbs right after the psalms. This clearly indicates its importance, for it is given precedence over even the Book of Job, of which tradition has it that it was written by none other than Moses himself. The reason for this is that the Book of Proverbs contains not only wise sayings and aphorisms but also specific teachings concerning the proper keeping of the commandments of the Lord. It contains quite a number of sermons as indicated not only by the tone but also by the style. It is thus an important work on morals and ethics, which teaches the reader the fundamentals of Judaism. It shows man the way in which to conduct his life, teaches him to deal kindly with relatives and strangers alike, and even with his enemies. This, the highest level of moral teaching, is summarized here succinctly thus: "If thine enemy be hungry, give him bread to eat, and if he be thirsty, give him water to drink" (25:21). Simple words, but how exalted and uplifting!

It is therefore certain that the man who uttered these words must have been a person of high moral standards who strove for justice and righteousness in the world, and consequently it is reasonable to accept the traditional view that the Book of Proverbs is the work of a man of great wisdom, King Solomon.

❧ THE BOOK OF JOB

The third of the Sacred Writings, the Book of Job, is one of the oldest pieces of dramatic literature in the world. It deals with the question as to whether innocent men are ever unjustly punished by God, and is the first work to discuss the problem of why the righteous man suffers while the evil man prospers. It is the age-old enigma of why a righteous man who keeps the commandments of the Lord and deals kindly and justly with his fellow men should suffer from want, illness, and other misfortunes, while a scoundrel who scorns the Law of the Lord and does evil to men should enjoy wealth, vigor, and happiness. In other words, is there justice in this world, and does the Lord guide His world with righteousness or not?

This drama is in the form of dialogues, which are preceded by a preface or prologue, and involves Job, a righteous man who, despite his goodness, has suffered grievously, and his three friends. The cast of characters consists of God, Satan, Job, Job's wife, and Job's friends Eliphaz, Bildad and Zophar, and also a man named Elihu. The entire action takes place within forty-two chapters, of which the first two constitute the prologue, and the rest are written in free verse. The drama has three acts and a total of seven scenes, in addition to the prologue and epilogue. In the prologue we are told of Job's righteousness, of his reaction to a lost fortune, and finally of his affliction by a loathsome skin disease.

The plot is as follows: After traveling round the world, Satan comes before the Lord with all the other angels. The Lord says to him, "Hast thou considered My servant Job, that there is none like him in the earth, a whole-hearted and an upright man, one that feareth God and shunneth evil?" Satan replies, "Doth Job fear God for naught? . . . Thou hast blessed the work of his hands, and his possessions are increased in the land. . . ." Job has seven sons and three daughters, a great fortune, seven thousand sheep, three hundred camels, five hundred oxen, and five hundred asses, thus making him a very rich man. "But," Satan goes on, "put forth Thy hand now, and touch all that he hath, surely he will blaspheme Thee to Thy face." And the Lord grants Satan full freedom to afflict Job as he sees fit, to test him, with only the condition that Job himself must not be allowed to perish.

Soon Job is stricken by one catastrophe after another. He loses his oxen and his asses, a fire burns his sheep and his servants, the Chaldeans seize his camels, and, finally, a violent storm causes his house to cave in, killing all his children. Job arises, rends his garments in mourning, but does not blaspheme God.

Satan returns to the Lord, and again the Lord asks him, "Hast thou considered My servant Job? . . . he still holdeth fast his integrity although thou didst move Me against him, to destroy him without cause." And Satan replies, "But put forth Thy hand now, and touch his bone and his flesh, surely he will blaspheme Thee to Thy face." And again the Lord gives Satan freedom to afflict Job in whatever way he deems appropriate, without, however, causing Job to die.

Now Job is afflicted with a loathsome disease of the skin. He is covered with boils from head to toe. His wife, seeing his intense suffering, says to him, "Dost thou still hold fast thy integrity? blaspheme God, and die." But Job answers her, "Thou speakest as one of the impious women speaketh. What? shall we receive good at the hand of God, and shall we not receive evil?" And Job still does not blaspheme the Lord.

Now Eliphaz the Temanite, Bildad the Shuhite, and Zophar the Naamathite hear of his misfortunes and come to comfort him. When they see the grief-stricken Job, they rend their own garments and weep. Then they sit with him for seven days and seven nights without speaking because they see how cruelly he is suffering. At the end of the seventh day, Job breaks the silence. This is the beginning of the actual drama.

Act One, Scene One: Job curses the day on which he was born. The first discussion opens with Eliphaz speaking to Job, who does not answer. Thereafter Bildad addresses himself to Job, who again does not reply. Finally Zophar speaks, and this time Job answers. The discussion concerns the justice of the Lord.

Act One, Scene Two: Another discussion with participants the same as in Scene One. This time the question under debate is whether man can possibly understand the ways of God. In *Scene Three* the theme of the discussion is the remoteness of God from man and his affairs.

Act Two, Scene One: Elihu, seeing that none of the others knows how to answer Job, speaks up. He says he has not spoken before because he is still young while the others are all old men, but now he sees that even old men have no monopoly on wisdom. He refutes the argument of Job. Job still feels that the Lord intends only to test man if He afflicts him.

Act Two, Scene Two: Job's reply to Elihu.

Act Three, Scene One: God answers Job "out of the whirlwind," and asks him, "Where wast thou when I laid the foundations of the earth?" He asks him whether he knows the secrets of nature, the real meaning of life and death, the mystery of the beginning of life and matter, and, most important of all, whether he really knows who God is and whether he walked in His ways.

Act Three, Scene Two: Job makes a humble reply and bows down before the Lord.

Epilogue: Job finds favor in the eyes of the Lord. The Lord restores his fortune so that Job now has twice as much wealth as he had before calamity struck. He also heals his illness and Job lives out his life in great happiness and contentment.

As to the authorship and time of origin of this Biblical work, we find extensive discussion even in the Talmud. One authority claims that Job lived at the time of Abraham. Rabbi Eleazar ben Azariah held that Job lived during the time of Isaac, and that the Elihu mentioned in the book is actually none other than Isaac. Still another view is that Job was a contemporary of Father Jacob; a fourth opinion is that he lived during the period of Israel's slavery in Egypt. Some say that Job lived during the time of Moses while others place him in the period of the Pharaohs, and others again in the Era of the Judges. Then there are those who consider him a contemporary of King David, or of King Ahasuerus, or of Ezra the Scribe. And only after all these opinions have been duly enumerated does the Talmud bluntly assert that "Job never existed; the whole story is nothing but a parable" (Baba Bathra 14).

The opinions are just as much at variance as to the actual authorship of the Book of Job. According to the Talmud (Baba Bathra 14) Moses wrote it, but there are other views on the subject.

According to the theories advanced by some of the Bible critics, Job lived at the time of the first Tannaim, 450 years before the Christian era. However, this cannot possibly be correct. For if we examine the Hebrew style of the original text, it is evident that the language is the same as that employed during the Biblical era rather than that of the era of the Tannaim. The Talmud explicitly states that the style of the Book of Job is very similar to that of the Pentateuch (Baba Bathra 74). The Book of Job is an ingenious work concerning the ways of God in the life of man. Thus, by virtue of both content and style, it is not too farfetched to assume that this great work was the product of the most outstanding man of Jewish history who witnessed the birth of the Jewish people—Moses.

❦ THE FIVE SCROLLS

1. The Song of Songs

The Sacred Writings also include the so-called Five Megilloth (scrolls). These are a group of brief literary pieces which are read aloud in public in the synagogue at various specified occasions. They are: (1) the Song of Songs, which is read on the Intermediate Sabbath of Passover; (2) the Book of Ruth, which is read on Pentecost; (3) the Book of Lamentations, which is recited on the Ninth Day of Ab, the fast day commemorating the destruction of Jerusalem and the Temple; (4) the Book of Ecclesiastes, which is read on the Intermediate Sabbath of Succoth; and (5) the Book of Esther, which is read on Purim. The Book of Esther is also called "Megillath Esther" (the scroll of Esther), or, simply, "The Megillah." Of these five scrolls, two—Ruth and Esther—are historical narratives; two—the Song of Songs and Lamentations—are poetic works; and one—Ecclesiastes—is a philosophical treatise concerning God, the world, and man.

Let us study these five scrolls in the order in which they appear in the Bible.

The first, the Song of Songs, is a love-song of eight chapters, the song of a young woman who longs for her beloved. Most of it is written in the form of a dialogue between the maiden and her suitor, with the maiden carrying the conversation in some places, and merely answering her lover in others. The words of love and the outpouring of emotions in the Song of Songs are among the most beautiful and exalted in all of world literature.

It is difficult, however, to understand the moral of the story which is hidden behind this great poetry. For this reason, many religious thinkers have attempted to give their own explanations of the purpose of these highly poetic chapters. Actually, it should be accepted simply for what it is, the song of a maiden who loved a young shepherd. This maiden had the good fortune—or, in this case, the misfortune—to attract the attention of King Solomon who, enamored of her extraordinary beauty, ordered that she be brought to his palace in Jerusalem. The maiden, Shulamith, locked up in the gilded cage, sings her songs of yearning for her beloved and scorns the king and all his promises. When the king sees that he cannot win her heart because she has remained true to her own beloved, he commands that she be sent back to her home and to her sweetheart. The religious thinkers, however, were not content with this simple interpretation and first sought to relegate the book to obscurity in the Genizah. But another point of view, propounded chiefly by Rabbi Akiba, saved the book from oblivion and eventually brought about its incorporation into the Holy Scriptures. According to his interpretation the dialogue of love is between God and the Jewish people which is His beloved.

As we have said above, the book has been ascribed to King Solomon. At the very beginning we are told in the narrative itself that it is "The Song of Songs, which is Solomon's." It is related in the First Book of Kings, Chapter 5, Verse 12, that King Solomon wrote a total of 1005 songs and this one was truly his "Song of Songs," the most beautiful and stirring of them all.

Another school of thought, however, holds that only the first chapter was written by Solomon, and that the others were all popular love ballads which were collected and added to the Song of Solomon at a much later date. According to this view, the book has no special theme or moral and is simply a collection of love songs that were in vogue at the time.

Pious Jews, however, regard the Song of Songs as a portrayal of the love of God for the Congregation of Israel. It is for this reason that it became customary to recite the Song of Songs in the synagogue after the regular service on Friday nights. It was with this in mind that the poet Rabbi Shelomo Halevi Alkabetz wrote his famous hymn "Come my beloved, to meet the bride," also sung at Friday night services, which extols the Jewish people as the bridegroom of the radiant Sabbath Queen.

2. The Book of Ruth

The Book of Ruth, which is the second of the Five Scrolls and the fifth of the Sacred Writings, deals with an episode that happened during the period of the judges. It is a splendid idyll of rural life in those days, and a sort of prologue to the story of the founding of what was eventually to become the ruling dynasty of David. Ruth, who had lived in the land of Moab, had married a Jewish man, and embraced Judaism. After the death of her husband she was married to Boaz, a kinsman of her deceased mate. The sages question how it happened that Ruth, a Moabite, could have been permitted to marry a Jewish man and to be converted to Judaism, in view of the Biblical command that "No Ammonite or Moabite shall enter into the congregation of the Lord." The explanation given is that the original Hebrew of the verse nowhere employs the feminine form of "Ammonite" or "Moabite," but only the masculine. Therefore it was felt that, while a male national of Ammon or Moab could not be permitted to marry a Jewess and be taken into the Jewish fold, the law did not apply to women of those nations, so that they were free to take Jewish husbands and to embrace Judaism (Yebamoth 69).

According to Jewish chronology, the series of events described in the Book of Ruth came about during the year 2787 after Creation, at any rate, certainly not later than the year 2793 after Creation; in other words, sometime between the years 967 and 973 B.C.

But even though at the very beginning of the story itself we are told that "it came to pass in the days when the judges judged," the Bible critics still claimed that it had been written at a much later date. The first to advance this opinion was Abraham Geiger, who maintained that the book had been written at the time of Ezra and Nehemiah as an attempt by its author to justify and prove the propriety of the marriage of Jews to nationals of Ammon and Moab. This was in opposition to the view of Ezra who was against the marriage of Jews to women of Ammon and Moab, even if such women were to convert to Judaism (Ezra 9).

Still some others say that the Book of Ruth was written sometime after the destruction of the First Temple. However, we are rather inclined to accept the traditional position handed down through the centuries in preference to the conjectures of scientists, regardless of their religion. This tradition has it that the events in the story of Ruth took place during the days of the judges. The Talmud explains that the Prophet Samuel, who wrote the two books that bear his own name, as well as the Book of Judges, was also the author of the Book of Ruth (Baba Bathra 14).

The Book of Ruth is read aloud in all synagogues on the second day of Pentecost after the reading of the portion from the Law of Moses. Various communities have developed customs of their own in connection with the recital of the story of Ruth. For example, those Jews who follow the Spanish-Portuguese (Sephardic) ritual read part of the book on the first day and part on the second, with the cantor and the congregation alternating, verse by verse, in a responsive recital.

3. The Book of Lamentations

The Book of Lamentations or "the Scroll of Lamentations" is the third of the Five Scrolls and the sixth of the Sacred Writings. The book is known in

Hebrew as "Echa" after the first word of the first verse, *Echa yashva badad* ("How doth the city sit solitary").

This is an elegy upon the destruction of the First Temple and of the first Jewish state, and it contains five chapters. The first, second, and fourth of these, each with an alphabetical arrangement of the verses, have a total of twenty-two verses (corresponding to the number of letters in the Hebrew alphabet). In the third chapter there are three verses for each letter of the alphabet, making a total of sixty-six verses for Chapter 3. The fifth chapter, like Chapters 1, 2, and 4, has twenty-two verses, but there is no alphabetical arrangement.

In the first chapter, the "lamenter" deplores the fact that Jerusalem, once so great and splendid, a "city . . . full of people" and a "princess among the provinces," the city beloved by all, should have been so utterly destroyed. In the second chapter he deals with all the suffering that has come to Jerusalem and to its inhabitants. Chapter 3 is an account of the catastrophe and stresses that Israel must accept what has happened as part of the Lord's righteous sentence. But the Lord will yet have mercy upon His people and cause it to return to its own homeland. He will also send full retribution to Israel's foes. The fourth chapter attributes the destruction of Jerusalem to the false prophets and the corrupt priests who led the people astray. The fifth chapter takes the form of a prayer to God not to forget His people forever and to "renew our days as of old."

According to the Talmud, the Prophet Jeremiah was the author of the Book of Lamentations, but there are differences of opinion as to the time at which it was written. Some said that it had been set down during the time of King Jehoiakim, while others maintained that Jeremiah wrote it only after the destruction of the First Temple (Echa Rabathi 81:1).

But the Bible critics had quite a different opinion as regards the date and authorship of the Book of Lamentations. Some of them claimed that the second and fourth chapters were written long before Chapters 1 and 5 and that Chapter 3 is much more recent than any of the others. All these views, however, are simply conjecture and are not based on any concrete evidence. Some of them explain their view of the antiquity of Chapter 2 on the fact that, in the alphabetic arrangement of the verses of that one chapter, the Hebrew letter "Peh" precedes the letter "Ayin." They point out that this was the order in which these two letters actually occurred in a Hebrew alphabet employed in very ancient days, while the more modern Hebrew alphabet places the "Ayin" *before* the letter "Peh." Since the alphabetical arrangement of the other chapters followed this latter order, it was assumed that these must be more recent in origin than Chapter 2. But the Midrash ascribes this reversal in alphabetical order not to grammar or a different era, but to the intent of the author to use symbolism in Chapter 2 indicating that the men of Jerusalem spoke words with their *mouths* (the Hebrew word for "mouth" is actually "Peh") before they could see them with their *eyes*. (The Hebrew term for "eye" is "Ayin") (Echa Rabathi, 2:25).

4. Ecclesiastes

The Book of Ecclesiastes, or, as it is known in Hebrew, the Book of Koheleth, is the fourth of the Five Scrolls and seventh of the Writings. It is the first work in Biblical literature to set forth quite independent philosophical thoughts on God, man, and the world. Many of the ideas set down here are quite daring and even, in some cases, in contradiction with the fundamental tenets of the Jewish religion. For instance, the author of Ecclesiastes denies the existence of reward and punishment, saying that, in fact, man is no better than the beast and will have the same fate. This is only one of the many unorthodox ideas that appear here.

We are told in the Talmud that the compilers of the Bible had originally intended to eliminate Ecclesiastes from the list of Holy Books and to ban it because of some of the "heretical" statements it contained, but that in the end, it was decided to retain it as part of the Sacred Scriptures because the thoughts expressed both at the beginning and at the end of the book seemed religiously acceptable.

The author of Ecclesiastes begins his work with a statement of the conclusion to which he has come after much thought and soul-searching. He has come to believe that all things in this world are vain and trivial, and that whatever man may accomplish while he lives beneath the sun is transient and impermanent. But let the author speak for himself. He puts the question quite openly:

> "What profit hath man of all his labour
> Wherein he laboureth under the sun?"

And:

> "One generation passes away and another generation cometh;
> And the earth abideth for ever."

And this is true not only of the earth, but also of the sun, and of the rivers which keep running into the sea eternally, and of the world in general.

> "That which hath been is that which shall be,
> And that which hath been done is that which shall be done;
> And there is nothing new under the sun."

What is true of nature is true of man as well. Men are born and, in the end, they pass away. Generations come and go. And this is the tragedy of all human life that: "There is no remembrance of them of former times; neither shall there be any remembrance of them of latter times that are to come, among those that shall come after."

Such is the way of the world.

Koheleth tells us that he was king in Jerusalem. (We shall study this statement in greater detail a little later.) And then he continues: "And I applied my heart to seek and search out by wisdom concerning all things that are done under heaven."

And he came to the conclusion that man's life on earth: "is a sore task that God hath given to the sons of men to be exercised therewith . . . behold, all is vanity and a striving after wind.

> "That which is crooked cannot be made straight;
> And that which is wanting cannot be numbered."

Koheleth feels that man's life is meaningless, and, even if a man should devote all of his days to the study of wisdom and science, it would still be of no avail. "And I applied my heart to know wisdom, and to know madness and folly—I perceived that this also was a striving after wind.

> "For in much wisdom there is much vexation;
> And he that increaseth knowledge increaseth sorrow."

What, then, is left for man to do? Should he pursue joys and pleasures, sumptuous homes, gardens and many servants? Should he strive to amass fortunes in gold and silver or surround himself with gaiety and with "the delights of the sons of men, women very many?"

Koheleth has tried all these things. He feels he can truly say that: "whatsoever my eyes desired I kept not from them; I withheld not my heart from any joy," but: "I looked on all the works that my hands had wrought, and on the labour that I had laboured to do; and, behold, all was vanity and a striving after wind, and there was no profit under the sun."

The greatest tragedy of all of life, however, is that man departs it like a fool, however wise and learned he may have been. "For of the wise men, even as of the fool, there is no remembrance for ever; seeing that in the days to come all will long ago have been forgotten. And how must the wise men die even as the fool! So I hated life; because the work that is wrought under the sun was grievous to me; for all is vanity and a striving after wind.

"And I hated all my labour wherein I laboured under the sun, seeing that I must leave it unto the man that shall be after me. And who knoweth whether he will be a wise man or a fool?"

And if someone should say that the best way of life would be to eat, drink, and be merry, the author will reply that he, too, has tried to live in that manner, but that he has come to the conclusion that this, too, is "vanity and a striving after wind."

For this reason Koheleth is quite pessimistic in his view of human life. He finds that whatever man does on earth is of little meaning and that all of it is nothing more than an empty "striving after wind." In his opinion, it cannot even be said that man must fulfill some higher purpose after death, "For that which befalleth the sons of men befalleth beasts . . . as the one dieth, so dieth the other . . . so that man has no preeminence above a beast; for all is vanity. All go unto one place; all are of the dust, and all return to the dust. Who knoweth the spirit of man whether it goeth upward, and the spirit of the beast whether it goeth downward to the earth?"

These are bitter words, but they are not heretical. True, the Torah teaches the Jewish people to view life with optimism ("and thou shalt choose life"). But there has always been an undercurrent of pessimism in Jewish ideology. This is confirmed in the Talmud where we are told that, for two years and a half, the disciples of Hillel kept alive a dispute with the students of Shammai as to whether or not it would have been better for man if he had never been born. In the end, the two parties came to agree that it would indeed have been better if man had never entered this world.

If we turn to the more positive aspects of Ecclesiastes, however, we will note that its author has a strong sense of justice, and he demands of man that he practice justice as long as he lives in God's world. He is a ceaseless fighter for the rights of the poor and of the oppressed, and is gripped by fierce anger when he considers "all the oppressions that are done under the sun; and behold the tears of such as were oppressed, and they had no comforter." That is the jealousy of man to man.

It is a matter of grave concern to the author that "All things come alike to all; there is one event to the righteous and to the wicked; to the good and to the clean and to the unclean."

He declares, "Rejoice, O young man, in thy youth; . . . But know thou, that for all these things God will bring thee to judgment." In other words, man will eventually be forced to pay, through years of sorrow, for the few happy moments that he may have enjoyed in his youth.

According to tradition, Koheleth, the author of the Book of Ecclesiastes, is none other than King Solomon. The term "Koheleth" actually means "a collection," indicating that its author was a leader of a "Kahal," or "community," a molder of public opinion. The Bible critics, however, maintain that Ecclesiastes was not written until the time of the Second Jewish Commonwealth. Graetz is of the opinion that the author was not King Solomon but Herod. Leimdorfer, another Bible critic, names Simon ben Shetach as the author. Renan assumes that the book was written at a much later date, perhaps during the first century of the Christian era. S. R. Rappaport is of the opinion that the work stemmed from some member of the Essene movement. And there are countless other conflicting views as to the identity of the author of the Book of Ecclesiastes. One school of thought even maintains that it is a potpourri of the writings of three different authors at a later time. But it would seem to us that most of these conjectures are unfounded, because Ben Sirah, who lived three hundred years prior to the Christian era, quoted certain parts of the Book of Ecclesiastes as excerpts from Biblical literature.

Other Bible critics believe that it originated from a Hellenist source and that it contains many traces of Greek influence. However, Rabbi Nachman Krochmal vehemently denied this, saying that "the book [of Ecclesiastes] contains absolutely nothing that smacks of Greek lore." And many scholars were inclined to agree with this view.

One of the Jewish protagonists of the view that the Book of Ecclesiastes did not originate with King Solomon was Samuel David Luzzatto who pointed to some places in that work which seemed in direct contradiction to the Book of Proverbs which is attributed to Solomon. David Cahan and Israel Fried-lander, on the other hand, disagreed with this thesis, and they found a great many instances of similarity between Ecclesiastes and Proverbs, and therefore were convinced that the author was indeed the one traditionally accepted—King Solomon.

Many non-Jewish scholars agreed with this last view. Also, Koheleth's call for justice is strongly reminiscent of the prayer which Solomon uttered when he first became king, asking the Lord to help him mete out justice to his people.

In view of the above, it would seem more logical to accept the traditional view concerning the authorship of the Book of Ecclesiastes; that is, that the name "Koheleth" is simply a pen name employed by none other than King Solomon.

The Book of Ecclesiastes has twelve chapters, but many commentators claim that this division is not correct, since many verses which would logically seem to belong to a former chapter have been incorporated in a subsequent chapter instead. For this reason the Bible scholars have adopted the scheme of Moses Mendelssohn who divided the Book of Ecclesiastes into thirteen chapters with a brief epilogue at the end. He arranged the order of the chapters in a manner radically different from the original, standard version.

The Book of Ecclesiastes is read at synagogue services on the Intermediate Sabbath of the Feast of Tabernacles. In some communities it is read on the Feast of Solemn Assembly. Unlike other books of the Bible, Ecclesiastes has not been assigned a traditional, special cantillation for public reading.

5. The Book of Esther

This is the fifth and final volume of the Five Scrolls and the eighth of the Writings. It is a narrative of a historical event which occurred in Persia during the reign of King Ahasuerus. Haman, the king's first minister, had plotted to kill all the Jews residing in the land. The queen, a Jewish woman named Esther, managed to persuade the king to annul Haman's decree and, in the king's name, issued an order that the Jews had a right to defend themselves against the attacks of anti-Jewish hordes. In this manner the Jews were saved from annihilation and saw the defeat of their enemies. This happened on the thirteenth and fourteenth days of the month of Adar, and for this reason the fourteenth of Adar was declared a permanent holiday. Cities such as Susa celebrated liberation only on the fifteenth. The holiday is called "Purim" ("The Feast of Lots") because of the lots (*purim*) which Haman cast to determine the day on which he would carry out his evil scheme against the Jews. The thirteenth day of Adar was appointed as a permanent fast day (the Fast of Esther) and it was decreed that the story of Esther be read in public that evening and again the next morning, which is Purim Day. On the evening of Adar 14 it is customary to hold a festive dinner.

According to Jewish tradition, the men of the Great Synod were responsible for the final editing of this book, and perhaps even for its writing. There was considerable discussion as to whether or not the book should be included among the Holy Scriptures.

There is a difference of opinion among Bible scholars as to the age and authorship of the Book of Esther. More specifically there is disagreement as to the actual identity of Ahasuerus. Some say that Ahasuerus was King Artaxerxes I who lived in Persia from 465 to 425 B.C. Others claim that the Book of Esther was written at the time of King Antiochus Epiphanes of Greece, while still others say that it dates back to the fourth century of the Christian era. This assumption appears to be in error, because even the Talmud notes discussions as to whether or not the Book of Esther should be canonized.

There are, on the other hand, those who claim that the book is simply a Hebrew translation of a story written in another language, perhaps Chaldean, and that it was originally an account of the struggle between the god Marduk (Mordecai) and the goddess Ishtar (Esther) concerning the gods Human (Haman) and Mashti (Vashti). Another school of thought labels the book as a mere allegory, depicting the eternal hatred of the nations for the Jews living in their midst. All these views, however, are based on nothing more than hypotheses.

We therefore prefer to accept the traditional view which treats the Book of Esther as a historical account of the origin of the festival of "Purim" and of the struggle of the Jewish people against its enemies. If accepted in this spirit, the Book of Esther is only one of the many other Purim stories that have been told throughout Jewish history. For through the ages there have been many instances of whole Jewish communities defending themselves successfully against the aggression of the non-Jews among whom they dwelt. Many such Jewish communities subsequently ordained the anniversary of their miraculous deliverance from destruction to be celebrated as some sort of a local Purim. Such local Purims have been observed in many communities until this very day.

❧ THE BOOK OF EZRA

The Book of Ezra, fourth among the Writings (if the Five Scrolls are all treated as one unit), and ninth if each scroll is taken as a separate entity in the Scriptures, is named after Ezra the Scribe who was one of the great leaders of the Jewish people at the time of their return to Palestine from Babylonia. It was he who guided the Jews as they set about the task of rebuilding the Temple and establishing their independent life as a free nation once more. Ezra was of priestly descent and possessed a document in which his ancestry was traced back directly to Aaron, the first High Priest in Jewish history. His own life history is told in Chapters 7, 8, 9, and 10 of the book which bears his name, and in Chapters 8, 9, and 10 of the Book of Nehemiah which follows the Book of Ezra in the order of the sacred Scriptures.

Ezra was born in Babylonia, or, at least, he must have resided there during the early years of his life. At the time of the reign of Artaxerxes I of Persia, Ezra received royal permission to go to the land of Israel with a great number of Jews to help reconstruct religious life there. In all, 49,897 Jews returned to Palestine from Babylonia. Despite the fact that Ezra would have had cause to fear being robbed during his long journey, he did not ask the king for any special guard or escort to accompany his caravan on the trip. After a journey of four months Ezra and his party arrived safely in Palestine. The year was 3413 after Creation, or 347 B.C.

The Book of Ezra describes the state of affairs that prevailed in the land on the return of the Jewish exiles from Babylonia. At that time the Jews had begun work on the erection of the Second Temple. Some of the enemies of the Jewish people, however, told the king of Persia that the Jews planned a revolt against him. Once the king had investigated this slanderous report and found it to be untrue, the Jews were once more permitted to continue their construction work.

Ezra did much for the Jews and for Judaism as well. He instituted the public reading of the Book of the Law and expounded the meaning of the Law to his listeners. A major problem was posed by the presence of a great many non-Jewish women whom the exiles had married in Babylonia. Ezra made every effort to persuade these men to divorce their alien wives and to marry daughters of their own people instead. He succeeded in part. Ezra also instituted a great many modifications in Jewish law; part of these amendments served to effect reforms in Jewish family life.

The Book of Ezra has ten chapters. Originally, it formed one unit with the Book of Nehemiah, which continues the account of Jewish life in those days, and it was only at a later date that the unit was divided into two separate books.

Several chapters of the Book of Ezra are written in Aramaic. The reason for this is that these were actually verbatim excerpts from official documents, and Aramaic was the language generally employed in those days for such papers. Since all the Jews knew Aramaic at that time, it was not then considered necessary to translate these chapters into Hebrew.

The Talmud makes frequent mention of Ezra the Scribe as the great personality who helped give new life to Judaism at a critical period in its history. It was Ezra who inaugurated the Epoch of the Scribes who were to create the Masoretic edition of the Biblical text and who were the first Pharisees (the Tannaim). It is for this reason that Ezra has been given such a prominent place in the history of Judaism and that he is considered to have been one of the greatest intellects ever produced by the Jewish people.

🌱 THE BOOK OF NEHEMIAH

The Book of Nehemiah is sixth of the Writings, (or tenth if each of the Five Scrolls is taken as a separate unit). Nehemiah, the son of Hacaliah, was governor of the territory of Judah but, more important, he was the leader who helped rebuild the Jewish state when the Jews returned from Babylonia to a land of ruins and shambles. He had formerly served as cupbearer to Artaxerxes I of Persia in the capital city of Susa. At an opportune moment he persuaded the king to permit him to rebuild the wall around Jerusalem in such a manner that the city might be protected against invaders from the outside. Gradually the king gave Nehemiah more and more authority over Palestine so that, in the end, Nehemiah attained the position of viceroy. But Nehemiah did more than repair the walls of Jerusalem. It was he who brought into being an entirely new Jewish community in Palestine and who did much to improve the entire Jewish way of life in those days. He was one of those great minds who appeared on the scene just at the time when his people was truly in need of an outstanding leader. Those were the days when the Jews established their second Commonwealth and began to reconstruct the Temple. Nehemiah did a great deal to help introduce a new era in Jewish life in Palestine.

There is some disagreement in scholarly circles as to whether or not Nehemiah was a contemporary of Ezra the Scribe. One school holds that both men lived during the reign of Artaxerxes I. According to the Biblical account, however, Ezra came to Palestine in the seventh year of the reign of that king, while Nehemiah did not come there until the twentieth year of that reign, in other words, thirteen years after Ezra. Moreover, Ezra came to the land of Israel from Babylonia, while Nehemiah formerly lived in the Persian capital of Susa. According to the historian Josephus, Ezra had died by the time Nehemiah first came to Palestine, and in his opinion the statement "Nehemiah the governor spoke, and Ezra the priest" (Nehemiah 5:9) refers not to Nehemiah the son of Hacaliah but to another Nehemiah who lived in Palestine at an earlier date. Accordingly, it would seem that there were two men by the name of Nehemiah who were both governors of Palestine. Other scholars again hold an opposing view, maintaining that Ezra came after Nehemiah—much later, in fact. But of all the contradicting opinions, Biblical tradition seems the most valid. Hence we shall assume that Ezra preceded Nehemiah into Palestine by thirteen years. The rebuilding of the Temple was begun in the days of Ezra but the land still lay waste and the walls around Jerusalem were still in ruins. It was only Nehemiah, who represented the Persian authorities and had their backing, who could finally bring order to the land and improve its spiritual and economic situation. Ezra, lacking Nehemiah's viceregal powers, could not have accomplished all this alone. Nehemiah continued Ezra's efforts to banish the alien women whom the Jewish exiles had brought back from Babylonia as their wives, and relentlessly fought against mixed marriages. He also strengthened the Jewish religion in general, and Sabbath observance in particular. He relieved the misery of the poor by canceling their debts and forced the rich to make financial contributions toward the rebuilding of Jewish life.

We are told in the Book of Nehemiah that there were some who were bitter enemies of his work. There were Sanballat, the governor of the neighboring province of Samaria; Tobiah, an Ammonite; and Geshem, an Arabian; who were not pleased with Nehemiah's administration and managed to win over to their views such Jews as the High Priest Eliashib who did not want to see Jerusalem become too strong. These men brought false accusations to the King of Persia against Nehemiah. The king, however, did not pay much heed to their words. He had implicit confidence in his viceroy. Besides, he, too, was anxious to have both Jerusalem and Palestine become strong bulwarks against the archenemies of Persia, that is, Egypt and Greece, which presented a constant threat to his country.

The Book of Nehemiah has thirteen chapters and can be divided into three sections. The first part (1-7) is an autobiographical sketch of Nehemiah, written in the first person singular. In these chapters he tells of his career at the court of the King of Persia, and recounts how the king first gave him permission to rebuild the walls of Jerusalem and finally gave him the office of viceroy in that city. In the second part (8-10), he describes his efforts to get the Jewish people to observe their religious laws. In the final part (11-13), he tells how he left Jerusalem but returned there in the end as governor and instituted stricter religious observance in the land.

The Book of Nehemiah, immediately following that of Ezra in the Scriptural order, is an account of the rebuilding of the Jewish nation and the renaissance of the Jewish people after the Babylonian exile.

🌿 CHRONICLES, FIRST AND SECOND

The two books of Chronicles are seventh in order of the Holy Writings, or eleventh, if each of the Five Scrolls is counted as one separate unit. These are the two final books of the Bible.

The Book of Chronicles recounts the genealogy of the Jewish families who returned to Palestine from the Babylonian exile. It is divided into two volumes, of which First Chronicles has twenty-nine chapters and Second Chronicles thirty-six. If we treat both volumes as one unit, however, the Book of Chronicles may be divided into three main parts. Chapters 1 to 14 of First Chronicles, the first of these, list the generations of man from Adam down to the twelve Jewish tribes. The second part (Chapter 15 of First Chronicles through Chapter 9 of Second Chronicles) tells the story of David and Solomon. Part Three (Chapters 10-36 of Second Chronicles) deals with the Kings of Judah from Rehoboam down to Zedekiah. Taken as a whole, Chronicles is a recapitulation of the Biblical books of Genesis, Joshua, Samuel I and II, and Kings I and II with certain modifications.

The main purposes of Chronicles is to trace the genealogy of the tribes of Judah. The dynasty of David and the priestly families are discussed in great detail. Relatively little space, however, is devoted to the kings of Israel and the ten tribes of the nation of Israel.

The material contained in Chronicles consists of (a) material taken from other Biblical sources; (b) excerpts from genealogical records; and (c) original material found nowhere else but in the Book of Chronicles.

According to the Talmud, the author of the Book of Chronicles was Ezra the Scribe, but modern Bible critics are of the opinion that it was written by a later author, for some of the names mentioned are of men who lived at least seventy-five years after Ezra. It is also thought that the author must have been a member of the tribe of Levi, because he put so much stress on the Levites who officiated in the Temple.

At one time the two books of Chronicles were taken as one unit, but in the end the work was divided into two separate books because of its large size. Actually, the books of Ezra, Nehemiah, and Chronicles are all regarded as one separate group in Biblical literature because they all deal with the events of one and the same era in Jewish history, that is, that of the rebuilding of the Second Temple.

The Book of Chronicles concludes the series of the Holy Scriptures. The Jewish Bible as we know it today, consists of a total of twenty-four literary works. First, there are the five books of the Law: Genesis, Exodus, Leviticus, Numbers, and Deuteronomy. Prophetic literature consists of (1) the early prophets, including the books of Joshua, Judges, Samuel I and II, and Kings I and II; (2) the latter prophets, including the books of Isaiah, Jeremiah, Ezekiel, and the "twelve prophets" (Hosea, Joel, Amos, Obadiah, Jonah, Micah, Nahum, Habakkuk, Zephaniah, Haggai, Zechariah, and Malachi.) The final part of the Bible, the Writings, contains eleven books in all; that is: Psalms, Proverbs, Job, Song of Songs, Ruth, Lamentations, Ecclesiastes, Esther, Daniel, Ezra, and Nehemiah (these last two are regarded as one book), and then Chronicles. This gives us a total of twenty-four books. At times we find the designation "Esrim ve-arba," the Hebrew for "twenty-four" employed with reference to the Bible.

18. Other Literary Creations of the Biblical Era (Apocrypha)

A number of books failed to be included in the Holy Scriptures. They "remained outside" and are therefore referred to in Hebrew by the designation "Seforim Chizonim," meaning "books that have remained outside" the collection termed as the Holy Bible. The Greek term by which these works are known is "Apocrypha," meaning "hidden," for at that time apocryphal literature was concealed in the Hebrew Genizah, so it should not be read by the people at large.

The apocryphal writings represent a form of literature all to themselves. There are altogether over thirty works in this class. It is hard to give an exact number because there is some dissent in scholarly circles as to which books actually belong in this category. At any rate, we are sure that there are at least thirty pieces of literature that are universally considered part of the Apocrypha.

We may divide these books into two main categories: (1) those which had already been completed when the Bible was compiled and which were not judged as suitable for inclusion in the Holy Scriptures, and (2) those books which were written down only after the number of sacred books to be included in the Scriptures had been determined and fixed for all time.

The books which were deliberately "left out" of the Holy Scriptures were excluded because of the final verdict of the Great Synod which was the ultimate authority on the question of canonization. The reasons for exclusion were: (a) the book in question was not permeated by the same holy spirit as the other books which had been adjudged fit for canonization, and (b) the book seemed to be in contradiction with the spirit of Moses and the prophets. The Talmud makes mention of several books which fall into this category such as the book of Ben Sirah and the books of Ben Lenah. The book of Ben Sirah is known to us today. It contains aphorisms on the order of those found in the Book of Proverbs. However, the synod thought that it was nothing more than an inferior imitation of Proverbs and therefore superfluous. The books of Ben Lenah have not been preserved, but we may assume that they must have run counter to the spirit of the Law and of the prophets. The name "Ben Lenah" must have been a pseudonym, for the word "Lenah" is simply the Hebrew term for "bitter grass," thus indicating a writer who spoke in bitter terms of certain prime issues in Judaism. The other books of the

Apocrypha, such as those of the Hasmoneans and others, were written only after the Bible had been compiled in its final form.

Another division of apocryphal literature consists of works describing visions which are not on the same level as those described in the prophetic writings. These are referred to by the Greek term of "Apocalypse," and include such works as the Book of Henoch and the Sybilline literature. In addition, the Apocrypha also comprises other books, parables, and riddles which are not of great literary significance.

Thus apocryphal literature is divided into four main categories grouped in accordance with their content: (1) historical, (2) visions, (3) hymns of praise on the order of the Book of Psalms, and (4) parables and wise sayings.

The first division, that is, the works of historical import, would include twenty books as follows:

(1) The First Book of Hasmoneans and (2) the Second Book of Hasmoneans, which are an account of Mattathias the High Priest and his sons, the Maccabees, and of their struggle against the Greeks.

(3) The Book of Asdrom (Ezra) which comprises an addition to the Book of Ezra.

(4) An addition to the Book of Daniel, containing the Story of Susanna and other such tales.

(5) An addition to the Book of Esther.

(6) The Prayer of King Manasseh, according to Second Chronicles 33:18.

(7) The story of Judith and Holofernes.

(8) The story of Tobias.

(9) A third part of the Book of Hasmoneans describing the persecution of the Jews in Egypt and their deliverance.

(10) The Book of Jubilees, a kind of homily on the Book of Genesis.

(11) The life of Adam and Eve, homilies on the order of the haggadic portion of the Talmud.

(12) The Testament of Abraham.
(13) The Testaments of Isaac and Jacob.
(14) Testaments of the Twelve Tribes.
(15) The Testament of Job.
(16) The Testament of Moses.

} All on the order of haggadic literature

(17) The Testament of King Solomon, which contains Talmudic legends concerning that king.

(18) The Book of Asenath and Joseph.

(19) The ascent of Isaiah, a legend about the death of the Prophet Isaiah, based on the story in the Talmud to the effect that he was murdered by King Manasseh (Yebamoth 49).

(20) "These Are the Last Words of Baruch," a story of the time of the destruction of Jerusalem.

The second category of apocryphal literature includes accounts of visions such as (1) the Book of Baruch and the Letter of Jeremiah; (2) the Ascent of Moses, a story on the order of the Testament of Moses, except that it contains more accounts of visions than the latter; (3) the Prophecies of Eldad and Mildad (according to Talmudic legend). Into this category, too, belong the Sybilline books of which several have been preserved to this day.

The third category, Hymns of Praise, includes, (1) a Psalm 151 which is not contained in the original Book of Psalms where we find only 150 chapters; (2) Psalms by King Solomon, eighteen in all; and (3) three psalms written in the Syrian language. One of these three is identical with Psalm 151, the second is a prayer set down by Hezekiah, and the third is a prayer of thanksgiving offered on the occasion of the day when King Cyrus finally permitted the Jewish people to rebuild the Temple. There are also two other psalms, previously unknown, which are attributed to King David.

The fourth category consists of wise sayings and parables such as (1) the Book of Ben Sirah; (2) the Book of Wisdom of Solomon, which tells how Solomon urged the nations to abandon idolatry, and (3) the Fourth Volume of the Book of Hasmoneans in which the belief in God is extolled against rationalism. This category would include other books as well, such as the Letter of Aristas from the Jews of Alexandria concerning the translation of the Bible, and other works of minor importance.

The attitude of the Christian Church toward apocryphal literature differs from that held by Judaism. They have incorporated some of these works into the Bible. But even before Christianity canonized certain apocryphal writings, we find that fourteen of these works had already been incorporated into the Septuagintal version of the ancient Greek translation of the Bible which was completed some time during the epoch of the Tannaim. These fourteen books are (1) and (2) both parts of the Book of Asdrom (Ezra); (3) the Book of Tobias; (4) the Book of Judith; (5) the addition to the Book of Esther; (6) the Wisdom of Solomon; (7) the Book of Ben Sirah; (8) the Book of Baruch; (9), (10), and (11) the three additions to the Book of Daniel; (12) the Prayer of Manasseh; and (13) and (14) the first two books of Hasmoneans. These same fourteen works were also included in the Vulgate, the Latin translation of the Bible, which was made by the Christian Church during the first century of the Christian era.

It would appear that these fourteen books had been written in either Hebrew or Aramaic during the time of Ezra the Scribe and that they were well known to the general public at the time when the Septuagint was edited ("Septuaginta" is the Latin term for "seventy," indicating the seventy scholars who translated the Bible into Greek). Another school of thought holds that the Second Book of Hasmoneans and the Wisdom of Solomon were originally written in the Greek language and translated into Hebrew at a later date. According to Jewish opinion, most of the fourteen books mentioned above were written in Palestine and only a few, such as the Second Book of Hasmoneans, the Wisdom of Solomon, and the Book of Tobias, had their origin in Egypt where Greek was the official language at the time.

On the whole, a closer examination of apocryphal literature reveals that most of it is not of very high quality and that there is no reason to regret its exclusion from the Holy Scriptures. Still, one cannot say that it is all absolutely worthless. Some of these books, such as the four books of the Hasmoneans, the Books of Asdrom, and several others, have a historical value. Others have ethical significance, such as the Book of Tobias which extols the duty of affording a decent Jewish burial to the Jewish dead; the Book of Baruch which strongly attacks immorality, the Book of the Wisdom of Solomon which propounds the immortality of the human soul and the Book of Ben Sirah which commands respect for scholars and healers of the sick. Others contain some important prayers. Parts of the books of Tobias, Susanna, Judith, and others have literary value as the first works of belles-lettres in Jewish history.

We have stated above that Christianity incorporated parts of apocryphal literature into its Bible. This must be explained in more detail. In the beginning, those fourteen books which were included first in the Septuagint and then in the Vulgate version of the Bible, were regarded by the Catholic Church as integral parts of the Scriptures, in which they formed part of what Christianity calls the Old Testament. This remained so until the days of Luther and the Reformation, when the various Protestant denominations first appeared in history.

Today most of the Protestant denominations do not recognize these fourteen apocryphal books as part of the original Bible. In addition to the New Testament, they regard as holy only the twenty-four books which the Jewish people deem sacred.

As time went on, the Catholic Church, too, changed its views in this respect. The Church authorities dropped the Second Book of Asdrom and the Prayer of Manasseh, because these works had not been included in all the editions of the Septuagint and therefore were not considered too important. Hence the Catholic Church today has retained as sacred only twelve out of the fourteen books which it had originally canonized.

The Protestant denominations have also made some modifications. The Anglican Church, for example, has retained some of the apocryphal works while discarding others. Other denominations have also subjected these writings to a procedure of selection and elimination.

Hence it is evident that there is disagreement even among the various sects of Christianity as regards the importance of apocryphal literature and the propriety of the canonization of any of it.

This chapter would not be complete without a brief survey of the apocalyptic writings, a whole body of literature which deals with visions and was written in various nations at various times in history. The first of these were set down in Egypt. Some of the documents portray the future of the world and that of mankind, and predict that the world will come to an end because of man's sins. Others describe the life of the human soul after the death of the body, while still others deal with dreams and other mystical themes.

The apocalyptic writings may be divided into seven categories. As we have indicated above, the first of these had its origin in Egypt. The second category included Hebrew works, written prior to the destruction of the Temple. Next are (3) the works written after the fall of the Temple; (4) the creations of the early Christians; (5) new Hebrew works written in the early Christian era; (6) similar creations from Islamic literature; and (7) the medieval world literature.

Each of these reflects the spirit of the times in which it was written. Some are dominated by a mood of pessimism, visualizing the downfall of the world when corruption and wickedness will end and a new and better mankind will emerge from the ruins. Reflecting the mood of a different age, other apocalyptic writings discuss life after death and have preserved for us detailed descriptions of paradise and hell. Others again, particularly those produced in the Middle Ages, deal with the kingdom of Satan and the evil which he and his cohorts do to men.

Taken as a whole, the Apocalypse has no great significance. It includes mainly the writings of men who were fearful, superstitious, and afflicted with morbid imaginations. They are thus of little permanent value, but they certainly represent a type of literature worth studying as part of our survey of history.

The Talmudic Era

I. The Time of the Tannaim

1. How the Talmud Came into Being

The First Tannaim—The Five "Zugoth"—Simon Ben Shetach—Hillel and Sham-
mai—Shemayah and Abtalyon

When the Jews returned to Palestine
from Babylonia to rebuild their temple, their religious life took on a form
quite different from what it had been before the destruction of the First Commonwealth. It seemed that idolatry had lost its hold upon the people of Israel.
Prior to the destruction of the First Temple, idolatry had been rife in Palestine. There had been much assimilation, too, in Babylonia, the mightiest
pagan nation of those days. But when Babylonia fell in its turn, Judaism
experienced an unparalleled religious revival. Leaders arose who urged the
people to repent of their sins and to return to their God, and they found a willing audience which heeded their words, something that would hardly have
happened during all the years of Israel's former independence.

At that time, there arose among the Jews three different groups of teachers and scholars, each with a different mission but all with one aim, namely,
to build and strengthen Judaism. These were the later prophets (Haggai,
Zechariah, and Malachi, as well as such personalities as Ezra the Scribe, and
Nehemiah), the scribes as a group and the members of the Great Synod. The
first group, the later prophets, were a class to themselves. These were men
who, though regarded as prophets, no longer possessed that great and fiery inspiration with which earlier prophets had been endowed, and who, therefore,
were not as independent and outstanding as their spiritual predecessors had
been in the past. They realized that the great light of prophecy which God had
handed down to the Jewish people had grown dim and would soon go out
altogether. They therefore did not feel qualified to bear all by themselves the
crushing responsibility for what would now become of the Jewish people. For
Israel stood at the crossroads then, faced with the choice of whether or not
to go on through history as the one people which, among all the heathen
nations, would persist in remaining true to the One God. The later prophets
called upon the Jews to stop and think and to cast aside their idols. But the
complete abolition of paganism in the land of Israel entailed tremendous difficulties, economical, political, and even geographical, for Palestine was surrounded on all side by heathen nations. For this reason the prophets, though
they knew they had been sent by the Lord to teach and guide His people,
always took counsel with the leaders of the Jewish nation before taking action
on their own. Because of the great responsibility involved in counseling the

Jewish people, we see that, once the rebuilding of the Temple was well under way, the prophets withdrew from the picture altogether and were content to have other leaders take charge. It is for this reason that we find little mention of these later prophets in connection with the period of Jewish revival and renaissance which immediately followed the return from Babylonia.

The second group of teachers, the scribes, had been called into being by Ezra the Scribe. They were the original Pharisees. The scribes, in turn, were eventually followed by the first Tannaim. The scribes primarily occupied themselves with writing down the Law of Moses and explaining it to the people. They carefully studied every word and letter of the Scriptures and determined the exact manner in which each word of the Bible was to be spelled in all future editions.

The scribes were predecessors of a third group of scholars who had a profound influence upon Jewish life. These were the men of the Great Synod, a kind of "Constitutional Convention" which was called together to determine the fundamentals of Judaism.

This body made a great many new laws and modified much of preexisting legislation. Their decisions were considered binding upon all Jews. It was this Synod which first ordained that every Jewish religious community must have rabbis and religious judges who would teach the people the proper way to observe their laws and settle whatever disputes might arise among their flock. The Synod also wrote down many prayers, such as the Kiddush that is recited on Sabbath and holidays and the Habdalah service which marks the end of each Sabbath. In general, the Synod fixed the fundamentals of Jewish religious practice and ritual as we know it today. But the greatest achievement of this body by far was the "canonization" of the Bible, the gigantic task of determining which of the sacred books was sufficiently important to be incorporated into the Bible and which should be discarded and relegated to oblivion.

The men of the Great Synod were succeeded by the first and second groups of Tannaim. Their era extended from the time of Simon the Just, one of the last members of the Synod, down to the days of Rabbi Judah the Prince who edited the Mishna and gave it its present form. The era of the Tannaim ended around the year 219 after the birth of Christ, after having endured through a span of five generations.

The first group of Tannaim were the so-called "zugoth," "pairs" or "teams" of two scholars each, who would either set forth their opinions jointly, or else debate the fine points of Jewish law with each other. That kind of scholarly teamwork was quite in conformity with the spirit of those days. The last such famous pair was that formed by Hillel and Shammai, who lived during the reign of King Herod.

Let us proceed in order. We shall first study the first Tannaim, the chief personalities who left their mark on that epoch in Jewish history, and the principles for which they fought. Thereafter we shall make a survey of the era of the second Tannaim and of their achievements.

❧ THE FIRST TANNAIM

Without a doubt, the era of the Tannaim was the most glorious in Jewish history. As we have said before, this period began with Simon the Just who was one of the last surviving members of the Great Synod which had been formed at the beginning of the Second Jewish Commonwealth, and ended about a hundred and fifty years after the destruction of the Second Temple.

This great era in the history of Judaism may be divided into two parts, the period of the first Tannaim and that of the second Tannaim. The first Tannaim expounded the Law over a period of about three hundred years while the Second Temple stood in Jerusalem. The second Tannaim came at a later date, around sixty years prior to the destruction of the Second Temple. The beginning of the epoch of the second Tannaim almost coincides with the opening of the Christian era, and the date of its closing is generally put at the year 220 (some say 210) of the Christian calendar.

The listing of the first Tannaim in chronological order is given us in the Talmud itself. There we are told early in the tractate Aboth that "Moses received the Law from Mount Sinai" and handed it down to the elders (meaning the judges down to the time of Samuel). The elders, in turn, passed the Law on to the prophets, and the prophets bequeathed it to the members of the Great Synod, the body of leaders which first came into being at the time of Ezra the Scribe. Thereafter came the first Tannaim who, at the start, worked in teams of two, or pairs. One of the partners would be the Nasi, or president, of the Sanhedrin, and the other would occupy the position of chairman of the religious court, second in command only to the Nasi. After Simon the Just, the period of the first Tannaim or "pairs" began. Altogether there were five outstanding teams whose achievements on behalf of Judaism have made them immortal. First there were Jose ben Yoezer of Zeridah (president of the Sanhedrin) and Jose ben Johanan of Jerusalem (chairman of the religious court). The second pair consisted of Joshua ben Perachiah and Nitai of Arbela. Then came Judah ben Tabbai and Simon ben Shetach; Shemayah and Abtalyon; and finally Hillel and Shammai. The tractate Aboth in the Talmud has preserved for posterity many of the wise sayings and moral adages of these learned men.

The Talmud gives us little biographical material on the members of these teams, but it does contain several valuable references to each. We may find there quite a few of the utterances of Jose ben Yoezer of Zeridah and Jose ben Johanan of Jerusalem, particularly with regard to those laws concerning the interpretation of which the two failed to agree.

There is very little in the Talmud about Jose ben Johanan of Jerusalem, but we do know that he served as chairman of the religious court at the time when the other Jose was president of the Sanhedrin.

We have more information about Joshua ben Perachiah than we do concerning his assistant, Nitai of Arbela. The former was president of the Sanhedrin during the reign of King Yanai (also known as Alexander Jannaeus) and when that ruler began to persecute the scholars and actually murdered quite a few of them, Joshua managed to escape to Alexandria. Hardly any mention is made in the Talmud of Nitai of Arbela.

With regard to Judah ben Tabbai and Simon ben Shetach, there is some disagreement in the Talmud as to which of these two had been president of the Sanhedrin. One authority, Rabbi Meir, held that Judah had been president of the Sanhedrin and Simon the chairman of the religious court, but other sages insisted that Simon, and not Judah, had headed the lawmaking body.

Simon ben Shetach was the brother of Queen Shulamith (or Salome) who was also known by her Greek name, Alexandra, and was married to Alexander Jannaeus. Jannaeus (or Yanai) was generally hated because of his persecution of the intellectual and scholarly elements of his country. The people, who sided with the Tannaim, were about to revolt against him, and Yanai, in order to save the throne, abdicated and appointed his wife Shulamith Queen Regent a few years before his death.

Shulamith had a great respect for scholarship, and when her husband died she immediately appointed her brother Simon ben Shetach president of the Sanhedrin. Simon then sent for his friend Judah ben Tabbai, who had fled to Alexandria to escape murder, and asked him to return. Judah did not hesitate to follow the invitation of his friend, who then appointed him chairman of the religious court.

These two great Tannaim did much to strengthen Judaism. They formulated a great many new laws and modifications of preexisting legislation concerning legal court proceedings so that justice could be done to both sides in a dispute. They compelled the judges to examine all testimony with the utmost care and made it very difficult for a court to hand down a death sentence. They also decreed that widows had the right to be made the legal heirs of their husbands.

Of particular importance was Simon ben Shetach's institution of compulsory education for all children. A seminary was established in Jerusalem for the training of teachers. There had to be at least one school for the young in every town and village, and each school was to be accessible to every child. These institutions of learning were the first true public schools in history.

The Talmud gives us little information concerning Shemayah and Abtalyon. But we do know that they were descended from proselytes. The Talmud tells us that "the grandsons of Sennacherib have studied the Law with the Jewish people; they were Shemayah and Abtalyon" (Gittin 57). Some of their legal decisions and wise sayings have been preserved for us in Jewish literature. In their day, there was instituted the first regular system of tuition fees for those who attended the houses of study.

But the most important of the five teams was the fifth, that of Hillel and Shammai. Hillel held the office of president of the Sanhedrin while Shammai served as chairman of the religious court.

❦ HILLEL AND SHAMMAI

Without a doubt one of the greatest figures in Judaism during the era of the Second Temple was Hillel the Elder or Hillel of Babylonia (also known by that name because he had lived in Babylonia during his formative years). He was not only one of the greatest teachers ever to be produced by the Jewish people, but was also an outstanding personality who, both through his teaching and his own personal example, demonstrated to all men, Jews and non-Jews alike, the highest ideals of ethics and human relations. It was Hillel who gave a new original interpretation to the Biblical commandment "And thou shalt love thy neighbor as thyself.'" Couched in such terms, this commandment seems difficult to fulfill, because, after all, it is a human trait to love oneself most of all and to give first priority to one's own interests. So that the average person might not find it too forbidding and impossible of fulfillment, Hillel rephrased this injunction in negative terms, as follows, "Thou shalt not do unto another that which thou wouldst not have him do unto thee." This is much easier for an ordinary mortal to understand and to obey than if it were stated in positive terms.

Hillel truly practiced what he preached. He showed us by his own personal example how to practice in our everyday lives the religious and ethical commandments he expounded from the lectern.

Hillel was born about 140 B.C. and died in 65 B.C. at the age of seventy-five. In one place in the Talmud, however, it is claimed that he lived a hundred and twenty years, forty in Babylonia, forty as a student of the Law, and another forty as the leader of his people. But this seems to be nothing more than a legendary conjecture such as often surrounds great men. Legend also has it that he was of noble descent, a member of the tribe of Benjamin. Other sources hold that he was a direct descendant of King David. This last claim seems an exaggeration. Hillel had a brother, Shavnah, who was a merchant and gave Hillel some financial assistance.

Hillel's son Simon, his grandson Gamaliel and one of his great-grandsons who was also named Simon, were all presidents of the Sanhedrin in Palestine during a span of some one hundred years before the destruction of the Second Temple. Hillel himself occupied that exalted office for some thirty years.

Hillel had originally come to Jerusalem from Babylonia to study the Law with Shemayah and Abtalyon, who were outstanding teachers. When he first came to Jerusalem he was very poor. Half of his meager daily earnings went to feed his family, and the other half he gave to the porter of the house of study as an admission fee, as was the custom in those days. One day he did not even have enough money to be admitted to the house of learning and therefore climbed up to the chimney of the building and lay there to listen to the learned discussion that went on inside. It was bitterly cold and the snow was falling, but Hillel was oblivious of the weather. Hours later the porter found him on the roof, unconscious.

The Talmud is replete with anecdotes of Hillel's marvelous disposition and his infinite patience. He was willing to give every man the benefit of the doubt and hesitated to pass harsh judgment on any person. There is the story about the Gentile who had come to Shammai, declaring his willingness to become a Jew if he could be taught all there was to Judaism while he would stand on one foot. Shammai, enraged at what seemed to him an insolent request, threw him out. When the prospective convert turned to Hillel for advice, he was kindly received and told that it was indeed possible for him to learn all the essentials of Judaism while he stood on one foot. "Thou shalt not do unto another that which thou wouldst not have him do unto thee—that is the fundamental principle on which all of Judaism is based," Hillel explained. "All the rest is commentary. Now go thou and study."

Hillel used to say, "If I am not for myself, who, then, will be for me? And if I will be only for myself, then who am I?"

He also said, "Be one of the disciples of Aaron the priest, who seek to make peace among men, and love all men, and strive to bring them near to the study of the Law."

Hillel was endowed with so much humility that it was impossible to make him angry. It seems that one man wagered 400 zuzim, a coin of that time, that he would be able to accomplish the impossible and rouse the gentle scholar's ire. The man came to Hillel one Friday afternoon, just as Hillel was preparing to wash his hair in honor of the Sabbath, and shouted "Is Hillel there?" (He did not ask for "the president of the Sanhedrin," or even for "Rabbi Hillel.") He thought that this rude approach alone would be sufficient to annoy the sage, but Hillel came out and greeted him with a good-natured smile, and asked him, "What dost thou want, my son?" The man then asked him a foolish question, to which Hillel gave a calm and patient answer. The visitor then left, but soon returned, shouting once more, "Is Hillel there?

Where is he?" And again Hillel met him with a smile and asked him, "What dost thou wish to know, my son?" Once more the intruder asked him some trivial question and Hillel gently replied. The unbidden guest left, but not for long. The third time he shouted at the top of his voice, "Is Hillel there?" And once more Hillel came out with a friendly greeting and without a trace of anger tried to answer the insolent question with which the man now confronted him. This time the visitor turned upon him angrily and said to him, "Art thou indeed Hillel, the president of the Jewish Sanhedrin?" And Hillel replied, "That I am." "If this be so, then let there not be any more like thee," retorted the visitor. And when Hillel, with a smile, asked him the reason for his statement, he replied in fury, "Because of thee I have just lost 400 zuzim" and proceeded to tell him the entire story of the bet he had made that he would be able to make Hillel angry. But Hillel quietly answered him, "Be careful, my son, with what thou sayest. It is better that thou shouldst lose 400 zuzim and even double that amount than that Hillel should lose his temper."

When Hillel first came from Babylonia, Shammai already headed a large Talmudical academy, or Yeshiva, in Jerusalem. One year Passover Eve fell upon a Sabbath and no one knew whether it was permissible to bring the Passover sacrifice on a Sabbath. The legal dispute resolved around the question of whether the offering of the Passover sacrifice was a violation of the Sabbath and, if so, whether the holiday of Passover took precedence over the weekly Sabbath. The then president of the Sanhedrin asked that all those who felt qualified to do so report their findings to him. It was suggested that Hillel, the young newcomer from Babylonia, be consulted. In a scholarly dissertation, Hillel explained why it was permissible, according to Jewish law, to bring the Passover sacrifice even on the Sabbath day. The learned men of the academy were so impressed with Hillel's erudition that they eventually elected him president of the Sanhedrin. Eventually Shammai became the chairman of the religious court, second in command to Hillel.

We know of Hillel that he accomplished what Ezra had done at an earlier time, that is, he succeeded in spreading the knowledge and observance of the Law among the Jewish people. The Law had been forgotten during the Babylonian exile and Ezra saved it from oblivion. When the Law once more fell into neglect in Palestine, it was Hillel who came from Babylonia to revive it once again.

Shammai was of quite a different nature. He was a stern, angry man whose interpretation of Jewish law was much more stringent and narrow than Hillel's. And yet we know that Shammai enjoined his disciples to "receive all men with a kindly countenance." We are told in the Talmud, though, that "the sternness of Shammai almost drove us from this world, but the kindliness of Hillel brought us back to life." Hillel thought highly of Herod and prophesied that he would yet become king. Herod, in turn, had a great deal of respect for the gentle teacher and it is quite possible that Herod exerted his own influence to have Hillel elected head of the Sanhedrin.

Hillel and Shammai each created his own great academy, known as the "School of Hillel" and the "School of Shammai" respectively. The adherents of these two academies became the most important figures in Jewish life in their day.

There was constant controversy between the schools of Hillel and Shammai with respect to the proper interpretation of Jewish law, not only with regard to ceremonial legislation but also with regard to ethics. The School of Shammai was like Shammai himself, stern and inclined to give the law a narrow, strict interpretation, making the fulfillment of many precepts quite difficult. It was extremely conservative. The School of Hillel, on the other hand, generally tended to much greater leniency and liberalism. But it would not be entirely true to say that the School of Hillel was consistently more liberal than that of Shammai, for there were some issues, though few indeed, with regard to which Shammai actually held the more liberal view. The intellectual warfare between the adherents of the two schools began even while the masters, Hillel and Shammai, were still alive. At times, the disciples of Shammai were in the majority and thus the students of Hillel were compelled to abide by the decisions handed down by the opposing camp. But, in general, the school of Hillel would have more disciples than that of Shammai and it was therefore ordained that, in every dispute, the decision formulated by the School of Hillel would be binding upon all, except for certain isolated cases. The controversies did not cease, however, until Rabban Gamaliel called a meeting of the two parties. After three years of negotiations, it was decided that the decisions of the School of Hillel would be accepted as binding upon Jewry as a whole. Yet, during all those years of disagreement, the disciples of Hillel always had nothing but the greatest respect for those of Shammai and even allied themselves with members of the latter school through marriage.

One day the two groups officially met in secret in the attic of the home of Hezekiah ben Guryon, to discuss certain pressing issues of mutual interest. Those were the days of the Hasmoneans who were mostly Sadducees and therefore the adherents of both Hillel and Shammai, who were Pharisees were in constant danger of persecution or worse. In that day, Shammai's students outnumbered Hillel's because Hezekiah was an adherent of Shammai, and for this reason quite a few of Hillel's disciples hesitated to come to the conference called at his home. At that meeting, it was decided that the rulings handed down by the School of Shammai with regard to eighteen specified laws of the Torah would be accepted as binding upon all Jews. Among these eighteen precepts were some which the School of Hillel had felt should not be enforced upon the Jews because their observance would have been too difficult. It was agreed, however, to abide by the decision of the majority of the School of

Shammai, who considered them as important and mandatory for every Jew to keep. At the same conference it was decided that the Book of Ezekiel should not be relegated to burial in the Genizah. Some of those present maintained that the book contained a number of statements in direct contradiction to the Law of Moses, but Hezekiah, the host of the conference, pleaded for its retention among the Holy Scriptures.

Many important religious laws were laid down then which are still binding upon Jews who observe the Law to this very day. Among these was the institution of the marriage contract which the Jewish bridegroom gives to his bride at the marriage ceremony. (In this document the bridegroom promises to give the bride an adequate financial settlement in case he should divorce her, so that she should not be left without means. If the bride was a virgin, the sum given her, in those days, was 200 zuzim; if a widow, she would be entitled only to 100 zuzim.

The most important of Hillel's many disciples was Jonathan ben Uziel who later made a translation of the Bible into Aramaic, which became known by the title of Targum Jonathan. The youngest of Hillel's students at that time was Rabbi Johanan ben Zakkai. We shall soon see what an important role he, the most junior of all the disciples of Hillel, was to play in Jewish history after the death of his master.

With the death of Hillel and Shammai the era of the teams (or pairs) of scholars was concluded, but there were also other Tannaim such as the "Benei Betirah," the "early Hassidim," "Chony Hamagal," and many others. Also with the passing of these two masters, the era of the first Tannaim came to an end, and it was their disciples who started a new epoch in Jewish history, that of the second, or later, Tannaim.

But before we proceed to talk about the period of the second Tannaim, it would be well to make a survey of the three parties in Jewish life in those days, that is, the Pharisees, the Sadducees, and the Essenes.

2. The Three Parties: Pharisees, Sadducees, and Essenes

The Sadducees, the Progovernment Party—The Essenes, a Nonpolitical Religious Movement—The Role of the Sanhedrin in Jewish Life—The Temple

It was now fifty years since the Hasmonean dynasty had begun its reign in Palestine. The Hasmoneans had ruled with an iron hand and waged wars with neighboring countries, at times victoriously and at other times with less success. But through these wars the new generation became better acquainted with life in other countries, particularly in Greece. The younger generation thus came to admire the Greek way of life, which represented a high level of culture. They adopted Greek names, arranged sports events patterned upon those of Athens and Sparta, built Grecian-style homes, and, in general, constantly strove to imitate the Greek manner of living and thinking. Even King Johanan Hyrcanus erected a Grecian-style palace quite near the Temple, to which he gave the Greek name "Casistus" and which he used for public gatherings and entertainments. A bridge passing over a valley connected this edifice with the Temple, thus symbolically linking Jewish culture with that of Greece. Hyrcanus also built a huge courthouse where the city fathers of Jerusalem held their deliberations and where the national archives were kept.

This Graecophile attitude of the ruling class brought upon it the opposition of the teachers and the common people, particularly with regard to religious matters. Eventually the adherents of government policy rallied around a leader named Zadok, who gave the new party his name and which has been known in history since then as the Sadducee movement. This party recruited its membership from among those who were close to government circles and from those who had some personal grudges against the Pharisees. Most of the common people sided with the Pharisees, from the Hebrew word "perush" meaning "interpretation," for the Tannaim (the leaders of the Pharisees) were the interpreters of Jewish law. (To this party, beside the Tannaim, whom the people regarded as their true friends, also belonged the members of the Sanhedrin, the judges, and other scholars of the Law.) However, these two parties did not confine their activities to religious life only. They were political parties and made their influence powerfully felt in the affairs of the state. The Sadducees were extremely conservative; they followed the strict letter of Jewish law without allowing for any latitude in interpretation, and also unswervingly supported the government program, regardless of whether it was conducive to the welfare of the people or not. The Pharisees, on the other hand, became known as the people's party, which looked at all issues from one point of view only, namely, whether or not the best interests of the common man were being served. The Pharisees applied the same liberal views to Jewish law as well. To them the Law of Moses was not a sealed book, but a living, dynamic guide of which not the letter but the spirit was of prime importance.

But there was need also for another kind of movement which would limit its activities to the purely spiritual sphere. This void was filled by a sect whose adherents called themselves the Essenes. We are not sure of the exact origin of this designation. It may be derived from the Aramaic word "issa," meaning "healer," for some of the founders of this new movement were in the field of medicine. The Talmud does not have too much to say about the Essenes. It may be, however, that the groups to which reference is made in the Talmud by the designations of "early Hassidim" and such, might actually be identical with the Essenes. Whatever we know today about the Essene movement we owe to the records of Philo of Alexandria and of the historian Josephus. According to them, this party had no interest in politics or affairs of state, and occupied itself primarily with spiritual matters. It had its own beliefs and superstitions which at times bordered on the absurd.

As we see it now, the two parties, the Pharisees and the Sadducees, were half political and half religious in nature. They bitterly opposed each other in both fields and at times their warfare erupted in actual bloodshed. At one time, King Johanan Hyrcanus actually condemned many of the Pharisee leaders to death. Despite these basic differences, the Pharisees refused to make a complete break with the Sadducees, for they felt that such secession would rend the entire nation asunder into two hostile camps. The Pharisees wanted peace, even at a price. For this reason, they were eventually ready to surrender to the Roman conquerors rather than resist them, for they felt that a small army such as that of the Jews would stand no chance against the mighty Roman legions and that such fighting would result only in futile loss of life.

The Sadducees, on the other hand, hewed closely to the line of the Hasmonean rulers who, though they tried to court Roman favor at times, were by no means advocates of "peace at any price." The Hasmoneans were a warlike family, jealous particularly of their own honor and survival and caring little for the interests of the people over whom they ruled.

The Essenes adopted a policy of isolation from everything that smacked of politics. They longed for a world in which there would be neither ruler nor subject; neither oppressors nor oppressed; a world in which God alone would reign supreme. They therefore stood aloof from both parties, though, as we shall see later, their views had somewhat more similarity to those of the Pharisees.

Before we go any further, it may be well to mention the two institutions that played a dominant role in Jewish life at that time in Jerusalem, the Sanhedrin and the Temple.

The Sanhedrin, a body consisting of seventy-one members, was the pride of the nation. It was a kind of Supreme Court with much more authority than a higher court of law. Its function was to interpret the Law of Israel, and its decisions were binding upon all Jews; it was also the guardian of the Oral Tradition, of the laws which were not set down in writing in the Five Books of Moses but which had been handed down through the generations from father to son. Thus, at times, the Sanhedrin would separate into two groups, of which one would deal with day-to-day problems while the other was engaged in the study and interpretation of the Oral Tradition. Therefore there would often be two Sanhedrins, one holding court at the gate of the Temple Mount and the other sitting in the gates of the Temple antechamber. In cases which required the presence of all the members of the Sanhedrin, the two groups met together in what was called the "Great Sanhedrin" with judges from the lesser courts substituting for any of the seventy-one who might be absent.

The Great Sanhedrin would sit in the middle of the Temple area. The chamber where this body held court had two exits, one leading into the Temple and the other to the Temple's court; thus the Sanhedrin sat midway between the house of the Lord and the people. The Sanhedrin met every day except on the Sabbath, when its scholar members would lecture to students or address the public in the House of Study which stood upon the Temple Mount. An attendance of twenty-three out of the seventy-one members of the Sanhedrin was regarded as sufficient for discussion of less important issues.

The Sanhedrin was a most liberal and equitable court of law. In criminal cases involving a possible death sentence the younger judges were asked to state their opinions first, because it was felt that if an older judge advocated the extreme penalty for the defendant, not one of the junior justices might dare raise his voice in dissent. Members of the Sanhedrin were permitted to reverse their votes in favor of the mitigation of the original sentence, but they could not change their decision to a penalty more stringent than the one upon which they had previously agreed. These were only a few of the rules instituted for conducting the Sanhedrin to prevent miscarriages of justice.

The other institution upon which all of Israel looked with pride was the Temple, the holiest place in all the land. Upon the Temple Mount stood a number of resplendent edifices. In the center of these was the Temple itself, which contained the "Kodesh Hakodashim," the Holy of Holies, where the high priest could enter only once a year, on the Day of Atonement.

The High Priest embodied in his person the highest ideal of service to God. He wore special garments, a breastplate, an ephod and a golden plate on his miter on which was written the Ineffable Name of the Lord. In the

Talmud we find a most interesting account of the ceremony that took place in the Temple on the evening and morning of the Day of Atonement when the High Priest entered the Holy of Holies with the censer in his hand. The High Priest had supreme authority over all the other priests and also presided over a "special court for priests" which enforced the specific laws pertaining to priesthood.

Also serving at the Temple were the Levites who sang and played various musical instruments during the services, while the priests poured out their libation offerings upon the altar. The Levites would stand on the fifteen steps leading from the women's chamber to the main hall and sing psalms, accompanying their chanting with such instruments as the harp, the viol, and cymbals. On holidays and on Passover Eve when the Passover offering was brought, they would also play upon pipes, and a choir of children would supplement the regular group of Temple choristers. On the Sabbath day the Levites would chant the psalms for the Sabbath day which the Jews still recite in their Sabbath prayers now.

We shall now proceed to a survey of Jewish life during the last sixty years of the Second Commonwealth, and make a study of the lives and achievements of the second group of Tannaim who expounded the law in liberal terms.

3. Rabbi Johanan ben Zakkai

The Second Generation of the Second Tannaim—The Disciples of Hillel and Shammai—The Price for Surrender—The Academy at Yavneh—The New Sanhedrin—Prayer Instead of Sacrifice

The second group of Tannaim lived and worked over a period of about two hundred and ten years, that is, from about sixty years prior to the fall of Jerusalem until about one hundred fifty years after the destruction of the Temple.

The era of these Tannaim is divided into five generations (or six, according to other historical schools). Each generation produced a certain group of leaders who put their stamp upon the time in which they lived. Let us, therefore, study the lives and achievements of some of these principal Tannaim and see what role they played in Jewish history, not only as a group, but also as great personalities. The second group of Tannaim numbered one hundred and seventy-five scholars. Others place their number at more than one hundred and fifty and still others as high as two hundred. We shall confine ourselves to the study of the most eminent among them.

The group known as the "first generation" was composed chiefly of the disciples of Hillel and Shammai, but also included a few other scholars of note who were members of neither school.

The students of Hillel and Shammai were many; their ranks also included disciples who had been taught by the pupils of Hillel and Shammai but who themselves had never met the original masters. This was a difficult period in Jewish history, as it was also the very beginning of the Christian era. Besides this, Rome had taken over Palestine, and the land was filled with Roman soldiers. On Passover, Pentecost, and the Feast of Tabernacles, when Jewish pilgrims from all over the country converged upon Jerusalem, the Roman soldiers would not hesitate to show their contempt for the defeated nation and no such holiday passed without some bloodshed. The Sanhedrin, though still in existence, had been stripped of most of its autonomous powers. As early as twenty years after the death of Hillel, the Sanhedrin had already been divested of its authority to pass and execute death sentences.

In the meantime, the disciples of Hillel and Shammai were engaged in academic warfare as to the interpretation of Jewish law. In general, the School of Shammai was most conservative and its views were much stricter and narrower than those of the School of Hillel.

One of the outstanding personalities of that era was Rabbi Johanan ben Zakkai. He was the youngest of the disciples of Hillel, and none other than Hillel himself had said of him that he would be "the father of wisdom and the shining light of generations to come." This prophecy came true in full measure, for it was he who built up new, firm pillars for the spiritual edifice of Judaism when its Temple was destroyed. When the priests had been dispersed and Judaism had lost its Temple, ben Zakkai pointed out that Israel still had its Law, and henceforth the Law became the spiritual rallying point of the Jewish people. Even as the Ark had accompanied the children of Israel through their wanderings in the wilderness at the time of the Exodus, said Johanan, so would the Law now travel with them wherever they might be scattered.

Ben Zakkai carefully planned the course he was to take. When Rome laid siege to Jerusalem and no one could leave the blockaded city, ben Zakkai managed to get out and to see the Roman commander Vespasian whose encampment was located directly outside Jerusalem. He told Vespasian that all the teachers and intellectual elements of the Jewish people would be willing to submit to Roman authority, without further resistance, if only Vespasian would grant him one request. Vespasian prepared himself for some kind of trick on the part of the Jew, but before he could think of a reply, ben Zakkai stated his terms.

"Let me have Yavneh with the scholars that dwell here," he said. "All I want of you is that you let no harm come to the scholars who study at the Academy of Yavneh. If you fulfill this my request, all my disciples will be ready to do your bidding."

The Roman soldier did not believe his ears. That the great leader of the Jews would be willing to surrender to Rome in return for one paltry village school seemed to him incredible. But Rabbi Johanan knew better. It was his plan to take this little school, which had already attained note as an institution of Jewish learning, and make it a center to which all Jews would be able to turn for spiritual guidance, and which would train teachers who would follow their people into exile and expound the Law to the sons of Israel wherever they would be scattered.

The village of Yavneh is not far from the Mediterranean. It is situated between Jaffa and the ancient Philistine city of Ashdod. It was to this place that Johanan summoned all the scholars of the Law and, indeed, hundreds of them followed his call, and a new center of Judaism was born. But even as they all labored to perpetuate the Law, they were filled with anxiety for the future, and their worst fears were soon confirmed by the news that the Temple had been burned, Jerusalem destroyed, and thousands of dead were lying in the streets of the City of the Lord.

Johanan ben Zakkai rent his garments, and he and his disciples wept aloud for the fallen glory of Israel. The first to speak was Rabbi Akiba, who said: "Alas for us that the place where our sins were forgiven is laid waste."

But Rabbi Johanan replied: "Do not despair, my son. We shall do something which will serve even better for the atonement of our sins. Let us deal kindly with one another. This will be sufficient, for has not the prophet said in the name of the Lord,[6] For I desire mercy, and not sacrifice.' "

Then one of the disciples asked how the sacrifices would be offered now that the Temple was no more.

And ben Zakkai replied: "The Lord, God, needs no offerings. All He requires of us is prayer. See to it that your prayers come from a humble and contrite heart, for the Lord will hear only the prayers of those who come before Him humbly and in sincerity."

Thus Rabbi Johanan ben Zakkai proceeded to turn Yavneh into a fortress of Judaism. He established a Sanhedrin of which he himself became chief justice, for Rabbi Gamaliel, the son of the last president of the original Sanhedrin, was still too young to hold that exalted office. Johanan was so zealous for the prestige of the new spiritual center he had created that he always referred to the new Sanhedrin as the "Great Court of the Law."

Rabbi Johanan realized, however, that certain changes had to be made in the form of Judaism if it were to survive under these new conditions, and he proceeded to set aside certain laws which seemed impossible to fulfill under the prevailing circumstances.

Of Johanan's many disciples there were five outstanding scholars: Rabbi Eliezer ben Hyrcanus, Rabbi Joshua ben Chananiah, Rabbi Jose the Priest, Rabbi Simon ben Nathanel, and Rabbi Eleazar ben Azariah. Johanan had words of high praise for every one of them. Of Rabbi Eliezer he said that his memory was like a cistern which retained every drop of water that was ever poured into it and let nothing seep out. Of Rabbi Joshua he said, "Happy is the woman who bore him." He praised Rabbi Jose for his fear of the Lord and Rabbi Simon for his dread of sin. Of Rabbi Eleazar, Johanan said that he was like a mighty stream, growing stronger in wisdom and virtue as the years went by.

And yet, despite all his active work in behalf of Judaism, Johanan ben Zakkai never ceased to mourn for Jerusalem and the Temple. One day, as he rode through Jerusalem on a horse to visit a friend in the territory of Judah, he beheld the daughter of the man who had formerly been the wealthiest of the land gathering up grains of barley from the ground to satisfy her hunger. Rabbi Johanan, seeing this, cried out bitterly to his disciples.

"Do you see this woman gathering up barley there? I myself signed her marriage contract. Alas, in those days she was a wealthy maiden. She brought 1000 golden trinkets as dowry from her father's house, and this in addition to the gifts she received from her father-in-law. Alas, my poor people, you refused to serve the Lord and now you must be slaves to Rome. You were loath to donate half a shekel as your contribution to the Temple, now you must pay fifteen shekels as tribute to Rome; you declined to clean the land at festival time, now you must scrub the streets for the conquering soldiers. Ah, it is written 'Because thou didst refuse to serve the Lord thy God with joy, thou art now compelled to serve thy enemies with sorrow.' "

Yet the situation was not hopeless. Israel still had its own king, Agrippa II, whose sister Berenice had captured the heart of no less a person than the Roman Emperor Titus himself, and it appeared that Berenice might even become the Empress of Rome. In those days Rome did not oppress the vassal state of Judea too severely and even allowed it a certain amount of autonomy in managing its affairs. Eventually, however, Berenice lost the favor of Titus and had to leave his court, and then things changed rapidly for the worse in Palestine. No one knows what became of the remaining members of the royal family of Judea. Legend has it that the Jewish princes and princesses went abroad and married into the ruling houses of other nations.

We do not know exactly how long Rabbi Johanan ben Zakkai was able to carry on his work at Yavneh. It was probably a period of less than ten years. But even during that short time he managed to accomplish what he had set out to do, that is, to build up a new spiritual center to replace Jerusalem and a new abode for the Law to replace the Sanctuary. In years to come, centers modeled upon the pattern of Yavneh were to spring up not only in many cities of Palestine itself, but in Jewish communities throughout the world, even in those countries where Jews were persecuted and paid dearly for their persistence in retaining the faith of their fathers. It was all attributable to the farsighted action of Rabbi Johanan ben Zakkai who, even in his lifetime, was known as the "Light of Israel" because he gave his people a new spiritual foundation built upon the ruins of the old.

Legend has it that Rabbi Johanan lived one hundred and twenty years. Before his death he told his assembled disciples, "It is my wish that you fear the Lord no less than you would a king of flesh and blood." His passing was widely mourned and it was said that when he died the beauty of wisdom vanished from the earth.

Johanan's approach to Jewish Law and its practical application was much like that of Hillel. His outlook was broad and liberal. Many of the interpretations formulated by Johanan ben Zakkai are still the basis of decisions rendered by the expounders of the Law.

Now came a new generation of scholars who carried on the work begun by their teacher. They were: Rabbi Chananiah; Rabbi Zadok who was a disciple of the School of Shammai; Rabbi Nahum who had been a member of the religious court of Jerusalem prior to the fall of the Temple; Rabbi Dossa ben Hyrcanus, an outstanding adherent of the School of Hillel, a man of great wealth, and a profound thinker; Abba Saul ben Batnith, a Tanna who sold wine for a living; and Rabbi Nechuniah ben Hakana. Finally there was

Rabbi Nahum of Gimso who was well known for his firm faith and persistent optimism. Over and over again he would avow his conviction that all things were for the best. But most outstanding among them all was Rabban Gamaliel, the son of Simon, a giant intellect who was better known as Rabban Gamaliel of Yavneh.

4. Rabban Gamaliel of Yavneh

Rabban Gamaliel and His Relationship with His Students and Scholars—His Dispute with Rabbi Joshua ben Chananiah—Why Rabban Gamaliel Was Relieved of the Chairmanship of the Sanhedrin

The new chairman of the Sanhedrin, Rabban Gamaliel, was the son of Rabbi Simon, who had held the same office, and a grandson of Hillel. Gamaliel was great in both wisdom and wealth. His official title was "Rabban," a designation implying greater authority than that of "Rabbi." More popularly, he was known as Rabban Gamaliel of Yavneh, because he diligently strove to carry on the work of his teacher, Johanan ben Zakkai, and because of his untiring efforts to enlarge the authority and scope of the academy and spiritual center at Yavneh. His generation, which spanned the period of 80-120 A.D., was the second in the era of the second Tannaim.

Gamaliel was a man of broad erudition. He was well versed in the sciences, such as mathematics and astronomy, and he made use of them in his study of Jewish Law. He was also a man of rare human qualities. Thus, for instance, he would refuse to accept gifts or favors of any kind from persons to whom he had lent money so that it might not seem as if he were accepting such services in lieu of interest from his debtors. He treated his servants generously and though he was immensely rich he was completely free of snobbery. He had great compassion for others, and he would often say, "He who has compassion upon his fellow men on earth will himself receive compassion in heaven."

Rabban Gamaliel wielded the powers that came with his high office with an iron hand, to show to his people and to the rest of the world that even though they no longer had a state of their own, the Jews still possessed some measure of independence. For the sake of greater unity, he made every effort to effect a reconciliation of the differences between the schools of Hillel and Shammai. Through his good offices, an agreement was finally reached whereby the interpretation of the Law as given by the School of Hillel would be the one that would be binding upon all Jews.

Gamaliel was a strict disciplinarian, and ordered the doorkeeper of his academy not to admit any student who came to the school only to while away the time or a student whom he, Gamaliel, deemed to have little interest in serious studies. Many of the young scholars were opposed to this arbitrary procedure but they had too much respect for their master to refuse to comply with his orders.

Despite his basic kindness, Rabban Gamaliel relished power and could not tolerate opposition or criticism in any form. He employed a form of excommunication to render harmless anyone who opposed his wishes. At that time the penalty took the form of an enforced isolation for a maximum of thirty days. In order to be recognized as such, the person under this temporary ban had to dress in black. Gamaliel imposed this punishment even upon his own brother-in-law, Rabbi Eliezer ben Hyrcanus, because Eliezer had insisted upon following the interpretation of the School of Shammai with regard to a certain point in Jewish law. This high-handed action aroused much opposition. A short time later, Gamaliel excommunicated Rabbi Jose of Tiberias, one of his disciples. As a result, even Rabbi Joshua ben Chananiah, a great friend of his, openly rebelled against him. Joshua was unable to persist in this opposition, however, because he was only a poor blacksmith who worked hard to earn a living and had little time for engaging in long-drawn-out quarrels. Finally, though, the two men met in open argument. The direct cause of the dispute was a question as to the proper dates for the celebration of the New Year and the Day of Atonement which, in those days, was determined each year by the examination of witnesses as to the exact time they had first seen the New Moon. Rabban Gamaliel and Rabbi Joshua differed in their findings. Siding with Rabbi Joshua in the argument were men of such prominence as Rabbi Johanan ben Nuri and Rabbi Dossa, the son of Hyrcanus. Gamaliel stubbornly refused to consider that he could have made an error. In the end Joshua ceded to Gamaliel in order to preserve peace and unity, and Gamaliel assured him of his continued friendship and respect. Joshua, however, could not quite forget that, while Gamaliel had poured out his wrath and indignation upon him, he had shown more consideration for Rabbi Dossa who had sided with him against Gamaliel. Joshua felt certain that Gamaliel had spared Dossa only because the latter was a wealthy man, unlike Joshua who had to struggle to make a modest living. The story soon spread among the other sages of the Sanhedrin, who did not take a favorable view of Gamaliel's action in this matter.

On another occasion, at a session of the wise men of the Sanhedrin, Gamaliel publicly differed with and insulted Rabbi Joshua in a matter of Law. Since Joshua was generally regarded as a great scholar in his own right, this met with vehement protest. As a result, a vote was taken to determine Gamaliel's fitness for office as chairman of the Sanhedrin and he was relieved of his position. On that very same day, some three hundred new disciples came to the House of Study. They had all been considered ineligible for admission during the administration of Rabban Gamaliel.

The wise men now had to elect a new chairman. Rabbi Joshua himself was not a satisfactory candidate because he had been the cause of the entire upheaval. Rabbi Eliezer was also not qualified because he was quick to anger and, besides, he was an adherent of the School of Shammai. Rabbi Akiba might have been a good choice because of his intelligence and erudition, but he lacked the distinguished family background which was considered essential for a president of the Sanhedrin. In the end the choice fell upon Rabbi Eleazar ben Azariah who was not only a great scholar but also of distinguished lineage and great wealth.

Now all the laws instituted by Rabban Gamaliel became subject to review by the entire Sanhedrin, and votes were taken to establish which of the laws were to be retained and which abrogated. On the very day of Gamaliel's dismissal, it was also decided that the book of Ecclesiastes and the Song of Songs should be incorporated into the Holy Scriptures and not, as some of the sages had wished, consigned to the oblivion of the Genizah.

Gamaliel, however, took his defeat with good grace. He remained at the House of Study and refused to speak ill of those who had voted for his dismissal. In fact, he even went to the home of Rabbi Joshua to ask him for forgiveness.

It is told that when Gamaliel came to Joshua's humble dwelling, he noticed that the walls were blackened with soot, and he said to Joshua, "One can see from thy walls that thou art a blacksmith."

Thereupon Joshua replied: "Alas for the people whose leader thou wert; alas for the ship at whose helm thou hast stood; for little dost thou know of the plight of the scholars; of how they spent their time and what they do for a livelihood."

Gamaliel bowed his head and begged Joshua for his forgiveness. Joshua remained silent. It was only when Gamaliel pleaded with him to pardon him for the sake of the memory of Gamaliel's illustrious parents that Joshua finally relented. The next day Rabbi Akiba suggested that he, Joshua, and Rabbi Eleazar, the new president of the Sanhedrin, go together to call on Rabban Gamaliel. At the meeting Rabbi Eleazar, out of respect for Rabban Gamaliel, renounced the office for which he had just been chosen. In the end, Gamaliel was restored to the presidency of the Sanhedrin, while Eleazar was made chief justice of the court of religious law. Gamaliel remained in office without interruption until his death.

In the meantime, the Emperor Titus had died in Rome. He was succeeded on the throne by his younger brother, Domitian, who ruled with a tyrant's hand and enacted laws designed to abolish Judaism altogether. Once again the Jewish people were faced with a crisis, and again there arose a leader to meet the challenge. This was Rabbi Akiba ben Joseph, a great leader who rendered valiant service to the Jewish people and to Judaism.

5. Rabbi Akiba

The Youthful Illiterate—His Love for Rachel, the Daughter of Kalba Shevua, Who Prevailed Upon Him to Go and Study—His Years of Study—His Fellow Students and Disciples—The Greatness of Rabbi Akiba—His Liberal Approach to Jewish Law—His Ethical Teachings.

One of the most illustrious figures of the third generation of the second Tannaim was Rabbi Akiba ben Joseph. We are not sure of the date of his birth; but we know that he met a martyr's death at the hands of the Romans in 135 or 136 A.D. Beyond the fact that his father's name was Joseph, we know little of Akiba's antecedents. It is generally thought that Rabbi Akiba was born in Lydda and that he had grown up more or less illiterate. He became a shepherd and was hired to tend the flock of Kalba Shevua, a wealthy Jewish farmer. It seems that Rachel, the beautiful daughter of his employer, fell in love with him. Upon her urging, Akiba decided to go away to the Academy and to engage in the study of Jewish Law. Rachel, who later became his wife, saw to it that he had no financial worries during this period, and her desire was that eventually he should become one of the greatest teachers and leaders of Jewish history. During the early years of Rabbi Akiba's career, the Temple was still standing in Jerusalem. Akiba was later one of that band of scholars who followed Rabbi Johanan ben Zakkai to Yavneh, where he was a member of the Great Court of Religious Law and enjoyed the high esteem of even Rabban Gamaliel. Later, Akiba made his home in the village of Bnai Brak and for thirteen years he studied with Rabbi Eliezer ben Hyrcanus and also with Rabbi Joshua ben Chananiah. Rabbi Akiba considered himself a disciple of Rabbi Nahum of Gimso. It was from Rabbi Nahum that Akiba had learned the maxim which he repeated so often, "All that God doeth is for the best."

Rabbi Akiba spent all his youth in poverty and remained poor even after his marriage to Rachel, for her father, Kalba Shevua, cut her off without a penny when she married the ignorant shepherd boy. It was only much later that the old man relented and gave a large share of his own fortune to his son-in-law who, by that time, had become famous throughout the land for his scholarship.

Rabbi Akiba enjoyed great respect in learned circles and, together with Rabbi Eleazar ben Azariah and Rabbi Joshua ben Chananiah, was a member of the delegation headed by Rabban Gamaliel which visited the Emperor Domitian in Rome to plead for the repeal of some of the harsh decrees which that ruler had enacted against the Jews.

His greatest friends were Rabbi Johanan ben Nuri, Rabbi Tarphon, Rabbi Jose of Galilee, and Rabbi Ishmael ben Elisha. Among his outstanding disciples were men like Rabbi Meir, Simon ben Azai and Simon ben Zoma, who all became great scholars in their own right. One of his disciples, Elisha ben Abuyah, later turned away from the Pharisees and therefore was referred to by the cognomen of "Aher," (the Hebrew term for "another") meaning another man.

Rabbi Akiba also took part in the uprising of Bar Kochba against Rome, which took place in the year 134 of the Christian era. He often engaged in verbal debate with Tyrannus Rufus, the Roman administrator of Palestine. We are told that he also made the acquaintance of the wife of the Roman official, and after the death of her husband, Rabbi Akiba, then himself a widower, married her following her adoption of the Jewish faith. Not long thereafter, however, the Roman authorities arrested Rabbi Akiba, because he had been one of the ringleaders in the revolt of Bar Kochba, and condemned him to death by cruel forms of torture. Even as he bore excruciating pain, Akiba did not forget his God. Over and over he repeated the words, "Hear, O Israel, the Lord, our God, is One," and with those words on his lips he finally died a martyr's death.

As to Rabbi Akiba's contribution to Judaism, it should be sufficient merely to state that Akiba laid the foundation for what is known today as the Talmud (the code containing in written form all those Jewish laws which originally had been handed down from father to son as the Oral Tradition of Judaism). We must remember that, until the days of Rabbi Akiba, all studying was done orally and the material committed to memory without the benefit of notes. The scholars had to remember a rather unorganized mass of civil and ceremonial law, which often made for some confusion. Rabbi Akiba was the first to classify all these laws under separate categories and headings to facilitate systematic memorization. He still made no effort to set them down in a permanent code. But on the basis of rudimentary notes made by other scholars, in the form of commentaries to certain verses of Biblical law, Akiba classified the Oral Tradition into divisions to bring some order into the study of the Law. And it was on the basis of Akiba's system that, many years later, Rabbi Judah the Prince was able to set down the Oral Tradition in writing, as a code for all future generations, easily accessible to the serious student, a work now known to us as the Mishnayoth. Very often we find in the Talmud references to "the Mishna of Rabbi Akiba" because, actually, Akiba had been the father of the Mishna which, of course, was the basis of the Talmud.

Akiba's attitude to the Law was liberal. To appease the Sadducees, who would not accept as binding anything that was not explicitly set down in the Law of Moses, Akiba demonstrated that no word in the Torah, not even a conjunction, was superfluous, and that many laws could be deduced and inferred even from cue words in the original text. In this manner he could exercise great latitude in the interpretation of what had been put down by him as law. Akiba's views, however, were opposed not only by the Sadducees, but also by some Tannaim, such as Rabbi Ishmael, who felt that the cue words of the five books of Moses, on which Akiba based so many of his theories, were there only for the sake of expression and not to be taken as a basis for hair-splitting. Gradually, however, Rabbi Akiba's method of study and interpretation gained recognition in Jewish scholarly circles.

Akiba was also the greatest ethical teacher after Hillel. He taught that man is worthy of love because he is created in the image of God. He constantly defended the poor and was opposed to the granting of special privileges to the rich. When, just before the destruction of the Temple, a law was under consideration which would have given additional privileges to the royal family, Akiba protested. "All Jews are the children of kings," he said, and he saw no reason why any one Jew should be given preference over another. Akiba also championed the rights of non-Jewish aliens in the Jewish state and, even in the face of opposition from other scholars, he stated that it was permissible for Gentiles to bring gifts to the Holy Temple. He established that documents drawn up by Roman courts and witnessed by non-Jews were valid testimony before any Jewish legal authority. The main principle of Jewish law, said Rabbi Akiba, could be formulated in very simple terms. "Love thy neighbor as thyself"—this was the fundamental of all the legislation of the Torah.

Two dominant qualities distinguished Rabbi Akiba as a teacher. First, the bond of mutual affection that united him with all his disciples, and second, his persistence in his studies. He curtailed his studies on only two days of the year, the eve of Passover and the Day of Atonement. He regarded the diligent study of the Law as so important that he refused to interrupt his work even during the serious illness of his son. He stopped only when he was told that the boy had died, and then not to weep and wail, but solely to pay proper respect to the dead as required by the Law of the Lord.

His outstanding disciple was Rabbi Meir, a man who truly walked in the ways of his great teacher.

6. Rabbi Meir

The Situation in Palestine After the Uprising of Bar Kochba—Rabbi Meir's Personal Tragedies—His Conservative Interpretation of the Law—His Parables— His Liberal Views on Other Nations and Mankind—His Friend Rabbi Simon Bar Yochai—The End of the Third Generation of the Tannaim

The revolt of Bar Kochba against the tyrannical power of Rome had ended in defeat. For a period of two and a half years, Bar Kochba and his small band had managed to hold a small corner of Palestine. Rabbi Akiba had been almost the only one of the Tannaim to espouse wholeheartedly the cause of the rebels and to urge his disciples to take up arms against the Roman oppressors. Most of the other Tannaim felt that the struggle of Bar Kochba's band would be a hopeless one. Rabbi Akiba, however, could no longer see his people submit to the brutalities of the conqueror. When Bar Kochba was defeated, Akiba and many of his disciples and friends were arrested by the Romans and condemned to death.

Rabbi Akiba numbered among his friends men who were outstanding scholars in their own right. There was Rabbi Tarphon of Lydda, a profound thinker, quite wealthy and a great philanthropist, who delighted in engaging in debates with the early Christians. (For this reason, he is treated with derision in works of early Christian literature, particularly in the writings of Justinus Martin.) Then there was Rabbi Eleazar of Modin, a scholar well versed in haggadic lore. Another contemporary was Rabbi Jose the Galilean, a man of execeptional nobleness and generosity. (It is told about him that when he divorced his wife with whom he found life impossible, and she married a very common man who could not provide for her, Jose took both of them, his former wife and her new husband, into his own home and saw to it that they lacked for nothing.) Among Akiba's friends were also Rabbi Judah ben Baba; Rabbi Chanina ben Teradyon; Rabbi Eleazar ben Chasmah; Rabbi Chalaphta and his sons, Rabbi Judah and Rabbi Jose. Many of these were murdered by the Romans.

One of the men named above who was to die a martyr's death was Rabbi Judah ben Baba. A farsighted man, he foresaw the disaster that would befall the Jewish people and that, once dispersed throughout the world, the Jews would be left leaderless. He therefore called a meeting at which he conferred rabbinical authority upon six of the disciples of Rabbi Akiba; namely, upon Rabbi Meir, Rabbi Judah the son of Rabbi Ilai, Rabbi Simon ben Yochai;

Rabbi Jose ben Chalaphta, Rabbi Eleazar ben Simon, and Rabbi Nehemiah. When the Roman authorities were told of that meeting—perhaps by an informer—they surrounded the home of Rabbi Judah with soldiers. Rabbi Judah ben Baba now told the newly ordained rabbis to flee for their lives. When they asked him what would become of him, he replied, "I am an old man and cannot save myself, but you are young and can still run away." Thus all six of the new rabbis managed to escape, each in a different direction. When the Romans finally broke into the house, they found Judah there alone and stabbed him to death.

The first of this group, Rabbi Meir, had already suffered much at the hands of the conqueror. His father-in-law, Rabbi Chaninah ben Teradyon, had been burned at the stake and his mother-in-law executed by the sword. A sister of Beruria, his wife, was sentenced to spend the rest of her life in a house of prostitution in Rome. The shadow of death constantly trailed Rabbi Meir himself, because the Roman authorities were well aware of the fact that Meir had been the first of the group which had received rabbinical ordination from Rabbi Judah ben Baba. Roman law on the subject was very brief and to the point: anyone giving or receiving rabbinical ordination was punishable by execution. Rabbi Meir, in fear for his very life, fled to Babylonia. It was only when the situation grew a little better, and the Romans seemed to have relented somewhat, that Rabbi Meir returned to Palestine. Then at the request of his wife, Beruria, he went to Rome to rescue her sister from the house of prostitution to which she had been taken by the Roman authorities. After first posing as a stranger to find out whether she was still virtuous, Meir succeeded in getting her released by bribing the guard. When the superintendents of the house of ill repute pursued him, he posed as a non-Jew and once more managed to escape together with his sister-in-law whom he brought back to her family in Palestine.

The Talmud contains many stories of the personal greatness of Rabbi Meir. But we know, too, that his wife was truly worthy of him. One Sabbath afternoon, while Rabbi Meir was away at study with his disciples, both of his sons were suddenly taken ill and died. Their grief-stricken mother took the bodies to a small room in the attic where she laid them on a bed and covered them with a sheet. When Rabbi Meir returned in the evening and inquired as to the whereabouts of the boys, his wife calmly told him that they must have gone to the house of study. When he replied that he had not seen them there, Beruria, without a word, gave him a cup of wine so that he might recite the prayer ushering out the Sabbath. It was only after he had said his prayers and eaten his dinner that Beruria quietly came to him and said: "Rabbi, there is a question to which I must have your answer. Someone has given me a precious jewel to keep for him and now he has asked me to return it. Must I give it back to him?"

Rabbi Meir replied, "To be sure you must. Return the treasure to him at once."

It was only then that Beruria led her husband to the little room upstairs, raised the sheets from the bed and showed him the bodies of their children. When Rabbi Meir burst into bitter weeping, his wife said to him: "Have you not just said that one must return that which has been loaned him for safekeeping? Do not mourn now, for behold, the Lord has given and the Lord has taken."

Rabbi Meir lived very simply and was always accessible to people from all walks of life. The Talmud tells the story of a woman who so enjoyed hearing his learned public discourses that she was late in returning to her home. Her irate husband threatened to divorce her unless she would go to Rabbi Meir and spit in his face. When Rabbi Meir heard of this strange command, he immediately sent someone to her with the message that he, the Rabbi, was suffering from severe eye trouble, and that his physicians had said he could be cured only if a woman would spit in his face and eyes. The woman immediately went to the home of Rabbi Meir and did as the messenger had told her. After she had done so, Rabbi Meir told the surprised lady, "Now go home to your husband and tell him that you really spat in my face, not only once, but, in fact, seven times."

Rabbi Meir had a sharp mind, and employed a method of study and exegesis that was most difficult even for his colleagues to understand. It was said of him that, through hair-splitting and casuistry, he could even explain that a commandment explicitly set down in the Bible was not a commandment at all but a prohibition. Actually, Meir always interpreted the Law in such a manner that it was made more difficult, rather than easier, to observe. For example, he decided that if a bill of divorcement had not been executed in exact accordance with the stipulations laid down by the scholars, the entire divorce was illegal and any children issuing from a subsequent marriage of the wife would be illegitimate. He also declared that if the amount of money promised by the bridegroom to his bride in the marriage contract was less than usually customary, the entire marriage was invalid. If there was the slightest doubt as to the permissibility of a certain act, it was to be regarded as forbidden. Moreover, if a person was suspected of having sinned even once, he could no longer be given credence even with respect to other matters.

Because of his inflexible attitude, Rabbi Meir did not enjoy great popularity with his colleagues, most of whom were of a much more liberal turn of mind. He continued the work begun by his master, Rabbi Akiba, that is, to collect and classify the many sayings of the Tannaim. Therefore, wherever a law or decision is mentioned in Mishnaic literature without the name of a specific scholar linked with it, that law or decision originated from Rabbi Meir.

Rabbi Meir had his own house of study in Chamtan, a small place near Tiberias. It seems that there was little love lost between him and Rabban Gamaliel, then the president of the Sanhedrin. Rabbi Meir earned a living as a scribe, copying down scrolls of the Law, and executing the parchment scrolls which were inserted into phylacteries and mezuzoth. Altogether he earned three shekels a week, of which he spent two for the needs of his family, and donated the third to charity.

He had a nearly inexhaustible collection of parables which he would cite during arguments. It is told of him that he had composed at least three hundred such parables having foxes as main characters, of which, however, only three have been preserved.

The Talmud also tells us of his respect for his teacher, Elisha ben Abuyah, who had originally been one of the disciples of Rabbi Akiba and had later left the Pharisees. Rabbi Meir was still willing to learn from him although the latter had become a kind of heretic and was given the name of Aher (another), as we have mentioned before. Meir explained his attitude by saying that, to him, the knowledge of Elisha was like a pomegranate filled with seeds (of wisdom) of which he, Meir, would pick out the good, and discard the bad.

As to Elisha ben Aubyah, who was regarded as an outstanding rabbi, we do not know whether he discarded only the teachings of some sages or whether he had actually ceased to believe also in the Law of Moses. In the Jerusalem Talmud it is said that he would burst into the houses of study and call out to the students of the Law, "Why sit here and study? Better go out and learn a trade so that you may make a living." Such statements in themselves do not necessarily constitute heresy, for not everyone really can or should devote all his time to study. But it seems that he belonged to the Gnostics (a philosophical sect of mystics). It is also said that Elisha sang Greek songs all the time.

As the Talmud indicated, Elisha made light of Jewish Law. It is told that one day he saw a man climb a tree to catch some birds and, in accordance with the Biblical command, first send away the mother bird before taking her young away with him. As the man descended from the tree with the fledglings, a snake curled around the stem of the tree bit him and he died instantly. Elisha is supposed to have said, "The Bible tells us at the end of the verse that all those obeying this command will be assured of long life and prosperity. How then can it be explained that this man died?"

Though Rabbi Meir was most conservative when it came to the interpretation of Jewish Law, he was surprisingly tolerant, particularly toward non-Jews. He said, for example, that a non-Jew who engaged in the serious study of Jewish Law could be said to be as great as the High Priest himself, for the Scriptures say, "And *man* shall observe these commandments so that he may live." Accordingly, the benefits derived from the study and observance of the Law, Rabbi Meir pointed out, were not restricted to the High Priest or even to the Jews alone, but were available to all men and that, of course, included Gentiles.

Among his friends was Rabbi Simon ben Yochai, a great scholar and ardent patriot. He, too, hated Rome with all his heart and soul and called upon all to take up arms against the oppressor. One day, after he had delivered a particularly vehement speech against the conqueror, he was denounced and with his grown son escaped arrest only by hiding in a cave, where they remained for thirteen years until it became safe for them to emerge. Unlike Rabbi Meir, Simon regarded Jewish law from a liberal point of view. He had many disciples and lived to see the rise of the fourth generation of Tannaim, among whom was Rabbi Judah the Prince, simply known as "Rabbi," the compiler of the Mishna in its final form.

7. Rabbi Judah the Prince

The Fourth Generation of Tannaim—Persecution by Rome—Rabbi Judah Ha-Nasi (Rabbi Judah the Prince)—His Broad Powers—He Opens His Larders to All during a Period of Famine—His Masterpiece, the Mishna

The era of the fourth generation of the Tannaim, which extended from the years 170 to 219 A.D., was a difficult period for those Jews who remained in Palestine. Once it had quelled the revolt of Bar-Kochba, Rome kept an eagle eye on the little vassal state of Palestine to make sure that such uprisings would not recur. At that time, Rome was ruled by a team of two emperors, Lucius Verus and Marcus Aurelius. While the latter contented himself with women and wit, Verus took a perverse delight in persecuting minorities. In Palestine he abolished the autonomous Jewish courts of law and prohibited the appointment of Jewish judges.

Because of the great pressure from Rome, the Jewish spiritual center was moved from Yavneh to a place named Usha. By this time the Sanhedrin, though still in existence, had lost nearly all its former civil authority. Verus later enacted laws prohibiting the observance of the Sabbath, the law of circumcision, and many other basic Jewish religious practices. It was only after the death of the Emperor Verus that a delegation of scholars, headed by Rabbi Simon ben Yochai, succeeded in persuading Marcus Aurelius to repeal some of the intolerant legislation enacted by Verus. At that time, the center of Jewish learning moved again, and this time to Shafaram, near Sepphoris.

As always in time of distress, there was a need now for a man who would win the confidence and respect of his entire people and serve as a leader to see them through the new crisis. And the Jewish masses found a person fully qualified for this task in Rabbi Judah, known as Judah Ha-Nasi, ("Judah the Prince").

Four generations earlier, Rabbi Johanan ben Zakkai had built up the academy at Yavneh to make sure that the Law of Moses would not pass into oblivion. The new leader, Rabbi Judah, sought to perpetuate all the wisdom that the sages had taught through the centuries. To accomplish this, he took a step that seemed revolutionary. He decided to set down the Oral Tradition in writing, in the form of an organized code, a procedure that had never before been considered permissible.

The Talmud has little to say about the early life of Rabbi Judah. It is known that he was born in the year 150 A.D. and that he had as his teachers the greatest scholars of his day, Rabbi Simon ben Yochai and Rabbi Eleazar ben Shamua. Eleazar had a great many disciples and it is told of him that seven students would share one single bench in his house of learning.

Rabbi Judah was descended from a long line of scholars who had all served as presidents of the Sanhedrin. His great-grandfather was none other than Hillel and his father, Rabbi Simon ben Gamaliel, was also his immediate predecessor in office as president of the Sanhedrin. Judah inherited a large fortune from his father and it was often said that he combined in his person both wisdom and wealth. In his day, the center of Jewish learning was shifted once again, this time to Beth Shearim, but eventually was moved back to Sepphoris. Judah Ha-Nasi was known to all scholars in Israel by the simple title of "Rabbi" which became his popular title. During the lifetime of Rabbi Judah, the Sanhedrin once again had its original full quorum of seventy-one members and once more possessed broad powers.

When a famine broke out in the land, Rabbi Judah opened his personal larders to all. Originally, though, it had been his intention to supply only scholars and not the general public. But when Rabbi Jonathan, one of his disciples, said to him, "Rabbi, feed me even as you would a raven or a dog," implying that even these lowly animals all had certain rights as creatures of the Lord, Judah consented to make his stores of food accessible to anyone in need, regardless of erudition or social status.

Judah enjoyed the respect and confidence of all. In fact, the Sanhedrin decreed that it was subject to the veto of its president (meaning Rabbi Judah) with regard to the conferment of rabbinical ordination, while the president could ordain anyone he chose without needing the approval of the Sanhedrin for this purpose. Thus it came about that Judah was the sole and final authority for the appointment of all teachers and religious leaders in Israel.

Thus, for a long time, Rabbi Judah had the power to ordain rabbis not only for Palestine but also for service in many communities abroad. He also appointed the judges and members of the Sanhedrin. Unlike his predecessors, Judah did not fill the office of chief justice, for he felt no need for an assistant or associate.

While the Talmud is generous in its praise of the virtues of the Rabbi Judah Ha-Nasi, it does not attempt to conceal his many failings. We are told that, despite his basic goodness, he was excessively sensitive and could not forgive any attempt at levity or jest regarding his person.

It is said that Judah once boasted to one of his favorite students, Rabbi Chiya, that if the Rosh Ha-Golah, Rabbi Huna of Babylonia (the "Head of the Exile," whose authority was recognized by the Babylonian government, and whose powers over Babylonian Jewry were even broader than those wielded by Rabbi Judah) should ever come to Palestine, he would give him all the honor due a man of his position, but not the presidency of the Sanhedrin. Eventually, Rabbi Huna died and, in accordance with his request, his remains were transferred to Palestine. Rabbi Judah knew nothing of this, but Rabbi Chiya, his disciple, had heard the news from a man who had come from Babylonia just a short time before. Chiya, desiring to play a joke on his master, told him, "Rabbi Huna has come here from Babylonia."

When Chiya saw Judah's consternation, however, he hastened to add that Rabbi Huna had not come alive, but that it was only his corpse that was being brought to Palestine from Babylonia for burial. Judah was relieved, but he was slow to forgive his disciple for the jest, and the latter was forbidden to come into his presence for a period of thirty days.

Bar Kappara, the great rabbi and scholar, also incurred the wrath of Judah. Bar Kappara, the author of witty parables in Hebrew, wrote a kind of satirical epigram aimed at Eliezer, Judah's son-in-law, who was wealthy but ignorant and therefore not taken seriously in scholarly circles. Rabbi Judah, furious, shouted at Bar Kappara, "Who art thou? I do not know thee." And Bar Kappara was never given rabbinical ordination by Judah.

Another one of Rabbi Judah's disciples, Samuel, a physician and astronomer who had once cured Judah of a serious illness, was denied ordination for the sole reason that he had shown him his superior knowledge of the secular sciences. Rabbi Hanina, another eminent scholar, never received ordination from the master because he had once dared to tell him that he, Judah the Prince, had made an error in the reading of a word in the Book of Ezekiel.

Somehow it seems strange that a man of Judah's stature should show such pettiness. But the very real and lasting services which this great rabbi rendered to Judaism outweighed these failings by far.

Rabbi Judah the Prince was the first to gather together all the Oral Tradition and record it in an organized code of law. This was considered a daring leap, because all the scholars before him had felt that this part of Jewish tradition, which they regarded as having been handed down orally from Mount Sinai simultaneously with the Written Law, must never be set down in writing but was to be committed to memory and passed on from one generation to another by word of mouth. Judah, however, feared that, if this state of affairs would continue, the Oral Tradition would eventually be altogether forgotten, and he therefore believed that the only way in which its preservation could be assured, even in exile, would be to write it down. It was fortunate that the initiative to do this was taken by a man of the stature and authority of Rabbi Judah, for no one else would have been permitted even to broach the subject, much less to take action.

Judah then proceeded to collect the many scattered notes made by the Tannaim. He classified all the existing laws under the headings originally formulated by Rabbi Akiba and by the latter's disciple, Rabbi Meir, and divided them into sections and categories. In this manner, he eventually brought into being the Mishna, a work of six books, each of which is divided into a series of "Masechtot," or parts. The first book, Zeraim (Seeds) deals with legislation on planting and agriculture; the second, Moed (Assembly), with religious holidays; Nashim (Women) with marriage and the specific laws applicable to women; Nezikin (Damages) with legislation on civil tort and indemnity; Kedoshim (Holy Things) with the laws connected with the sacrificial ritual in the Temple; and Taharoth (Purity) with the regulations on priestly and personal purity.

Judah made many important changes in Jewish law and ritual. He established a definite calendar to eliminate the need for fixing the dates of holidays each year by determining the exact position of the moon. He also abrogated some of the laws which had been valid only during the time of the Temple, such as those of tithing. He wanted to abolish the Sabbatical year, but his associates did not permit him to do so. At one time, he even wanted to abrogate the Fast of the Ninth Day of Ab which commemorates the destruction of the Temple.

The permanent compilation of the words of the Tannaim put an end to the great epoch of the Tannaim for all practical purposes. The one generation of Tannaim that followed Judah the Prince has no real historic significance. History records that "The era of the Mishna came to an end with the completion of the work of Rabbi Nathan and Rabbi Judah the Prince." Rabbi Nathan had valiantly assisted Judah in the gigantic work of compilation and editing.

Rabbi Judah lived about seventy years, of which he spent thirty as president of the Sanhedrin. Before his death, he asked that his son Gamaliel be appointed to succeed him, and the Sanhedrin complied with his wish.

The Mishna compiled by Rabbi Judah became the cornerstone of the giant compendium of Jewish law which is the Talmud.

The Tannaim were succeeded by the Amoraim in Palestine and Babylonia who, in their turn, interpreted the utterances of the Tannaim and gave their explanations to the laws of the Oral Tradition. The sum total of their work became known as the Gemorah. Written between the years 219 and 500 A.D. the Gemorah, together with the Mishna, forms the Talmud, which is second only to the Bible in Jewish literature.

8. The Structure of the Talmud

Two Laws: the Written Law and the Oral Tradition—Is It Enough for a Jew to Observe Only One?—What Is the "Masorah"?—The Ancient Jewish Laws

The Talmud is that gigantic work which encompasses the laws for everyday life that had been compiled by the Tannaim and Amoraim, who lived and worked over a period of some 850 years. The Talmud can be said to have had its beginnings at the time of the return of the exiles from Babylonia and the rebuilding of the Second Temple under the leadership of Ezra and Nehemiah; that is, in the year 3408 after Creation, or 350 years B.C., and was not completed before the year 500 A.D.

As we have stated before, the Talmud consists of two parts: the Mishna (or Mishnayoth) which was created by the Tannaim, and the Gemorah, which was compiled by the Amoraim. The last group might be called the spiritual heirs of the Tannaim.

The term Tanna (Tannaim is the plural form) is the Hebrew designation for a teacher of Jewish Law. It is generally assumed that there were altogether some hundred and seventy-five scholars in that category. Some scholars would add the names of all the persons mentioned in the textbooks of those days other than the Mishna, and accordingly place the total number of Tannaim at two hundred, or even more. This era concluded with the final edition of the Mishna, when all the Mishnayoth of the Tannaim were compiled by Judah the Prince into one unified code in the year 219 A.D.

The era of the Amoraim began at that time and continued until the year 500 A.D. Their masterpiece, the Gemorah, is simply comprised of discussions or discourses upon the Mishna, even as the Mishna was a commentary on the original Law of Moses. The task of the Tannaim had been to discuss the original Biblical text and to give what they thought to be the proper manner to construe and execute each law. The Amoraim confined their deliberations to the explanation of the Mishna; however, they did not consider it to be within their province to take issue with the opinions set down by the Tannaim, in the Mishna, concerning the Law of Moses.

The number of Amoraim, whose era extended over six generations, from 219 to 500 A.D., was much greater than that of the Tannaim. Altogether, it is assumed that there were a total of eighteen hundred Amoraim. Some of these were giant intellects; others were less gifted, but all of them had a share in the creation and final compilation of the Talmud.

The literal meaning of the word "Amora" (Amoraim is the plural form) is "interpreter," or "lecturer in Talmudic Law." While the Tannaim lived in Palestine, most of the Amoraim dwelt in Babylonia. These latter created the so-called "Babylonian Talmud." Those few Amoraim who expounded the Law in Palestine (altogether some three hundred scholars, whose era spans three generations, from 219 to 359 A.D.) produced their own Gemorah to the Mishna which is known today as the "Jerusalem Talmud." We will talk about this later.

From the very beginning, the Tannaim strove to have their interpretation of the Law of Moses accepted by the entire Jewish people as an integral part of Jewish learning and, in fact, wanted it to be treated with the same respect as the Bible itself. They therefore taught that the body of Jewish Law consisted of two parts, each as important and binding as the other; namely, the Written Law, which is explicitly stated in the Biblical text, and the Oral Tradition, the official appendix and interpretation of the Law of Moses, which had been communicated orally to Moses on Mount Sinai at the time of the revelation of the Written Law. It was also decreed that the text of the Written Law must never be committed to memory, while the Oral Tradition must never be set down in writing and had to be memorized and passed on in this manner from generation to generation. When Rabban Gamaliel was asked by a nobleman how many books of Law the Jewish people had, he replied, "Two, one written and one oral." In the Gemorah (Gittin 60), Rabbi Eleazar states that most of the Law of Moses had been written down (in the Bible) and only a small part, also deriving from Mount Sinai, had been handed down orally from generation to generation. Rabbi Johanan, on the other hand, felt that the Written Law actually was only a very small part of the legislation given the Jewish people by Moses, and that the bulk of the law lay in the Oral Tradition. Since no agreement could be reached as to which opinion was correct, it was generally felt that none of the traditions communicated by word of mouth should ever be recorded permanently, while no part of what had been received in writing through the Bible should ever be committed to memory and passed on in that manner.

Shammai, the great opponent of Hillel, once rejected a Gentile applicant for conversion to Judaism when the prospective convert told him that, while he was willing to abide by the Written Law, he saw no reason why he should observe the requirements set by the Oral Tradition. When the inquirer turned to Hillel, Hillel first agreed to accept him into the Jewish fold but later explained to the convert that, actually, the Written Law and the Oral Tradition were one and inseparable and neither could be properly observed without the other (Shabbat 31).

The Written Law, then, consists of the original Five Books of Moses; that is, Genesis, Exodus, Leviticus, Numbers, and Deuteronomy. Prophetic literature is not included in this category since it contains no legislation. The Written Law was not to be committed to memory but studied only by means of word-by-word reading, for the Mosaic Law explicitly stated that "Ye shall not add unto the word . . . neither shall ye diminish from it" (Deut. 4:2), and memorization might have brought about the inclusion of extraneous material or the omission of important parts of the text.

The Oral Law, on the other hand, was taught by the method of memorization and, until the coming of Judah the Prince, no systematic effort was made to compile all this wealth of material into one written code. It was explained that the Oral Law, while also an integral and essential part of Jewish legislation, had not been given to the Jewish people in writing so that they would not become enslaved by the written word; that their Law should not be static in nature, but living, dynamic, and capable of development. The Law was not to degenerate into a series of dogmas which would gradually have stifled freedom of thought. For this reason, only one part of Jewish Law, that is, the Five Books of Moses, was communicated to Israel in written form to serve as a kind of basic constitution for the Jewish people, not to be memorized, and to be used for the purpose of ascertainment of the exact wording of the original Law. The other part, the Oral Tradition, was to be a dynamic force that should serve to adapt the basic constitution of the Written Law to the changing conditions of life. It was felt that, if the Oral Tradition were to be set down in writing, it would soon become a fossilized mass and not capable of growth. Moses knew that all things existing in life must go through a slow process of evolution if they are to survive. He knew that some of the laws he had given to the Jewish people would have to undergo reinterpretation, adaptation, and perhaps even modification. For this reason, he set aside the Oral Tradition as a sort of "unwritten constitution" which allowed for additions and amendments much more readily than a written one. In this sense, the Mishna asks, "What was created for what; Israel for the Law or the Law for Israel?" And the answer given is, "The Law was created for Israel because, had there been no Israel, there would have been no place in the world for the Law."

But in addition to all of this, the Jewish genius has created a concept that is unique, namely, the Masorah (tradition). Masorah, however, is more than mere tradition—it is something handed down orally from generation to generation. Masorah, therefore, is the *unbroken* spiritual thread which has gone through the history of the people of Israel since the days of Moses and on through the ages.

The "Ethics of the Fathers" begins with an introduction as follows: "Moses received the Law on Mount Sinai and passed it on to Joshua; Joshua passed it on to the Elders; the Elders to the Prophets; and the Prophets in turn handed it down to the Men of the Great Synod."

It has ever been thus throughout Jewish history. The preservation of the element of continuity was considered so important at the time of the Tannaim that it was enough that a scholar say with regard to a certain Law "so-and-so is my Masorah," or even "this I have heard," and his opinion would carry decisive weight; and not only in the past but to this very day, the concept of Masorah is the most precious ideal of the Jewish people, for it guarantees the inner, spiritual continuity which extends from Mount Sinai down to the very last Jew to live on earth. At times that tradition may be difficult to understand, but it will always be cherished, almost like a sacred testament left by a grandfather to his descendants. Yet Masorah has never become synonymous with blind dogma, for it may be explained in a variety of ways and is neither static nor immune to reinterpretation.

The Oral Tradition is composed of several parts as follows: (1) *Ancient laws,* which were actually observed among the Jewish people long before the giving of the Law on Mount Sinai. (2) *Traditional interpretations,* which went hand in hand with the laws as written in the original Biblical text. For example, we are told by the Written Law solely that Jews can eat only such animals as have been slaughtered and not such as have died either a natural or accidental death. The Written Law does not, however, explicitly state the exact manner in which the animal must be slaughtered to render it fit for consumption by Jews. The details concerning the proper slaughtering and the other qualifications which determine the animal's fitness for consumption are given in the Oral Tradition. (3) *Interpretations* of Biblical Law by the scholars. (4) *Modifications* in the Law also made by scholars. (5) *Decrees* handed down by the Supreme Court of Religious Law in Jerusalem which have retained their validity to the present day.

The sages of the Jewish people placed the Oral Tradition on the same level of sanctity as the Written Law; in fact, at times, Oral Tradition actually modifies and sometimes even abrogates the former. In explanation of what seems a paradox, the scholars of the Law have said that, at times, even the abolition, by authority, of a law in the Law of Moses, is actually a fundamental of that very Law. Tradition has it that, when the Lord told Moses to hew out new Tablets of the Law to replace those which he, Moses, had broken, special emphasis had been put in the Biblical narrative on the phrase, "which thou hast broken." The sages explain this to mean an indication of divine approval of what Moses had done, and that, under certain conditions, it was just as meritorious to break a law as to make one. If we look at the issue from this point of view, certain changes, or even abolition of certain legislation, do not constitute violations of the basic Law of Moses, but are, in fact, quite in accordance with the spirit in which that Law had originally been given.

In the beginning, the commandment that the Oral Tradition must never be written down was strictly kept by all the authorities. Eventually, however, it became impossible to commit to memory the wealth of material that had accumulated as part of the Oral Tradition for centuries. The sages therefore ruled that the commandment in the Written Law stating "Ye shall not add unto the word . . . neither shall ye diminish from it" (Deut. 4:2) does not prohibit interpretation or explanation, and that therefore, there was nothing in the Law that would prohibit the taking of brief notes as an aid to memorization of the Oral Tradition.

This new approach was then considered revolutionary, and it paved the way for the eventual compilation of the entire Oral Tradition into the permanent code which became the Mishna. At first, a verse from the Biblical Law would be set down, to which would then be added the interpretation, meaning the details that would be part of the observance of the law, and the manner in which that law should be construed. Thus there gradually grew up a mass of legislation which was later called Mishnayoth. Eventually the sages no longer cited the original Biblical text verbatim, but set forth the interpretation alone without the basic text to which it applied. Often only the first words of the pertinent verse from the Bible would be quoted, for it was assumed that the serious student of the Law would know to which verse the statements given referred.

The code which we know as the Mishnayoth has six books, but only four, or rather three and one half of these contain laws that are still of practical validity today. The other part contains the legislation on sacrifices and certain aspects of priestly purity which could be observed only while there was still a Holy Temple, *and an independent Jewish state.* The same is true of much of the eleven divisions of the first volume dealing with agricultural procedure. The Law in the land of Israel after the Mishnayoth is the Gemorah, which is simply an elaboration and a commentary on the Mishnayoth, written down in the form of minutes of discussions among the Amoraim (interpreters of the Law). But not all of the six books of the Mishna contain Gemorah material as well. There is no Gemorah for the tractate called "Zaraim" except the first section of it; there is Gemorah for all of the twelve divisions of the tractate dealing with the ceremonial law pertinent to religious holidays; for all of the seven divisions of the tractate on marital relationships; and for all of the eight divisions of the tractate dealing with tort and damages. There is Gemorah for the Mishnaic laws on priestly purity and for most of the precepts on sacrificial ritual, because, for the most part, these tractates contain laws which have no practical validity or interest for Diaspora Jewry.

Mishnayoth are written in pure Hebrew, for Hebrew was the language of Palestine, where the Mishna was born. The Gemorah, on the other hand, was put into writing in Babylonia and was therefore written in Aramaic, which was the language of that country. (Actually, the Aramaic employed in the Gemorah is not pure, but mixed with Syrian. The Syrian language, akin to Aramaic, was used by the masses in everyday conversation, while pure Aramaic was the vehicle of communication associated with the social and intellectual elite of those days.) Most of the Amoraim conducted their learned discussions in the language of the people, which was, of course, Syrian.

However, the Gemorah does not consist solely of learned discussions on the material found in the Mishna. Actually, the contents of the Gemorah can be classified into two categories; first, "Halacha" which is legal material, the actual interpretation of the Mishna, and the "Haggada" which is a written record of talks by scholars on a variety of topics, interspersed richly with parables and legends.

Of these two parts, the Halacha, of course, is the weightier and more difficult to understand. It occupies a full two thirds of the entire Gemorah. The Haggada, which comprises about one third of the Gemorah, is easier to read and understand, and affords the reader some insight into the ideas and ways of the masses of the Jewish people who lived during the period from the second to the fifth centuries of the Christian calendar.

The halachic material takes the form of a word-for-word record of discussions which took place in the houses of study, or elsewhere, among a group or groups of scholars concerning the proper interpretation of the laws set down in the Mishna. Altogether there were some eighteen hundred participants in these debates, but no more than a hundred of them seem to have been so important that their names recur over and over again. These scholars, as we have explained elsewhere, are known as the Amoraim and their period in Jewish history extended over three hundred years. As we study the Gemorah, we may come upon discussions between "pairs" of Amoraim, and each of the six generations of Amoraim produced at least one outstanding pair of debating scholars.

The Halacha is divided into "sugyot," meaning discussions of certain issues from several vantage points. The language of the Gemorah refers to such debates as "Shakla-ve-taryah" (an Aramaic term meaning assumptions and rebuttals) indicating the procedure typical of any learned discussion.

The Haggada consists of legends, ethical teachings, parables, and wise sayings. The word "Haggada," an Aramaic term, has the same roots as the Hebrew word "Hagadda"; both words denote the concept of "telling" or "relating."

The material of the Haggada is divided into eleven categories as follows:

1. *Legends* concerning righteous men or the Jewish people in general. For example, there is the tale of the worm that burrowed its way into the brain of the Emperor Titus, and the story about Chony Hamagal who slept for seventy years. These legends were folk tales, originally devised by men of great imaginative skill in order to emphasize some important point.

2. *Debates* on Jews and Judaism, carried on by Jewish scholars against kings, Jewish heretics, and non-Jews. Among the many Amoraim who conducted such debates was Rabbi Abahu who lived in Caesarea, Palestine. It seems that he engaged in such verbal fights with the Christians, attempting to refute their basic beliefs such as, for example, that dealing with the bodily

ascension of Jesus into heaven. He explained that Judaism knows of no human being who had physically ascended into heaven. Such a statement, he said, could not even be made of Moses and of the Prophet Elijah (Succah 5). When the opposition cited the example of Enoch, of whom it appeared to have been said that his body actually did go to heaven from earth, Abahu postulated that the words in the original text "and the Lord took him" indicated a natural death as opposed to one by violence, rather than physical ascension into the lofty regions.

3. *Philosophical talks* on a variety of topics, such as whether Adam had first been a dead clay figure before God breathed the breath of life into him, or whether God had created and destroyed any other worlds before establishing our own earth. Others deal with the idea advanced by Thales, the Greek philosopher, that water had been the original substance from which everything else had then been formed.

4. *Parables* in the form of fables from bird and animal life. Rabbi Meir alone, for example, is responsible for some three hundred such parables. Other parables deal with human figures such as kings.

5. *Wise sayings* commonly employed by the people of the time. These are usually introduced by a remark to the effect that "this is what people say."

6. *Medical advice* on the prevention and cure of certain ailments, and also on amulets and charms.

7. *Phantasies,* weird products of a fertile imagination, such as the tales of Rabbah bar Bar Chana, who was a master at devising such strange stories as "come and I shall show thee the place where heaven and earth kiss each other."

8. *Witty puns.* The explanation of Biblical verses by means of puns in order to put stress on a particular thought in connection with the text.

9. Interpretations through the *analysis of words.* Called "Gimatrioth" in the Talmud, these are based on the fact that the Hebrew language employs the letters of the alphabet also for numerals, so that the numerical value of each word can be found by adding the sum totals of the numbers represented by each letter of the word.

10. An *interpretation of the wording of a Biblical verse in support of the Halacha.* For instance, we are told in the Bible in the account of the creation of Eve that, *"va-yiven* et ha-tzela," meaning, "the Lord *built"* the side which He had removed from Adam's rib so that it took on the form of a woman, Eve. But the Hebrew term "va-yiven" can be construed as being phonetically related to "havanah" which is the Hebrew word denoting "understanding." This fact is taken by the sages to indicate that the Lord endowed woman with a special intelligence which causes her to mature earlier than man.

11. *Satires and humor.* At times the Haggada also employs satire and humor, for example, in the account of the manner in which Korah ridiculed the Law of Moses.

Even in those days, there was a marked distinction between those scholars who occupied themselves with Halacha and those who gave most of their time to the Haggada. The "men of the Halacha" were generally on a higher intellectual level than the devotees of the Haggada.

In the days of the Mishna, spiritual guidance came from the scholars who had written the Halacha and who had a tendency to look down upon those interested in the haggadic material. When, for example, Rabbi Akiba, whose name was always linked with the Halacha, showed signs of interest in haggadic literature, his colleagues said to him, "How does a man of thy greatness come to pursue the Haggada? Go back to the Halacha."

Yet the Haggada grew and developed, and, in fact, the editors who put the Talmud in its final form gave a prominent place to haggadic material.

If we should examine an actual folio of the Gemorah, we will find a great deal of difference in appearance between one containing only haggadic material and one comprised of Halacha only. A folio of Gemorah devoted entirely to Halacha actually has only a small part of text in the middle of the page. This text is surrounded on all sides by commentaries, such as those of the famous Rashi, and those of the Tosafists, the disciples and descendants of Rashi, and statements by later authorities who not only give their commentaries but also pose pertinent questions, and give their answers to these self-posed queries. On the folios containing haggadic material only, however, there is very little commentary and the page is dominated by the original text. The reason for this disparity between Halacha and Haggada is explained by the sages who compare the Talmud to a vast ocean. The Halacha represents the body of water most difficult to negotiate, so that the would-be navigator needs the assistance of experienced pilots such as Rashi and the Tosafists who, with their explanations and commentaries, safely steer the student through the troubled waters. The Haggada, on the other hand, is compared to a calm and placid sea where the navigator does not need to rely so heavily upon the aid of the "pilots" as he did in traversing the waters of the Halacha. The style of the Haggada, unlike that of the Halacha, is clear and direct, with every thought explicitly set down in plain words, and if a person understands the language in which it was written he needs no other help for understanding. It is only in a very few instances that the wording of the haggadic material resembles the "shorthand" style of the Halacha.

Most of the Halacha was written in Hebrew and Aramaic, because the discussions that are part of it were carried on by the intellectual elite which preferred these two languages. The Haggada, on the other hand, is a mixture of Aramaic and Syrian, and some of its portions are entirely in Syrian, which was the language of the masses at the time.

9. The Contribution of the Tannaim to Judaism

Must Man Adjust Himself to the Law, or the Law to Man?—The Liberal Interpretations of the Law by the Tannaim—The Conception of Juadism as a Better Way of Life as Held by the Tannaim

Even in the very early days of Jewish history, Israel's scholars gave a great deal of thought to the question: "What, actually, is Judaism?" Was Judaism a mass of legislation which every Jew was bound to observe unquestioningly, regardless of whether or not it served his best interests, or was it a teaching designed to guide man how best to live in God's world? Must man always bow to the Law, regardless of how difficult it may be to observe? Or were the laws created for man, to be interpreted and construed in such a manner as to be compatible with the conditions posed by changing times? And the sages decided that it was the Law that must be adjusted to man, and should not be reduced to a static code. This attitude is evident from an explanation given by the Tanna Rabbi Simon ben Menassiah who was a contemporary of Rabbi Judah the Prince. He construed the Biblical verse "the Sabbath shall be holy *unto you*" to mean that "The Sabbath was given *to you,* and *not you* to the Sabbath" (Mechilta 80 Ki Thisah). This is of great significance for it shows the liberal spirit that guided the religious leaders of the Jewish people. They considered that the Law had been made for man, and therefore felt that, in those cases where the actual law seemed unduly harsh or difficult to comprehend, the scholars of Jewish Law had the right and the authority to reinterpret it in such a manner as to make it conform with the needs and best interests of the people.

The sages understood that, had the Law been given all in one rigid piece which could not be changed, it could not have survived. They compared the Law to a living plant which grows new branches constantly. This means that the Law, rather than being static and immovable, is capable of growth and development. It is dynamic and therefore subject to change, much like a plant which sheds old leaves while it grows new ones.

It was in this spirit that the sages reinterpreted not only single verses but also entire portions of Biblical Law. The sages have found ways of reinterpreting the Law without actually abrogating it. Take, for instance, the portion in Chapter 21 of the Book of Deuteronomy dealing with the "stubborn and rebellious son." In brief, the law there is as follows: If a man has a son who refuses to obey his parents and all punishments have proved of no avail, the parents must bring the son to the elders of the city and tell them, " 'Our son is stubborn and rebellious; he doth not harken to our voice; he is a glutton, and a drunkard.' " . . . And all the men of his city shall stone him with stones, that he die. . . ." (Deut. 21:21).

This seems a harsh judgment. Exactly what sins does the epithet "stubborn and rebellious" cover? How much may a son eat if he is not to be considered "a glutton," and how much must he have drunk before he can be called "a drunkard"? In order to make the issue clearer, the sages decided to establish some kind of standard for enforcing that law, so that there should be no miscarriage of justice which, in this case, might involve actual murder which is repugnant to the Law. For this reason it was decided that the consumption of an amount equivalent to two pounds of meat at one time could be considered gluttony, while the term "drunkard" as employed in the law could refer only to one who had imbibed an amount equivalent to one quart of wine at one time. However, this in itself is not sufficient reason to condemn a young man to death. Hence the wise men went on to establish a total of other criteria which must all be found in a son before he could be called "stubborn and rebellious." The last and the twenty-seventh of these points was such as to make sure that the drastic punishment could actually *never* be carried out under any circumstances, as the wording of the original text is ". . . he does not listen *to our voice*," and not "he does not listen to *our voices*," as it should be. This, the sages explained, shows a son could be accused and condemned only if the voices of both parents had been "as one voice," meaning identical voices, so that, the authorities maintained, not only the voices, but even the parents had to be alike and of equal physical stature before such charges could be brought against their son. In this manner, while the actual harsh law was not repealed, the conditions for its execution were rendered so as to make it impossible of fulfillment. Accordingly, the authorities established that "actually, there can never be, nor will there ever be, a 'stubborn and rebellious son' " (Sanhedrin 71).

Another example: There is a law in Chapter 13 of Deuteronomy concerning false prophets. This law reads as follows: "If there arise in the midst of thee a prophet . . . saying: 'Let us go after other gods, which thou hast not known, and let us serve them' ; thou shalt not hearken unto the words of that prophet . . . thou shalt surely smite the inhabitants of that city with the edge of the sword, destroying it utterly, *and all that is therein* and the cattle thereof, with the edge of the sword. And thou shalt gather all the spoil of it . . . and shalt burn with fire the city . . . it shall not be built again."

It seemed difficult to understand why an entire city of innocent men and beasts should be destroyed just because a few of its inhabitants had sinned.

And were the houses of the city also accomplices in the crime that they had to be razed as well?

Again, the sages came to the rescue. They based their argument upon the phrase ". . . and all that is therein." Would this not mean that even such sacred objects as scrolls of the Law and phylacteries would also have to be destroyed if they were in that sinful city? But holy objects could never be burned and therefore had to be excepted from that rule. Now if an exception had to be made in this case, then it would not be true that "all that is therein" could be burned in the city. Now, therefore, since "all that is therein" could not possbily be burned, it was decided that the law actually referred only to the eradication of all guilty elements, but not of the innocent. Thus, once again, the sages took a law of the Bible and construed it in such a manner that it was impossible to enforce.

The scholars of the Law had the courage to assume authority to construe the entire Biblical law in such a way that it would be in conformity with practical life. Laws were not to be followed blindly but in accordance with the dictates of reason.

In addition, at times they even took it upon themselves to make outright changes in the Law, without any effort at reconstruction or reinterpretation, whenever they considered such a drastic step necessary.

For instance, there is a law in Deuteronomy, Chapter 21, reading "if one be found slain in the land . . . lying in the field . . . thy elders . . . shall come forth, and they shall measure unto the cities which are round about him that is slain. And it shall be, that the city which is nearest unto the slain man, even the elders of that city shall take a heifer of the herd . . . and shall break the heifer's neck. . . . And all the elders . . . shall wash their hands over the heifer whose neck was broken in the valley . . . and say, 'Our hands have not shed this blood, neither have our eyes seen it.' "

In time, however, it was noted that the number of murders increased in the land. The wise men understood that the law had been made at a time when murder was a rarity and that the ceremony was meant to stress the seriousness of the isolated instances when foul play did occur. However, when murder became an almost daily occurence, this ceremony was discontinued because it no longer made any sense. In the Mishna it was then established: "When murders increased in frequency, the entire ceremony of breaking the heifer's neck was abrogated" (Sota 49).

Or take the law in Numbers 5:12-31 concerning the wife suspected of adultery where it is said: "If any man's wife go aside, and act unfaithfully against him [her husband] . . . and he be jealous of his wife . . . then shall the man bring his wife unto the priest, and shall bring her offering for her. . . . And the priest shall take holy water in an earthen vessel; and of the dust that is on the floor of the Tabernacle the priest shall take, and put it into the water." Thereafter, the hair of the woman had to be uncovered, and the priest had to have the woman swear that she had never been unfaithful, and write down her oath on a piece of paper which was then also immersed in the water. After she had sworn, she was to be given to drink from the bitter water so prepared by the priest. If she was innocent, the water would not harm her. Had she perjured herself, however, her belly would swell and her thighs fall away.

The Talmud devotes much discussion to this issue, but Rabbi Johanan ben Zakkai abrogated the entire law, as can be seen from the Mishna, where it is said, "when sexual iniquities increased, Rabbi Johanan ben Zakkai abrogated the law to give the suspect woman bitter water to drink."

But of special interest is the liberal manner in which the sages construed the laws concerning Sabbath observance.

After the ideal of monotheism, the Sabbath is the second greatest concept to have been given to the world by the Jewish people. While much of the rest of the world was enslaved without respite, Moses was the first to proclaim the law: "Six days shalt thou labour and do all thy work; but the seventh day is a sabbath. . . ."

Some Bible critics maintain that the Jewish people were neither the first nor the only one of the ancient nations to have a Sabbath day. They point to the "Sabbatu" of the ancient Babylonians in support of their argument. But the fact is that the "Sabbatu" was a day of mourning, having nothing in common with the joyous day of rest established among the Jewish people, which entails not merely physical rest from labor for all, but also spiritual recreation. It is to be a day of rest for body and soul, a day of holiness and elevation of the spirit.

Over and over again there is mention of the Sabbath in the Bible and in prophetic literature. The three most important statements on the Sabbath are found in Genesis 2:1-3; Exodus 20:8-11 (The Fourth Commandment); and Deuteronomy 5:12-15. In Genesis, we are merely told that the Lord completed His work of creation within six days and rested on the seventh "and God blessed the seventh day and hallowed it." No mention as yet of any commandment that man, too, should have a Sabbath, because the Lord had rested on the seventh day after six days of Creation.

In Deuteronomy, the commandments are repeated in brief. This time, however, the reason given for the Sabbath law is not that the Lord Himself had rested after six days but that "thou wast a servant in the land of Egypt, and the Lord thy God brought thee out of there by a mighty hand and by an outstretched arm; therefore the Lord thy God commanded thee to keep the sabbath day."

Thus we are given two motives for Sabbath observance, one with the spirit in mind, and the other relating to the needs of the body. In the Fourth Commandment we are told that the day should have spiritual significance for us as well. In Deuteronomy, on the other hand, we read that, since the Jew had been a slave in Egypt and the Lord had freed him from that bondage, he should observe the Sabbath so that he might remember that he was no longer physically enslaved. However, the sages said that both motives are really one, as it means not only for the body but for the soul as well.

The sages of the Jewish people made the Sabbath commandment into the most important of all the Biblical commandments. To them, the Sabbath was the "be-all and end-all" of Judaism. They sang its praises in extravagant terms and symbolically endowed it with the crown of "The Sabbath Queen." The scholars even went so far as to say that a person who observed the Sabbath in the proper manner would be forgiven even if he should lapse into idol worship (Sabbath 110:8). Of course this statement would seem paradoxical, but it does show the overwhelming importance which the authorities attached to the Sabbath day.

Isaiah the Prophet says, "And call the Sabbath a delight" (Isaiah 58:13), and the sages state, "The Sabbath was given only for the purpose of delight," and that "therefore he who rejoices in the Sabbath is deserving of having everything his heart desires" (Sabbath 110:8).

In view of this attitude held by the scholars, it is not surprising to note the liberal manner in which they interpreted the Biblical and Mishnaic legislation pertaining to Sabbath observance.

Let us take, as an example, the Biblical law, "let no man go out of his place on the seventh day" (Exod. 16:29). Literally construed, this would mean that a person would have to spend the entire Sabbath day at the place where he happened to be when the sun set on Friday night. But such Sabbath observance would hardly serve to make that day one of delight.

The question of the proper interpretation of that law hinged upon the words "from his place." Some of the sages took "his place" to mean "within four ells." Others said that it meant the house in which one lives. A later authority opined that the commandment referred to the "courtyard," and later still it was agreed that "his place" meant the city in which a person dwells. In the end, it was established that the commandment should be interpreted to mean that a person was permitted to walk a distance of 2000 ells in any one direction outside the city in which he lived. At a later date, this was extended to mean "anywhere within a radius of 2000 ells outside the city," and finally it was decreed that a person would be allowed to walk another 2000 ells, in addition to the distances mentioned above, if he would perform a ceremonial act known as "the laying of an Erub."

Now the Bible itself does not explicitly state the kinds of work that must not be done on the Sabbath. It only says "Thou shalt not do any labor" on the Sabbath day. This posed another great task to the expounders of the Law. The Hebrew term "melachah" is employed in the original commandment to denote "labor." This same term had been used in the Bible also in connection with the types of work involved in the building of the Holy Tabernacle.

For this reason, the sages decided that the law applied to all those activities which were entailed also in the erection of the Sanctuary. It was established that this would include a total of thirty-nine specified types of work, and these came to be the main classifications for work to be forbidden on the Sabbath.

To these explicit prohibitions, however, the scholars amended many provisions which were most liberal in nature:

(1) A deliberate violation of the Sabbath was punishable. But many violations of the Sabbath really involved two separate acts. The carrying of packages, for instance, which was forbidden on the Sabbath, involved first the lifting of the bale from its original place and then its deposition elsewhere. If the person took the package away from one place, but did not deposit it elsewhere during the Sabbath day, it was considered only half of the labor performed and therefore no violation at all.

(2) Only that work which is done for the sake of the work itself, and for no other purpose, was considered an outright violation of the Sabbath. For instance, it was forbidden to dig a pit in order to derive some benefit from the pit. But if one should dig the pit not in order to make use of the pit itself but only for the purpose of taking the earth thus excavated, he was not considered a Sabbath violator.

(3) If a person purposely performed the work in a manner different from that in which he would do it during the week, for example, if he should carry a load on his head, instead of in his hands or on his shoulders as is the usual practice, he was not considered a violator of the Sabbath.

(4) If his original purpose in doing the work had been different from what he had actually done, he was considered innocent. An example of this would be if a person had intended to cut a certain vegetable for his consumption but, inadvertently, had cut off another which he had not intended to eat then (Sabbath 72).

(5) Any kind of work done for the sole purpose of destroying was not considered a direct violation of the Sabbath. If, for example, a person were to tear a garment for the sole purpose of tearing it, with no thought of its reuse or alteration; in other words, if the labor performed would bring the performer no personal gain whatever, it was not considered "forbidden work."

We went into all this detail only to show how anxious the scholars were to keep the law within reason and to prevent it from becoming inflexible. If every kind of work would have been categorically prohibited without explanation, it would have been most unreasonable and the law could not possibly be observed in its entirety by anyone.

It was in this spirit, too, that the sages established that "the saving of a human life outweighs the Sabbath." In cases of illness it was not only permitted, but actually mandatory, to violate the Sabbath, because the Sabbath had been created for the welfare of man, and not man for the Sabbath. And under the definition of "illness," the scholars included even ailments as trifling as a cold.

For this reason, too, they established that, in time of war, it was permissible to fight against the foe even on the Sabbath. They based their decision on the Biblical commandment to fight against a foe until he is annihilated. This, they reasoned, could certainly not be done if all fighting were to cease one day each week.

Such was the liberal spirit that influenced the sages in their construction and interpretation of Biblical Law. They allowed pure reason to guide them in determining what was good for man and what was not, and it was upon this firm but flexible foundation that they built up Judaism.

As we have already said, Jews consider the Sabbath to be more than merely a day of respite from physical labor. The Jewish Sabbath is a unique institution. It is meant to be holy, for the Bible states that God made the Sabbath day holy and commands man to "remember the sabbath day, to keep it holy" (Exod. 20:8). This means that, if properly observed, the Jewish Sabbath includes not only physical rest but also spiritual recreation. It means that, on the day when the Lord rested from His labors of creation, man, too, should turn aside from all the hustle-bustle of his own everyday activities and turn to higher, spiritual spheres. The Sabbath should be a day which will cast all its aura upon our spiritual lives for the entire week, a day of joy and inspiration.

Because of the many benefits inherent in the Sabbath, the sages decreed that, even if a traveler should lose track of the calendar, he could still observe a Sabbath of his own by counting six days and then resting on the seventh. In this manner, even though he might not observe the spiritual Sabbath, he could at least be able to enjoy the physical respite that any day of rest affords.

Thus Judaism, so interpreted, became not merely a religion, but a teaching, a guide for universal application; and that is, after all, what the actual translation of the Hebrew term "Torah," used to denote "the Law," means: a teaching.

10. *The Ideologies of the Three Parties*

THE PHARISEES

It is self-evident that, in order to be properly understood, ancient historic documents must be provided with some sort of commentary. Any document bears the indelible impress of the time at which it was written and needs explanation in order to give future readers a background and frame of reference enabling them to understand it correctly.

This is true particularly of codes of law. For laws, too, are the products of a specific period of time, and provision must be made for both elucidation and reinterpretation if they are to remain meaningful and applicable to future generations.

The same would also apply to any religion that is based on a code, and particularly to constitutions of national entities, beginning with the Magna Charta which was signed by King John of England in 1215, down to the charters of the most recent member of the United Nations. All these legal documents need or eventually will require commentary, elucidation, and canons to aid in reinterpretation.

In the United States the Founding Fathers foresaw this need when they formulated our Constitution, and provided for a Supreme Court whose function it would be to interpret the constitution so that it would continue to be a living, dynamic force throughout the subsequent history of our nation.

The Law of Moses was nothing less than the constitution by which the Jewish faith and the Jewish people lived. As such it, too, was in need of interpreters, of acknowledged authorities who would explain to the people the correct manner in which the terse sentences and generalizations found in the original text of the Law should be construed. A great many of the commandments contained in the Torah actually cannot be understood at all unless such aid is given. We need to know why it is that some of these commandments, for instance, recur several times in the Scriptures, but with a different motive cited in each place. Many commandments, moreover, are difficult for modern man to comprehend unless we know their background.

This is a gigantic task and requires men of broad learning whose authority is accepted by the people at large. In the case of Jewish law, this function was fulfilled by the Tannaim who put the finishing touches, as it were, to the edifice of Judaism as we know it today. The epoch of the Tannaim was the great and glorious era in Jewish history which produced such giant intellects as Hillel and Shammai, Rabban Gamaliel the Elder and his son, Rabbi Simon, Rabbi Johanan ben Zakkai and Rabbi Akiba, Rabbi Meir, and Rabbi Judah the Prince, to name only a few. This period, dominated by men of outstanding moral character, of profound insight and remarkable liberalism, was second in historic significance only to the period of the prophets.

The Tannaim and their adherents and disciples soon became known by the Hebrew name of "Perushim," meaning "interpreters of the Law," from which we derive the designation by which history refers to them today—the "Pharisees." They enjoyed great popularity among the people at large and exercised much influence in Jewish life. Josephus, the great historian, had this to say on the ethical and moral standards of the Pharisees:

"The Pharisees content themselves with little; they have no desire for luxuries either in food or in dress. They do not pursue pleasures; they choose the path of better understanding and they conduct themselves accordingly. They are most industrious and quite respectful of their elders. Pride and arrogance are alien to them and they are endowed with a great many other virtues. It is for this reason that they found such favor in the eyes of the people" (Antiquities, Chapter 18).

It is strange that, in view of all this, the word "Pharisees" should have the unsavory connotation that it does in the English language. In Webster's Dictionary, the word "Pharisee" is defined as referring to: (1) making a show of religion without the spirit of it; (2) hypocritical; (3) self-righteous.

It seems that this prejudice against the Pharisees was derived from the New Testament where the Apostles speak of the Pharisees as hypocrites. It is interesting to note that the very Apostles who thus attack the Pharisees had actually never seen any Pharisees themselves because they, the Apostles, were not born until about one hundred or one hundred fifty years after the founder of Christianity and therefore were a century removed even from the second generation of the Tannaim. For example, the Apostle Matthew, in relating the sermons of Jesus to the Pharisees, constantly refers to the group as "ye hypocrite Pharisees" (New Testament, Matthew 23:23).

It was not until recent times that a great Christian scholar, Trevers R. Herford, resolved to find out the truth about the Pharisees. He undertook the task of studying the Talmud in its original language and soon realized that his coreligionists had grossly misunderstood the Pharisees. He then became convinced that these scholars and their disciples had not been hypocrites at all, but, instead, had been of high ethical character and the greatest intellects of their age. In 1912, he published his findings in a work entitled *The Pharisees,* in which he states that the Pharisees were great men, men with great souls, who lived a higher sort of life. They feared God and did that which is just and right in His eyes, and they engaged in higher pursuits. "It is my desire," he said, "to give my readers a clear idea of what the Pharisees actually were, what they fought for, so that the reader may see how very far the Pharisees were from being hypocrites."

This book had profound repercussions in scholarly circles. A short time later, Herford published another volume entitled *The World's Debt to the Pharisees,* in which he further documented the views concerning the Pharisees that he had advanced in his first book on the subject.

Many other Christian scholars followed suit and reexamined their own attitude toward the Pharisees in the light of the new evidence that had been presented. In his book entitled *Judaism in the First Centuries of the Christian Era,* Professor George Foot Moore said that "It is disgraceful to say that the Pharisees were hypocrites because, in fact, they were men of great nobleness. They were the great minds of their time, and the creators of Judaism."

Thus, gradually, Christian scholars discarded their prejudices against the Pharisees and began to regard them not as hypocrites but as the great men that they actually were.

Let us now make a brief study of the views of the Tannaim, or the Pharisees, who were men of sincerity and intelligence, and amazingly liberal in their outlook.

To the Tannaim, or Pharisees, Judaism was not a religion but a teaching, a teaching applicable to practical, everyday life, in short, "a law of life." For this reason, they adopted as their chief device the Biblical verse "and he shall live by them," meaning, of course, that man should live by the laws. Conversely, they said "and he shall not lose his life through them." The laws of Judaism, they maintained, must be such that they should improve the people's way of life rather than stunt and narrow it.

Based on this view, the sages took upon themselves the right to amend quite a number of laws by means of exegesis. As an example, the ancient law "an eye for an eye," on which the Tannaim commented that it should not be taken literally but construed to mean merely that in cases of physical injury caused by another, appropriate financial restitution must be made to the injured party. Similarly, the Tannaim always asserted that it required a great deal more intelligence and wisdom to amend an existing law than it did to accept its letter without question. It is an easy thing to lay down a categorical imperative or prohibition, but it requires profound knowledge and study to be able to interpret the law from a broader, liberal vantage point.

Thus those who expound the Law of Israel have been given a basic principle by which to guide themselves in their decisions—namely, to attempt to find the most liberal possible interpretation within the framework of the ancient Law.

❦ THE SADDUCEES

As we have said earlier in this book, Jewish life during the days of the Second Temple was dominated by several parties. After the party of the people, the Pharisees, which numbered among its members the expounders of the Law and their disciples, came the Sadducee party which included most of the military and social elite of the land, and, aside from both, the Essene group, which was actually not a political party at all and consisted of mystics and visionaries. The Pharisee movement enjoyed the support of the masses, while the Sadducee party, representing men of high rank and great wealth, exerted a powerful influence in the affairs of the country. The membership of the Essenes, on the other hand, consisted mainly of those who sought a means of escape from reality and had no great desire to play an important political role in national issues.

Thus the intellectual warfare concerning the manner in which the Law should be construed was carried on between only two disputing factions: the Pharisees and the Sadducees. We have already given a brief survey of the Pharisee ideology. Now let us study the views of the Sadducees, which were more conservative. This was so because the Sadducees viewed the Written Law of Moses as a finished, closed unit to which nothing further could be added, not even through inference or interpretation. It was a static thing, and not subject to commentary or change. Their device was "Thus it is written"; in other words, these are the explicit words of the original text of the Law, which must be obeyed to the letter and cannot be reinterpreted. It was not permissible, they maintained, to deviate in any manner from the literal wording and intent of the ancient Law.

Accordingly, they maintained that the ancient law "an eye for an eye," for instance, meant precisely what it said. If a person were to put out the eye of another, he must be punished by being deprived of his own eye. The Sadducees preached obedience to the strict letter of the law, and refused to accept the explanation of the Tannaim that the purpose of the Law was not to exact physical vengeance from the wrongdoer, but to emphasize the importance of payment of a satisfactory indemnity to the injured party.

Among examples of the literalistic attitude of the Sadducees is the stand they took regarding the law of "levirate marriage." This law provides that a man must marry the widow of his deceased brother if she should be childless. If, for some reason, he should be unable to do so, the law says that a ceremony called Chalitza shall take place in which the widow, by taking off her brother-in-law's shoe, symbolically expresses her contempt for him for not wanting to perform his duty toward her. The literal wording of the law is that, as she takes off his shoe, she has to "spit full in his face." The Tannaim or Pharisees interpreted this as merely a figure of speech indicating the attitude of contempt which the woman should have for the man who refused to aid her in her plight. However, the Sadducees took the command quite literally and said that the entire ceremony would be invalid unless the woman had actually spat in the face of her brother-in-law. In the end, the Tannaim, in order to appease the opposition, ceded that the woman "might spit on the floor during the ceremony to show her contempt but not into the face of the man." The Sadducees, however, adamantly refused to accept this decision as binding.

The Sadducees were unwilling even to adopt those unwritten laws which had been accepted by the entire Jewish people for generations before. They recognized neither the ancient Masorah, the tradition handed down orally from father to son, nor the recent amendments introduced by the Tannaim. They stubbornly maintained that only the literal word of the original law had final, binding force, and that there was no such thing as an Oral Tradition that was as much part and parcel of Jewish legislation as the Written Law.

It remains for us now to compare the broad and liberal interpretation of the Law as advanced by the Pharisees with the narrow view held by the Sadducees, because only then shall we see what profound and liberal thinkers the Pharisees actually were, and how unduly narrow-minded and conservative the Sadducees were.

However, it would be an oversimplification to say that all the Pharisees always sought to make the Law easier, while the Sadducees constantly strove to make it more stringent and difficult to observe. Not all the Pharisees attempted to make the law simpler to observe. The School of Shammai, for instance, reinterpreted the Law by adding many restrictions which the adherents of Hillel considered unnecessary. But the stern view was the thesis that those laws which were difficult to understand could be reinterpreted and explained. The difference between the School of Shammai and that of Hillel lay solely in the fact that the reinterpretation given by the former was stricter, while that advanced by the latter tended to be more liberal. But, unlike the Sadducees, neither school was literalistic. They both accepted the concept of an Oral Tradition which would serve to reinforce and explain the Written Law, to which the Sadducees accorded no validity at all. The Sadducees knew only of the written text of the original Law as a living organism. They would have turned Judaism into a narrow set of dogma, a mass of difficult laws that must be observed without any explanations or reasons given, and that was binding upon every Jew, regardless of whether he understood it or not.

And in this narrow view lay the downfall of the Sadducees. The people were against them, even as practical life ran counter to their rigid concepts. Not long after the destruction of the Second Temple, the party disappeared entirely from the stage of Jewish history.

But there were other issues, too, with regard to which the Sadducees differed from the Pharisees. The Pharisees had advanced a new set of ideas concerning redemption and the reward of righteousness. They felt that all good men would be rewarded in afterlife, while the wicked would then receive their just deserts. They also viewed the future with confidence, for they be-lieved in the coming of a Messiah, an "anointed one," who would rebuild the Jewish kingdom so that it would regain all its former glory, and that the Messianic era would inaugurate better days not only for the Jewish people, but for all the rest of the world as well. Finally, the Pharisees taught that death is not final, but only a long sleep from which the dead would eventually be resurrected to a new life. All these ideas were vehemently opposed by the Sadducees, for the simple reason that none of them were explicitly spelled out in the original text of the Law of Moses.

As we read in the Talmud (Sanhedrin, 90-94), the sages attempted to prove that this new set of ideas was indeed based on several statements in the Pentateuch, the Prophets, and the Holy Writings. But whatever verses the Pharisees would cite in their support would be refuted by the Sadducees who felt that no meaning should be read into the text of the Bible other than that which was plainly and explicitly stated in the original wording.

The new beliefs had adherents as well as opponents, even outside the partisan ranks, among the rank-and-file population. The debates centered around the theory of the resurrection of the dead in particular, a theme we will elaborate later.

But even more fervent than the opposition of the Sadducees was the manner in which these ideas were espoused by a new movement, the Essenes. Their belief in them proved much stronger than even that of the Pharisees, and they embellished them with their own fantasies and daydreams. Inclined as they were to mysticism and metaphysics, the Essenes found these new be-liefs very much to their liking, as we will see in the following pages.

❧ THE ESSENES

We are not quite certain how the third party in Judaism came by its name. Pliny, a Roman writer, referred to them by the Latin term "Esseni." The Mishna and Gemorah, in making mention of the movement, employ such terms as the "First Hasidim," "the faithful ones," or even, "those who prac-tice morning immersions" as it was their custom to perform a ritual immer-sion in water very early each morning. While these texts do not contain much historic data concerning the Essenes, we can learn a good deal about them from the account left by the historian Josephus, and even more from the writings of Philo, the Alexandrian Jewish philosopher.

Let us first investigate the information we can obtain from reading the works of Philo. Philo, who resided in Alexandria, Egypt, about thirty years prior to the destruction of the Second Temple, lived twenty out of the total sixty years of his life before the birth of Jesus. He is also known as "Yedidiah of Alexandria." In one of his books, written in Greek, he gives a detailed account of the Jewish sect or party which called itself the "Essene" movement. During his own day, he says, the party had some four thousand members dispersed through Palestine and Syria, and had an important place in Jewish life. It was a sect that followed a path peculiarly its own. The Essenes felt that one could serve the Lord not by bringing sacrifices but only by keeping one's person holy and pure. They preferred village life to the hustle-bustle of metropolitan commerce, for to them barter and trade were simply theft and fraud. They preferred to work the soil and to live a pure, honest life as plain farmers or simple artisans. Their wants were few and they disdained gold and silver. None of them was wealthy, for they refused to engage in trade. They did not believe in war and did not possess arms. They neither worked as servants themselves nor employed any of their own, for they believed that no human being should exploit the work or services of another. All men were equal in the sight of the Lord and thus there could be neither servant nor master among them.

The Essenes had three basic principles; namely, to serve the Lord with devotion, to love all men, and to suppress certain physical desires and impulses. They never took the name of the Lord in an oath and were careful never to utter an untruth. They firmly believed that, whatever the Lord did, He did for the best. They avoided all physical enjoyments and lived an extremely simple life. Some of them never married for they felt sexual contact with a woman to be defiling. They were friendly to all, received all people with joy, and were happy to accept new adherents. Some of them banded together to form small collective settlements, living together and pooling their earnings in a communal treasury with each member receiving enough money for his basic needs. If one of the members became ill and was unable to work, he still continued to receive this allowance, and every effort was made to secure proper medical care for him. The Essenes were also noted for the profound respect they had for their elders.

So much for the account given by Philo. Josephus, the historian, who was a contemporary of Philo, also gives a detailed description of the Essenes in his book *The Wars of the Jews*. Most of this account corresponds to that given by Philo. Josephus, however, did contribute a few new facts. First of all, he explained that the Essenes were deeply religious and gave an extremely strict interpretation to Jewish Law. On the Sabbath, for example, they did not move objects from place to place, nor did they themselves walk about much. Some even went so far as to refrain from attending to their natural wants on the Sabbath. They did not regard it as a day of delight and ate only bread and water on that day. They frequently performed ritual ablutions in cold water. Josephus also states that some of those who refrained from marriage dressed in white garments only, being careful not to stain them in any manner.

From the information given us by Philo and Josephus, it is quite clear that the interpretation given to Jewish Law by the Essenes was much more narrow even than that of the Sadducees. Actually, the Essenes never attempted to engage the Pharisees in debate, but they accepted for themselves the most stringent and literal interpretation of the Law, observing practices which were not only unnecessary but actually in contradiction to the spirit of the Law as such. The Pharisees disapproved of these ways, but they left the Essenes to their own devices knowing that the latter, in accordance with their teaching never to engage in any quarrel, would not attempt to refute their arguments. Thus the sages simply looked upon the Essenes as dwellers in a world of fantasy, who preached a doctrine that was far removed from reality, and said that those who followed their teachings were simply "pious fools."

Other Tannaim, more aggressive, charged the Essenes with misinterpreting the Law of Moses. The Essenes, they said, had taken a Law which had been intended as a Law of life, a way of life that would be good for all men to follow, and turned it into a kind of cult which only made life more difficult, a mass of dogmas which crushed the spirit and demanded the negation of the essential physical functions of human life.

It would be well here to give only a few examples of the extremes to which the Essenes carried the practical implementation of their views. The sages, believing that the Sabbath was a day of joy, were willing to modify some of the stern prohibitions in order to make that day more pleasant for its observers. The Essenes, on the other hand, prohibited even a great many things which were explicitly permitted according to the original law. For example, while the sages decreed that it was permissible on the Sabbath to move about freely within a certain radius, even outside the limits of the city in which one resided, the Essenes clung to the literal wording of the law, "let no man go out of his place on the seventh day," and remained almost immobile on the Sabbath. According to the Essenes, it was not even permissible to remove a knife from the table on the day of rest. They forbade their women to employ cosmetics or to put on beautiful garments during their monthly unclean periods. This was certainly not in accordance with the spirit of the Law. The Tanna Rabbi Akiba strongly opposed this practice, for he felt that a woman who would neglect her personal appearance, even at such a time, would become repulsive to her husband and might thus destroy her marriage. In fact, Akiba tended to relax some of the restrictions to which women were subject during their ritually unclean days (Sabbath 64).

Particularly, the Tannaim opposed the views of those Essenes who preached isolation from women and practiced celibacy. The advocates of this doctrine felt that he who was capable of suppressing his sexual impulses could attain true holiness. But the Tannaim retorted that the glory of God dwelt only among married couples, that he who had deliberately refused to marry was as if he had shed blood (Yebamoth 63), and that a teaching which would destroy the institution of the Jewish home and thus ultimately spell the end of the Jewish people must be false and dangerous.

In addition to their strange attitude toward Jewish Law, the Essenes had a strong mystical bent and grossly exaggerated notions of the new beliefs that had been advanced by the Pharisees concerning the coming of the Messiah, reward and punishment in afterlife, and the resurrection of the dead. In general, it was their tendency so grossly to distort all things to the point of absurdity as to make Judaism actually seem ridiculous to an outsider.

Their notions concerning the fate of man seem odd. They claimed, for instance, that every movement made by man was predetermined in heaven. The Tannaim did not share this opinion and believed that man was endowed with a free will and could act as he chose. The Tannaim felt that there were two dominant forces in the world, first, that of heaven which was divine providence, and, secondly, the strength of man who is endowed with freedom of choice. Thus, the Tannaim reasoned, certain things are predetermined by heaven, but man himself is free to choose between the path of good and that of evil. If everything were to be predetermined by divine decree, the Tannaim argued, then those who sin would only carry out a divine decree by so doing. Thus there would be no sinners, but there would also be no righteous men, because every act of righteousness, as well as every crime, would have been carried out involuntarily, in blind submission to a compelling force. For this reason, the sages pointed out, man must be endowed with a certain amount of self-determination. And if he is thus free to choose between good and evil, he is also fully responsible for his acts and thus subject to reward and punishment.

Of course, all this gives rise to an obvious question: If the Lord knows in advance what man will elect to do, is it not then true that man acts involuntarily in accordance with God's decree and that free will is fiction? Centuries later, the medieval Jewish philosophers were to spend a great deal of time and thought on that problem. According to the Talmud, however, the answer is as follows: "The Tannaim felt that man does indeed have the free choice between good and evil. If he chooses to be righteous, he will receive his reward, while he will be subject to punishment if he elects evil. The Lord, however, who knows all things, also knows in advance what choice each man will make, but He does not attempt to influence man in his decision. Man, however, does not share this advance knowledge with his Maker, and therefore what God knows has no bearing whatever upon the choice which man makes of his own free will."

The Sadducees, on the other hand, maintained that nothing was predetermined in any manner by God and that man is endowed with unlimited free will. At the same time, they declared that all reward and punishment take place in this world and that there is no such thing as reward or retribution in an afterlife.

The views of the Essenes concerning the coming of the Messiah and reward and punishment were even more extreme than those of the Pharisees. They shrouded these concepts in mysticism and surrounded them with an abundance of fantasy.

In view of the foregoing, it would be well for us to study in detail the views of each of the three parties in Jewish life concerning the Messiah, paradise and hell, and the resurrection of the dead.

11. The Messianic Ideal

❧ THE BEGINNING

The new beliefs first advanced by the Tannaim (or Pharisees) were accepted by the majority of the Jewish people. This ideology could well be divided into three parts: first, the hope for the redemption of the Jewish people as a whole, embodied in the Messiah; second, justice for the individual in the form of due reward and punishment; and third, the eventual resurrection of the dead.

The belief in the Messiah, who would come to save the entire nation, arose from the very depths of the spirit of the Jewish people. The theory of reward and punishment in the hereafter and the resurrection of the dead, on the other hand, originated in cultures other than that of the Jews.

Let us, then, begin our survey with a study of the Messianic ideal and how it came into being.

Jewish legend and homily give us a psychological explanation based on the drive for self-preservation which is common to both men and nations. In Midrash Echa Rabati 33, we are told that the Messiah was born at the very moment the Temple had been destroyed. In other words, the time of the greatest national catastrophe in Jewish history gave birth to the hope for eventual redemption. Stated in simple terms, the Messianic idea is the belief that a scion of the House of David will redeem the Jewish people from exile. The Jews will then return to the land of Israel, the Temple will be rebuilt, and a Jewish king will once again sit upon the throne in Jerusalem.

The prophets, who sought to give renewed courage and hope to their people, communicated such ideas to them in order to keep their spirits high.

Jeremiah, who had lived during the days of the First Temple and who mourned its fall in his classic Lamentations, and Ezekiel, who lived in exile in Babylonia soon after the destruction of the First Temple, were the main protagonists of the Messianic ideal. Earlier, similar hopes had been advanced by Isaiah. The concept of a Messiah stemmed from the hope that all the Jews would return from Babylonia to Palestine, and that the states of Israel and Judah would be reunited to form one Jewish kingdom such as had existed during the days of David and Solomon. The prophets imagined that the leader who would be able to effect such a reunion would have to be a descendant of the Davidian dynasty, a "sprout from the stock of Jesse," for the House of David had enjoyed great popularity in days past and only a scion of that family would be able to voice a call which all Jews would gladly and enthusiastically follow. That man would then be the logical person to become king of a new state thus constituted. For this reason, the prophets referred to this person as the "Mashiach" (Messiah), literally, "the anointed one," a term employed in the Bible to denote the Jewish kings.

Jeremiah says: "In those days the house of Judah shall walk with the house of Israel, and they shall come together out of the land of the north to the land that I have given for an inheritance unto your fathers" (Jer. 3:18); "I will raise unto David a righteous shoot, And he shall reign as King and prosper . . ." (Jer. 23:5), and "I will make a new covenant with the house of Israel, and with the house of Judah" (Jer. 31:31).

In the Book of Ezekiel, we read that the Lord will "cause a horn to shoot up unto the house of Israel" (Ezek. 29:21). Ezekiel sees the day when Judah and Israel will be united, for the Lord says: "I will take the stick of Joseph, which is in the hand of Ephraim, and the tribes of Israel his companions; and I will put them unto him together with the stick of Judah, and make them one stick, and they shall be one in My hand" (Ezek. 37:19). In his description of the valley of dried bones, he envisions also the resurrection of the dead.

Isaiah devoted a total of twenty-seven chapters (40-67) to the Messianic era and to the reunion of the states of Judah and Israel into one kingdom, through a scion of the house of David.

Similar words are found also in other works of prophetic literature, and there is no doubt that they expressed the same hopes that were cherished by the entire Jewish people, the masses in both Judah and Israel.

Hopes, however, are not always fulfilled, and so the expectations of the prophets, too, fell far short of fulfillment. True, the Jews did return to Palestine after the Babylonian exile, and they rebuilt the Temple, but a reunion of the two separate kingdoms under the scepter of a scion of the house of David never came to pass. Actually, the land of Israel never became truly free again, and he for whose coming the Jewish people had so fervently hoped remained as far away as ever. This caused widespread despondency among the Jewish masses. For this reason, the later prophets attempted to reinterpret these expectations by explaining that they were not meant to be fulfilled in the foreseeable future, but only at a time so far distant that it was still veiled from view. This new thought is expressed in the prayer of Ezra (Chap. 9) and in the Book of Daniel (Chap. 11 and 12), for example, "Shut up the words, and seal the book, even to the time of the end" (Dan. 12:4). The later prophets did not want to predict a definite date for the hoped-for redemption lest the people, failing to see their dreams come true during their lifetime, give way to utter despair and cease to believe in prophecy altogether.

The new interpretation of the Messianic idea soon spread among all the people. The masses were anxious and willing to retain the hope for redemption. The Messianic idea, thus reinterpreted, was basically as follows: Some lay in the remote and indefinite future, there will rise up a descendant of the house of Jesse who, by the persuasive power of his words, will be able to unite the Jewish people upon the soil of their ancient homeland. At that time, all the Jews will return to Palestine from the diaspora. This scion of the house of David will be the "Mashiach" (Messiah), the anointed one, who will then reign as king over all the people of Israel.

The men of the Great Synod who, at the beginning of the era of the Second Temple, selected those sacred books which were to be incorporated into the Holy Scriptures, supported this new belief which had already been accepted by the vast majority of the people. Therefore, they could not very well include in the Scriptures any of those books which preached other ideas concerning the Messiah than those set forth by the later prophets. Writings not meeting this standard were discarded. Some of them, however, have been preserved for us to this very day as part of apocryphal literature. Several contain references to a Messianic era according to the lights of the author, but not in accordance with the teachings of the later prophets.

❧ THE MESSIAH OF THE PHARISEES

The Pharisees did not approve of these excesses. They expected that the confident hope in the coming of a Messiah would give new strength and courage to the people; distorted in this manner, however, it could only do serious harm. When the Tannaim saw the way in which the dream had been exploited by the mystics and even heretics, their enthusiasm waned and they sought to dissociate themselves entirely from the belief in a personal Messiah.

But there was still another reason why the Messianic belief no longer seemed so attractive to the Pharisees. At that time, they suffered greatly from persecution at the hands of the Sadducees who comprised the ruling class of the land. The Sadducees aired their opposition to the Pharisees not only through verbal debate, as is normally the custom among scholars, but also through physical persecution. The Sadducees were responsible for the brutal execution of a great many adherents of the Pharisee party. It became quite clear to the sages, therefore, that the continuation in power of the Hasmonean dynasty, which was supported by the Sadducees, spelled disaster for the country. They knew, however, that the Jewish military and social elite were hostile to every form of study, and therefore did not feel that the liberation of the land of Israel from Roman rule would be a great boon to the Jewish people, for once the foreign conquerer left, there would be another enemy waiting, this time the remaining members of the Hasmonean dynasty, who were tyrants in the true sense of the word. Why, then, they reasoned, instill into the people the hopeful expectation of the coming of a Messiah who would unite the states of Judah and Israel beneath the scepter of one Jewish king? What if the king should be a member of the Hasmonean dynasty and would rule over the men of learning with an iron hand?

The Tannaim pondered what stand they should take. They could not very well entirely eradicate the belief in a Messiah from the minds of the people, for it had been so firmly implanted into the spirit of the masses that its forcible uprooting would be dangerous, if not impossible. They therefore explained that the Messiah could not possibly be expected to come within the foreseeable future. The Messianic era could come about only at some very distant time still obscured to the human mind. But they could not bring themselves to describe the Messiah as a scion of the House of David, because the tyrannical Hasmonean rulers, for whom they felt nothing but hatred, also claimed to be descendants of that king.

The aversion felt by the Tannaim against the further dissemination of the belief in a Messiah can be seen from the fact that Rabbi Judah the Prince, the editor of the Mishna, did not see fit even to make mention of this belief in his master work. In fact, it is even said that this scholar at one time sought to abolish the Fast of the Ninth of Ab, the day of mourning in commemoration of the loss of the Temple and of the Ten Tribes of Israel, for he felt that days of mournful commemoration such as that would only serve to keep awake the hope for a Messiah in the hearts of the people. Another great teacher, Rabbi Akiba, actually said that the Ten Lost Tribes would never return to the fold of the Jewish people (Tractate Sanhedrin 10:3). Since the return of the Ten Lost Tribes was such an integral part of the Messianic dream, Akiba felt that, by categorically and authoritatively writing off the Ten Tribes as a permanent loss, as it were, he would be able to eradicate the hope for a Messiah from the minds of the Jewish people.

It was fortunate that, on the whole, the people sided with the Pharisee platform. To begin with, the average Jew disliked the idle fantasies of the "lunatic fringe," some of the adherents of which had given rise to the early Judeo-Christian sects. Moreover, the people, too, had a strong dislike for the Hasmoneans, their oppressors. Since they were thus not too fond of their own Jewish rulers, they had no great desire for the immediate advent of a Messiah. Hence it was easy for them, eventually, to conceive of the Messianic era as a vague ideal of political deliverance which would come to pass at some time in the remote future, brought about not by miraculous acts, but by a ruler who would bring all the Jews back to their homeland and reign over them in justice and mercy.

Such was the concept of the Messiah held by the Tannaim and they passed it on to the Amoraim, their spiritual heirs. In Berachoth 34, Samuel, one of the Amoraim, stated flatly that the only difference between the present day and the era of the Messiah would be that, in the days of the Messiah, all the Jews would be redeemed from exile and returned to their ancient homeland—nothing more.

Or, as it is quite clearly stated in Pesikta Rabati (Chap. 30), the second redemption will not be like the first one. Whereas the redemption from Egypt involved miracles, the deliverance from exile will proceed in a very ordinary fashion. The second redemption will be of greater significance than the first only in view of the fact that, while the first deliverance was eventually followed by years of exile, the second will be permanent and the Jewish people will never again have to leave their land.

This concept of the Messianic era as one of political, rather than miraculous, redemption remained the accepted opinion of all the scholars whose names are associated with the Halacha. Of course the Talmudic era, which spanned a period of many hundred years, produced plenty of dreamers and haggadists who held different views, and mystics whose imagination ran riot but these were in the minority. The Messiah, as portrayed by the rabbis of the Halacha, became the ideal of the redeemer to the majority of the Jewish people.

❧ THE HEZEKIAH GROUP

Among the various minority groups with ideas of their own on the subject of the Messiah, we might mention the adherents of Hezekiah, who are mentioned in several places in the Talmud. This group, which existed through the era of the Tannaim down to the advent of the Amoriam, believed that King Hezekiah, a scion of the house of Jesse, was the true Messiah. It is told of him in the Book of Chronicles (30:16) that he destroyed all the heathen places of worship in the land, reintroduced the worship of the One God in the Temple of Jerusalem, called upon all the Jews to observe the law of Moses, and endeavored to reunite the kingdoms of Judah and Israel into one nation. It was also said that when he celebrated the feast of Passover in Jerusalem there was such joy in the land as had not been since the days of Solomon. Hezekiah reigned for a period of twenty-five years and, even during his lifetime, was proclaimed by his friends and adherents as "the anointed of the Lord." But when, at the end of his reign, the Ten Tribes of Israel were driven into exile, the majority of the people ceased to believe in him as the Messiah. A small minority, however, tenaciously clung to the belief in him, and we read in the Talmud, that the Amora Hillel said "Israel no longer has a Messiah, because he had already come in the days of Hezekiah" (Sanhedrin 98). Bar Kappara, in Sanhedrin 94, said "The Lord sought to make Hezekiah the Messiah. . . ." These statements, set down many years after the death of Hezekiah, proved the strong persistence among a group of people that Hezekiah had indeed been the Messiah.

🌺 THE QUALITIES OF THE MESSIAH

The Tannaim, then, did not conceive of the coming of the Messiah as a miraculous event which would change the entire world, but considered the Messiah simply as the Redeemer chosen by God, who would come some day in the distant future and lead the Jews back from exile into their own land. This Redeemer would not have the power to forgive past sin, nor would he have to suffer because of the transgressions of others. The Jewish Messiah would redeem the Jews from exile, but not from past error. It would be a purely political act of redemption, and nothing more.

This was the view of the Tannaim as expressed in the Mishna and the Gemorah. Even the haggadists, some of whom left free rein to their imagination in their dreams of the Messiah, did not openly oppose the authoritative opinion. They confined their speculations to the "days of the Messiah," that is, to the Messianic era rather than to the actual person of the Messiah.

With regard to the "days of the Messiah," the haggadists emphasized that the days immediately preceding his coming would be difficult. Israel would go through a period of economic crisis and spiritual travail which they chose to call "the birth pangs of the Messiah." The generation which would witness his advent would have few scholars; both prices and impudence would be on the rise, wisdom of no worth, truth forbidden. The young would laugh at their elders, sons would insult their fathers, daughters their mothers, and wives would speak insolently to their mothers-in-law. The entire generation would be on a low moral level indeed (Sota 49).

Unlike the Tannaim, the haggadists conjectured that, besides redeeming the Jews from exile in the political sense of the word, the Messiah would also bring about their redemption from moral chaos. They felt that long exile would have to have a harmful effect upon the people of Israel, and that Israel would be ready for a moral rebirth at the time. This renaissance, however, could take place only when Israel would be upon its own home soil again. It was only there that its moral fiber could be strengthened and refined.

🌺 THE NEW VIEWS

At that time, these writers constituted a minority group. Later on, however, some of their views received the support of men whose names are associated with the Pharisees. This school of thought maintained that the Messiah would not be a human being at all but the Lord Himself. In other words, at the appointed time, the Lord Himself would personally act to redeem His people. This idea, of course, met with violent protest from the Pharisees who still insisted that the Messiah would be a human being, a descendant of the House of David, who would appear whenever it pleased God to send him.

However, the believers in a direct divine act of redemption could not quite agree among themselves as to what that deliverance would be like. Some felt that God would confine His work of redemption strictly to the Jewish people. Others, less nationalistically inclined, envisioned a divine deliverance of the entire world together with the people of Israel. Among the adherents of the more nationalistic view were the authors of such apocryphal works as the Sybilline Books (particularly the third part), the Book of Jubilees, Ethiopians, the Book of Henoch, the Psalms of Solomon, and the Book of Baruch. In the Sybilline Books, for instance, we read that "the Lord will send a king from the east, who will put an end to all wars, and He will create the kingdom of Justice. But at that time the true king will be the Lord, and the king of flesh and blood will merely carry out His will." In Chapter 29 of the Book of Jubilees, on the other hand, we are told, "The Lord will be the Messiah for the entire world." Much the same thought, though couched in different terms, is expressed at the end of the Book of Henoch, in the Psalms of Solomon, and in the Book of Baruch.

Some of the haggadists approved of these views. One of them said that the second redemption from exile would be quite the same as the first. Even as God had brought about Israel's deliverance from its first exile, so would He also put an end to its second period of subjugation. The thought that God Himself would be the Messiah also found its way into the Jewish prayer book. "And Thou, O Lord, wilt rule alone over all Thy creatures, upon Mount Zion, the abode of Thy glory." But the men of the Great Synod quickly amended it by adding the plea ". . . and mayest Thou speedily establish the throne of David in its midst." Philo, also, was an adherent of the belief that God Himself would be the Messiah, and he believed that the Lord would redeem the entire world while at the same time delivering Israel from exile. The later aprocryphal works, however, such as the Ethical Wills of Abraham, Isaac, Jacob, the Twelve Tribes, Moses, and Solomon, which are legendary in nature, envision God as a kind of nationalist Messiah who would redeem the Jews only. Many of the ideas propounded by these writers were later adopted by some of the Essenes who preferred fantasy and mysticism to reality.

❧ IDEOLOGY OF THE GNOSTICS

The trouble and unrest that were rife in Palestine during the rule of the Romans proved fertile soil for the rapid growth of all sorts of strange movements. Preachers throughout the land broadcast new beliefs based on mysticism and will-of-the-wisp ideas. They found no audience among the Pharisees, who accepted straight reasoning as their only guide through troubled times. Nor could they win converts from the ranks of the Sadducees, who categorically refused even to consider any ideas that could not be found in the straight original text of the Bible. But they did find adherents among the Essenes, those strange visionaries who combined the down-to-earth cultivation of the soil with views and ways founded on dreams and fantasy. Unlike the Pharisees or the Sadducees, the Essene movement did not represent one single ideology but comprised a hodgepodge of sects and denominations, as it were. Some of them tended to asceticism, and abstinence from all worldly pleasures. Others advanced views which would be called communistic today; they lived in collective settlements whose earnings were equally distributed among all the members. Still others believed in celibacy because they felt that intercourse with a woman would taint their purity. The only bond that united all these varied sects was their common inclination to mysticism rather than to faith based on reason.

We know today that the group known as the "Gnostics" played an important role in the Essene movement. This sect went through a great many changes until, some time during the third century, it was absorbed into the then new religion called Christianity. In fact, some Christian scholars claim that the Gnostics were actually the forerunners of the Christian faith. This, however, is not true, because Gnosticism was originally a Jewish movement numbering in its ranks pious Jews who differed from their brethren only in that they tended to mysticism. The term "Gnostics" comes from the Greek and denotes "knowledge," but the knowledge which this group sought was not that of man and the world. It was supposed to consist of strange revelations from Heaven itself which were not ever accorded to outsiders.

This sect began its activities in the ranks of the Essene movement about a hundred and fifty years prior to the destruction of the Second Temple. They gave much thought to such abstract questions as the nature of God and creation, and eventually they adopted views from the Persian and Greek cultures which were quite alien to Judaism, for they conceived of God not as one single Being, but as one of many faces and personalities. As a result, the Tannaim officially refuted their beliefs in the words that are found in the "Ethics of the Fathers": "To know, and to make oneself and others know that He is One God, that He is the sole Creator and Shaper of all things." This statement was specifically directed against the idea advanced by some factions in the Gnostic movement that, while it was true that God was the Creator of all things, the final shape was given to His creatures not by Him but by another being delegated by Him for this purpose.

The Gnostics themselves did not present a united front, but were split into countless factions which greatly differed from one another. One such group was led by Simon Magi, who was of Samarian descent. Another leader, Menandes, preached to his adherents that he himself was the Messiah and that the Lord had created the world not by Himself but with the assistance of His angels. Then there was Malchi, a contemporary of Rabbi Akiba, whose views on Judaism were very definitely colored by the mysticism which then prevailed in India, and in the end the Gnostic movement came to contain groups whose teachings were entirely foreign to Judaism.

🌿 THE BEGINNING OF CHRISTIANITY

At about that time, there began to spread among the Essenes a new concept of the Messiah. The Messiah was to be a martyr who would have to suffer for the sins of the Jewish people, and who himself would be able to give absolution for all transgressions. This was not at all in accordance with the spirit of Judaism. As the Talmud ironically puts it, "Why should Sigud receive a beating for the sins of Tobias?" Judaism has always held that each man must suffer for his own sin and that no one man was meant to suffer for the errors of another. Nor does Judaism accept the theory that anyone other than God Himself could impart absolution for wrongdoing. The Jewish point of view on this subject is simple: "Only the Holy One, Blessed be He, can forgive sin." True, a righteous man can intercede with God on behalf of a sinner, but the choice of whether or not to forgive rests with the Lord alone, and no human being, however righteous, has the power to impart forgiveness or absolution on his own. And, for that matter, the Lord pardons sin only if the sinner comes before Him with a contrite heart, truly repents of his wickedness and highly resolves never to go astray again. In fact, we are told that there are at least two serious transgressions for which there is no divine forgiveness at all in this world, namely, sinning and persuading others to sin as well, and weakening the prestige of the Name of the Lord on earth. In such extreme cases, not even the solemn repentance engendered by the Day of Atonement is sufficient for absolution, and only the actual death of the transgressor can eradicate his guilt (Yoma 85).

So it happened that the beautiful vista of the future, which was to serve as a source of hope and comfort for the Jewish people, was distorted in the hands of the mystics into a mixture of strange beliefs which had little in common with the original Messianic ideal.

However, the concept of the martyr Messiah rapidly gained ground among the Jewish masses, who came to believe that the Temple would be destroyed because of the sins of the Jews, that God was wroth with His people, and would therefore lay waste His sanctuary and scatter Israel to the four corners of the earth. According to some of the haggadists, God's anger was so great that He cried out, "O, would that the Jewish people had forsaken Me, but kept My Law." When the Temple and Jerusalem actually did fall to the Romans, it seemed quite clear that this disaster had come to pass only because the people of Israel had sinned against their God. At that time, the Jewish people were divided into two camps of opposing views: One faction, the Zealots, mostly young people, fought against the Romans to the bitter end. The defeatists, on the other hand, claimed that it would be of no use to resist the conqueror, for the Roman legions, they said, were strong and mighty and the Lord would not be at the side of His people because they had sinned; and, finally, when Rome had subdued all of Palestine and turned the splendid Temple into rubble, most of the Jewish people firmly believed that this was nothing but just punishment for their sins.

Thus, some of the Jewish masses were quite willing to adopt the concept of the Messiah, the idea that he, Messiah, would cleanse the Jewish people and rub out its trangressions before the Lord. This new idea originally developed within a small Essene group known as "Evyonim" ("the poor"). To this sect, a Messiah who would gather all the Jewish people and reunite them into one single Kingdom, which would include the Ten Lost Tribes of Israel as well, had little meaning. Instead, they hoped for a Messiah who would cleanse the souls of all the people of Isarel, who would institute the kingdom of God on earth and who would cause all sin to be forgotten.

This group, however, was divided into two camps, one universalist and one more nationalist in character. The universalists were concerned not only with the sins of the Jewish people, but also with those of all the rest of mankind. They felt that as long as sin existed anywhere in the world, God would have no peace, and that the world could be redeemed only after the Messiah had come to absolve all men, regardless of creed or nationality, of their guilt. The nationalists, on the other hand, felt that God was concerned particularly with the Jews, and that therefore He would send the Messiah only to His people so that Israel, and Israel alone, might be cleansed of its taint of sin and thereafter redeemed.

The Essenes, then, could not agree to any one view of the Messiah. The Pharisees all believed that the Messiah would bring about the reunion of the kingdoms of Judah and Israel into one mighty nation. The Sadducees, for their part, were united in the belief that there was no Messiah at all. But the Essene movement had room for a great many different and often divergent opinions on the subject.

Given this historic setting, we can quite readily see that some of the masses were quite eager to listen to a person who would declare that he himself was the Messiah who had come to redeem Israel and the entire world, and this happened in the appearance of Jesus of Nazareth. Thus began Christianity, a new faith in the world arena.

❦ THE JEWISH VIEW AS OF TODAY

Maimonides, who had explicitly set down the opinions formulated by the sages of the Talmud, presented in his *Yad Hachazakah,* gave a complete and clear picture of the days of the Messiah according to the Halacha. In Hilchoth Melochim, Chapter 12, he says: "Let no one believe that when the Messiah will come anything in the world will be destroyed, or that there will be some change in Creation. This will not be so. The world will go on then even as it had before. The Tannaim said that there will be no difference between the present day and the days of the Messiah, except for the fact that the Jews will cease to be subject to alien domination. That is all."

12. The Ideology of Reward and Punishment

❦ THE REWARD AND PUNISHMENT IDEOLOGY IN THE BIBLE

The Pharisees, who had been the first to disseminate the original Messianic ideal, also gave some thought to the fate of the individual. The Messiah would be sent by the Lord to redeem the entire nation, but each individual, too, was a source of concern to the Lord by himself. The Pharisees explained that every single person would receive a reward for his good deeds and just punishment for his sins.

Now came the question of what was meant by "reward" and "punishment."

The Five Books of Moses have a great deal to say concerning reward and punishment but there is nothing to indicate that these would be given man in a place other than right here on earth. Let us read, first, the words of some portions of the Holy Writ with regard to the reward or punishment which would be meted out to the Jewish people as a whole, depending upon its collective conduct: "If ye walk in My statutes and keep My commandments, and do them; then I will give your rains in their season, and the land shall yield her produce, and the trees of the field shall yield their fruit. . . . and ye shall eat your bread until ye have enough, and dwell in your land safely. . . . And ye shall chase your enemies. . . . And I will set My tabernacle among you. . . . and will be your God, and ye shall be My people" (Lev. 26:3-4, 5, 7, 11-12).

These, then, are the blessings promised the Jewish people by Moses, if, as a united nation, it would keep the Law of the Lord: an abundant harvest; peace in the land and, in case of war, victory over all enemies; physical growth and increase, and finally, the establishment in its midst of the presence of the Lord who would be a God to it even as it would be His people.

If, however, the Jewish people should disobey the Law of the Lord, it would receive punishment that would have an impact much more powerful than that of any reward it might obtain for loyal obedience. This punishment, Moses declared, would culminate in the expulsion of the Jews from their land. They would then remain in exile until they repented of their sins and the Lord would redeem them once more (Lev. 26:37-40).

As far as the individual Jew is concerned, he is called upon to cleave to

218

the Law of God first "that it may go well with thee," and "that thy days may be long" (Deut. 5:16). Long life is promised explicitly as a reward for the observance of the law concerning the proper respect due one's parents, and for compliance with the commandment to send the mother bird away before removing any of her young from her nest (Deut. 22:6).

To impress upon his people the importance of obeying the Law of the Lord, and the dire consequences inherent in disobedience, Moses had them go through a special ceremony as they were about to cross the Jordan and enter the Promised Land. He commanded the chieftains of the tribes of Simeon, Levi, Judah, Issachar, Joseph, and Benjamin to stand on Mount Gerizim and, from the top of the mountain, to enumerate to the people of Israel all the blessings which would come to them as a reward if they would abide by God's commandments. At the same time, Moses bade the leaders of the other six tribes, Reuben, Gad, Asher, Zebulun, Dan, and Naphtali to stand atop Mount Ebal and, from that vantage point, to proclaim the curses that would befall the Jews if they broke faith with the teaching given them by the Lord.

So much for the words of Moses, the Man of God, concerning reward and punishment. All the rewards and punishments of which he speaks are of this world. There is nothing in the Bible that would imply the existence of a "world to come," an "afterlife" where the good would rejoice and the wicked would be made to suffer.

In the beginning, the promises given by Moses of reward and punishment in terms of prosperity and famine, life and death, were generally accepted by the people. But eventually, as the Jewish people attained maturity as a nation, they began to have doubts, even as young individuals approaching adulthood begin to question the facts taught them by their elders.

Thinking Jews began to ask themselves the question: "If it is indeed true that all the good will receive their reward and the wicked will be punished, then why is it that we so often see righteous men suffer while sinners prosper?" We find evidence of these doubts even within the pages of the Bible itself, particularly in the Book of Job, which has this problem as its central theme. When Job's three friends commiserate with him upon the terrible calamities that have blighted his life, a discussion develops as to whether there is really a reward for the righteous and punishment for the wicked, and whether the Lord is indeed a just God.

The Book of Ecclesiastes speaks even more bluntly. "All things come alike to all; there is one event to the righteous and to the wicked; to the good and to the clean and to the unclean . . ." (Eccles. 9:2). In other words, it does not pay to be righteous since, in the end, the fate of the righteous man will be identical with that of the sinner. Or take the statement, "For that which befalleth the sons of men befalleth beasts . . ." (3:19). This is an open declaration of disbelief in the special purpose of man, and in reward for the righteous and punishment for the wicked.

In the Talmud (Chulin 142) we are told of a man who fell to his death as he descended from a tree with some young birds which he had just removed from their nest. Before taking the fledglings he had complied with the divine commandment to send their mother away first. Now the Talmud asks: "We were explicitly promised that those who would obey this commandment would be rewarded with a long life. This man acted in full accordance with the law. He sent away the mother bird before removing her young from their nest. Why, then, did he have to die?"

❦ BEGINNING OF THE NEW IDEOLOGY

The sages were thus faced with the task of reinterpreting the word of God so that the people should not cease to believe in it because of these statements which, apparently, could not be reconciled with reality. When a similar problem arose in connection with the redemption of the Jewish people from exile, the scholars met the emergency by explaining that the Messiah could not be expected to come within the foreseeable future but only at a time still far distant. Now the sages taught that reward, and punishment too, would not come immediately, but would be given to each individual only at some future date; in fact, it would not even be given here on earth at all, but in quite another world.

The Sadducees who, as we know, never accepted any idea that could not be found in the Biblical text itself, responded to this new thought with stubborn disbelief. But even the Tannaim and their supporters, the Pharisees, were not quite sure of just what was meant by "another world." No one as yet thought in terms of "paradise" and "hell." This was a later invention, but people asked if the term "another world" meant that man lived on elsewhere after his death, that part of him would live on even after his body had rotted away. If so, how would the soul manage to go on living? Could the soul, detached from the body, do good or evil? Could the spirit enjoy pleasures or suffer from pain and anguish once it had left the body?

In the Talmud (Chulin 142) we find some explanation at the same place where there is the question concerning the man who had died, even though he had obeyed a law which carried the promise of long life as its explicit reward. We find the following assertion: "We are told in the Bible, '. . . so that your days may be long and so that it may be well with you.' This means, '. . . so that your days may be long *in a world that is long-lasting* and so that it may be well with you *in the world which is nought but good.*'" This shows that, originally, the world to come was viewed as a place for reward only. It was taught that all those who would obey the law of the Lord would come after death to a world in which all things were good and where they would partake in pure, unalloyed pleasure. The punishment of the wicked would simply be that they would not be able to enter this world of pure joy once they leave the earth. This is the meaning of the Mishna, "All of Israel has a portion in the world to come" (with the exception of some who do not) (Sanhedrin Portion Chelek).

This new idea, however, did not quickly gain universal acceptance because no one was quite sure just what was meant by the saying that the soul of the good would not die together with their bodies. The Pharisees, therefore, had to go into greater detail in their explanations to the broad masses.

The Pharisees based their entire concept of a "world to come" on the postulate that the human soul would not die, but this was not enough to prove their theory and the idea met with strong opposition, not only on the part of the literalistic Sadducees, but also from their own followers who were not willing to accept the promise of a "world to come" as an arbitrary answer to their doubts concerning reward and punishment. However, the Pharisees insisted that their theory was the only answer to the problem, and in reply to the arguments of the Sadducees, the Tannaim even explained that the Holy Writings must be construed not literally but in accordance with four aids which would help the human mind to understand the terse thoughts set down there. These four aids were: (1) *Peshat*. The original text as is; (2) *Remez*. An intimation in the text; (3) *Drash*. The study of one Biblical verse in comparison with another; and (4) *Sod*. An approach akin to mysticism.

Thus, in dealing with the question of the immortality of the soul, the sages pointed out that, while there was no explicit statement in the original text of the Bible to the effect that the soul would never die, the text did intimate the eternal nature of the soul. They pointed out the phrase, "and [he] was gathered to his people," which is used as a euphemism for death in the Biblical account of the lives of the Patriarchs. This, the scholars declared, meant that when the Patriarchs died, their souls were joined to those souls which had already come to the "other world" before them. They also cited I Samuel 25:29 ". . . yet the soul of my lord shall be bound up in the bundle of life with the Lord thy God; and the souls of thine enemies, them shall he sling out, as from the hollow of a sling." They pointed out that even the author of Ecclesiastes, who viewed the whole idea of reward and punishment with considerable skepticism, said, "And the spirit returneth unto God who gave it . . ." (12:7). These verses, and many others, could be construed as intimating the possibility of a life after death, even though they do not explicitly state that this is so. The Sadducees, however, were not impressed by these arguments. They continued to maintain that death was permanent and that any thought of a "world to come" in which the human soul would go on living after having left the body was idle folly. The Tannaim, however, stood firm. In order further to instill this idea into the minds and hearts of the people, they wrote beautiful prayers, the Eighteen Benedictions which are a part of the daily morning and evening services, where all these new ideologies are mentioned.

❧ THE VIEW OF THE MYSTICS CONCERNING THE NEW IDEOLOGY

In contrast to the Sadducees, the mystics, including the writers of the books of the Apocrypha, did believe that the soul was indeed immortal. In the book "The Wisdom of Solomon," for example, we read, "The body is of earth, but the soul is from heaven and it is divine. The soul was in existence long before the body was put into the world" (*ibid.* 8:19, 20), and further "The body is a burden for the soul, and therefore, after the body has died, the soul hastens to return to God" (*ibid.* 6:20). Mention of the immortality of man's soul is found also in Chapters 23 and 31 of the Book of Jubilees, in Chapters 4 and 31 of the Book of Henoch, in Ben Sira, in the Book of Hasmoneans, and many others.

The Essenes, in particular, espoused the new idea with their customary fervor and added to it their own exaggerated notions. Josephus, the historian, tells us some interesting details. The Essenes claimed that all souls were kept in a heavenly treasure chamber from which they were expelled against their will to enter the bodies of human beings on earth. The soul regarded the period of its confinement to the human body as a prison sentence, and suffered greatly because of man's falseness and his physical lusts. It yearned for the day when it would be permitted to leave the mortal body and to return to its original source. For this reason, they claimed, the death of man's body brought great joy to the soul which, liberated, then hastened to soar heavenward to its Maker.

The concept of the soul as an organism that lived even before it was sent earthward to enter a human body and that would return to heaven after the body's death is not strange to the non-Jewish ideology. We find similar views in the writings of Plato, the Greek philosopher, in the works of those Greek thinkers who lived long before him, and in the sacred literature of the Hindu religion. The Essene concept of a heavenly treasure chamber in which the souls dwell before being sent down to earth, for instance, is given mention in the works of Plato. In fact, Plato even discusses in some detail the idea of a "soul-mate," explaining that souls are paired off in Heaven to test whether or not they would be a compatible couple if they should meet on earth and be married to each other. Similar ideas are mentioned also in the Talmud.

Thus we can readily see that a great many foreign influences and non-Jewish teachings are evident in the formulation of the concept of the "immortal soul" and "the world to come."

❧ WHO'S WHO IN THE "OTHER WORLD"

The next question to be studied is also readily apparent. Exactly what is the nature of the "world to come" which the souls of the good will enter after death? And what will be the joys that the righteous will experience there?

Truth to tell, the creators of this new ideology were not quite sure of the answers themselves. Generally speaking, they agreed that the pleasures of the "world to come" would not be physical but spiritual. There would be neither food nor drink, neither envy nor hatred; there would be no trade and commerce, and no physical love between man and woman. In Berachoth 16 we are told that "the righteous men will sit with crowns upon their heads and will delight in the purity of God's glory." The exact meaning of this, however, is not clear, but we read in the Ethics of the Fathers that "one hour of the delights of the world to come is better than all of life on earth." The sages have also said that he who pursues the pleasures of this world will not be able to enjoy the delights of the world to come. On the other hand, we are told that great spiritual leaders such as Rabbi Judah the Prince, who certainly had every right to a place in the world to come, also had a liberal share in the wealth and luxuries that the world here below has to offer. However, it is stressed that not every human being is worthy of having the best of both worlds. In other words, though no one was quite sure of the exact nature of the pleasures that were in store for the righteous in the world to come, it was agreed that the good would indeed receive a reward in the afterlife in which the wicked would have no share.

The Law of Moses stipulates that certain grave sins are punishable by the sinner's soul being "cut off." This, according to the sages, simply means that the soul of the wicked man would be "cut off" from the roster of those souls who would be privileged to savor whatever delights the world to come would hold for the righteous.

As we have already noted, the broad masses, who usually were inclined to accept the views advanced by the Pharisees, were slow to adopt the new theories on the immortality of the soul and of a "world to come," in which the righteous would receive their just reward. There were even Tannaim who were not at all sure that they believed in these novel concepts. Scholars like Bar Kappara felt that there was no need at all for reward in a world to come, because "the performance of a good deed is its own reward." The man who has done a good turn, he felt, is more than amply rewarded by the knowledge that he has been able to help his fellow man. The sinner, on the other hand, is more than sufficiently punished by his chagrin at the thought that he has harmed another or violated the Law of the Lord. Antigonus of Socho said, "Be not like servants who minister to their master upon the condition of receiving a reward, but be like servants who minister to their master without the condition of receiving a reward . . ." (Ethics of the Fathers 1:3). And other sages commented on the verses in Psalm 112 which read: "Happy is the man that feareth the Lord, that delighteth greatly in His commandments," that the type of person referred to "delighteth greatly" in the Law of the Lord, not because of any recompense he might have expected for such obedience, but because he considered obedience to that Law to be its own reward.

The Talmud contains many similar statements, thus indicating that there must have been quite a number of scholars who felt that it should be sufficient for man to obey the Law because he knows it is the will of his Maker, and not because of any specific reward he might expect for his good conduct. Most of the Tannaim, however, supported the theory of the "world to come."

The people, though, had to be given some clearer details before they could be expected to believe in what the Tannaim had told them to be true. The Tannaim, therefore, further elaborated upon the concept of reward and punishment and they explained it to mean that while the righteous would enjoy the delights of a world to come, the souls of the wicked, in addition to not being included in these joys, would go to a place where they would suffer tortures.

Thus additional concepts were made part of the original theory, namely, the new concept of "paradise" and "hell," or in Hebrew "gan eden" and "gehinnom" (or "gehenna").

❧ PARADISE AND HELL ("GAN EDEN" AND "GEHENNA")

The Pharisees realized that the vague promise of a "world to come," in which the righteous would "delight in the purity of the glory of God" would not be sufficient to make the plain people believe in divine justice, and the masses would have to be told something that would be more concrete and more appealing to their imagination. After giving the matter considerable thought, the Pharisees propounded that the human soul, which was immortal, would be assigned to an "afterlife," the nature of which would depend upon the life the person had led on earth. There would be a place for the righteous where they would partake of heavenly joys and delights, and quite another locality where the souls of the wicked would suffer untold tortures. They reasoned that while joy, of necessity, was limited in scope, suffering knew no bounds. Even the fact that one did not have to suffer was in itself a source of joy to man. The ills that man might be called upon to endure were far greater in number than the pleasures he might be granted. If, therefore, a person were told that he would experience great joy as a reward for being good, that measure of joy would be well defined and could be described within the framework of a few words. On the other hand, it was not necessary to give an exact description of the suffering he would have to endure as the result of sin. A good illustration of this can be found in the Biblical account of the blessings which Moses promised his people if they remained loyal to their God and the curses which he said would befall them if they went astray. The blessings he enumerated were few, but the list of curses was extensive indeed. This was the basis for the new concept which the sages now sought to disseminate among the masses, namely, that there was a paradise in store for the righteous while gehinnom (or gehenna) awaited the sinner. The joys of paradise were well defined, but the sufferings of gehenna would be limitless.

The "world to come" had now taken on a new form. Whereas originally that designation had been employed only to describe the place where the righteous would get their just reward and to which the sinners would not be permitted to go, it now became the term to denote the "afterlife" in general, during which the good would reap the delights of paradise and the wicked the anguish of gehenna.

Again, the Sadducees refused to have anything to do with such new-fangled un-Biblical ideas. The Essenes, on the other hand, eagerly accepted the new notion of the world to come and surrounded it with products of their own fertile imaginations.

The plain people, who ordinarily accepted the views of the Pharisee school of thought, did not show too great enthusiasm at the beginning. But gradually they grew interested, for unlike the "world to come" the terms "paradise" and "gehenna" were historical realities and not philosophical abstractions. The sages had done well to choose these two places as the localities in terms of which to describe the afterlife to the ordinary folk.

❦ WHERE IS PARADISE?

Let us now see why paradise and gehenna had historical significance to the broad masses.

Regarding paradise, the answer is quite simple. Any one with even an elementary knowledge of the Bible was familiar with the account of Adam and Eve, who had been given paradise as their dwelling place, but had forfeited it by partaking of the forbidden fruit. Paradise, then, was an apt designation for a place reserved for those who had never sinned. Now since the sages had defined a righteous man as "one who had never known the taste of sin," it was quite logical that all righteous men would be entitled to a portion in paradise.

But the Biblical account explicitly states that the original paradise was not in a world to come but on earth itself. It even gives us a detailed description of the geographical location of the Garden of Eden, as follows: "And the

Lord God planted a garden eastward, in Eden; and there He put the man whom He had formed. And out of the ground made the Lord God to grow every tree that is pleasant to the sight, and good for food; the tree of life also in the midst of the garden, and the tree of the knowledge of good and evil. And a river went out of Eden to water the garden; and from thence it was parted, and became four heads. The name of the first is Pishon; that is it which compasseth the whole land of Havilah, where there is gold, and the gold of that land is good; there is bdellium and the onyx stone. And the name of the second river is Gihon; the same is it that compasseth the whole land of Cush. And the name of the third river is Tigris; that is it which goeth toward the east of Asshur. And the fourth river is the Euphrates." (Gen. 2:8-14). Now "Cush" (Ethiopia), Tigris, Asshur, and Euphrates were geographical locations not too far away from Palestine and therefore places with which the Jews were familiar. How, then, could the sages explain that the paradise which would be the portion of the righteous in afterlife was located not in Asia Minor, nor even anywhere else on earth, but only in a sphere beyond the physical world?

The scholars soon found a solution. They said that while it was quite true that the original paradise had been situated in Asia Minor, man could no longer hope to behold it. When Adam and Eve had been expelled from there, the Lord decreed that no descendant of theirs could ever come to the Garden of Eden, for there was no guarantee that other humans would not sin there also, seeing that the very first man and woman to live on earth had succumbed so easily to temptation. The Lord had therefore created a "heavenly" paradise, which would be open only to the souls of those who had never sinned. Since the soul, once separated from the physical body, was incapable of sin, that heavenly Garden of Eden would eternally remain pure and untainted by transgression, and therefore was eminently suitable as a place where the righteous of this world would receive their reward in afterlife.

The sages could not agree, however, as to the actual nature of this "paradise above," nor could they all give an authoritative definition of the pleasures which would await the righteous there. In later years, however, the haggadists evolved numerous legends dealing with this theme, and one of them, Rabbi Joshua ben Levi, even took his listeners upon an imaginary stroll through that heavenly garden and gave a detailed description of what would be found there.

❦ WHERE IS GEHENNA?

Now let us leave paradise and turn to gehenna.

The original Hebrew word "gehinnom" is derived from the Biblical Valley of Hinnom mentioned in the Book of Joshua as part of the description of the tract of land allocated to the tribe of Judah when the people of Israel first entered the Promised Land. In the Book of Nehemiah, Hinnom is named once more, this time as one of the places in which the returning exiles from Babylonia settled. In general, "gehinnom" was quite well known during the days of the Second Temple. Called "Vadi el Rabba" by the Arabs, Hinnom is located southwest of Jerusalem. In ancient days, gehinnom ("the Valley of Hinnom") was employed by the heathens as a site for the altars upon which they sacrificed their first-born to the Moloch (Jer. 32:35). It was said that a huge fire was constantly kept burning there for this purpose. Gradually there began to grow up the legend that the idolaters had picked this place for their barbaric sacrificial cult because a mighty natural fire steadily glowed far beneath the surface of the valley, a fire that seemed well suited to accept the human offerings cast before Moloch (Erubin 19). Later there evolved the belief among the Jewish masses that sinners falling into the valley would be burned to death by that fire while righteous men meeting with the same accident would emerge unscathed. It was quite obvious, then, that the choice of gehinnom as a kind of hell was quite apt. And even as there was a "paradise above," so there was not only a physical "gehinnom" that men could see, but also a "gehinnom above" which would serve as the place where sinners would receive their just deserts in afterlife.

But even as the sages were not sure of the nature of paradise above, so they could also not agree upon what, exactly, gehenna would be like. They could not define the form which the sufferings of the wicked there would take, nor could they establish whether or not that punishment would be eternal, and, if it were not, where the souls would go after they had served their term of atonement.

Again, the Jews were not the only ones to occupy themselves with these concepts. The ancient Indian religion had built up an elaborate repertoire of legends about a paradise for the righteous, and about a place where the sinners would suffer for their wickedness. The Hindus, the Egyptians, and the Persians, to number just a few of the ancient nations, all had their own notions of the cruel fate which would await the wicked after their bodies departed this life.

The plain people were not all of one mind concerning paradise and gehinnom. Perhaps this was partly owing to the fact that the sages themselves, who had originally taught them these new ideas, had been unable to agree on standard definitions and details. But, primarily, it was because the average people were very much of this world and could not muster such intense interest in what would become of them in a world which they did not know and could not see. Most of them still felt that reward would have meaning to them only if they could obtain it during their lifetime on earth, and that punishment would be effective only if administered not in some far-away gehinnom, but in the world in which the sins were perpetrated.

For this reason the sages, who had given much thought to the issue, now evolved a new concept of reward that would be closer to the people—namely, the eventual *resurrection of the dead.*

13. The Ideology of the Resurrection of the Dead

❧ VARIOUS OPINIONS ABOUT RESURRECTION

To satisfy the ordinary folk, the sages now proceeded to explain to them that there would indeed be a reward for them in the very world in which they were now living. This reward, however, would not come in the immediate future but only at the time of the coming of the Messiah, and it would take the form of the resurrection of all those who had died. In fact, they said, life itself consisted of two parts, with the first, man's sojourn on earth, constituting only an antechamber, as it were, to the true life which would begin only when the dead would be resurrected after the coming of the Messiah.

Again, however, the scholars were not certain of the nature of that eternal resurrection, and whether the wicked, too, would rise again from their graves. Some said that while the righteous would rise to an eternal life, the wicked would return to a life of eternal shame, even as the prophet Daniel seemed to have indicated in his statement, "And many of them that sleep in the dust of the earth shall awake, some to everlasting life, and some to reproaches and everlasting abhorrence" (12:2). In the Book of Henoch, which is part of apocryphal literature, we are told that "When the Messiah will come he will sit upon a throne and judge mankind. He will awaken all the dead and summon them forth from their graves, and they will all come to life. He will then separate the righteous from the wicked and will reward each in accordance with his deeds."

Other authorities maintained that the punishment of the wicked would consist of the fact that they would have to remain in their graves while the righteous would all be summoned forth from death to life eternal. Others still claimed that while both good and wicked would be resurrected, only the good would then live forever, while the evil would eventually have to return to the grave, even as it is said in the Talmud "The righteous whom God will revive from among the dead will not have to return to the dust" (Sanhedrin 92).

❧ ARE THERE BIBLICAL SOURCES FOR THE BELIEF IN RESURRECTION?

In view of the lively debate that went on among the sages themselves on the issue, it should not be surprising to us that this, the most recent reinterpretation of the concept of reward and punishment, should call forth a storm of protest against the sages from their constant opponents, the Sadducees. As long as the Tannaim had only spoken of "another world" and engaged in discussions of paradise and gehenna, the Sadducees were content to dismiss their talk as that of idle dreamers who dabbled in fantasy. But when the scholars who led the Pharisee school began to propagate the idea of a resurrection of the dead which would take place in this very world and not in some unknown region, the Sadducees became greatly disturbed and angrily demanded that the Tannaim show them any one place in the Bible which explicitly foretold the coming of such a miraculous event in the history of the world. The scholars replied that, while the original text of the Bible did not actually spell it out, it did contain many statements that could be construed as allusions or intimations of such a place.

The fact of the matter is that the Five Books of Moses make no mention whatever of anything that might indicate a future resurrection of the dead. There are several statements in the rest of the Bible, however, which could be cited to show a belief in the eventual quickening of the departed. There is a verse in the First Book of Samuel reading "The Lord killeth, and maketh alive; bringeth down to the grave, and bringeth up" (2:6), and one in the Book of Isaiah to the effect that "Thy dead shall live, my dead bodies shall arise—Awake and sing, ye that dwell in the dust" (26:19). But, strange as this may seem, the same prophet says elsewhere that "The dead live not, the shades rise not" (26:14). There are also numerous verses in the Psalms, in the Book of Job, and in other Scriptural works which would indicate disbelief, rather than belief, in resurrection.

The Sadducees kept pressing the Pharisee leaders for concrete evidence in support of the views advanced by the Tannaim. Of course, the scholars were unable, most of the time, to cite direct quotations from the Bible to prove their point, and had to resort to the device of reading new meanings into the original Biblical text, which the Sadducees refused to accept. These arguments between the Pharisees and the literalistic Sadducees continued for many years.

🌺 DEBATES AMONG JEWS AND NON-JEWS ABOUT RESURRECTION

We can see in the Talmud that such discussions took place not only between the Sadducees and the Pharisees, but also between Jews and non-Jews, the latter including illustrious personalities, such as Cleopatra, who showed an interest in the possibility that the dead might indeed be resurrected to eternal life. Of course, the arguments which the Jewish scholars employed in dealing with non-Jewish inquirers were based not on Biblical exegesis but on attempts at proof by logical reasoning.

It seems that the entire idea did not for a long time find general acceptance among the masses, perhaps for the reason that here, too, the sages could not agree upon one standard doctrine. In the end the scholars flatly stated that, while it was uncertain what form the resurrection would take, it was incumbent upon all to believe in it, and that those who would not so believe would eventually be punished by not receiving a share in that eternal life themselves. Naturally this did not greatly frighten the nonbelievers, who felt they had no reason to fear being proved wrong in their skepticism.

🌺 WHAT IS THE JEWISH BELIEF?

The Jewish philosophers who lived at a later date gave much thought to the issue of resurrection. Maimonides wrote a booklet on the issue, and Rabbi Saadia Gaon before him had published a volume in which he had attempted to cite logical evidence in support of this belief. Even those philosophers who did not feel that the belief in the quickening of the dead was an essential part of the Jewish religion viewed the matter as being of such importance that it merited detailed discussion and deliberation.

In the end, the Jews at large came to accept the doctrine of resurrection, and finally accepted the entire ideology, namely, that there would be a Messiah; that there were indeed such places as paradise and hell; and, finally, that the dead would all eventually be revived and enjoy eternal life from that moment onward.

The Talmudic Era

II. The Time of the Amoraim

14. Rav, the First of the Amoraim

Rav's Arrival in Babylonia—His Appointment as Head of the Academy at Sura— His Friendship with the King—His Colleague, Samuel, with Whom He Carried on Debates on the Law

Our study has now taken us to the era of the Amoraim, the creators of the Talmud, who lived and worked during a period extending from about 219 to 500 A.D. Altogether, there were about eighteen hundred such scholars who were engaged in the development of the Halacha and in the fabrication of haggadic material.

The first generation of the Amoraim, which bridged a period of about forty years (from the year 219 to 259), could boast of two scholars who can well be viewed as the outstanding figures of their time: Rav and Samuel. Although they could never agree on many issues of Jewish law, these two were great friends. However, before we go on to learn about their lives, it might be well to make a brief survey of Jewish life in the Babylonia of those days, where Jews enjoyed a large measure of religious autonomy and took full advantage of the opportunity thus afforded them to establish and develop outstanding institutions for the dissemination of Jewish learning.

Palestine had been conquered by Rome. While the Romans had not actually driven the Jews out of their land and had even permitted them a certain measure of political autonomy, conditions in the country were such that most Jews felt that, if they had to live under the rule of a foreign king or emperor, they would prefer to live abroad rather than watch their own country slowly being absorbed by an alien conqueror.

At that time the only great nation to receive the Jewish emigrants from Palestine with open arms was Babylonia. The Babylonian government permitted the new arrivals to preserve and cultivate their ancient traditions. The Jews found, too, that Babylonia held much greater opportunities for a decent livelihood than did their own land which had been impoverished by war and defeat. Hence, we see that during the third century of the Christian era not only the Jewish masses, but also their leaders and teachers, streamed into Babylonia. There they found an ancient Jewish community with thriving institutions which had originally come to Babylonia at a time of the destruction of the First Temple, and those members had done so well in their new country that they did not return to Palestine when Ezra and Nehemiah called upon their people to go back to their homeland. This Jewish community had quietly existed and grown throughout the four hundred years of the Second

Commonwealth in Palestine. Though it had always regarded the Holy Land as its spiritual center, Babylonian Jewry had prospered quite independently, both economically and spiritually, so that the Jews who now came into Babylonia found that they had not come into a wilderness, but could join an ancient and well established religious community.

In former years Babylonia had been a large empire composed of many vassal countries. During the period of the compilation of the Talmud, however, the Jewish people were largely concentrated on a small strip of land on the east of the river Euphrates with a capital called Pumbeditha. In the north of that district was the city of Nehardea; in the south the city of Sura (also known as Moso Mechasia), and, not far away from Sura, there was the city of Machuza. Of these centers of Jewish settlement, Nehardea was probably the most beautiful and the most distinctly Jewish. Close by was the fortress city of Perus Shevor, and also the capital of Pumbeditha, which was located on a branch of the river Euphrates and which ranked second only to Nehardea in Jewish population. As we have said before, the city of Sura was on the other side of the district of concentrated Jewish settlement, about twenty-two miles away from Pumbeditha. Youngest of all the centers was Machuza on the River Tigris, a flourishing city which in many ways competed with the older cities of Pumbeditha and Nehardea.

Among the many Jewish scholars who followed the masses to Babylonia there was one learned man named Abba, who had been a disciple of Rabbi Judah the Prince. Abba (also known as Abba Aricha, meaning "Abba the Tall" in Aramaic) eventually came to be called by that name by which he is known to this very day to any student of the Talmud—*Rav,* which was actually not a name but a title, much like "Rabbi" in Palestine.

Rav had come to Babylonia in the year 219 A.D. from Jerusalem. His uncle, Rabbi Chiya, who had also been a disciple of Judah the Prince and had made a name for himself as a most diligent student of the Law, suggested that, before leaving for Babylonia, Rav obtain rabbinical ordination from his former teacher, Rabbi Judah. Judah acceded to his pupil's request at least in part, conferring upon him the authority to answer inquiries pertaining to the Law and to conduct certain arbitration cases.

The news of Rav's arrival was greeted by Babylonian Jewry with great rejoicing, because it was felt that he would be a most valuable addition to Jewish life in the country. The Babylonian rabbis therefore went in a body to meet him and received him with all the honor due a scholar of his kind. After that, in order to acquaint himself with the Jewish community of Babylonia, Rav made an extended tour of the land. When Rav, in the course of his travels, arrived in Nehardea, he found there a flourishing academy, headed by Rabbi Shila, who immediately offered to resign and yield his place to him. Rav, however, declined the honor, saying that his friend Samuel, who had come to Babylonia before him and who had actually lived in Nehardea all the time, was much more qualified for the position. Rav then decided to settle in Sura and established an academy of his own in that city.

The Jewish community of Babylonia in those days enjoyed a great measure of religious autonomy. The entire Jewish community was headed by an Exilarch. When Rav first came to Babylonia, this exalted position was held by Anan, a man of great wealth and influence. Since Rav needed some additional funds to supplement his meager income from his academy, influential friends prevailed upon the Exilarch to appoint Rav as overseer of the market places in the city. Rav, a man of great generosity, refused to enforce certain regulations by punishing the violators. When taken to task by Anan for his laxity, Rav replied that he would continue to act in accordance with the dictates of his own conscience rather than blindly obey another official. In the end Anan, whose executive powers included the authority to make arrests, had Rav put into prison. It was only after Karna, the judge in the case, had reminded Anan of the unpleasant repercussions the circumstances of the scholar's arrest might have in Palestine, that Anan relented and released Rav. Rav was reinstated in his position and eventually his authority was extended to include the inspection of weights and measures throughout the land.

On one of his journeys in connection with his work, Rav met Artaban III, the King of Babylonia, who was greatly impressed by Rav's knowledge. The two men soon became close friends and the king presented the scholar with a bag filled with precious pearls as a token of his affection.

On that journey, Rav noticed that the Jews of the provinces had gradually come to neglect the Law, with regard to both religious ceremony and morals. Jewish women flouted the dietary laws without shame. It was a widespread custom among Jewish men to marry a woman one had never seen before, spend the night with her and then drive her out without giving any reason. He returned to Sura, firmly determined to bring some order to Jewish life in his adopted country.

Rav then raised the standards of his academy, and eventually the number of his disciples grew to twelve hundred, of whom at least one hundred distinguished themselves in their studies. The school expanded until it became the largest of its kind in all Babylonia. At that time Rav was given the mansion of a convert to Judaism who had died without heirs. He turned it into an annex for his academy and it came to be known as "The Garden of Rav's Disciples."

The personal prestige of Rav grew apace when it became known that the king was ready at all times to grant whatever request the scholar would make of him. Eventually, Rav was given the authority to inflict penalties of excommunication or stripes upon any person who would disobey his orders. Thus supported by the power to enforce his will, he soon set down rules designed to increase religious observance and to raise the moral standards of his fellow Jews in Babylonia. Then he forbade spur-of-the-moment marriages and decreed that the couple must be permitted to decide between themselves whether or not they would want to marry. A father was no longer permitted to marry off his daughter before the girl had attained sufficient maturity to decide on her own whether the bridegroom chosen by her father would be a good husband for her. The wedding itself had to be conducted as an official ceremony. Husbands could not divorce their wives without good cause, nor were they allowed to invalidate a divorce once given, for without a divorce the wife was neither maid nor widow and could not remarry. Anyone violating any of these regulations was subject to the penalty of stripes. If a rabbi sent for a person and that person disobeyed the summons, the latter was subject to excommunication for thirty days. If, after thirty days, the person still refused to come to the rabbi, he was to be given a certain number of stripes. All these arbitrary regulations and punishments had to be instituted to restore order and decency among the rank-and-file Jews of the land.

Rav was very wealthy and owned a great deal of land. He tilled the soil himself and insisted that his disciples also engage in agricultural work, permitting them to come to the academy only during the month preceding Passover and the month before the High Holidays when there would be nothing for them to do in the fields. It was his custom to preach to the public on the Sabbath preceding each religious holiday.

The Babylonian Talmud is replete with explanations given by Rav, many of which begin with the introductory comment "We have learned. . . ." He had frequent differences of opinion with his friend Samuel. Eventually it was decided that Rav's views would be binding in all questions regarding religious issues, while those of Samuel would be given final authority in all questions involving civil law. Rav's name occurs over and over again in the pages of the Talmud. Besides being the first of the Amoraim, he also had the distinction of being regarded as one of the last Tannaim. Whereas the other Amoraim were permitted only to interpret the words of the Tannaim and not to amend or oppose them, such action on the part of Rav was justified in the Talmud by the statement, "Rav is a *Tanna* himself and therefore has the right to disagree with the opinions set down by the *Tannaim* in the Mishna."

But even though Rav was a man of great wealth and was in a position to wield great authority, he remained quiet and humble throughout his life. It is told of him that he refused to permit the punishment of a rude butcher who had publicly insulted him, stating that he would wait until the Eve of the Day of Atonement to see whether the ruffian would come to him and ask for his forgiveness. When it was almost time for the evening services to begin and the man had not yet appeared, Rav himself went to his house and told him that he, Rav, had forgiven the insult.

His married life was anything but happy. His wife had so little concern for his comfort that she would deliberately prepare foods that she knew her husband disliked. Eventually, Chiya, their son, decided that he would take matters into his own hands and tell his mother to cook the very dishes which he knew his father disliked, knowing that she would do the contrary, and in this way his father would have what he liked best. For a while this worked out quite well, until Chiya one day revealed his stratagem to his father. Rav thanked his son for his concern, but asked him to refrain from this in the future because even mild forms of deception, such as these, might lead to the habit of telling deliberate falsehoods.

Rav died in the year 291 at the age of seventy-two, after having served as head of the Academy at Sura for twenty-eight years. He left distinguished progeny. His son Chiya became a great scholar in his own right. One of his daughters was married to a son of the Exilarch and two of his own grandchildren, Akiba and Nehemiah, became Exilarchs themselves.

15. Rabbi Samuel: Physician, Jurist, and Astronomer

His Liberal Legal Principles Which Attained Universal Recognition—Why He Did Not Receive Rabbinical Ordination—His Death at the Age of Ninety-seven—His Spiritual Heritage

Samuel ben Abba, the greatest friend of Rav, was quite a different type. While Rav had been immersed in Jewish learning almost to the exclusion of all other branches of knowledge, Samuel was a man of broad and liberal education who was familiar with medicine, secular law, and astronomy.

Samuel came to Babylonia some time before his friend Rav and settled in Nehardea, where he eventually succeeded Rabbi Shila as head of the academy when the latter died.

Samuel had little patience with the mystic tendencies that had somehow crept into Jewish practice and ideology at that time. While he believed in the coming of a Messiah, he did not for one moment think that the advent of the Anointed One would be accompanied by miraculous events as the mystics preached. He said: "The days of the Messiah will be no different from the present except for the fact that the Jews will then no longer be subjected to the rule of foreign princes."

Samuel set down certain legal principles which have come to be accepted by Jews and non-Jews. He asserted also that Jews were obligated to observe the law of the land in which they lived. "The law of the land is the law to be obeyed" ("dina de-malchusah dina"), he declared. In this manner he sought to persuade the Jews not to fight or rebel against the laws of their adopted countries, for disobedience would only incur them the hatred of their non-Jewish neighbors. At the same time his dictum was intended to make it quite clear to the non-Jewish rulers that there was nothing in Jewish law which would command a Jew to disobey the orders of the government in the land in which he happened to dwell. This was quite in the spirit of the prophet Jeremiah who, many years before, had told his people when they first went into exile, "And [ye shall] seek the peace of the city whither I have caused you to be carried away captive, and pray unto the Lord for it; for in the peace thereof shall ye have peace" (Jer. 29:7).

Samuel enjoyed great respect and popularity among the non-Jewish Persian intelligentsia who listened to his words of wisdom with great interest.

Samuel often said that he was as familiar with the nature of the orbits of the stars as with the streets of his city, Nehardea, but he admitted that he knew little about the paths of the comets. His extensive knowledge of astronomy enabled him to establish a fixed Jewish calendar, eliminating the necessity for consultation with the authorities in Palestine to determine the dates of the holidays anew each year. Samuel practiced medicine as well, and prepared a number of healing ointments. He also believed that most diseases were caused by "bad air" (Baba Meziah 107).

As to Jewish Law, while his friend Rav was stringent in his insistence upon the observance of minutiae, Samuel tended to be more permissive in his interpretation of the Torah. For example, he ruled it permissible to extinguish on the Sabbath burning coals which had been thrown out inadvertently, so that passers-by should not be endangered (Sabbath 42). While Rav decreed that all everyday kitchenware could not be used on Passover and had to be broken before the holiday, Samuel decided that it would be permissible to subject certain utensils to such treatment as to render them usable on Passover (Peschim 54). He even went so far as to declare that the Jews of Babylonia needed to observe no other fasts than the Ninth of Ab and the Day of Atonement.

With regard to business law, Samuel asserted that, in suits involving an outstanding debt, it was the creditor who had to prove that money was indeed due him and the debtor could not be summoned to show proof that he owed nothing (Baba Kamah 47). Moreover, Samuel declared that money matters must be decided in accordance with the dictates of fairness and equity, rather than by the views of a majority.

In reply to a query, Samuel stated that a woman who received full financial support from her brothers was under no obligation to turn over to them whatever money she might earn by her own efforts (Ketubah 43). Funds left in trust for orphans might be invested in return for interest. The Biblical law forbade the collection of interest on loans, but Samuel felt that an exception could be made in such cases so as to better the financial situation of the youngster who no longer had parents to provide for him.

In addition, Samuel formulated much new legislation to protect the rights of women in cases of marriage and divorce. In these efforts he met with stern opposition from his friend Rav, who felt that women should be entirely dependent upon the good graces of their husbands.

When Babylonia was conquered by Persia, Rav lost all the privileges he had enjoyed during the reign of the Babylonian king who had been his friend. Samuel, on the other hand, was greatly respected by the new Persian rulers for his worldly wisdom and became a good friend of Sapphor, the king of Persia, so much so that he, the Jewish scholar, was at times actually called by the name of the king himself (Baba Bathra 115). In one instance, his friendship with King Sapphor caused him to act in a manner which the people interpreted as being against the best interests of his Jewish brethren. When Sapphor, in one of his Western Asian campaigns, conquered Masako Caesarea, the capital city of Capodoria, he slew all its male inhabitants, even though most of them had surrendered and would therefore have been entitled to the courtesies ordinarily accorded to prisoners of war. Among the men slain, there were several thousand Jews. This catastrophe plunged Babylonian Jewry into deep mourning, and protest meetings were called in every Jewish community to give expression to the sense of outraged justice that filled every Jew throughout the land. Samuel, however, stopped the proceedings, asserting that there was no need for the Jews of Babylonia to mourn the loss of Jews wicked enough to attempt to resist his friend, the king of Persia. This arbitrary action on the part of Samuel aroused violent protests throughout the Jewish community, for it appeared that Samuel had become blind to the atrocities committed by the king and had shown that he would place the interests of the king before the welfare of his own people.

Despite the fact that Samuel came to enjoy great prestige among both Jews and Gentiles, he never could overcome his chagrin at having been refused full rabbinic ordination at the hands of his teacher, Rabbi Judah the Prince. All his life he made every effort to secure such ordination from a scholar in the land of Israel, but to no avail. This was the result of a certain caprice on the part of his teacher.

Samuel died at the advanced age of ninety-seven. He left only daughters, but his heritage was carried on by his students, who perpetuated the broad and liberal views of their master.

16. The Second Generation of Amoraim

The Generosity of Rabbi Huna—Rabbi Judah's New Method of Study and Interpretation—Rabbi Sheshet the Blind—Rabbi Nachman, Erudite but Arrogant

The situation of the Jews in Babylonia at the end of the first Amoraic era (about 300 A.D.) was not very favorable. The Babylonian empire itself was constantly at war, engaged in campaigns to subjugate all neighboring nations. And both the Jews and the Christians who lived in Babylonia now came to suffer religious persecution for the first time. The Persian overlords of Babylonia followed the faith of Zoroaster, which preached the belief in two opposing gods, the god of darkness and the god of light. The latter could be worshiped only by the lighting and careful tending of fires, and the fanatical priests of the new cult could not bear to see fire used for purposes other than those which they considered sacred. They therefore did not permit the Jews to kindle lights on the Sabbath and on Jewish holidays. The pious worshipers of Zoroaster would go about on those days and extinguish all the lights in every Jewish home.

At about that time, a certain Papa bar Nazor of Palmyra gathered about him a band of warriors whom he placed at the service of the Roman authorities who were hard put to keep order in the territories they had conquered. Papa's plan was to help the Roman legions annex Persia and Babylonia. For this purpose he received additional personnel from the Roman army itself and, with their assistance, managed to lay seige to the city of Nehardea and to destroy it. As a result the students of the Academy of Nehardea had to leave the city and eventually settled in Sura, Sechanzib, and Pumbeditha.

The endeavors of Rav and Samuel to bring order to Jewish life in Babylonia had met with success. Observance of religious law increased, as did the thirst for Jewish learning and knowledge.

The disciples of Rav and Samuel loyally carried on the work begun by their masters. Rav had been succeeded at the Academy of Sura by Rabbi Huna, and Rabbi Judah ben Ezekiel became the head of the Academy at Pumbeditha. Other well known and popular scholars at the time were Rabbi Nachman ben Jacob, who eventually established a small academy of his own in the city of Sechanzib, and the Amoraim, Rabbi Sheshet and Rabbi Seira.

Rabbi Huna ruled the Academy of Sura with an iron hand. Though he was a close relative of the Exilarch, Huna had spent his youth in relative poverty, cultivating with the labor of his own hands the small plot of land which at the time had been all that he possessed. Eventually he became quite wealthy and acquired vast fields and gardens which he turned over to hired help while he devoted himself to his educational work.

Rabbi Huna always remained humble, and was generous to all those who were in need. Whenever he sat down to eat, his servants would first open all the doors of his house and call out, "Let him who is hungry come and eat." He supported out of his own pocket some eight hundred students who would come to his academy at stated periods of the year and attend the classes of thirteen lecturers who interpreted for them the wise words of Huna, their great teacher.

Huna lived to see not only a renaissance of Jewish learning, but also the restoration of the high moral standards which had gradually come to be disregarded by the generation before him. He drew a great many new students to his academy, at whose head he remained for a period of forty years until he died at the venerable age of eighty.

Judah ben Ezekiel, the new head of the Academy of Pumbeditha, had also been a disciple of Rav, but had chosen to follow the way of Samuel, whose approach to Jewish law had been far more lenient than that of his colleague. Under Judah's administration, the Academy of Pumbeditha became the most important institution of Jewish learning in all of Babylonia, surpassing even the famed Academy of Sura, not only in the number of students but also in importance and prestige.

Rabbi Judah was known for his sharp and ingenious mind. We are told that he considered study more important even than daily prayer, and that he would recite his prayers only once in thirty days (Kidushin 70). He was the first to introduce the method of "Pilpul" (literally meaning "sharp and peppery debate") into the study and interpretation of the Mishna. This approach was based on ingenious dialectics and casuistry that bordered upon hair-splitting. Judah's particular forte was the interpretation of laws dealing with money and finances. He showed little interest in that legislation which had lost its practical validity when the Temple was destroyed. He painstakingly cited the source of every interpretation he mentioned in his own lectures, and was frank to admit his lack of knowledge when he could not answer a question asked by a disciple.

Judah came from a noble family and attached great importance to having his own offspring marry only into families of equal social status. When his son expressed the desire to marry a certain maiden of his own choice, Judah at first would not hear of it. It was only upon the persuasion of the Amora Rabbi Ulla that he finally relented and permitted the young man to wed the girl.

Because of his wisdom and honesty, Rabbi Judah enjoyed great respect and popularity throughout Babylonia. After the death of Rabbi Huna in Sura, Judah was requested to assume the leadership of the academy there, but he declined the offer. The choice then fell upon the Amora Rabbi

Chasdai Ha-Kaphri, a veteran scholar who, like Judah, had been one of the disciples of Rav.

Though he had been a friend and colleague of Huna, Rabbi Chasdai was an adherent of the views of Judah. He, too, had a sharp mind and the Pilpul method of study was therefore greatly to his liking. When he died at the age of ninety-two, he could look back upon a peaceful and happy life. While he had been poor in his youth, he eventually acquired great wealth and left a large fortune to his numerous descendants. We are told that he lived to see his grandchildren's grandchildren, and that he witnessed the weddings of sixty of his descendants in his own home.

Even as the first generation of Amoraim produced "pairs" of scholars who would study together and debate the law with each other, so Rabbi Chasdai too had a colleague, team-mate, and opponent, as it were, in the person of Rabbi Sheshet.

Rabbi Sheshet, who had also been a student of Rav and a colleague of Rabbi Huna, was totally blind. Yet he managed to overcome his handicap to the extent that he became one of the great Amoraim of his day. He was gifted with a phenomenal memory which enabled him to retain not only the entire Mishna, but even those gems of wisdom that had never been written down but passed on by word of mouth to the Amoraim. Sheshet was an outspoken foe of the casuistry and hair-splitting that were part of the "Pilpul" approach to the study of the Law and would refer to the adherents of that method as "one of the company of Pumbeditha who delight in leading elephants through the eye of a needle." Beyond the fact that Sheshet emigrated to Shilo after the destruction of Nehardea, and died there at a ripe old age, we know very little about his personal life. The Talmud has no mention of either the date of his death, or the exact age at which he died.

Rabbi Nachman ben Jacob, the third outstanding master of the generation, was the youngest of them all. The son-in-law of the Exilarch—he married Yalta, the widowed daughter of the latter—Nachman lived as befitted a member of the aristocracy. He surrounded himself with servants and so made himself inaccessible to the general public except by appointment. His father-in-law made him head of all the rabbis in the Jewish community of Babylonia. It seems that all this power went to Nachman's head, for the Talmud tells us a great many things about him which do not cast a favorable light upon his conduct and personality. For example, he would refuse to debate any point of the Law with another scholar, for he maintained that his knowledge was greater than that of any other rabbi and that therefore only his decisions could be regarded as binding. Another time, he took wood for the erection of a succah from an old woman without offering her any compensation for her property. When the lady came to him and protested against his arbitrary action, he first refused to listen to her pleas altogether, and finally dismissed her with a mere pittance in payment for the wood. Nachman also showed little consideration for his servants and even interfered in their private lives, forbidding them to marry. His arrogance did not stop short at his inferiors; he did not hesitate to insult and humiliate even the greatest scholars of his day. Yalta, his wife, was no better than her husband. We are told that she once drove from her home one of her husband's guests, the Amora Rabbi Ulla, simply because that sage had declined to drink a toast to her health. And yet, despite his many faults, Rabbi Nachman occupies an important place in Jewish history. He was a man of great erudition and scholarship, and he left the impress of his learning on a great many laws which are well known to students of the Talmud even at the present day. He died at the age of eighty-nine.

No study of the second generation of Amoraim is complete without the mention of at least the name of the Amora Rab Seira, who eventually left Babylonia for Palestine, where he acquired great fame. Like Sheshet, Seira too was not in agreement with the Pilpul method of study, and it is said of him that when he came to Palestine he actually prayed to God that he might forget whatever he might have learned of the Pilpul approach during his years in Babylonia.

17. Abbaye and Rabba

Virtues and Faults—The Two Cobbler-Scholars—High Office vs. Scholarly Endeavors—Rabbi Joseph, the Blind Scholar

As time went on, Babylonia gradually came to replace Palestine as the spiritual and economic center of Judaism. Though it had become part of the Persian empire, Babylonia was by no means a conquered vassal state and, since it was situated at the crossroads of Central Asia, it played an important part in international commerce. For this reason, Jews left Palestine in increasing numbers to settle in Babylonia, and there created centers of Jewish life and learning.

The academies at Sura and at Pumbeditha grew and flourished. Each represented an approach to Jewish law all its own; Sura stood for conservatism, retaining the old method of simple and plain study without the artificial dialectics so dear to the Pilpulists. The Academy of Pumbeditha, on the other hand, was a school of dynamic scholarship, and attracted the keen, ingenious minds which delighted in the Pilpul approach that had been introduced by Rabbi Judah.

This new generation produced three giant intellects who left the mark of their knowledge and erudition on Jewish Law: namely, Rabba bar Nachmani, Abbaye, and Rabba. There is evidence of their keenness and sagacity on nearly every page of the Talmud.

Rabba bar Nachmani had originally come from a town called Mamala in Galilee. This town was unusual in that all its inhabitants were descended from the priestly family of Aaron. There was documentary evidence to the effect that they all were descendants of Eli, who had been the spiritual mentor of the prophet Samuel. The family of Eli, however, had been afflicted for generations with the curse of premature death, so that Mamala was a city in which there were no old men. As if this alone were not enough, the town seemed to be cursed with poverty as well. Yet two of Rabba's brothers, the scholars Chanina and Ushaiah, found that they were even worse off in Babylonia and therefore decided to return to Palestine where they made a meager living as cobblers.

Rabbi Johanan, who was an important figure in scholarly circles in Palestine, wanted to confer rabbinical ordination upon these two pious men, but somehow he never carried out his intention. The two brothers viewed their failure to obtain ordination as just another one of the curses which were the lot of their distinguished but unfortunate family.

Rabba, however, had emigrated to Babylonia at an early age and remained there, engaging in study at the Academy of Pumbeditha. He spent all his days in illness and dire poverty, and yet he modestly declined the honor, when, upon the death of Rabbi Judah, he was asked to take over the leadership of the academy.

The Academy of Pumbeditha finally chose Rab Huna bar Chiya as its new head. Rab Huna was a wealthy man, and we are told that he put gold coverings on the benches of his disciples, but his administrative qualities were not outstanding. Hence the reins of leadership were actually held by Rabba bar Nachmani and his friend Rabbi Joseph. Rabba by then enjoyed fame far and wide for his keenness of mind and for his clear and orderly system of study. He had committed much of the legal material to memory.

Soon it became known that Huna bar Chiya had not come by his fabulous wealth by honest means. It seems that he managed to obtain a government appointment as tax collector and employed arbitrary procedures in the collection of taxes, such as confiscating the household effects of those unable to pay and selling them, probably with some profit to himself. When these facts came to light, his outraged colleagues demanded that he either give up his lucrative source of income or else resign from the rectorship of the academy. Rabbi Huna chose to remain at the academy, and there were many who had high praise for his willingness to give up government office in favor of continued leadership in educational endeavors. Rabbi Joseph, however, a man of high ethical standards, felt that Huna had not become a better man by the simple act of refraining from conduct which had been considered questionable, and declared that he could no longer be associated with the academy while Huna was at its helm. This contention cost the academy a considerable amount of prestige which it did not regain until after the death of Huna.

When Huna died, the learned men had two candidates from whom to choose a successor. They were Rabba and Rabbi Joseph. Rabbi Joseph modestly declined the candidacy. It is said, though, that modesty was not the sole motive behind his refusal to serve. It seems that he had consulted a soothsayer who told him that, if he were to accept this exalted office, he would die in the course of a period no longer than two and a half years. It seems strange that a man of the caliber of Rabbi Joseph should have stooped to this practice which was explicitly forbidden by Biblical law, but it appears that he was not then the only Jewish scholar to follow the advice of soothsayers, who enjoyed much popularity among the people of Babylonia at that time.

Thus, in the end, the academy was turned over to Rabba, who had originally declined to become its head. It was he who regained for the academy of Pumbeditha some of the prestige which it had lost as a result of Rabbi Huna's conduct. It was Rabba's practice to make study more palatable to his pupils by beginning each lecture with a witty, humorous introduction. During his administration the enrollment at the academy rose to a total of twelve hundred disciples.

Rabba died under tragic circumstances. During a period of political unrest, he was denounced to the Babylonian government as a revolutionary and he had to remain in hiding in Pumbeditha to escape arrest. One day he lost his way in the woods round about the city. As he wandered about through the deserted forest, he suddenly heard behind him a rustle which he mistook for the steps of pursuing men. The resulting fright caused him to suffer a stroke which was immediately fatal.

Rabba's successor as head of the Academy at Pumbeditha was his friend Rabbi Joseph. Joseph was a wealthy man, but his health deteriorated with the passing years and in the end he became totally blind. His illness caused him to become moody and irritable so that it became difficult for his students to get along with him. Once he lost his self-control to such a degree that he struck one of his disciples, Nathan bar Assa, for some minor misdemeanor. Eventually he lost his memory so that he could not remember the laws which he himself had taught to his classes.

After the death of Rabbi Joseph there were four men who could be considered as candidates for the position left vacant by his passing; namely, Abbaye, Rabba, Rab Seira, and Rabba ben Mathanah. Since they all seemed of equal merit and scholarship, it was decided that the final choice should be made on the basis of an oral questioning period to which all four would be subjected at the academy. The answers given by Abbaye seemed the most logical and plausible, and thus he emerged as the victor in the contest.

Abbaye, surnamed "Nachmani," was an orphan and was raised at the home of his uncle, Rabba ben Nachmani, who had served as head of the Academy of Pumbeditha. Both Rabba and the nurse who acted as the boy's foster mother treated him with parental love and kindness.

Abbaye often suffered from poverty and want during his youth, but eventually he became wealthy and owned much landed estate. It soon became evident that he had in him the makings of a great scholar and he was greatly admired and respected by all. Yet the enrollment at Pumbeditha fell to two hundred during the five years of his tenure as head of the academy. The cause of this drop in attendance may have been Rabba, who then served as head of the great rival academy at Sura and by the force of his magnetic personality drew most of the young men to him. This greatly disturbed Abbaye, and he sought means to make his own academy more attractive to prospective students.

After Rav and Samuel, Abbaye of Pumbeditha and Rabba of Sura and Machuza are the two dominant figures in Talmudic literature. Their ingenious debates, set down there for posterity in the form of clever dialogues, are known in the Talmud under the title "The Discussions of Abbaye and Rabba."

After the death of Abbaye, Rabba's fame grew greater still, but he had acquired wealth and authority in his own small community of Machuza, where he then resided, and had no desire to give up everything in order to assume the leadership of the Academy of Pumbeditha. We are told that Rabba was eager for riches and recognition and that as a result he lost the favor of a great many of the better elements in his city. One of his own students, Rav Papa, openly denounced Rabba for an act which he, the student, felt had been unethical.

Yet Rabba had done a great many good things and had instituted many measures to ease the lot of the student of the Law, such as, for example, the exemption of all scholars from the payment of taxes. He was an outstanding orator and an excellent teacher so that he never lacked for a large audience.

The successors of Rabba were Rab Nachman bar Isaac, Rav Papa, and then Rav Chamah of Nehardea. None of these three, however, could compare to their great predecessor. Nachman bar Isaac, though a man of great honesty and sincerity who was well liked by all, never could attain the measure of scholarship associated with Rabba. Rav Papa spent his youth in poverty but eventually became a wealthy brewer. His successor, Rabbi Chamah, was also a man of average accomplishments. It was apparent that the golden age of Babylonian Jewry was nearing its end.

18. Rav Ashi, Who Completed the Talmud

A Task upon Which Rav Ashi Labored Fifty Years but Could Not Complete—Bar Rav Ashi, His Son, Continues the Work—Other Scholars—The First Jewish Martyrs in Babylonia—The Final Compilation of the Talmud

The fourth generation of the Amoraim in Babylonia was witness to the intellectual and spiritual decline which was a reflection of the chaotic conditions that prevailed throughout the Ancient World as a result of the downfall of Rome. It was at the end of the fourth and the beginning of the fifth century of the Christian era that the far-flung Roman empire first showed signs of decay, and the repercussions of this gradual process of dissolution were felt in all of Asia Minor and hence in Babylonia as well. It was at that time that the wild Huns and Goths first swarmed over Europe to begin their rule of vandalism and destruction which was a prelude to the Dark Ages.

Jewish learning in Babylonia, too, seemed on the wane. There were no outstanding new scholars to take the place of the giant intellects who had been part of the third generation of Amoraim. But even while it seemed that the lights were going out, one by one, upon the horizon of Jewish scholarship, there arose a new star that was to shine on down through the ages to come. This was Rabbana Ashi, the son of Simlai of Sura, the scion of a family of eminent students and scholars, who dedicated his life to the rescue and preservation of the values taught by past generations.

Ashi was fortunate enough, also, to have been born to wealth so that he had no financial worries. When he was only twenty years old, he was chosen head of the great Academy of Sura which had been closed for some time because of the lack of proper leadership. Ashi reestablished the academy, improved its physical facilities, and drew many disciples from all over the country.

Because of his remarkable erudition and outstanding scholarship, Ashi had been given the unusual title of Rabbana (the Aramaic for "our teacher"). During the period of fifty years that Rabbana Ashi had charge of the Academy at Sura, the Academy of Pumbeditha had a rapid succession of seven deans, none of whom had more than average ability. There was also a new academy at Nehardea, to replace the one which was disbanded at the time that city was destroyed, but Maremar, its dean, could not compare with Ashi by any stretch of the imagination. It thus came to pass that the Academy of Sura played a dominant role in Jewish cultural life in Babylonia and attained the same position of importance which it had occupied during the days of Rav many years before. Not since Judah the Prince, it was said, had so much wisdom and greatness, learning and wealth been combined in the person of one human being as could be found in Rabbana Ashi. Even the Exilarch would come to the Academy at Sura to pay his personal respects to the great teacher.

Many years before, Rabbi Judah the Prince, sure of the confidence of his people, had undertaken the gigantic task of compiling the Mishna. Now Rabbana Ashi, who was also certain of the support of his brethren, felt that he was the person upon whom by right devolved the responsibility of setting down the Talmud in its final form. This meant that he had to gather all the material which the Amoraim, beginning with Rav and Samuel, had taught their disciples by word of mouth, and classify it according to subject matter in order to facilitate study by future generations.

Ashi was well aware of the danger that all this wealth of scholarship and knowledge might be forgotten altogether if it were to remain entirely unrecorded, and he labored mightily at his task for a period of well over fifty years, until the day of his own death.

At the same time, Ashi was ever mindful of the ancient prohibition against putting into writing that which was actually part of the Oral Tradition. For this reason he could not, and would not, make the Talmud serve as a verbatim presentation of the wise sayings of the Amoraim. Instead, he conceived of the Talmud as nothing more than a compilation of the notes made by the Amoraim of each generation, a kind of shorthand guide to aid the future student in the memorization of all the views, laws, and legal decisions that had accumulated over a period of generations. In this manner he made sure that the Oral Tradition would never be forgotten, while at the same time he preserved the essentially "oral" character of that tradition. His students, who helped him and continued his work after his death in 427 A.D., were also guided by the same principle in their endeavors.

The disintegration of the Roman Empire, which now proceeded apace, lent added impetus to the work, for the scholars feared that if Babylonia should become involved in the chaos that was fast enveloping the rest of the ancient world, the labor begun by Rabbana Ashi might never be completed and the wisdom of the Amoraim would eventually be lost and forgotten.

Rabbana Ashi was succeeded at Sura by Maremar, an old scholar who himself died after serving only five years as head of the academy. His successor, a student of Ashi, held office for a period of twenty years but left little in the way of scholarly achievement for which he might be remembered by posterity. Rav Nachman bar Huna, the next dean of the academy, also does not seem to have been an outstanding personality, for there is very little mention of him in the Talmud. At any rate, he stood at the helm of the Academy of Sura for only three years.

Thus during the thirty years that had now passed since the death of Ashi, the Academy of Sura once more experienced a period of general decline. The Academy of Pumbeditha fared even worse.

After the death of Nachman bar Huna, one Acha of Diphta was elected to succeed him. Ashi's own son, known as Bar Rav Ashi, would have been much better suited for the office, but at the time there was a powerful opposition which refused to countenance his election. In the end, however, he was chosen to succeed his opponent as head of the Academy at Sura.

Bar Rav Ashi was a great scholar who enjoyed the esteem and admiration of his colleagues and of the people in general, but it was no longer possible for him, or anyone else, to restore the academy to the position of eminence and prestige which it had occupied at the time of his father. It was clear that the trend of decline could no longer be reversed.

Seeing the gradual but obvious deterioration of Jewish life, and the decrease in new recruits who would study at the academies and form the spiritual elite of the next generation, Bar Rav Ashi was all the more anxious to complete the great work begun by his late father. He was the one person with sufficient authority to supervise the task, for all his decisions concerning Jewish Law (save for only three exceptions during a lifetime of study and teaching) had been accepted as binding upon all Jews. He thus proceeded to continue the immense task of compiling, collating, and classifying the wealth of legislation that had come down through the generations.

By now Babylonia was constantly involved in warfare and revolutions so that there was little time left for spiritual and scholarly pursuits, and Babylonian Jewry also was no longer capable of producing giant intellects such as those in whom it had taken such just pride in generations past.

After serving as head of the Academy of Sura for a period of thirteen years, Bar Rav Ashi died and was succeeded by Rabba Yospah, a man little known in the world of the Law.

By that time the Jews of Babylonia had come to feel the pain of religious persecution. King Jesdigert III (to whom the Talmud refers by the epithet of "the evil Persian") bore some inexplicable hatred against the Jews and made it difficult for them to observe their religious practices, particularly the Sabbath and congregational worship. In the end the Exilarch, Rab Huna bar Mar Sutra, was arrested and executed. A great many other scholars shared his fate. They were the first martyrs to die in Babylonia for their faith. The situation now grew worse by the day. The Babylonian authorities closed all the autonomous Jewish courts of justice. Jewish children were kidnaped and turned over to Persian priests to be indoctrinated in the Persian pagan mode of worship. As a result there began a wave of mass emigration of Jews from Babylonia to other lands such as the Arabian Peninsula, and to the east as far away as India.

After the death of Jesdigert, however, the persecutions ceased and the life of the Jews who remained in Babylonia reverted to a semblance of normalcy. The two great academies were reopened, Sura under the leadership of the Amora Rabina (Rabbana Abina), whose name is found in many places in the Talmud, and Pumbeditha under that of the Amora Rabbi Jose.

However, both Rabina and Jose knew well that the days of the Jewish center at Babylonia were fast coming to an end, and therefore they were more than anxious to continue the work of compilation which the son of Rav Ashi had left undone. They enlisted the aid of their disciples, and that of the last of the Amoraim, Rabbi Samuel ben Abahu of Pumbeditha, Rab Rechima, Rabbina of Omza and many others and, with their assistance, completed the masterpiece which we know today as the Talmud, the second great work created by the genius of the Jewish people after the Holy Bible itself.

19. How to Understand the Talmud

🌱 THE HALACHA

Is the Talmud really a sealed book to all but those who have devoted decades to its intensive, painstaking study? If this is so, what, actually, is it that makes the Talmud unique among legal codes, and what are the difficulties which the prospective student meets in its perusal? More specifically, is the entire Talmud difficult to understand, or are some parts more intricate than others? And if the Talmud contains some parts that are easier to understand than others, how do these differ from the more difficult passages?

These questions are not new. They have been asked by thinkers in every generation ever since the Talmud was first set down. The main question, however, is whether or not the Talmud was written in a definite style, and if so, just what that style is. This problem has been studied by many scholars, both Jewish and non-Jewish. Non-Jewish scholars such as Darmstaedter, Moore, and others label the Talmud as a mass of allusions and half-sentences, and some Jewish students agree with them, without knowing or understanding that the Talmud was written in this manner deliberately and not because of any mental quirks or deficiencies on the part of its compilers.

As we have pointed out elsewhere, the legal code of the Talmud could not possibly have been written out verbatim because there existed a specific prohibition against the detailed recording of what was actually an "oral" tradition, originally intended to be handed down by word of mouth through the generations and thus capable of growth and reinterpretation.

Gradually, during the period from the second down to almost the end of the fifth century of the Christian era, the academies, with which the eighteen hundred Amoraim were affiliated, evolved a system of taking notes on what their masters had taught them, notes which would serve as an aid to memorization of what had been taught, but not as verbatim records, for that was forbidden.

We have already seen how the Tannaim, the actual builders of Judaism as we know it now, compiled the Mishna, which was based on interpretations of the original text of the Bible itself. The Amoraim, however, no longer dealt directly with the Biblical text. Their authority was confined to the explanation and interpretation of the comments found in the Mishna. Again, a detailed written record of the teachings of the Amoraim would have been a violation of the prohibition against the writing down of the Oral Tradition.

Yet something had to be done to make sure that these teachings would not be forgotten. With this in mind, the Amoraim through the generations came to develop a system of shorthand note-taking which gradually was accepted by all students and commentators of the text of the Mishna. These notes, as we have stressed throughout, were never meant to be anything more than cues to aid in the memorization of that material which could not be written down verbatim, if the Oral Tradition was to remain oral in nature.

If we take time to study the pages of the Talmud, we see that this system of note-taking was based on ten guiding points as follows:

1. The use of one single word to represent an entire statement, a long discussion, or to ask a question or to supply an answer. The Amoraim created a special terminology of about five hundred words to fill this need, of course all in Aramaic.

For example, if the rabbi had posed a question pertaining to a certain Mishna and found that he had a second question to add to the first, he first used the word "ve-su" (and another thing). As the students were not permitted to note down the entire discourse, they wrote down the one word "ve-su" to help them remember that the teacher had had two questions on that particular subject. Also, if there was a debate as to whether the Mishna had not been too explicit on a certain point of law, the rabbi might then proceed to explain why the Tannaim of the Mishna had been within their rights to express themselves as fully as they did, despite the prohibition against the detailed "writing out" of the Oral Tradition. The rabbi would introduce his explanation beginning with the word "itztrichi" (they had to explain it in this manner). Thereupon the students would put down that one word in order to indicate that this discussion had taken place. Just that word "itztrichi" (they had to explain) was enough for the students to remember the whole discussion.

Perhaps there was a point of law on which the Tannaim had been unable to agree. The rabbi might have taken time to explain to his disciples the various views and opinions. Now, it was the task of the students to remember what their teacher had said. But, again, they did not take down any part of the learned discussion, and wrote down only one word "pligi" (there were conflicting views). The details they retained in their memories.

2. At times the students would employ two words to help them remember an issue, such as "ko omar" (he has said) to indicate that at that particular point there had been a discourse of profound significance by their teacher. The discourse itself went unrecorded, but the students made it their business to remember it. Or perhaps the rabbi of the academy might have discovered that one Tanna had made a statement which was in contradiction to something that he himself might have said in another portion of the Mishna. The rabbi would give elaborate illustrations, but to aid them in remembering these dis-

courses, the students would write down just two words "hal'mai tani" (why have we learned it differently?).

3. On less frequent occasions, the students would employ a term consisting of three words. Their teacher might have wondered how it came about that a Tanna had come to advance a certain view. The disciples would follow the rabbi's reasoning, and write in their notes "ko salko datoch," meaning "how did this occur to thee [to the Tanna]?"

4. A shorthand device of making one new word out of a phrase consisting of several words, for example, when the rabbi asked a question about the Tannaim and said "do minain lon" which means "from where they got it," the student shortened this to one word, "minolon," with the same meaning; or the two words "bechlal shloma" which they shortened to one word "bishloma," and so with many others.

5. The mnemonic device of using the initial letters of words to indicate the main points of a legal discussion.

6. The use of Hebrew, Greek, Latin, or Persian terms to indicate what it was that the rabbi had said. The students would use the first such word that would come to mind as conveying the approximate meaning. This is the reason why the Talmud contains so many foreign words.

7. The use of abbreviations for words, e.g., "Gem." for "Gemorah" or "Shen." for "She-ne-emar" (it is said).

8. The use of standard abbreviations in note-taking so that the notes of any student might be intelligible to any other reader. In time this would serve as standard terminology in note-taking.

9. Eventually, even the shorthand terms devised by the teachers and students were no longer written out in full but were only indicated by the use of abbreviations or initial letters.

10. All the foregoing is applicable only to the halachic portion of the Talmud. The Haggada was not regarded as part of the Oral Tradition and therefore any such homiletic or legendary material could be written out in full without the use of shorthand or mnemonic devices.

Now we can begin to understand why it is that a page of the halachic portion of the Talmud contains so little text and so much commentary. If the student was to understand the material, he needed the assistance of commentators like Rashi (Rabbi Solomon Yitzchaki) to wade through it. The text of the Haggada, however, is plain and to the point, and hence easily understandable without too much extraneous commentary. For this reason, a folio of haggadic material will contain more actual text than commentary.

Let us now return to the question which we posed to ourselves at the very outset; that is, whether the Talmud has a definite style. In the light of what we now know, we can answer it quite easily: Yes, indeed, there is such a thing as a definite Talmudic style. It is unique and was created especially for the Talmud and for the Talmud only. It is a style based on shorthand and mnemonic devices, designed as an aid to memorization rather than as a vehicle for a detailed record. Hence the student desirous of understanding the Talmud must first make himself familiar with the specific terminology employed by the Talmud. In this respect the Talmud is no different from any other learned text, for every science has its own terminology which must be studied before the text itself can be properly understood.

Hence, the Talmud is not a sealed book to those who are willing to study and to understand it.

❦ THE HAGGADA

We might do well to bear in mind that the haggadists had a good deal more freedom in their work than those who dealt with the Halacha. The latter had to confine their endeavors to an interpretation of the Mishna, and were not at liberty to have direct recourse to the Bible, prophetic literature, or, in fact, any other text than the Mishna. The haggadists labored under no such restrictions. They were free to base their tales and parables on the Pentateuch, the writings of the prophets, or any part of the Holy Scriptures; or to dispense with those texts entirely and to rely upon their own imagination.

We might therefore say that the haggadists can be viewed as the first literary writers to be produced by the Jewish people. They were the authors of an endless wealth of tales and parables, sketches and stories. Some of their works dealt with past history, and others with the time in which they lived, and still others with heroes of the Jewish people. Some writings were in the form of verse or even song, others as monologues or dialogues. There are in the Haggada elements of humor and satire on strictly religious issues, and on human life in general as well. Thus it would not seem at all far-fetched to designate the haggadists as the original creators of belletristic literature for the Jewish people. Of course, the purpose of the Haggada, like that of all the other literary works written at the time, was not so much to entertain the reader as it was to bring out a certain moral for his spiritual edification. Yet there are some tales in the Haggada that seem to have been put there simply because of the beauty of the story itself, and with no other motive.

Let us look at a few samples from that treasury of legend, story, poetry, and homily. Take, for instance, a story about the wisdom of King Solomon, which seems a little strange at first glance, but has a moral which we will discuss at the end. Here, in brief, is the tale:

Once Ashmodai, the king of Demons, came to King Solomon and said to him:

"O King, men have said of thee that thou art wiser than all men. Now I shall show thee that there is at least one thing of which thou wilt not know what to say."

Solomon accepted the challenge. Ashmodai then led into the throne room a freak with two complete heads, two pairs of eyes, two noses, two mouths, and two tongues.

"Tell me now, O King," said Ashmodai, "is this one man or must he be treated as two men?"

Solomon could not answer. He called in his faithful adviser, but the latter fainted with fright at the sight of the strange creature and could not say a word.

Finally Solomon decided to subject the freak to a detailed examination himself.

"Who art thou?" Solomon asked.

"I am a man," replied the monster.

"Whence hast thou come?" asked the king.

"I am a descendant of Cain, the son of Adam."

"Where is thy dwelling place?"

"I dwell in a place called Hevel, O King."

"Do the sun and the moon shine there?"

"Indeed they do, O Solomon. Our sun, however, rises not in the east but in the west, and it sets in the east and not in the west like your sun."

"And how do you spend your days?"

"We work in the fields and we tend our sheep and cattle."

"Do you pray to God?"

"Yes, we pray to Him."

"And how do you pray?"

"We say, 'How great are Thy wonders, O Lord, in wisdom hast Thou made all things.' "

Thereafter Solomon offered to have the man returned to his homeland. Ashmodai, however, said that this could not be done. The freak therefore remained in Palestine where he eventually married and had seven children. Of these, six were normal, but the seventh was a monster, resembling his father in every detail.

After the death of the strange creature, his children began to quarrel about the inheritance he left them. The six normal children reasoned that their father's estate should be divided equally among all the seven children, but the seventh son, the two-headed monster, maintained that the inheritance should be divided into eight equal parts, and that he would be entitled to two-eighths of the estate since he was not one person, but two.

The matter was placed before the Sanhedrin. The Sanhedrin, however, declined to take the case, and King Solomon had to assume the responsibility for deciding it.

All night long before the trial Solomon prayed to God to give him the wisdom necessary to come to a fair and equitable decision. His prayer did not remain unanswered. Suddenly he realized what it was that he would have to do the next day when the disputing parties would appear before him.

When all those concerned were assembled to hear the King's verdict, Solomon declared:

"There is a simple way to establish whether the freak before us is one person or whether he is actually two. If one head should feel the pain felt by the other, he is one man. If, however, the second head will not be sensitive to the hurt of the first, then we know that we have before us two creatures, each entitled to a separate share of his father's inheritance."

The king then ordered his servant to bring in boiling water and to pour it over one of the heads. Both of the mouths of the freak immediately began to shriek in pain, and his hands touched both his heads in anguish.

"Dost see now?" said Solomon. "Both thy heads feel the pain of the one. Therefore thou art not two men, but only one man, and only one share of thy father's property is due thee."

All those assembled agreed and they believed that Solomon was indeed wiser than all men on earth.

The moral of this rather lengthy tale is simple: Man is one and indivisible, and the pain or illness which affects one of his limbs or organs will have an effect on the rest of his body as well.

One of the greatest haggadists was Rabbi Joshua ben Levi who had actually been an Amora, but a member of the first generation of Amoraim in Palestine at the beginning of the third century of the Christian era. He pursued the Halacha and served as dean of the Academy of Lydda for some years. At the same time, however, he was the author of many tales which were included in the haggadic portion of the Babylonian Talmud.

Joshua ben Levi said once that he had devoted much of his time to helping those afflicted with scabies. When he was asked why he was placing his own health in jeopardy, he replied, "The Lord will help me and His Law will protect me." Eventually, however, he himself fell ill and the angel of death came to his bedside. Joshua said to the apparition:

"I am prepared to die, but before I depart this life I wish to see the place I will occupy in the Garden of Eden."

The angel of death was willing to accede to the scholar's request and asked Joshua to come with him.

"I shall go with thee," replied Joshua, "but let me hold thy sword, for how shall I know that thou wilt not smite me with it while we are on the way to see my place in paradise?"

The angel of death then turned over his sword to the rabbi and took him to a high place from which he could see the dwelling which he would occupy in the Garden of Eden. When Joshua beheld his future home, he leaped down into paradise and refused to leave. When the angel of death saw that all his entreaties were in vain and Joshua would not return to him, he pleaded with Joshua that he might at least return his sword which he, Joshua, had taken with him when he descended into the Garden. Joshua stubbornly clung to the weapon. Finally the Lord Himself commanded him to surrender it to the angel of death.

The moral of the story is that death is often a good thing for a man, and that the sword of the angel of death is not only an instrument of pain and sorrow, but also an indispensable tool which the angel of death must have to wield in the service of man.

Another story told by Rabbi Joshua ben Levi deals with the Messiah. Joshua met the Prophet Elijah on the road and asked him when the Messiah would come. Elijah suggested that Joshua turn to the Messiah himself for the answer. The Messiah, he said, could be found sitting at the gate of the city of Rome.

"But how shall I know him?" asked Joshua, perplexed.

"He will sit among the sick and the poor within the gate of the city. When all the others change the bandages that cover their wounds, they unbind them all first, and then bind them all up fresh. But Messiah will uncover each wound separately and put on the new bandage immediately thereafter so as not to lose time if he should suddenly be called by the Lord to redeem the Jewish people."

Rabbi Joshua ben Levi did as he was told and really found Messiah at the place where Elijah had said he would be. He respectfully greeted the scion of David and asked him when he would come to redeem his people. The Messiah replied, "This very day."

The next morning Joshua ben Levi again came upon the Prophet Elijah and angrily complained, "The Messiah has deceived me. He told me yesterday that he would come this very day, but he has not come."

The prophet replied, "The Messiah has not deceived thee at all. What he meant was to quote to thee the verse from the Bible, where the Lord said, This very day, if only you will hearken to my voice and repent of your sins.' "

To close the chapter, let us look at a piece which stands like a song in free verse, describing the sorrow which God Himself felt because He had been compelled to exile His beloved people from their land.

"Rabbi Jose says, 'One day I went to a synagogue to pray to God. And I heard a voice which was like that of a dove, saying:

"Woe is Me for the sufferings of My children
  Because of whose sins I have destroyed My own House,
  Burned My own Palace
  And dispersed them among the nations.

Woe is Me, woe is Me!
Woe to the father who has exiled his children
And woe to the children who have been driven from
their father's house!" ' "

This is a thought which was to be thoroughly discussed in the Cabala many years later; that is, that the glory of God itself went into exile when the Jewish people were driven from their land. Exile carried with it more than mere physical suffering. The Jewish spirit itself, the genius of the Jewish people, was affected by the loss of independence, and would revive only when the Jews would be able to return to their own country.

20. Parables and Allegories in the Talmud

Parables and allegories have had a major place in world literature ever since men have been able to tell tales. The greatest masters in this skill were the scholars whose names occur over and over again in the pages of the Talmud, the halachists as well as the haggadists.

Actually the parable, the story with a moral, was the father of the short story and hence of all the forms of literature that came thereafter.

It was quite natural that the Jewish religion, which is basically a guide of morals and ethics, should have made extensive use of the parable. Many scholars such as Landsberg, Baeck, and others believe that the Jewish people, in fact, had been the originator of the parable. Of course other civilizations have also made their own contributions to the world treasury of classic allegories, but they lacked the moral teaching of those of the Jews, nor were they produced in such great volume.

Biblical writings of such diversified character as the Book of Proverbs, the Song of Songs, Ecclesiastes, and the Book of Job have one characteristic in common; namely, that they all either are allegories or else are replete with parables. Even in the Pentateuch (Numbers 21:27) we find a statement ". . . .Wherefore those that speak in parables say . . ." which is evidence that even in the days of antiquity there were men among the Jewish people who cultivated that art. We see another allegory in the Book of Judges, where Jotham, desirous of having his kingdom returned to him from Shechem, tells the allegory of the trees which went out to seek a king whom they could anoint as their ruler. When Nathan the Prophet seeks to castigate King David for his sin with Bathsheba, he also employs the parable to bring home to the king the enormity of his sin (II Sam. Chap. 12). The woman whom Joab sends to King David to speak with him about his son Absalom is commanded to convey Joab's message to the king by way of a parable (II Sam. 14:1-7). And when the Bible extols the virtues of King Solomon, it tells that the king had devised three thousand parables. Perhaps this is a slight exaggeration, but it is proof that parables enjoyed great popularity with the Jewish people even in those ancient days and that the authors of parables and allegories were generally respected and admired for their wisdom.

The Talmudic epoch gave birth to a wealth of such tales which have been preserved for posterity in the pages of the Talmud and which may be divided into four main categories, as follows:

1. *Parables dealing with kings.* In his work, "The Royal Parables" published in 1903, Ziegler lists ten subjects with which these parables deal, namely, (1) the honor of the king, (2) his might, (3) his authority to reward the good and to punish the wicked, (4) his wealth and the great number of servants at his command, (5) his friends and advisers, (6) his family life, (7) his palaces and gardens, (8) his amusements, (9) his sense of justice, and (10) his wives, concubines, and children. It is estimated that Talmudic literature contains about one thousand such "royal parables."

2. *Parables employing the fox as their central figure.* For some reason it was assumed that the fox was the wisest of all beasts, and many fables were evolved in which all sorts of clever ideas and plans were attributed to that animal. Rabbi Johanan tells that Rabbi Meir had devised and told three hundred different fables in which the hero was a fox. Unfortunately all but the three recorded in Sanhedrin 38 had been forgotten by the time the Talmud was compiled.

It is told of both Bar Kappara and Rabbi Akiba that they, too, told a wealth of such stories, all with the fox as the hero.

3. *Fables in which animals other than the fox are employed to convey a moral.* In these, the lion is portrayed as the king of all the beasts; the tiger as an aggressive creature; the snake as cunning; the deer as the swiftest of animals; and the camel as the most patient. Of the domestic animals, the dog is described as man's best friend; the cat as a false creature; the rooster as the herald of dawn; and the duck as a bird which, though it walks about with its head bent, can see farther than most other animals.

4. *Fables centering about plants, trees, and flowers.* These are discussed by August Wunsche in the work *Plant Fables in World Literature* where he devotes a special section to the plant fables found in the Talmud.

The Talmud also contains parables in which tradesmen such as launderers and millers play the main part.

Let us look at some samples from each of these categories.

First, we have here two stories dealing with kings.

The first tale centers about the relationship of the king to his own children, demonstrating that while he has the power to punish anyone he chooses to punish, he still will be lenient when it comes to members of his own family.

It seems that a king had cause to be very angry with his son. He saw a boulder lying on the ground and swore that he would throw that rock at his son. As his wrath abated, however, he realized that this would be tantamount to murdering the boy. But a promise once given by a king is irreversible and his word is law. Therefore the king commanded that the boulder be broken up into tiny pieces. It was these fragments which he then threw at his son. In this manner he fulfilled his oath without actually harming his offspring.

Another tale illustrates the just treatment which any master should accord his servants:

A king entrusted his beautiful garden to the care of a servant. When, some time later, he came to inspect his garden, he found that all the trees there had died, the flowers had faded, and the garden itself was filled with thorns. The king was furious at his servant and the man was forced to flee for his life. He then called in workers to clear away the thorns. One of these workmen found a beautiful flower hidden among the thorns. The king plucked the flower from the ground, inhaled its perfume, and exclaimed: "For the sake of this one fragrant flower I will richly reward him who caused my garden to be laid waste."

The following fable shows the cunning of the fox:

One Friday a fox met a wolf who seemed hungry. The fox, fearful for his life, offered to take the wolf to a Jewish home where there would be much good food to satisfy his hunger, since it was the eve of the Sabbath. The fox then took the wolf to a farmyard where there was a well, above which hung two buckets. These were attached with cords around a piece of wood suspended above the well in such a manner that, if one of the buckets would be lowered, the other would rise. The fox jumped into one bucket and lowered himself into the well. He pointed to the reflection of the full moon on the sparkling waters of the well and called out to the greedy wolf, "See the lovely yellow cheese down here in the well! Why not join me for dinner?" On the invitation of the crafty fox, the foolish wolf then jumped into the empty pail which hung above the well. Since the wolf was heavier than the fox crouched in the other pail, the fox rose to the surface as the wolf descended, and the clever animal escaped from his enemy while the latter still thrashed about in the waters of the well.

In the third category, there is the story of the lion who had devoured a smaller animal. One of the bones of his prey became lodged in the big cat's throat. The lion offered a generous reward to the one who would be able to remove the splinter. Soon there came an Egyptian who had had extensive experience in dealing with animals. The man commanded the lion to open his mouth. Putting his head into the lion's maw, he searched for the bone, sighted it and pulled it out with his hands. The beast, relieved, thanked its benefactor, but said no word of a reward. When the Egyptian demanded the promised payment, the big cat laughed, "Why, thou hast already had thy reward. Is life itself not sufficient recompense for thee? Remember, thou hast put thy head into the maw of a lion and he has let thee retrieve it from there safe and sound."

And then we have the short but clever tale of the snake. It seems that the snake's tail complained to the head of the reptile as follows, "O head, why dost thou always go ahead of me? Why cannot I lead thee instead?" The head agreed to cede its position of leadership temporarily to the tail. The result was that the tail first struck water, then crept into the midst of a wood fire and finally became entangled in a mess of thorns. At last the head ruefully exclaimed, "If only I had not consented to follow my tail I could have spared myself all this trouble."

We might end this brief collection of parables and allegories with a plant fable. It seems that the stem, the chaff, and the grain had an argument, with each claiming that it was the most important part of the wheat plant. In the end, the ear of wheat said, "Let us wait until we shall be brought into the barn. There we shall see which one of us is indeed the most important." At harvest time, the farmer first separated the chaff from the rest of the plant, and the chaff was driven away by the wind. Then he cut away the stem and spread it out to dry. But it was the grain which he took away to the miller, where it was turned into the flour from which bread, man's staple food, is made.

21. Debates with Unbelievers

The Talmud also contains in the haggadic portion a great many debates and discussions which the Tannaim and Amoraim carried on with non-Jews and with Jewish unbelievers. These discussions dealt with philosophical themes such as Creation, providence, the Jewish religion, the belief in the coming of the Messiah, and the resurrection of the dead. These subjects provided bones of contention also among the various sects within the fold of Judaism: the Pharisees, the Sadducees, and the Essenes. The Talmud has preserved a great many of these debates. Now, we shall study just a few of them in order to understand their nature and character.

First, let us take the philosophical discussion which the famed Rabbi Akiba had with an unbeliever.

"Who created the world?" asked the unbeliever.

"God," replied Rabbi Akiba.

"Prove it to me," demanded the other.

Rabbi Akiba asked the unbeliever to return to him the next day so that he might give him the desired evidence. The following morning Rabbi Akiba asked the other man how the material for his cloak had been made.

"It is woven," replied the unbeliever. "The stuff of which my cloak is made was woven by weavers."

"I cannot believe your words," retorted Rabbi Akiba. "I must have clear proof first."

"What proof do I need to give you?" asked the inquirer. "Is it not quite obvious that the stuff was made by a weaver?"

"Quite true," Rabbi Akiba answered, "But is it not obvious to you also that the world was made by God?"

After the unbeliever had left, Rabbi Akiba's disciples asked their master, "But where is the clear proof which you promised to show him?"

Rabbi Akiba replied:

"My sons, each house attests to its builder; each bolt of cloth bears witness to the skill of its weaver. In the same manner, the whole world affords testimony of the greatness of its creator, which is none other than the Lord."

Then there is the debate of Rabban Gamaliel and the Roman emperor on the question of whether there is indeed only one God, or whether the Zoroastrians had been right when they taught of the existence of two divinities.

"Why do you say that there is only one God, when your own Bible speaks of two? Does not your own Bible say 'He that *forms* the mountains and He that *creates* the wind?' " the pagan emperor asked. "Does this not prove that the deity that formed the mountains is not the same as the one that created the wind?"

The wise Gamaliel instantly replied: "But the terms 'and He formed' and 'He created' are used interchangeably also in the Biblical account of the creation of man. Hence, if your assumption would be correct, it would mean that man could not be the harmonious being he is, for then one god would have created one eye, and the other god the other; one deity would have made one ear, and the rival deity the second. Since this is obviously not so, we know that "the One who formed' and the 'One who created' are one and the same God, and anyone who seeks to use the Bible to prove otherwise is wrong."

Here is another debate involving a verse from the Bible.

Tyrannus Rufus, the Roman governor, asked Rabbi Akiba: "Why should your God hate us? It is written in your Bible, 'I have come to hate Esau' (Mal., Chap. 1) and we Romans are descended from Esau. This must mean that your God has hatred for us also. Why should this be so?"

Rabbi Akiba asked him to return the next day, at which time he, Rabbi Akiba, would have his answer ready.

When the Roman official came back the morning after, Rabbi Akiba began to tell him of a dream which he had had during the night and in which he had seen two dogs, one named Rufus and one named Rufina. Before he could finish his account, the governor angrily interrupted him:

"How dare you call your dogs by my name and the name of my wife! You shall be put to death for this insult to the authority of Rome!"

Rabbi Akiba calmly replied:

"Basically, wherein are you different from these two dogs? They eat and drink and so do you; they produce offspring and so do you; you are but mortal, even as they are. And yet you are angry because I called two dogs by your name and that of your lady. How, then, should our God, who made the sun, the moon, and the stars, who gives life to all and reigns over all things, deal with men who insult Him by taking an inert, powerless piece of wood, calling it by His own Name and worshiping it?"

There were other discussions in which the sages employed action to prove their point to their opponents. An example of this would be the verbal encounter which took place between Rabbi Judah the Prince and a ruler whom the Talmud calls Antonius but who, we assume, is actually Marcus Aurelius, the Roman emperor-philosopher. The emperor asked the Jewish scholar whether man could say the prescribed prayers at any time that would be convenient to him. When Judah said that this could not be done, the emperor seemed surprised, and asked the reason why this was so.

"Prayer would be too cheap otherwise," replied Judah.

When Judah saw that the emperor was still not convinced, he evolved a method of his own to prove his point to the emperor.

Early the next morning, Judah came to the palace, called out a reverent greeting to the sovereign and then left. An hour later, he returned again and said, "My humble greetings to the emperor" and once more departed. At the end of the next hour, Judah again appeared at the palace gates and voiced his "respectful greetings to the great king." By this time Antoninus was angry and accused Judah of ridiculing the authority of the emperor.

But Judah merely said, "Let your own ears perceive the profound truth which your mouth has just uttered. You, a mere human, are angry because you feel that such constant tribute from your subjects is not tribute at all but actually constitutes a jest at the expense of the emperor. Do you not see, then, why it would certainly be improper to constantly disturb the King of Kings with your importunings?"

Whether Judah actually made this experiment, or whether he had only told the story by way of illustration is not known. But we do know that it could convince any doubter of the correctness of Judah's reasoning.

Other discussions involved questions more specifically Jewish, such as whether Israel really was the chosen people of God and did God truly take a personal interest in the fate of Israel? Would the Jewish people really live forever?

A philosopher asked Rabbi Eliezer: "We read in the Book of Malachi that 'they will build and I will destroy'; in other words, we are told that God will destroy whatever the other nations will build up. But this is not true, for do we not see everywhere the magnificent edifices which the enemies of the Jewish people have reared?"

Eliezer explained to the doubter that the Biblical verse did not refer to structures of stone and wood, but only to spiritual machinations such as the plans devised by the nations against Israel. The nations of the world could plan the destruction of Israel in intricate detail, but the Lord would thwart all their efforts, so that they would meet with no success.

Then there were the endless debates between the Sadducees and the Pharisees about the resurrection of the dead.

A Sadducee questioned Rabbi Ami as follows: "You may say that the dead will come to life again, but we know that the dead all return to dust. How can clods of earth assume new life?"

Rabbi Ami's answer came in the form of the following parable:

"A king commanded his servants to build for him a palace on a site where there was neither earth nor water. The servants searched for a long time until they found such a spot and then began the construction work. But the structure collapsed. The king now ordered them to erect a palace on a site where there would be soil and water. The servants claimed that they could not do the work. The king became angry and said, 'You were willing and able to build me a palace in a place where there was neither soil nor water. Why is it, then, that when I ask you to make me another upon a site where soil and water are both present, you cannot do it?' The moral of the story is as follows: Man is made from nothing, and yet he can create life. Cannot God then create new life from clay, which has substance?"

Another Sadducee said to a Tanna: "Woe to you, Pharisees, who say that the dead will come to life again. If even living creatures must die, how, then, can the dead return to the realm of the living?"

The Pharisee teacher replied:

"Woe unto you, O wicked men, who say that the dead will not be revived. Behold, those who never lived before are given life in this world; would it not then be an easy thing for those who actually have spent a lifetime on earth to return to new life?"

22. *Tales, Folk Medicine, and Wise Sayings*

In addition to the material we have studied in the previous chapter, the Haggada is replete with other bits of fantasy and practical wisdom of which we shall attempt to give a few examples here.

First let us look at this type of literature which has been known in the world down to the present day but for which we actually have no special name. It can best be characterized as a type of travel story, richly embellished with fantasy and subtly flavored with satire. Writers blessed with a fertile imagination and with the gift of an acid pen would clothe their ridicule of certain aspects of human conduct in tales dealing with journeys through lands that existed only in their minds. Through the centuries there have been only a very few authors who might be classed as masters in this field.

One such king of fantasy and satire was the famous Baron von Munchausen (1720-1797), a member of the Hanoverian aristocracy, who fought in the cavalry on the side of the Russians against Turkey. This soldier spent his spare time writing quite a series of fantastic travelogues of a satirical nature. We know them today in the English language as *The Tales of Baron Von Munchausen.*

Another outstanding figure in this field was Jonathan Swift (1667-1745), an English clergyman who poked fun at the real world and its inhabitants in his immortal *Gulliver's Travels,* the story of an ordinary human being who traversed lands that existed only in the fantasy of the author.

The Jewish people also had two such masters of satire. These, however, lived long before either Munchausen or Swift; they are part of the Talmudic era of Jewish history. The first, a Tanna named Aba Saul, lived during the period immediately following the destruction of the Second Temple. Aba Saul, a giant of a man, made his living as a baker in the employ of Rabbi Judah the Prince, but offered his volunteer services to the community as a gravedigger. He wrote down a good many of the truths of human life which he had formulated as he examined the dead bodies entrusted to his care. But of even greater interest for our purposes are his little fantastic tales, liberally laced with satire, in which we can also detect, of course, the influence of the activity to which he devoted many of his leisure hours. Let us study only a few samples of his strange imagination:

It seems that one day, as he was walking on a road, the ground opened up beneath his feet and he fell into a cavity which turned out to be the eye socket of a corpse. When he finally managed to extricate himself, he was told that the eye socket had belonged to no less a person than Absalom, the son of King David. What Aba Saul meant to intimate by this eerie tale was that Absalom, who had sought to deprive his father of his kingdom, had "giant" eyes; in other words, that the range of things which his eyes coveted was limitless.

Another time, Aba Saul pursued a running stag and somehow managed to crawl into the hollowed-out bone of what had once been a huge human leg. He ran inside the strange tunnel for three whole miles, but the bone never came to an end, nor did he capture the object of his pursuit. Later on, he was told that the bone had been that of none other than Og, the King of Bashan. This was intended to point out in graphic terms the wild desire with which that ruler pursued his ambitious aim to conquer the rest of the world.

The second Jewish satirist of a later period, Rabbah bar bar Hanna, had first gone from Babylonia to Palestine where he became a disciple of Rabbi Johanan. Some time later, however, he returned to Babylonia and enrolled at the Academy of Pumbeditha during the administration there of Rabbi Judah bar Ezekiel.

Besides being a great scholar, Bar bar Hanna was a lover of fantastic tales, and has left us a great many such stories. Some of these have a distinct satiric undertone. Others, again, are so involved and unreal that it is difficult to tell exactly at what he had intended to poke fun. Yet they are so absorbing that they cast a spell upon any reader, even though he may not understand their true intent.

Here we shall just attempt to glance at a few of his tales. Most of them begin with prefatory remarks such as "I have seen" or "Once upon a time."

Now, let Rabbah bar bar Hanna speak for himself:

"Once upon a time, as I was sailing on a ship, I saw a giant fish and noticed that a tiny worm had burrowed its way into the nostril of this monster. As a result, the huge animal died. Now the ocean, which abhors dead bodies, spewed out the fish. The immense weight of the dead beast, thus thrown upon the land, caused the destruction of sixty cities. But the inhabitants of sixty other cities gathered up vast pieces of the carcass, which they preserved in salt and upon which they fed for months. One eye alone yielded three hundred barrels of oil. When I returned twelve months later, I saw that men were busily sawing away at the bones of the fish, and I was told that the bones were being used to rebuild the sixty cities which had been crushed beneath the weight of the carcass when it first was cast ashore."

Another tale:

"Once upon a time I met an Arab wanderer who said to me, 'Come with me, and I shall show thee the place where heaven and earth kiss each other.' I took a basketful of bread and put it down there where the heavens lower themselves to touch the earth, and then I turned aside to say my prayers. Afterwards I went back to look for the basket but could find it no longer. I demanded of the Arab, 'Are there thieves here?' but he replied, 'Wait for the heavenly wheel which slowly turns round and round; come back tomorrow and by that time it will have returned to its old position and thou wilt find thy bread.' "

The idea which the scholar intended to express here was that there can be no heaven without an earth below, and in the same manner there can be no spiritual existence without physical life. Heaven and earth really do "kiss one another." The spirit and the body are one and inseparable.

The Haggada is also replete with medical advice. Some of these cures had been tried and proved effective for generations. Others were new, set down for posterity by some Amoraim, such as Samuel, who, in addition to being outstanding scholars of the Law, were also practicing physicians.

Here again we shall have to limit ourselves to only a few examples of the preventatives and cures that are mentioned in the pages of the Talmud:

Rabbi Joseph said: "There are three things that are harmful to the eyes: combing one's hair while it is dry; drinking water that flows forth from an unknown source; and lacing one's shoes while one's feet are still wet."

Samuel said that any wound should be regarded as dangerous and that therefore any measure employed to hasten healing should in no way be construed as a violation of the Sabbath.

That the sages of that day were well acquainted with human anatomy is readily apparent to anyone studying their laws concerning ritual slaughter, the examination of animal carcasses to determine their fitness for consumption, and the precepts on ritual purity and impurity which are found in the halachic section of the Talmud. Of course a good deal of what we read in the haggadic literature does not seem to be in agreement with what we know about medicine today, but the fact remains that the men whose names recur many times in the Haggada had a knowledge of medicine that was quite advanced for the day and age in which they lived.

Finally, let us examine a few of the many, many wise sayings that have been perpetuated for us in haggadic literature. This study should afford us an interesting glimpse into the life and thought of those who then lived in Babylonia and in Central Asia in general. For most of these sayings were not exclusively Jewish but were part of the lore of the Asiatic nations in whose midst the Jewish people dwelt. Most of them are prefaced by the statement, "This is what people say." Bialik and Ravnitzky, in their monumental work, *The Book of the Haggada,* have set down about two thousand three hundred such adages, but these do not by any means constitute the sum total of the sayings found in haggadic literature. We shall list here only a few of them:

"Man usually worries about his money."

"Man may kindle a new flame from an old light, but this will in no way decrease the power of the original light."

"Man is too close to himself to be objective about his own person."

"Man prefers one measure of his own to nine measures of another's wealth."

"One man's belief in himself is stronger than that of a hundred others."

"We would say to the bee, 'I do not desire thy honey; neither do I want thy sting.' "

"The treatment of a doctor who charges no fee is of no value."

"When in Rome, do as the Romans do."

"The walls have ears."

"Woe to him whose defender turns into a prosecutor."

"Woe to those who see but know not what it is they see."

"Who is a hero? He who can overcome his evil inclination."

"Who is a hero? He who can turn an enemy into a friend."

"Who is wise? He who can learn from all men."

"Who is respected? He who gives honor to every man."

"Who is rich? He who is satisfied with his own portion."

"Who is a fool? He who loses that which is given him."

"There are some who are satisfied with vinegar and do not yearn for wine."

"A man never sins without a motive."

"A man and a viper cannot live together" (the "viper" is in this case a shrewish wife).

"Man cannot testify in his own behalf."

"A man cannot incriminate himself."

"No man can be held responsible for his actions while he is in pain."

"In death a man is truly missed only by his wife, and a wife only by her husband."

"There is nothing worse in this world than poverty."

"Only that which man earns for himself is truly blessed."

"The evil inclination tempts man only to do that which is forbidden."

"When it comes to matters between man and woman there is no judge."

"No prisoner can unchain himself alone."

"There is no evil inclination in the grave."

"Invisibility is not proof of nonexistence."

"Opportunity knocks at least once for all men."

Of course, these are only a very few samples from a vast collection, but these words of practical wisdom should be sufficient to afford us a general idea of their character and tenor.

23. The Code of Jewish Ethics

❧ THE CREATORS OF JEWISH ETHICS

The code of morals and conduct which comprises what we call "Jewish ethics" was not created all in one day. As we shall see later, it was the product of many generations. To begin with, it was brought into being by the Tannaim and the Amoraim, who based their own lives also upon high standards of character and morality. In addition to laying the foundations for Judaism as we know it today and expounding ancient law to their people, these wise teachers also set forth for all posterity a code of ethics and morals which eventually came to be accepted by many other civilized nations. Bits of this code, which might be called the third component of the Talmud, are scattered throughout the Haggada and the Halacha, the other two portions of that gigantic encyclopedia of knowledge.

The teachings that constitute Jewish ethics encompass every aspect of human life. They govern man's conduct as an individual in matters such as personal cleanliness and clothing. Others deal with the relationships of the individual with his fellow men—his friends and his neighbors and fellow citizens. Still others regulate his relations with his parents, his wife, his children and relatives, and his behavior in society as well. Here, too, we find suggestions on how to acquire virtues and how to break bad habits, and on how a man may win for himself a good name which will live on long after he has departed this life.

We shall present some choice examples of this wealth of teachings, beginning with those regulating man's personal conduct.

❧ PERSONAL CONDUCT

It is told that the disciples of Hillel and the students of Shammai spent over two years debating whether or not man would have been better off if he had never been created. In the end they came to the conclusion that it would indeed have been better if man had never been born. Since it was too late to change that, however, the scholars agreed that the best thing for man was to do good deeds all the days of his life, so that some good should come of his stay on earth.

Rabbi Meir said: "When man is first born, his hands are closed, as if to say, 'I shall take the entire world as my own'; but when he dies, his fingers are spread apart, as if to say, 'See, I've taken nothing from this world.' "

Rav said to Rav Hamnunah: "My son, if thou hast wealth and possessions, enjoy them while thou livest, for there is no pleasure in the grave, and worry not over much, for death comes swiftly and does not tarry. Perhaps thou wilt say, 'I must leave my wealth for my children,' but once thou art in thy grave, dost thou know what thy children will do with thy wealth? Man is like grass. It sprouts up only to wither away in the end."

Samuel said to Rabbi Judah: "O wise man, eat and drink thy fill, for this world is like a wedding. Once the feast is over, it all is at an end."

Rabbi Eleazar the Caphirite said: "With regard to the Nazirite (the abstemious man) we are told 'May he be forgiven for having sinned against himself.' In what manner has he sinned against himself? By abstaining from wine. Now, if a person is called a sinner merely because he refuses to drink wine, how much more so is he a sinner who abstains from other lawful pleasures as well?"

"Who is a pious fool? He who sees a ripe date and says, 'I shall give this to the first person I meet on the way' [instead of eating it himself]."

The following is attributed to Rabbi Judah the Prince: "When man reaches the world to come he will be asked to render accounting for every luscious fruit which he saw but did not eat and for every beautiful garment which he might have been able to procure but never bought."

The sages also taught their people that it was man's duty to enjoy the beauty that life affords. In fact, they even instituted a special blessing which was to be recited in thanksgiving to God at the sight of fragrant flowers, verdant trees, and even men or women of exceptional beauty.

It is told of Rabban Simon ben Gamaliel that he once laid eyes upon a heathen woman of unusual physical charm and immediately praised his Maker for her beauty, saying, "How great are Thy creations, O Lord."

When Rabbi Akiba first sighted the wife of Tyrannus Rufus, who was of rare beauty, he first spat upon the ground, then laughed, and finally wept. He spat upon the ground at the thought that she was the wife of a wicked heathen. Then he laughed because he knew that she eventually would mend her ways and become his wife after the death of her evil husband. Finally, however, he shed bitter tears at the thought that even a woman of her beauty would one day have to rot away beneath the ground.

❧ ON FOOD AND TABLE MANNERS

The sages had much to say on the subject of the wise use of food and drink.

"Before the age of forty, it is better to eat; after that, it is better to drink."

"Man must eat, because he must gain strength. But he must refrain from gluttony."

"Make proper use of your teeth (chew your food well) and you will find that what you eat will give strength to your legs."

"He who eats slowly will live long."

"One may even borrow money in order to be able to eat well, but this must not be overdone."

"It is man's duty to take care of his body."

"Be on your guard against drinking. Too much drinking is bad, particularly when a woman drinks too much wine."

"A woman may take one cup of strong drink. If she takes two cups, she will be too light-headed. If she drinks three, she will be entirely out of her mind."

"A man must not eat the soft part of his bread and leave the crust behind, nor may he tear a piece of bread apart. He who does so is a glutton. A man may not drink up his cup in one draught, lest he be called a sot. Instead, he must quaff his drink slowly."

"A man should not eat garlic or the bulb of the onion; he should content himself with the sprouts of these vegetables."

"A man should not lick his platter clean or gather up crumbs from the table in order to eat them."

"If two people sit at a table, the younger of the two must wait for the elder to begin eating before he himself partakes of food."

Rabbi Akiba made it a practice to have his meals together with his students in order to teach them good table manners.

A well bred person, the sages said, must not take a bite from a piece of bread and then give what is left to another. Nor must one return to the table bread from which he has bitten off a piece, for the sight of the marks left by his teeth are not conducive to the enjoyment of the meal by others.

One must not criticize the food one eats.

One should not throw bread around, nor should one clean up one's platter with a piece of bread.

If a host invites a guest it is not proper for the former to finish eating before the latter. It is an even worse breach of etiquette for a guest to bring with him a guest of his own. Even more boorish is he who eats before the scholar in the house where he happens to be has been served. But worst of all is the guest who deliberately makes things unpleasant for his host.

One should not talk while eating.

One should not drink from a cup and then pass it to another.

Rav said to his son Chiya, "Rinse out your cup before you drink from it. After drinking, rinse it once again before putting it aside. If you should drink water and then desire to give others to drink also, rinse out the cup before passing it on to the others."

❦ ON DRESS

Rabbi Uriah said: "It is permissible to eat and drink less than one's fill, but one must not thus restrict oneself in matters of dress."

Rabbi Jose ben Chanina said: "He who wears ugly clothes will never derive pleasure from himself."

The beauty of a person depends on his dress.

There is an Aramaic saying as follows: "In my own city my name alone suffices, but once away from there, the impression I make is determined by my garments."

He who has no more than one garment is not really living.

Rabbi Judah said that Rav had commented as follows: "One must sell even the fixtures of his dwelling if necessary, in order to buy shoes for himself."

❦ PERSONAL CLEANLINESS

It has been said in the name of Rav: "One must not live in a city where there is no bath."

There are three kinds of perspiration: sweat from physical work; the sweat of a sick person; and the sweat in the bath. The sweat of honest toil serves to give man his daily bread; the sweat of the invalid brings him healing; but the sweat during a bath is the healthiest of all.

We have learned: "A man must wash his hands, face, and feet each day."

Samuel said: "A cold bath upon rising and a hot bath before retiring at night are the best medicine of all."

One should not eat before washing his hands.

Samuel said: "A head long unwashed may be the cause of blindness; unwashed garments may lead to insanity; and an unbathed body may cause pocks."

One must take a bath at least once a week.

❦ ON LABOR

The great teachers of the Jewish people have always attached much importance to work. They not only urged everyone else to learn a trade, but actually practiced what they preached. Most of the Tannaim and Amoraim were simple artisans or farmers, and only a very few engaged in trade and commerce. Gradually they evolved a code of ethics to govern both labor and business practices which is of great importance to this very day.

We shall make a brief survey here of the statements of these wise men which have been preserved for us in the Talmud.

The sages taught: "There are three kinds of persons of whom it can be said that their existence is no life at all; namely, he who is dependent on the charity of others; he whose wife rules over him; and he who suffers pain and anguish."

It is said: "When a person eats of that which is his, he is comfortable and content, but if he must eat off the bounty of others, even if they be his own parents or children, he can be neither happy nor content, and he certainly cannot be so if he must depend on the charity of strangers for his food."

The sages taught: "He who is dependent upon his wife's earnings will never attain happiness."

It is better to treat the Sabbath like any other weekday than to be dependent upon the charity of others.

Rather do work that is not pleasing to you than be dependent upon the charity of others.

A poor man is always unhappy, even on the Sabbath and on holidays, because his stomach is not accustomed to holiday fare and even if he can afford better food for those occasions, it will not agree with him.

Poverty pursues the poor.

There are many kinsmen and friends at the rich man's gate, but there are none at the door of the poor man's hovel.

Abbaye said: "To our mind only he who is poor in spirit is truly poor."

It is written in the Book of Ben Sira: "Worry not about the morrow, for it may be that by tomorrow thou wilt no longer be here, and then thou wilt have worried in vain."

Man must not treasure money more than his body.

It is written: "May the Lord bless thee and keep thee. . . ." This might be construed to mean that the Lord will bless man even if he is idle. But in order to avoid such misconstruction, we are told soon after that the Lord will "bless thee in everything that thou doest." This means that the Lord will give His help if man does his share; but if man should sit idle, the Lord will also not assist him.

A man must never say, "I need not work, for God will help me." Instead, man must work diligently, for only then will the Lord help him.

If a man prepared not his meal on Friday what would he have to eat on the Sabbath?

If a man will not till his soil, sow his seed, and reap his harvest in the summer, what will he eat in the winter?

Rabbi Tarphon said: "Do not refuse to do a task that seems difficult or that never seems to come to an end. Take the case of a man who was hired to drain off water from the sea and to pour it onto the dry land. He said, 'But the waters of the sea will never grow less, neither will the dry land change. Why, then, should I do that work?' " But Rabbi Tarphon replied, "Foolish man, this is none of thy concern. Dost thou not get wages each day for the work? Go ahead, then, and do it."

Rav Sheshet said: "Work is a great thing because it is good for man."

When entering the house of study, Rabbi Judah would bear a pitcher on his shoulder in connection with his work. When he was asked why he did that, he replied, "Work is great, because it makes man important."

Rabbi Simon spoke in the same vein of the heavy packages which he would carry on his back on the way to his house of study.

The students of Rabbi Ishmael said: "The Bible tells us to 'choose life.' That means we are all to learn a trade."

Rabban Gamaliel said, "He who has learned a trade is like a garden surrounded by a fence so that neither man nor beast can enter it and do damage there. But he who knows no trade is like an open garden which any man or beast can enter and destroy." An unskilled laborer is likely to be exploited and underpaid.

"There was a famine in the land for seven years, but it did not cross the threshold of the worker's home" (Aramaic proverb).

Shemaya said: "Love work and hate ruling over others." Rabbah said to his disciples, "Do not come to me during the months of Nisan and Tishri when men must work in the fields. To interrupt your work in order to come and study during those months would affect your harvest and you must live a whole year from the produce of your soil."

"The Bible says, 'It is good that man should bear a yoke in his youth.' This means actually, three yokes: the yoke of the Law—to study it; the yoke of a woman—to marry one; and finally the yoke of a trade—to learn one."

Rabbi Judah said: "He who does not learn a trade is as if he had learned to become a robber."

Rabbi Meir said: "A man must teach his son a clean and easy trade. The rest he should entrust to God, for trade, too, may bring either wealth or poverty, and which of the two man shall have is determined by the Lord alone."

The sages taught: "Those whose work brings them into contact with women; that is, those who sell jewelry, who dye dresses, dress women's hair and manicure their nails, and those who supervise women's baths are of little worth. None of them has ever become a king or a high priest, for the work they do is not nice."

Rabbi Judah the Prince said: "There is no such thing as work that is not needed, but happy is he whose parents have a nice trade, and woe to him whose parents ply a trade that is not nice. The world needs both perfume sellers and ditch diggers, but he who sells perfumes rejoices, while he who digs ditches is sad."

Rav said to Rav Kahane: "Better strip off the hide of a carcass in the street than depend on the charity of others. Say not that thou art a great man and the work is not fit for thee."

If a man should say, "I am of noble birth and it is not seemly that I should work," he should be told: "Even God Himself worked six days and rested only on the seventh. Could it be that thou thinkest thyself nobler than thy Maker?"

Rabbi Jeremiah said: "A trade is of greater worth than even the greatest nobility."

❦ ON AGRICULTURE

The Jewish sages also had high regard for the agricultural trades.

Rabbi Eleazar said: "There will be a time when everyone will want to work the soil, for this kind of work is needed always."

Resh Lakish said, "If a man will engage in working the soil, he will have bread to eat; if he does not do this work, he will have no food."

Samuel would visit his fields once each day. He would say: "I am not as good as my father. He would inspect his fields twice each day. He who visits his fields at least once each day will profit from them."

Abbaye would go to inspect his fields once each day. Once he met his gardener carrying a load of wood on his shoulders. He asked him, "Where art thou taking this load?" The workman replied, "To thy home, o master." Abbaye realized that this was a lame excuse and that the gardener would have taken the wood to his own house had he not met his master. He therefore said to him, "We have caught thee in the act."

Rabbi Isaac said: "A man should divide his wealth into three parts. With one he should buy land, the second he should use for business, and the third he should keep in cash."

Man should not invest all his money in only one venture, for if that venture should fail, he will lose all he has.

Cattle-dealing is better than work in the fields.

Rabbi Johanan said, "He who would grow rich should raise sheep and calves, for this is sure to bring him money."

❧ ON BUSINESS AND COMMERCE

This is what the sages had to say concerning business and commerce:

"In times of depression buy as much merchandise as you can, for in the end prices will rise again."

"He who buys in times of depression has gained; he who sells at such times has incurred loss thereby."

Rav said to his son: "I wanted thee to become a teacher but I did not succeed in making thee one. Become a merchant, then, and take this my advice: If thou hast merchandise in stock, sell it quickly, as long as thou hast customers. But remember that once thou wilt have sold thy goods thou wilt regret it because thou wilt think that thou mightest have gotten more money than thou didst. But do not be troubled. The only sale thou wilt never regret is that of wine, for wine left standing long will grow sour and spoil. When thou sellest merchandise, first take the money from the customer before turning the goods over to him. It is better to earn little, but to earn quickly, than to expect a huge profit some time in the distant future."

"When prices fall, that is the time to buy."

"Merchandise is carried only where there is demand for it. Such is the way of the world."

Rabbi Johanan said: "He who has inherited money from his father and is anxious to spend it quickly should dress in flaxen garments (which tear soon), use glass dishes (which break easily), and not oversee his workers (for they will be idle without supervision)."

"Business is a good thing, but only if one is honest. He who is honest in business will be respected by his fellow men."

Rabbi Gidal sought to buy a plot of ground. In the meantime Rabbi Aba came and purchased it himself. Rabbi Gidal went to Rabbi Seira and told him the story. Rabbi Seira in turn told it to Rabbi Isaac Niphchah, who said: "Let us wait until Rabbi Aba will come to the city for the holidays."

When Rabbi Aba arrived, Rabbi Isaac asked him: "If a poor man should wish to buy something and another man comes and buys it first, what kind of a man is that person?" Rabbi Aba replied: "He would be a scoundrel."

"Why, then, didst thou buy the land that Rabbi Gidal sought to purchase?" asked Rabbi Isaac.

"I did not know that he wanted to buy it," Rabbi Aba answered.

Rabbi Isaac then asked him: "Wouldst thou turn it back to him now?"

"I do not wish to sell it now because it is the first plot of ground I have ever bought and it is well known that he who sells the first piece of land he ever purchased will fare badly. But if Gidal should want to have it, I shall be glad to give it to him as a gift." Rabbi Gidal refused to accept the generous offer. Rabbi Aba left the land to lie fallow and in time it came to be known as "The Scholar's Acre."

"If you sell, sell with a smile."

Samuel said: "One must not sell at a profit of more than one-sixth of the original price."

One should not engage to buy when one has neither the money nor the intention to do so.

If someone should have made a bad purchase, one must not tell him that he has been cheated. Instead, tell him that he bought well, for it is of little use to make him unhappy.

He who engages in moneylending for interest will lose all his fortune in the end.

A man should rather hire out his daughter as a maidservant than borrow money from a moneylender.

The overly cordial greeting a would-be borrower gives a lender is also a kind of interest.

❦ ETHICS OF FAMILY LIVING

Both the Tannaim and the Amoraim devoted a great deal of time to the discussion of the problems of marriage and family living. They regarded physical love as a normal, natural thing, stressing, of course, that all such love must lead to marriage and the raising of a family, for the family is the basis of all human civilization. They had a remarkable insight into the psychology of both men and women and so, though some of them did not hold the weaker sex in great esteem, they insisted that husbands were obligated not only to supply the material wants of their wives, but also to spare their feelings and to protect their honor.

It should be interesting for us to read some of the statements of those scholars, many representing differing points of view on the subject. First we shall see what they had to say about beauty and physical love.

"A woman who has beautiful eyes is beautiful altogether."

Resh Lakish said: "A tall man should not marry a tall woman, for their children would be giants, nor should a dwarf take a small wife, because their children would then be dwarves also. If a man with blond hair should wed a woman who is also blonde, their offspring would be light, and therefore such a marriage would not be advisable. The same applies to a marriage of two dark-haired persons, for children of such a union would be so dark as to be almost black of hair and complexion.

"A man who has no wife has no joy, no happiness, and no contentment."

"It is the man who must search for a wife, not the woman for a husband."

"A man should marry when he is eighteen years of age."

Rabbi Chasdai said: "I am better than my friends, for I married when I was sixteen years old."

Rav Chunah said: "If a man is not married by the time he is twenty years of age, his mind will constantly dwell on thoughts of sin."

Rabbi Chiyah bar Aba said: "Our Scriptures say that hopes left unfulfilled too long are nothing but heartbreak. This statement particularly applies to one who is engaged to marry but must wait an indefinite period of time before he can be wed. Once a man is engaged to a woman he should wed her at the earliest possible moment."

But it seems that not all the sages were in complete agreement with this last statement. We are told that "Our sages taught that a young man must first go away to study the Law and marry only after that. If this is not possible, let him marry first and go forth to study thereafter. But Rabbi Johanan said, 'What? Do you think he'll still go out to study after he has the millstone tied around his neck?' "

"Forty days before our birth it is decreed in heaven whom we shall marry. It may happen that we then meet our predestined mate quite by accident, but it may well be that we must go out and search for him or her."

Rav Papa said: "When you wish to sell a plot of land, do not delay, but do not be hasty in choosing a wife. Be willing to compromise in your expectations in marriage, but take a good look at those who lead her to the marriage canopy." (In other words, give careful consideration to her family background.)

"Before marrying a woman, first see what her brothers are like, for most children take after the brothers of their mother."

"A calf takes after the cow and the daughter takes after her mother."

"He who marries for money will not have good children and he will have no profit from the money."

"A man must sell all he has, if necessary, in order to marry off his daughter to a scholar."

"One must not marry off one's daughter while she is still a child. Parents should wait until she is sufficiently mature to decide for herself whom she wants for a husband."

Rabbi Judah attributed these statements to Rav: "A man must not marry a woman without having seen her first," and: "He who marries off his daughter to an old man or he who takes an older wife for his young son brings down a curse upon his house."

Rabbi Eliezer said: "Do not lead thy daughter into prostitution." This, the sages said, means that one should not marry off a young girl to an old man.

It was an ancient custom to sing the praises of the bride on the eve of her wedding day. The sages discussed the proper procedure to follow in this time-honored rite. The disciples of Shammai said that one should be entirely truthful in "praising the bride," but the school of Hillel maintained that every bride should be told on her wedding day that she is beautiful and charming, even if, in fact, she should be lame or blind. When the students of Shammai rejected this view, pointing to the Biblical injunction against telling a falsehood, the adherents of Hillel replied: "If we are to go by what you say, then we should have to tell the unvarnished truth to him who purchased a garment which is not worth the money he spent for it. Instead, when we see a person who, in our opinion, has not made a wise purchase, we tell him that he has obtained a bargain so as not to make him unhappy. This should also be permissible in the case of an ugly or shrewish bride. Such praise is not falsehood but merely a means of keeping the groom happy and content."

The scholars of the Talmud also had well defined views on the duties of the wife toward her husband and on the husband's responsibilities toward the woman he married. They figured out in detail how much money a husband should give his wife for household expenses and clothing. These figures, of course, were based on the purchasing power of Babylonian money in those days.

A woman must grind the wheat and corn into flour, bake bread, wash the laundry, cook the food, nurse her babies, make the beds and, in general, take care of her husband's household. If he is wealthy and should be able to hire a servant, the wife may delegate the work of flour-making, baking, and washing to that paid help. If her husband should be able to afford two servants, the wife may turn over to them also the kitchen and the responsibility of caring for her children. If she has three servants, she need no longer make the beds herself or occupy herself with household matters, and if she should have four she is free to sit in her boudoir and do nothing. But Rabbi Eliezer said: "A woman must do some work even if her husband could afford to hire a hundred servants for her, for if she sits idle she will eventually go mad."

Here are some of the sayings of the sages concerning peace and harmony in the home.

"If man and wife live together in peace and happiness, the glory of God Himself rests upon their home."

Rabbi Eleazar said: "The literal translation of the Biblical verse stating God's intention to create a wife for Adam is 'I shall create *for* him a *helpmate against* him.' This is to teach us that if the marriage is happy, the wife is a helpmate, but that if the couple is mismated, the wife is not 'for' her husband, but only 'against' him."

"He who has a wicked wife grows old before his time."

When Rav said farewell to Rabbi Chiyah, he said to him: "May the Lord preserve thee from a fate worse than death; that is, from a wicked wife."

"A man must protect and guard the honor of his wife."

"A home can be truly happy only if the husband loves his wife and gives her even more honor than he demands for himself, and if the children are taught to honor both parents."

It is said: "If your wife is small, bend down and whisper into her ear" (that is, in order to seek her advice).

Rav said: "A man must not cause his wife grief, for a woman weeps easily and the punishment for making a woman weep is great. But it is not good to give in to one's wife too often."

"The wives of the scholars distinguish themselves by the manner in which they take care of their husbands. They will stay awake all night long in order to be able to greet their husbands when they return from the house of study."

"A man should not keep his wife from going to visit neighbors in order to borrow whatever she may need at the moment in her household. But if she should neglect both her husband and her home, he may divorce her and any claim she may have upon him for support on the basis of the marriage contract is invalid."

The disciples of Shammai, however, said: "A man can divorce his wife only if he has found out that she has sinned with another man."

The views of some of the other sages were far more radical, in fact, amazingly so. The disciples of Hillel said that a man could divorce his wife even if she allowed his food to burn, and Rabbi Akiba asserted that he could divorce her as soon as he found someone more beautiful.

Rabbi Meir said: "Even as people have varying tastes regarding food and drink, so men are not all of one mind concerning women. A man who has so little confidence in his wife's virtue that he locks her up in the house as soon as he leaves is like one who breaks a cup simply because he finds a fly in the water that the cup contains. A man who trusts his wife and knows that she would never deliberately deceive him even when he is away may be compared to one who, finding a fly in his drink, pours out the fly but keeps the cup. But he who does not care even when he sees his wife misbehave before his very eyes is like one who is not repelled by the fly he finds in his cup, but actually devours it with great relish."

"It is a man's duty to divorce his wife if she is wicked."

On the other hand: "If a man puts aside the wife of his youth, even the altar at the Temple sheds bitter tears."

Rabbi Johanan said: "He who loses his first wife in death is as one who has witnessed the destruction of the Temple in his own day."

Rabbi Alexander said: "All the world grows dark before the eyes of him whose first wife has died."

Rabbi Samuel, the son of Nachman, said: "All things, once lost, can be replaced, save for the wife of one's youth."

Rabbi Judah said to his son Isaac: "A man finds true contentment only with the wife of his youth."

"He who hopes that his wife will die before him so that he may inherit her money will die himself and be survived by her."

❦ ETHICS OF CHILD-REARING

The sages of the Talmud have left to posterity a wealth of advice on child-rearing and on parent-child relationships, practical wisdom which is as valid at present as it was in the days of our ancestors.

First of all, the scholars emphatically stated that no person may deny himself the privilege of parenthood.

The Prophet Isaiah once told King Hezekiah that he, the king, was as good as dead in this world and would not even live on in the world to come because he had not begotten any children. In reply to the king's plea that he had been afraid of begetting bad children, Isaiah scolded him: "Why dost thou meddle in God's own concerns? It would have been thy duty simply to beget offspring and to leave the rest to Him."

"The world was created on the basis of procreation, so that he who does not beget offspring actually destroys the world order."

"The glory of God rests only upon that home where there are children."

Rabbi Joshua said, "He who married in his youth and had no children should wed again in later life and perhaps he will have offspring then. But as for him who had children in his youth, he is certain to have children in later life as well."

"It is good if one's first child is a daughter, because she will then help her parents in caring for the younger children."

It is written in the Book of Ben Sira: "A daughter is a constant source of concern to her father. When she is still a child, the father worries lest she be raped. As she grows older, he is afraid that she may get into trouble willingly. When she becomes a woman, he frets lest she will remain an old maid; and once she is safely married, her father fears that she may have no children."

"True, the world cannot exist without either men or women. And yet, happy are the parents who have sons and woe to those who have only daughters."

Here is a bit of ancient advice that seems rather quaint today:

"If a pregnant woman eats meat and drinks wine, she will have healthy children. If she eats eggs, her children will have large eyes. If she eats fish, the baby will be pleasant; if she eats vegetables, the child will be noble. If she consumes a lot of fat, her children will be fat themselves."

And then another statement that contains a bit of eternal truth:

"He who begets a child but does not care for him is not truly his father. A child's true father is the man who rears him."

"It is incumbent upon every father to provide for the sustenance of his offspring while they are young."

As for the training and discipline of the young, the sages of the Talmud said:

"Children must be trained, because most of them are wild by nature."

"Everything that was made during the six days of Creation is in need of being perfected. Man is no exception."

It is written in the Scriptures: "Train the boy in the way he should follow." In this connection, Rabbi Eliezer said: "If you have trained the boy to study the Law diligently, he will continue to study when he is grown." Rabbi Joshua said: "A cow that is not trained to work in the fields will be of no help when it is mature, and the twig must be bent early in the direction in which it is to grow. The same is true of the child."

"A father must devote himself to the training of his son until the boy reaches the age of thirteen. It is only then that he may thank God (at the Bar Mitzvah ceremony) for having relieved him of the direct responsibility for the actions of his son."

What is youth? Rabbi Judah said, the years from sixteen to twenty-two; Rabbi Nehemiah said, the years from eighteen to twenty-four.

"As soon as a child begins to speak, its father must teach him to study the Law. If he does not do so, it is as though he would bury the child alive (for the child will then grow up to be a useless ignoramus)."

The wise men enumerated the duties of a father toward his son as follows: "First he must circumcise him. As he grows older, the father should either study with him himself or else send him to a school. Later on, the father must see to it that his son learns a trade, and thereafter he must find him a wife." Others say that a father is duty-bound also to teach his sons how to swim.

Ben Azai said: "A father must study the Bible also with his daughters."

Rabbi Eliezer, on the other hand, did not have too high an opinion of the intelligence of the female sex and maintained that a father would only waste his time trying to teach the Bible to his daughters.

Rabbi Abahu said in the name of Rabbi Johanan: "A father may teach his daughter the Greek language, because it is an added accomplishment for her."

Rabbi Akiba said: "A son inherits his father's handsomeness, his strength, and his wisdom."

"A wise man's son is half of a wise man himself."

"Like mother, like daughter."

"The child will repeat in the street what he has heard his parents say at home."

The Talmud contains a variety of differing opinions on child discipline. The Bible itself has a law pertinent to the treatment of a "stubborn and rebellious son" but the sages had some difficulty in arriving at a universally accepted definition of the terms "stubborn" and "rebellious," and they had many differing theories on punishment and discipline.

The sages said, first of all, that a child should be trained in the correct manner so that there should be no need at all for punishment.

Rabbi Chasdai said: "A man must not force his household to live in fear and trembling of him, because no good could come of such a state of affairs."

The Talmud tells also of incidents where fathers, instead of punishing their children on the spot for some offense, left the threat of severe discipline hang over their heads. The children, unable to stand the fear, drowned themselves. Therefore, the sages advised that a father should not threaten his son that he would beat him some time in the future for his misbehavior. If he wished to chastise the boy, he should either do so at once, or else let the child go unpunished.

Rabbi Isaac said, "A father must be patient with his son (if he disobeys) until the boy is twelve years of age. After that, he must punish him severely for any misbehavior."

It is written in the Bible: "Thou shalt not put a stumbling block . . . before the blind man." This, the sages pointed out, was applicable also to a father who would beat his adult son.

"One must not treat one child differently from the rest."

"If a man bequeaths all his fortune to others and disinherits his own children, his testament cannot be changed, but the fact remains that he has done wrong." But Rabban Simon ben Gamaliel said that such action on the part of a father was justified if the children did not conduct themselves properly.

Samuel said to Rabbi Judah: "O wise man, thou shouldst have scant regard for those who would disinherit their children. Fathers should not even disinherit a bad son and give all their possessions to the good son, for the wicked son may yet present his father with good grandchildren. And it is certainly wrong to disinherit a son in favor of a daughter."

The scholars of the Talmud were anxious to make sure that children give parents the respect and honor justly due them. They compared the commandment to honor one's father and mother to the injunction to obey God Himself.

Rabbi Ulla said: "Why does the commandment 'Honor thy father and thy mother' precede the commandment 'Thou shalt not kill'? The answer is simple. The Bible meant to point out that he who would be in a position to support his parents and failed to do so should be regarded as if he had murdered them."

"A man has three parents; namely God, his father, and his mother. Therefore if a man honors his father and mother it is tantamount to honoring God Himself."

In the words of the sages: "to respect one's parents" means that the son should not sit in his father's seat, that he should not interrupt the words of his parents or voice stubborn opposition to their wishes. "To respect one's parents" means also that the son should provide his father and mother with food, drink, and clothing and with a home of their own.

If a person sees that his father has transgressed a law of the Torah, he must not tell him, "Father, you are sinning." Instead, he must remember his obligation to respect his father, and tell him without an overtone of reproach or ridicule, "Father, is there not a verse in the Bible in which it is written that we must (or must not) do such and such?"

Rabbi Ulla was asked to what lengths the duty of respecting one's parents should be carried. In reply, the Rabbi told the following story: One day the wise men went to a non-Jew in Ashkelon in order to purchase from him a precious stone for the breastplate of the High Priest. The owner of the stone, however, happened to be asleep when the sages came to his home and the keys to the chest where the stone was kept were beneath the head of the sleeping man. The son, who would have stood to earn sixty thousand shekels for the stone, decided to send the would-be purchasers away rather than disturb the sleep of his father.

Rabbi Dimi once sat among the great men of Rome. He was dressed in a costly robe of gold brocade. Suddenly his mother rushed into the hall, tore off the garment from him, beat him and spat in his face. But the son had been taught from earliest childhood to honor his mother, and so he made no move to fend the woman off.

Rabbi Eliezer said that a son must never resist his parents, not even if they should take a bag of his money and cast it into the water.

Once the mother of the great scholar Rabbi Ishmael complained to the sages that her son did not give her the respect properly due her. In response to the amazement of the learned men at her complaint, she explained that her famous son would not let her wash his feet when he returned from the house of study. The sages then called Ishmael and explained to him that even if others might think that a son should not permit his mother to perform so servile an act as washing his feet, a respectful son must not interfere if it is his mother's wish to care for him in this manner.

"If both father and mother should ask their son for a drink of water at the same time, the son must wait upon the father first, because the mother is obligated to honor and obey her husband."

This statement was attributed to Rab Chasdai, "If a father wishes to waive the respect properly due him, he may do so."

Many of these rules seem arbitrary and stern. But we shall find that the sages were no less strict when it came to formulate rules that man was to follow in his relationships with his fellow humans, particularly with his friends.

🌿 ETHICS OF FRIENDSHIP

Friendship has always occupied a position of great importance in Jewish ethics and the sages of the Talmud viewed sincerity, devotion, and loyalty as indispensable virtues in human relations.

Rabbi Eliezer said, "The honor of thy friend should be as precious to thee as thy own honor."

It is written in the Bible: "And thou shalt love thy neighbor as thyself." Rabbi Akiba said that this was the most important basic principle of the entire Torah. Ben Azai, on the other hand, felt that the basic tenet of the Bible was framed in the verse: "This is the book of man's creation—he was created in the image of God." Therefore, "Say not 'I shall insult my friend even as I was insulted' or 'I have failed, therefore let my friend fail also,'" since, as Rabbi Tanchuma put it, "If thou wilt act thusly, thou shouldst remember whom it is that thou dost insult, because every man was created in the image of God."

Scholars such as Rabbi Johanan and Rabbah showed the courtesy and respect due to old age, even to old heathens.

Ben Azai said: "Do not put any man to shame, and do not say of anything that it is unnecessary, for there is no such person of whom one may not need a favor one day, and there is no such thing on earth that does not have a place in this world."

The sages taught: "A man should be as pliant as a reed by the water and not as hard as a nut."

The disciples of Rabbi Nechuniah ben Hakanah asked their teacher to tell them the reason for his longevity. He replied: "I was never happy when my friend was insulted; I never gave a friend cause to curse me, nor have I been miserly in money matters when it came to helping a friend."

"He who puts his friend to shame will eventually be put to shame himself." An Aramaic proverb says: "If one spits upward, the spittle will fall down upon his own face."

Resh Lakish said: "A person who raises his hand against a friend is called a wicked man even if he does not actually strike him."

"A man should have friends as loyal as the friends of Job, or else he is better off dead."

What is the best thing a man can find in life? Rabbi Joshua said, "A good friend," Rabbi Jose said, "A good neighbor." And what are the evil things that a man should avoid? Rabbi Joshua said, "A bad friend," and Rabbi Jose said, "A bad neighbor."

The sages said: "Avoid ugliness and even such things as border upon ugliness. In fact, one should avoid even what is remotely reminiscent of things bordering upon ugliness."

Abbaye said: "If a wicked man is badly off, his neighbor is badly off also. But when the righteous man prospers, his neighbor prospers as well."

"A man must know with whom he sits, with whom he stands, with whom he breaks bread, with whom he is speaking, and particularly he must know the person in whose favor he draws up a bill."

We have been told: "A man should not bring too many friends into his home, because such excessive hospitality cannot be good."

"He who attaches himself to men of ill conduct will suffer even as the latter do, though he himself may not actually have followed their evil example."

"To each his own—good to the good and evil to the wicked."

Rabbi Mattiah ben Heresh said: "Greet everyone whom thou wilt meet when thou comest out from thy home."

"A man should not visit his friend without having told him in advance of his coming."

"One must not even enter one's own home unexpectedly, lest he startle the members of his own household."

Rav said: "Do not drive into a city unexpectedly or enter a house without warning."

Shammai said: "Greet everyone with a smile."

"There are three things which will endear a man to his friends; namely, a generous hand, a table that is ready at all times, and good cheer."

"A man should not praise his friend's virtues too highly, because in this manner he might come to reveal his own shortcomings."

"If someone does you a favor, do not spread the word around, for then everyone else will also ask him for favors and he will stand to lose thereby."

Rabbi Jeremiah ben Eleazar said: "It is proper to praise a man to his face, but do not extol all of his virtues until after he has left."

Rabbi Abahu said: "If you speak well of your friend, tell also the source of the good report. But if you must speak ill of him, merely say that 'this is what people have said.'"

Rabbi Simon ben Eleazar said: "Do not attempt to ask a friend's forgiveness while he is still in anger, do not try to comfort him while grief is still heavy in his house, and do not attempt to watch him while he does a foolish thing."

"Do not be wicked if you can be good."

"If a person can have pleasure from something belonging to another without the other losing anything by giving it to him, and the other should nevertheless refuse to lend it to him, that other is no better than an inhabitant of the wicked city of Sodom and can be forced to act more generously."

"If you receive a person as your guest in your house, you are obliged to guard his honor even more zealously than you would that of your parents."

"Do not cast stones into the well from which you have once drunk water. In the same manner, never speak ill of him who once did you a favor."

The Bible says: "He who repays good with evil shall never have evil leave his own home." Rabbi Simon ben Abba said that the same applied even to those who merely rewarded evil with evil.

It is written in the Bible that the three angels who were Abraham's guests asked their host: "Where is Sarah, thy wife?" From this the sages infer that a courteous guest always inquires after the well-being of the wife of his host.

It was said in the name of Rav: "Do not give a gift to anyone without letting him know in advance."

Rabbi Simon the son of Rabbi Gamaliel said: "If you give a piece of bread to a child, you must tell it to his mother."

"He who has made his friend angry must ask his forgiveness."

"God will forgive man those sins which man has committed against God, but He will not pardon the wrong which man may do his neighbor, until the sinner will have obtained the forgiveness of the injured party."

"He who prays to God in behalf of his friend and does not pray for himself, though he, too, needs help, will be helped even before his friend receives Divine aid."

With regard to those who would deceive or fool their friends, the sages say:

"There are seven kinds of thieves; the first of those is the one who would steal his friend's mind" (one who would fool his friend).

Samuel said: "One must not fool even a stranger."

"One must not even pretend the desire to purchase merchandise if one actually has no intention to buy at all."

"One must never tell a sinner who has repented and mended his ways: 'Remember the wrong thou didst do in the past.'"

"One must not remind the convert of the fact that he had once been a heathen."

"If one sees a person who suffers, one must not tell him that his sufferings are punishment for his sins."

"To deceive a man with words is an even greater sin than to defraud him in business."

Rabbi Meir said: "A man should not invite someone to his home for a meal without wanting him to accept the invitation, nor must he give a gift to him who he knows would refuse a present, because that would be verbal deceit."

Rabbi Chasdai said: "Towards the end of the Day of Atonement, all the gates of heaven are closed, but that gate which receives the prayers of those who beg to be forgiven for deceit and fraud remains open longer than the rest."

Rabbi Eleazar said: "God sends a messenger to punish men for all their sins, except for the sin of fraud and deceit, for which He Himself will exact retribution without an intermediary."

Rabbi Abahu said: "There are three prayers that God is ready to answer at all times: namely, the prayer of one who has been deceived; that of one who has been robbed; and that of one who is being forced to bow to idols."

However, the sages concede that while one should not deceive a person or lie to him, one may "sugar-coat" the truth for the sake of peace, for Hillel said: "Be like the disciples of Aaron. Take delight in peace and endeavor to make peace among others. . . ."

The best example of this "endeavor to make peace" was demonstrated by Hillel's own disciples. Though engaged in constant intellectual warfare with the School of Shammai on basic questions of Jewish Law, the adherents of Hillel maintained most cordial personal relationships with their opponents throughout.

❦ VIRTUE AND VICE

Of great significance are the teachings concerning virtue and vice which the Talmudic scholars have left as a legacy for posterity. Talmudic literature contains a wealth of wise sayings on truth versus falsehood, hypocrisy, gossip, jealousy, arrogance, falseness, and levity.

We shall attempt to present here only a few of these aphorisms so that we may get some idea of the views of the sages with regard to virtue and vice in man.

"We have learned that the sin of causeless hatred leads to discord in the home."

"A home in which there is discord will gradually destroy itself."

"Nothing good has ever come of discord."

Hillel said: "Do not condemn thy friend until thou thyself hast been in his situation."

Joshua ben Perachyah said: "When judging others, give them the benefit of the doubt." (Or, as we might say it today, "Innocent until proved guilty.")

Rabbi Eleazar said: "He who accused a friend of sin without just cause must ask his forgiveness."

Resh Lakish said: "He who accuses an innocent man of a crime will be punished for his false accusation."

"Love him who punishes thee, and hate those who praise thee."

"Purify thyself before attempting to cleanse others."

Rabbi Nathan said: "Do not criticize in others a fault which thou thyself hast."

Abbaye said: "If thou shouldst see a scholar who is well-liked in his city, know that the people love him not because of his great knowledge but because he does not punish them for their wrongdoing and lets them do as they please."

Rabbi Eli quoted Rabbi Eleazar, the son of Rabbi Simon, as having said: "It is a good thing to utter words to which men hearken, but it is even more important not to address them to those who will not hear."

King Yanai said to his wife: "Fear not the Pharisees, nor their opponents, but only those false men who pretend to be pious even though they actually are rascals."

Rabban Gamaliel declared, "A student who is not what he pretends to be must not be permitted to enter the house of study."

Ben Azai said: "It is an easier thing to rule over the entire world than it is to change those men who are wicked but wrap themselves in a cloak of piety."

"When a swine lies down upon the ground, he will stretch out his legs to show that he has a cloven hoof," thus deliberately, as it were, deceiving the passer-by, for in order to be fit for consumption by Jews, a beast must not only have a cloven hoof but must also be a ruminant.

Rabbi Chanina said: "If ill befalls a man, it came to him because he indulged in vicious gossip."

Rabbi Judah quoted Rav as having said: "Had King David not listened to vicious gossip, his kingdom would never have been destroyed; had the children of Israel not bowed down to idols, they would never have been driven out of their land."

In answer to a query by one of the Exilarchs as to whether he should denounce to the government certain people who did him deliberate harm, Rabbi Eleazar stated, "It is written in the Bible: 'I shall put a guard over my mouth when the evil man is against me'; this means that one should be silent even if the enemy should actually stand face-to-face with him." When the Exilarch replied that he could no longer tolerate the excesses of his enemies, the scholar answered: "It is also written in the Bible, 'Be silent before the Lord and put thy trust in Him.' Therefore do not attempt to have thy foes punished by denouncing them to the authorities. Their punishment will come of itself." And it happened that Rabbi Eleazar's prediction actually came true.

Rabbi Eleazar, the son of Rabbi Simon, held a municipal office which carried with it the duty of ferreting out thieves. Rabbi Joshua ben Karchah wrote to him: "O thou vinegar begotten of wine" (a derisive epithet for the unworthy son of a great father), "why dost thou deliver Jews, children of the people of God, into the hands of death?" (for in those days theft was subject to the death penalty). Rabbi Eleazar replied, "All I do is weed out the thorns from the garden." But Rabbi Joshua retorted: "Let the owner of the garden (i.e., God) attend to the weeding Himself."

Rabbi Jose said: "I have never said one thing and then done the opposite."

"The liar's punishment is that men will eventually cease to believe his words even if, perchance, he should be telling the truth."

"Examine thy speech carefully before it goes forth from thy mouth."

"Teach thyself the art of saying 'I do not know' lest thou shouldst come to make an untrue statement."

Rabbi Seira said, "One should not tell a child, 'I will give thee bread' and then not keep his promise, for in this manner he teaches the child to utter falsehoods."

"True words are easily recognized."

"It is written in the Bible, '. . . and he who speaks the truth in his heart.' How can this best be illustrated? Rabbi Safra had some merchandise to sell. A customer came to him just as he was saying his prayers. The customer offered to buy the merchandise and to pay the rabbi the amount he had requested. Safra did not answer because he would not interrupt his prayers. The customer, however, interpreted Safra's silence as meaning that he wanted more money than he had offered and therefore said that he would be willing to pay a larger sum. Still the rabbi did not react. When he had finished his prayers, he turned to the customer and sold him the merchandise for the amount that had been originally stipulated. He told the amazed buyer, 'I cannot take more money from thee than I had originally wanted, for when thou didst name the first amount, I was ready in my heart to sell thee the merchandise for that sum as soon as I would have finished my prayers.' "

"Twice 'yes' or twice 'no' is tantamount to a vow."

"A decent person will not utter a vow even concerning things that are true."

The disciples of Rabbi Ishmael taught: "Man must always speak in a decent fashion."

Rabbi Joshua ben Levi said: "A man must never allow a filthy word to escape his lips."

Rabbi Chanina bar Rabba said: "All men know what a couple do on their wedding night, but he who would cheapen it by obscene jokes will forfeit whatever good may have been decreed for him."

"The sages of the Jewish people always were refined of speech."

Rabbi Eliezer said, "Thou shalt not be quick to anger."

"There are four kinds of tempers: he whom it is easy to provoke but easy to pacify, his loss disappears in his gain; he whom it is hard to provoke but also hard to pacify, his gain disappears in his loss; he whom it is hard to provoke and easy to pacify is a saint; he whom it is easy to provoke and hard to pacify is a wicked man."

Resh Lakish said: "Even a wise man loses all his wisdom at the moment of his anger."

"Angry men make mistakes."

"Man should not be as humble as was Hillel, but also not as quick to anger as Shammai."

Rabbi Akiba said: "He who, in anger, casts bread or money to the ground, will have to depend on the charity of others before he departs this life."

Bar Kappara said: "An angry man has nothing but his anger" (meaning that he will achieve nothing by his violent temper).

"Our wise men have taught as follows: 'There are three kinds of people of whom it can be said that they never truly enjoyed life: those who constantly pity others; those who perpetually bewail the injustice that has been done them; and those who are too critical of food.'"

"In three situations can a man's true character come to light: when he is drunk, when he must part with money, and when he is angry."

"Happy is he who can hear and remain silent, for he saves himself much trouble thereby."

Rabbi Meir said: "O man, be humble before all other men."

The sages taught: "Man was created only on the sixth day, so that, in case he should become overly proud, he can be reminded that he has no reason for arrogance since even the humble worm was created before him."

"The brier from the midst of which God spoke to Moses was chosen only because a brier is the lowliest of all plants."

Rabbi Akiba quoted Rabbi Simon ben Azai as having said: "Sit two or three seats below the place where thou shouldst be seated, for it is better that thou shouldst be invited to take a choicer seat than that thou shouldst be told to take a humbler place."

"A pitcher rattles even if it contains only one single coin."

On the other hand: "There where they know thee not, thou canst say who thou art."

And: "While some say it is better to be the head of a fox than to be the tail of a lion, Rabbi Matthis ben Heresh said that it is better to be the tail of a lion than the head of a fox."

Rabba said: "A learned man may make himself known and ask for all the privileges usually accorded scholars."

The sages of the Talmud attached so much importance to the teaching of ethics that they devoted to it a special section which is known as the "Ethics of the Fathers" and which is recited by Jews every Saturday afternoon during the summer months. There is also in the Talmudic collection another tractate known as the "Aboth de Rabbi Nathan," maxims on ethics collected by Rabbi Nathan of which we have cited some.

❧ HOW TO UNDERSTAND MEN, WOMEN, AND CHILDREN

As we have just seen, the sages whose names figure in Talmudic literature were anxious to raise the moral and ethical standards of all men, and particularly those of their own people. But in addition to being men of both virtue and erudition, they also had a profound insight into the psychology of their fellow humans. They presented their views in the form of aphorisms which they sketched briefly, but in a clear-cut way, expressing the intellectual and emotional profile of men and women as they saw it.

We might begin our study of their sayings in this connection with a survey of the views held by them concerning women.

We are told: "It is written in the Bible that the Lord chose to create Eve, the first woman, from the rib of Adam. It was like this: The Lord had reasoned, 'If I should create her from the head of man, she will be too proud; if I should make her from Adam's eye, she will be plagued by curiosity; if I should form her from his ear, she will want to hear too much; if I should shape her from his mouth, she will be a chatterbox. Nor can I make her from his heart, because she may then bear a grudge in her heart against all others, nor from his hand, lest she touch everything, nor from his foot, lest she walk about in an unseemly manner.' The Lord therefore at last decided to create her from Adam's rib, a part that is usually hidden by garments, so that she might be modest, virtuous, and good." Many of the Talmudic scholars talked about the virtues of women so they agreed that women were endowed especially with the virtue of compassion.

Yet many of the sages do not seem to have too high an opinion of the weaker sex. For example:

One rabbi said: "Women have four faults. They eat overly much, they are overly curious, they are too lazy to work, and they are prone to excessive jealousy." Rabbi Judah ben Rabbi Nehemiah said, "They are quick tempered, quick to anger and they talk too much." Rabbi Levi went so far as to say that "women number in their ranks many thieves and prostitutes."

Other sayings:

"Why is it that man can be pacified much more easily than woman? It is because man was made from the dust of the earth which is soft and pliant, while woman was made from one of man's bones which is tough and inflexible."

"The world was allotted ten measures of speech, of which the woman took nine, thus leaving only one to the rest of the world."

"Women want to know everything."

"We have just cause to suspect a woman of uncovering her neighbor's pot just to see what she is cooking that day."

"Women are frivolous."

"Woman's mind is not clear and hence one cannot rely on what she says."

"A woman would rather have an elegant home and beautiful clothes than eat fatted calves."

Rabbi Joshua said: "A woman would rather have little food and much extravagance than to eat much but live modestly."

"What are the ornaments of woman? The color with which she paints her face, the lotion with which she colors her eyelids, and her hair-do."

Rabbi Chiya taught: "A woman exists only for beauty and for bearing children."

"Woman wants to wed man much more than man wants to marry woman."

Rabbi Samuel bar Uliyah said in behalf of Rav: "A woman is a piece of property which belongs to him who employs it for creating something new of it." (In other words, woman belongs to the man who lives with her.)

Of man in general, we are told:

"Poverty makes a man be that which he does not want to be."

"Poverty is tantamount to death, for a poor man has no opinions of his own."

"All parts of man's body are dependent upon his heart, but the heart in turn is dependent upon his purse" (that is, the amount of money he has to provide for his needs).

"There are three lacks that are hard to bear: insufficiency of the heart, from which the whole body must suffer, inadequacy of the digestive system, which is worse, but the worst deficiency of all is lack of money."

But wealth is also not an unmixed blessing.

"Lack of money can lead man to do evil, but man is even more likely to go astray through the temptation offered by great wealth."

"A little wealth is a good thing, but too much of it is dangerous."

The disciples of Rabbi Yanai said: "A dish of straw cannot make a lion roar, but a dish of meat can." (He becomes dangerous only if he overeats.)

Rabbi Sheshet said: "A full stomach is the beginning of all evil."

Rabba said: "The length of one's life, the way in which one's children turn out, and prosperity in worldly goods are purely a matter of luck. Take the example of the teachers Rabbah and Rav Chasdai. Both these men were righteous. But Rav Chasdai lived to be ninety-two, while Rabbah died when he was forty. Rav Chasdai could always celebrate weddings at his home, while Rabbah always had dead to mourn. Rav Chasdai had so much fine flour that his household was surfeited and threw it to the dogs, while Rabbah did not even have barley bread." Thus it was concluded that all this was a matter of sheer luck.

"No man ever attains all he wants before he dies, for he who has a hundred pieces of gold wants two hundred and once he has two hundred he yearns for four hundred."

"God was asked why He created jealousy and envy. The Lord replied that, but for these two vices, the world would long since have ceased to exist. For a man marries only because his friend has just wed too, and he wants to show him that he was able to win the heart of a maiden more beautiful than his friend's bride. When he sees that his friend has built a house, he, too, builds a home of his own because he wants to prove that he can make a better home than his friend, and thus every other human achievement is motivated by nothing else but jealousy."

Rabbi Levi, another Amora, saw the world from another vantage point. He said: "Six organs are at the service of man; three of these are under his control, while the other three are not. He has no control over his eyes, his ears and his nose, for he may be forced to see that which he does not care to see; to hear what he would not want to hear; and to smell what he would not wish to smell. But he does have full mastery over his mouth, his hands, and his feet, for he can say what he wants to say; he can touch whatever he wishes to touch; and go wherever it may please him to go. It is a good thing if one employs these organs to do good, but it is sad indeed when one makes them serve evil purposes."

"A man's true character can be recognized from his business dealings, from his behavior when under the influence of drink and from the way in which he speaks."

"There are four kinds of men whom we call 'wicked': he who raises his hand to strike another; he who borrows money and does not pay it back; he who is too impudent; and he who constantly quarrels with others."

"There are four kinds of men who are unbearable: a poor man who is arrogant; a rich man who should be honest but tells lies instead; an old man who runs after women; and an official in a charitable organization who publicly boasts of the fact that his services are purely voluntary."

Rabbi Johanan said: "Even if we had never received the Law, we could have learned the virtue of modesty from the cat (which always hides its excrements); we could have learned to refrain from stealing through the example of the ant (for every ant enjoys the fruit of its own labors only and does not seek to take that of its brother creatures). We could have learned faithfulness in marriage from the dove (which permanently cleaves to its mate); and as for winning a lady's heart, we can learn much from the cock who preens himself before the hen of his choice before he takes her as his own."

The sages have also stated that there are certain situations in human life in which a person cannot be made responsible for what he says or does. Yet they also taught us that man must be able to accept trouble even as he accepts good things.

Rabbi Meir and Rabbi Akiba were both quoted as saying: "A man must acquire the habit of telling himself that whatever God does, he does for the best."

"God tries men. When they are rich, He tests them to see whether they will be generous to the poor, and when they are poor He tries them to see whether they will rebel against Him."

"There is no person who is entirely free from pain or illness. Therefore we must learn to live with our ailments and keep them to ourselves."

"A man should rather be one of the persecuted than one of the persecutors, for the Lord is always at the side of the oppressed."

24. Other Creations of the Talmudic Era

🌼 THE JERUSALEM TALMUD

While the Amoraim who lived in Babylonia developed their own interpretation of the Mishna, which eventually was written down in the giant legal encyclopedia known today as the Talmud, those Amoraim who still resided in Palestine had also not been idle. The Holy Land could boast of three academies, one in Tiberias, one in Sepphoris, and the third in Caesarea where every item of the Mishna was discussed with the same zeal and assiduity as it was in the schools in Babylonia. The commentaries of the Palestinian sages were eventually set down in a smaller code which we know today as the "Jerusalem Talmud," as distinguished from the larger work which is called "Talmud Bavli" or the "Babylonian Talmud."

The "Jerusalem Talmud" deals with only four of the six main divisions of the Mishna; namely Zeraim (agricultural laws), Moed (ceremonial laws pertaining to festivals), Nashim (laws applicable to women and marriage), and Nezikin (torts and damages). It contains commentaries to the first chapters of the Tractate of Niddah and to parts of the tractate dealing with Sabbath observance. There are some tractates, of course, which have no commentary at all, neither in the Babylonian nor in the Jerusalem Talmud. On the other hand, there are some parts of the Mishna which received far more detailed elaboration in the Jerusalem Talmud than in the Babylonian code. It is quite possible, too, that the Jerusalem Talmud actually was much more extensive than would appear to us today, and that some of the parts simply got lost in the course of the centuries. Even as the Jewish community of Babylonia produced Amoraim of the caliber of Rav Ashi and such, the remnants of the Jewish people in Palestine also could boast of great intellects, the men who compiled the Jerusalem Talmud. Most important among them was Rabbi Johanan.

The era of the Jerusalem Talmud, meaning the span of time during which the Palestinian Amoraim lived and worked, was brief compared to that of the Babylonian Talmud. Altogether it extended over only three generations, from about 219 to 359 A.D., a total of not more than a hundred and forty years. Since the Babylonian Talmud was completed much later than its Jerusalem counterpart, it is generally assumed that the scholars who compiled the former must have had a more extensive knowledge of the Law and its application, and as a consequence the rulings of the Babylonian Talmud are accepted as binding rather than those of the Jerusalem code. The Babylonian Talmud is much more profound and ingenious than the other. It also contains much more legend and homily.

The following were the principal Amoraim of Palestine:

First generation (219-279): Yanai the Elder, Johanan the Elder, Rabbi Hoshaya Rabbah, Levi bar Sisi, Rabbi Chanina bar Chamah, Hezekiah, Rabbi Johanan bar Napchah, Rabbi Simon ben Lakish, Rabbi Joshua ben Levi, and Rabbi Simlai.

Second generation (279-320): Rabbi Eleazar ben Pedath, Rabbi Ami and Rabbi Assi of Tiberias; Rabbi Chiyah bar Abba, Rabbi Simon bar Abba, Rabbi Abahu of Caesarea; and Rabbi Seira.

Third generation (320-359): Rabbi Jeremiah, Rabbi Johanan, Rabbi Jose ben Sabdah of Tiberias.

In contrast to the Babylonian Talmud, the Jerusalem Talmud does not devote much discussion to the exact meaning of certain Hebrew terms found in the Mishna, for it had been written in the country in which Hebrew was still spoken, whereas the Babylonian code originated in a Jewish community where Hebrew was gradually falling into disuse as an everyday language.

The Palestinian Amoraim were generally titled "Rabbi" (meaning "my teacher") while those in Babylonia styled themselves as "Rav" (teacher) or simply "Mar" (the equivalent of the English "Mr." or "Master").

Since the Jerusalem Talmud was not studied to so great an extent as its Babylonian counterpart, it is also not as filled with commentary as the former and therefore it is customarily printed in one or two volumes. The fact of the matter is that there never was a so-called "standard edition" of the Jerusalem Talmud with each page having its own definite length and form as has the Babylonian code.

This does not mean, however, that the Jerusalem Talmud is not considered a valuable part of Jewish sacred and legalistic literature. There are a few good commentaries on it; one of the best of such commentaries is by the noted Rabbi of Slutzk, the "Ridvaz," published only recently. All the scholars of the Gaonic era were well conversant with the Jerusalem Talmud and many later masters made it a practice to cite the rulings laid down in that work and to compare them to corresponding legislation in the Babylonian Talmud.

The Jerusalem Talmud gives quite an accurate reflection of the somber spirit which prevailed in Palestine at the time of its compilation. Whereas the Babylonian code contains flashes of wit and banter, the Jerusalem Talmud is written in a dead serious vein, devoid of all humor. Perhaps this is so because, while Babylonia was a flourishing Jewish community on which the pain of exile did not weigh very heavily, the Jewish remnant in Palestine was still very much under the impact of the ruin and destruction of its ancient homeland.

🤿 THE "SABORAIM" GROUP

The teachers and scholars who were the spiritual heirs of the compilers of the Talmud were known as "Saboraim" (a term denoting men capable of reasoning). It was the Saboraim who took on the task of completing the collection of the sayings of the Amoraim in the compilation of the Talmud.

The exact time span of the era of the Saboraim has never been determined. The Jews in those days suffered so much from oppression at the hands of the Persians that they had little time or energy left for the compiling of records that might have shed some light upon the activities of these scholars of the Law. One scholar known as "the Ravad" claimed that the era comprised five generations, extending through the period of some hundred and seventy years. This, however, would not seem entirely accurate, for we know that Rabbi Hanan of Iskivan, for example, whom the Ravad calls a member of the third generation of the Saboraim, is generally regarded as one of the first of the Gaonim whose era followed that of the Saboraim, so that it would seem to us that the scholars whom the Ravad classes as fourth and fifth generation of the Saboraim were actually Gaonim who belonged in the next era of Jewish history rather than to that of the Saboraim.

We would assume, therefore, that the era of the Saboraim hardly exceeded two generations. Accordingly, we would establish its beginning as having been in the year 500, shortly after the conclusion of the Talmud and after the death of Rabina, the last of the Amoraim, and that it came to an end about 560 A.D.

The main personalities of this era were Rav Jose of Pumbeditha; Rav Amma of Bei Chetim; Rav Sama the son of Rav Jodah; Rav Rabai; Rav Samuel ben Judah of Pumbeditha; Rav Rechumai; Rabbina of Umazia; Rav Acha the son of Abu; Rav Tachna; Rav Sutra; Rav Simona of Pumbeditha; Rav Gira in Sura; Rav Ahadibui the son of Katinah and, finally, Rav Sutra, the son of Rav Chanah, who was the last of the Saboraim group.

As we have indicated before, the main work of the Saboraim consisted of the elucidation of the Talmud and its final editing so as to make it clearer to the reader. This involved the addition of certain new notes and the elimination of others. The student can find traces of their editorial work wherever he sees in the Talmud a notation such as "and the law in this case is . . ." or "he asked him all these questions and then studied with him" (an explanation of the reason a law is interpreted in that particular manner). The Talmud as set down by the Amoraim was a record of the debates concerning points of Law and often did not plainly indicate the exact nature of the final decision that was to be binding upon future generations. The Saboraim remedied this deficiency by adding at times specific notations to point out the explicit decisions arrived at as a result of the deliberations of the Amoraim.

❦ THE GAONIM

The period immediately following the era of the Saboraim and extending down to the year 1000 is called the "Era of the Gaonim" or "The Gaonic Period" after the heads of the great academies which then played a dominant role in Jewish life in Babylonia.

As we already know, the Jewish community in Babylonia in those days enjoyed a certain amount of autonomy. Its supreme civil authority was vested in a Jewish Exilarch who had quasi-viceregal powers. Its spiritual affairs, however, were subject to the jurisdiction of the presidents of the Talmudic academies who were known as the "Gaonim," a title which might be translated by the term "Eminences."

This era of Jewish history lasted about four hundred and fifty years. The first of the Gaonim was the Gaon Hanan of Ishkivan, who was at the head of the Academy of Pumbeditha; the last was Rav Hai, one of Hanan's successors at Pumbeditha, who died in the year 1038. During that time in the Academy of Pumbeditha there was a total of forty-eight Gaonim. There were also Gaonim in the Academy of Sura (only thirty-six) and three in the Academy of Nehardea.

The Gaonim sought to propagate the study of the Law by creating a number of smaller yeshivas or "academies" in towns and villages throughout Babylonia and facilitated the practical application of this legislation by arranging the laws of the Talmud in a definite order more readily accessible for reference purposes. The Gaonic era brought forth important legal works such as the book "Halochoth Gedoloth" (which is of uncertain authorship, ascribed by some to Rav Simon Caro and by others to Rav Yehudai Gaon); "The Questions of Rav Ahai Gaon" and many others. Another great masterpiece of the period was the wealth of "Questions and Answers" in which the Gaonim attempted to give authoritative answers to questions on the interpretation of the Law. We can readily see, then, that the era of the Gaonim was one of the most important in the history of the Jewish people.

❦ THE SECTS AGAINST THE TALMUD

During the time of the Saboraim and then later during the era of the Gaonim, there arose certain sects in Babylonia who revolted against the Talmud. According to a historical work by Jacob Karkasani (in Arabic) dealing with that period in Jewish history, there were about seventy such sects during a span of two centuries. We shall attempt to give here a brief description of several of these movements and their founders as listed by Karkasani.

The first of these were the Isaists, named after their founder, Abu Isa Obadiah of Ispahan. We are told that this man, though he was a simple tailor and could not even read or write properly, somehow managed to publish quite a number of books and was viewed by his adherents with veneration bordering upon actual worship. He declared that he was the Messiah sent by God to redeem the Jewish people from exile and actually rallied round him an army of ten thousand men to fight against the Arabs. Unfortunately he and his soldiers were eventually done to death by the wild Arab tribes against whom they attempted to go to war. Abu Isa was the first to voice open opposition to the rabbis and to give his followers new decrees which were in contradiction to the spirit of the laws of the Talmud.

Another such sect was founded by one Yodgan whom some believe to have been a disciple of Abu Isa. Like Abu Isa, Yodgan, too, claimed that he was a prophet and the Messiah. He forbade the consumption of meat or wine and stated that Jews were under no obligation to observe the Sabbath or other holidays while they were in exile. He also frankly declared his opposition to certain laws in the Talmud.

After him came one Mushchah who, like Abu Isa, also claimed to be a Messiah and assembled a band of warriors to fight against the Arabs. Some contemporary historians claim that he and his army also met with the same fate as did Abu Isa.

Not long thereafter a man named Shadgan rallied round his person a sect of his own with much the same views as those already mentioned. It is told of Shadgan that he commanded one of his adherents who had sinned to atone for his transgression by fasting for forty days, for he interpreted the Biblical punishment stipulating forty stripes for sinners as referring not to physical chastisement but to abstention from food.

Then there were the Achborites named after Ishmael the Achborite of whom it is said that he was well conversant with the Law and actually dared make changes in the Torah. He, too, was opposed to much of Talmudic legislation.

Then the Belbakites, named after their founder, Mashoi of Belbaki, had similar objections to the Talmud.

But the most important of all these rebel sects was the Karaite movement which was the largest of all and which has survived to this very day in certain parts of the world.

🌸 THE KARAITES

The Karaite movement began as a group which endeavored to eliminate from Judaism certain superstitions which had crept into it from the ancient Persian religion.

In the year 750 Mohammed first began to broadcast his new teaching of Islam. He and his followers zealously sought to eradicate every vestige of the old Persian cult, particularly the superstitions that had grown up among its adherents through the centuries. It may well have been that this "reformation" was the factor which lent impetus to liberal elements within the Jewish people to endeavor to cleanse their own religion of all foreign accretions. The leader of this new movement within Judaism was one Rav Anan ben David, who later was to engage in bitter intellectual warfare with the rabbis and to found the Ananite sect which captured more adherents than any other revolutionary group within the Jewish faith. This group was later united with the Karaites who were already in existence. The followers of Anan did not stop at the extirpation of foreign elements from Judaism; they gradually came to make changes in Jewish law and published many scholarly works contrary to the spirit of Talmud. This brought upon them the wrath of the Gaonim, particularly Rav Saadia Gaon, who waged a bitter fight against them.

Karaite literature, however, did not deal only with law, but also included poetry, Hebrew grammar, and new commentaries on the original text of the Bible. Indeed, the interest of this new sect in the Bible was so great that it took its name from that sacred source. (The term "Karaite" is derived from the Hebrew "Kriah" or "Mikrah" which refers to the five books of Moses.) There were periods when the influence of the Karaites was so great that a considerable number of Jewish communities sided with them.

After the tenth century, when the Jews emigrated from Babylonia en masse to the countries of Eastern and Western Europe, however, the Jews who regarded the Talmud as binding broke all relations with the Karaites. Eventually the latter became a heretic splinter group which had little in common with the main stream of Jewish tradition such as developed among the rest of the Jewish people.

The rabbis promulgated stern decrees against the Karaites, and in the end no adherent of rabbinic tradition was permitted to marry a Karaite or to become related to one by marriage. Thus the Karaites who were by then dispersed throughout the world in small groups had no other choice but to marry one another and thus eventually their number decreased greatly. Others, particularly those in Egypt, finally gave up the struggle against the dominant element within Judaism and once again submitted to the authority of the rabbis.

Today there are about three to four thousand Karaites in the entire world, many of them living in the new State of Israel where they are making an effort to reconstitute their ties with the main trunk of the tree of Judaism.

❧ THE MASORAH

The Bible is accompanied by extensive supplementary notes called "The Masorah" ("tradition") which indicates the manner in which the text of the Pentateuch, the Prophets, and the rest of the Holy Scriptures should be read and written "in accordance with tradition."

First, there are instructions for nearly every page of the Biblical text showing the proper way in which certain words should be read. Then there is a system of musical notes which indicate the manner in which the portions of the Bible should be chanted when read aloud in public. There is a certain traditional "trope" (system of notes) for every book of the Bible which must be used by the cantor or worshiper who reads it to the congregation as part of the synagogue service.

The "instructions" governing the proper reading and copying of the Biblical text include ten major points, as follows:

1. A listing of every letter and word of the entire Bible.

2. The vowels which appear in the form of lines or dots beneath the consonants and which determine the pronunciation of words.

3. The "crowns," ornaments, and which letters in the text are to be adorned by them.

4. Instructions on how to read certain words and how to interpret them.

5. Instructions regarding the pronunciation of words whose spelling is at variance with the manner in which they should be pronounced when read aloud.

6. How to pronounce the Name of God.

7. The division of the text into "verses" and "weekly portions."

8. Instructions as to the interpretations of certain words occurring in the middle of a verse in the original text, that is, whether the word is part of the phrase preceding it, or rather part of the thought expressed in the second half of the verse.

9. Inequalities in the size of the letters to be considered in the writing of the text.

10. The "final consonants." In the Hebrew language, certain consonants have two forms; one when they occur at the beginning or in the middle of a word, and quite another if they come at the end of a word.

The Talmud (Nedarim 33) states that these Masoretic instructions had their origin at the time of the Revelation on Mount Sinai. According to this view, Moses actually bequeathed to his people two editions of the five books that bear his name; one without any instruction, which is the one from which ordinary scrolls of the Law are copied, and one with all the detailed explanations necessary for its proper understanding, which was turned over only to certain chosen scholars and teachers who handed it down to their spiritual heirs.

Another school of thought attributes the origin of the Masorah to Ezra the Scribe and to the Great Synod. Some say that Ezra had merely brought back the system which had originally been communicated to the chosen few by Moses, but had gradually been forgotten. Others give Ezra and the Synod full credit for devising it.

A third opinion holds that the Masorah was created only after the conclusion of the Talmud and that it was completed only during the days of the Gaonim. The adherents of this view maintain that this endeavor was the achievement of grammarians who lived in Babylonia and Palestine during the ninth and tenth centuries.

The fact of the matter is that the Masorah as we know it today was indeed given its final form during the Gaonic era.

With regard to the traditional "trope," it would seem that at least the system of musical notations, if not the chant itself, originated in the Jewish community of Babylonia, for most of the notes have Aramaic names. There are certain variations in the trope with the "Ashkenazic" congregations (those following the Eastern or Western European Jewish ritual) differing in this respect from the "Sephardic" communities (which follow the ritual of the Spanish-Portuguese Jews).

Another opinion claims that the trope is very old indeed; that the original notes were all in Hebrew and were supplanted by Babylonian designations only at a later date. Those who would agree with this view cite in their support the notes that still have Hebrew names even to this day.

At any rate, the notes which indicate the trope to be followed in the public reading of the Biblical text are the oldest form of musical notation. This art of reading the Bible with a chant that should not only be appealing to the ear but also in accordance with the meaning of the text is called "cantillation" today and is an extensive field of study in itself.

❧ THE JEWISH PRAYER BOOK

The traditional Jewish prayer book is a collection of prayers to be recited daily and on various special occasions. The most important of these are the Morning Service (known in Hebrew as "Tefillath Shacharith"), the Afternoon Service ("Tefillath Minchah") and the Evening Service ("Tefillath Maariv"). Most of the major prayers are those of ancient origin, dating back to the Mishnaic Era. Others, such as the blessings to be recited before partaking of food and drink (all of them begin with the words "Blessed art Thou, O Lord . . .") originated at the time of the Amoraim.

The earliest known Jewish prayer book was compiled by Saadia Gaon who lived from the end of the ninth century to the middle of the tenth. Saadia gave the name of "Siddur" (from the Hebrew "seder" meaning "order") to what he called his "order of prayers." Later there came to be other prayer books, with some variations in order and text, depending upon the ritual followed in the locality in which they were published.

Perhaps the oldest of all the prayers is the classic "Hear, O Israel" and the "Prayer of Eighteen Blessings." The custom of praying three times daily was first introduced during the lifetime of Ezra the Scribe to take the place of the offerings which could no longer be brought after the destruction of the Temple. At that time, too, it was ordained that the prayers, when recited at the synagogue, should be said aloud by one man chosen for this function by the congregation. Eventually this purely honorary office gave rise to the profession of "cantor" as we know it today.

At first public prayer meetings were not held regularly, but eventually they came to take place each day. Chapters from the Book of Psalms were added to the ordinary daily services, as were certain portions of the Mishna dealing with the ritual of sacrifice to recall the ceremony which now could no longer be performed. At that time, too, we find that the "Talith" (fringed "prayer-shawl") was first worn by men in the synagogue to comply with the commandment given in the Book of Numbers concerning the fringes to be attached by all male members of the House of Israel to the corners of their garments to remind them of the Law of the Lord when they are tempted to go astray. The Hebrew name for these fringes is "Tzitzith."

The custom of putting on phylacteries each weekday morning also originated at about that time. These capsules containing portions of the Law, which Jewish men don each morning, one on the forehead and one on the arm, had been in use long before then, but no specific time had been set for the performance of this act. In fact, during the twelfth century the practice had fallen into disuse in many Jewish communities to such an extent that scholars were no longer quite sure as to the exact manner in which the parchment pieces on which the pertinent parts of the Law were written should be inserted into the capsules. There was a heated controversy on the subject between the famous scholar Rashi who wrote the classic Hebrew commentary on the Pentateuch, and his grandson Rabbenu Jacob Tam. The opinion of Rashi prevailed so that it became the accepted practice followed by all Jews. A few men of special piety, however, employ two sets of phylacteries even today, one adjusted as recommended by Rashi, and the other in accordance with the view of Rabbenu Tam.

❦ THE HOLIDAY PRAYERS—LITURGICAL POETRY

A large part of the special prayers recited on holidays such as the New Year, the Day of Atonement, Passover, Pentecost, and the Feast of Tabernacles is taken up by liturgical poetry.

The oldest of these, known as "yotzroth" or "piyutim" in Hebrew, came into being at about the end of the eighth century. These early works were written in blank verse and the names of their authors are not given.

The first known writer of such religious poetry was Jose ben Jose who is also called "the Orphan," and whose name is mentioned in the works of Chia and Saadia Gaon. It appears that he lived some time during the ninth century. Leopold Zunz, the famous Jewish scholar, believes that Jose came from either Palestine or Syria. At any rate, Jose ben Jose was the author of some of the best known and most beautiful poetry that is part of the service for the Day of Atonement; one of these is written in the form of an acrostic employing the letters of the Hebrew alphabet in succession twice over as the initial letter of each verse.

Another such poet was Rabbi Eliezer Ha-Kalir. His father, Jacob, seems to have come from the old Palestinian town called Kiryat Sefer. Some scholars, however, hold that he came from the city of Cagliari in Italy, while others maintain that the land of his origin was Mesopotamia. It is believed that he lived some time during the ninth century because his name is mentioned in the works of the later Gaonim. Eliezer was the author of some 165 liturgical poems for the various major holidays, for Purim, the Fast of the Ninth of Ab, and other occasions. They are recited in nearly every Jewish community, though some of them have been shortened by the various congregations because they seemed overly long.

Among the writers of liturgical poetry are numbered men like Saadia Gaon, who wrote piyutim that are still part of the Pentecost service today; the famous poet Abraham ibn Ezra of Spain who was responsible for a hundred and fifty such poems; Rabbi Moses ibn Ezra, author of two hundred such poems and Rabbenu Bachya, Maimonides, Nachmanides, Solomon ibn Gabirol, and particularly Rabbi Judah Ha-Levi who created a total of three hundred such prayers. Zunz believes that the number of "paytanim" (or "liturgical poets") was about fifteen hundred and mentions the names of some five hundred, most of them from Spain and Portugal. Many of these writers had published whole books of poetry of which only part have been accepted into the Jewish prayer book.

Not all of the piyutim are recited by every Jewish congregation today. There has been considerable freedom of choice so that, while some of the most important poems are part of the service of almost every traditional synagogue in the world, others are said only in certain communities, with each community selecting those it considers most suitable for its service. The Chassidic group has little use for piyutim, so that their synagogues have reduced that part of the service to bare essentials.

Some of the most famous piyutim are those which form the Selichoth services that are recited a week prior to the High Holidays. These are not part of any weekday or holiday prayer book but are a service all to themselves, reflecting the spirit of introspection and penitence that is the keynote of that solemn season.

🌿 MIDRASHIC LITERATURE

It is not generally known that most of the homilies that are part of Midrashic literature were created during the era of the Gaonim, that is, between the seventh and tenth centuries.

This wealth of material, numbering hundreds or perhaps even a thousand homilies and sermons, can be divided into seven main categories as follows:

1. Midrashim on Jewish Law, such as the "Mechilta" which is based upon the Book of Exodus; "Sifra" based on the Book of Leviticus, and "Sifre" based upon the books of Numbers and Deuteronomy.

2. Midrashim dealing with Haggada based on the Pentateuch in general, such as the Midrash Rabbah and others.

3. Midrashim based on prophetic literature and the Holy Writings, such as the Midrash on Samuel, the Midrash on Proverbs, the Midrash on Psalms, the Midrash on Isaiah, the Midrash on Jonah, and the Midrash on Job.

4. Smaller Midrashim dealing with sundry matters such as the Midrash Tanchumah, Agadath Bereshith, and so on.

5. Midrashim viewing the Messiah and the world-to-come from the vantage point of mysticism, such as the Pirkei de Rabbi Eliezer, Seder Eliahu Rabbah, Sota, and the Zohar.

6. Midrashim compiled from fragments of preexisting Midrashim, called "yalkutim" (the Hebrew for "pocket" or "gleanings"), such as Yalkut Reubeni, Yalkut Shimoni, and Midrash Hagadol.

7. Other minor Midrashim.

Not all of the authors of these Midrashim appended their names to their creations. Some of them signed the names of great Tannaim to their works to give them greater prestige in the public eye. An example of this would be the collection entitled "The Alef-Beth of Rabbi Akiba" which actually had nothing at all to do with that famous scholar. Many Midrashim are not original creations at all, but only repetitions and recastings of previously existing material, or enlargements on things to which brief allusion was made in the Gemorah.

Perhaps the most popular of all the Midrashim are the Midrash Rabbah based on the books of the Pentateuch, the Midrash Tanchumah, the Midrash Socher Tov, based on the Book of Psalms, the Seder Eliahu Rabba and Zuta, the Yalkutim, the Pesiktas, and some others. Of the rest of the Midrashim in existence, only parts have been printed; others are still in manuscript form, preserved in the archives of various national libraries. Dr. Adolph Jellinek published six volumes of minor Midrashim, and Judah David Eisenstein, the editor of the classic *Otzar Israel* (*The Treasury of Israel*) also compiled an *Otzar Midrashim* (*The Treasury of the Midrash*), which includes two hundred small Midrashim, arranged in alphabetical order.

🌺 THE BEGINNINGS OF THE CABALA

The era of the Gaonim also saw the beginnings of the Cabala, a new philosophical-mystical approach to the inquiry into the nature of God. Actually, the Cabala had much more ancient roots; for the very first cabalists were certain Essene groups which were part of the era of the second-generation Tannaim, and other splinter movements which flourished during the days of the Amoraim. These first groupings, however, have gone unrecorded, and it is only in the eighth and ninth centuries, during the age of the Gaonim, that we can find the first works of cabalistic literature, such as Sefer Yezirah, Shier Koma, The Book of the Angel Raziel, Hicholah, the Homilies of Rabbi Nehuniah ben Ha-Kanah, and Sar Hatorah. These books were not published under the names of their true authors. Some of them, such as The Midrash of Rabbi Nehuniah ben Ha-Kanah were titled after great personalities who actually had had nothing whatever to do with the theme or authorship of the works that bore their names.

The Cabala begins with logic and reasoning, but then it leads the student into the realm of mysticism and has a terminology all its own. The Lord Himself is titled "En-Sof" (The Never-Ending One or The Infinite One). Then there is a fantastic description of ten forces which emanate from Him and through which we are told He created the world and still rules over it. These ten Sephiroth (spheres) are as follows; in descending order: (1) The Crown (of the Most High), followed by (2) Wisdom, (3) Insight, (4) Mercy (justice), (5) Might (judgment), (6) Glory (the compromise between mercy and might), (7) Eternity, (8) Fame, (9) The Fundamental (an intermediate degree to reconcile eternity and fame), (10) Kingship (splendor, brilliance).

All these forces, however, are not equal, and therefore they are grouped in two columns, right and left, with Wisdom, Mercy, and Eternity listed in the right-hand column, and Insight, Might, and Fame on the left. The Crown of the Most High is placed in the center above the two columns, while

Glory and Fundamental are given an intermediary position in the roster. The two columns are also known as Abba (Father) and Ima (Mother) to indicate that the divine attributes listed there are the "parents" of the world and mankind, as it were.

The Cabala also divides the universe into four worlds of Creation, of which our own earth is the last one.

Such were the beginnings of the Cabala, the science of mysticism which was to be in full flower during the Golden Age of the Jews in Spain. After the expulsion of the Jews from that country, however, it declined into a set of teachings to which were attributed magic powers of healing and miracle-making.

✣ THE REVIVAL OF THE HEBREW LANGUAGE

The advent of Mohammed and the rise of Islam brought many changes to Babylonia and even a new language. Aramaic was replaced by Arabic, the language of Mohammed the Prophet, which was now employed not only by the government but also by educated circles in general. Aramaic took second place and was used by the less erudite masses.

Since Arabic is so closely akin to Hebrew, it was not at all strange that, as Arabic grew in popularity, efforts should be made among the Jews to revive their own Hebrew language. Particularly the Karaites who had little use for the Talmud and concentrated on the Bible showed great interest in the language in which this sacred Book was written. The Karaite movement could boast of many eminent Hebraists, poets and grammarians. In order to prove to the people that the Hebrew language was by no means the monopoly of the Karaites, Rabbi Chiya Gaon and, somewhat later, Rabbi Saadia Gaon, published Hebrew grammar texts of their own. Chiya's work unfortunately has been lost, but Saadia's text, entitled *Agron,* is still known to the scholarly world today.

A considerable contribution to the revival of Hebrew was made also by the paytanim, the bards of liturgical poetry. They coined entirely new words which were eventually generally accepted into the Hebrew language. When it was difficult to find or create a Hebrew word properly to convey their thoughts, they would turn to Arabic, but not too often, for most of the Jewish scholars did not have a high opinion of Arabic. (Maimonides, for example, labeled Arabic as a corrupted Hebrew dialect.) Most frequently they would find the words they needed in the Mishna where the Hebrew is pure and unadulterated.

Such were the first efforts of the Jewish community in Babylonia to make the Hebrew language live again. Their work was continued by their descendants in Spain who produced a great number of poets and grammarians, as we shall see later on.

Gradually the scholars of the Law, too, began to use Hebrew once more for the writing of their treatises, and discarded Aramaic which for centuries had been the language of Jewish scholarship. The sole exception was the text of the questions and answers of the Gaonim, which is in Aramaic, the language of the Gemorah. All other books, decisions, and theses on Jewish law, however, were henceforth written in Hebrew. Thus Hebrew now replaced Aramaic as the official language of Jewish life.

The Era of the Philosophers

I. The "Golden Age" in Spain

1. Who Were the Jewish Philosophers?

Jews Have Always Inquired About God—Moses Has a Dispute With God in the Holy Scriptures—Ecclesiastes and Job—The Difference Between an Ordinary Philosopher and a Religious Philosopher—Rabbi Saadia Gaon, the First Jewish Religious Philosopher

The Jewish people have always felt at home with the Lord; they have always felt free to ask questions and to press Him for redress of grievances. It can safely be said that the Jewish people were never afraid to ask even basic questions, touching upon fundamental problems of Judaism, for Judaism is no faith at all, but a body of knowledge, and knowledge can be obtained only by asking questions about points that are obscure.

Therefore we find a great many questions throughout the Bible concerning God, His guidance of men, reward and punishment, and many other such basic points. Judaism never required blind faith of its adherents. Jews have always been expected to study, to understand, and to know rather than merely to believe. For this reason, questions were welcomed rather than silenced, so that Jews might come to know more about God and His ways.

When the Jews made the Golden Calf and God threatened to destroy the entire people in punishment for its sin, Moses prayed to the Lord and said, ". . . Lord, why doth Thy wrath wax hot against Thy people, that Thou hast brought forth out of the land of Egypt . . . ? Wherefore should the Egyptians speak, saying: "For evil did He bring them forth, to slay them in the mountains, and to consume them from the face of the earth? Turn from Thy fierce wrath, and repent of this evil against Thy people." (Exod. 32:11-12). And finally, in desperation, Moses cried to the Lord, ". . . if Thou wilt forgive their sin—; and if not, blot me, I pray Thee, out of Thy book which Thou hast written" (Exod. 32:32).

And in a similar manner countless other Jewish leaders have pleaded and reasoned with God Himself. They demanded of Him that justice be done and they insisted that He be good to His people. We see this questioning of even God's justice run like a red thread throughout Jewish history, through the books of the prophets, in the writings of the Tannaim and sages after them, up to Rabbi Levi Isaac of Berditchev who rebelled even against God and cried out: "What dost Thou want of Thy people Israel? Why art Thou wroth with Thy people? Always it is only 'Speak unto the people of Israel' or 'Command the people of Israel.' Why, O Lord, always 'Israel'? What dost Thou want of Israel?"

Of course it is quite a different thing when men come to God directly and question His ways than if they go to other men and complain about God's seemingly unjust acts. If a son goes directly to his father and tells him that he feels that justice has not been done, that the father has failed him, the father will readily understand and will be more than glad to explain the reasons for what he had done which displeased his offspring. But if the dissatisfied son should go to his friends first, and tell them all of his father's behavior which he thought unjust, then the father would indeed have cause to feel resentment, for such conduct on the part of the son would be a direct insult, an act of disrespect against a father whom the son should honor and defend against all critics from without.

In the Jewish religion, too, it is perfectly proper to express one's doubts directly to God. What Judaism considers heresy is that kind of doubt that men discuss with one another, when men discuss with each other whether there is really such a thing as God, or Divine justice, or reward for the righteous and punishment for the wicked. For such questions indicate not a quest for divine redress, but a refusal to acknowledge that there is a God at all.

But the Jewish religion has always permitted its adherents to question God directly, and even to remonstrate with Him for not sending help and deliverance in time of trouble. The writings of many of these pious remonstrators have actually been canonized and have thus become part of the sacred literature of the Jewish people. Two such documents of indignant questioning of divine righteousness are the Book of Ecclesiastes and the Book of Job.

The Book of Psalms is filled with such pleas and demands that justice be done. In Psalm 88, David cries out in anguish: "For my soul is sated with troubles, and my life draweth nigh unto the grave. . . . . I have called upon Thee, O Lord, every day. . . ." The psalmist asks: "Wilt Thou work wonders for the dead? Or shall the shades rise and give Thee thanks?" Shall Thy mercy be declared in the grave? . . . Shall Thy wonders be known in the dark? And Thy righteousness in the land of forgetfulness? . . . Lord, why castest Thou off my soul? Why hidest Thou Thy face from me?" (4, 10-13, 15).

These are pleas of the first order, but there are pleas of another order as well, such as "For what vanity hast Thou created all the children of men?" (Psalm 89:48). In other places too, the Lord is called upon to answer whether there is really any hope for divine justice, whether the righteous man may indeed expect his just reward, and whether the wicked will receive the punishment they deserve. The writer of the Book of Ecclesiastes exclaims: "Who knoweth the spirit of man whether it goeth upward, and the spirit of the beast whether it goeth downward to the earth?" (3:21). He even concludes that "For the living know that they shall die; but the dead know not any thing, neither have they any more a reward; for the memory of them is forgotten" (9:5). He states that there are many righteous men who are cut down in their youth, while many wicked men live to a ripe old age. Hence, "Go thy way, eat thy bread with joy, and drink thy wine with a merry heart" (9:7) because the dead who have died are better off than the living who are still alive.

The Book of Job contains much the same questions, in equally poetic language. This book, which consists of 42 chapters, contains 37 chapters in which Job and his three friends, Eliphaz the Temanite, Bildad the Shuhite, and Zophar the Naamathite, question God's justice. The last three chapters of the book then, contain the Lord's own answer to the pleas of these four men.

These documents of righteous indignation paved the way for later expressions of questioning as found in the literature of the philosophers who lived in Spain during the Golden Age of Jewish culture there, a period which actually began in Babylonia, in the tenth century, with Saadia Gaon who was born in Egypt in 892 A.D., served as head of the Academy at Sura and died there in 942 A.D.

And throughout the ages since then, Jewish philosophers the world over have made it their task to search deeply into the teachings of Judaism and to attempt to understand them and to make clear their significance to the Jewish people.

However, as we go on to discuss the various Jewish philosophers, let us first make clear that the definition of a Jewish philosopher is not synonymous with that of an ordinary philosopher who just happens to be Jewish.

A philosopher, in the sense of the word as we know it, is one who asks questions and seeks answers concerning the existence of a God, the manner in which the world evolves, the way in which life first came into being on earth, and, above all, the real sense and meaning of life itself. Hence, if he is to obtain satisfactory answers to all these questions, the ordinary philosopher must be free from all biases, prejudices, or beliefs. Nothing must stand in the way of his free and unfettered thinking processes so that his trend of thoughts is not blocked or deflected in any manner. This kind of philosophy is best represented by the thinkers of ancient Greece. It is quite a different matter, however, when the philosopher is firmly rooted in a religious faith, such as Christianity or Mohammedanism, or any other faith, for that matter. Such a philosopher will find that his religion will have set certain definite bounds for him, beyond which his thinking must not and cannot go. Unlike the philosopher who has no religion of his own, he cannot arrive at the conclusion that there is no God. He must base all his logic on the fundamental premise that there is, indeed, a God, and he must ascribe to that God all the attributes assigned to Him by the religious faith of which the thinker happens to be an adherent. Therefore the trend of thought of the "religious philosopher" is, of necessity, a circumscribed one, as opposed to the vastly greater freedom of thought enjoyed by the thinker who is not bound by any religious belief.

Thus, when we study "Jewish philosophy," and "Jewish philosophers," we must keep in mind that these thinkers were all "religious philosophers," with few exceptions such as for example, Baruch Spinoza, who attempted to be a "free" philosopher and thus came to leave Judaism behind him.

2. *Saadia Gaon and His Views*

How Saadia Became Head of the Academy of Sura—His Fight with Ben Meir of Jerusalem—His Stand Against the Resh Galuta—The Enlightenment Among the Arabs—The Ten Points of Saadia Gaon

Rabbi Saadia Gaon was one of the outstanding personalities in Jewish history. He was a great Talmudist and in his time rabbis the world over turned to him for advice and decisions in problems concerning Jewish law. He also was one of the first philosophers among the Jews who published a philosophical treatise which has enjoyed widespread fame even to this very day. He knew a great many languages in addition to Hebrew and Arabic. He was a Bible exegete, the author of prayers and liturgical poetry, a lexicographer, and the first to make an orderly compilation of the synagogue rituals in his famous "prayer book." In many ways he resembled another great personality in Jewish life, Maimonides, who lived several generations after him. Saadia Gaon's influence on Jewish life was so profound that it still affects us.

Let us therefore study first his life and his work, and then his philosophical approach to Judaism. But before we proceed, let us examine the environment in which he lived so that we may gain a better understanding of the influences that molded Saadia Gaon.

Our setting is the land of Babylonia. The "Babylonian Talmud" was completed in the year 500 A.D. The completion of the Babylonian Talmud was followed by a brief epoch dominated by Jewish scholars called Gaonim (from the word "Gaon"—"eminence").

In those days the Jews in Babylonia had a certain degree of autonomy. They had a leader called "Resh Galutha" or Exilarch, who had final authority over all civil matters of the Jewish population. Co-regent with him was the "Gaon," the head of the Academy of the city of Sura who was the supreme religious authority for the Jews of the land. It was these two leaders who were rulers over all Jewish life in Babylonia. The Exilarch appointed the "Gaon" of the Academy of Sura and, in general, had powers approximating those of a viceroy.

At that time there was another great Talmudical Academy in Babylonia, the academy of Pumbeditha, but the "Gaon" of that institution of learning was only second in rank to the head of the school at Sura.

The Gaonic era began in the year 589 A.D. and extended for some four hundred and fifty years thereafter. During these years Pumbeditha had forty-eight Gaonim who succeeded one another in holding that office in the academy. The last of these was Rabbi Hai Gaon, who died in the year 1038 and after whose demise the academy was disbanded. Sura had a succession of thirty-six Gaonim who ruled there until the year 943 A.D. There was also a third academy, much smaller than either that of Sura or the one at Pumbeditha. This school was in the city of Nehardea and existed only for a short period of time before it merged with the Academy of Pumbeditha.

Rabbi Saadia Gaon was the last Gaon of the Academy of Sura. How he attained this position and how he waged his bitter struggle against the Exilarch is an account of profound interest from which we can see what a strong personality he really was. He was not the man to bow before the wealthy or the powerful in his community; he fought and he suffered until victory came to him in the end, and his erstwhile enemies had to come to him to beg forgiveness.

Saadia was the only Gaon of that era who was not a native of Babylonia, but of Egypt. He was born in a village called Dilaz in the province of Payum, in the year 882. His father was both a businessman and a scholar in the Law. Saadia had studied at the feet of the great rabbis of Egypt and also became a disciple of the outstanding Arab scholars of the day, among whom there was the eminent historian Massoud. Several years later he went to study at the academies of Palestine. He began to write works of his own at a very early age. His first publication was entitled *Agron,* a dictionary for poets. He also put out a series of polemical broadsides against the Karaites, who at that time played an important part in Jewish life in Palestine, Egypt, and even Babylonia. These publications were distributed widely and soon Saadia had made himself a name in the learned circles of his day. Therefore he was received with a great deal of respect when he came to Babylonia. At that time the Exilarch in that country was David ben Zakkai, who was a great scholar and Talmudist in his own right and therefore had acquired some familiarity with the works of the youthful writer. The older man often invited Saadia to his home and had long discussions with him about many aspects of learning, both Jewish and secular. Since the position of Gaon of the academy at Sura was vacant, the Resh Galuta, who had come to respect Saadia's intellectual integrity, appointed him to that office.

Soon after Saadia had taken charge of the institution at Sura, world Jewry was well-nigh split into two warring factions by an issue that shook Jewish unity to its foundations. In 921 A.D. a great scholar from Jerusalem, Rabbi Aaron ben Meir, advanced a theory that the calendar followed by Jews throughout the world, which had been created in Babylonia, was in error by two days. Rabbi Aaron, therefore, felt that every Jewish holy day should be observed two days earlier than stipulated in the calendar, which he thought inaccurate. Thus it came to be that world Jewry was divided into two factions, with the Jews in Palestine celebrating the festivals two days sooner than their co-religionists in Babylonia and the rest of the world. This discrepancy in Jewish observance went on for two years before the head of the Academy of Sura intervened. Saadia, who was also a mathematician and astronomer of note, wrote several treatises in which he proved that Rabbi Aaron's theory was not founded on fact and therefore was entirely invalid. These works made a profound impression because of the scholarly approach evidenced in them, and it was generally conceded that Rabbi Aaron had made a mistake in his calculations.

Now Saadia turned all his energies to the fight against the Karaites, and his Hebrew and Arabic treatises against the Karaite sect did much to weaken the influence of the Karaites in the Jewish world, particularly in Palestine and in Babylonia.

It was the custom in those days, much as it is at present, for institutions of higher Jewish learning to send out emissaries to collect funds for their maintenance. In Babylonia the monies thus gathered had to be turned over to the Exilarch. Once Saadia Gaon went to David ben Zakkai and demanded an accounting for the amounts brought in. The Exilarch, however, was reluctant to comply with the Gaon's demand. Finally David ben Zakkai admitted that the annual revenue of the academy was 70,000 pieces of gold, and said that he desired to keep 10 per cent of the total amount for other purposes. Saadia, however, pointed out to the Exilarch that the money had been intended for the academy only and that, therefore, the Exilarch had no right to withhold any of it.

The Exilarch refused to discuss the question any further. He terminated the audience with Saadia and sent his son to the academy with a paper for the Gaon to sign, stating that the Exilarch was entitled to keep 10 per cent of whatever funds had been collected for the institutions of Jewish learning in Babylonia, to spend it as he saw fit. Saadia refused to sign such a document and told the young man to tell his father that he would not be partner to such a misappropriation of the funds. The Exilarch's son became angry at these words and would have struck Saadia, if the students had not quickly ejected him from the academy.

Thus began a bitter struggle between the Gaon and the Exilarch. Ben Zakkai demanded that Saadia sign the document or else be removed from office. Saadia replied that he would not bow to wealth or power. Thereupon Ben Zakkai carried out his threat, dismissed Saadia, and appointed a young student, Joseph ben Yaakov, in his place. Saadia then declared that he did not recognize the authority of Ben Zakkai, and announced that henceforth the Resh Galuta should not be Ben Zakkai, but Joshua Hazon, the younger brother of the latter. Rabbi Saadia was supported in his struggle by the scholarly circles, but Ben Zakkai had behind him all the wealthy Jews of the land. This went on for some two years. Then Ben Zakkai declared that Saadia was not even qualified to be head of the academy of Sura since he was a citizen of Egypt and thus an alien in Babylonia. Even so, the Exilarch made a last-minute attempt to make Saadia agree to his way of handling the academy's funds but Saadia replied that he would rather starve than be part of a practice which was against his principles of right and honesty. As a result, Saadia was forced to leave the country, and he settled in Bagdad, where he lived with his wife and two children in abject poverty for some four or five years. He subsisted on alms doled out by generous friends, but it was during those years that he created a great many of the works that remained part of our eternal Jewish heritage. He wrote a scientific commentary on the Bible in Arabic, the first such attempt in the field of Jewish scholarship, entitled *Kitav al Amanat Ve-al I-tikadat* (*A Treatise on Beliefs and Opinions*). This book was subsequently translated into Hebrew by Ibn Tibon under the title of *Ha-emunot Ve-hadeoth*. The Hebrew translation made the work accessible to Jews the world over and it aroused such interest that it had to be copied many times over. When the art of printing was invented, *Ha-emunot Ve-hadeoth* was one of the first books to be printed. The first printed edition appeared in Constantinople in 1562 and has been reprinted many times since then.

The greatest event in Saadia's life, however, was the moment when Ben Zakkai came to him in Bagdad, asked his forgiveness, and begged him to return to Sura to resume his leadership of the academy there. The Exilarch told Saadia that he had looked far and wide and had not been able to find anyone even approaching Saadia in greatness and scholarship who would be fit to take the position at Sura. There was a reconciliation between the two leaders and Saadia returned to Sura on the eve of Purim of that year. Ben Zakkai invited Saadia to be his guest at the Purim dinner, but the latter insisted that he should have the honor of receiving the Exilarch at his home for that festive meal. To settle this dispute, they resorted to the drawing of lots and it was determined that Saadia was to accept Ben Zakkai's invitation.

Professor Henry Malter, author of the most comprehensive biography of Saadia, tells us that Saadia wrote no less than a hundred works in Hebrew and two hundred in Arabic.

Not long after Saadia's return to Sura, the Exilarch ben Zakkai died and, a few months later, his son Judah, who had attempted to strike Saadia that day long ago, also died. Judah left behind a small son eleven years of age, whom Saadia took into his own home and raised as a foster child. Unfortunately, Saadia himself was not destined to live much longer. His health failed him and he died in Sura at the age of fifty, on the 26th day of Iyar in the year 942 A.D.

Now we are coming to the time when we devote some study to Saadia's book *Ha-emunot Ve-hadeoth* in which he had attempted, for the first time, to explain Judaism in scientific terms. The thoughts contained in this book are as intelligible and pertinent today as they were when first set down over a thousand years ago.

Saadia Gaon's *Beliefs and Opinions* was written with the specific intent to support the Jewish point of view with scientific logic. Its aim was to resolve, by philosophical reasoning, certain doubts about some aspects of Jewish belief. Many religions have produced works of similar character, for nearly every religion has a theology, but not all theological writings are of equal character. The caliber of such a treatise depends on the extent to which the author makes use of logic and philosophy to defend his religion, whether he makes his philosophy subordinate to his religion, or whether he has religion accommodate itself to his philosophy. There are theologians who regard religion itself as all-important and give philosophy a secondary place. In other words, they will tailor their philosophy to suit their religious beliefs. And then, of course, there are others who are inclined to perform the same operation upon religion to reconcile it with the philosophy they hold. If we examine the philosophical literature of our own Jewish religion, we shall find samples of both methods. Now the question before us is to which category Saadia Gaon belonged.

Before we can determine this, we must first discover what philosophy Saadia Gaon expounded in *Beliefs and Opinions*. Was it an original philosophy, or was it an approach derived from some other thinker, and if the latter was true, then who was the philosopher on which Saadia based his own treatise? It is also important for us to know whether Saadia's philosophy was in any way molded unconsciously by the works of Arab thinkers or by any one teacher.

In this connection, we ought to devote some thought to the renaissance in Arab culture that took place at just about that time. This era of revival began around 750 and ended sometime between 1250 and 1258. It was one of the happiest chapters in the history of the Arab world. Let us attempt to gain some insight into the causes of this renaissance and its significance for the Jewish people.

Until the advent of Mohammed, the descendants of the Ishmaelites were pagans, living a nomadic life in the desert and knowing nothing of culture or scholarship. The cultural awakening of the Arab peoples came about only after the entrance of Mohammed and his new religion on the proscenium of world history.

Mohammed, the founder of the Islamic religion and the author of the Koran, started out in life as a poor illiterate camel driver, but he was possessed of a high degree of intelligence, which enabled him to overcome the handicap of a lack of education. He was clever enough to surround himself with Jewish scholars who familiarized him with the treasures of the Bible and Talmudic and Midrashic literature. Some of these men of learning even became his secretaries, as it were, and it has been discovered that they were responsible for major parts of the Koran which is, of course, attributed to Mohammed alone.

Whatever one may think of Mohammed, he must be given credit for having abolished idolatry among the Arab nomads, partly by the force of his word and partly by the use of the scimitar, and for having replaced paganism with the belief in one God who created Heaven and earth. Mohammed did not claim to be a god himself or the son of a deity, but assumed a more modest position as "Allah's" prophet. He taught his followers to repeat five times daily the basic doctrine of the newly founded faith: "Allah il Allah, Mahammed razul Allah" ("There is no God beside Allah and Mohammed is His Prophet"). This new concept of the Deity, together with the treasures of Jewish literature which had been revealed to Mohammed and which he communicated to his disciples, served as a stimulus to the Arab masses who, despite their seemingly uncivilized way of life, had great potentialities for absorbing knowledge. The new religion awakened them from centuries of sleep; they threw away their stone idols and looked about them to discover new horizons.

At this time the Arabs developed a sudden interest in literature and science, and made tremendous progress in the fields of medicine, mathematics, alchemy, and other branches of scientific scholarship. They also came to discover the heritage of the philosophers of ancient Greece, a treasure which had been buried in the dust first by the conquering Romans and then by Christianity. They became particularly interested in the ideas set forth by the philosophers of the Socratic era, Plato and Aristotle, and translated many of their works into Arabic.

As far as religious dogma was concerned, the Arab world still lived in a spiritual vacuum. The old idols had been destroyed but the new faith taught by Mohammed had not as yet taken firm root. There were, as yet, no spiritual leaders, no explicit religious precepts, no prescribed ritual, and no express injunctions as to what a loyal Mohammedan should or should not do. No wonder, then, that the more enlightened element among the Arabs turned to the works of the Greek thinkers to fill the vacuum, for the latter had lived in a period that was much like the one in which the Arab world now found itself. In those days, too (as we have already explained in the section on the Prophets), there was a general casting off of old idols and a search for a new and better form of worship.

As we have said before, the Arabs favored mostly the works of the disciples of Socrates, Plato, and Aristotle. Plato contributed much to the development of logic, psychology, ethics, and public administration, but he dwelt upon a more academic plane. Aristotle had a more practical mind and made a systematic analysis of the ideas advanced by Plato. He developed his own doctrines concerning the nature of the world and human relations. The Arab thinkers of the era with which we are dealing here had as yet developed no original philosophies, and adhered to the ideas which they had derived from their readings in Greek thought. These they reinterpreted to suit the needs of their own time and within the framework of their new Islamic religion. These three hundred years of cultural reawakening (from 900 to 1200 A.D.) were an outstanding chapter in the history of the Near East. During the first century of this epoch that part of the world was dominated by the kingdom of Persia; then, from about 1000 A.D. to 1200 A.D., the Caliphs of Spain held sway.

During that era there evolved two schools of philosophy in the Arab world; the Neo-Platonist and the Neo-Aristotelian. The Neo-Platonists did not produce great thinkers. The Neo-Aristotelians, however, had in their ranks men like Ibn al Rashid, his son Harun al Rashid, Mansun, and later, Avisena, the greatest philosopher of all the Renaissance (b. 980, d. 1037). Avisena was not only a gifted thinker, but also a most skillful physician. Some say that he was a Jew. He devised his own philosophical approach with which he tried to effect some sort of compromise between the teachings of Plato and the ideas of Aristotle.

Saadia Gaon was a disciple of the above-mentioned Arab philosophers, particularly of Ibn al Rashid who had the greatest influence upon his thinking. Saadia had high regard for Ibn al Rashid's ideas and sought to incorporate them into Jewish ideology. His aim in doing so was not to change Judaism, but merely to strengthen it. When it came to the reconciliation of religion with philosophy, Saadia, who was on the side of religion, made the necessary changes at the expense not of religion but of philosophy. It was Saadia's intention to employ Rashid's ideas to strengthen Jewish faith, even in those points that did not represent the basic principles of Judaism, such as the belief in the resurrection of the dead. To him even such secondary concepts were essential parts of the whole of Judaism and he was anxious to apply the logic of philosophy to the elimination of all doubt regarding these beliefs. Of course, many of the opponents of his approach were to declare subsequently that he did not succeed very well in his efforts to do so.

In *Beliefs and Opinions* Saadia Gaon sets forth ten points which he thinks are the basic principles of the Jewish faith and which every Jew must acknowledge as true and binding upon him.

Saadia Gaon wanted to make clear to the Jews of his day what it means to be a Jew in the true sense of the word. It was with this view that he studied and delved into the treasures of Jewish lore and then abstracted from the results of his research the ten cardinal principles which he held to be basic to Judaism. Saadia's philosophical approach was a combination of the views of Aristotle and Plato, and this was the guide upon which he based his formulation of the ten points. Before he lists these articles of faith, he sets forth for his readers what he considers the four essential rules for rational thought. He states that the first kind of knowledge man can come to possess is what he derives through his own five senses: sight, touch, hearing, taste, and smell. The second kind is obtained from what man's intelligence tells him, as, for example, that justice is good while injustice is evil. The third source of knowledge is actual experience; for example, if one touches a pot full of hot water, the resulting pain teaches the human being not to touch a pot of water standing on a heated stove. However, Saadia adds, there is a fourth source that tells us how to manage our lives and that is the chain of tradition, handed down from generation to generation. This, too, is an important source of human knowledge.

The above four kinds of human knowledge serve as the basis for Saadia's formulation of his ten points in his great work *Beliefs and Opinions*. Briefly, the ten principles are as follows:

1. *God created the world.* The world was made by a Creator. Greek philosophy showed three different views concerning the origin of the world. Aristotle held that the world was never "created"; it had no beginning and has no end, and even as one does not ask about how God came into being, so it also does not behoove man to ask how the world came into being. Plato believed that the world was brought into being by a Creator, but that it was created from a mass which was in existence prior to the creation of the world. What the Creator did was take the preexisting mass and alter it to make the universe as we know it today. Socrates said that the world and man were created by the fusion of two elements, the material and the spiritual.

Saadia Gaon does not accept any of the above three doctrines. He claims that a Jew must believe that God created the world out of nothing and even if the universe was indeed formed from a preexisting mass, that mass was also created by God.

Saadia seeks to corroborate this thesis by means of logic. He proves that everything that lives must eventually die. This shows that all things have a beginning and an end. If this is true of living creatures, Saadia feels that it must, of necessity, be true also of the world in which they live. This means that the world began by means of an act of creation, and also that it will end one day.

Saadia states that, actually, there was no reason to believe that God needed to use a preexisting material from which to create the world. For to assume that God made the world from a mass that already existed before creation would be to limit His power, implying that, without the mass, He could not have proceeded with His creation of the world. If, indeed, the world was not created "out of nothing," then one would have to assume that it was not the Creator of the world, but whoever made the basic material from which the world was formed, that was the true God. Therefore it is quite clear to Saadia that a Jew must know and understand that God created the world "out of nothing," even as it is stated in the Bible, "In the beginning God created the Heavens and the earth." God created it all with the breath of His mouth.

2. *God is One.* If we believe that the world was indeed created by God, then we must also believe that there is only one God. Saadia refutes the doctrine of those who, like Zoroaster, say that there are two gods, the god of light and the god of darkness, the god of good and the god of evil. There is only one force in this world, consisting of such positive factors such as light and goodness. The negative elements such as darkness and evil, says Saadia, are not forces at all but are just symptoms of the lack of light or goodness. If a house lacks light then it is dark; darkness is not a force in itself but merely the result of the absence of light; therefore, as soon as a lamp is brought into the house, it is no longer dark.

The same is true also of good and evil. Saadia declares that God created good, but not evil. He created food to eat and water to drink. When a person eats not at all, or too much, it is bad for him. The same is true of drink. But the Lord did not make evil. Evil is only the lack of good or indiscriminate use thereof. There is no war between light and darkness, or good and evil. The basic forces created along with the world are goodness and light, and nothing else.

3. *A Jew must believe that every man is endowed with a soul.* For when a human being dies, his body remains the same as when he was alive. What then, Saadia asks, does the living body possess that the corpse lacks? What in man's body makes the difference between life and death? Saadia's answer is that it is the soul that leaves the body when life departs. As long as man has his soul within him, he is alive, he is able to move, speak, walk, act, think, or dream. Once the soul has gone, man's body still looks as it did when he was alive, but he can no longer move, speak, think, or walk. This shows that man has a soul, or spirit, created by God, given to man when he is born. As long as he has his soul, he is alive; when the soul leaves him, he dies.

4. *A Jew must believe that the Torah was given to us by God.* For the Torah, which will live forever, cannot be the product of a human being. Man is mortal, and only God is eternal. Saadia divides the commandments of the Torah into two distinct categories, namely, those laws the basis of which man can readily understand, and those the reasons for which we cannot comprehend. The former need no explanation, because any thinking person can understand them. As for the latter, we must believe that since God, who ordained them, is possessed of infinite wisdom, far beyond the limited intelligence of man, we must simply accept the fact that God knew the rea-

sons for these laws, and that it is our duty, therefore, to obey them. As for the basic premise that the Torah was indeed divinely revealed, we know this to be true from the tradition that has been handed down to us through the generations. Therefore it is a regular part of our general knowledge.

5. *A Jew must know that the Torah will never be abolished.* There is, of course, the argument that all things created by God must have a beginning and an end, and that, therefore, the Torah, too, which has been created just as man and beast, must eventually come to the end of its existence. Saadia explains, however, that the Torah cannot be compared to the rest of creation. All other creatures of the world go through stages of development; they have a birth, prime of life, and, in the end, must die. Man, for instance, goes through the stages of youth, middle age, senescence, and, finally, death. Objects are first new, then used, and, finally, obsolete. The Torah, however, has no youth, prime, or old age, and therefore it cannot die.

6. *A Jew must believe that the prophets were sent by God* to communicate His message to men. God does not want sinners to perish, but desires that they repent, and for this purpose He appointed the prophets to call sinful man to repentence. One example of this is the mission of Jonah the Prophet, who was sent by God to the city of Nineveh, where sin and godlessness prevailed.

7. *A Jew must believe that man is endowed with a free will,* and therefore has the choice of doing what is right or wrong in the eyes of God. Therefore, too, he will receive a reward for doing good and will be punished for doing evil. There is the question whether or not God knows of man's intentions in advance. If we are to assume that God does not know in advance whether man will do good or evil, we thereby place a limit on our concept of God's infinite knowledge. On the other hand, if we should believe that God is aware of what man will do, then we would have to infer that man can act only in accordance with what God has determined. If this is so, then man has no choice at all, and no free will, and is therefore deserving neither of reward for good, nor of punishment for evil. Saadia solves this dilemma by explaining that man does, indeed, have free will, but that, at the same time, God is well aware in advance of the choices men will make. The will of God, however, makes no attempt to influence that of man. For instance, if a man is wicked, God, even though He knows that the person will choose to do evil instead of good, will not intervene directly to make the wrongdoer mend his ways. He will permit him to choose evil instead of good. God has the knowledge, but does not use it to influence man.

8. *Reward and punishment.* If, based upon the foregoing, we believe that man does have free will, it is obvious that man will receive a reward for goodness and punishment for evil, in accordance with his acts. The reward is in store for the soul when it leaves the body, and the nature of the reward is such that we cannot comprehend it, for we are a product of the union between body and soul. The same is true as regards punishment.

9. A Jew must believe that redemption will eventually come to the Jewish people. Saadia even set a date for this liberation. (That date has long since passed.)

10. A Jew must believe in the resurrection of the dead. Saadia attempted to prove the truth of his assumption by means of logic. If we believe, said Saadia, that God indeed created the world from nothing, then we must infer that He can certainly give life to a human being; this would be "creation from previously existing matter." This means to restore life to a body that once possessed it.

It can readily be seen that not all the points of logic cited by Saadia can actually be borne out. But it is obvious to us from the foregoing that Saadia made every effort to prove the validity of his beliefs by methods of logic.

Here, then, we have had a basic outline of Saadia Gaon's beliefs as he formulated them in his *Beliefs and Opinions.* In that great book he goes into considerable detail on each of his ideas. *Beliefs and Opinions* had a great impact not only upon the Jews, but also upon all the enlightened Arab world.

It is interesting to note that while Saadia's approach to the Torah in *Beliefs and Opinions* is very conservative, his viewpoint seems much more liberal in his commentary on the Torah in Arabic. In the latter work he states, for instance, that the story of Eve and the serpent is not to be taken literally, but only as an allegory. The story of Jacob's ladder, he says, is an allegory portraying the attempt of the soul to rise heavenward; likewise, angels are not winged creatures, but symbols of thoughts.

Several decades after Saadia's death, the Arab philosopher Avisena incorporated parts of Saadia's phiolsophy into his own. Avisena had a talent for assimilating the philosophies of others and communicating them to his readers and listeners as his own. He had done the same with Plato and Aristotle. A crass example of this kind of plagiarism is his medical treatise *Canon of Medicine,* in which he set down the words of the great physicican Galen as if they were actually his own. And the *Canon of Medicine* was considered the standard text for all physicians and universities until well into the seventeenth century.

Avisena was born in 980 A.D. some thirty-eight years after Saadia's death, in a Persian village near Bokhara. His real name was Abu Ali al Hussein ibn Abdallah ibn Sina. He was a child prodigy and was regarded as a genius all his life. (He died in 1037, at the age of fifty-eight.) He was from a poor family and was largely self-educated. Still, he grew to be the most erudite man of his day. In addition, he was not averse to wine, women, and song. He was politically active and came to be the prime minister of his nation. At other times he was imprisoned for political reasons and was sentenced to death several times but always somehow managed to escape execution. During his active life he wrote countless works on philosophy, astronomy, mathematics, and other sciences, and was known far and wide as the greatest physician of his time.

The story of Avisena is as fascinating as any modern novel. He had adventures without end. He moved among courtiers and noblemen, as well as among servants and prostitutes, all this while authoring some hundred books on a variety of scientific subjects. His works had a strong impact upon the later Jewish philosophers, particularly Rabbenu Bachya Hadayan, author of *Duties of the Heart,* whose life we shall discuss in the next chapter.

3. Rabbi Bachya and His "Duties of the Heart"

Ethical Teachings Clothed in Philosophy—The Relationship of Man and God—Monastic Orders in Judaism—A New Philosophical Approach

Toward the end of the tenth century we see that the center of enlightenment and culture of the Arab world shifted from Babylonia to Spain. Perhaps it may be that as Mohammedanism gained strength in Babylonia, an established clergy gradually came into being which fought against all secular education and free intellectual development. But the situation of the Jews in Babylonia, too, had undergone a radical change. The great academies of Sura and Pumbeditha were no more; they had fallen victim to a wave of anti-Semitism which the Jews of that country hitherto had not known existed, and which poisoned some of the best minds of the Arab world. Jewish scholars and other Jews of note now left Babylonia and settled in Spain which, at that time, was also ruled by Arabs. There the Caliphate reigned supreme and the atmosphere was still one of freedom, as compared to that of Babylonia.

Soon it was evident that Spain was to produce some of the greatest Jewish intellectual giants in history. There began the so-called "Golden Age" of the Jews in Spain which was to last for nearly five hundred years (from the end of the tenth century until the expulsion of the Jews from Spain in 1492). This era saw the rise of quite a number of Jewish philosophers, each of whom endeavored to strengthen the Jewish religion in his own way. There were also outstanding Talmudists and Bible exegetes. One of the first such philosophers in Spain was Rabbi Bachya the Judge.

Rabbi Bachya (pronounced "Bachaiah" by the Ashkenazic Jews and "Bachya" by the Sephardim) was the son of Joseph ibn Pakuda. His full name was "Rabbi Bachya, the Judge, the son of Pakudah." He lived in Spain, first in Saragossa and then in Cordova during the first half of the eleventh century. The exact dates of his birth and death are unknown. All we know is that his monumental work, *Ktav Pi Hadiaiah Praiz Alklub* (In Hebrew—*Hovoth Halevovoth—Duties of the Heart*), was written in 1040 and subsequently translated into Hebrew by Judah ibn Tibon. In addition, he was the author of many other works, but *Duties of the Heart,* in which he stated his own philosophy of Judaism, is by far the greatest of all his literary achievements.

Rabbi Bachya was regarded as one of the most outstanding philosophers, not only by his own people, but also among the Arabs. It is interesting to note that he did not find it necessary to prove the existence or the oneness of God. He felt that greater minds had dealt with that subject before. It was his conviction that the existence of God was a fact in which one must simply believe and, if one should not so believe, no amount of logic would be able to influence the nonbeliever to change his views. Rabbi Bachya was quite familiar with the works of the Arab thinkers, particularly with those of Avisena who, in general, shared the views of Rabbi Saadia Gaon. Bachya, however, had little use for Greek philosophy or any of the schools of thought derived from it. To him the issue of supreme importance was the feeling for God which the human being bears in his heart, and it was for this reason that he named his masterpiece *Duties of the Heart*. His approach, as manifest in this work, is philosophical-poetic or poetic-philosophical. He speaks to the heart of man rather than to his intellect, and therefore *Duties of the Heart* reads like a beautiful poem, a song rising from the depths of the soul, a hymn to God and a song in praise of better understanding between man and man.

Rabbi Bachya divided his book into ten parts in which he dealt with various concepts of the relationship of man to God and of man to man.

The first part of Bachya's treatise is entitled "Shaar Ha-yihud" ("Unity of God"). In this chapter Bachya attempts to prove that the belief in One God is the basis of all ethics and moral teachings. After proving the existence of God, Bachya discusses His unity and here he makes use of the trend of thought as followed by Saadia Gaon and formulated by Avisena. He was the first to state a parable which was later to be used by philosophers such as Maimonides and others. The parable ran as follows:

A man came to visit a friend. The friend greeted him with great joy and told him, "Come and see what a beautiful song I have here." The guest read the song and was duly impressed. "Wonderful!" he cried out. "A beautiful song. Who wrote it? Did you compose it?" "No," replied his host, "No one composed the song." "Then, how did such a splendid song come into being?" asked the guest. "Very simply," his friend replied. "There was a white sheet of paper on the table and next to it there stood an inkwell filled with ink. The inkwell turned over on the paper and here is the song." "Nonsense!" said the guest angrily. "Do you really think I could believe such a stupid explanation? Who would ever believe you?" The same, says Bachya, is true of the creation of the world. All of creation, too, is a wondrous song. And how could such a splendid song have been created by mere accident?

The second part, "Against the Personification of God," deals with the expressions in the Bible about God that were put into human terms for the sole purpose that mortal man might be able to understand God better. He discusses such expressions as "the hand of God," "and God spoke," and so on. Of course, Bachya says, God is not human, and therefore He does not "speak" to man with a "mouth" as humans do. Such expressions, therefore, are all merely allegorical, intended to portray God so that man in his limited intelligence may have some conception of Him. Bachya cites the place in the Talmud in which it is said, "The Torah has spoken in the language of man."

In the third part "The Way of Understanding," Bachya points out that every individual must come to understand God in his own way and formulate his own concept of Him. Bachya sets down seven different ways in which man may sense the spirit of God within him and in which he may recognize the Lord and serve Him."

The fourth chapter, "How to Serve God," deals with the manner in which man must serve his Maker. It is in the form of a dialogue between the intellect and the soul concerning the way in which man can come to know God. It is written in a highly philosophical-poetic vein, and its conclusion is that man must recognize God by himself and within his own spirit.

In the chapter called "The Way of Trust," Bachya stresses the importance of having faith in God. Man must do his share in achieving his goal, but he must trust in God at all times. He proves that faith in God can banish all care and worry.

In another part, "The Way of Doing Things," the author praises the virtue of honesty, integrity, and sincerity and condemns all falsehood and hypocrisy.

In "The Way of Modesty," Bachya discusses the vice of pride and sings the praises of modesty and humility. He emphasizes that man must not be proud and must deal kindly with all men, regardless of social position. Man must not think highly of himself nor must he praise himself for doing good.

The chapter "How to Be Moderate," teaches man to be moderate in all things, be it food, drink, sleep, or sexual relations. Man must not run after pleasures, for a life of greed may please the body, but do irreparable damage to the soul. Similar things he discusses also in the next two chapters.

In the final chapter, "How to Love God," Bachya teaches the reader how to love God. He states that it is the duty of our heart to serve God and to love Him, for it is only thus that man may become "complete" and attain the goal and destiny for which he was created.

Thus we see that Bachya, instead of engaging in philosophical discussions, which he felt would not lead to any practical conclusions, desired to teach man how he must conduct himself on God's earth. His *Duties of the Heart* was the first textbook of morals and ethics ever written in Jewish literature, and it is unique in its type. It reads like a song and is a source of inspiration to all who study it.

There is one rather strange idea which Bachya advances in *Duties of the*

Heart. In the chapter in which he exhorts man to avoid luxury and greed, he suggests that there be established among the Jewish people, a group of men who would remain celibate.

As a matter of fact, it was at about that time that the Christian religion created its orders of monks and nuns who took vows of celibacy, believing that man could become holy and serve God with all his heart, only if he would forego all pleasures of the flesh including sexual relations. Under the influences of this movement in the Catholic Church, the Mohammedan religion soon set up similar orders among its own followers.

It seems that Bachya, too, was attracted to this idea of monasticism. In one place in *Duties of the Heart,* he advances the opinion that the sexual drive was a great obstacle to man in his search for God. He suggests that the Jews, too, set up celibate orders for men and women. It might be added here that, at that time, the great Arab philosopher Algasali left his home and secluded himself in a monastery to write his scholarly treatises. At any rate, Bachya suggests that the Jews establish "orders of ascetics" similar to the "Sons of the Prophets" and the "Sons of Yonadab ben Rachab," in olden times.

It is interesting to note that the idea advanced by Bachya was advocated also in a work by the Jewish philosopher Rabbi Abraham ben Rabbi Chiya of Barcelona (known in world literature as Abraham Judas), who lived from the end of the eleventh century into the beginning of the twelfth. In his treatise *Hegyon Hanefesh,* Rabbi Abraham speaks out in favor of the idea of creating such monastic orders for men and women.

Rabbi Bachya employed the tools of philosophy solely to strengthen the Jewish faith. His chief interest lay not in man's intellect but in the emotions of the human heart and the relationship of man to his fellows and to God. Spanish Jewry, however, was soon to produce a philosopher of a different type, one who attained great fame among both Jews and non-Jews through the new views, which he sought to incorporate into Judaism. This was Rabbi Shlomo ibn Gabirol.

4. The Doctrine of Rabbi Shlomo ibn Gabirol

The Prosperity During the Rule of Samuel Ha-Nagid, Grand Vizier—How Samuel, Originally a Grocer, Became Viceroy of the Land—Samuel's Aid to Rabbi Shlomo ibn Gabirol, the Poet-Philosopher—Ibn Gabirol's Philosophy, a Mixture of Philosophy and Cabala (Mysticism)—The Opponents of Shlomo ibn Gabirol and His Defender, Abraham ibn Ezra

The first half of the eleventh century saw Jewish culture in full bloom in Spain. In general, the Jews in Spain at that time were secure and prosperous and this led to the immigration of thousands of Jews, merchants and scholars, not only from Babylonia but from Northern Africa and Palestine.

At the head of the Hispanic Jewish community at that time stood a man of whom it was said that "both knowledge and wealth were united in his person." He was immensely rich, a merchant prince and at the same time thoroughly versed in Talmudic lore, the outstanding rabbi of his generation, and also a scientist of note. His name was Samuel Ha-Nagid ("Ismael ibn Yosef bin Nagdila" in Arabic).

The life story of Samuel Ha-Nagid reads something like a fairy tale, but the facts have been confirmed by all the historians of that era. He was born in 993 in the city of Cordova. His father came from a small town in southern Spain. He had studied Jewish lore and Talmud at the feet of the most eminent rabbis and scholars of that day, but had also acquired the knowledge of Arabic and other languages, and was particularly interested in the sciences. When he was about twenty years of age, a civil strife broke out in Cordova between the Berbers (a North African tribe) and the Arabs who had lived there before. The situation became so strained that the Jews of the city, and Samuel among them, had to flee for their lives. Samuel went to northern Spain and settled in the city of Malaga, where he made a meager living by running a small grocery store. However, he still continued to devote a good part of his time to the study of Jewish law, foreign languages, and the sciences and thus, within a relatively short time, he became an accomplished linguist and could converse and write with ease in Arabic, Latin, Spanish, and Berberic.

Samuel's store was not far from the palace of Abu al-Kasim, the Grand Vizier. This gentleman served as viceroy in behalf of King Habus of the province of Granada. (Spain had not yet become a united empire, and each province was ruled by a king of its own.) One day the Grand Vizier sent his maidservant to Samuel's store to procure food for the palace. The maid asked the grocer if he would write a letter for her. Samuel complied with her request and from that time on she sought his aid in all her correspondence. Once she asked him to write several Arabic letters for her. Impressed by Samuel's linguistic ability, the maid showed these letters to her master who was amazed by the eloquent style and the exquisite handwriting.

The Grand Vizier sent for the Jewish grocer, and when he saw that he was a man of erudition and scholarship, he asked him to give up his store and become Secretary to the Grand Vizier instead. The viceroy soon found out that Samuel was a man of wisdom and great political acumen and often discussed crucial issues with him. In advising the king, the Grand Vizier, in his turn, leaned heavily upon advice given him by Samuel.

One day the Grand Vizier became ill and he knew that he would not live much longer. The king himself came to call upon his trusted minister and asked him whom he would recommend that he, the king, appoint as the new Grand Vizier. The Grand Vizier confessed to his king that, during recent years, he had placed great confidence in his secretary and entrusted many of his responsibilities to him. He recommended that the king appoint that secretary, Samuel the Jew, as the new Grand Vizier.

The Grand Vizier died soon thereafter and the king asked Samuel to fill the vacant position. At that time the Grand Vizier was invested with almost unlimited powers, for the king took little interest in the management of his country and left all administrative duties to the Grand Vizier. Under Samuel's leadership, the province of Granada flourished and prospered and became one of the most powerful provinces of all the Spanish lands.

Samuel, however, had his share of enemies. Among them was an Arab who had purchased Samuel's grocery store when the latter was first appointed secretary to the former Grand Vizier. This man envied Samuel's rapid rise to power and, whenever he would see the Grand Vizier on the street, he would berate him with the crudest epithets. One day Samuel passed by with the king himself and, when the latter heard the Arab's vile outburst, he commanded that Samuel punish the disloyal subject by cutting out his tongue. Samuel, however, proceeded in a manner quite different from that recommended by his king. He called the Arab grocer and asked him why he was so disgruntled. The Arab replied that he was deep in debt, whereupon Samuel gave him enough money to discharge his obligations and to buy some new merchandise so that he might enlarge his store. From that day on the Arab had only words of praise and blessing for the Grand Vizier who repaid evil with good.

Not very long after this incident, the king and Samuel once again passed by the little grocery store and the king asked the Grand Vizier whether he had carried out his command to cut out the tongue of the little merchant within. Samuel replied that he had indeed done so, but in a manner slightly different from what the king had suggested. He had extirpated his enemy's evil tongue by dealing kindly with him, and the latter had now acquired a new organ of speech that was full of praise for his benefactor.

Samuel was the author of many works on the Talmud, the Hebrew language, and also of a philosophical treatise entitled *Ben Koheleth*. But Samuel is remembered most of all for the support he gave to Jewish scholars, particularly to Rabbi Shlomo ibn Gabirol whom he supplied with the necessities of life so that he could devote all his time to writing and study.

Rabbi Shlomo ibn Gabirol, or, as he was known in Arabic, Abu ibn Suleiman ibn Yechiya ibn Gabirol, was one of the greatest philosophers of the "Golden Era" of Spanish Jewry. His Hebrew works, particularly the poem entitled "Keter Malchuth," were all familiar among his people, but, strange to say, his masterpiece, *Mekor Chayim* was totally unknown. This latter work was translated from Arabic into Latin and was preserved in the National Library of Paris for close to eight hundred years under the title of *Fons Vitae* (*The Source of Life*). The author's name was listed as "Aviebron" and also "Avensebrol." The translators of the work were a monk and a Jew who had embraced Christianity. The monk's name was Dominicus Gundisolvi; the Jewish renegade was one Johann Hispalenis whose original name was Abraham ben David. It was only recently that the Hebrew translation of the original Arabic manuscript was found. That translation was made by the scholar Rabbi Shem Tob Falaquera in 1260.

Mekor Chayim had a great impact on medieval philosophy, particularly upon the Christian world. It is a profound philosophical work written in a lofty poetic style.

Before we go into the study of this book, however, we will do well to learn more about the life of the author. No one knows the exact date of his birth. But it is known that Ibn Gabirol was in Cordova at about the same time as Samuel Ha-Nagid and that he, too, was forced to flee Cordova and then settled in Malaga where he eked out a bare living. Despite his extreme poverty he was able to devote much of his time to the study of Talmud, Hebrew, Arabic, and other languages and also to the sciences. When still a very young man, Ibn Gabirol had already written quite a number of Hebrew songs and liturgical poems, which were incorporated into the Jewish High Holiday prayer book. One of these is "Ascharot," a hymn about the 613 commandments, which is still recited on Shevuoth today. In it there is a line in which the author states, "I am only sixteen years of age but I have acquired the wisdom of one of eighty."

Ibn Gabirol composed both religious hymns and secular songs. Outstanding among them is his "Keter Malchuth," in which he states his philosophy of God. He also wrote a book entitled *Muvchar Peninim,* in which he set down, in Hebrew, excerpts from the works of several Arab philosophers concerning ethics and human conduct.

Shlomo ibn Gabirol never married because, despite the support given him by Samuel Ha-Nagid and other patrons, he found that he would never have enough to support a family. The date of his death is not known for sure. According to contemporary historians, such as Judah Alharizi and Rabbi Moses ibn Ezra, Shlomo ibn Gabirol died before he reached the age of thirty. According to Arabic source material, however, he was born in 1021 and died in 1058 and thus lived to the age of thirty-six or thirty-seven.

The cause of his death is also a mystery. It is said that he did not die a natural death, but was murdered. Legend has it as follows: Ibn Gabirol had written a splendid song which he then read to a friend, a Turk, who himself was the author of some Arabic hymns. Envious of the far superior talent of Ibn Gabirol, the Turk murdered him and buried the body in his own garden, planting a fig tree over the grave.

There were many other fig trees in that garden, but the one planted over the grave of Ibn Gabirol came into bloom much earlier than the rest of the trees. This phenomenon was reported to the king who asked that a study be made of the soil on which that particular plant was growing. The terrified Turk then confessed his crime and received the death penalty.

Now as to Ibn Gabirol's philosophical approach as revealed in "Keter Malchuth" and also in *Mekor Chayim.* The poem "Keter Malchuth" deals with God, as Ibn Gabirol, the poet-philosopher, saw Him. In it, like Plato, he states that the Lord created the world from material that was in existence prior to creation. Actually, Ibn Gabirol felt that every Jew must believe that the world was created without the aid of any preexisting material. However as a follower of Plato, he attempts to resolve his conflict in the following manner:

"The Lord," says Ibn Gabirol, "created His world from nothing, and created matter from nothingness. He set up huge pillars and none other has done like Him." But, Ibn Gabirol adds, "He had ordained a green strip of land, stones of 'tohu va-vohu' (void and formless) and it is from there that the waters of the surface came forth." The author means to say that he does agree with Plato that, before the creation of the world, there did exist material which had no shape or form and that this was the basis used by God when He made the heavens and the earth. How, then, can Ibn Gabirol reconcile this point of view with the belief, professed at the same time by him, that the world was made from nothingness?

In part, however, Ibn Gabirol based his philosophy also upon the works of the Cabalists, such as "Sefer Ha-Yetzirah." He believes that God created ten "emanations" of Himself by means of which He rules the world. The Cabalists conceive of these "ten emanations" as symbolizing the various aspects of culture such as wisdom, beauty, and strength. Ibn Gabirol, however, interprets these emanations as being ten stars which form the basis of the universe. He calls them "wheels" or "worlds." First and lowest of all, is the earth on which we live. Then, in ascending order, comes the "world of stars." This is Mercury, the "wheel of wisdom and understanding." Then comes "Nugah" (Venus); then the sun, and after her, "Madim" (Mars) is fifth, "Zedek" (Jupiter) is sixth, and hereby he refers to Jupiter as the force that "awakens man to the fear of God, righteousness, and repentance." The seventh world is "Shabthai" (Saturn), "which rouses man to war, pillage, and hunger." The eight "wheel" is the one that moves all the others, but the highest of them all is the tenth one, which is the intellect. Ibn Gabirol calls this tenth world the "wisdom of the universe" ("intellectus universalis"). To this he adds that there are two additional forces that rule the world, first, "the soul of the world" ("anima universalis") and "universal nature" ("natura-generalis"). Thus Ibn Gabirol has divided the universe into ten worlds in ascending order, all ruled by the "wisdom of the universe" which is aided by "the soul of the world" (spiritual power) and "universal nature" (natural forces).

We can see, then, that Ibn Gabirol has taken much of his philosophy from the mystic writings of the Cabala which he attempts to combine with other philosophies not exactly in accordance with the accepted Jewish spirit.

It is for this reason that, while his hymns and songs were incorporated into Jewish liturgy, his philosophical treatises were given scant regard in those days. When his essays were first translated into Hebrew, many eminent scholars of his day openly spoke out against them. Among his opponents was the famed Ravad (the author of "Ha-emunah Ha-ramah") who explicitly stated that Ibn Gabirol's book ran counter to the Jewish spirit and to the Jewish faith.

One generation after Ibn Gabirol, however, saw the rise of another Jewish philosopher, Rabbi Abraham ibn Ezra, who proved to be a great defender of the views held by Ibn Gabirol. The next chapter will deal with his life and the ideas he advanced.

5. Abraham ibn Ezra and Moses ibn Ezra

Abraham ibn Ezra's Great Erudition, Knowledge, and Broadmindedness—The Tragedy of His Son's Apostasy and His Wanderings Through the World—His Belief in the Limited Power of God—He Maintains, However, That Everything Is Possible for God—Moses ibn Ezra's Book Ha-Tarshish *and His Philosophical Treatise* Arugath Habosem

The beginning of the twelfth century marked the setting of the sun of enlightenment in the Arab world and particularly in Spain. The great interest in culture and knowledge gradually waned. At this time Christianity first strengthened its hold in southern Spain, and with it Latin, which was the language of Christian civilization and scholarship, came to power.

As Arab interest in the sciences decreased, the rest of the world no longer paid much attention to the Arabic language as a medium of culture. Spain was filled with unrest and civil strife between cities and provinces. Some of the Islamic rulers attempted to convert the Jews living within their provinces, and in many instances the Jews could avert such coercion only through huge bribes.

Even so, southern Spain still was a center of Jewish culture. There were still great rabbis who were masters in Talmudic lore; inspired poets wrote their greatest works in the Hebrew language, and, above all, Jewish philosophy still flourished and developed. One of the outstanding Jewish philosophers of those days was Rabbi Abraham ibn Ezra (His full name was Abraham ben Meir ibn Ezra). He came from a distinguished family and was one of four brothers, each of whom attained eminence in his own field.

Rabbi Abraham ibn Ezra is the author of a commentary on the Bible which is included in many editions of the Pentateuch. He was a man of versatile interests: a poet, a philosopher, a Bible critic, an authority on Hebrew grammar, an astronomer, and well versed in many other sciences. Unfortunately such versatiliy often has little financial reward, and so it was with Abraham ibn Ezra. He remained a poor man all of his life, which he did not mind, however. Being possessed of an excellent sense of humor and the ability to laugh at his bitter fate, he wrote satirical songs in which he poked fun at the misfortunes with which his life seemed to be filled. In one such ditty, he describes his efforts to ask for financial aid from the wealthy.

As far as we know, Abraham ibn Ezra was born in 1092 in the city of Toledo, in Spain. We have no account of whom he married and how many children he had, but in one of his works he himself states that his family consisted of a wife and five children. His first son, Isaac, was the most talented of all his children and a famous poet. However, the young man embraced Christianity and from that day forward his father mourned him as though he were dead.

Rabbi Abraham ibn Ezra lived in Spain until 1140. Then, because of the tragedy of his son's apostasy, he could no longer remain at home and began to travel around the world. He was one of the most widely traveled Jewish scholars of his day. His life can be divided into two parts: from 1092 to 1140, the years he spent in Spain, and from 1140 to his death in 1167, the period in which he remained abroad. He traveled through France, Egypt, and Babylonia and also saw India, North Africa, and Palestine. During these wanderings he never ceased to add to his knowledge and erudition, but, because of his personal misfortunes, he became interested in the pseudo-science of astrology and came to believe in it.

While wandering through the world he produced many scholarly works. In his first book, *Moznayim,* he dealt with the Hebrew language. Then he fell ill and was nursed back to health by devoted friends. Upon his recovery he decided to write a book on cabalistic problems, particularly concerning the "Ineffable Name" of God. His work was entitled *Sefer Ha-Shem* (*The Book of His Name*) and was considered a great literary treasure by the students of the Cabala. Thus far it would seem that Abraham ibn Ezra inclined strongly toward mysticism, but there was another aspect to his scholarship which found little appreciation with the mystics or even with most religious Jews. We are referring to his commentary on the Pentateuch where he inserted remarks which really could be called the first examples of modern Bible criticism. He was the first scholar to dare state the opinion that certain parts of the Pentateuch were added to the Bible at a later date and therefore the Bible was not a uniform work. Moreover, he made several changes in the Biblical text, which, of course, were repugnant to the religious, who felt that every word of the Bible was revealed to Israel by God, and must never be altered.

The mind of Abraham ibn Ezra must have been filled with many conflicting ideas. He wrote a book entitled *Yesod Morah,* which is based in its entirety upon the philosophical approach of Plato, whose thinking is quite foreign to the Jewish ideology. Plato believed that God created the world from preexisting material, contrary to the Jewish belief that the world was created by God from nothing. Abraham ibn Ezra agrees with Plato, who advanced the proposition that the material of which the world was created was already in existence, waiting for God to shape it into the universe as we know it today. This is not a Jewish view. On the other hand, Abraham ibn Ezra wrote a treatise entitled *Iggeret Ha-Shabbat* where he sharply attacks those who would keep the Sabbath only on Saturday instead of beginning its observance on Friday evening. Here his approach seems somewhat like that of a religious fanatic, bitterly condemning all those whose beliefs differed from his own. He denounces those who would negate the Oral Tradition, who would approach the Torah in a nontraditional manner; and all this at the same time that he was the author of a book and a commentary on the Bible which were very definitely not in accordance with accepted views and beliefs. Abraham ibn Ezra was a great astronomer and authored a book on the science of astronomy, but at the same time he was interested in the very primitive art of "star gazing" and believed in the thesis of astrology which holds that the fate of every man is influenced by the constellation under which he was born. Abraham ibn Ezra was also the first one to state that the Book of Isaiah was not written by one prophet. He declared that Chapters 40-66 were of authorship other than that of the first half of the book. Naturally, these views did not find favor in the eyes of the orthodox. Ibn Ezra was also the author of a great variety of poems and songs. Some of these were religious in nature and were incorporated into the Jewish prayer book for the High Holidays; others were love songs and poems on various subjects. He also wrote a textbook on Hebrew grammar and devised a table dealing with the orbits of the stars.

So far, we have talked about his writings in general, but now we shall pay particular attention to Abraham ibn Ezra's philosophical work where he most plainly states his way of thinking. It is the book mentioned before entitled *Yesod Morah* (*The Foundation of Reverence*). Much like Ibn Gabriol, the poet-philosopher who, like Ibn Ezra, spent most of his life in poverty, Abraham was an advocate of Plato's view that it is true that the world was created by God, but from preexisting material. Naturally, his opponents posed such questions as who, then, was the creator of this material which existed before the creation of the world, and what was the stuff from which the material was created; and why did not the creator of the material create the world? Ibn Ezra replied in the vein of the great Greek philosopher, Plato, that God only changed the form of the basic stuff itself because the basic material existed long before the world was ever created. However, the origin can not be questioned, just as we can not ask, "Who created God?" It seems to him that the creation of the world is thus more plausible. Again, like Ibn Gabirol, Ibn Ezra believed that all men were subject to the influence of the stellar constellations. He believed that there are ten spheres through which man must pass, and the soul of man is ruled by the constellations until it reaches the tenth and highest level of perfection, at which time it passes to the sole jurisdiction of God. But here he begins to mix cabalistic ideas into his purely rational philosophical approach. For example, he says that if one knows how properly to pronounce the "Ineffable Name" of God, one can use it to cause miracles to occur. He raises the question of whether God's direct interest and rule affect only the course of the universe in general, or whether His concern extends to every single individual, so that no man can do anything that is not in accordance with the will of God. Jewish philosophers have been of divided minds as regards this issue. However, Ibn Ezra's attitude in this matter is not too clear as he sometimes is in agreement with both sides of the argument.

As to the question whether man has a free will, Ibn Ezra says: God does determine the acts of man, and even He does not know what man will do in the future. Therefore man has been given complete freedom of action, to do as he pleases.

Thus we can see that there is a conflict in Ibn Ezra's mind, even as regards the basic nature of God Himself. On one hand, he believes that nothing is impossible for God to do, that He can create all things and knows the course of events from the very beginning, but, on the other hand, he places a limit upon God's power, maintaining that He could fashion the world only from stuff that was present before Creation, also that God knows everything, and yet the future of individual man is unknown to Him. In this book, Ibn Ezra also discusses the Biblical commandments and attempts to set down his own interpretations of them. Unfortunately, however, he did not succeed very well in what he set out to do. In general, *Yesod Morah* does not rank among the outstanding treatises that came out from the "Golden Age" of Jewish culture in Spain.

Just as Ibn Ezra's works present a puzzle, so does his personal life, particularly as regards his relationship with a relative, Moses ibn Ezra, the great poet-philosopher who as a poet, towered far above him. Moses fell madly in love with the beautiful daughter of Abraham's brother, Isaac, and she reciprocated his affections. But Abraham was against permitting the girl to marry Moses and, instead, married her off to his younger brother. This marriage was to end in tragedy.

Moses ibn Ezra was known as one of the greatest Jewish poets of the Golden Age in Spain. In addition, he was a linguist and philosopher of note. The Ibn Ezra family, in general, produced many distinguished men. Abraham's brothers were, Isaac, the eldest, then after Abraham came Aaron, and last and youngest, Joseph. (The Arab names by which they were known were Abu Yitzchak, Abu Ibrahim, Abu Harun, and Abu Chadzazh). Their father, Judah, occupied a high position at the court of King Habus. Moses ibn Ezra studied Talmud with his cousin Isaac, who was a great Talmudic scholar. At that time Moses was still a young man and fell madly in love with his relative's daughter, Shoshana, who was only a year younger. Rabbi Isaac refused to hear of any talk of marriage between the two. Abraham ibn Ezra and Rabbi Joseph sided with Isaac in the matter. Moses, however, felt it would be impossible for him to live without Shoshana.

It was then that Moses began to write his famous love songs, in which he declared that Shoshana had been predestined for him in heaven, and that their souls were part of each other so that, apart, he and his lady love each had only half a soul.

However, all of Moses' pleas were in vain, despite his fervent avowals that he would either marry Shoshana or not marry at all. Finally, Isaac married off Shoshana to Joseph ibn Ezra, much against her will. She died in childbirth with the name of her true lover upon her lips.

When Moses learned of Shoshana's death, his grief knew no bounds. He wrote a heart-rending elegy which he sent to her father. Reading this outpouring of sorrow, Rabbi Isaac and his brothers realized their share in the blame for Shoshana's early death and regretted their refusal to permit the girl to marry the man she loved. They begged Moses' forgiveness, but Moses was unwilling to have anything to do with them. He left Spain and traveled first through Portugal and then through many other lands.

Moses ibn Ezra wrote many songs. Some are in tribute to his lady love, others lament the falseness of relatives and the disloyalty of friends. He sings of the beauty of nature and of women, particularly in his epic *Ha-Tarshish*. (The numerical value of the word "Tarshish" is 1210, corresponding to the number of verses in the volume). The book is called *Sefer Anak*. It was written in accordance with an Arab form of rhyming, and the verses represent the most eloquent expressions of poetry, philosophy, imagination, epic drama, emotion, and meditation. In addition, Moses wrote many religious hymns that have become part of the Jewish Holiday services. Best known among these is the prayer "Ashrei Ayin" (Happy is the eye that has seen all this). This is recited during the Day of Atonement and describes the service as performed by the High Priest on that day in the ancient Temple of Jerusalem.

Broken by tragedy and grief, Moses ibn Ezra saw the world and creation in the darkest of colors. Hence his philosophical treatise, which was translated from the original Arabic into Hebrew and entitled *Arugas Habosem* is in anything but an optimistic vein. Neither the Arab nor the Hebrew version was ever set in print and the manuscripts are to be found in the manuscript departments of the National Libraries in Leningrad, Hamburg, and Oxford. According to the catalogue of the Oxford Library, *Arugas Habosem* is composed of seven chapters. The first chapter deals with God Himself; the second with monotheism, the third with the attributes which men ascribe to God, that is, expressions like, the "hand" of God and the "eyes" of God. The other chapters discuss nature, the world and man, and what man's relationship should be toward his fellows. According to the abstract, Moses ibn Ezra shares Plato's views concerning creation. On the whole, *Arugas Habosem* is filled with pessimism and is a work of little joy.

Later in life, Moses ibn Ezra was to derive some measure of comfort from the great poet Judah Ha-Levi, whom he met and who told him that he, too, had been cruelly deceived in his love for a maiden. Judah poured out his own grief in a song which he dedicated to Moses ibn Ezra.

Moses ibn Ezra died in 1138 at the age of sixty-eight.

6. Rabbi Judah Ha-Levi

Judah Ha-Levi's Opposition to Greek Philosophy—His Own Nationalist View Concerning Jews and Judaism—His Book, The Kuzari—*The Debate Involving a Philosopher, a Christian Clergyman, a Mohammedan Religious Leader, and a Rabbi—The Legend About Judah Ha-Levi's Death*

Judah Ha-Levi (his Arabic name was Abu al Hassan al Lavi) was born in Toledo, southern Spain, at the end of the eleventh century. Some of his biographers state that the year of his birth was 1085, while others claim that it was 1088. He was the only son of Samuel of Castile and was sent to study at the then famous academy of Rabbi Isaac Alfasi. In addition to Jewish lore, Judah also studied sciences, particularly medicine. He perfected his knowledge of Arabic and read all the Arabic translations of the works of the Greek philosophers, as well as the outstanding works of the Arab thinkers. Thereafter he went to Cordova in western Spain, which at that time was the cultural center of the entire country.

Judah was still young when he began to write the many religious poems and hymns that later became part of the Jewish Holy Day prayer books. It is thought that he wrote more than three hundred religious poems, prayers, and lamentations. He was also the author of a great number of more worldly songs, dealing with nature, women, and earthly pleasures.

After a thorough study of Greek philosophy, Judah Ha-Levi came to the conclusion that Greek philosophy was utterly foreign to the Jewish spirit, because it was sterile. "It has only flowers but bears no fruit," said Judah. He gave expression to his opinion in a song which soon became famous throughout the Jewish world and contained the basic thought of his philosophy. The following is a rather free rendition:

> Do not succumb to the charm of Greek wisdom,
> For it bears only flowers, but no fruit.
> And it teaches that the earth was never created
> And that God has not spread out the skies above it.
> It knows of no beginning of creation,
> Nor an end to time,
> Therefore, O man, heed my words, their thoughts are confused
> And built on sterile ground.
> All it will do is confuse and confound you.
> Therefore, why walk upon crooked paths
> And leave the one true way?

This song is mainly an attack upon the philosophy of Plato who claimed that the world was created from some preexisting material and also on that of Aristotle, who maintained that the story of divine creation was a piece of fiction. Judah Ha-Levi offers a substitute philosophy which is based on Judaism rather than upon the ideas advanced by the Greek thinkers.

Judah Ha-Levi explains his philosophy in a book entitled *The Kuzari*. We shall speak later of the reason for the title of the book and the exact purpose for which it was written. For the present, however, let us study the main points which the author advanced in this outstanding work.

1. God gave the Torah to the Jewish nation and made the people of Israel His people. Why did God choose the Jewish people? Well, this is just like asking why God created the sun, the moon, and the stars. It should be sufficient to say that it was God's will to do so. And even as it was His will to bring the universe into being, so was it also His desire to elect the Jewish people to be the bearers of His Torah to the rest of mankind. The logical explanation for the choice of Israel would simply be that God wanted one nation in the world to be His very own and to proclaim His name to all the other peoples. And His choice fell upon the Israelites, the children of Jacob.

2. If we believe that Israel is indeed the chosen people, we should readily see that we do not need to draw upon Greek philosophy to strengthen our own religion. For the history of the Jews has taken a course quite different from that of any other nation. No other nation has been saved from slavery and made God's people as was Israel, nor has any other tribe received a divine law on Mount Sinai, and partaken of food from heaven during forty years of wandering in the wilderness. Therefore, says Judah Ha-Levi, the other peoples cannot compare themselves to Israel nor can Israel regard itself as being like the rest of the nations of the world.

3. "And I will walk among you, and will be your God, and ye shall be my people." (Lev. 26:12)—these words were communicated by God through Moses to the Jewish people alone and not to any of the other nations. Therefore even the wisest words of the thinkers and scholars of other peoples have no appreciable impact on us. Since God has chosen Israel above the rest of the nations, it is the latter that must learn from Israel, and not Israel from them.

The Kuzari was written in Arabic, as it was customary in those days to set down all scholarly works in that language. Judah ibn Tibon translated it into Hebrew and changed the original lengthy Arab title of the book to the much briefer form of the *The Kuzari*.

The purpose of the book was, as stated before, to set forth the views held by its author concerning the faith and philosophy of Judaism. Judah Ha-Levi set down his ideas in the form of a discussion, much like the Book of Job, which presents many important thoughts concerning reward and punishment and the divine influence upon human fate. It is in the form of a debate among three friends who came to commiserate with the unfortunate

Job. Judah Ha-Levi chooses as his characters a philosopher who believes in no religion whatever, a Christian priest, a Mohammedan scholar, and a rabbi, each of whom gives the views of his school of thought on God and man. He based the book upon an event that had actually occurred not very long before. The pagan king of the Khazars, desirous of changing his religion, invited the representatives of the leading faiths of the civilized world to explain their beliefs to him, so that he might choose the religion which would appeal to him most of all. The result was that the king of the land of the Khazars embraced Judaism in the year 740 A.D. and then commanded all of his subjects to do likewise. What Judah Ha-Levi attempted to do in *The Kuzari* was to retell in his own words the debates among the various religious leaders, as he imagined them to have taken place before King Bulan, and to show what it was that led the king to choose Judaism in preference to any of the other religions.

The book begins with an account of a dream of the king of the Khazars, a vision which he saw several nights in succession. In this dream the heathen king beheld an angel who told him that his mode of worship was not the right one. The angel made it clear to Bulan that God was well pleased with his honesty and with his good intentions, but disapproved of the polytheistic religion held by him and his subjects. Much perturbed by these visions, Bulan resolved to find a new faith, but he was by no means sure which of all the religions of the world would be the proper one for him to adopt.

To help him solve his problem, the king summoned a philosopher who was thoroughly conversant with Greek thought. He asked the scholar many questions concerning the relationship between man and God, what man must believe in order to be truly God-fearing, and what his relations should be with his fellow men. The philosopher told the king that there was indeed a God, but that He was so far away from the earth that he knew little of mankind or its needs and therefore prayer was of no avail. God was indeed the Supreme Being, the thinker continued, but he had no hand in the creation of either earth or man. Man, descended from a more primitive form of life, had fallen heir to all the baser desires and traits of his natural ancestors and therefore was not entirely free to be his own master. The philosopher admitted that man could exercise a limited control over his baser urges by using his intellect, but intellect was not dependent upon any religion, and a human being could be on a very high moral level without believing in any form of deity.

The king was not entirely satisfied with what the expounder of Greek philosophy had to offer. He then decided to call upon one representative each of the Christian and Moslem faiths to explain their views to him. He had no intention at that time to summon a Jew, because he regarded the children of Israel as a "fallen and depraved nation." First the priest was brought into the king's presence and thoroughly questioned on the beliefs of Christianity. After the priest had ended his presentation, the king asked him on what Christianity was based. The churchman replied that his religion was derived in its entirety from the Bible and the words of the prophets. The king then asked, "And to whom was the Bible first given?" "To the Jews," replied the priest. Somewhat taken aback, the king said that he failed to understand why he had to be given a lecture on Jewish philosophy from a second-hand source, and he dismissed the clergyman curtly.

Next came the spokesman for the faith of Islam, who carefully expounded the bases of his religion to the king. Again the king asked for the source from which Mohammedanism was derived. When the Moslem replied, "From the Bible," and when the king had ascertained that this was the same "Bible of the Jews" from which Christianity had also drawn the basic tenets of its philosophy, the Mohammedan too was dismissed.

At last, after much troubled deliberation, the king came to the conclusion that, if two major religious faiths were dependent for their philosophy upon the Bible of the Jews, it would be best, after all, to call upon a Jew to present the views set forth in the teachings of Judaism.

And thus it came about that Rabbi Isaac Sangari, the most prominent among Jewish scholars, was brought to the king of the Khazars and questioned in detail about his religion. This learned man then proceeded to give to the king a brief explanation of Judaism, set forth in seven cardinal points as follows:

1. There is a great difference between ethics as acquired from childhood through the teachings of religion, and ethics as taught on the basis of philosophical reasoning. Philosophy alone cannot teach a person good habits. Morals and proper behavior must be instilled into the human mind from earliest childhood through religious teachings, if the person is to maintain such habits throughout later life.

2. The Torah tells us that God created the world and everything in it from nothing, and that He used no preexistent materials in their creation. This eliminates the need for debates as to what the "preexistent" material was and who was its creator. And since it was God who created the world, He is eternal. He existed before the world came into being, and He will continue to exist even if He should see fit for some reason to destroy the world. This means that God can have no body, since a physical body cannot endure forever.

3. The above shows us the unique nature of God which the human mind cannot grasp. God cannot be described or pictured as having human characteristics. If, notwithstanding, the Bible uses such expressions as "God spoke," "the hand of God," it does so only to make Him more comprehensible to the human mind.

4. In order to give us some understanding of Himself, God gave us prophets to show us some of His divine guidance of the world. The prophets carry

within them a spark of the divine. It was for this purpose that God chose one nation, the Jewish people, and descended to Mt. Sinai to give them the Torah.

5. Every living thing in the world is endowed with a soul, a force that keeps it alive. The nature of this "soul," however, is not alike in all creatures. Lower forms of life are possessed only of the power to grow and develop, and to reproduce their kind. Men were given the additional gift of the ability to think. And certain human beings, a chosen few, have been endowed with the faculty to rise above their human limitations and come close to God Himself.

6. Man has the freedom of choice to do as he pleases, and, therefore, he is entitled to reward when he does good, and liable to punishment for evil acts. God does have advance knowledge of what will happen in the future, but does not attempt to influence man in his actions, so that man has absolute freedom of will, and the opportunity to choose for himself between good and evil.

7. The Jewish religion is not universal in character. God gave the Torah only to the Jews and to no other group. The Jewish religion, therefore, is national rather than international in character. Other nations and other religions also serve a definite purpose in helping advance the development of mankind. But the promises and prophecies contained in the Bible apply only to the people of Israel, and the land of Israel is supreme over all other countries of the world.

The spokesman for the Jewish faith then continued to enlighten the king of the Khazars on the various commandments contained in the Bible pertaining to the manner in which God must be served, and to human relationships. He also told the heathen ruler that some of these commandments could be explained by logical reasoning, while others seemed to have no logical basis and were given to us in order to test whether we would follow the dictates of God's word even if we were not given any acceptable reason for so doing.

Judah Ha-Levi enjoyed equally great fame as a poet. He was the author, as we said before, of more than three hundred poems, hymns, prayers, and elegies which became part of the Jewish Holy Day prayer book. He is particularly known for his "Songs of Zion" which he wrote during his later years.

We are told that when he was about sixty years of age, Judah Ha-Levi decided to leave Spain and go to Palestine. It must be remembered that such a journey entailed great difficulties in those days. The Second Crusade had just ended in failure, and the defeated Christians vented their anger upon the Jews, and frightful pogroms took place all over the Christian world, particularly in Germany, so that most Jews did not dare travel. Nevertheless Judah Ha-Levi together with his only daughter and his grandson Judah, with whom he lived, was determined to settle in the land of Israel. It was at that time that he wrote his famous "Songs of Zion," in which he pictured Mother Zion as the second great love of his life; and which secured him a place among the great Jewish poets of Spain.

The first stage of Judah's long journey took him to Egypt, where he was summoned to the residence of the "Nagid" Samuel Abu Mansur, the physician of the Caliph, who had the power of viceroy in the land. Abu Mansur offered Judah some money for the long trip to Palestine, but Judah refused it with these words: "Why should I take money from you? What have I done for you to deserve it?"

All we know about the rest of Judah's journey is that he spent some time in Damascus. Nothing was heard of him thereafter. Legend has it that Judah was crushed by the horse of a Mohammedan rider as he knelt down upon the soil of the Holy Land to kiss it. How much truth there is to this report, no one knows.

7. Maimonides, the Giant of Jewish Philosophers

The Jews in Spain in the Early Days of Maimonides—His Wanderings with His Father Before Settling in Fez (North Africa)—Maimonides as a Philosopher and Physician—Maimonides as Personal Physician to the Caliph of Egypt—The Significance of His Book Yad Hachazakah—*His Philosophical Views—What Is the* Guide for the Perplexed—*Objections to the Ideas of Aristotle Concerning God and the World—Does Maimonides Contradict Himself in His Works?*

The second half of the twelfth century was a difficult time for the Jews living in Europe and Asia. The Jews were persecuted in southern Spain, where the Mohammedans ruled, as well as in the northern part of the country, which was under Catholic dominion. Those were the days of the Crusades which resulted not in any victory for the Christians, but in persecutions of the Jews.

In southern Spain where, for centuries, the Jews had lived in peace with their Mohammedan neighbors, life now became impossible for them. The fanatical elements among the Moslems seized the seat of power and demanded that all the "infidels" in the land convert to Mohammedanism. All the famed Talmudical academies were closed and their teachers and students had to move elsewhere. At that time the situation was still somewhat better in the north, for the Catholic rulers there were not yet very powerful. However, they, too, hated the Jews and were already planning to set up the dreaded Inquisition which was to present the Jews in Spain with two alternatives: baptism or death.

It was in those days, when the economic and spiritual fortunes of Spanish Jewry were on the decline, that a new light arose in Israel which was to shine not only upon Spain, but upon all the rest of the world. This was a leader whose name was to become known not only to that generation, but to men throughout the ages. He was Moses ben Maimon, better known as Maimonides.

In discussing Maimonides, we must first decide which aspect of his knowledge and talents we shall study, for Maimonides was a man so versatile and gifted that it is hard to imagine that so many gifts and abilities could have been combined in a single person. Therefore, if we speak of "the Rambam" (Rabbi Moses ben Maimon), we see before us the great Jewish scholar, the authority on Biblical and Talmudic Law who compiled all of Jewish legislation into one gigantic work, *Yad Hachazakah,* which consisted of fourteen parts and became the one supreme authority on Jewish law save the Talmud itself. A statement that "the Rambam decided thus," meant that the decision was final with no recourse to appeal. Indeed some scholars debated the reasons that might have been the bases for Maimonides' decisions on such matters, but the validity of the decision itself was never questioned.

We get quite a different picture of Maimonides, however, when we study him as one of the greatest Jewish philosophers in the history of the Jews of Spain, and as the author of the famed work *Guide for the Perplexed* in which he presented one of the most profound and original approaches to Judaism that has ever been attempted. Here we have a man who has definite opinions of his own as regards both God and man, views with which even those who regarded him as their supreme Talmudical authority often violently disagreed.

Maimonides was also an eminent physician who wrote a number of works concerning cures for a variety of ailments.

In addition, he was the author of a book entitled *A Commentary on the Mishnayot* on which he worked for seven years and which takes a prominent place in Jewish scholarly literature.

Maimonides also found time to send out brochures and messages of comfort to his brethren throughout the world, in which he addressed his fellow Jews much as a devoted father would address his children. In these letters he gave much encouragement and renewed hope to the Jewish communities throughout the world, wherever they suffered persecution. He told them that the people of Israel would live forever, and that, if they would only have faith in God, their troubles would eventually come to an end.

Maimonides accomplished a great deal in his lifetime. He died when he was seventy years of age, after much hardship, labor, and personal tragedy. At his death he was mourned far and wide as a great Talmudist, an eminent philosopher, as the leader of the Jewish community of Egypt, and as physician to the Caliph, Ibn Saladin, the pride of the Arab world.

Rabbi Moses ben Maimon (his Arabic name was Abu Amran Mussa ben Maimon Obed Allah was born in Cordova, Spain, on Passover, 1135 A.D. During his youth he studied with his father who was a Talmudic scholar of note and served as judge of the religious court of the city of Cordova. He also devoted much time to the secular sciences and became adept in the Arabic language. It soon became apparent that the boy Moses would some day be a great scholar. He was a child prodigy, with a photographic memory, and he could immediately repeat by heart whatever his father and his other instructors had taught him but once.

When Maimonides was thirteen years old, the Almohades, a fanatical sect of the Islami faith, came to power and immediately issued an order to the effect that all Jews must either convert to Mohammedanism or leave the city. Rabbi Maimon and his family left Cordova and for ten years wandered around both northern and southern Spain in search of a place to live. At last the older Maimon decided to leave Spain altogether, and the family settled in Fez (Morocco) around 1159. There Moses soon became the student of Rabbi Yehuda ibn Shushan, a noted Talmudic scholar there. Soon, however, the Almohades extended their rule from southern Spain to Morocco and the Jews of North Africa also became the victims of persecution. Moses, then still quite young, began to send out messages of hope and comfort to his hounded brethren, telling them not to lose their faith in God, to try to study the Torah, and to observe Jewish law as much as possible. He asked them to be careful to pray three times each day, or at least to say a short prayer once a day if that should prove impossible.

According to some scholars (such as E. Carmoly, Heinrich Graetz, and M. Munk), Maimonides was forced at one time to conceal his Jewish faith and to profess the Mohammedan creed. They base this assumption upon the reports of Arab writers of that day. Others, however (such as S. Steinschneider) cite proof to the effect that this is not true.

At that time a zealous rabbi decreed that any Jew who would even only pretend to embrace Mohammedanism, ceased to be a Jew by so doing. This ruling affected a great many Jews in Morocco and other countries where Jews had been forced to accept the faith of Islam, if only under pretense. The Mohammedans did not demand that these Jews take part in any religious observances; all they required was that the convert declare his intention to become a Moslem by reciting the tenet, "There is no other God beside Allah, and Mohammed is Allah's prophet." Therefore, because such conversion did not involve actually abandoning Judaism in practice or adopting a new ritual of worship, many Jews pledged allegiance to Mohammed simply to escape persecution at the hands of the true followers of Islam. Naturally, consternation reigned among the sham converts when the rabbi's opinion was communicated to them. Thereupon Maimonides sent out letters to the Jewish communities of all the countries where Jews had been forced to embrace Mohammedanism under similar circumstances, telling them to disregard the judgment of the rabbi and to consider themselves good Jews as before. This circular letter, entitled "Iggeret Ha-Shmad" or "Maamor Kiddush Ha-Shem," set out to prove that Mohammedans were not idolators. Since the Mohammedans were monotheists, like the Jews, it was not a deadly sin or treason against Judaism if, when faced by danger of death or exile, a Jew would declare that he, too, acknowledged Mohammed as being the prophet of Allah. After all, Allah was nothing but the Mohammedan name for the One God in whom the Jews also believed, and while Jews could not in all sincerity believe that Mohammed was God's prophet, the mere recital, under duress, of the basic tenet of Mohammedanism was in itself neither apostasy nor idolatry.

But the time came when the Mohammedans in Northern Africa became still more violent in their fanatical hatred for Jews, and the life of Maimonides was in real danger. He was saved by a friend, the Arab poet Ibn Mussa, who, one dark night, on the 4th of Iyar, 1165, put Maimonides, his father, and the rest of his family on a ship bound for Palestine. After storms and many hardships, the boat landed in Acre, where the Jewish population turned out to receive Maimonides, who had already acquired great fame. Maimonides then visited Jerusalem, Hebron, the cave of Machpelah, and other holy places. However, he found it impossible to remain in the land of Israel and went to Egypt where he settled in the city which today is called Cairo. It was there that, a few months later, Maimonides' father died and was buried.

Maimonides had a brother, David, who was also well versed in Talmudic literature, but who, instead of delving further into study, became a merchant of gold and precious stones and achieved great wealth. It was he who provided financial support for both his father and his brother Moses. Unfortunately David met an untimely end. The ship on which he was sailing on a business venture was lost at sea, and so Maimonides lost not only a beloved brother but also his one provider. Maimonides was offered the position of chief rabbi of Egypt, but he refused the honor and, in general, was averse to entering the rabbinate. Thus, in order to support himself, he turned to the field of medicine and soon came to be known as an able physician.

It was not long after that he was invited by the Caliph of Egypt to become his personal physician, and after that his fame grew rapidly in medical circles throughout the ancient world.

The position at court was a demanding one. Maimonides had to be at the palace each day, and the palace was outside the city. Yet he found the time to write his two greatest scholarly works, first the *Yad Hachazakah* and then the *Guide for the Perplexed*.

Yad Hachazakah is, as we have said already, a monumental work consisting of fourteen parts. (The numerical value of the letters in the Hebrew word "Yad" is fourteen). It contains all the commandments and prohibitions according to both the Bible and the Talmud. It was a most difficult undertaking, because it is complicated by the fact that it is hard to determine just what is permitted and what is prohibited in accordance with the discussions set down in the Talmud. In the Bible we find, enumerated quite explicitly, both "Mitzvoth" (commandments) and "Averoth" (transgressions). There, however, they are set down briefly, in very general terms without any particulars. Then came the Tannaim, the great teachers in Israel who expounded the Torah in the beginning of the Era of the Second Commonwealth, and explained the manner in which this Biblical legislation was to be interpreted and applied. Their teaching was the Mishna.

After the Tannaim came the Amoraim, teachers of the Law both in Palestine and in Babylonia, who sought to interpret and clarify the Mishna. These questions and answers, by which they attempted to arrive at the proper interpretation for each law of the Mishna constitute the "Gemorah." Thus, in a volume of the Talmud, we find that every Mishna is joined by an entire treatise of Gemorah, summarizing the discussions and debates that took place on a particular point in the house of study or at one of the Talmudical academies. But the Gemorah does not make at all clear just what the decisions of the teachers and expounders were. There is no statement to the effect that "the Law" is such and such, or that the teachers arrived at a definite decision concerning some obscure point.

Hence, we can readily see that it is quite difficult, and often impossible, to make decisions on Jewish law simply by reading the Talmudic text, because most of the statements in the Gemorah are nothing but a "Shaklo Vetaryah" (Talmudic expression for a debate on a certain issue). In order to come to a decision, using the statements contained in the Talmud as a basis, then, it would have been necessary to set up a rabbinical court of men, great rabbis, a sort of miniature Sanhedrin, or else to institute a rabbinical academy which would spend years of labor and study to find out the proper interpretation of Jewish Law, taking as a basis the opinions offered in debate by the greatest minds in the field of Jewish legislation.

This gigantic work, however, was all done by one man, Maimonides, during a decade of toil under most unfavorable living conditions, from 1170 to 1180. The completed volume was written in a classic Hebrew.

True, attempts at such a work had been made before. There was, for instance, the *Sepher Halochoth Gedoloth* compiled in the ninth century by a scholar whose name is not known, and also the *Sepher Halochoth* by Rabbi Isaac Alfasi who, as we mentioned in the last chapter, had been a teacher of Maimonides. But none of these efforts could compare with *Yad Hachazakah,* in which all the laws are set down in separate sections, such as those dealing with religious life, and those applicable to civil order, all in a clear and easily intelligible manner.

However, like many other spiritual giants, Maimonides, too, had to suffer much at the hands of those little men who could not appreciate his greatness. Several objections were raised to *Yad Hachazakah*. Some criticized its author for not citing the exact source in the Talmud from which he derived the laws stated in his work. Others felt that he had so simplified the study of Jewish law that his book, which is also called "Mishne Torah," could be understood by anyone who had studied no more than the Bible, and therefore the Talmud itself would soon come to be neglected. One of his opponents, Rabbi Abraham ben David (Rabad), actually succeeded in having his critical remarks recorded in the book itself. But regardless of all this petty opposition, *Yad Hachazakah* has come to be regarded by all Jews as the authoritative work on Judaism. It is the book which contains all the laws, commandments and prohibitions, customs and rulings on ethics, clear and concise for all to understand. It is a colossal volume which only a man of the spiritual caliber of Maimonides could have completed alone and during such a relatively short span of time. As he himself wrote to one of his pupils, he had worked on it "day and night for all of ten years."

Hence we can readily understand that, even if Maimonides could never have produced any other scholarly treasures, this one work alone would have earned him the greatest title of honor that is in the power of the Jewish people to bestow upon its most brilliant minds, namely, that of "Rabbi and leader in Israel." But *Yad Hachazakah* was only one of Maimonides' works on the subject of Talmudic research, for he had also written two volumes entitled *Sepher Ha-Mitzvoth* and the *Commentary on the Mishnayot* which are also of great importance in the field of Jewish scholarship. As a matter of fact, the *Sepher Ha-Mitzvoth,* an enumeration of all the 613 Biblical commandments and prohibitions, was written before *Yad Hachazakah.* The *Commentary on the Mishnayot* is an attempt to set down the proper interpretation of the Mishna, for often the Mishna appears in quite a different light after one has read the pertinent Gemorah statements. In order that all might understand the book, it was written in Arabic and only subsequently translated into Hebrew.

What were the conditions under which Maimonides labored to complete his scholarly works? Some insight into his life at the time can be obtained from the perusal of his correspondence with Rabbi Judah ibn Tibon, the translator of Maimonides' *Guide for the Perplexed* from the original Arabic into Hebrew. When Maimonides asked Rabbi Judah to accept this task, the latter replied that he would like to be his disciple and come to live with him to study at his feet. Rabbi Judah at that time lived in southern France, but was prepared to spare neither hardship nor expense to come to Egypt where Maimonides resided. Maimonides advised Judah not to undertake the strenuous journey because the trip would be fraught with danger and besides, he, Maimonides, was so busy with his own work that he would hardly have any time to spare for a prospective disciple. The following is part of the letter in which Maimonides sets forth his reasons for suggesting that Samuel remain at home:

I am living in Egypt, in Fostat [now Cairo]. The king lives in Alcairo which is quite a distance from my home, and I have a position at Court which requires that I spend much time there. It is absolutely necessary that I be there early every morning, even under normal conditions. But if one of the king's many sons, daughters, or concubines should be taken ill, I must be at the palace all day long. If nothing happens, I can go home to Fostat at noon. By that time I am quite hungry, but my halls are already filled with patients, Jews and Gentiles, rich and poor, judges and police, friends and even enemies, all of whom expect me to give them medical aid. I dismount from my donkey upon which I am wont to ride home from the palace, I wash my face and hands, and then I beg my patients' indulgence while I get my noonday meal, which is the only food I take within a span of twenty-four hours. Then I go out to see my patients and to prescribe medicines for them, and I am kept busy until midnight. . . . By that time I am so weak and weary that I am hardly able to speak. This means that the only time one of our Jews can speak to me is on the Sabbath. Then the entire Jewish community comes to me after synagogue services and I advise them as to what they should do during the week that is to come. After that I study with them and then they go home, but they return for more study in the afternoon. . . .

It seems miraculous that under those trying conditions Maimonides was able to find the time to complete his many works of such profound scholarship. Should this alone not be sufficient to awaken within us a deep and abiding respect for this great scholar and teacher?

Thus far we have discussed the works of Maimonides to show what an unusual man he was. But what should interest us even more greatly is Maimonides' own philosophy of Judaism. He stated his ideas on his religion in his *Commentary on the Mishnayot* (in the Portion Chelek of Tractate Sanhedrin), in part of *Yad Hachazakah,* but particularly in his work entitled *Moreh Nebuchim (A Guide for the Perplexed)*. We will discuss that work later on.

What kind of work is *A Guide for the Perplexed,* what does it contain, and what was Maimonides' purpose in writing it? To formulate his own views on Judaism, Maimonides wrote a book in Arabic, the language which the average Jew spoke in those days. Its title was *Dalalat Al Ha-Yirin*. When it was translated into Hebrew, it was given the title of *Moreh Nebuchim,* meaning "Teacher (or Guide) for the Perplexed." He dedicated it to his beloved student, Rabbi Joseph ibn Aknin.

A Guide for the Perplexed consists of three parts, and is divided into a total of 178 chapters. In the first part, Maimonides discusses the concept of monotheism. He emphasizes that God must be understood as being free of the physical characteristics usually attributed to Him. The Jew should not think of Him as having the form of a human being. When we read in the Scriptures that "God spoke," it should not be thought that He actually has a mouth with which to utter sound, and when we are told that "God raised His hand" in order to punish the wicked, we must not imagine Him as smiting sinners with a stick held in His hand, for such things as hands and mouths belong to men, but cannot be attributed to God.

True, the Torah does contain myriads of such expressions to the effect that "God spoke," "God did with His hand," and so forth. But Maimonides tells us that the Talmud had already set forth the explanation that "the Torah spoke in the language of man," because it would be difficult for anybody to conceive of God without such human terms. Nor can man understand the ways of God, for they exceed by far the scope of our own limited intelligence.

And since not everyone can conceive of God upon a purely intellectual level, Maimonides suggests that those not capable of doing so had best not occupy their minds with such mental search as to the nature of God (Chapters 33 and 34).

The second part of *Guide for the Perplexed* is even more profound. It constitutes a discussion aimed against the views held by Aristotle concerning God and creation. Aristotle had said that the world was not created by God, but has always existed. And even if it was created at all, we cannot know how it came into being. Even as we cannot ask, "Who created God?" it also does not behoove us to question, "Who made the world?" But actually, if one maintains that the world has always existed, this premise automatically excludes any concept of divine omnipotence. In the days of Maimonides, Aristotle was still regarded as one of the greatest thinkers of all time. (Maimonides himself was profoundly interested in the works of Aristotle.) He strongly disagreed with him, however, in regard to his views on God.

Maimonides devotes much space to a thorough discussion of the ideas advanced by Aristotle. He refutes Aristotle's view on the eternal nature of the world by stating that it contradicted the statement in Genesis: "In the beginning God created heaven and earth." This, says Maimonides, clearly shows that God was the creator of the world. Indeed, if Aristotle had been right, he (Maimonides) would have been able to reinterpret the word of the Bible in the light of the findings of Aristotle, but he sees no necessity for so doing, since Aristotle was unable to prove that he was correct, and he himself said that he had stated his opinion without being supported by any concrete evidence or proof. Since this was so, Maimonides feels that we have every right to persist in the traditional interpretation of the word of the Bible. And if it should seem illogical that God should have created the world, how much more contrary to logic would be the statement that the world was never created, but has always existed (Part 2, Chapters 15 and 16). And if one should maintain that God has indeed created the world, but has done so not from "nothing" but from some preexisting material, then there would be more unsolved questions as to what was the nature of that material, and who brought that material itself into being. For all these reasons, Maimonides sees no other solution to this problem than to admit that the world was the result of an act of creation, that God was it creator, and that it was created "from nothing." Maimonides also points out that, if one should maintain that the world has always existed, such a view would leave no room for any religion or moral code (*ibid.*, Chapter 25), and therefore we must conclude that the idea of divine creation is the cornerstone and foundation of all the Torah and hence of our religion (*ibid.*, Chapter 27).

In the third part of the book Maimonides speaks of the concepts of "substance" and "form." He points out that only "substance" is subject to decay. "Form is indestructible, and lives on eternally, even though it may not be in the same shape. Then Maimonides deals with the question of "free will," and the problem of reward and punishment, and discusses the problem posed by the fact that so many good men are afflicted by misfortune while the wicked enjoy all earthly happiness. He turns to the debate on that subject which is set down in the Book of Job.

The last chapters of the book are devoted to the interpretation of the divine commandments. The work ends with a discussion of human virtues such as nobility, modesty, humility, and, primarily, the importance of understanding God and walking in His paths, for God Himself is righteousness incarnate.

In his *Guide for the Perplexed* Maimonides touches upon many things which he had already discussed in previous works such as *Yad Hachazakah* and his commentary on the Mishnayot. Some of the opinions set forth by Maimonides met with violent opposition on the part of a number of rabbis and scholars of his day.

In *Yad Hachazakah,* Maimonides states (Hilchoth Teshuvah 83-87) that whoever maintains that God has a physical form or body is a "heretic." This is in accordance with his view that God must not be conceived as having physical form. But Rabbi Abraham ben David, a great scholar who lived in Piscaria, in Provence, France, who was Maimonides' opponent, said, "Greater and better men than he have held to that idea," meaning that one cannot brand a person a heretic simply because he pictures God Himself as having a physical form, much like a human being. Many good Jews, said Rabbi Abraham, hold such views without being traitors to their faith. In like manner, Rabbi Abraham expressed his opposition to many other opinions on Jewish law as set forth by Maimonides.

In some instances, too, it seems that Maimonides contradicts himself, voicing one view in one work, and one diametrically opposed to it in another. For example, regarding three basic issues, namely, reward and punishment (heaven and hell after death), the coming of the Messiah, and the resurrection of the dead. He voices entirely different concepts of each in his three works, *Yad Hachazakah, Commentary on the Mishnayot,* and *Guide for the Perplexed.* Take the issue of "reward and punishment." In *Yad Hachazakah* and in *Guide for the Perplexed,* Maimonides speaks of the "world to come" not as a place where physical pleasures, such as food or drink, are given to the righteous man as a reward, but as the place where the soul will receive spiritual recompense in the form of enjoying the glory of God. The punishment for the wicked is that they will be unable to reach this exalted level. They will be denied the joy of the revelation of God which will be granted to the righteous. (*Guide for the Perplexed,* III, Chapter 27) In like manner, Maimonides speaks of the revival of the dead as the "awakening of the soul" to a new spiritual life, which will be denied to the wicked.

With regard to the "days of the Messiah," Maimonides states in *Yad Ha-*

chazakah that "when the Messiah will come, there will be no change at all in the world," save the fact that the Jewish people will be redeemed from exile and restored to the land of Israel. He counsels men not to pay attention to the many legends that have sprung up through the ages as to what will take place when the Messiah will appear on earth. In other words, he visualizes the Messianic era in such a way that we might say that the Jews of our present state of Israel are living in it today, since the governments of the nations have conceded that the Jews have a right to an independent homeland and state of their own.

But in his *Commentary on the Mishnayoth,* in the section entitled "Sanhedrin," in his preface to the portion of "Chelek," Maimonides declares that there are thirteen Principles of Faith in which each Jew must believe. Among these thirteen, he lists "reward and punishment," "the coming of the Messiah," and "the resurrection of the dead," and the interpretation he gives to them is exactly that which legend has given them through the ages, without any of the redefinition which he has set down in the *Yad Hachazakah,* and *Guide for the Perplexed.*

This would make it appear as if he had a variety of opinions on one and the same subject, but if one examines these seemingly contradictory statements more closely, it can readily be seen what it was that Maimonides attempted to accomplish in stating such opposing views in his own works. Maimonides had a good deal of insight into the human mind and knew that men differed from one another in their capacity to understand abstract thoughts. Much as one must promise a small child the reward of a piece of candy so that he will be willing to study, the simple man must be promised a reward for good or threatened with punishment for evil in terms that he can understand, in terms of a Garden of Eden filled with beauty, food, and drink, or else of an actual hell which is a place of physical pain and suffering. As for the person of average intelligence, one can appeal to his mind by promises on a higher level. He will do good and refrain from evil if he is told that his reward for righteousness will be spiritual pleasures which he will be denied if he should choose the path of evil on earth. To a person of superior intellect, however, the mere knowledge that he has done good is his reward, and his punishment is the heartbreak and chagrin which he feels when he realizes that he has sinned. As the Talmud states it, "The good deed is its own reward, and sin its own punishment" (Aboth, Part 4). We see, then, that Maimonides actually felt that each person may conceive of these basic beliefs of Judaism, such as the Messiah, reward and punishment, and resurrection, in such terms as are accessible to his own level of intelligence and ability to understand. Regardless of the manner in which he perceives these concepts, he is still a good Jew and cannot be called a heretic.

The life of Maimonides was filled with sorrow, illness, and privation. When he grew old, however, his situation improved somewhat. He was held in high esteem by the Sultan's Grand Vizier who paid him a munificent salary. When his wife died, he married the daughter of a man who was a favorite at court. He was considered the spiritual leader of Egyptian Jewry, and in many Jewish communities, the phrase "and during the lifetime of our lord and teacher Rabbi Moses ben Maimon" was inserted in the Kaddish prayer. Maimonides died on December 13, 1204, at the age of seventy in Tiberias, Palestine, where he was visiting. His death was widely mourned throughout the world, and his epitaph read, "Here lies Moses the son of Maimon, the best among all men." And Jews the world over said, "From Moses [the giver of the Torah] unto Moses the son of Maimon there was none like Moses."

8. Nachmanides and His Teachings

The Author of an Outstanding Talmudical Work When only Sixteen Years of Age —The Debate with an Apostate in the Presence of the King, Which Begins in the Royal Palace, Continues in the Cathedral, and Ends in the Synagogue—His Clever Answer to the King Concerning the Birth of Jesus—His "Ten Sephiroth"

We now turn to the beginning of the thirteenth century in Spain. The period of enlightenment in the Arab world had come to a close. The days when Jews and Arabs worked together in every field of the arts and sciences were over. The Jews were being persecuted by the Arab religious fanatics in all the provinces of Spain where the Mohammedans were still in power. It seemed as if the Arab tribes were to sink back into a state of benighted lethargy and ignorance, with the one difference that while prior to the period of enlightenment they had been in the clutches of the fanaticism of idolatry, they were now ruled by the intolerance of a new creed, founded by one of their own, Mohammed, the camel-driver. They came to understand the superficial aspects of his teachings, but the deeper meaning, which Mohammed had derived from Judaism, remained a closed book to them.

The situation in the Christian part of Spain was somewhat better. Christianity had not yet gained a firm foothold, and its adherents had not yet become fanatics in their religion. Two hundred years were to pass before they, too, came to persecute all the "infidels" and to burn them at the stake. For the present, the Jews still lived in peace in Christian Spain.

It was at about that time that Maimonides died and Jews the world over felt as if a brilliant light had been extinguished and they were plunged into darkness. Then a new star rose upon the horizon, not quite as great as Maimonides, but still a light for Israel for generations to come. This was Rabbi Moses ben Nachman of Gerona, in Christian Catalonia.

Rabbi Moses ben Nachman (called "Nachmanides" in world literature) was born in 1194, ten years prior to the death of Maimonides. He studied with the most eminent rabbis of that day, particularly with the great Talmudist Rabbi Judah ben Yakar. He also was trained in the field of medicine by Rabbi Nathan ben Rabbi Meir, one of the outstanding physicians of that time. But from his earliest youth, Moses had still another wish; namely, to penetrate the mystic secrets of the Cabala, and for this purpose he availed himself of the knowledge of Rabbi Azriel, one of the greatest Cabalists of that period.

Before we go any further, let us make one thing clear concerning the study of the Cabala. We have seen that all the Jewish philosophers whom we have studied thus far, beginning with Rabbi Saadia Gaon through Maimonides, were rationalists who did not spend too much time on mysticism and metaphysics. It would be wrong, however, to say that mysticism and Cabala were unknown to all but a very few. Because of the worsening of the situation of Jews all over the world, many sought refuge in the realm of metaphysics. It is a known fact that, in time of danger, one seeks escape in the study of occult forces.

Mysticism and Cabalists were found among the Jewish people as early as the latter days of the Second Temple. The study of metaphysics was in full flower in the seventh, eighth, and ninth centuries A.D. when secret books such as the *Sepher Yetzirah, Sepher Ha-Behir,* and *The Book of Angel Raziel* were written.

The activity of the mystics diminished somewhat during the first two centuries of the new millennium which marked an era of prosperity and of the rationalists and philosophers. But when the Arabs began to exchange enlightenment for fanaticism and attempted to force all those of different belief to embrace Mohammedanism, mysticism started to flourish again. A great many outstanding Jewish leaders became interested in the Cabala then, but because Jewry was still very much under the influence of the era of the philosophers, mysticism had to be clothed in the garbs of rationalism and logic. This was the period of the philisophical Cabala, and Rabbi Moses ben Nachman, or Nachmanides, was both a Cabalist and an adherent of rational philosophy.

When Nachmanides was forty years of age, he was the rabbi of Gerona, the city in which he was born. (Some called him "Gerandai" after his birthplace.) Later on he was to become the chief rabbi of all of Catalonia.

Nachmanides was a genius from his earliest youth. When only sixteen years of age, he had already written a treatise in defense of the work of Rabbi Isaac Alfasi (who was known as "Rif" by his initials), one of the greatest Talmudists of that day, against the attacks hurled upon it by Rabbi Zerachyah Ha-Levi Geronda and Abraham ben David. Nachmanides showed such an immense knowledge of the Talmud that even the greatest scholars were flabbergasted. When he was in his twenties, he wrote a commentary on the Pentateuch which is still printed in a great many editions of the Hebrew Bible, and also a commentary on the Talmud. Also, while still in his twenties, Nachmanides started to practice medicine and soon became known as one of the competent authorities in this field as well.

Nachmanides might have spent the rest of his days amidst great honor and success, and might have had ample peace to write all his outstanding works in Spain, had it not been for an event that put an end to his peace and resulted in his being driven from his home.

This happened in 1263. A certain Jew who had acquired some knowledge of Jewish lore embraced Christianity and joined the Dominican order which occupied a position of great importance at that time in Christian Spain. This apostate, who took on the name of Paulus Christiani upon baptism, and was better known as "Fra Pablo" or Brother Paul in the Dominican order, was incited by his fellow monks to call upon the Jews to engage in debate with him regarding the truth of the Christian religion. The Jews were then asked to show cause why they did not embrace Catholicism. Such debates were held all over the country, much to the distress of the Jews. For while the advocates of Christianity were free to say whatever they pleased, the Jews were not permitted to do so, with the result that the Jewish side always lost the argument, and anti-Semitic persecutions ensued. The Dominicans were well aware that the Jews were becoming reluctant to engage in further debates voluntarily, and hence they appealed to King James I of Aragon to decree that such debates be held at regular intervals. They asked the king to order the chief rabbi of Catalonia, which was part of Aragon, to represent the Jewish point of view against Fra Pablo. The discussion was to be held in Barcelona.

When Nachmanides saw that he could not avoid participating in the debate, he requested the king to grant him full freedom to make whatever statement he should see fit during the discussion. The king granted his request.

The debate took place in the presence of the king and lasted four days. Nachmanides spoke openly, and incisively attacked the views of Fra Pablo and of his order. At the end of the fourth day Fra Pablo begged the king to stop the proceedings, and the king declared Nachmanides the victor. Nachmanides was rewarded with a prize of three hundred golden ducats and sent home with the king's blessing.

The Dominicans, loath to admit defeat, spread the word that they, and not the Jew, were the actual winners. Nachmanides then decided to publish the proceedings of the entire debate which had been recorded by the king's scribes in the presence of the king himself. He readily gained access to these documents and distributed copies widely among both Jews and non-Jews. Thereupon the Dominicans clamored that the Jewish rabbi had insulted the Christian faith and they haled him into court on the charge of insulting the Christian religion. Nachmanides testified that these documents contained nothing but the very statements, word for word, made by both Fra Pablo and himself. But the Dominicans could ill afford to acknowledge defeat and finally succeeded in driving Nachmanides out of Spain. Thus, in 1267, Nachmanides left his home and decided to settle in Palestine.

Nachmanides found the land of Israel in a deplorable state. The Crusaders had marched through the land and destroyed and looted everything that came their way. The Jewish communities were destitute. Nachmanides set to work reorganizing the scattered remnants, creating new institutions, and bringing back to Jerusalem those who had fled during the period of war and unrest. He established a Yeshivah where he taught his disciples and wrote his scholarly works.

Unlike many of our other great thinkers, Nachmanides did not write any one specific work in which he set down his personal philosophy of Judaism. Instead, we find his thoughts scattered in various places in his writings, particularly in his commentary on the Torah. We shall therefore attempt to learn about his philosophical approach by examining his scholarly works.

But before we do so, let us devote a few moments to the debate in which Nachmanides engaged with Fra Pablo. This debate is worthy of study, not because of the opinions voiced then by Nachmanides—because any other Jewish scholar in his place might have presented much the same arguments —but because of the way in which he expounded his point of view.

Imagine the scene of this tournament of minds. The debate was held in the royal palace. The king presided, seated on his throne and dressed in all the trappings of royalty. Behind him stood his ministers and the greatest churchmen of his day, bearing crosses and crucifixes. Then there was a large audience of eminent generals, bankers, and leaders of society. In other words, the audience consisted of Christians, and Christians only. And in front of them all sat Fra Pablo, the apostate, surrounded by his brother monks, all bearing crosses.

And opposite them stood Nachmanides, the chief rabbi of Catalonia. It may be that a few Jews stood behind him as if to give him moral support, so to speak. It was his task to debate not merely with the one apostate alone, but with the entire audience, to tell them truths they did not like to hear. Now he had to muster the strength and courage to speak as he must at such a time.

And Nachmanides rose to the occasion. He spoke out firmly and relentlessly. He spared the feelings of no one, and certainly not those of the apostate. He told the truth as he saw it, and did not shrink from telling the truth even to the king. After four days of strenuous discussion, the resistance of Fra Pablo wavered and he begged the king to stop the proceedings.

Here we see what kind of a person Nachmanides was. He came before the king like a prophet, speaking out freely and without trepidation, lashing out at bishops, priests, and government officials alike, in church, palace, and synagogue.

It would be impossible to set down here all the things that were said in the debate. Suffice it to state that Fra Pablo repeated over and over again that the Messiah had already come, and he attempted to cite places in the Bible and Talmud to prove his point. Some of the statements he made in support of his views were anything but logical or intelligent, but Nachmanides had to provide answers for them all. He followed the counsel of the Book of Proverbs, "Answer not a fool according to his folly, lest thou also be like unto him" (Prov. 26:4), except for a few instances when he lost his patience and said that he refused to answer pure nonsense. He did not hesitate to say this even to the king, when the latter attempted to intervene in support of Fra Pablo.

Pablo cited the place in the Talmud where it is stated that the Messiah was born on the day when the second Temple was destroyed. It was obvious, said he, that this referred to none other than Jesus. Nachmanides replied that Jesus was actually born sixty-seven years prior to the destruction of the Temple, so that he could hardly have been the Messiah to whom reference was made there.

Then the apostate asked whether it was not true that all the sages whose names appeared in the Talmud thought highly of Jesus. Why, then, did the rest of the Jewish people not acknowledge Jesus as their redeemer?

Thereupon Nachmanides pointed out that there was no basis at all for the assumption that our sages regarded Jesus as a messenger of God. The Talmud was completed some five hundred years after the birth of Jesus and there is no mention of his name in any part of the writings of the Talmud.

Fra Pablo now attempted to cite chapters and verses from Talmudic literature, twisting their true meaning to suit his own ends. He said that the Talmud told the story of one Rabbi Joshua ben Levi, who asked Elijah the Prophet when the Messiah would come. Elijah is supposed to have replied, "Go ask him yourself." Thereupon Joshua ben Levi asked, "Where is he?" "Within the gates of Rome," answered Elijah. This, said Fra Pablo, seemed definite proof that the sages of the Talmud felt that the Messiah had already come.

"But," said Nachmanides, "did not Rabbi Joshua ben Levi ask Elijah when the Messiah would come? Does this question not make it very plain that the Messiah was not yet here when the question was asked?"

In one instance, when James I of Aragon attempted to participate in the discussion about whether or not Jesus was the son of God, Nachmanides replied: "Your Majesty is a Christian, a son of Christian parents. Your priests have told you all your life that Jesus was the son of God, so that it does not even occur to you that it could be otherwise. This is simply your belief. But is it not contrary to all logic to think that God, if He wanted to have a son on earth, would allow such a son to be born of a human mother, to grow up like any ordinary child, to reveal himself as the son of God only as a grown man, and then to be killed by human hands, only to be resurrected? Could not God have sent down a son to earth in such a manner that all men would have known that this was indeed a supernatural being?"

Fra Pablo finally asked that the debate be stopped. But Nachmanides was told to remain in the city because the king and some of the religious leaders wished to meet him again in the synagogue that Sabbath. On the next Sabbath the king and his nobles appeared in the synagogue, together with Fra Pablo who, attempting to redeem himself, posed nine questions to be answered by Nachmanides. The latter, however, now had the additional advantage of being on his own "home ground," as it were, and again he had no difficulty in defeating the Jewish apostate. When the king again attempted to come to the aid of the Dominican friar, Nachmanides told him politely but firmly that, if Jesus had indeed been a son of God, he should have been able to prove that fact in the days of the sages of the Talmud who had felt that the Messiah had not yet come. As a matter of fact, Jesus was unable to save himself from death upon the cross, and was executed together with a band of common criminals. How, then, Nachmanides continued, could one prove now, after all these centuries, that despite all these arguments to the contrary, Jesus was indeed the son of God?

The next day Nachmanides was allowed to return home. The king praised him for the tactful and eloquent manner in which he had conducted the debate and, as a token of friendship and appreciation, gave him a reward of three hundred golden ducats.

The philosophical approach set forth by Nachmanides was a harmonious combination of emotion and logic. Nachmanides was against the pure rationalism of Maimonides, Ibn Ezra, and the other philosophers who advocated the ideas of Plato and Aristotle. He was rather in agreement with Judah Ha-Levi, who felt that Judaism should be derived not from alien thought, but from the original sources of our own religion. He felt that Judaism was a matter of the heart and the emotions, and not of rational logic. A certain amount of logic would be in order in our religion, but too much would be useless.

Nachmanides was thus the first to incorporate the concepts of the Cabala into the philosophy of Judaism. He was one of the first to create a sort of philosophical Cabala. He stated that Judaism had three cardinal principles: first, that the world was created "out of nothing"; second, that God knows the future of men and the universe; and third, that He governs all things (Sermons of Nachmanides, p. 55). Nachmanides believed literally in the miracles mentioned in the Bible. He also believed in devils (whom he conceived as being the opposite of angels), in physical reward and punishment in the world to come, and in reincarnation (though he held that the soul could go through this process only three times). He also speaks of the "Ten Sefiroth" through which God governs the world and supplies all men with all their needs.

In addition to his commentaries on the Pentateuch and on many parts of the Talmud, he also wrote a book entitled *Haemunah Ve-Habitochon, (Faith and Trust)* in which he discussed a variety of cabalistic problems. He also composed much religious poetry which is still recited during holiday services today.

Nachmanides died in 1270 in Acre. Some say that his grave is in Haifa next to that of Rabbi Jehiel of Paris. Others maintain that he was buried in Hebron, near the cave of Machpelah.

9. Rabbi Abraham Abulafia

The Period of Mysticism in Jewish Life—Abraham Abulafia and His "Philo-sophical" Approach to the Cabala—Abraham's Audience with Pope Martin IV

In the thirteenth century, Christianity grew strong in Spain and, as its followers increased in number, the zealous Christians were quick to emulate the fanatical Mohammedans in their un-relenting persecution of the Jews. Naturally, this had a profound impact not only on Jewish life but on the spiritual growth of the Jewish communities in Spain as well. Despair was widespread, and it seemed that unless a miracle happened soon, the people could not hold out much longer. It is not surpris-ing, therefore, that Jews now again began to delve into the Cabala and mysticism to see whether these secret writings might not contain some veiled hint as to the date when deliverance would come to them. As this trend now attained a dominant role in Jewish life, the Cabalists, anxiously awaiting the coming of the Messiah, pored over the sacred writings of the Bible and actu-ally sought to bring redemption nearer by devising ingenious interpretations of the various verses of the Scriptures and by finding countless combinations for the letters that spell out the Ineffable Name of God.

In those days there lived in Castilia a wealthy Jew, Todros Abulafia, of an ancient and noble family which had originally come from Tunis. Todros soon became a favorite at the court of King Sancho IV of Castalia and was particularly close to the queen, Maria de Molina, whose physician he was. Eventually, through the good offices of the queen, Todros Abulafia was ap-pointed Minister of Finance and took an active part in most of the affairs at court. Thus he attended the royal couple when they traveled to Bayonne to meet with King Philip of France to make a peace treaty. Eventually, how-ever, the king became suspicious of Abulafia's friendship with his queen and had him arrested. It was only thanks to the pleas of the queen that Abulafia was spared from execution and released from prison. Whether or not he was reinstated in his old position at court is not known.

At any rate, Todros, because of his wealth and the high esteem which he once enjoyed at court, was an influential figure in Jewish life. Since he and his sons Levi and Joseph were fervent adherents of the Cabala, the interest of much of the Jewish community soon turned to that branch of mysticism which then quickly became the vogue, taking the place formerly enjoyed by philosophy in the Jewish scholarly world.

Perhaps the most outstanding intellect in the family of Todros Abulafia was his relative Abraham Abulafia who was born in Saragossa in 1240 and brought to Toledo when he was still a child. His first teacher was his father, who taught him the Hebrew language and Talmudic literature. When young Abraham was eighteen years of age, his father died and he was left an orphan. Abraham nevertheless continued his studies, for he possessed an ingenious mind and much imagination. He soon distinguished himself in the field of Talmudic lore. Following in the footsteps of the other members of his family, he familiarized himself with the Cabala. Eventually he set out on a journey through the world in order to find the Ten Lost Tribes of Israel. For this purpose he decided that he had to find and cross the river Sambatyon, the body of water which, as legend has it, casts off stones all week long and rests only on the Sabbath Day.

The first leg of his journey took him to Palestine. On the way there he stopped in Greece where he married. He arrived in Palestine at the most inopportune time, for those were the days of the Fourth Crusade, and the land was a battlefield on which Christians and Mohammedans fought a bloody war.

Abraham saw that he could hardly continue his journey. He decided to return to Greece and from there proceeded to Italy, where he became a disciple of Rabbi Hillel of Verona, who then lived in Capua, not far from Rome. He became interested once more in Jewish philosophy, particularly in Maimonides' *Guide for the Perplexed.* Finally he returned to Spain and settled in the city of Barcelona. It seemed now as if he had abandoned mysticism and was ready to devote all his time and energies to the exploration of logic and rational philosophy. This phase, however, was short-lived, for soon Abraham returned to his old love, the Cabala. Eventually he came to imagine that the Lord Himself had spoken to him, and that he, Abraham, was therefore a holy man and perhaps even the Messiah.

Yet we must not conclude that Abraham Abulafia was nothing more than a madman, for had he been simply a "crackpot" he would never have come to occupy the important place in Jewish history that he does. He was a great thinker, a profound philosopher, and a caustic wit. He made a critical analysis of all the Jewish movements of his day and was not afraid to voice his own views, which at times were quite radical, on the Talmud, the Cabala, and philosophy. He formulated a novel approach to Jewish thought and a kind of "philosophical" approach to the Cabala. He went so far as to say that those who spend all their time studying the Gemorah were dry and withered and knew nothing except the dead letter of the Law. In fact, he derisively pointed out that the initial letters of the Hebrew words "Chacham muflag ve-rav Rabbanan" ("a man of great wisdom and a teacher of teachers"—a title accorded by the rabbis to eminent scholars of the Law) formed the highly uncomplimentary Hebrew epithet of "Chamor," meaning "donkey."

Nor did Abraham spare the Cabala. He ridiculed the theory that the Cabala was of a prophetic origin and derided the Cabalists for their apparent inability to explain the exact nature of the ten "Sephirot" (divine forces) which they claimed aided God in His creation of the world. It seems that there was no definite agreement among the Cabalists as to whether these "Sephiroth" were actual physical bodies or merely spiritual concepts.

Abraham had particularly sharp words for Greek philosophy. He mercilessly pointed out the flaws in Greek philosophy and had little regard for those Jews who became its adherents. He claimed that it was sterile and had nothing to offer. The philosophers of Greece, he said, maintained that the Biblical account, reading, "In the beginning the Lord created heaven and earth," was a fairy tale, intended to deceive man, that there was no such thing as divine providence, that reward and punishment were figments of the imagination, and that there was no life after death.

And so Abraham Abulafia came to formulate his own personal approach to Jewish thought. He discussed it in twenty-six works which he called *Books of Prophecy*. Some of these books have been lost, but most of them can still be found in manuscript form in certain libraries.

Actually this would be the place for a detailed study of the "philosophical approach" to the Cabala. But this would be a difficult task. The reason for my reluctance is not because I think that the Cabala is unintelligible to the reader. Not at all. Any idea or teaching devised by man is created for other humans and can be made clear, if only it is explained properly. The Cabala is no exception. However, the "philosophical approach" to the Cabala constitutes not a separate entity, but a link in a huge chain. Therefore, if we should attempt to explain it, we would have to discuss it together with the entire history of the Cabala, which extends over a period of two thousand years. We shall therefore, at least for the present, study only those main points of the "philosophical" or "theoretical" approach to Cabala that we need for our purposes right now in order to see how the "theoretical" approach differs from the "practical" view of Cabala, and, particularly, what Abraham Abulafia had to say on the subject.

The first principle of the Cabala, of course, was the concept of the "Ten Sephiroth," the ten forces that emanated from God and through which He created and governed the world. God, the Cabala maintained, was Infinity ("En Sof") who could not be defined in terms of human concepts such as time, space, will, goal, and purpose. How, then, could it be said that the perfect, infinite God created a world that is limited in scope and definitely not perfect? The answer to this question is that the Lord must have delegated some of His powers to perform the work of creation and providence. These are the "Ten Sephiroth" which we discussed in a previous chapter.

A second basic principle is summarized by the term "The Secret of

(Divine) Limitation." It is written in the Bible, "The whole earth is full of His glory," (Isa. 6:36) and we are also told that there is no place in the world where God is not, for He is the force of life and of action and hence there would be no life in the place where God would not be present. But, the Cabalists asked, what about the filthy places that are filled with impurity and sin? Is God there also? And, if not, how, then, can there be life in those places? They found an answer which seemed to be satisfactory. The Lord, they said, "limited His presence" to the areas that were pure and unsullied by sin. In other places the task of governing and providence was delegated to the ten Sephirot which, of course, were emanations of none other than God Himself.

This is as far as we may go here, for if we should proceed further in our investigation, we should digress beyond the scope of this work. We will merely add that, in addition to this philosophical interpretation, there is also a "practical" application of Cabala, a system which does not deal in abstract matters but employs all sorts of mystical devices to attempt to force the hand of God to bring about some desired, concrete result, such as recovery from an illness or perhaps even the coming of the Messiah.

Now let us return to the specific views of Abraham Abulafia. Abulafia did not think that God could be explained or understood with the help of philosophy. Man, he said, can reach God only by accepting Him and taking Him to his heart. Often this perception of the Divine comes to man like a flash of lightning, as happens in the case of prophetic inspiration. But it may also happen that such persons will suddenly lose the way to God. Eventually, however, they are bound to return to Him, because, as Abulafia sees it, "The divine is truth and the absence of truth is falsehood."

Abulafia then set down these ideas in a book entitled *Seven Paths to Wisdom,* or *Seven Paths to the Law,* in which he explains seven different paths by which man can reach God, and the last of these seven paths to God is the divine inspiration which is part of prophecy.

As we have indicated earlier in this chapter, Abraham Abulafia also devoted much time to "practical Cabala" and, as a result, became so deeply enmeshed in mysticism that he began to have strange ideas. Thus, for example, he thought that he was the expected Messiah, and that he was duty-bound to meet with the Pope and convert him to Judaism.

Abraham communicated his intention to his disciples, who heartily approved of the venture. The pontiff who occupied the Holy See at the time was Martin IV who reigned from 1280 to 1285 and who, like his predecessor, Nicholas III, was a notorious Jew-baiter. However, Abraham felt that he was called upon to convert him to Judaism.

For a whole month Abraham and his disciples fasted, prayed, and devised magic formulas to secure the help of God, so that the Pope might indeed listen to the words of the Jewish scholar, embrace Judaism, and thus bring peace and happiness to the entire world. The date for the crucial audience was set for the eve of the Jewish New Year.

The audience took place as scheduled. The Pope, of course, felt that the Jew was not in his right mind, and had him arrested, so that Abraham spent the entire holiday season in prison subsisting on a diet of bread and water. After a period of twenty-eight days he was released.

From then on Abraham never had a permanent home again. He wandered from city to city in Italy and was constantly in want, for he could get along with neither student nor liberal nor Cabalist. He died in about 1292.

After Abraham Abulafia's death the beacon of scholarship and intellectual enlightenment moved to France where it was held high by the great Talmudist, philosopher, and inventor, Rabbi Levi ben Gershon, known as "Gersonides" or in Hebrew, the "Ralbag" (from the initials of his name).

10. Rabbi Levi ben Gershon (Gersonides)

The Excommunication of His Grandfather, and Its Effect upon the Grandson—
A Great Philosopher Who Was Born One Hundred Years Too Late—Rabbi Levi
ben Gershon and Pope Clement V—His Liberal Views

We now come to the end of the thirteenth century. In Spain the era of the Inquisition was just about to begin, and the fear of persecution at the hands of religious fanatics stifled all free thought, both Jewish and non-Jewish. At that time a number of Jewish scholars managed to escape from Spain and settled in Provence, France, where, even though Catholicism was dominant, there was still more religious freedom than across the border.

One of the learned men who fled from Castilia to France was Rabbi Levi ben Abraham, who had written a great many books on astronomy and the natural sciences. He was also the author of a goodly number of philosophical works in which he expressed thoughts on Judaism that seemed quite radical. For that reason he incurred the wrath of the rabbis. To escape their persecution he went to Narbonne where he stayed at the home of a friend, Rabbi Solomon Shulami, a man of great wealth, who was also a poet and scholar of note. However, upon the urging of the eminent Talmudist, Rabbi Solomon ben Adret, Shulami had to tell Levi ben Abraham to leave his house. Levi then went to stay with his cousin, Rabbi Samuel ben Reuben. But even there Solomon ben Adret gave him no peace. At about that time, Rabbi Levi, who by then had become a widower, fell in love with a young woman of good family to whom he dedicated songs to show his affection and esteem. She, however, was not anxious to become involved with a man such as her suitor, who was the target of so much persecution and hostility from his fellow Jews, and turned down his marriage proposal. Rabbi Levi now wandered through France, but was unable to escape the wrath of Rabbi Solomon ben Adret, who finally excommunicated him.

His son, Rabbi Gershon, who was born in France, and eventually married a daughter of the great Nachmanides, is remembered as the author of the book entitled *Shar Hashamaim* (*The Gate of Heaven*), which dealt with natural sciences.

Rabbi Levi ben Gershon, the son of Gershon and namesake of his grandfather, was seventeen years of age when the latter was excommunicated. The impact of this action upon the young man was profound. He resolved then not to be afraid of religious fanaticism and to voice his own views and opinions freely and without fear, and he remained true to his intention. Many years later, he wrote a commentary on the Pentateuch which he entitled *Milchamos Hashem (The Wars of the Lord)*, which contained views that were considered more than radical at the time. In the end, however, the work was accepted by all Jews and today can be found in the Hebrew editions of the Pentateuch alongside commentaries by such authorities as Rashi.

Rabbi Levi ben Gershon, who was known among Jews by the initial letters of his name as "Ralbag," and in the non-Jewish scholarly world as "Gersonides," or as Leon de Bagnois, and Magister Leo Hebraius (Master Leo the Hebrew), was born in Bagnois, France, in the year 1288. He studied the Torah with some of the most eminent Jewish scholars of his time and also perfected his knowledge in such worldly sciences as astronomy and medicine. The brilliant young man soon made a name for himself as an outstanding Talmudist, philosopher, and inventor.

Rabbi Levi ben Gershon could well be called a Jewish Leonardo da Vinci, for, like the latter, Levi, too, was a man of many talents and of a most versatile turn of mind. He might have become the rabbi of a large congregation, but he had no desire for a pulpit. As a philosopher, some say, he surpassed even Maimonides, who was considered, in his time, a unique genius in Jewish scholarship and philosophy. It seems that Levi ben Gershon was born one hundred years too late, for had he lived a century earlier, when Jewish philosophy was in flower, he would have received much more appreciation during his lifetime than he did. He was much more frank in stating his views than Maimonides. It is therefore safe to say that he was the most liberal intellect of his time. For example, in his Biblical commentary, he expressed such radical views that the fanatics changed the title of his book *Wars of the Lord* to read *The Wars* Against *the Lord*. Yet, as we have said before, this work eventually was to be accepted as authoritative by even the most orthodox of his brethren.

Before we go on to study the details of his philosophy, it would be well for us to look at Levi ben Gershon, the man.

Rabbi Levi ben Gershon spent most of his life in the city of Avignon, in the district of Provence, France. This city achieved prominence as the seat of the Papacy, for King Philip the Fair of France managed to exile the Holy See from the Vatican, so that, beginning with Pope Clement V, the heads of the Catholic Church dwelt under the jurisdiction of the French sovereign. Clement V was a worldly man who loved to entertain at balls and concerts, so that the city of Avignon became known as a town of gaiety and gracious living. Avignon also harbored a large Jewish community. It seems that the Jews preferred to live under the direct supervision of the pleasure-loving Pope rather than under the vigilant eyes of the fanatical bishops and lower clergy.

When the fame of Levi ben Gershon, the prominent scholar and physician, reached the ears of Clement V, the Pope summoned him to an audience and, as was his custom, engaged the visitor in a discussion on religion. The Pope expressed his amazement at the fact that a man of Levi's intelligence did not embrace Catholicism. However, Levi diplomatically countered the Pope's question by a simple parable. A father and a son, he recounted, were walking on a road when they came upon a beggar. Instead of giving the poor man money, the father insulted him and drove him away. Shortly thereafter, the wealthy man heard that the beggar had complained bitterly about the way he had treated him. The wealthy man asked his son not to remain silent but to defend his father against the accusations of the beggar. But the young man replied: "Father, the best thing for me to do is to keep quiet. Were I to say that you were in the wrong, I would be insulting my own father. Were I to say that you were right, it would be an untruth. Therefore, it is wisest for me not to speak at all."

The Pope was clever enough to understand the point of this tale. It was obvious to him that Levi ben Gershon was afraid that whatever reply he might give to the question of Clement V might be used to incriminate him or the entire Jewish people. The Pope wisely refrained from pressing his visitor further. However, as he was impressed by Levi's wisdom and erudition, he appointed him as his personal physician. He also told him that he was willing to discuss with him the merits of both Judaism and Christianity and that he, Levi, should feel perfectly free to state his views on both faiths.

To this Rabbi Levi ben Gershon replied, "I am afraid that not much good could come of such an interchange of opinions. If you should manage, by the strength of logic, to open my eyes to some of the faults inherent in my religion, and if I should be able to point out to you some of the shortcomings of your faith, the end would be that I would no longer be a good rabbi and you would no longer be a good pope. Therefore, let us leave things as they are and remain friends."

Nevertheless, the Pope often attempted to broach the subject to his physician. In the end, Levi ben Gershon agreed to have such discussions with the Pope, but only on the condition that they must never take place in the papal throne room, and that at such times the Pope must be dressed in ordinary clothes and not in his official vestments. Clement V accepted the terms posed by the rabbi and had frequent talks with him on religion on a man-to-man basis, with the Pope speaking not as the Head of the Church from his throne, but as an ordinary adherent of the Christian faith.

Legend has preserved for us quite a few accounts of the debates that went on between the two men.

So it is told that one day the Pope asked Levi ben Gershon: "Do you believe that religion is a staff which will guide man to the straight and right path?"

"Not always," replied the rabbi.

Clement V, somewhat surprised at the answer, asked Levi how it was that he, a religious leader among the Jews, did not believe that religion served such a purpose.

"There are two different paths," answered Levi ben Gershon. "There is the straight path and then there is the crooked path. There is also a path that leads through dry land and another that leads through the ocean. If we walk on a straight path, we need no staff to guide us; if our path is crooked, the staff would be of no avail. If we walk on dry land, a staff might serve some purpose, but what good would it do to attempt to use a staff when walking through the ocean?"

"Does this mean, then, that you do not believe that God is able to lead man upon a straight path, even when he walks through the water?" queried the Pope.

"Of course I do believe it," replied the rabbi, "but yet I think that if captains of ships at sea could have a staff to guide them as they sail upon the waters, such a device would be of better use to them at that time than religion."

"If you are so clever, then why don't you get to work and invent the kind of machine that would serve as a staff to guide the seafarer?" the Pope asked bluntly.

Levi ben Gershon accepted the challenge and returned to the Pope three months later bearing in his hand the instrument which he had invented to indicate to the navigator the direction in which he was sailing. He called it "Jacob's staff," referring to the statement of our Patriarch Jacob in the Bible "For with my staff I passed over this Jordan" (Gen. 32:11). The efficiency of the device was later tested and proved, and soon it was in great demand in the maritime world. In addition, Levi ben Gershon devised maritime maps which indicated the paths to be followed by navigators as they plied the ocean in their ships. So much for the legend.

Now that we know something about the personality of Levi ben Gershon, it may be of interest to acquaint ourselves with his approach to Judaism and its philosophy.

We have already said that he was the most liberal among the Jews of his day. Of course, we might add that he never went beyond the framework of the Jewish religion, but, within that range, he did not hesitate to formulate questions and opinions never expressed before. It is enough to say that Rabbi

Levi ben Gershon was almost completely in agreement with the views of Plato as regards God and the World. Like Plato, Levi maintained that the Lord had created the world not "out of nothing" but from some substance which he called "chomer" (material) and which already existed prior to creation. Thus the Lord did not actually create the substance but only gave it shape and form. Plato, however, claimed that this basic substance was not inert, but mobile (even before creation), and that all God did was channel its motion in specific paths such as the orbits of the sun, the moon, the planets, and the stars. Here Levi ben Gershon disagreed. He believed that the basic substance was originally inert and that, at the time of creation, God lent it not only form, but also life and motion. It is difficult to understand why Rabbi Levi ben Gershon should have imposed a limit on the omnipotence of the Creator and maintained that God created the universe not out of nothing, but out of a substance which existed long before the time of creation. In answer to arguments that his views contradicted the statement in the Bible that "In the beginning God created the heaven and the earth", Rabbi Levi ben Gershon declared: "There should be nothing that should hinder us in our search for the truth, not even the Torah itself. For it is after truth that we strive, and we shall stop at nothing, even if we were to find that the truth differed from tradition." No Jewish philosopher prior to Rabbi Levin ben Gershon had ever dared to express such thoughts.

We find other radical thoughts in his commentary on the Bible. For example, Rabbi Levi interprets the Song of Songs not in its literal sense, but as an allegory to portray the struggle which man must wage against his own self. "Solomon," represents human reason, "Jerusalem," man himself, and "the daughters of Jerusalem," the talents of man. He gives a similar interprestation to the Book of Ecclesiastes. In his commentary on the Book of Job, he voices his own questions in connection with the doubts expressed by the friends of Job, who had come to comfort him in his hour of grief.

Despite all his radicalism, however, Levi ben Gershon believed in the immortality of the human soul. He also regarded the Torah as a work of divine revelation, and literally believed in the truth of the accounts of the miracles as given in the Pentateuch and in the books of the prophets.

As regards divine omniscience and human free will, his views were as follows: Everything that comes to pass is within the realm of possibility, a possibility which may or may not become reality. The Lord has the advance knowledge of whether or not such and such thing will happen. Man, on the other hand, has no such prescience and, therefore, has the free choice of what course he will follow.

Levi's ideas of reward and punishment coincide with those advanced by Maimonides; that is, that reward and punishment are spiritual rather than physical. These views of Rabbi Levi ben Gershon met with bitter opposition, not only from the pious rabbis, but also from such Jewish philosophers as Rabbi Samuel ben Yehuda of Marseilles.

Some historians state that Levin ben Gershon died in 1344, at the age of only fifty-six. Other scholars, however, such as Abraham Zaccuto, set the date of his death at 1370. If this is true, it would mean that he attained the venerable age of eighty-two.

11. Rabbi Hasdai Crescas

The Situation of the Jews in Spain at the Time of the Inquisition—Mass Baptisms —The Rabbi Who Wanted to Become Pope—The Civil Autonomy of Jewish Courts of Justice in Spain—Crescas' Works in Which He Stated His Opposition to Maimonides and Rabbi Levi ben Gershon

By the end of the fourteenth century, Christianity had won over all of Spain. The land was filled with Catholic orders. Most prominent among these was the Dominican order whose members believed it was their duty to win as many souls as possible for the Church. This they attempted to do by means of debates with prominent Jews, or even by the outright bribing of Jews with money or offers of high political office. It seems that a great many Jews were willing to sell their souls. But this should hardly come as a surprise, because by that time the spiritual and intellectual life of Spanish Jewry was very much on the decline because of the constant persecutions of the Jews, not only by the Christian majority, but also by the Mohammedans that still remained in the land. Some Jewish converts also made every effort to prove their fervent loyalty to their new creed and outdid even the Christians in devising ways and means of making the lot of the Jews even worse.

Among the many converts there was even a rabbi, Solomon Ha-Levi from Burgos, who was a diligent student of the Law and conducted a lively correspondence with Rabbi Isaac bar Sheshet, one of the greatest Talmudists of that day. By the time he was forty years of age, he had become famous in Jewish circles, and perhaps it was for this reason that the Dominicans bent every effort to win him over to the Church. They offered him riches and the promise of a position as minister in the government, and it seems that Solomon succumbed to the temptation. After he had undergone baptism and adopted the name of Paulus de Santa Maria, he was given sumptuous apartments near the royal palace, horses, carriages, and servants. Soon the former rabbi became a frequent visitor at the court of the king. However, he soon saw that he was not likely to attain a ministerial appointment and, opportunist that he was, he now aimed, not for a government position, but for nothing less than the Papacy itself. He therefore moved to Paris to study for the priesthood. After completing his studies, he went to Avignon, which was at that time the residence of the popes. Because of his familiarity with the Old Testament and Jewish Law, he became quite important among the priests who formed the court of Pope Benedict XIII. Eventually his efforts to ingratiate himself with the Pope met with some success. Paulus de Santa Maria, formerly Solomon Ha-Levi, was made a bishop in the Catholic Church. But he was not yet satisfied. If he was to become a Cardinal and eventually a Pope, he felt that he would have to attract attention by excelling in the persecution of his erstwhile co-religionists, the Jews. He therefore sent letters to all the outstanding rabbis, calling upon them to convert to Christianity. At the same time, he also denounced a great many rabbis and Jewish communal leaders to the government as traitors and called for their execution.

The conversion of the former rabbi had strong repercussions on the Jews, particularly on the Jewish youth. It also had an adverse effect upon the Marranos, those Jews who had converted to Christianity under duress, but still observed, under cover, whatever they could of Judaism. Now that they saw that a famous rabbi had accepted Christianity, a great many Marranos gradually abandoned their plan to become Jews again at the earliest possible opportunity.

At that time there lived in Spain a great Talmudist, philosopher, and diplomat known as Rabbi Hasdai ben Abraham (some say that his father's name was not Abraham but Judah) Crescas. Born in Barcelona in 1340, Rabbi Hasdai studied Jewish Law with some of the greatest rabbis of that day and eventually was ordained, but he refused to accept a rabbinical position. At the same time he also attended the lectures of the most brilliant philosophers of his time and became well versed in that field. When he was in his late twenties, Hasdai entered business and became fairly wealthy. Because of his wit and erudition, he was often invited to the royal court and consulted on various affairs of state. Frequently the king would send him abroad on special missions.

Unfortunately, Hasdai's position at court was not of very long duration. In 1380 Don Joseph Pichon, a Jew who enjoyed the high esteem of King Enrico II of Castillia, and who had the high position of Chief Tax Collector, was denounced by Jews, who envied him, as having been guilty of malfeasance in office. The king promptly had him arrested, but eventually Joseph was able to prove his innocence and was released and reinstated at court. Joseph, seeking to exact vengeance from his fellow Jews for the wrong they had done him, denounced many of them to the government. Since many rabbis and respected members of the Jewish community were affected by Joseph's treachery, the Jewish court of law, which was vested with wide powers by the government and could even pass death sentences upon Jews, decided to decree the maximum penalty for Joseph Pichon. He was tried *in absentia* and sentenced to death for treason. In the meantime, King Enrico II had died. On the eve of the coronation of Enrico's son, Juan I, the functionaries of the Jewish court of justice persuaded the chief of police to carry out their sentence on Pichon. He sneaked into Joseph's palatial home and beheaded him with one stroke of the sword. When the new king learned of what he viewed as the murder of his father's friend, he ordered the arrest of all the leaders of the Jewish community of Barcelona and sentenced them to death. Hasdai Crescas was among those arrested.

The King first carried out his sentence upon those who actually participated in the execution of Pichon. After much pleading on the part of the Jewish community, the king eventually released the other leaders on condition that they leave the country. After five months of imprisonment, Hasdai, too, was freed and emigrated to Saragossa, in Aragon. Before he left, his son, who was barely twenty years of age, died a martyr's death. The Dominicans, eager to exact vengeance for the death of Pichon who had given them much financial support, arrested the boy and placed before him the choice between immediate execution and conversion to Christianity. Hasdai's son chose to die rather than abandon his religion.

Hasdai Crescas was the author of many important works on Jewish philosophy. Perhaps the most important among them was his book *Or Hashem* (*The Light of God*). He also wrote a rebuttal of Maimonides' *Guide for the Perplexed*. In his foreward to *Or Hashem* he stated his intention eventually to publish a huge work which would include all aspects of Jewish belief, but it seems that he never managed to write it.

Crescas was definitely opposed to those who sought to cite the Greek philosophers in order to strengthen Judaism. His book *Or Hashem,* was particularly aimed against Maimonides and Rabbi Levi ben Gershon, both of whom had lived before his time. He maintained that the Bible and Jewish Law could do very well without the support of Platonian or Aristotelian philosophy. He declared, too, that Jews should believe that God created the world "out of nothing" and not from some preexisting substance. He specified, however, that a Jew did not cease to be a Jew, even if he refused to believe in either of these two postulates.

According to Crescas, Judaism does not have thirteen fundamental principles, as stated by Maimonides, but only six, as follows:

1. There is a God.

2. Divine providence rules over all things, both over the universe in general and the life of the individual in particular.

3. God is omnipotent and He can act in accordance with His will.

4. God inspired certain people with the divine gift of prophecy so that the prophets actually did speak in the name of God.

5. God left the choice between good and evil in the hands of man.

6. The world was created for a definite purpose or end.

As regards the questions of divine omniscience and free will, Hasdai concurred with Nachmanides, who said that while God knows exactly what will happen in the future, He exerts no influence upon man to act in any particular way. Thus man, who cannot forsee the future, has a free choice between good and evil. God, however, knows in advance which of these two paths each man will choose.

Hasdai believed in the God's election of the people of Israel, and that Palestine, the land of Israel, was indeed a blessed land which enjoyed a status higher than that of the other countries of the world.

He also attempted to find an answer to such questions as the purpose of the world in general and of human life in particular; the reason why God had created the world and all that is in it; and man's role on earth.

In answer to the above questions, he had this to say: There are three worlds—the upper, the middle, and the lower. Man has to strive to rise from the lower level to the middle and eventually to the upper sphere. The lowest level is that of common clay, the next is more of the spirit and the highest is that of Godliness. Man must regard it as his goal to acquire Godly virtues and, in general, to come as close to God as possible. According to Hasdai, this end could best be attained by observance of the Torah.

Hasdai believed in the immortality of the soul, and in spiritual reward and punishment. But he did not insist that belief in either of these constituted a basic requirement which a Jew had to fulfill if he was to be regarded as a Jew. Nor was the belief in the coming of a Messiah and in the revival of the dead an absolute essential. Yet he felt that a Jew ought to believe in some sort of resurrection, particularly in that of the righteous.

In general, he asserted that Judaism was not a true "belief" with a fixed set of indispensable articles of faith, but demanded only an understanding of God. For this reason one could not label a Jew a heretic or excommunicate him simply because he did not "believe" in any one of the six principles which he, Hasdai, had enumerated.

Hasdai Crescas died in 1410 at the age of seventy. His spiritual heir was his disciple, Rabbi Joseph Albo.

12. Rabbi Joseph Albo and His "Book of Principles"

The Epidemic of Mass Baptisms in Spain—The Debate of Joseph Albo with a Convert, a Former Rabbi—Joseph Albo's Three Principles of Judaism

The situation of the Jews in Spain deteriorated with each passing day. The persecutions increased and led to bloody pogroms. The second half of the fourteenth century also saw the epidemic of the black death which came after the era of the crusades and wrought havoc throughout Europe.

The epidemic itself lasted about three years (from 1347 to 1350), but its effects were felt even well into the fifteenth century. The disease, which is known in medical science as the "bubonic plague," and is spread by the rat flea, killed some 25 million people in Spain, Germany, Italy, France, and most of the rest of Europe. Naturally panic reigned everywhere and the priests took advantage of the situation to stir up the hysterical populace against the Jews. The plague, they explained, was the work of the Jews who had poisoned the wells so that the water might become polluted and the Christians would die from it. The Jew-baiters, to support their false claims cited in their support the fact that the disease had claimed a much smaller percentage of victims in Jewish quarters than among the Gentiles. This proved to be true, but the reason for this phenomenon was simply that the Jews had a healthier way of living, because they complied with the hygienic laws of the Torah. At any rate the Christian masses, incited by the rabble rousers, took speedy action. In May of that year, twenty Jews were murdered in Barcelona. A few weeks later, three hundred Jews lost their lives in the city of Triga. Then the entire Jewish community of Sibillia of some four thousand souls was destroyed. Murder and terror also stalked the Jewish communities in Cordova, Burgos, and Valencia. Aiding and abetting the Gentile masses were some Jewish converts who had sold their souls to the Dominicans and were eager to prove their loyalty to Christianity by bringing harm to as many Jews as possible.

During that sad period in Jewish history, in the year 1380, to be exact, there was born to a poor couple in Monreal a boy who was to be known as Rabbi Joseph Albo, noted Jewish philosopher and physician. He not only studied with the greatest Talmudists of that day, but also had the advantage of being able to attend the lectures of some of the eminent philosophers of that time. In addition, he was a disciple of Rabbi Hasdai Crescas. According to some historians, Joseph Albo was a famous preacher who exhorted the Jewish masses to cling to their Judaism and not to succumb to the threats and temptations of the Christian agitators. As time went on, Albo became one of the most important figures of Jewish life in Spain.

At that time Pope Benedict XIII decreed that the rabbis and scholars of the Jews were to be challenged to a debate on Judaism by Maestro Geronimo de Santa Fe, formerly Rabbi Joshua of Lorqui, who had been converted to Christianity and had become a stanch ally of the Church. It is interesting to note that when the infamous Rabbi Solomon Ha-Levi had undergone baptism as Paulus de Santa Maria, Joshau of Lorqui had written him an angry letter, denouncing him for his defection from Judaism. It seems that a correspondence developed between the two and that, in the end, probably with the help of the Dominicans, the former Rabbi Solomon Ha-Levi was able to influence Joshua to embrace Christianity himself. It was upon suggestion of Maestro Geronimo that Pope Benedict ordered the debate which was to take place at Tortosa between Geronimo and some of the rabbis and leaders of the Jewish community. Among the Jewish participants was also Rabbi Joseph Albo.

The great dispute began on February 7, 1413, and continued for four days. Among the many Jewish leaders who took part, there was also one Don Vidal ibn Labi. The debate ended in defeat for the convert, and the Pope himself was forced to admit that the convert was no match for the Jewish scholars.

The debate, which was attended not only by the Pope himself, but also by the king of Aragon, took place in the palace of the Bishop of Tortosa at the command of King Ferdinand of Castillia on behalf of the Pope. A day before the debate, we are told, the Pope assured the Jewish participants that they had nothing to fear. He said that Maestro Geronimo would only attempt to prove that even the rabbis of the Talmud were convinced that the Messiah had come, but that the burden of proof rested upon Maestro Geronimo.

When the Jewish delegation arrived at the palace the next morning, they found the hall festively bedecked. There were seventy chairs for the members of the Christian hierarchy, and some thousand places for lay Christians. The King of Aragon and the Pope sat on thrones on a dais overlooking the entire gathering.

Pope Benedict XIII took the stand. He stated that as far as he was concerned, there was no doubt in his mind that the Christian faith was superior to Judaism and that Judaism had, in fact, lost its validity with the advent of Christ. He said, however, that it was the intention of Maestro Geronimo to prove that even the Talmud itself contained statements to the effect that the Messiah had already come. With that, he called upon Geronimo to make his presentation.

The former Rabbi Joshua of Lorqui began to cite places in the Talmud which referred to the Messiah and from which he attempted to prove that the rabbis of that time had already believed that the Messiah had come. The discussion went on for four days. The members of the Jewish delegation were able to refute Joshua's every point and in the end both the King and the Pope were compelled to acknowledge the superior debating skill of the Jewish side.

On the last day, however, Geronimo asked the Pope for permission to have a debate with Rabbi Joseph Albo alone on the comparative merits of the Jewish and Christian faiths. His request was granted.

In his famous work, *Sefer Haikarim (The Book of Principles)* Chapter 25, Section III, Joseph Albo describes what went on during that crucial discussion. It is interesting to note that this chapter appears only in the oldest editions of the book. Later on it was deleted by the censors of the Church.

According to this account, the argument of Geronimo ran as follows:

It is my intention to prove that the level of the teaching of Christ is much superior to that of the Torah of Moses: The Torah of Moses only tells legends of patriarchs and such, but the teaching of Christ speaks of higher things. It explains in great detail the nature of the Trinity, Father, Son and Holy Ghost, while your Torah contains only veiled references to the Deity; your Torah speaks only of reward and punishment in this world, but our Gospels hold a promise of recompense and retribution in the next world. Your law commands the sacrifice of animals, but the teaching of Christ has no need for primitive animal slaughter and demands only symbolic offerings of bread and wine.

Joseph Albo then refuted Geronimo's theses one by one. First, he explained, that one could not very well call the Gospels a "teaching" in opposition to that of the Torah, for Christ himself said that he did not come to add or detract even a hair's breadth from the Torah.

Secondly, he said that it was quite wrong to say that the Torah of Moses was only a book of legends, while the Gospels dealt with higher things. Actually, it is the Gospels that are full of hymns of praise for Jesus, while the Pentateuch does not by any means glorify a human being even such as Moses was.

As for reward and punishment, Joseph Albo maintained that it was an easy thing for anyone to guarantee reward or punishment in a world beyond this life, for no person could prove him wrong. For this reason Moses, who had no wish to tell his people anything beyond the certainty given him by divine promise, confined his prophecies to the tangible rewards and punishments of this world.

Finally, as for Geronimo's argument about sacrifices, Joseph said that the offerings of bread and wine in the Christian ritual were meant to symbolize the body and the blood of Christ and seemed just as illogical to the Jew as the slaughter of animals upon the Temple altar would seem to the Christian.

In a similar manner Joseph Albo managed to counter every one of the arguments advanced by Geronimo, so that, in the end, Geronimo, defeated, asked the Pope for permission to leave the chamber.

Just the same, the Jewish community of Spain suffered from an epidemic of mass baptisms. Because some of the more prominent converts were men of broad wordly education, the pious extremists felt that the study of secular science should be shunned altogether, because it only led to baptism. What they failed to consider was that, as a matter of fact, there were more renegades among those learned in Jewish Law than among those who were more interested in worldly culture and knowledge. It was this sad state of affairs that impelled Joseph to write his famous work *Sefer Haikarim* (*The Book of Principles*), so that it might be made quite clear to his fellow Jews just what was an essential principle of Judaism and what was not, and that secular learning, rather than leading to baptism, actually would point up some of the doctrinal flaws of Christianity.

In this book, which was published in 1425, Joseph Albo declared his opposition to the thirteen principles of Judaism set down by Maimonides. He came to the conclusion that there were only three basic principles in which he felt Jews should believe; namely: (1) that there is a God; (2) that God gave the Torah to the Jewish people; and (3) that all good deeds would be rewarded and all evil punished. True, he said, these three basic tenets could be accepted by any monotheistic faith, including Christianity and Mohammedanism. However, the difference consisted in the inferences and concepts that are derived from each of these principles.

Albo then discussed the ideals which the Jewish faith derives from each of the three fundamentals. From the belief in God, Judaism drew three inferences: (1) there had to be a moral code; (2) there had to be a code of civil justice; and (3) men must strive to improve both themselves and the society in which they live so that truth and goodness should be universally acknowledged and respected. The belief in the divine revelation of the Torah to the Jewish people includes the recognition of God Himself and the understanding of the meaning and importance of prophecy. Reward and punishment, Albo asserted, have been promised us for four different periods of time: that is, in this world, in the world to come, at the time of the advent of the Messiah, and at the time of the resurrection of the dead. Albo sincerely believed in all the eight conclusions which he drew from the three basic principles, but he did not feel that anyone who denied any of the eight inferences thereby ceased to be a Jew. To him only the three actual fundamental tenets seemed absolutely essential. He could not agree with the implication of Maimonides that a person who did not believe in the Messiah could not be a Jew.

13. Don Isaac Abrabanel

Behind the Scenes Before the Inquisition—The Inquisition and the Dominicans—Don Isaac Abrabanel Comments on the Works of Maimonides—His Explanations of "Basic Principles" and "Axioms"

By the second half of the fifteenth century, the zealous Dominicans were ready to make practical use of the permission given them by the king to set up the tribunal which was to go down in history as the "Bloody Inquisition." They could no longer stomach the prosperity of the Marranos, whom they contemptuously called the "New Christians," and who played an important role in the cultural and economic life of Spain. The Jews who were active in trade and commerce had done much to bring wealth to the country, and those of them who accepted baptism rose quickly in Spanish society. They lived in palatial homes in the most exclusive residential sections of the large cities and still enjoyed great wealth and universal respect. This the Dominicans resented bitterly, for they themselves had, for the most part, come from poor homes, lived in poverty, and did not take kindly to the thought that the "new Christian" upstarts should have the best of everything while the Dominican brothers and the true original Christians had to content themselves with a much lower standard of living. It was only natural, then, that the Dominicans should actively seek ways and means of discrediting the new converts. An opportunity to do so soon appeared.

Most of the "new Christians" were still Jews at heart and secretly observed the customs and ceremonies of their faith. They had accepted conversion only to make life somewhat easier for themselves, and had no desire to become devout Catholics. They saw the inside of a church only rarely, and then only in order to satisfy their curious Christian neighbors. The zealous monks proposed to set up a court of inquest, or "Inquisition," which would investigate the religious loyalties of the Marranos, and take drastic action wherever it seemed advisable. It was not such an easy thing for the Dominicans, however, to put this plan into practice. King Ferdinand would gladly have signed the necessary decree, for his head was filled with visions of the silver and gold which would be confiscated from the Marranos, pouring into the coffers of his own treasury. His wife and co-ruler, Queen Isabella, however, though a devout Catholic and very much under the spell of the Dominican Thomas Torquemada, was more cautious. She was shrewd enough to realize that with the elimination of the rich Jews, the Marranos, who constituted the backbone of the merchant class of the country, Spain would lose much of her wealth and the position of power which she then held among the nations of Europe. The queen therefore stalled and kept postponing her own decision on the matter. In the end the royal couple decided that they would consult the Pope and abide by whatever he would say. Sixtus IV, who then occupied the Holy See, loved money, and, seeing the possibilities for increasing the wealth of his own Vatican State by the monies to be confiscated from those to be condemned by the Inquisition, quickly declared himself to be in favor of such a court, which would try and punish those "new Christians," who seemed lax in the observance of their adopted faith. The Pope released his approval on November 1, 1478, but it was not until January 2, 1481, that the first victims of the Inquisition were burned at the stake. By November of that year, some two hundred and eighty of the most prominent Marranos had been burned to death as part of the program of "Auto-da-fes" ("Acts of Faith"), instituted by the fanatical and wicked Dominicans. The victims marched to their doom with the ancient Jewish declaration "Hear, O Israel" upon their lips.

Such was the time in which Don Isaac Abrabanel, the Talmudist, philosopher, and statesman, grew to maturity.

The Abrabanels were an old and noble family who could trace their descent directly to King David. Don Isaac ("Don" was a Spanish title equivalent to the British "Sir") was the son of David Judah Abrabanel who had escaped from Spain to Lisbon where Isaac was born in 1437. The boy received an extensive education in both Jewish lore and secular sciences. He entered the field of business and finance and became wealthy. Eventually King Alfonso V appointed him minister of finance.

At about that time Alfonso conquered the city of Arsila in Morocco, taking many captives, among whom were two hundred and fifty Jews. Don Isaac used his wealth and influence to secure their release, and then took care of all their needs for two years until they could fend for themselves.

When Alfonso died, his son, Juan, made what we would call today a "purge" among his father's servants and ministers because he had been told that they were all conspiring against him. Don Isaac managed to escape to Spain and settled in Toledo, but he had to leave behind all his fortune, which was promptly confiscated by King Juan.

The newcomer did not remain unnoticed for long, however. He attracted the attention of Ferdinand and Isabella who asked him to become their minister of finance. During the eight years of his tenure in this position, Spain grew greatly in power and wealth. It is believed by some people that Don Isaac and other Jewish benefactors gave Columbus the funds he needed for his historic journey which resulted in the discovery of the New World.

When, in 1492, Ferdinand and Isabella finally signed the decree ordering the expulsion of all Jews from Spain, Don Isaac Abrabanel implored them to rescind the order. However, the royal couple remained adamant, although they assured him that the decree would in no way affect him and that they wanted him to continue serving them as minister of finance. But Don Isaac felt that his place was with his people, and, when all the other Jews began their exodus from Spain, he, too, left the country and settled in the then free city of Naples where he served as advisor to its king. He continued in the same position during the reign of Alfonso II, the son and successor of that ruler. When King Charles I of France annexed the city of Naples and Alfonso had to flee to Sicily, Don Isaac went into exile together with his master and remained with him until the king's death in 1495.

Don Isaac Abrabanel was a prolific author. His two best known works are his commentary on the Bible and his book, *Rosh Emunah,* which deals with matters of Jewish philosophy. In his Biblical commentary he did not hesitate to quote Christian sources, such as the works of Hieronymus, Nicolai de Lira, and others, wherever he felt that their views coincided with his own. He was one of the first Bible commentators to write an introduction to each sacred book, and in his prefaces to works of prophetic literature, such as Isaiah, he gives a detailed analysis of the historical background, style, and ideals of the writers.

While Don Isaac was quite at home in the field of philosophy, he himself made no original contributions to Jewish thought. He was very pious and had no patience with those who admired Greek philosophy, or even attempted to use it in support of Judaism. Yet he defended Maimonides against the attacks of such men as Hasdai Crescas, and Joseph Albo. He explained that the thirteen principles of faith set down by Maimonides were not all of equal importance, and that Maimonides himself had never meant to imply that a person who had doubts concerning one or more of them thereby ceased to be a Jew. When Maimonides referred to his thirteen points as "principles," said Abrabanel, he simply meant to indicate that these were thirteen of the most important theses of Judaism, but by no means basic to it.

This explanation of Abrabanel's stirred up a good deal of controversy in the Jewish scholarly world. One eminent teacher quoted verbatim to Abrabanel the words which Maimonides himself had appended to his thirteen principles, namely: "He who does not believe in even one of these principles thereby reads himself out of the community of Israel; he is called an unbeliever and a heretic. Such a man should be hated; he should be denounced publicly, and should be destroyed." It seems that Don Isaac was not able to offer a comment of his own on this explicit statement made by Maimonides himself. The same scholar pointed out that Joseph Albo was quite right in taking exception to the ideas of Maimonides, for even the Amora Hillel had not in any way been labeled a heretic when he flatly stated that the Messiah would never come, although Maimonides had declared the belief in the Messiah to be one of the thirteen principles of Judaism. Those who had protested against Hillel's views said that they only hoped the Lord would forgive him for his rash statement, but it did not occur to any of them to excommunicate him, and certainly not to destroy him.

Abrabanel, however, did not give in. In his writings he explained that Maimonides had only followed the practice then in vogue with most of the non-Jewish philosophical writers of his day, which was to posit a specific number of "principles" or "axioms" as the basis of their treatises. Don Isaac argued, however, that actually there was no reason why Maimonides or any Jew should ape non-Jewish thought or style, because "The Torah of God has its own way and we need not imitate non-Jewish scholars, when it comes to such things. For this reason we need not take too literally the word 'principle,' as used by Maimonides."

In his old age Don Isaac Abrabanel left Sicily and lived first in Corfu, then in Minopol and, finally, after eight years of moving from place to place, settled in Venice. There he played an important role in the negotiations between the rulers of Venice and the King of Portugal concerning commerce in spices and he was close to Venetian government circles until he died in 1508 at the age of seventy-one. He was buried in Padua, but a year later the city was besieged and conquered by a hostile power and the Jewish cemetery was destroyed so that no one now knows his burial place.

The death of Don Isaac Abrabanel may be said to represent the end of the Golden Age of Spanish Jewry, which we call the first epoch in the Era of the Philosophers. But now a discovery was made, which was to be the basis for new views and ideas in the philosophy of Judaism, namely the *Book of the Zohar,* which we shall discuss in Chapter 14.

14. The Discovery of the "Zohar"

Rabbi Moses de Leon Who Published the Zohar *as the Work of Simon ben Yochai—The Tale of His Widow and His Daughter—What Is the* Zohar?*— Six Main Points—How the* Zohar *Anticipated Copernicus—A Brief Summary of the Golden Age of Spanish Jewry*

As the situation of the Jews in Spain deteriorated, clear and rational thinking came to hold less interest for them than mysticism and metaphysics. The persecuted Jews sought the promise of deliverance in the pages of cabalistic lore and even philosophers of formidable reputation devoted their talents to the exploration of mystical literature. The most outstanding among these thinkers were Rabbi Isaac ibn Latif (also known as Al Latif); Rabbi Joseph ben Abraham Giktalia, a disciple of Abraham Abulafia, and Rabbi Moses ben Shem Tov de Leon. The latter, who was born in 1250, traveled about the Spanish countryside, interrupting his journeys only for temporary stops in various cities, where he engaged in the writing of books with mystical themes, such as *Shoshan Edoth* (*The Rose of the Testimony*), *Sepher Hermon* (*The Book of Hermon*) and others, in which he sought to give the Biblical commandments a new interpretation, strongly colored by the mysticism of cabalistic literature.

One day he announced the publication of a book which he entitled the *Zohar.* The title page named the Tanna Simon bar Yochai as the author of this book. This rabbi was a scholar who lived in the era of the Mishna, shortly after the destruction of the Second Temple, and was a favorite disciple of the martyred Rabbi Akiba. Simon and his son Rabbi Eleazar had hidden in a cave for thirteen years to escape the wrath of the Roman conquerers, remaining there until the accession of the Emperor Andronius. The anniversary of Rabbi Simon's death which falls on the minor Jewish holiday of Lag B'Omer, is still celebrated today in Israel by the lighting of torches and the singing of hymns in Meron (near the ancient town of Safed) where he died around 148 A.D. Thus, if the book of the *Zohar* was really the work of Simon bar Yochai, it was not published until some eleven hundred years after the passing of its author.

When Moses de Leon was asked how he had come into the possession of the book, he explained that Nachmanides, having discovered it on one of his journeys to Palestine, had promptly dispatched it to him by special messenger. The ship on which that messenger sailed had been caught in a storm and forced to seek shelter in the harbor of Alicante, in Valencia, Spain. In the end, however, the book was safely delivered into his hands.

The book aroused much interest both in cabalist circles and among Jews in general. Some scholars believed de Leon's story that it was indeed written by none other than Rabbi Simon bar Yochai. Others were rather inclined to think that de Leon himself was the author. Still others attributed its authorship to some unknown Cabalist who had lived in Babylonia during the ninth or tenth century and that de Leon, in publishing it, had named the famous Bar Yochai as the author so that the work might sell more readily.

Shortly after the publication of the *Zohar,* there arrived in Spain from Palestine one Isaac of Acre, a refugee from the bloody battles of the Crusades. A Cabalist himself, Rabbi Isaac had been a friend and disciple of Nachmanides, and was therefore somewhat surprised that this teacher should never have told him about the work which, according to de Leon's story, he was supposed to have discovered and sent on to Spain. When he questioned de Leon, the latter swore to him that he had told the truth and that he would shortly show him the original copy of the manuscript. However, before he could carry out his promise, Moses de Leon was taken ill and died in the town of Arbela where he had stopped on the way to his native city of Avila. But de Leon's death (in 1305) did not deter Isaac of Acre from continuing his quest for the true author of the *Zohar.* He went to Avila and contacted two of the most esteemed members of the Jewish community there, Rabbi David Rephan and Rabbi Joseph de Avila, who, he hoped, could shed some light on the mystery. Rephan was quite sure that de Leon never received any sort of manuscript from Nachmanides and that he must have written it himself. De Avila went to visit the widow of de Leon who lived in great poverty with her unmarried daughter. He promised the woman that if she would tell him the whole truth about the book which her husband had published as the work of Simon bar Yochai, he would give her a considerable sum of money and also take her daughter for his daughter-in-law. The widow and daughter then admitted that Moses de Leon had written the book himself, without the aid of any preexisting manuscript or document, and that he had ascribed it to bar Yochai only because he felt that the name of the famed scholar on the title page would attract many more purchasers than his own name would have.

Of course no one knows whether the two women told the truth. At any rate, the Cabalists revered the *Zohar* as a holy book. Many others, however, had their doubts about its authorship. The first to express his views openly was Rabbi Joseph Vicar, a philosopher and Cabalist, who lived in the early part of the fifteenth century. Later Rabbi Eliahu Delmidiga argued, as did many other later scholars (particularly Rabbi Jacob Emden who attacked the *Zohar* and maintained that it had been written not during the era of the Mishna, but some time after the Talmud was completed), that the book contained the names of scholars who lived long after bar Yochai, and that it made mention of events which occurred after his death. Moreover, they declared that the *Zohar* contains laws which definitely run counter to the spirit of the Talmud and that, in general, the book is too full of inaccuracies to be the work of the great scholar to whom it was ascribed.

Modern scholars generally agreed that the *Zohar* was not the creation of Rabbi Simon bar Yochai who lived eleven centuries prior to the publication of the book. For one thing, the *Zohar* is written in the Aramaic-Syrian dialect, which was not commonly used by the scholars of the time of Simon bar Yochai, who employed Hebrew as their vehicle of communication. If, in addition, we consider the other chronological factors, it would seem that the *Zohar* was not written in Palestine and not during the days of the Mishna, but by some Cabalist in Babylonia during the eighth century or perhaps early in the ninth, in the early days of the Cabala and Jewish mysticism. It was in these days that the mixture of Aramaic and Syrian, in which the *Zohar* and many works of post-Talmudic literature were written, was commonly used in Babylonia. Hence the confusing fiction that for some unknown reason the book was never published in that country and remained unknown until it came into the hands of Rabbi Moses de Leon, who, desiring to make a sensation and also to obtain some material profit from it, announced that he had discovered an ancient work of the great Simon bar Yochai which he was now willing to turn over to the public.

Actually, the *Zohar,* as we know it today, is not just one book, but a whole series of volumes. In addition to the main work, there are the *Tikunei Zohar,* the *New Zohar,* then two books entitled *Idra Rabba* and *Idra Sota* (*Great Assembly of Wise Men* and *Small Assembly*) respectively, the *Book of Modesty,* another one entitled *The True Shepherd,* and many others. There are some editions in which all these works are printed in one volume. In others, each is printed separately. There is no doubt that a great many other later writings of unknown authorship, similar in style and tenor, have been added to this anthology at a later date and have become a part of what we now know as the *Zohar.*

Even though the *Zohar* is actually a book of mystical philosophy, we are going to make a brief survey of its contents, since it does contain certain views which had a profound influence upon the development of the philosophy of Judaism. Let us, then, list the six basic ideas that run through the *Zohar.*

1. The stories contained in the Bible, such as the accounts of Abraham, Isaac, Jacob, and others, are not simple stories to be taken at face value but contain a great many profound mysteries which not everyone can perceive. "Woe to him who views them only as ordinary stories without perceiving the profound theme that is hidden in them" (*Zohar, Portion Bethaalothecha*).

2. Before the creation of the universe, God was in a state of semiexistence ("existing and yet not existing"). At that time His name was simply "Mi" (the Hebrew word for "who"), and it was only after creation that the prefix "Eloh" (meaning "these") as added to His appellation to make it "Elohim."

Allusion is made to this in the Biblical verse reading "lift up your eyes and see *who* created all *this*" (*Zohar,* Parshat Terumah, 162:72).

3. The *Zohar* also accepts the cabalist theory concerning the ten spheres, beginning with "En Sof" ("God, the Infinite One") (*Zohar,* Idra Sota, 288).

4. The human soul is immortal and when the body dies, the soul returns to the heavenly treasure chamber of souls whence it originally came. There it is received with great joy by its fellows, if it returns free, or almost free of sin (*Zohar,* Idra Sota).

5. In addition to the ten spheres of holiness listed in the Cabala, there are ten spheres of impurity, which fall under the dominion of Satan. In other words, the strength of evil is equal to that of virtue and man must wage a fierce struggle if he is not to succumb to the temptations of evil.

6. The *Zohar* contains accounts of the coming of the Messiah and the resurrection of the dead which will follow his advent.

It would seem that the philosophy of the *Zohar* is neither extraordinary nor particularly profound. But the student will be amazed to find in the *Zohar* the following statement. "The entire world revolves like a sphere; some men are on the top of the sphere while others are at the bottom thereof. Hence while the light of day shines on one half, the other half is dark, and there are places on earth where the hours of darkness are very few." In other words, the author of the *Zohar* here refers to the fact that the earth revolves around the sun, which was acknowledged by the rest of the world only after its discovery by Copernicus in the second half of the fifteenth century. Today we know that this theory was known in Babylonia during the eighth and ninth centuries, having been advocated by Persian scholars who derived it from ancient Indian sources.

Eventually the *Zohar* was recognized as a sacred book, particularly by the hassidic sect, and it was translated into other languages, including Latin, French, and English.

15. Were the Jewish Philosophers Free-Thinkers?

The End of the Golden Age of Spanish Jewry—Debate and Philosophy as an Intellectual Pastime—Plato, Aristotle, and the Arabs—Scholasticism

The Golden Age of Spanish Jewry extended over a period of more than five hundred years. It was an era of intensive intellectual, spiritual, and scientific activity, of poetry and invention, science and theology, of Biblical research and scholarly studies of Jewish Law. It is now advisable to make a summary of that important period in Jewish history, and particularly of the intellectual achievements for which it is best remembered.

In previous chapters we have studied the lives and works of fourteen great Jewish philosophers: Rabbi Saadia Gaon, Bachya, Shlomo ibn Gabirol, Abraham ibn Ezra, Moses ibn Ezra, Judah Ha-Levi, Maimonides, Nachmanides, Abraham Abulafia, Levi ben Gershon, Hasdai Crescas, Joseph Albo, Isaac Abrabanel, and Moses de Leon. It would be erroneous to assume, however, that these were the only great intellects produced by the Golden Age, for actually there were many, many more Jewish thinkers and scholars, each of whom contributed something to that great era. Each left his mark upon that particular period in the history of his people. The Golden Age left to the Jewish people a better understanding not only of its Laws and its literature, but also of the best in Jewish thought and ethics.

In order to do justice to the many lesser known philosophers of that era whom we have not discussed in the preceding chapters, it might be well to make a brief list of just a few of them and to obtain some knowledge of their intellectual contributions to Judaism. Proceeding in chronological order, we will begin with Rabbi David Almkametz and Rabbi Donesh ben Tamim, who were both contemporaries of Rabbi Saadia Gaon. The works of Almkametz, who was a disciple of Saadia, have been lost, but quotations from his writings may be found in those of other philosophers. It is generally agreed that his views were largely in agreement with those expressed by his teacher in his book entitled *Ha-emunoth Ve-hadayoth*. Little is known about his ancestors. Some claim that he was an Arab, a follower of Mohammed, who embraced Judaism; others class him as a Karaite, but there is no historical proof for either claim. The works of Donesh ben Tamim suffered a fate much the same as those of Almkametz, but the quotations from his writings that have been preserved in various sources indicate that he published a philosophical commentary on the cabalist book *Sefer Hayezirah* (*The Book of Creation*) and that, like Almkametz, he was an adherent of Saadia Gaon.

Rabbi Joseph ben Zaddik, a contemporary and friend of Judah Ha-Levi and Abraham ibn Ezra, served as rabbi in the city of Cordova. The work for which he is best remembered is entitled *Olam Katan* (or *A Little World*). The "Little World" refers to man. Joseph ben Zaddik agreed with the view of Judah Ha-Levi, who believed that Jews should seek the answers to their problems, not in the works of Greek philosophy or in other alien ideologies, but only in the Law of the Torah.

Another scholar of that time was Rabbi Abraham ben David Ha-Levi (or Abraham ibn Daud, as he was known in Arab circles), who wrote a book entitled *Ha-emunah Ha-ramah* (*The Exalted Faith*). This was a refutation of the views advanced by Shlomo ibn Gabirol in a book called *Mekor Chayim* (*The Source of Life*). In that work Ibn Gabirol expressed his admiration for the philosophy of Plato. Ibn Daud preferred the way of Aristotle, as expounded by the Arab scholar Ibn Sina and in his treatise compared the views of Aristotle with those of Plato to the advantage of the former. The work makes no pretense to depth or originality; it is simply a collection of talks and discussions.

A little later on we meet with the Allegorists, a group of thinkers who gave allegoric interpretations to stories in the Bible. For example, they explained that the Biblical characters of Father Abraham and Mother Sarah actually were meant to represent "chomer" ("material") and "tzurah" (form), and that the twelve sons of Jacob symbolized the twelve heavenly constellations. The creative period of the Allegorists in the beginning of the fourteenth century was of brief duration.

Rabbi Hillel of Verona, a contemporary of Rabbi Solomon ben Abraham ben Samuel, defended the philosophy of Maimonides against its opponents. Rabbi ben Samuel wrote a book dealing with such themes as God and reward and punishment, but it is not considered an outstanding literary work.

Finally we might mention Rabbi Aron the Karaite; Rabbi Joseph ibn Caspi; Rabbi Shem Tov ben Shem Tov; Rabbi Isaac Arema; Rabbi Yehiel Ish Pisa, and Rabbi Joseph Solomon Delmedigo of Candia. Their works did not represent ventures at new or original thought, but these men, as well as many, many others too numerous to be mentioned here, have all made important contributions to Jewish knowledge.

Reading some of the amazingly radical views expressed by the philosophers of that era, we might be led to believe that these thinkers were agnostics, or at least not orthodox in the accepted sense of the word. This is simply not true. These scholars might have taken considerable liberties in their critical research and thought, but for all that they never deviated from the observance of the Jewish faith, as set down in Biblical and Talmudic Law.

As a matter of fact, they were not even so very unorthodox in thought. It is quite erroneous to class such men as Maimonides and Levi ben Gershon as freethinkers simply because they said or implied that they would not cease to search for truth even if the truth would contradict the Torah. What they actually meant was that the Torah was not so narrow that it could not allow for reinterpretation in the light of newly discovered truths. Hence those who would quote the words of these philosophers in order to prove that they were freethinkers are making a serious error, for they are basing their assumptions on a false premise. The best proof that they are wrong is that orthodox Jews today revere Maimonides as a great scholar and saint and accept all his decisions on Jewish law as binding, even if they happen to disagree with some of them. His *Guide for the Perplexed,* which gave rise to so much controversy when it was first published, has assumed a place of secondary importance.

Rabbi Levi ben Gershon, whose views, as expressed in his works, seem to outspokenly radical, is acknowledged by all orthodox Jewish scholars as an outstanding authority on the Law, and his commentary on the Bible is printed next to that of the famous Rashi in Hebrew editions of the Pentateuch. Somehow the intelligence of the Jewish people, through the ages, has retained the ability to make the distinction between the radical statements of the philosophers on one hand, and their basic views, which were essentially orthodox, on the other. For actually all the involved theological discussions on God and creation, on free will and reward and punishment, and on the future and purpose of mankind, which are found in the works of these thinkers, represent nothing more than a kind of play of the mind, an indulgence in intellectual gymnastics that was then the vogue among both the Jewish and non-Jewish intelligentsia.

Don Isaac Abrabanel quite openly said that in our study of Jewish thought we must not take too literally the points which the philosophers delighted in setting down as "basic principles." The method of philosophical discussion on the basis of set principles was simply an imitation of the practice then prevalent among Arab thinkers to base their treatises upon a definite and explicit number of "axioms." The "principles" set down by men such as Maimonides were never really meant to be construed as "basic" or "fundamental" to Judaism. They were therefore subject to free discussion, and neither the men who formulated them, nor those who disagreed with them, were to be considered in any manner as being outside the fold of orthodox Judaism.

We see, then, that the extensive philosophical discussions of the great Jewish thinkers were not formulations of dogmatic doctrine, but rather exercises of the mind in the Arab style. Likewise, the interest that Jewish scholars took in the Greek philosophers, Plato and Aristotle, was nothing more than a natural outgrowth of the profound impact which the ideas of the two Greeks had upon the Arab world in which the Jewish intellectuals of that day lived.

Why the Arabs should have taken such a fancy to Plato and Aristotle can be easily understood, if we take into consideration certain similarities in historical background.

Plato and Aristotle lived at a time when Greece was in a state of spiritual and intellectual change. Idolatry no longer satisfied the more educated people. The philosophies advanced by Plato and his disciple Aristotle, though somewhat at variance with each other, served well to fill the spiritual vacuum in which the better minds of Greece now found themselves. Plato taught them for the first time that there was only one God who created the world and all that is in it. But having been accustomed to polytheism, neither Plato nor the rest of the Greeks were ready to accept the Jewish view of God as an omnipotent being of infinite might who could make an entire universe out of nothing. Hence Plato reasoned that even though God was indeed the Creator of all things, the material which He used for this purpose was already in existence prior to creation, and possessed life and motion, and God simply shaped it in accordance with His will.

Now, centuries later, the Arab world was in much the same state, culturally and spirtually, as the Greeks had been in the days of Plato and Aristotle. The educated classes could no longer accept the ancient cult of idolatry, but they were not yet ready to follow the teachings of Mohammed, the camel-driver, which were actually based upon pure, monotheistic Judaism. The religious vacuum in which they now found themselves needed to be filled, and, still lacking original thinkers of their own, the Arabs turned to the ideas which had been advanced by the ancient Greek philosophers in a similar situation long ago.

The Jews who lived in their midst actually had no need to do so, because the Jewish view of God and creation was much more plausible and readily explainable than the theses advanced by Plato and Aristotle. However, at about that time the Arabs became interested in the pseudo science of astrology, the belief that the stars in heaven could influence and determine the course of human life on earth. Here again the Jews aped them to such a degree that even such rational thinkers as Maimonides, Ibn Ezra, and Levi ben Gershon actually spoke of the influence of the starry constellations on man's life on earth.

In recapitulation we might say that the philosophies that prevailed in the ancient world from the ninth to the fifteenth century were mainly lengthy discussion, questions and answers, indulged in simply for the exercise of the mind and leading to no absolute conclusions. To the minds of that era, in the history of both Judaism and the rest of the world philosophy was a sort of intellectual pastime with no end in view other than the sharpening of the mind. This type of speculation, which is known today as "scholasticism," ruled supreme among thinking men until the advent of Descartes who propounded an entirely new approach to logic and thought.

One of the outstanding disciples of Descartes was a Jew, Baruch Spinoza, who inaugurated the second era of Jewish philosophy, which extends down to the present day. This new era differed from the first period in that, while the first epoch was confined to Spain, the creative activity of the second took place, not in a single country, but all over the world, wherever Jews settled in religious communities. We shall discuss these new ideas in the following chapters on the second part of the Era of the Philosophers.

16. Other Creations of the First Part of the Era of the Philosophers

❧ THE COMMENTATORS

During the first part of the era of the philosophers, the genius of the Jewish nation produced a group of scholars who have gone down in Jewish history as the "meforshim" or "commentators." These men, who are considered outstanding authorities in the field of Jewish literature, were the authors of the classic commentaries on the Bible and the Talmud, which are still studied intensively by scholars and seminarians.

The most important of the commentators was Rabbi Solomon Yitzchaki (better known as Rashi) who wrote a commentary on the Pentateuch, on the prophets, other holy writings, and the Talmud. It is generally conceded that, were it not for the explanations given by this eminent master, certain passages, both in Biblical and Talmudic literature, would be almost impossible to understand and would certainly have presented almost insurmountable hurdles to the serious student.

Rashi, however, was not the first of the commentators. Before him there were "expounders" such as Rabbi Hananel and others. But the commentary of Rashi is the one that has been accepted as authoritative by all Jews, and it forms an integral part of the study of the Pentateuch and the Talmud even in elementary institutions of traditional Jewish learning.

Immediately following Rashi in the order of importance is Rabbi Obadiah MiBartenura, who wrote commentaries on both the Mishna and the works of Maimonides.

All in all the number of commentators is some three hundred. Among the most important commentaries after Rashi's were those written by Abraham ibn Ezra, Levi ben Gershon, Maimonides, Isaac Abradanel, Rabbi Moses Elishach, the works known as *Siphorno* and *Or Hachayim* (*The Light of Life*) and the commentaries of Rabbi Obadiah MiBartenura on the Bible and the Mishna.

The existing commentaries on the Bible can be classified in three categories as follows:

1. Brief notes which confine themselves to simple explanations of the original text.

2. Lengthier comments which draw upon haggadic and homiletic material.

3. Discussions in which the commentators state their personal opinions on the text.

Perhaps the most important and universally accepted of these commentaries are the ones in the first category, the most important of which is, of course, that of Rashi.

If we study a page of the Talmud we will find that there are two commentaries flanking the text on either side. The one on the right-hand side of the folio is that of Rashi and that on the left, entitled "Tosafos" (additions or supplements), is the work of a whole group of scholars known today as the "Tosafists."

Most of these "Tosafists" were either descendants or students of Rashi and are numbered among the greatest rabbinic minds of Germany and France during the period immediately following that of Rashi. Some, but not all of them, are explicitly quoted by name in the commentaries. The French Tosafists are represented in the commentary mainly by Rabbi Eliezer of Touques (or Tuch), with a number of other, unnamed French rabbis contributing their own remarks. Among the first Tosafists were Rashi's own sons-in-law, Rabbi Meir ben Samuel and Rabbi Judah ben Nathan. But the most important of all was Rabbi Jacob ben Rabbi Meir (also known as Rabbenu Tam), a son of Rabbi Meir ben Samuel and a grandson of Rashi.

Rabbi Isaac ben Asher Ha-Levi was the chief of the Tosafists in Germany. Eventually, however, a group of three French rabbis formed a kind of editorial board to arrange the commentaries known as "Tosafos." These were Rabbi Moses of Evreaux, Rabbi Eliezer of Touques, and Rabbi Peretz ben Eliahu of Courville.

The Tosafos were written and compiled during a period extending over more than two centuries. The number of Tosafists, as cited in the commentaries themselves, is forty-four. Many of the notes must have been written by disciples of Rabbi Jacob ben Meir ("Tam"), for, as we are told by Rabbi Solomon ben Yechiel Luria in his foreword to his book *Yam Shel Shlomo* (*The Sea of Solomon*), there was a time when Rabbenu Tam, as Rabbi Jacob was popularly known, had eighty disciples, each one of them himself an ordained rabbi. Those explanations in the Tosafos to which is appended a note saying "written in a notebook," evidently originated with Rashi himself because it was his habit to set down his commentaries in small notebooks. The Tosafos is replete with a type of discussion and reasoning that sheds much light upon the manner in which the sages, whose names appear in the Talmudic text, debated the fine points of Jewish law.

And even as there were commentators on the original Biblical and Talmudic texts, so there were also supercommentators who explained the commentaries. The commentary of Rashi, for example, was annotated by Rabbi Eliahu Mizrahi; Rabbi Judah Liva of Prague; Rabbi Mordecai Jaffe, and

Rabbi Shabse Bass and others. Rabbi Joseph ben Eliezer Ha-Sephardi and others rendered the same service for the commentary of Ibn Ezra.

The commentators have an important place in Jewish religious literature, for it is their explanations that have made even the most difficult portions of the Bible and Talmud accessible to the student of Jewish lore.

❧ THE "POSKIM" AND THE RESPONSA

The "Poskim," (literally meaning "codifiers") were scholars few in number, but of universally accepted authority whose decisions on matters of religious law were considered final and binding upon all Jews. These masters of Jewish law attained their position of final authority not by appointment, or by some other standard procedure, but solely by and through the general respect which they enjoyed among the masses of the Jewish people.

The first Poskim were the great scholars who laid down decisions on Jewish law, some in the form of the extensive legal documents known as "Responsa" and some by writing codices of the laws. As to the first group, it was quite simple; if there was a question on some fine point of the Law, the natural person to be consulted would be one who was reputed to be thoroughly versed in every aspect of that Law, both written and oral. Hence if a local rabbi could not answer a query of a congregant or disciple, he would address the inquiry to a scholar who had a reputation of vast knowledge and wisdom, and he would abide by the decision handed down by that sage. The first scholars to hand down such authoritative answers, or Responsa, were the Gaonim, the heads of the great Talmudical academies in Babylonia. Eventually, their decisions were published in the work entitled *The Responsa of the Gaonim*. In this manner, certain Rabbinic scholars gradually came to enjoy an international reputation for the soundness of their thinking and judgment, and were widely consulted by their less prominent colleagues the world over.

A later scholar of such stature was Rabbi Hananel who lived in the Province of Cyrenaica in Africa, where there was a great academy that was founded by Rabbenu Hushiel. Another such authority was Rabbenu Nissim, author of the legal treatise entitled *Megilath Setharim*. When the center of Jewish culture moved from Babylonia to Spain and to certain parts of France, we find a good many Poskim in both these countries. There were Rabbi Samuel Ha-Nagid (who died in 1055); Rabbenu Isaac ben Judah ibn Giaf who, in 1089, published a work entitled *Sefer Ha-halachoth* (*Book of Laws*), and Rabbi Isaac Alfasi, whose book *Sefer Ha-alfahs* created something of a sensation in scholarly circles. Of other Poskim, the most outstanding was Maimonides whose book, *Yad Hachezakah (The Strong Hand)*, is universally acknowledged as a standard and authoritative guide to Jewish law and its practical application.

Later on there was Rabbenu Gershon (know as the "Light of the Exile") who lived in Germany and died there in the year 1040 and who immortalized his name in Jewish history by the extensive "Takkanoth" ("ordinances") which he established for all future generations to follow. The most important of these are: (1) The abolition of polygamy; (2) A change in divorce laws preventing the husband from divorcing his wife arbitrarily, if she did not desire the dissolution of the marriage; (3) A decree providing that a man whose wife dies during the first year of marriage must return to her father whatever goods and chattels she might have brought to her husband's home at the time of the marriage; (4) A prohibition of the purchase of Christian religious articles from Christian clergy or laymen; (5) A prohibition against opening or reading letters addressed to another without the express permission of the latter.

To this were added codes of law such as the work entitled *Baalei Nefesh* (*Masters of the Soul*) by Rabbi Abraham ben David of Posquires, France, which dealt with the ritual laws pertaining to the marital relationship; the *Sefer Ha-ator* by Rabbi Isaac bar Abba Mari of Marseilles (d. 1222); a book on rules regarding permission and prohibitions by Rabbi Eleazar ben Nathan (d. at the end of the twelfth century); *Hilchoth Nedarim* (*Laws pertaining to Vows*) and others by Nachmanides (d. 1270); *Torah ha-Bayit* (*The Teaching of the Home*) by Rabbi Solomon ben Adret (d. 1310); *Sefer Ha-chinuch* (*Book of Education*) by an unknown author; the *Sefer Mitzvoth Gedoloth* (*Book of Great Commandments*) by Rabbi Moses ben Jacob of Coucy (d. 1260); a work by Rabbi Samson ben Zaddok (d. at the end of the fourteeth century); the book of *Ribash,* by Rabbi Isaac ben Shesheth at the end of the fourteenth century; the book of *Rush* by Rabbi Asher ben Yehiel (d. 1328); *Mordecai* by Rabbi Mordecai ben Hillel of Nuremberg (who died a martyr's death in 1398); *Sefer Mitzvoth Katan* (*The Small Book of Commandments*) by Rabbi Isaac ben Joseph of Corbeil (at the end of the thirteenth century); the *Responsa of Rabbi Meir ben Baruch* (Rabbi Meir of Rothenburg) and many others.

At the end of the thirteenth century there appeared a work entitled *Responsa from Heaven* by Rabbi Jacob Ha-Levi, a French scholar who stated in the foreword to the book that the questions enumerated therein were inquiries which he, Jacob Ha-Levi, had made of God and that the answers given to each were the decisions actually handed down to him from heaven.

The most important books of Jewish law are as follows:

1. The *Turim* (*Rows*) by Rabbenu Jacob ben Rabbenu Asher (d. 1340), consisting of four volumes: (*a*) *Orach Chaim* (dealing with commandments concerning ritual symbols such as the phylacteries, prayer shawls, and mezuzoth), (b) *Yoreh Deah* (dealing with dietary laws and related legislation),

(c) *Choshen Mishpat* (dealing with civil legislation), and (d) *Even Ha-ezer* (laws pertaining to marriage and divorce).

2. The book entitled *Beth Joseph* by Rabbi Joseph Caro (d. 1575). Originally intended only as a commentary on the *Turim* by Jacob ben Rabbenu Asher, it eventually became a new code, entitled *Shulchan Aruch* (*The Prepared Table*), which is accepted today as the standard code to which all rabbis refer in handing down decisions on Jewish Law.

Another commentary on the *Turim,* entitled *Bayit Chadash* (*New House*) and known as the *Bach* by its initials, was written by Rabbi Joel Sirkis. A similar work was published by Rabbi Joshua Falk (at the end of the seventeenth century).

Commentaries on the *Shulchan Aruch* were written by the following rabbis: Rabbi David ben Samuel Halevi (d. at the end of the seventeenth century); Rabbi Abraham Gumbiner (a contemporary of Halevi); Rabbi Moses of Vilna (showing the sources from which the author of the *Shulchan Aruch* derived the laws listed in the code); Rabbi Hezekiah ben David Da Silva (end of the seventeenth century); and more recently by Rabbi Shabati ben Meir Ha-Cohen (known by his initials as the Schach); by Rabbi Jonathan Eybeschutz and Rabbi Aryeh Leib Ha-Cohen.

One of the most important Poskim of more recent times was Rabbi Moses Isserles who maintained his own Talmudical academy in Cracow, Poland, and supported its students with his own funds. He was considered the greatest authority in Jewish law in Poland, and all traditional rabbis abide by his standards in handing down their own decisions in these matters.

❧ THE RENAISSANCE OF HEBREW LITERATURE IN SPAIN

The renaissance of the Hebrew language which began in Babylonia during the ninth and tenth centuries was in full flower during the Golden Age of Spanish Jewry from which date beautiful works of poetry, both religious and secular.

It was at about that time that Arab bards first introduced the rhyme in song and poetry. Before that time most songs were written in blank verse in the form of acrostics. The best examples of acrostics in Biblical literature may be found in the Book of Psalms, and the entire Book of Lamentations is one great acrostic.

The first Hebrew rhymes were penned by Yanai and Eliezer Ha-Kalir, who lived in the days of the Gaonim and who wrote much liturgical poetry. Saadia Gaon also wrote quite a number of poems which have been preserved to the present time. Among the outstanding Hebrew poets during the Golden Age in Spain were Rabbi Abraham ibn Ezra, Moses ibn Ezra, Solomon ibn Gabirol, and Judah Ha-Levi.

The first Hebrew poems of that era of renaissance were hymns and prayers that have become part of synogogal liturgy, and the famous "Zemiroth" which are still sung by Jewish families during the Sabbath meals at home. Eventually, however, the poets of the Golden Age also came to employ secular themes such as lullabies and love and romance. Moses ben Ezra (d. 1139) published a whole volume of love songs. Many were prolific in both religious and secular poetry. The Golden Age of Spanish Jewry produced about one hundred poets in Spain alone. At the same time, similar activity went on also in certain other countries. Among the best known non-Spanish poets to write on secular themes were Emanuel the Roman (d. 1330) and Rabbi Israel Nagarra of Turkey. The latter also wrote quite a number of hymns.

At the same time the first attempts were made to formulate fixed rules for the grammar of the Hebrew language. This work, which also began in Babylonia, was actively continued in Spain by the following rabbis: Rabbi Samuel Ha-Nagid; Rabbi Donesh ben Tamim; Rabbi Menahem Surok; Rabbis Isaac and Moses Gikatilla; Rabbi Judah ibn Bileam; Rabbis Moses and David Kimchi, Rabbi Joseph Caspi, and others. These grammarians searched into the fundamentals of the Hebrew language and on that basis set down the grammatical rules that serve as standards for both spoken and written Hebrew today.

❦ FALSE MESSIAHS

Jewish history and Jewish literature are both replete with accounts of "false Messiahs."

When Jews went through periods of persecution and oppression and it seemed to them that they could no longer stand the suffering, they felt certain that the time had come at long last for God to send them their Messiah, His Anointed One. When at such times a man would proclaim that he was the Messiah sent by the Lord, he would always find a willing and attentive audience who believed in him and looked to him as their redeemer, and whenever such a "false Messiah" was exposed for what he really was, his adherents were gripped by a wave of despair. Yet there were always some stanch partisans of the pseudo redeemer who not only continued to believe in him themselves, but who passed on their belief to their children and descendants.

We might divide the "false Messiahs" into two distinct categories. First, there were those who really believed that they were chosen by God to redeem His people. Then there were others who knew well that they were not redeemers but just ordinary men. Their desire, however, to feel important for even only a short time was so great that they cared little about the price they might have to pay for their folly. Perhaps some of them really believed that by so doing they eventually might be able to better the lot of their people. The nuisance of "false Messiahs" started very early in Jewish life.

Flavius Josephus, in his *History of the Jews,* tells us that there were false Messiahs even in the days prior to the destruction of the Second Temple, and that these pseudo redeemers prevented the Jewish people from making peace with the Roman conquerors. Another such pretender was one Theodos, who appeared about 44 A.D. and in 55 A.D. there was one in Egypt who rallied around him a small Jewish army to fight against the Romans. However, he and his soldiers were quickly done away with by Felix, the then Roman governor.

In the Gaonic era there were quite a number of false Messiahs, each of whom had enough adherents to form an individual sect. We know of one Abu Isai of Ispahan (705 A.D.); of his disciple, Yoddgan (750 A.D.) and one Sirioni (about 740 A.D.). Later, during the time of the Crusades we find one in France (1087 A.D.); one in Cordova, Spain (1117 A.D.), and one in Fez, Morocco (1127 A.D.), and many others. Some of them are mentioned by Maimonides in his work *Letter to Yemen.*

In 1160 David Alroy, who came from Kurdistan, announced to the Jews of Persia that he was the Messiah and that he would lead them in a war against the despotic king of their country. He managed to rally an army for this purpose but he and his troops were defeated and killed. After his death some of his adherents claimed that Alroy had risen from the dead, and they formed a sect which they called "Menahamim" (the Comforters).

In 1502 one Asher Lemlin in Germany proclaimed himself as the one chosen by God to redeem the people of Israel. He seems to have truly believed in his mission, for he assured his followers that they would all bake their unleavened bread for the following Passover in the Holy City of Jerusalem, rebuilt in all its former glory and splendor. Unfortunately, Lemlin died quite suddenly. Many of his adherents, disillusioned and despondent, then forsook Judaism and embraced Christianity.

In 1524 there appeared one David Reubeni who said that he was a brother of an Arabian king and that the many Jews who dwelt in that kingdom had entrusted him with the mission of seeking the support of the Pope and of all the rulers of Europe for a campaign against the Mohammedans. He was actually received by Pope Clement VII and by the King of Portugal. But eventually Reubeni was apprehended by the Inquisition and taken away to Spain. He finally committed suicide by poisoning himself in a Spanish prison.

At about the same time there was another pseudo Messiah by the name of Solomon Molcho, who was eventually burned at the stake.

Perhaps the most famous of them all was Sabbatai Zvi, who was born in Smyrna, Turkey, in 1626. Among his adherents were numbered a great many eminent rabbis and scholars. In the end he embraced Mohammedanism.

Many of his followers believed in him even after his death. Some of his disciples themselves made attempts at playing Messiah, but without much success. However, one of Sabbatai's pupils, Jacob Frank, who was born in Podolia in 1726, was successful in gaining large numbers of followers. He was the founder of the Frankist movement which appealed primarily to the simple masses. But in the end, Frank, together with a thousand of his adherents, deserted Judaism, even as his master had done many years before, but whereas Sabbatai Zvi had espoused Islam, Frank chose Christianity.

The Era of the Philosophers

II. From Spinoza to the Present Time

17. Baruch Spinoza and His Philosophy

The Jewish Community of Amsterdam in the Middle of the Seventeenth Century —Its Four Rabbis—The Excommunication of Spinoza and Its Effect upon Him— The Influence of Descartes' Philosophy on Spinoza—Spinoza's Theological-Political Tractate *and* Ethics—*His Attacks on Jews and Judaism*

The Jews were finally expelled from Spain in 1492. It was not until well over a century later that world Jewry was to make some recovery from the spiritual upheaval caused by the dissolution of the greatest and most prominent Jewish community of the Middle Ages. Most of the refugees from Spain went to Italy, Turkey, and Holland. Some also went to Poland and some gained entry elsewhere. Eventually a few even settled in the newly discovered territories across the Atlantic.

Holland, in particular, accepted the Jewish newcomers with open arms. Soon Amsterdam had a flourishing Jewish community with four splendid synagogues, each with its own rabbi or "Hacham" ("sage"), as he was called, and a Talmudical academy with seven classes, known as "Yeshiva Etz Chaim." This institution of learning was an outstanding school. Particular emphasis was placed on the study of the Bible and the Hebrew language, and the young men in the graduating class conducted their conversations in Hebrew even outside of school. Etz Chaim differed from similar schools in Poland and Russia in that its course of study did not put so much stress on later Talmudic literature as did the Eastern European academies.

One of the outstanding alumni of the Yeshiva Etz Chaim was Baruch (or Benedict) Spinoza, who even in his boyhood had already acquired the reputation of being an "Illui" (a term for "Talmudic genius"). But before we proceed with the life and philosophy of Spinoza, we would like to throw some light on his surroundings, namely the early Jewish community of Amsterdam, the first new community to be formed by the Jews who had been expelled from Spain, for this was the environment in which Baruch Spinoza grew up.

Together with whatever possessions they were able to take with them, the Jews of Spain and Portugal had also brought to their new homes certain ways and customs which they had cherished for centuries. So the Jewish community in Amsterdam, as those of their former homes, was headed by lay leaders, called "Parnassim" who were mostly men of wealth but of little Jewish learning. The refugees from the various communities of Spain and Portugal formed synagogues in accordance with "nationality groupings," as it were. Hence, of the four synagogues of Amsterdam, three were "Spanish" and one "Portuguese," and like those in Eastern Europe, the Jewish communities in Holland did not have one rabbi for the entire community, but a separate rabbi or Hacham for each synagogue. In the days of Spinoza, Amsterdam had four such spiritual leaders; Rabbi Isaac Aboab; Rabbi Menasse ben Israel; Rabbi Saul Morteira and Rabbi David Pardo.

The first of these, Rabbi Isaac Aboab, was born in Portugal in 1606 and brought to Amsterdam by his mother when he was only seven years of age. He studied with Rabbi Isaac Uziel, one of the most outstanding rabbinic minds of that day. To the disappointment of his teacher, Aboab did not become a great scholar. But he gave early indications of a remarkable gift of oratory, and soon became known as a fiery, fascinating preacher. It was probably this talent that won him the pulpit of the Portuguese synagogue when he was still a very young man. He died at the venerable age of eighty-eight. He left no works of great scholarly significance. One of his contemporaries wrote of him, "Aboab was weak of character, and sought to curry the favor of others by flattery."

Menasse ben Israel was born in 1604, the son of Joseph ben Israel, a Marrano who, together with a hundred and fifty Marrano families, had escaped from Portugal in 1603. They were saved from execution by the Inquisition only by a last-minute offer of King Philip III to give them their freedom in return for a considerable sum of money to be paid by them to the government and ecclesiastical treasuries. This Jewish family arrived in Amsterdam with not much more than the clothes they wore. Some years after that, Menasse began to study the Talmud and the Responsa of the Poskim with Rabbi Isaac Uziel and took instruction also in secular subjects and languages such as Spanish, Portuguese, Latin, and Dutch. He was a diligent student, but hardly an outstanding one.

Like Isaac Aboab, Menasse soon showed signs of oratorical talent, and it was due to his reputation as a preacher that he was appointed Hacham of one of the Spanish synagogues to which Jews from all over Amsterdam flocked on Sabbaths to hear him speak.

Manasse ben Israel is best remembered as the man who helped reopen the gates of England to Jews. Oliver Cromwell and the Puritans, who ruled England at the time, were sympathetic to Judaism. Some of the Puritans even believed that the English people were originally part of the Ten Lost Tribes of Israel. Menasse explained to Cromwell that the Messiah would come to redeem the people of Israel and the rest of mankind only after the Jews had indeed been dispersed "to all the corners of the earth" and that therefore the divine promise could be fulfilled only if there were some Jews in England too. Before coming to England himself, Menasse sent to the British Parliament a copy of his book *The Hope of Israel* in Spanish, entitled *Esperanza de Israel,* in which he recounted the heroism of Israel's martyrs. In 1656 Menasse ben Israel appeared before Parliament in person, and in a brilliant speech convinced that ruling body that the Jews would prove to be a blessing to England, if only they were to be readmitted. Not long thereafter, Oliver Cromwell yielded to Menasse's plea and permitted Jews to enter England once more for the first time since they had been expelled from there in 1290.

In addition to *Esperanza de Israel,* Menasse wrote several other works in Hebrew such as *Nishmath Chaim* (*The Soul of Life*) and *Teshuath Israel* (*The Salvation of Israel*). He died in 1657.

The third of the Hachamim, Rabbi Saul Morteira, was born in Venice, Italy, of Portuguese parents and came to Holland quite by accident. It happened that he was a childhood friend of Rabbi Eliahu Montalto, the famous physician, who ministered to Queen Maria de Medici of France. When the doctor died suddenly while traveling with the royal household, the queen asked Saul Morteira, who was the closest friend of the deceased, to take his body to Amsterdam so that he might be buried in the Jewish cemetery there. The nature of his mission drew the attention of the Jewish community to him, and he made such a profound impression upon the Jews of Amsterdam by his bearing and personality that he was soon appointed Hacham of one of the synagogues there. He left a small volume containing a collection of his sermons. However, he could not match the oratorical skills of either Isaac Aboab or Menasse ben Israel.

The fourth of this group of rabbis, David Pardo, seems to have been the least important. He left no scholarly works whatever. But, like the other three, Rabbi David Pardo taught at the Yeshiva Etz Chaim at the time when Baruch Spinoza, the main subject of this chapter, was a student there.

Baruch Spinoza was born in Amsterdam on November 24, 1632, the son of Michael de Spinoza. The elder Spinoza, who had come to Holland from the Spanish town of Spinoza, was neither learned nor wealthy, but he enjoyed the respect of the entire community because of his uprightness and honesty. Baruch was a child of extraordinary intelligence, and he became one of the star pupils at the Etz Chaim Academy. When he was six years of age, his mother died. Soon thereafter his father remarried and it seems that Baruch was none too happy with his stepmother. He had always been a taciturn lad, but now he became almost abnormally introverted. When he was twenty-three years old, his father died, leaving him a modest inheritance on which Baruch managed to live for a long time—some say for the rest of his life— for his material wants were few.

After his graduation from the Talmudical academy, Spinoza continued to study by himself. He acquired a fluent command of Spanish, Latin, and Dutch, and he had some knowledge also of engineering, but his chief interest lay in the field of Jewish philosophy. He was thoroughly familiar with the writings of the Jewish philosophers of the Golden Age of Spain, particularly with those of Maimonides, Ibn Ezra, and Levi ben Gershon. In addition, Spinoza studied the works of non-Jewish thinkers, especially those of René Descartes, the French philosopher who had opened a new era in thought, and who had made a particularly profound impression upon the young intellectuals of his day. One of Spinoza's professors was the famous Franz Van den Enden, who liked to poke fun at religion. It is probable that Van den Enden's views might have influenced the young student's attitude, but there is no evidence that Spinoza, at that time, had either voiced or written any opinions that might have been regarded as heretical. As a matter of fact, Spinoza frequently attended the synagogue during his student days. It is known that nine months after the death of his father, he was regularly seen at daily services where he recited the mourner's Kaddish and even made a small donation in memory of his parent. This was in 1655.

How, then, is it that only one year later, in 1656, Spinoza was solemnly excommunicated by Amsterdam Jewry? It is difficult to imagine what Spinoza, a learned but modest young man of twenty-four, who was well liked by his contemporaries, might have done to incur this extreme penalty. At the time of his excommunication Spinoza had not as yet published any writings or voiced any ideas that might have been classed as heretical.

Some say that the youthful Spinoza was in love with the daughter of Van den Enden, who, of course, was not Jewish. But this could hardly have been true, since the girl was only thirteen years old at the time and an ugly, gawky youngster at that. Others maintained that Spinoza had expressed antireligious views to two of his friends. But even if these assumptions had been more than hearsay, neither of these peccadillos was serious enough to warrant so drastic a measure as excommunication. It should be remembered, too, that even after he had solemnly been read out of the fold of Israel, Spinoza did not abandon the faith of his fathers, and continued to view himself as a Jew.

What, then, caused his excommunication, and who was responsible for it?

One thing is certain; the idea did not originate with the rabbis. Of the four Hachamin of the Jewish community, Menasse ben Israel had gone to London, and a son of Isaac Aboab testified to the Protestant clergy that his father had nothing to do with the excommunication of Spinoza. The third rabbi, Saul Morteira was too fond of his pupil to wish to humiliate him in this manner. In fact, if we look at the document attesting to the excommunication, we find that it does not bear the signature of any one rabbi, but only the notation "with the consent of the rabbis" at the end.

And so the question remains: Who excommunicated Baruch Spinoza? If we are to attempt to answer it, we must study the historical material available with regard to the time and place in which Spinoza lived.

As we have already indicated, the structure of Jewish life in Holland was quite different from that of Eastern Europe, where there was only one rabbi for the entire Jewish community, and he was the only authority in all Jewish matters.

In the Spanish Jewish communities in Spain, Portugal, and Holland, the authority was not vested in the rabbis but in the lay leaders or Parnassim who had the veto power over the rabbinate. The rabbi was a servant of the community rather than its leader.

This system had had its origin in the ancient Jewish community of Babylonia which was ruled by a lay exilarch, whose absolute authority over Babylonian Jewry was recognized even by the government of the land. The exilarchs possessed quasi vice-legal prerogatives and could even pass and execute death sentences. When the bulk of Babylonian Jewry migrated to Spain, the lay leaders of the new communities which were established there appropriated to themselves many of the privileges formerly enjoyed by the exilarchs. The same system of administration was then carried over by the Jews into the countries that offered them refuge after their expulsion from Spain in 1492. Subsequently this form of Jewish communal government was established also on the American continent by the Spanish Jews who settled there, so that the old Spanish way to a large extent accounts for the dominant role which the American Jewish layman plays today in synagogue leadership while the influence of the rabbi is limited to that of a teacher and preacher.

Unlike the ancient exilarchs, the Parnassim of Holland did not have life-and-death powers over their communities. But they did appropriate for themselves a most potent weapon to use upon those who incurred their displeasure—excommunication. The Parnassim, who dominated Dutch Jewry in the days of Spinoza, made free and often unjust use of this extreme penalty, and the rabbis had no choice but to assent to the decree of the lay leaders. Ten years prior to the excommunication of Spinoza, the Parnassim pronounced a similar ban upon one Uriel Acosta, with the explanation that he did not agree with the accepted beliefs in the immortality of the soul and the resurrection of the dead. But this explanation is insufficient, for such doubts were also expressed long before Acosta by men such as Levi ben Gershon, who certainly were not regarded as heretics, but venerated as saints and scholars instead. It is generally believed, therefore, that the true reason for the excommunication of Acosta was that he had somehow neglected to pay the Parnassim that respect and honor they felt was due them. At any rate, Acosta was excommunicated not only once, but actually twice. In the end he suffered a mental breakdown and committed suicide when he was only forty-four.

Eventually these abuses on the part of the Parnassim led many of those affected to institute legal proceedings in the civil courts of Holland. Finally the

Dutch government imposed an injunction upon the Parnassim, forbidding them to make further use of the penalty of excommunication.

In view of the foregoing, it would seem most probable that the ban on Spinoza, too, was pronounced not on the initiative of the rabbis, but by decree of the powerful lay leadership to which the rabbis were forced to give their assent.

And yet we doubt that it was quite as simple as that in the case of Spinoza. For the document of excommunication, written for him explicitly, states that the punishment was given him because he had disseminated "heresy and unbelief." It is possible that Spinoza might have made some remarks to a friend here and there which seemed rather unorthodox. The first measure taken against him was a mild form of the ban, which did not entail the public humiliation of actual excommunication, and was in force for only thirty days. The rabbis, who actually thought highly of the young man, hoped that at the end of the thirty days Spinoza would come to them and admit that he had been wrong. In order to save him from further humiliation, they informed him that if he would admit his error, he would receive an annuity of one thousand pieces of gold from the community. All they asked in return was that he refrain from critical comments on Judaism and that he come to the synagogue from time to time. But Spinoza had too much pride to give in so easily.

One day when Spinoza was leaving a theater, he was attacked by some wild fanatics and narrowly escaped death. Then and there he decided that he could no longer live in Amsterdam and moved to a small village not far from the city, where he took lodging with some Christian family. It was only then that the Parnassim excommunicated him.

Actually, the excommunication, when it did come, did not upset Spinoza too greatly. Excommunication meant that he could no longer be asked to come to the synagogue to complete the required quorum of worshipers, that no one would be permitted to circumcise any sons he might have, and that he could not be buried in a Jewish cemetery. But all this mattered little to Spinoza. He had not been to a synagogue for a long time now; he had no children since he had never married, and he did not particularly care where he would finally be buried.

After this Spinoza lived in various small towns near Amsterdam until 1670, when he moved to The Hague, where he resided until his sudden death on February 21, 1677. During the last years of his life he suffered from consumption. He worked at lens grinding, but it seems that he did not do this for the sake of making a livelihood, for the inheritance left him by his father was sufficient for his material needs. In addition, he received gifts of money from various friends. During his lifetime he published only one book entitled *Theological-Political Tractate*. Written after his excommunication, this work caused much excitement in the Christian world, because it represented as sharp an attack on religion in general as had ever been written.

The clergy finally managed to suppress it and prohibit its sale. For this reason Spinoza declined to publish any other works during his lifetime, and asked in his will that his writings, among them his book *Ethics,* be published after his death.

Spinoza was a warm adherent of the philosopher Descartes, and one of his first works contained a detailed explanation of the latter's reasoning. It is worth while, therefore, to learn more about this eminent thinker and about the philosophy which he propounded in the days of Spinoza.

As far as is known, René Descartes (or Cartesius) was born in France in 1596 of devout Catholic parents. He was enrolled in a Jesuit school and, even though he later led a lonely life, cut off from all others, he remained a pious Catholic all his days. In fact, it was his custom to pray to the Virgin Mary for help in the formulation of his thoughts. He was also a great believer in the significance of dreams and visions. And even as Columbus inaugurated a new era in geography and Bacon discovered a new field in physical science, Descartes opened new vistas in thinking, and he became known as "the father of modern philosophy."

The principal forte of Descartes' approach was that he helped turn philosophy into a true science based on firm foundations. Originally a mathematician, Descartes sought to establish a set of basic principles and axioms for philosophy, even as there were fundamentals and axioms in the science of mathematics with which he was familar. His best remembered principle, of course, is the famous statement, "Cogito, ergo sum" ("I think, therefore I am"), implying that man's ability to think is the best proof of his reality and existence.

Descartes asserts that the world is composed of two elements, matter and mind. Matter, which is incapable of thought, is limited to a definite place. Mind, on the other hand, is not confined to any one locality. Therefore, it is obvious that there must be an over-all mental force of which the human mind is part, and since mind is thus a concept that cannot be defined in terms of time or space, it is equally obvious that mind is above matter. Hence, Descartes reasoned, there must be a spiritual force which rules the entire world and which has no physical form or shape. In other words, this supreme spiritual force, Divinity, cannot be described in human terms, for man is a mixture of mind and matter, and God is purely spiritual.

This is the basic premise upon which Descartes built up his original philosophy. His disciple Spinoza went one step further. As against the "dualism" of Descartes, he asserted that the world is not composed of two elements, but is one single whole, for mind and matter are actually only two different forms of one and the same substance. Hence, mind cannot be above matter, and both the physical and the spiritual elements go hand in hand. Therefore, reasoned Spinoza, God and the world are one and the same. This is the basic principle upon which is based the ideology that is known today as pantheism.

Actually, Spinoza may well have obtained the first impetus for his new trend of thought not from the writings of Descartes, but from the works of the Jewish philosophers of Spain, particularly from the book *Mekor Chaim* (*The Source of Life*) by Solomon ibn Gabirol, which contains a detailed discussion of this concept of the oneness of God and the world. Or perhaps he might have been influenced by the works of the Cabalists who advanced the idea that there is no place in the world in which God is not. In Genesis 21:23, where it is told that Abraham made peace with Abimelech in Beer-sheba, it is also said that he called upon God as "El Olam" ("God of the world"). The Cabalists explained that Abraham had thus meant to imply that "God" ("El") was "the world" ("Olam") and that, conversely, "the world" was "God."

As regards the human mind, Spinoza knew of three distinct kinds of perception; namely *imagination* (which, of course, may be misleading), perception *through the senses* (which may bring man closer to the truth than mere imagination), and *intuition* (which usually is equivalent to the truth). Thus Spinoza acknowledged the power of intuition long before the famed French-Jewish philosopher Henry Bergson.

These basic concepts were the foundations for Spinoza's views on the role of religion in human life, and particularly on the part played by Judaism in the life of the Jew. But it seems that Spinoza, who originally had posited the axiom "not to laugh, not to weep, but only to try to understand," when viewing the phenomena of life and the world, could not remain entirely objective when it came to his own religion. It seems that, after all, he had not accepted excommunication with complete indifference, but had come to bear a grudge against the Jewish community as such.

Spinoza may have had good cause to resent the arbitrary action of the leaders of the Jewish community of Amsterdam, but this certainly was no justification for his hatred for all the Jews and even for Judaism as such.

Actually, had Spinoza been true to his own philosophy, he should have suppressed his feelings of rancor and ill-will, for after much thought, he himself came to the conclusion that there was no place for emotion in reasoning, since any feeling, be it hatred or love, served only to becloud the issue in question and to obstruct clear and logical thinking. But it seems that Spinoza could not be so detached and objective with regard to the things that affected him personally. The ideas advanced by Spinoza show that the philosopher's reason was rent asunder by a conflict between subjective emotion and objective thought. At times he allows his reason to rule and speaks well of Judaism, but then he will suddenly break away and spin a new thread of thought colored by blind resentment. In other instances he begins with a bitter tirade and then suddenly checks himself and, using his reason, sees good in the faith of his own people. Such was the ambivalent attitude of Spinoza regarding his fellow Jews and Judaism in general.

In his work *Theological-Political Tractate,* which was originally written in Latin, Spinoza asserts that philosophy is not incompatible with pure belief.

For this reason it is not only permissible, but actually mandatory, for a religious person to pursue philosophy, for "if he does not do so, he actually robs the society in which he lives and thus disturbs the pure and true fear of God." Spinoza further states that "we can perceive that we are in God and that God is in us only if we understand that He has imparted to us some of His own spirit, namely, the capacity for higher thought." It is interesting to note that these words were taken from the sermons of none other than John the Baptist. It is quite obvious then, that here was one instance in which Spinoza allowed his emotions to rule over his reason.

Then Spinoza turns to an analysis of magic and superstition. He explains that man is never entirely happy in God's world and is constantly torn between fear and hope. For this reason, he is apt to give credence to anything that might hold out to him a promise of deliverance from his continuous state of anxiety. He recalls that even so illustrious a soldier as Alexander of Macedonia believed in magicians and consulted an oracle to inquire as to the outcome of a war which he planned to make upon an enemy nation. Spinoza thereafter turns to the place that superstition occupies in religion, and explains that Mohammedanism contains more superstition than any other faith. However, Spinoza adds, this is not the fault of the religion itself, but only of the religious leaders. The clergy of all religions are apt to spend so much time on secondary and trivial issues and on criticizing one another, that they lose sight of the basic principles of their faith. He says, "They make pretty speeches about the Bible, but they do not take the trouble to understand the true meaning of the Bible and to teach it to the people." Spinoza has some bitter words for those Jewish philosophers who employed the thoughts of Plato and Aristotle in their interpretation of the Biblical literature of Israel. "It was not enough for them to imitate the Greeks and their follies," he wrote. "They had to take the foolish words [of the Greek philosophers] and put them into the mouths of our prophets." Here Spinoza simply paraphrases the words of other great Jewish thinkers, such as Judah Halevi, who bitterly opposed the interpretation of the Jewish Bible in accordance with the tenets of Greek philosophy.

Spinoza's views on prophecy and revelation seem somewhat contradictory. He does not agree with Maimonides' definition of prophecy as a revelation of God Himself to a man in a dream. But he does believe quite literally that God spoke to Moses and revealed Himself to the people of Israel on Mount Sinai. He insists that the Biblical accounts of such divine revelation must be taken literally and not reinterpreted in any manner.

If we should stop our study of Spinoza at this point, we would have good cause to think that he was a pious Jew in the accepted sense of the word and to wonder how a man of such orthodox beliefs could possibly have been excommunicated. But if we look further, we shall soon see another side of Spinoza's mentality.

Spinoza goes on to deal with the various phases and degrees of prophecy, and here he and Judaism come to the parting of ways. He comes to the conclusion that the pinnacle of prophecy was attained not by Moses, but by none other than Jesus of Nazareth, because Jesus was the only one to whom God had revealed Himself undisguised, in all His glory. For this reason, Spinoza says, "The words of Jesus Christ are the words of God Himself," and "The Holy Spirit was embodied in human form by Jesus who became the light of the nations." The other prophets, he asserts, saw God only in a disguised form and therefore could not truly understand Him. It was for this reason that they employed the many parables and the veiled language found in much of prophetic literature. Jesus, on the other hand, received clear instructions directly from God, teachings which he could then communicate to his disciples and to the masses.

It is quite obvious that when Spinoza wrote these words, his pen must have been guided not by his reason but by bitter hatred for his own faith and people. Nor can we say that Spinoza is objective when he writes that "it took Moses twenty-four hours to comprehend that which Jesus was able to grasp within one hour."

Spinoza's aim, as we can see, was not to prove the merit of the Christian faith or of any other religion, but merely to attack his own people and to belittle the spiritual achievements of the Jewish genius.

In his second chapter the same Spinoza who in the first chapter had attacked those who would corrupt the words of the prophets by the use of Greek philosophy in their interpretations suddenly turns against all the prophets who lived before the coming of Jesus, and claims that their range of perception was narrow and that the later philosophers came much nearer to attaining the truth than did the prophets of the people of Israel. "The prophets did not understand God," says Spinoza. The philosophers, he asserts, came much closer to Him through their accumulation of knowledge which could not be wrong or false. He claims that the prophets were embittered bigots and that kings such as Pharaoh and Ahab could hardly be blamed for not heeding their words.

Spinoza did not believe in the selection of Israel above the other nations. The Lord loved all the nations and desired the welfare of all of them. When the Lord gave the Law to the Jewish people, Spinoza points out, He did not even promise them the bliss of a heavenly afterlife if they fulfilled His commandments. The only rewards He guaranteed were such as could be had only during life on earth. Spinoza does not believe that the fact that Israel was chosen of all peoples to receive the Torah indicates any special divine predilection for the Jews. Long ago, he says, the Prophet Ezekiel employed words of bitter irony to convey to his people the wrath of God at their laxity in the observance of the Law and said in the name of the Lord, "Wherefore I gave them also statutes that were not good and judgments whereby they should not live" (Ezek. 20-25). Spinoza, rendered blind by his hatred for Judaism, takes this statement literally and cites it in proof of his view that God had given Israel a law which was harsh and designed only to make the Jews suffer.

According to Spinoza, the survival of the Jewish people throughout the ages was not due to any special grace of God, but solely to the hatred of the other nations. It was only anti-Semitism, says Spinoza, that has caused Israel to endure. "The more I study," Spinoza writes, "the more convinced I become that the Lord purposely gave harsh laws to His people in order to exact vengeance from them for their sins." He says that Tacitus, the Roman writer, had held the same opinion centuries before him. In fact, the laws of the Torah were so difficult to observe and wrought such hardships upon those desiring to keep them, that it could be easily understood why the Jews of the days of the judges and the era of the First Temple did not comply with the Law of the Lord, but turned to idolatry instead.

It is almost impossible to believe that, earlier in the same book, this man could have declared that the Lord spoke with Moses face to face. The same thinker who had spoken so admiringly of the Torah, now attacked its laws as cruel and impossible to observe.

Now another statement that seems more than strange, a kind of twisted prophecy in the third part of Spinoza's book, reads as follows: "If it were not for the Jewish religion which saps the strength of the Jewish people, I might truly have come to believe that a time might come when, due to changed circumstances, the Jews would return to their homeland, establish an independent state and once again become the chosen people of the Lord." Then he adds: "If the Jews really believe that they are truly a chosen people, I have no objections. But there is absolutely no difference between the Jews and the other nations of the world as regards spiritual and intellectual achievements."

And so the entire book is a battleground reflecting the struggle between calm reason and blind hatred that was fought out in the soul of Baruch Spinoza.

The Christian clergy naturally greeted with joy what Spinoza had to say about their faith as compared to Judaism. But eventually the teachings of Spinoza were relegated to the background and almost fell into oblivion until they were rediscovered and resurrected by the German author Herder and by the classic poet Johann Wolfgang von Goethe, who might well be called a prime advocate of Spinoza's doctrine. Since then, thousands of books and essays have been written on Spinoza and his views. The scholars seem unable to come to an agreement in the interpretation of his words. Some maintain that Spinoza was a true believer in God; others label him an atheist. However, it is generally thought that the doctrine of Spinoza can best be classified as a theory of pantheism.

After the death of Spinoza there was a long pause in the development of Western Jewish philosophy until the advent of Moses Mendelssohn who ushered in a new era in the history of the Jews of the entire world.

18. Moses Mendelssohn and the New Era

Moses Mendelssohn and the Beginning of a New Era—German Jewry in Mendelssohn's Day—His Friendship with Gotthold Ephraim Lessing—His German Translation of the Pentateuch and His Commentary on the Bible—Phaedon and Jerusalem—*The Relationship of Immanuel Kant and Mendelssohn—Mendelssohn's Philosophy*

After the death of Spinoza, creative Jewish thought almost came to a standstill. Since Holland was able to absorb only a limited number of Jewish refugees from Spain and Portugal, many Jews went on to seek new homes in other countries, such as Germany, Poland, and Russia, and some settled in England, after Oliver Cromwell had permitted their entry. Generally speaking, the Jews did not now make economic progress, and Judaism entered a period of spiritual stagnation. The rabbis and teachers of the Talmud did not bring forth new or original ideas in the new Yeshivas in Poland and Russia. They were busily engaged in hair-splitting debates on fine points of Jewish Law in rabbinical academies. The same could also be said about the Talmudic academies of Germany. Or else they buried themselves in the Cabala and mysticism to which the Jews had always turned at times of stress and oppression from without. The Jewish people were too busy trying to keep alive to be able to devot attention to such creative intellectual pursuits as the study of Hebrew literature, the writing of Hebrew poetry or the formulation of new thoughts. But throughout its history, Israel has never stood still for long. And so now too the genius of Judaism, after a period of rest that extended for almost a century, came to life again.

The centuries that were now to come were to see a new era of bustling activity in Jewish life. First, the beginning of the religious movement of Hassidism; then the other extreme, the "Haskalah" or "Intellectual Enlightenment." These stirrings, however, were not confined to the Jewish community of any one country, but had an impact on Jewish communities throughout the world. It would therefore be quite proper to say that this new era which begins with Moses Mendelssohn was one of the most fruitful in the history of the Jewish people.

Moses Mendelssohn, also known as "Moshe ben Menahem" or "Moses of Dessau," was born on September 6, 1729, of pious Jewish parents in the town of Dessau, Germany. His father, Menahem, was learned in the Torah and a scribe of scrolls of the Law and of Mezuzoth. During his boyhood Moses studied with his father. When he grew older, his parents sent him to Rabbi David Frankel, the spiritual leader of his city, to study. This great Talmudic scholar taught Moses not only the Talmud, but also such works of Jewish philosophy as the *Guide for the Perplexed* by Maimonides.

In his early youth Mendelssohn developed a disease of the spine which left him a hunchback for the rest of his life. It may well be that the sedentary mode of living and his constant study without exercise aggravated the condition. Eichel, a contemporary and biographer of Mendelssohn's, wrote of him, "He was small in stature, with large feet and a high chest, a thin body, pitch-black hair, and a face of dark complexion with no particular charm." Yet he made a profound impression on all who saw him, because his brilliance was visible in his large, fiery eyes. He spoke softly, slowly, briefly, and to the point, and he enjoyed being in company.

In 1743 Rabbi Frankel was called to Berlin to assume the rabbinate in that city, and his pupil, Moses Mendelssohn, followed him there. One of the members of Frankel's congregation, Haim Bromberg, permitted the young student to live in the attic of his house rent-free and gave him also free board for years so that he could devote all his time to his scholarly pursuits. During those years Mendelssohn applied himself diligently not only to Jewish learning, but also to secular studies, such as the sciences, French, English, and Latin.

At that time Mendelssohn made the acquaintance of one Berman Zilz, a wealthy merchant who had an abiding interest in the study of Jewish lore. Mendelssohn made a profound impression on him and he engaged the student as a tutor for his children. This was the beginning of a new life for the young man from Dessau. His employer, who saw that Mendelssohn was versatile, and also that he had a good handwriting, hired him as general manager of his paint and dye concern. Eventually Mendelssohn became a partner in the firm and grew to be quite wealthy, but he never ceased to study. His days were spent at business, but his nights were devoted to learning. It was about that time that Mendelssohn first met Gotthold Ephraim Lessing, the famed German writer, who was to become his close friend.

In 1762, when Mendelssohn was thirty-three years old, he married Fromet Guggenheim, the daughter of Abraham Guggenheim, a wealthy man who lived in Hamburg. The match was proposed by a matchmaker, in accordance with the custom of the day, so that the bride and groom did not meet in person until the latter came to the bride's home to sign the formal contract of engagement. Legend has it that when Fromet saw the man to whom she was about to become engaged, she ran to her father and begged him not to force her to marry the ugly hunchback. Guggenheim had no other choice but to go and break the news to Mendelssohn who was waiting in another room. Mendelssohn, however, did not take "no" for an answer, and asked to be permitted to speak to the girl, after which she would be at liberty to make her own decision as to what she should do.

"Madam," he said to the maiden, "It is written that forty days before a baby is born, Heaven already decrees who his marriage partner will be. When I was still in heaven and heard the name of the woman I would eventually marry, which was none other than your own, I asked the angel whether I might be permitted to see my future bride. This had never been done before, but in the end my request was granted and I saw you, and I noticed then that you had a hunchback. I was filled with pity for you and, since a good husband protects his wife and takes upon himself all her burdens, I asked the angel whether he could not make you straight and let me have your hunchback instead. He agreed, and here I am. Now I leave it to you to decide whether or not you will do me the honor of becoming my wife, because if you should decide in the negative the hunchback has to go back to you."

Fromet was impressed by her suiter's plea and, being a young woman of more than average intelligence, she realized that physical beauty was not all-important in marriage, and certainly not more important than a good character and personality. It was quite obvious from the manner in which Mendelssohn phrased his appeal that here was a man who would be considerate of his wife at all times, a man with a steady character, on whom a woman could rely. And so Fromet Guggenheim consented to become the wife of Moses Mendelssohn.

We would do well to stop here and make a brief survey of the situation of the Jewish community of which Mendelssohn was a part at that time. The kingdom of Prussia, in which Mendelssohn lived, was ruled by King Frederick II, who called himself a great liberal, but who certainly showed no such liberalism in his attitude to his Jewish subjects. In 1750 he had promulgated a decree dividing the Jews of Prussia into two distinct categories: Jews who enjoyed the special protection of the government, and Jews who were merely tolerated in the land. The "Schutzjuden," the "protected" Jews, who were given certain privileges in return for large payments, were classified in accordance with three sub-categories: (1) "Generally privileged" Jews, who could go about freely as they chose. The same privilege was also extended to their families and all the members of their household. (2) "Protected Jews in Ordinary," who could live freely within a certain territory circumscribed by imperial decree, and work at trades permitted them by the Directorate General of the Prussian Ministry of the Interior, which was in charge of the enforcement of these regulations. These privileges, however, were not extended to all the children of the "Protected Jew in Ordinary." (3) "Protected Jews in Extraordinary", who themselves had certain freedoms but whose children were not permitted the same privileges. This last category included professionals and artists. Rabbis, cantors, and other Jewish religious functionaries were classified as "tolerated Jews." "Tolerated Jews" could not legally engage in any other type of work or trade except their own and were not even permitted to marry in accordance with German law. In addition, the Jews had to pay "protection taxes," "military taxes," "income taxes," "excise taxes," "community taxes," "fire protection taxes," and other such levies without end. Then there was a sales tax, called the "china tax", which only Jews had to pay with every purchase they made. These funds went for the upkeep of the king's porcelain factory. The registration of the birth of a child involved the payment of a tax, as did the simple act of traveling from one town to another. Those who married without permission from the government were subject to huge fines. "Tolerated Jews" could not engage in trade or commerce, nor could they own land or real estate. They could not be seen in a tavern, nor were they allowed to deal in foods or groceries. Married men had to grow a beard as a special sign of identification. Such was the well-nigh intolerable situation of the Jews in Prussia in the days of Moses Mendelssohn.

Mendelssohn continued to read and to study. The boy who spoke the Judeo-German dialect at home now became a master of a pure German style, and together with his friend Lessing, he published a book entitled *Pope, the Metaphysician,* which was an answer to a query from the British Academy as to whether the metaphysical visions described by Alexander Pope, the famous English poet, had any truth or merit. At the same time, Mendelssohn prepared another brochure for the British Academy, dealing with the question of whether metaphysical concepts could be confirmed by factual proof or demonstration, such as by methematics. For this work Mendelssohn received a fee of fifty ducats. In the course of his research in this connection, Mendelssohn met the Marquis d'Argance who introduced him to all of his friends as "the Jewish philosopher." The Marquis, although a devout Catholic, was interested in philosophy, and he was anxious that as much freedom as possible be allowed to Mendelssohn, so that the latter could carry on his studies undisturbed. Hence he wrote a petition to King Frederick on behalf of Mendelssohn, in which he stated, "I, a Catholic philosopher, beg the Protestant philosopher [Frederick regarded himself as one] to grant permission to a Jewish philosopher to go about freely wherever he chooses." The King approved, and Mendelssohn was free to come and go at will. He was later invited to collaborate in the publication of *Literaturbriefe,* an important literary journal of that day, and his name as a writer and thinker soon spread all over Germany.

Now we are ready to examine the works of Mendelssohn, and the question arises whether he was just a writer on subjects pertaining to philosophy, or whether he was a Jewish philosopher in the true sense of the word in that he developed new and original thoughts.

Mendelssohn was best known for his German translation of the Pentateuch which he annotated with a commentary to explain the more difficult passages. This work was published under the title of *Paths of Peace*. Mendelssohn also wrote a scholarly introduction to the Pentateuch. He was assisted in his preparation of the Biblical translation and commentary by Naphtali Hartwig Wessely, one of the eminent Jewish scholars of the day, and by Rabbi Salomon Dubno, a great Talmudist who frequently visited the famous "Gaon of Vilna" and enjoyed his high esteem.

Mendelssohn himself was strictly orthodox in his religious practices. Even those who attacked him for his views, which seemed unorthodox to some, had to admit that Mendelssohn was most punctilious when it came to his own personal observance of Jewish Law. Yet he was accused of having paved the way for Reform Judaism, for it was claimed that he, Mendelssohn, advanced the theory that Judaism was only a religion without any nationality, a view which was to become the basis for the philosophy of Reform and assimilationism. We shall see later on whether or not this charge was well founded. However, even his opponents could not deny the tremendous impact which his German translation of the Pentateuch, the first such rendering ever made, had upon his people, particularly the young. In fact, the fame of this work spread eastward beyond the borders of Germany to Poland, Russia, and Lithuania, where hundreds of rabbinical students learned the German language by comparing Mendelssohn's translation with the original Hebrew text. Once they knew German, the young Jews of the East eagerly devoured also the secular literature written in that language, and thus Mendelssohn and the group that rallied around him became the initiating force of the "Haskalah," the movement of intellectual enlightenment that quickly spread among Jewish youth first in Germany and then in Eastern Europe, a movement that was the forerunner of secularist Jewish socialism and of Zionism.

Mendelssohn discussed his thoughts in great detail in the works he wrote and published. It would be interesting for us, therefore, to acquaint ourselves with some of his principal writings.

Mendelssohn's first important book, *Phaedon,* was published in 1767. It was written in response to the many inquiries he had received from non-Jewish scholars concerning life after death. Over two thousand years earlier Plato, the Greek thinker, had written a treatise on that subject in the form of a discussion between Socrates and his disciples, with the philosopher answering the questions of his students. Mendelssohn made use of this form when he gathered material for his own work.

Mendelssohn's book, which was written in a splendid German poetic style, became what we would call today a best-seller. During the first three years after its publication, three editions of *Phaedon* were printed, one after the other, and it was translated into many languages. The discussion of the actual problem is objective. Mendelssohn stated that since there was no definite proof of the existence or nonexistence of an afterlife, there was room for a great deal of latitude in thought on the subject and both those who believed in a life after death and those who did not were each free to adhere to their own views. *Phaedon* made a profound impression upon the scholarly world, and soon Mendelssohn became known as the "German Plato," since Plato was the philosopher with whom Mendelssohn had agreed in a great many instances regarding the problem which was the theme of this work.

In 1777, ten years after the publication of *Phaedon,* Mendelssohn met Immanuel Kant, the German philosopher. A contemporary writer left us an account of that first meeting which should prove of interest to us and which we will therefore set down here in brief.

After reading *Phaedon,* Immanuel Kant wrote a letter to Mendelssohn saying that he was anxious to make his acquaintance. Kant led a very withdrawn life. He had never married, he never left the city of Königsberg in which he lived, and he never went farther away from his home than the few blocks he had to walk each day to the University where he taught. Hence, anyone desirous of meeting Kant had to come to Königsberg. Mendelssohn undertook the long journey and, immediately upon his arrival, hurried to the university so that he might be able to hear the great thinker lecture.

Mendelssohn diffidently entered the university building and humbly sat down near the door of the lecture hall. When the students noticed the little hunchbacked Jew with the pointed goatee, a wave of tittering went through the classroom. Soon the hall resounded with catcalls and raucous remarks about Jews in general. Mendelssohn remained calm, deliberately pulled over a chair and sat down on it. When some of the students came over to him and asked him what he wanted, he quietly replied that he was waiting for Professor Kant. This answer was the signal for a new burst of laughter and stamping of feet which went on until the professor entered the lecture hall. The noise immediately subsided. The students, raptly engrossed in the lecture of their master, soon forgot about the little Jew who still sat quietly near the door. At the end of the session, Mendelssohn rose from his chair and rushed up to Kant. Again there was loud jeering, but the laughter yielded place to stunned amazement only a moment later, when the master went to meet the Jew with outstretched hands and the joyous exclamation, "Why, Moses Mendelssohn!" As if by magic, the mood in the classroom changed. Awed whispers went through the hall. "That's the Jewish philosopher." "It's our German Plato." And the students arose as if by command, and arranged themselves in two lines between which the German philosopher and the Jewish scholar passed out of the room arm in arm.

The second important book to be written by Mendelssohn was *Jerusalem* or *On the Power of Religion and Judaism,* which was not published until 1883. Once it appeared in print, however, it sold rapidly and several editions were published, including many foreign translations. This book, which is mainly a discussion of Judaism, is a statement of Mendelssohn's own philosophy, which is based primarily upon the teachings of Leibnitz and Wolf, two thinkers who were his contemporaries.

In order that we may better understand the philosophy of Mendelssohn, let us briefly study the personalities and views of these two non-Jewish philosophers. Actually, the ideas of Wolf were nothing but a supplement to the teaching of Leibnitz, so that what we have before us is not two separate philosophies but only one which is known as the "Leibnitz-Wolf doctrine."

Gottfried Wilhelm Leibnitz (b. Leipzig, July 6, 1646; d. Hanover, 1714) had the opportunity of making the acquaintance of Baruch Spinoza and of discussing philosophical concepts with him. Leibnitz wrote a book in which he thoroughly refuted the philosophy of Spinoza. At a later date, at the request of the Baroness Sophia Charlotte (who was to become the queen of Frederick I of Prussia), he published another book, this time in French, in which he explained his own philosophy in a simpler, more popular style. Leibnitz believed that the Lord had created the world solely for the benefit of mankind. True, he conceded, the world is far from perfect, but it is as good as it could possibly be under the given circumstances. In fact, if the world were indeed perfect, man would not be ready for it or capable of accepting it. Hence the world is in a state of constant progress and evolution toward eventual perfection. God deliberately created evil in order to punish the wicked among men. True, the righteous also suffer from these ills, but this is unavoidable. Leibnitz bases the belief in God, in free will, and in reward and punishment on scientific fundamentals. In this respect, Leibnitz' thesis closely resembles that of *Faith and Reason,* the classic work of Rabbi Saadia Gaon. But Leibnitz goes a step further. He believes that man marches on toward perfection not only in physical and technical things, but also in his ethical, moral, and spiritual development. He asserts that the spirit is capable of rising to a very high plane. It may retrogress for a while, but then it will again resume its upward course and rise once more to its former lofty level, if not higher.

The philosophy of Leibnitz spread quickly among the German intelligentsia and eventually was supplemented by the views of Christian Wolf, who was thirty-three years younger than Leibnitz.

Wolf (b. Breslau, January 24, 1679; d. Halle, 1754) was a famous and popular professor of philosophy at the University of Halle. Because of his known influence on young people, Frederick William I of Prussia suspected Wolf of having something to do with the large number of desertions of young men from his armies. The king therefore ordered that Wolf be dismissed from the university and that he leave the city at once. Fearing for his life, Wolf immediately complied with the king's decree. It was only after the death of Frederick that Wolf returned to Halle and was reinstated in his old position, which he retained until the day of his own death.

As we have indicated before, Wolf based his philosophy on the main thesis of Leibnitz, namely, that God created the world for the benefit of the human race. Hence, Wolf added, whatever life may bring to us, though it may seem unpleasant or even tragic, actually is good and intended only for our own welfare. It is incumbent upon man, therefore, to strive to improve his personality and character at all times, in order thus to strengthen the forces of good in the world. He who does evil abets the powers of evil and thus disturbs the divinely instituted order of the world.

Although Immanuel Kant was not at all in agreement with these views, his friend Mendelssohn based much of his own philosophy concerning the world in general, and Judaism in particular, on the doctrine advanced by Leibnitz and Wolf.

Thus Mendelssohn's approach to Judaism was founded both upon the ideas formulated by German philosophers and upon the views of the Jewish thinkers of the Spanish era, particularly Maimonides.

Much of Mendelssohn's *Jerusalem* is devoted to proving the existence of God, in accordance with the views of the Jewish philosophers of the Golden Age in Spain. He flatly rejects the thesis of Spinoza that God and the world are one. Delving into the question of whether or not man is truly free to choose good or evil, seeing that God has prescience of what man will do, Mendelssohn agrees with Saadia Gaon, Hasdai Crescas, and other Jewish philosophers of that period that man does indeed have that freedom. Although the Lord knows in advance what choice each person will make, and even whether or not the sinner will repent and mend his ways, He makes no attempt to impart this knowledge to man or to influence him in his decision.

Mendelssohn rejects the materialistic theories in vogue in his day according to which man was nothing more than a machine that lived until it wore out and disintegrated. Man, says Mendelssohn, being capable of thought and perception and endowed with talents in art, music, and literature, must be something more than a mere automaton.

Finally Mendelssohn formulates his definition of Judaism. To him, Judaism is not a religion like all others, because the law upon which Judaism is based is called "Torah," meaning "teaching" or "knowledge" and not "faith" or "belief." Mendelssohn holds that "a Jew need not believe in anything that is not compatible with his intelligence; nevertheless he must not transgress any of the basic laws of his Judaism" (*Jerusalem*, Part II). "Nowhere in the Torah," he continues, "is there a commandment to believe. Even the Ten Commandments themselves begin with a simple statement of fact, 'I am the Lord your God. . . .' " Being a doctrine that is intended to appeal to reason and intelligence, the Torah contains no such statements as "Thou shalt believe." Indeed, we read in the Pentateuch, "And ye shall *know* that I am the Lord your God." What the Torah says to the Jew concerning God is meant to be *known* and *understood,* not blindly believed. And the principles which Jewish thinkers such as Maimonides attempted to formulate as binding upon all Jews who desired to be regarded as such, never attained universal recognition in world Jewry.

Mendelssohn then proceeds to destroy Spinoza's argument that the laws of the Torah were harsh and cruel and were given to the Jews only to cause them suffering. He agrees with Leibnitz and Wolf that whatever comes from God is good and designed to further man's happiness. He points out that since they were God-given, the laws of the Torah must be good also. Although at times it may seem unfathomable, God's world order is always good. Whatever is, is right, because God has willed it to be so.

Even as it was the will of God to create the world, so it was His will also to give the Law of the Torah to the people of Israel. The Torah, then, is a good doctrine, simply because it is His. It is by the Torah that the Jewish people have lived for centuries, and survived and grown in spite of oppression and persecution. Yet, though it is God-given, the Torah does not impose on the Jew the yoke of blind, unreasoning belief. The Law teaches the Jew that there is a God, a Supreme Being who created heaven and earth, who gives life to every living thing, and who chose the people of Israel to give them His Law. But this the Jew is expected to understand and to know, rather than to believe, for blind belief would run counter to reason, and Judaism is a teaching, a doctrine of knowledge, and not of blind belief.

Mendelssohn emphasizes that, in view of the above, a Jew does not cease to be a Jew merely because he finds that he cannot accept for himself a belief such as that in the resurrection of the dead or in the coming of the Messiah.

In a subsequent chapter, Mendelssohn touches upon a difficult question; namely, the validity and purpose of the laws of the Torah in the present day. He explains that the Torah originally was not only a teaching, but a code of law designed as a constitution for a theocratic state, and that it could not be subdivided into two parts, one entitled "civil" and the other strictly "religious" (*Jerusalem,* p. 460). When the Jews still lived in Palestine as an independent nation, the Torah was the law of the land. If a Jew there disobeyed any of the laws of the Torah, he transgressed against the law of the land by so doing, and was subject to punishment by the law-enforcing arm of his government. Since the Jews have lost their state, however, they have been subject to the political authority of the countries in which they have resided, and therefore there is no longer such a law-enforcing authority that has the power to impose penalties upon them for the violation of the laws of the Torah. Therefore, the Torah has ceased to be for the Jew the "law of the land" and has become only a religious law to be followed by him in accordance with the dictates of his conscience, rather than in obedience to the authority of a Jewish state.

If, then, the Torah was meant to be a constitution for a politically independent nation, Mendelssohn asks, what value is there in its observance today, when the members of that nation are scattered to the four corners of the earth? Hence he points out that certain laws of the Torah, which can be observed only in an independent Jewish state, have really lost their validity. These laws, however, Mendelssohn feels, are nevertheless binding upon all Jews wherever they may be, not only because they are part of the heritage that has come down to the Jewish people through the ages, but also because they are good and conducive to their spiritual welfare.

Mendelssohn is viewed as the father of the Haskalah movement, which stood for intellectual enlightenment and did much to break down the spiritual barriers that had grown up together with the physical walls of the ghettos of Europe to separate the Jews from their non-Jewish neighbors. Particularly his translation and commentary on the Bible had a noticeable impact on Jewish youth all over Europe, and especially in the East. Even as it was said of Peter the Great of Russia, that he "opened a window to the culture of Western Europe," so it can truly be said of Mendelssohn that he did the same thing for the Jews. Certainly, with his German rendering of the Bible, Mendelssohn was the first to show the Jews of Poland and Russia a glimpse of the world of secular learning that lay in the West beyond the walls of their ghettos.

Of course, Mendelssohn's view of Judaism as a body of knowledge is nothing new as such, for Maimonides had expressed similar opinions several centuries before. But to the young Jews, who for generations had been taught by scholars who stressed Talmudic legislation or cabalist mysticism rather than philosophy, Mendelssohn's approach to Judaism, even though it was, in the main, a restatement of ideas that had been formulated long before his day, seemed novel and unusual.

Naturally the rigidly orthodox, who viewed all new ideas with suspicion, feared that Mendelssohn's philosophy might lead to a weakening of Judaism. They pointed out that although Mendelssohn himself was a pious, observant Jew, his attitude toward Judaism was such that some of his own children grew lax in its observance and finally adopted Christianity. Some of his disciples, too, followed the same path. Of course this accusation seems ridiculous to us, for it is well known that, throughout Jewish history, there have been cases of apostasy even among the children of the greatest rabbinic minds, particularly during the Golden Age of Spanish Jewry. So we find among the converts even the sons of the most rigidly orthodox rabbis, of parents who certainly could never have been charged with having liberal views on Judaism, and who in many cases had had no other education than that afforded by the Talmudical academies.

But the rigidly orthodox were not the only ones to regard the philosophy of Mendelssohn as dangerous to Judaism. The pioneers of the Jewish nationalist movement, the forerunners of modern Zionism, particularly Peretz Smolenskin, felt that Mendelssohn, in *Jerusalem,* had implied that the Jews were no longer a nation, but were held together only by bonds of a common religion.

It is difficult to understand how Smolenskin, for one, could have arrived at the conclusion that Mendelssohn had denied the nationhood of Israel, for, actually, that question was acute neither in the days of Mendelssohn, nor in the mind of Mendelssohn himself. The problem which occupied Mendelssohn, and which constitutes the main theme of *Jerusalem* and of his other works, was not whether or not the Jews were a nation, but whether or not it was possible for a Jew to remain loyal to Judaism while at the same time taking an active part in the modern life and thought that were part of the world about him. This latter question he answered in the affirmative. The concept of modern nationalism had not yet been born in his day, and so he could hardly have discussed it, or even made any statements that could be construed as being either in favor of Jewish nationalism or opposed to it.

Moses Mendelssohn was not a philosopher, but a philosophical writer. His greatness did not lie in creating new and original ideas. His abiding merit was that he reinterpreted the ideas of the great thinkers of the past in the light of his own day. In *Phaedon* and *Jerusalem,* he brought the thoughts of both the ancient Greek philosophers and the medieval Jewish masters not only to his fellow Jews, but also to the German-speaking public. He also restated Jewish theology in terms of science and portrayed Judaism as a science rather than as a body of beliefs to be blindly accepted.

At about that time, however, there grew up quite a different movement in Jewry beyond the borders of Germany, in Podolia, Poland, where there lived a mystic who had spent his days in the perusal of the Cabala, and who was the father of a new approach to Judaism. It was the saintly Israel ben Eliezer, better known as "Israel Baal-Shem Tov," who has gone down in Jewish history as the founder of Hassidism.

19. Rabbi Israel Baal Shem Tov, the Founder of Hassidism

The Meaning of the Title "Baal Shem"—Who Was Israel ben Eliezer, the "Baal Shem Tov"?—The Strange Legend Concerning His Birth—His Seven Lonely Years as a Clay Digger—How Learned Was the Baal Shem Tov?—His Philosophy: Naturalism—His Teachings Concerning Man

Let us now go back several decades before the birth of Moses Mendelssohn. After the expulsion of the Jews from Spain at the end of the fifteenth century, when some three hundred thousand Jews had been uprooted from their ancient communities and had been forced to look for new homes in other countries, some settled in Poland. It is interesting to note that each country received a different type of Jewish immigrant. Somehow those Jews who had a glimmer of interest in secular science and learning gravitated to Germany. Turkey played host to those who had a penchant for mysticism, as exemplified by the Cabalists. Poland came to be the home of those Jews whose main concern was with the study of Talmudic lore. It was Polish Jewry that gave to its brethren in the rest of the world some of the greatest Talmudic scholars even known in Jewish history, and it was in Poland, too, that there now arose a new spirit, which, though deeply rooted in the Talmud, was also interested in the Cabala, and constituted in itself a new philosophy of Judaism, an entirely new movement in Jewish life. This was the Hassidic movement which was founded in Poland by Israel ben Eliezer, better known as the "Baal Shem Tov," (Master of the Good Name) or, simply as "the Besht." We shall discuss here not so much the Hassidic movement as such, but the life and personality of the Baal Shem Tov as the creator of a new philosophical approach to Judaism.

First of all, let us make clear why Israel ben Eliezer came to be known as "the Baal Shem Tov." Ever since the tenth century, those mystics who attempted to heal the sick by means of cabalistic formulae and incantations had been accorded that title by the Jewish masses who believed in them. Some say that the "Shem" refers to the Ineffable Name of the Lord, the letters of which, if interpreted and used in the proper manner, were believed by the Cabalists to have magic, curative powers. Others claim that the title simply meant to indicate that its possessor had a "good name," that is, that he enjoyed widespread popularity and respect as a saintly healer. Jewish history tells of some twenty outstanding savants who were accorded that title.

For example, there was Rabbi Elijah ben Rabbi Judah Aaron, the rabbi of the town of Chelm, the great-grandfather of the great Rabbi Zvi Ashkenaz, who wrote a famous treatise in the sixteenth century. Another "Baal Shem," who also lived during the sixteenth century, was Rabbi Elijah ben R. Moses Linz who was a rabbi in the famous Jewish community of Worms, Germany. Other "Baalei Shem" lived during the seventeenth and eighteenth centuries. Israel ben Eliezer, however, differed from most of these in that he was not a rabbi. In fact, he was regarded for years as an ignoramus in Jewish studies and it was only much later that he was proved to be otherwise. Eventually he came to be so much loved and venerated by the simple Jewish masses that he was called not simply "Baal Shem" (Master of the Name) but "Baal Shem Tov" (Master of the Good Name). We shall later attempt to find out who he was, whence he came, and how it was that this simple, unknown figure attained immortality in Jewish history as the creator of an entirely new philosophy of Judaism.

Not long after the death of the Baal Shem Tov there was published a book entitled *Shivchei Ha-Besht* (*In Praise of the Baal Shem Tov*), an anthology of legends concerning his life. Most of these legends are not of great literary value; in fact, they are crude and primitive. As an example we shall cite here the strange tale given in this book as regards the circumstances of the birth of Israel ben Eliezer. According to this tale, Rabbi Eliezer and his wife, the parents of the Baal Shem Tov, who lived in the province of Wallachia, had been quite old when their son was born. The legend has it that a band of robbers invaded the town in which they lived, and ransacked the old couple's home. The old lady managed to escape to another city where she earned a meager living as a midwife. Eliezer, however, was captured and taken away to a far-off country where he was sold as a slave to a wealthy man. Soon the Jew gained his master's confidence and he became the manager of the entire household. Eventually, however, Eliezer was given away to the viceroy of the province. One day the viceroy was consulted by the king on an important matter of state, and he was unable to find an acceptable solution to his ruler's problem. Sadly the viceroy returned home and told his servant Eliezer of his humiliation. Eliezer begged to be permitted to give his own views on the matter. His master found his suggestion so good that he informed the king of it. The king, impressed by the evident wisdom of the Jew, thereupon made him his principal adviser and, when the viceroy died, the Jewish servant was appointed the successor of his former master. What was more, the king offered Eliezer the hand of his beautiful daughter in marriage. Since the princess was not Jewish, Eliezer declined the honor. It was then that the Prophet Elijah appeared to him, praised him for resisting the temptation offered him by the king and promised him that as a reward he would yet have a son of his own who would be a light for the entire world. Soon thereafter

Eliezer was reunited with his wife whom he had believed to be dead, and a son was born, Israel, later known as the great Israel Baal Shem Tov.

Actually, we have no historical material to document the life of the Baal Shem Tov in detail. This lack of documentary sources led one nineteenth century writer, Ephraim Dinard, to deny altogether that there had been such a person as the Baal Shem Tov. This theory seems untrue, however, because, though we have no actual material on the life of the Baal Shem as such, there is historical evidence that a man such as he did indeed live some time between the end of the seventeenth century and the middle of the eighteenth.

Let us see, then, what historians have managed to find out concerning the life of this unusual figure in the story of Judaism.

It seems that Israel ben Eliezer was born either in 1696, 1697, or 1698 in the town of Okupy (or Tlust), near Kamenetz-Podolsk, Poland, which was situated near what was then the border between Poland and Turkey. His parents died when he was still very young. Most probably someone in the community took the youngster in and gave him a home. In the work *Shivchei Ha-Besht* we are told, "It was his way to study for a few days at a time and then to run away from the Heder (classroom). After some searching, he would be found sitting alone in the forest, and he would be brought back to his teacher. But he did not sit in class long and soon ran away again into the woods." It may be that the youngster, not being interested in the intricacies of the Talmud and filled with all kinds of dreams and visions instead, preferred solitude. Eventually he became an assistant to a teacher. This meant that he had to take the children to and from the Heder, and also recite certain prayers with them. The youngsters loved him for his sweet voice and his kindness. Later on he became an assistant to the sexton of the synagogue, and gradually he evolved a way of life all his own. During the day, when the synagogue was filled with worshipers and students, Israel would sit immersed in his own thoughts. It was only at night, when everyone else was asleep, that he would rise from his bed and study in the tomes of Jewish law.

We are futher told in *Shivchei Ha-Besht* that when Israel was fourteen years of age he was visited by a stranger whose name was Rabbi Adam (a name which had never been in use among Jews). Rabbi Adam turned over to the boy a package of manuscripts which Adam said that, according to his father's last will and testament, were to be turned over to one Israel ben Eliezer, because "they belong to the very root of his soul." The story tells in detail how the stranger met the boy as he spent his nights praying to God; how the written material was turned over to the boy, and how the two spent a long time alone together, poring over the papers and interrupting their studies only for immersions in the ritual pool for purification. They observed a set of fast days all their own.

Elsewhere, we are told that when Israel was about fifteen, the elders of the community married him off, as was the custom in those days. Unfortunately he lost his young wife soon after the wedding. After the death of his bride, Israel went away to eastern Galicia and settled in the vicinity of the city of Brody, making his living as a teacher of the young. He soon became known for his honesty and sincerity, and was often called in to arbitrate simple disputes among the townsmen. It seems that in the course of these activities the young man met Ephraim, father of the famous Rabbi Abraham Gerson of Brody. Ephraim took an immediate liking to him and offered to him in marriage the hand of his daughter, who had been previously married and divorced. Israel accepted the offer but asked that he be allowed a certain period of time to spend alone before the wedding. His request was granted and the bridegroom left for parts unknown. Eventually Ephraim died and his son Rabbi Abraham Gerson found among his father's papers the engagement contract drawn up for his sister and Israel ben Eliezer, but no one knew the whereabouts of the bridegroom-to-be.

One day Israel suddenly appeared at the rabbi's house, dressed in a short fur coat bound by a broad belt, and in a rude tone asked the rabbi to give him his bride. Rabbi Abraham Gerson, perplexed and shocked, called in his sister and asked her whether she would really agree to marry this uncouth man. The young woman replied that since it had been the will of her late father, she had no other choice but to become the stranger's wife. Before the day of the wedding, the bridegroom revealed to his bride who he really was, but adjured her to keep his story a secret until such time as he himself would be ready to reveal it publicly. His future wife promised him the strictest secrecy.

After the wedding, Rabbi Abraham Gerson realized that his new brother-in-law was a total ignoramus as regarded the Talmudic studies which he valued so highly. Ashamed that he should have married his sister off to such a peasant, he asked her whether she did not wish to divorce her new husband. When she declined to do so, her brother bought the couple a horse and carriage and told them to move and settle elsewhere. Eventually the newlyweds settled in a village near Kasov in the Carpathian Mountains. There the two led a strange life. Israel would spend most of his time wandering in the mountains in lonely reverie. Twice a week his wife would come to him from the town with their horse and carriage, and he would dig up clay, fill the carriage with it, and have his wife take it back to town to sell. In this way he managed to secure the bare essentials of a livelihood. He himself did not need much except some water and bread to keep body and soul together and often he did not require even that, because he fasted very frequently. This went on for seven years. Finally, his wife could no longer stand this way of life and appealed to her brother, the rabbi, for help. The latter then called them back home and hired his brother-in-law as his sexton, but he soon found out that Israel had little talent for that type of work. In the end the rabbi decided to rent an inn for the two not far from Kotev which his sister ran while her husband continued his accustomed mode of living. Eventually Israel settled in his native town of Okupy and once more took up teaching. Thus he remained until he was thirty-six years of age. At that time he decided to tell the people who he really was, or, as the Hassidim had it, to "reveal his true identity."

The teachings of the Baal Shem Tov quickly spread among the simple Jewish masses and he rapidly gained adherents. Eventually he attracted not only the plain village Jews, but also scholars who originally came to scoff at what they thought would be ridiculous nonsense, but who came under the spell of the Baal Shem's personal magnetism and became his fervent admirers. It is certain that the Baal Shem Tov could not have drawn these scholars to him by any striking ability to debate the fine points of the Talmud since they were much superior to him in that respect. However, one does not need to be a Talmudic scholar to formulate a new approach to Judaism. In *Shivchei Ha-Besht,* we do not once find mention of any great masters under whom he might have studied. And the subordinate positions he held during his younger years hardly required outstanding ability in the study or interpretation of the Law. On the other hand, we read in one place in *Shivchei Ha-Besht* that Israel served as a "shochet" or ritual slaughterer. If this is true, he must have had some knowledge of the Law, for no man could serve in this capacity unless he had been certified by an ordained rabbi as a man of at least some Jewish learning. Some historians even claim that shortly before his death he participated with two other rabbis in a debate against the heads of the Frankist movement in Lemberg in the presence of members of the Christian clergy. His adherents, the Hassidim, cite this assumption as proof of the Baal Shem's great learning. Others, however, point out that he was chosen to take part in the discussion solely because he knew Polish and therefore could be understood by the Christian spectators.

At any rate, it is quite clear that the Baal Shem Tov was definitely not a great Talmudic scholar. Be that as it may, it is certain that many of his contemporaries knew vastly more than he did. Legend has it, however, that the Baal Shem Tov was quite well versed in the lore of the Cabala, and that he managed to communicate with the spirit of the long-departed sages as Ahijah the Shilonite and the Prophet Elijah and to study with them the secret writings of mysticism. This we may or may not believe as we choose.

Looking at the Baal Shem Tov from a more rational point of view, we may classify him as a naturalist, a philosopher who went directly to the phenomena of nature, the trees and flowers of field and forest, the birds and animals, sunrise and sunset, to learn about the truths of life. History tells us of many such thinkers, some learned in book knowledge, others quite ignorant of such matters, who consulted nature, that greatest teacher of them all, to find out more about the basic phenomena of living. We cannot digress here to enumerate all the philosophers who were adherents of the school of naturalism. We might mention, however, the best known naturalist of comparatively recent times, Henry David Thoreau (1817-1862), who lived in the United States. A graduate of Harvard University (class of 1837), and a close friend of Ralph Waldo Emerson, the sage of Concord, Massachusetts, Thoreau was irresistibly drawn to nature. In 1845 he settled near Walden Pond, where he lived a solitary life, completely absorbed in the wonders of creation. He worked at odd jobs only when he needed money. The rest of his time he spent observing nature and writing books describing what he had learned from the great outdoors. The most important of Thoreau's works is the classic *Walden.*

The Baal Shem Tov, too, was less interested in book learning than in studying the secrets of nature. Israel ben Eliezer was also much influenced by the mystical teachings of the Cabala which were widespread in those days.

The Baal Shem Tov's approach to Judaism may be classified in two separate parts—his concept of God and his teachings as regards mankind. The Baal Shem Tov's view of God was somewhat akin to pantheism which holds that God and the world are interchangeable concepts. Of course, every form of pantheism has its original roots in the Cabala, where it is stated that there is no place where God is not and that He is present, to some degree, even in places of filth and sin. But even within the realm of pantheism, the Baal Sham Tov was by no means in agreement with Spinoza, the other early Jewish advocate of that philosophy. While Spinoza believed that God was *in* all things, the Baal Shem asserted that God was directly *above* everything in creation. In other words, instead of saying, like Spinoza, that each tree, stone, brook, or worm has God within it, the Baal Sham Tov believed that the Lord was the Almighty Force above them all, giving each and every one of them the strength to exist. All things were created by God and all things live through Him alone; hence God is everywhere and His almighty power is evident in every work of creation.

Such is the teaching of the Baal Shem Tov as regards God, which was so beautifully set down by Rabbi Nahum'ke Chernobiller in his book *Meor Ainaim (A Light for the Eyes).* As the basis for the concepts developed by the Baal Shem Tov in relation to the way in which man must walk with his Maker and worship Him, these are his principles:

1. Man must serve the Lord with gladness. Man, instead of mortifying his body, should be glad at all times and banish every care from his heart. Sadness and dejection are even worse than idol-worship. Man must have constant and serene faith in God and in His help, and it is permissible for man to use stimulants such as wine to gladden his heart, as it is said in the Psalms, "Wine which gladdens the heart of man." Though he was an optimist who called upon man to rejoice in his life, the Baal Shem Tov still felt basically that the evil in the world far outweighed the good. It is precisely for this reason that man must make a determined effort to be of good cheer at all

times, for once he stops to contemplate the misery in the world, he may as well mourn all the time.

2. Man must acknowledge truth at all times and cleave to it. The Baal Shem Tov once said, "If a man is in doubt, he no longer has God with him."

3. Man is one family, and men should remain close to one another in brotherly love. This spirit of brotherhood was strong among the adherents of the Baal Shem Tov. They knew no difference between rich and poor; it mattered not whether a man was a scholar or an ignoramus. The Hassidim of the Baal Shem Tov viewed themselves as one large family. They formed a truly democratic society.

4. The Baal Shem Tov created the institution of the "Tzaddik," the saintly man to whom the Hassidim could turn in times of stress. A Tzaddik (literally "righteous one") was one who, unlike ordinary men, had kept free of sin and therefore was considered to be closer to God than ordinary men. It was thought that he could therefore intercede with the Lord on behalf of his followers. Eventually the Tzaddik became a combination religious leader and psychological counselor. There was a big difference between the rabbi of the town and the Tzaddik. The rabbi of the town was consulted only for problems connected with the practical observance of Jewish law, whereas the Tzaddik filled an important need in the community, namely, that of adviser in personal problems such as illness, financial crisis, marrying off a son or daughter, or a married woman's barrenness. He gave comfort where he could; he rendered advice and aid to the helpess and lent new courage to the despairing.

Thus the Baal Shem Tov soon won the hearts of the masses who until then had sought in vain for help and spiritual guidance.

Of course the Baal Shem Tov based his teachings upon the firm foundation of Judaism. He founded his view of God on the words found in the Biblical passage, "The whole earth is full of His glory" (Isaiah 6:3) and on the interpretation which the Cabalists had made of this Biblical quotation. His teaching of "serving the Lord with gladness" was derived from the Biblical injunction, "thou shalt be altogether joyful," (Deut. 16:15), while his institution of the Tzaddik had its origin in the Talmudic statement to the effect that "the righteous man commands and the Lord does his bidding."

The Baal Shem Tov did not leave any writings, and most of the facts we know about him have been handed down by word of mouth through his disciples and their descendants. After he "revealed his true identity" to the people, he settled in the town of Medzibozh, Podolia (Poland) where he gathered about him a great number of adherents (or Hassadim), who established their own houses of worship, the so-called "shtieblach," (little rooms). Actually, they did not consider it necessary always to worship with a congregation, for they felt that the Lord hears all those who call upon Him, even if one prays alone and far from a synagogue. They did not adhere to a definite schedule of time for prayer, nor did they believe in decorum and discipline as we know it during worship; they felt that each worshiper must be at liberty to express his emotions freely as he prays to God. This meant that it was not considered irreverent or indecorous for a Hasid to sway, dance, or walk about as he prayed.

These strange new ways roused much opposition from the other Jews who were characterized as "mitnagdim" (opponents) of the Hassidim. One of the most articulate leaders of this opposition was Rabbi Elijah, the famous Gaon of Vilna. In addition, the new Hassidic sect was the target of bitter attack from the adherents of the Haskalah movement who stood for intellectual enlightenment and ridiculed what seemed to them to have degenerated into Tzaddik-worship.

After the death of the Baal Shem Tov in 1760, there arose another new star on the Jewish horizon, this time in Galicia, in the person of Rabbi Nachman Krochmal, who is best remembered as the author of the great book *More N'vukhe Hazman* (*The Guide for the Perplexed of Our Time*).

20. Nachman Krochmal and His Disciples

Early Youth in Galicia—His Marriage at the Age of Fourteen—The Outdoors Was His Classroom—Influence of Hegelian Philosophy on Krochmal—Krochmal's Interpretation of the Torah

In all Jewish history there has never been even one generation of which it could be said that it was entirely sterile as regarded Jewish learning. Each period in the history of the Jewish people has produced some outstanding leaders either in the study of ancient law and tradition, or in the development of scientific research into the spiritual treasures of the past. When one such giant intellect would pass on, another would take over where he left off, and thus carry on the eternal chain of study and learning. Thus the sun of Jewish culture did not set with the passing of Israel Baal Shem Tov, for not long after his death there arose a new leader in Galicia in the person of Nachman Krochmal. This great scholar and thinker not only achieved fame in his own generation but immortalized himself in the annals of Jewish history for the generations that were to follow.

Nachman Krochmal was born in Brody, Galicia, in 1785, some thirteen years after the death of Israel Baal Shem Tov. His father, Sholom, was a man of means who enjoyed the esteem of the entire community. Young Nachman's Jewish education was much the same as that of his contemporaries; he was taught the rudiments of Jewish learning in the traditional Heder and then pursued higher Talmudic studies in the Beth Ha-Midrash or house of study in his town. The spirit of the Haskalah, the movement that sought to bring to the ghettoes the new ideas and the knowledge that grew apace in the world outside, had already penetrated the Jewish quarter of Brody, and so Nachman, in addition to studying Talmudic law, was also given instruction in arithmetic and foreign languages by a private tutor whom his father had engaged for that purpose. As was customary among the Jews of those days, Nachman was married quite early. When he was only fourteen years old, a match was arranged for him with the young daughter of a wealthy man in the town of Zolkiev. After the wedding the youthful bridegroom was taken into the home of his father-in-law, who, as was the custom then, provided for the support of the newlyweds until the young husband completed his studies. It was then that Nachman first met Baruch Neu, a scholar who taught him the fundamentals of worldly science and philosophy. Nachman would sit for hours in his new friend's library, poring over the books that opened for him new vistas of what went on in the world outside the ghetto. Never strong by constitution, Krochmal's health soon gave way and after his recovery he remained frail and delicate for the rest of his life.

Young Krochman continued to board at the home of his father-in-law and of course he did not neglect his Talmud studies at the house of learning. But soon a time came when he was no longer content to remain just a student and felt the urge to impart to others the knowledge he had gathered in the course of the years. He rallied round him a strange group of disciples. Young men and boys who had buried themselves in the study of Talmudic lore to the exclusion of all else left their benches and followed Krochmal out into a new classroom, the fields and forests outside the little town. Here he taught them the new ideas he had gathered from his broad and extensive studies. His method of teaching was much like that of the ancient Greek philosophers; the students would ask questions, and Krochmal, the teacher-philosopher, would answer them even as Socrates and Plato had answered the queries of their disciples many centuries before. These outdoor classes would go on for hours. Krochmal's audience grew apace. At first there were only teen-age students from the Beth Ha-Medrash. These were soon joined by young husbands who, like Krochmal himself, were given room and board by their fathers-in-law so that they might continue their studies. Then came little boys, eleven years of age and younger, to listen to the words of the gifted young scholar. The pious men of the town, suspicious of any pursuit that took their young men away from the benches of the study halls, claimed that Krochmal was undermining the morals and religious loyalties of his followers. They went so far as to inspect his library to see whether it did not harbor books that contained views contrary to the spirit of Jewish law and Judaism as they saw it. Krochmal's father-in-law, however, never lost his confidence in the young man to whom he had married his daughter and protected him against the increasingly violent attacks of the extremists.

The great Talmudic scholar, Rabbi Zvi Hirsch Chajes, who was then the rabbi of the town, also thought highly of the youthful teacher whom he was quick to recognize as a genius. At about that time Krochmal made the acquaintance of the Hacham Kakusov, leader of the Karaite movement, and began a correspondence with him. This was grist for the mill of the extremists of Zolkiev, who now declared that Krochmal had joined the heretic sect of the Karaites who refused to accept the authority of the Oral Tradition in their observance of the Jewish religion. Actually, Krochmal had never thought even remotely of adopting the views of the Karaite with whom he liked to discuss certain points of Jewish law, but nothing more.

Gradually Nachman Krochmal reared a whole generation of scholars who considered themselves his disciples and felt deep admiration and respect for their teacher. Among them were a number of men who became famous in their own right. They included Rabbi Meir Halevi Letteris (1800-1871), the noted Hebrew writer and poet, who edited the Masorah of the Pentateuch for the English Bible Society and made an English translation of the Holy Day prayer book and Rabbi Solomon Leib Rappaport (1790-1867), an eminent scholar who served as Rabbi in Tarnopol and thereafter in Prague and wrote many works of great importance in Jewish historical research. It is said that he often traveled to Zolkiev to hear the words of his former teacher.

Krochmal's influence also extended beyond the confines of the country in which he lived. He maintained a regular correspondence with Leopold Zunz (1794-1886), the great scholar-founder of what became known as "The Science of Judaism" and who, throughout his active life, considered himself a student of Krochmal. Isaac Beer Levinson, the father of the Haskalah movement in Russia, was also among the many scholars and teachers who traveled great distances to see Krochmal and to talk with him.

All this time Krochmal and his family lived with his father-in-law who continued to give them food and board at his house. Ten years after Krochmal's marriage, however, his mother-in-law died, and soon thereafter his father-in-law lost his entire fortune and was no longer able to support an extra family, so that Krochmal was forced to think seriously about earning a living for himself, his wife, and his children. Eventually the Krochmals went to Brody, Nachman's home town. There he received several offers of pulpits, all of which he refused. He even declined to answer the call for the rabbinate in the Jewish community of Berlin, in far-off Germany, on the grounds that he did not wish to be obligated to a religious community or congregation. During the last years of his life, Krochmal made his home with his daughter, who was married to Dr. Horowitz, a physician. It was in his daughter's home that he wrote a great many of the works for which he is famous until today in the world of Jewish scholarship, among them the *More N'vukhe Hazman* (*The Guide to the Perplexed of Our Time*) which was not published until after his death. He requested in his will that the manuscript be sent to Leopold Zunz, who published it in Lemberg in 1851, eleven years after the death of its author. *The Guide to the Perplexed of Our Time* had a profound impact upon the generation immediately following Krochmal, perhaps even more so than his personal conversations with his students. In this monumental work we may read Krochmal's personal approach to Judaism, which to a great extent was influenced by the philosophy of Georg Wilhelm Friedrich Hegel, the famous German thinker.

At this point, we might do well to learn a little more about the life and times of Hegel and attempt to gain some understanding of his basic philosophy. Hegel (1770-1830), the author of many philosophical works, served as professor in some of the greatest German universities, those at Jena, Heidelberg, and Berlin. Though philosophy was his main interest, Hegel also pursued other branches of learning such as history, religion, political science, political economy, and the arts. He attempted to formulate a synthesis combining all the knowledge contained in these sciences in one single theory. His philosophy is noticeably colored by theology and tinged with a marked predilection for Christianity.

According to Hegel, the human intellect is the main force in the world. The intellect, however, is not perfect at the very beginning, for every idea or "thesis," also bears within itself the seeds of a counteridea, or "antithesis." These two elements, "thesis" and "antithesis," must be reconciled to form a "synthesis," and it is only the "synthesis" that represents the true and correct idea. This, according to Hegel, is applicable to every phenomenon of world order, history, the arts, family life, and the workings of government. In the realm of nature this is best illustrated by the fact that the mineral kingdom and other, organic materials combined to form the vegetable kingdom which in combination with other elements created animal life. The highest form of animal life, of course, is man himself, who then evolved human intellect. Thus, Hegel explains, even the human intellect is a synthesis. Mind and matter are not two separate things, but actually one and the same. In human life this is represented by the family, which forms the synthesis between the individual (thesis) and society(antithesis). The family, in turn, combines with the larger society to form the state. This led Hegel to the conclusion that the state was the highest form of human life; and therefore the state has precedence over the individual and in case of conflict the individual is duty-bound to subordinate his own interests to those of the state.

Departing from this premise, Hegel goes on to say that the state must be governed by one individual, a dictator, rather than by a more democratic authority because only through subordination to the will of one person can the institution of the state become perfect. It was upon this Hegelian thought that the adherents of modern totalitarianism, fascist and communist alike, based their stand, regarding democracy as ineffectual and dictatorship as the only proper means of government.

As regards religion, Hegel established that Christianity was the synthesis of all religious faith and was therefore the highest form of religion in this world.

Now let us see what the thinking of Nachman Krochmal, the Jewish philosopher, could possibly have had in common with the very definitely non-Jewish ideology advanced by Hegel and his disciples. At that time Germany numbered among its citizens many other outstanding thinkers such as Fichte, Schelling, Schleiermacher, and Schlegel, who advocated views quite different from those of Hegel. We are then faced with the question of why, of all the philosophies then prevalent in Germany, Nachman Krochmal, the Jew, chose that of Hegel upon which to base his own personal interpretation of Judaism.

It seems that the philosophy of Hegel was quite the vogue among the younger intellectuals of his day. Jewish youth in particular was impressed by Hegel because, though his views were strongly colored by Christianity, he was not an anti-Semite. Other German philosophers were less kindly disposed to the Jews. Fichte, for example, openly opposed the giving of equal rights to members of the Jewish faith, and Schleiermacher frankly believed that Jews should be deported to some place other than Germany (though he himself rather liked Jewish women). Schlegel also was inclined more to Christianity. He had carried on an affair with Dorothea Mendelssohn, the daughter of Moses Mendelssohn, and prevailed upon her to leave her husband and two children and come to him instead. Thus it was on account of Hegel's benevolent attitude toward Jews as compared to the attitudes of these other thinkers that Nachman Krochmal became interested in Hegelian thought. But Krochmal, being a pious Jew, could hardly accept Hegel's religion. He solved that problem by saying that Judaism takes the place which Hegel had appointed in his philosophy for the faith of Jesus of Nazareth. This is the trend of thought which Krochmal followed, particularly in his seventeen-chapter masterpiece mentioned above.

In brief, the thesis advanced by Krochmal in this work was as follows:

The Torah is a synthesis between belief and knowledge. As long as the Jew is still intellectually immature, he must simply believe in what the law tells him and observe all of its commandments without inquiring into the reasons for them. As he gains in maturity, he will attain to reason, pure and refined, which is the spiritual source of religion.

In agreement with the thought formulated by Hegel, Krochmal says that a nation can rise to a very high plane, but that its very ascent bears within it the seeds of decline. This is followed by the synthesis between these two opposite states. The same theory is applicable also to the Jewish people. Unlike the other nations, however, Judaism has created not only strictly nationalist values, but also values that are valid for all mankind; Judaism is an integral part of the culture and civilization of humanity as a whole. It is a historical-cultural attempt to reach the spiritual absolute.

Such is the basic theme of Krochmal's *Guide for the Perplexed of Our Time*. In addition, the work contains a discussion of the various forms of Jewish religion, of the meaning of various Jewish laws, of the holidays, and of the Bible and apocryphal literature. We may read there also of the time of the Great Synod, the philosophy of Plato of Alexandria, the Cabala, and many other issues of Jewish thought. As the very title implies, Krochmal's book is patterned upon the historic *More N'vukhim* (*Guide to the Perplexed*) written by Maimonides. Though it is not quite as profound as the latter, it nevertheless had a powerful impact on Jewish youth in the ghettos of Galicia, Lithuania, and Poland.

Krochmal did not live to grow old; he died when he was fifty-five years of age. Soon after his death there came about a new attempt to reinterpret Judaism, this time an effort at radical change in the religion itself.

21. The New Idea—Reform Judaism

*The Declaration of the Synhedrion of Paris Regarding the Nationhood of Israel—
The First Attempt at Change in Synagogue Services in Germany—The Organ in
the Synagogue—Abraham Geiger and Samuel Holdheim, the Advocates of
Radical Reforms in the Jewish Religion*

For thousands of years, Judaism was regarded as one indivisible whole, from which nothing could be detracted without harming the entire body. When confronted with the problem of reconciling certain traditional beliefs and practices with contemporary thought, Jewish philosophers strove to interpret them so as to make them seem least objectionable. As regarded those beliefs which had originated in other cultures and had found their way into the fabric of Judaism, such as "heaven and hell" and "resurrection," such philosophers as Levi ben Gershon, Joseph Albo and later, Moses Mendelssohn, minimized their importance in Judaism, explaining that those who found themselves unable to hold them did not thereby cease to be Jews. But none of the thinkers and teachers prior to the nineteenth century had ever dared attempt to reconcile Judaism with contemporary ideas by means of radical surgery, as it were, by actually making changes in the basic structure of Judaism.

The movement for such far-reaching change, which became known as "Reform Judaism," originated in Germany. What it proposed to do was not simply to eliminate customs and practices which were of secondary importance in Judaism and which seemed offensive to contemporary thinking, but to make basic alterations in the fundamentals of the Jewish religion.

In the ordinary course of events, new laws are formulated and set down in writing first, and then carried out in everyday life. First comes the theory, and the practical application follows. What took place in Reform Judaism was quite the reverse. First the practical changes were made, and only then did the reformers seek to find justification for them. First let us meet the leaders of practical reform, David Friedlander and Israel Jacobson, and after them, Abraham Geiger and Samuel Holdheim, the first philosophers of the new movement.

Let us stop and examine the historical background against which Reform movement grew. At the end of the eighteenth and the beginning of the nineteenth century the term "emancipation" was first applied to Jews in the Western world. Emancipation, in this case, meant granting to Jews all the rights of citizenship in the countries in which they lived. This was an outgrowth of the French Revolution of 1789, which was fought under the device of "liberty, equality, and fraternity" on the premise that all men were created equal and should therefore also enjoy full equality before the law. However, this era of general liberalism was followed by a wave of reaction during which the Jews lost whatever ground they had gained in equality with their gentile neighbors. In all, modern history to date can be divided into four such eras of emancipation and reaction.

The first of these, which centered in France, extended from 1789 to about 1815. During that period, the newly created Republic of France accorded equal rights to Jews. This policy was upheld by the Emperor Napoleon and extended by him to Holland and certain parts of Italy and Germany when his armies occupied these territories. With the downfall of Napoleon, however, we come to the beginning of the first era of reaction, which lasted from 1815 to 1848, and during which time all the Jews of the Western world, with the exception of those residing in France and Holland, once again lost the rights they had so recently obtained.

The Revolution of 1848 marked the beginning of the second era of emancipation. It was during this era that the Jews of far-off Russia also began to agitate for the rights they had never enjoyed in the past. The year 1881, however, marks the start of the second era of reaction. It was a period of new anti-Semitic movements in Western Europe and pogroms in Russia, a bloody epoch that did not end until 1917, the year of the Russian Revolution, when Kerensky and other liberals strongly advocated equal rights for all citizens, regardless of race or religion.

Now that we know some of the historic events which took place during the past century and a half, it will be easier for us to understand the conditions which gave rise to the new movement of Reform Judaism that began in Germany.

In the French Parliament and in the legislative halls of the other nations where the proposition of equal rights for Jews was raised, the debate centered around the question, "What, really, are the Jews?" Were the Jews a separate nation, an alien entity in each country where they resided, or did they regard themselves as part and parcel of the communities in which they lived? If they were indeed an independent nation, then the Jews could quite properly be classed as foreigners and could hardly lay claim to the rights and privileges enjoyed by the citizens of the countries in which they resided. But if they were united only by ties of a common religion, then they could not be denied full citizenship with all the prerogatives enjoyed by their gentile neighbors. The opponents of emancipation argued that the Jews were, indeed, an alien element wherever they lived. The Jews, they claimed, had always kept apart from the others; they prayed three times each day for the coming of a Messiah who would lead them back to Palestine, which they still revered and loved as their homeland, and they regarded the countries in which they lived as places of no more than temporary sojourn.

In 1807, this question of whether or not the Jews were a nation was placed squarely in the laps of the Synhedrion, a council of seventy-one French Jewish leaders (two-thirds rabbis and one-third laymen) which the Emperor Napoleon had convened in Paris to act as spokesmen for his Jewish subjects. Desirous of putting an end to the constant persecution that had been the lot of their fellow Jews, the Synhedrion reluctantly replied that the Jews were not a people but were held together only by a bond of common religion. The natural consequence of this pronouncement was that the French government then asked the Jews of France to give up every vestige of communal autonomy and to subordinate themselves entirely to the authority of the state of which they claimed to be citizens. This same attitude was later adopted also by other countries in which Jews claimed and received equal rights.

At about that time, David Friedlander, a student of Moses Mendelssohn and president of the Jewish community in Berlin, declared that all prayers implying the nationhood of Israel and dealing with the return of the Jewish people to Palestine should be eliminated from the Jewish prayer book. What is more, he asserted that the language of prayer in his community should no longer be Hebrew but German, the tongue of Prussia. Finally, he urged changes in the structure of synagogue edifices so that they might look more like the houses of worship of the dominant faith. By 1812, the Jews of other German provinces such as Westphalia, Brunswick, and the city of Frankfort had attained equal footing with their gentile neighbors. At that time Friedlander gained an important ally in his quest for reform in Judaism, Israel Jacobson of Brunswick.

Jacobson, a man of means, occupied a prominent position in the government of Westphalia. Originally minister of finance at the court of Grand Duke Charles Ferdinand of Brunswick, he was appointed minister of finance for all of Westphalia when Brunswick was incorporated into that state by King Jerome Bonaparte, the brother of Napoleon. Jacobson made every effort to demonstrate to his gentile neighbors that the Jews were anxious to be like them. For this purpose he set up a new synagogue in his own home in which he put into practice some radical reforms in the religious service. Certain prayers were recited in German rather than in Hebrew, and a preacher delivered eloquent, formal sermons in German after the manner of Protestant pastors. Whereas women traditionally had no part in the synagogue service, Jacobson had a choir consisting of both men and women officiate in his temple. Instead of having the boys celebrate the traditional Bar-Mitzvah upon attaining the age of thirteen, Jacobson established the practice of confirmation for both boys and girls after the manner of the corresponding Protestant ceremony. In general, it was Jacobson's desire to have the Jewish synagogue resemble as closely as possible the churches of the Protestants who were in the majority in his country. In the meantime, David Friedlander had founded a similar synagogue in Berlin at the home of Jacob Beer, the banker who was the father of Giacomo Meyerbeer, the famous composer. But Friedlander had gone one step further than Jacobson; he had installed an organ in his new temple to be played during the services. This was a radical reform indeed, because the rabbis had decreed centuries before that there should be no instrumental music in the synagogue.

Friedlander's experiment in Berlin did not last long. The Prussian government, suspicious of any movement that smacked of radicalism in any aspect of life, closed down his temple in 1816. But this was not to be the end of Reform Judaism. In 1818 there was opened a new Reform temple in Hamburg, for which two scholars evolved a special prayer book. In this order of worship there were many new German prayers. In fact, only the most essential parts of the liturgy were retained in the original Hebrew. Many of the old Hebrew prayers, particularly those relating to Zion and Jerusalem, were eliminated. In addition there were German sermons, and the organ had an important role in the service.

Naturally these reforms aroused much opposition from those who adhered to the traditional form of Judaism. The rabbis of Hamburg, Altona, and the communities near these great cities asserted in a joint declaration that, according to Jewish law, it was forbidden for any Jew to pray in such houses of worship. The reformers, on the other hand, managed to secure the support of Eliezer Lieberman, a Talmudic scholar from Austria, who in turn persuaded four other rabbis, two in Hungary and two in Italy, to endorse the new mode of worship. The leaders of traditional Judaism now marshaled their forces and drew up a document roundly condemning the Reform movement. This declaration was signed by forty rabbis, among them the famous Rabbi Akiba Eiger, Chief Rabbi of Posen, and his equally eminent son-in-law, Moses Sofer, who was Chief Rabbi of the Jewish community of Pressburg, Austria (now Czechoslovakia).

The Temple in Hamburg, however, secured many new members and eventually other houses of worship patterned upon it were established in other German cities such as Leipzig and Karlsruhe, and, soon after, in Copenhagen, the capital of Denmark.

Friedlander and Jacobson were succeeded as leaders of Reform by Abraham Geiger and Samuel Holdheim. These two were the pioneer thinkers of the Reform movement and devised theories to justify that which had already been carried out in practice.

Geiger (1810-1875) was born in Frankfort-on-the-Main. He received a traditional Jewish education at a rabbinical college, and then took courses in philosophy and Semitic languages at the universities of Heidelberg and Vienna. When he was only seventeen years old, he published a new commentary to the Mishna. His approach to the subject was critical and scientific rather than traditional. In 1832, soon after he had enrolled at the University of Heidelberg, Geiger published a treatise entitled "Was hat Mohammed aus dem Judenthum aufgenommen" (Bonn, 1833), on the elements of Judaism that Mohammed had incorporated into the faith of Islam. This work aroused great interest in scholarly circles. When Geiger completed his studies, he accepted a pulpit in the German city of Wiesbaden. Eventually Geiger began to occupy himself with the question of the necessity of reform in Judaism. He envisioned a new Judaism built upon scientific bases and set up a journal entitled *Wissenschaftliche Zeitschrift für Juedische Theologie* (*Scientific Journal for Jewish Theology*), which served to propagate his views. Later on he settled in Breslau, where he became a preacher. In his sermons he vigorously defended the reforms introduced by Friedlander and Jacobson which by then had already spread to a great many synagogues.

Geiger's chief ally in these endeavors was Samuel Holdheim (1806-1860) who had been a student at the rabbinical college in his birthplace, Kempen, near the city of Posen, Prussia. After finishing his Jewish studies, Holdheim enrolled at a university, and it was then that he first became interested in the problem of reform. When, some years later, he became chief rabbi of Mecklenburg, he introduced the new Reform prayer book into the synagogues there, but he met with strong opposition from the traditionalists, now known as the "Orthodox."

By 1844 there were enough rabbis in the Reform camp to warrant the calling of a conference of Reform rabbis in Brunswick. Geiger and Holdheim served as the principal speakers. The first question that came before the conclave was whether it was indeed permissible to use a language other than Hebrew in the synagogue service, as had already been done in the temples. In a long discourse, Geiger asserted that the use of the vernacular in the synagogue was not contrary to Jewish law. In support of his argument he cited a passage in the Talmud to the effect that the declaration of faith beginning with "Hear, O Israel" could be recited by the worshiper in whatever language he could understand best. The second question, whether it was at all expedient to retain Hebrew as the language of prayer, was answered by Geiger in the negative. The retention of Hebrew as the language of prayer, he asserted, ran counter to the spirit of the declaration of the Paris Synhedrion which stated that the Jews did not constitute a nation but simply a religion; the use by Jews of a language other than the vernacular would indicate that the Jews still felt themselves to be a separate national entity. Holdheim supported Geiger's stand, explaining that the average Jew would better understand the prayers he was reciting if he were premitted to say them and hear them said in the language he was accustomed to use in everyday life. At the end of the meeting, the conference framed four resolutions as follows: (1) that they wholeheartedly endorsed the declaration of the Synhedrion that the Jews did not constitute a separate national entity; (2) that it was permissible for a Jew to marry a gentile, provided that the gentile partner believed in One God. Unitarians, for example, would come under this classification; (3) that the new prayer book set down by Samuel Holdheim in Mecklenburg should be the standard prayer book for the new movement; and (4) that the ancient "Kol Nidrei" which is an important part of the service of the Eve of the Day of Atonement should be eliminated from the prayer book.

The three years that followed saw many such conventions. At the last one, Geiger asked for changes in the laws governing Sabbath observance, urging that the prohibitions against certain types of work on the Sabbath be abolished. This proposal was the subject of much heated debate. In the end the conference decided to abolish the observance of the second days of the holidays of Passover, Pentecost, and the Feast of Tabernacles, retaining only the first day of each.

One of the young leaders of the Reform movement, Rabbi Isaac Mayer Wise (1819-1900) left Europe in 1846 and settled in America where he first accepted a pulpit in Albany, New York. His attempts to introduce his type of Reform Judaism into the Albany synagogue were unsuccessful, and in 1854 he moved to Cincinnati where he became the spiritual leader of a synagogue which was more receptive to his ideas. There, too, in 1875 he founded the Hebrew Union College which is the training school for Reform rabbis in the United States.

We have now learned of one movement in Judaism which was largely an outgrowth of the emancipation of the Jews in Western Europe. But emancipation gave rise to another current in Judaism as well, a drive for a renaissance of Jewish studies and learning.

22. "The Science of Judaism" in Germany

"Conservative Judaism," Midway Between Orthodoxy and Reform—The Four Great Thinkers: Zacharias Frankel, Leopold Zunz, Marcus Jost, and Heinrich Graetz—Ten Other Great Jewish Philosophers

The eighteenth century, particularly the second half of it, represented an era of political renaissance in Europe. The sixteenth century had seen the first stirrings of a renaissance, a shedding of the dust of the Middle Ages from European civilization. This rebirth was manifest first in the arts. At the end of the sixteenth century and the beginning of the seventeenth century, it became evident in religion as well, when Martin Luther and his followers first sought to rid Christianity of the yoke of the papacy of Rome. By the eighteenth century, Europe strained also at the fetters of political tyranny, a struggle which found its most forceful expression in the French Revolution of 1789. This revolution, which had a profound impact on the rest of Europe, helped stir up much intellectual activity which had remained dormant for years, and led to a host of new movements and ideas, in the Jewish world as well.

One of the first new movements in Judaism, as we have learned in the last chapter, was Reform, which was attracting a great many young Jewish intellectuals. But even as the Christian Reformation gave rise to a counter-reformation in the other camp, Reform Judaism was countered by a new philosophy which eventually came to be called "Conservative" Judaism and held a position midway between Orthodoxy on one hand, and Reform on the other.

There emerged a new trend in Jewry, the application of modern scientific methods of research to the study of the vast spiritual heritage of the Jewish people and its history. Thus began an era whose intense cultural and intellectual activity was reminiscent of that which had characterized the Golden Age of Spanish Jewry centuries before. Historians designate this entire period in Jewish history as the "Epoch of the Science of Judaism."

The main figures of this epoch, which had its origins in Germany, were Zacharias Frankel, Leopold Zunz, Marcus Jost, and Heinrich Graetz. These four Jewish scholars, who could not identify themselves with Reform Judaism and its total break with the past and tradition, but also could no longer accept Orthodoxy, each made an important contribution to Jewish learning. Actually, they cannot be classed as philosophers, for they did not intend to continue the chain of original thought and reasoning that had been forged during the Golden Age in Spain to determine what Judaism was and what it was not. Their contribution to Jewish thought was more practical than philosophical in nature. Frankel helped contemporary students gain a better understanding of the Mishna. Zunz published important studies on Jewish liturgy. Jost and Graetz devoted their energies to the field of Jewish history. These four men, though each specializing in a different area of study and research, also served as builders of that counterreform movement now known as Conservative Judaism.

The first of this group, Zacharias Frankel, was born in Prague, in 1801. After an intensive Jewish education, which culminated in his ordination as a rabbi, he engaged in secular studies at universities in Prague and Budapest and received the degree of Doctor of Philosophy. Shortly thereafter he accepted a pulpit in the city of Teplitz, in Bohemia, which carried with it the title of District Rabbi. Later he occupied a rabbinate in Dresden. The Jewish community of Berlin wanted Frankel to become its chief rabbi. However, since one of the functions of the chief rabbi was to serve as a spokesman of the Jewish community before the authorities of the state, the Prussian government had some voice in the election of this official. It was the Prussian government that disqualified Frankel because he was not a citizen of Prussia. Thus Frankel remained in Dresden. Eventually he moved to Breslau, where he founded a rabbinical seminary which he headed until his death in 1875.

Frankel is regarded by present-day Conservative Jews as one of the first founders, leaders, and thinkers of their movement. No longer able to accept the old forms of Orthodoxy, he was also repelled by the radicalism of Reform. He had attended the rabbinical convention at which Abraham Geiger had declared that there was no reason or necessity for conducting synagogue services in the Hebrew language. Frankel followed a more moderate course. He openly stated that the use of Hebrew in the synagogue ritual was an essential feature of Judaism, and confined the changes in the services in his own synagogue to the omission of some of the more obscure liturgical poems and to the addition of a few German prayers.

Frankel's most important contribution to Jewish learning, however, consisted in his studies of the various translations of the Bible that had been made in ancient times into Aramaic, Syrian, Greek, and Latin. He was actually the first Jewish scholar to delve into this vast field of knowledge. Frankel also engaged in diligent research on the Mishna and Talmudic Law and published many important works on the subject. Here, too, Frankel was a pioneer, blazing a trail for others to follow after him.

Leopold Zunz, who was born in 1794 in the German town of Detmold, also received an extensive education, both in Jewish learning and in secular subjects. His friend Marcus Jost was his close companion in his studies. Zunz received his doctorate in philosophy from the University of Halle. During his youth he often suffered from dire poverty, but his economic difficulties were alleviated when, at the age of forty-six, he became principal of the Teachers' Seminary in Berlin, where he lived until his death in 1886 at the venerable age of ninety-two.

Zunz, too, may be called a Conservative Jew since he rejected Reform, but at the same time believed that some minor changes had to be made in the orthodox interpretation of Judaism.

One of Zunz's most important contributions to the science of Judaism is his work entitled *Die Gottesdienstlichen Vortraege der Juden* (*Sermons of the Jews*) which is an exhaustive study of the development of synagogue homily throughout Jewish history from ancient days until Zunz's own time. It is a thorough analysis of the various types of sermons, showing their value in the spiritual education and moral edification of the audience.

Even more important is his monumental work entitled *Synagogale Poesie des Mittelalters* (*Liturgical Poetry of the Middle Ages*), dealing with the liturgical poetry that forms an important part of the Jewish Holy Day prayer book. Here Zunz traces the history of each poem and gives biographical sketches of the authors. In addition, he gives an explanation of the many customs that are followed in traditional worship at the synagogue.

Isaac Marcus Jost was born in Bernburg (Germany) in 1793; thus he was the senior of his friend Zunz by one year. Like Zunz, he studied both at Yeshivoth and at institutions of higher secular learning. When he first entered the university he actually suffered from want, and Israel Jacobson, the leader of the Reform movement, offered to subsidize his studies if he would become a Reform rabbi. Jost, however, had no desire to join the ranks of Reform. Judaism, he asserted, must be built or reconstructed on the basis of scientific, critical research rather than through arbitrary changes in the order of worship. Later Jost became a teacher at the famous "Philanthropin" school in Frankfort-on-the-Main, a position which he kept until the day of his death in 1860.

Jost's contribution to Jewish learning was in the field of Jewish history. During the period from 1820 to 1828 he published a nine-volume history of the Jews beginning with the ear of the Maccabees and ending with his own day. Even though the work contains a great many inaccuracies and thus is far from perfect, it was widely read and has value for us today in that it was the first Jewish history textbook of its type ever to have been written.

Jost also wrote a work entitled *Geschichte des Judentums und seiner Sekten* (*A History of Judaism and Its Sects*), a three-part volume which was considered to be of great importance in the field of Jewish scholarship. Another one of his writings, titled *Die Geschichte der Juden in der Neuen Zeit* (*The*

History of the Jews in Recent Times) deals with the period from 1815 to 1845, which was part of his own lifetime.

The last of these four scholars, Heinrich Graetz, was born in 1817 in the town of Xion near Posen. He, too, studied both at Yeshivoth and at universities. In his youth Graetz was a fervent believer in Orthodoxy. Later he was to deviate considerably from this point of view, but he never approved of Reform, particularly of the views of Abraham Geiger. Thus Graetz, like his three colleagues, may also be called a Conservative Jew.

Graetz's youth was made difficult by poverty. It was only years later that he joined the faculty of the Rabbinical Seminary of Breslau headed by Zacharias Frankel. In 1869 he became a professor at the University of Breslau, a position he held for the rest of his life. He died in Munich in 1891.

From his very early youth it was Graetz's ambition to write a comprehensive history of the Jewish people. He began this work seriously in 1853 and the first volume was published not too long thereafter. But it was not until he had obtained the position in Breslau that he could devote all his spare time to writing, and it was not until 1871 that the entire work, which comprised eleven volumes, was completed.

Graetz's *History of the Jews* is of great significance. In compiling it, the author utilized every possible source of information that was accessible to him. He consulted not only Jewish literature but non-Jewish writings wherever mention was made of Jews and Judaism. The book is written in a German literary style that is beautiful, almost poetic, and yet so simple that the ordinary reader can easily understand it. Of course the work has weaknesses too. For example, it would appear that Graetz had little understanding of the life of the Jews in Eastern Europe and that he did not know too much about the history and nature of the Hassidic movement. However, there is no question but that Graetz's *History of the Jews* represents a most valuable contribution to Jewish learning.

Of course the era of the science of Judaism produced many other thinkers and teachers. It was a brief period in Jewish history that was confined to Germany and lasted barely a century. But it was a time of phenomenal intellectual creativity and occupies an important place in the history of the Jewish people; it was an era which saw the publication of great works and the beginnings of the Conservative movement in Judaism. It gave Jewry no less than ten philosophers who each formulated their own interpretation of Judaism, some guided by the philosophies of non-Jewish thinkers, and others basing their stand on Jewish thought alone.

23. The Four Philosophers of Reform Judaism

The Teachings of Ludwig Steinheim, Salomon Formstecher, Moritz Lazarus, and Samuel Hirsch—The Idea of a Union of Juadism and Christianity

During the first half of the nineteenth century there evolved within German Jewry three different interpretations of Judaism, each formulating its own doctrine in accordance with systematic logic and reasoning. The first movement thus to become articulate was Liberal, or Reform Judaism which produced several outstanding thinkers and made an important contribution to the field of "The Science of Judaism." The second, which called itself Conservative, was rooted in traditional Judaism, and allowed for only those small changes in worship and ritual practice which seemed absolutely essential in making Jewish tradition acceptable to the modern mind. Finally, there was Neo-Orthodoxy; this was the philosophy (restated in terms of modern thought) of those who remained steadfastly loyal to ancient tradition and refused to accept the admissibility of changes in the practice and interpretation of Judaism.

The eminent thinkers of that period who cast their lot with Reform Judaism were: Ludwig Steinheim, Salomon Formstecher, Samuel Hirsch, and Moritz Lazarus.

Ludwig Steinheim, who was born in 1790 in the city of Bruchhausen, Westphalia, was not a teacher but a physician and practiced in the German city of Altona, near Hamburg. Together with his good friend Gabriel Riesser, he fought in his youth for the equal rights of the Jews of Germany. Steinheim is remembered today for a number of works in which he set forth his personal interpretation of Judaism. His *Gesaenge Obadiahs Ben-Amos aus der Verbannung (Songs of Obadiah Ben-Amos from Exile)* express in poetry Steinheim's own idea of the mission of the people of Israel to spread light and goodness among all the nations of the world. Another work, entitled *Sinai*, is a series of articles dealing with various Jewish problems of his day. Perhaps the most famous of all is the four-volume book entitled *Die Offenbarung nach dem Lehrbegriff der Synagoge (The Revelation According to the Concepts of the Synagogue)* which was published in 1835. It was this book that placed Steinheim in the ranks of the great thinkers of Jewish history. In it he attempted to resolve the conflict that plagued him throughout his life. It seems

464

that Steinheim, though powerfully attracted to Reform Judaism, had had enough training in his early years in Biblical and Talmudic literature to sense that the Reform movement was not the answer to the problem of reinterpreting Judaism to the generations of modern times. It was this conflict that led him to write this work in which he sought to reconcile the two opposing tendencies in his thinking.

Steinheim was an adherent of the view of Immanuel Kant that spiritual concepts, since they are abstract, cannot be scientifically proved, but that it is nevertheless necessary for man to believe that such concepts do exist. For instance, it is good that man should believe that there is a God, that man is endowed with a soul, and also that he has been given by God the ability to make a free choice between right and wrong. To Kant's thesis, Steinheim added a concept of his own, namely, that the Law of the Bible was truly the Teaching of God Himself, which He had desired to make known to all of mankind through the Jewish people to whom He gave it on Mount Sinai. This thought constitutes the basis of all of Steinheim's philosophy of Judaism. This, in brief, represents Steinheim's view:

"Whatever we know we know through our five senses. But we know, too, that our senses may deceive us, and furthermore we are aware of the fact that our five senses cannot perceive things abstract and intangible. In other words, it is only through our power to reason that we can understand the things of the spirit. But we must remember that our reason and intelligence are also not infallible. Therefore, we must turn to belief as it is not only good for us but is also quite compatible with reason. Why, then, should we not believe not only that there exists a God, but also that this God revealed Himself to man so that man might learn His ways?"

This revelation, Steinheim continued, took place on Mount Sinai in the form of the Ten Commandments and the other laws of the Bible which were given there to Moses. True, it cannot be proved that this miraculous event actually took place, but it is not by any means incompatible with reason to believe that it did. Thus we can perceive this abstract truth with our reason in quite the same manner as we employ our physical senses to perceive tangible phenomena.

But despite his intense loyalty to Judaism and his apparent belief in its tradition, Steinheim spent most of his days far away from Jewish communities and often sided with the adherents of radical reform. When he died in Zurich in 1866, he was buried not among his fellow Jews but in a Christian cemetery.

Like Steinheim, Salomon Formstecher, who was born in Offenbach, Germany, in 1809 and occupied the rabbinate of the reform temple there for a period of forty-seven years until his death in 1889, had also received a thorough grounding in both Jewish lore and the secular sciences.

Unlike Steinheim, however, Formstecher was very active in the practical work of the Reform movement and attended nearly every conference called by its leaders. His most important work, *Religion des Geistes* (*Religion of the Spirit*), which was published in Frankfort in 1841, is a statement of his own interpretation of Judaism. Formstecher based much of his philosophy of Judaism on the philosophy of Friedrich Wilhelm Joseph von Schelling, the German thinker who had been a close friend of Hegel's. Schelling asserted that the world and nature were designed and still existed in accordance with a higher plan, and that nothing in this world happened without a reason, even if we sometimes fail to understand it. Formstecher elaborated upon this theory in terms of Judaism. He stated that it was the purpose of religion to teach man to perceive and know more about the Divine Spirit which was manifest in that plan according to which the world exists. Judaism had been a religion that was designed to fulfill this function. This was true at the very beginning when Judaism fought against idolatry and proclaimed the supreme sovereignty of universal truth and justice. It was still true when Israel first went into exile and spread among the nations the ideals which Judaism had been intended to advance. But through the centuries of persecution which its adherents suffered in the ghettos of the alien nations, Judaism eventually stagnated, as it were, and the kernel of truth that it contained was not brought to full fruition. Now that the yoke of persecution had been lifted from the Jews, however, Formstecher felt that Judaism had more of an opportunity to make progress in its search for truth and to fulfill its mission of creating a better world for all mankind which would culminate in the Messianic era of universal peace and prosperity.

The daughter religions of Judaism, Christianity and Mohammedanism, derived their continued ability to exist from the fact that they contained in their make-up the basic truth of Judaism. Mohammedanism, Formstecher asserted, adopted certain elements of Judaism and incorporated them into Islam in substitution for the ancient Oriental forms of idolatry. Christianity attempted to combine some of the features of paganism with the monotheistic characteristics of Judaism, and thus early Christianity had a constant conflict between two ideologies which by virtue of their very nature were irreconcilable. Christianity had to be "reformed" by Protestantism to eliminate from it the elements of idolatry which Christianity had retained. And just as the Christian religion had to be cleansed of the undesirable features that had remained with it through the centuries, so too, Formstecher believed, Judaism was in need of reforms which would remove from it the accretions that had come to surround it as the years went by. Hence Judaism would once more be free to develop and make progress in its quest for truth and for a better world. Thus did Formstecher conceive of the role to be played by Reform Judaism.

Moritz Lazarus was born in 1824 in the province of Posen, Germany. His father, Rabbi Aaron Levin Lazarus, took great pride in the fact that he,

Aaron, had been a student of the great Rabbi Akiba Eiger, the giant intellect and champion of uncompromising Orthodoxy and spiritual leader of the Jewish community of Lissa, Posen. At first young Moritz was taught the rudiments of Biblical and Talmudic literature in the old Heder. When he was twenty years old, he entered the gymnasium in Brunswick. The ordinary age for entrance to the European gymnasium was ten, and the student was eighteen years of age by the time he was graduated, but Lazarus quickly made up the time he had lost, managing to complete the eight-year course in two years. He then entered the University of Berlin where he studied philosophy, psychology, and history. Subsequent to his graduation from the university as a doctor of philosophy, he married. After the death of his first wife, he wed a writer who had originally been a Christian, but had converted to Judaism and adopted the name of Nahida Ruth Naomi.

Moritz Lazarus devoted most of his intellectual energies to the creation of a new branch of psychology. He published a book called *The Psychology of Nations,* which is an inquiry into the psychology of national entities as such. His valued collaborator in this new field was his brother-in-law, Dr. Heymann Steinthal. Unfortunately the two scholars did not find much support for their views. In fact, many maintained that there could be no such thing as a "psychology of nations," since nations consisted of individuals, and the individuals were simply human beings and basically all were alike regardless of differences in nationality.

In addition to *The Psychology of Nations,* Lazarus wrote several important works which dealt specifically with Judaism. In his *The Ethics of Judaism,* of which only the first volume was published during his lifetime (the second did not appear until 1911, eight years after his death), he formulated his own theory with regard to the function of Jewish thought. There he declared that the teachings of Judaism had profound moral significance and he cited many selections from Talmudic literature and other Jewish sources in proof of his thesis. Many of Lazarus' own views in this connection were based on the teachings of Immanuel Kant, the non-Jewish philosopher, but Lazarus constantly emphasized that the ethical and moral teachings of Judaism were far superior to those of any other philosophy.

Lazarus asserted that the separate identity of the Jew was based not on race or nationality, but solely on religion. In keeping with his theory of "the psychology of nations," he believed that groups gradually acquired certain psychological characteristics through years of living together in national communities. Lazarus explained that the Jews, too, had acquired the psychological make-up of the nations among whom they happened to live. For instance, the Jews living in Germany, though they differed from their fellow citizens with regard to religion, were actually Germans, rather than Jews, in mind and spirit.

From 1868 to 1872 Lazarus served on the faculty of the University of Cologne. During that period he was quite active in Jewish communal life and held high office in various Jewish organizations and institutions. He was well known for his skill in the art of lecturing and oratory. He died in Merano, Tyrol, in 1903, at the age of seventy-nine.

Samuel Hirsch, the fourth philosopher of Reform, was born in Thalfang, Prussia, in 1815. After having completed his Jewish studies, Hirsch left his home and acquired his secular education at the universities of Bonn, Berlin, and Leipzig. In 1838 he was appointed rabbi of the Jewish community of Dessau but was soon forced to resign because he had adopted the principles of Reform Judaism. It was only in 1843, after the King of Holland had appointed him chief rabbi of the Principality of Luxembourg (which then was part of the Kingdom of the Netherlands) that Hirsch could embark openly upon a career in Reform Judaism.

In 1886 Hirsch accepted a call from America to become the rabbi of Temple Kneseth Israel in Philadelphia. There he introduced the holding of Sabbath services on Sundays instead of on Saturdays and other radical departures from traditional practice.

In addition to many other less important works, Hirsch wrote two books which should not be glossed over in a history of Jewish thought, namely, *Religionsphilosophie der Juden* (*The Religious Philosophy of the Jews*), which was published in 1842, and *Die Messiaslehre der Juden* (*The Messianic Doctrine of the Jews*), which appeared in 1843.

Dr. Hirsch was an adherent of Hegel's dialectic theory even as Nachman Krochmal had been about a generation before. As we have said in a previous chapter, Hegel had applied his so-called "dialectic theory" to religion, stating that Christianity, being the synthesis of idolatry and monotheism, represented the highest form of religion. Krochmal adopted Hegel's way of thinking in its entirety, except for the fact that he substituted "Judaism" for "Christianity." Hirsch, although employing the Hegelian form of "dialectics," differed with both Hegel and Krochmal in its application. According to Hirsch, the antithesis to idolatry was not monotheism, but Christianity. Jesus, Hirsch explained, sought to abolish idolatry by spreading the ideals of Judaism throughout the world. The concepts that Jesus had preached, Hirsch asserted, had not been in conflict with the spirit of Judaism at all. The "kingdom of God," of which he spoke, was a Jewish ideal. When he called himself a "son of God," Jesus had in no manner intended to claim special status for himself. He merely meant to imply that all the children of Israel were "sons of God" for the Talmud itself contained a statement to the effect that "ye are the children of God" and that he, Jesus, was a pioneer in the endeavor to break the idols of paganism and to bring about the speedy advent of the kingdom of God on earth. This, Hirsch pointed out, was the line of thought followed by the Gospel of St. Matthew. St. Paul, however, had given a literal interpretation to Jesus' statement and explained that Jesus had literally been the begotten son of God.

This was the basis of Catholicism. In his opinion, Protestantism represented some kind of return on the part of Christianity to the original Judeo-Christian tradition. Hence, Hirsch felt that the synthesis was neither Christianity (which to him represented the antithesis of idolatry) nor Judaism, but a union of Judaism and Protestantism, together advancing the coming of the kingdom of God. And yet Hirsch did not feel that Judaism should cease existing forthwith or even that the Jews should entirely discard their hope for an eventual return to Zion; he felt that the Jews had to retain their separate identity for the time being so that they could exert the greatest possible influence in behalf of the coming of the kingdom of God which was an ideal that was purely Jewish.

Hirsch died in Chicago in the year 1889.

While these philosophers of Reform Judaism propounded their theories, there were other movements in Judaism as well. Orthodoxy, which for a long time had refused to fight for its views with modern weapons, finally became articulate and made use of modern thought and reasoning in its endeavor to preserve the ancient traditions of Judaism. On the other extreme there were those who had little hope for the future of Judaism altogether and therefore abandoned it entirely.

24. Neo-Orthodoxy and Apostasy

Neo-Orthodoxy: Heymann Steinthal and Samson Raphael Hirsch—"The Nineteen Letters"—Three Apostates: Börne, Heine, and Marx

While many Jewish thinkers of the nineteenth century sought to reshape Judaism so as to render it more compatible, as they felt, with modern thought, the uncompromising adherents of tradition also began to muster their forces to give effective voice to their interpretation of Judaism. It was obvious to them that if they were to perpetuate Jewish tradition, they would have to restate these ideals in the language of the present day and establish some sort of strong organization to serve as the rallying point around which they could gather. We shall now study in some detail the lives of two of the most famous early expounders of what came to be called Neo-Orthodoxy, Heymann Steinthal and Samson Raphael Hirsch.

Steinthal was born in 1823 in the Province of Anhalt in Germany. He had strayed far from Orthodoxy in his younger days. After he had completed his Jewish studies, he went on to study philosophy and languages at the University of Berlin where he later became a professor of philosophy. It was then that he collaborated with his brother-in-law Moritz Lazarus on the development of the latter's theory of "the psychology of nations." Steinthal also delivered lectures on Biblical literature at the Lehranstalt für die Wissenschaft des Judentums (Institute for the Science of Judaism) which he had helped found in Berlin.

In those days Steinthal seems to have favored Reform Judaism, and many of his former students, such as Rabbi Emil G. Hirsch (who was to occupy a major pulpit in Chicago) actually became eminent Reform rabbis. In his book *Ueber Juden und Judentum* (*On Jews and Judaism*) which was printed in three editions, Steinthal asserted that if Judaism was to survive, the mold that it had accumulated on its structure through the ages would have to be removed and radical changes in Jewish thought and practice were urgently needed if the Jewish religion were to endure and grow.

In later years, however, there seems to have been a profound change in Steinthal's attitude toward Judaism; in a small brochure which he published shortly before his death, he wrote as follows: "The basis of the Jewish religion is the prayer, 'Our God and God of our fathers.' Religion is not valid only for a specific period of time; it is a force that becomes stronger with each new generation. Those who raise their children in the spirit of Reform

Judaism actually give their children no religion at all, and it would be better if they would teach their young some other religion rather than let them grope without any faith whatsoever. Religious training is fundamental to Judaism and no Jew has the right to deny it to his children."

As regards the desire of the Reform leaders for changes in prayer and liturgy, Steinthal wrote, "It is quite true that, we, too, could compose prayers and liturgical poems of our own and they might well be even more beautiful than the ones we already have in our Holy Day prayer book. But they will never be accepted by the people of Israel, because they do not bear the stamp of tradition. The language of our prayers must not be any other than Hebrew, our holy tongue in which our fathers, grandfathers, and great-grandfathers poured out their hearts to their God. We must remember that we were not born yesterday; we are the bearers of an ancient, historic tradition."

Steinthal died in Berlin in 1899, at the age of seventy-eight.

The position of practial leadership in the Neo-orthodox movement was held by a man quite different from Steinthal, a great rabbi, scholar, and philosopher, Samson Raphael Hirsch, who was born in Hamburg in 1808.

Hirsch, a grandson of Rabbi Mendel Frankfurter, a well known rabbi in Altona, was a student of Rabbi Isaac Bernays, of Hamburg, an uncompromising adherent of Orthodoxy. It was Bernays who taught young Hirsch the art of homiletics and who was the great influence that dominated the course Hirsch was to follow throughout his life. In 1825 Hirsch studied at the famous Yeshiva of Rabbi Jacob Ettinger in Altona. Thereafter he took up philosophy at the University of Bonn. It was there that he met Abraham Geiger, and the two young men were fast friends until Geiger became an outspoken advocate of Reform and he and Hirsch thus came to a parting of the ways.

Hirsch's first pulpit was the district of Oldenburg. There he took into his home Heinrich Graetz, the historian, who, then a very young man, was an ardent admirer of Hirsch and begged to be accepted as his student. Graetz stayed with Hirsch for about three years. Later Graetz was to hold views quite different from those championed by his former mentor, but in those early days the youthful Graetz felt a devotion for Hirsch akin to hero-worship.

In 1841 Hirsch left Oldenburg to become chief rabbi of the district of Baden. There he remained until 1846, when he was called to Nikolsburg, Moravia, to serve as chief rabbi of the province. In 1851 he returned to Germany. This time the call came from Frankfort-on-the-Main. His new flock was a small group of strictly orthodox Jews who did not feel at home in any of the synagogues already existing in Frankfort and had banded together to form a congregation of their own which they called *Israelitische Religionsgesellschaft* (Jewish Religious Society). Headed by the forceful personality of the new spiritual leader, this little group grew apace and soon numbered over five hundred members, including some of the wealthiest Jews of the city.

Hirsch's views were extreme and he became a controversial figure even in the ranks of Orthodoxy because of his refusal to allow his congregation to collaborate in any endeavor with other segments of the Jewish community, on the grounds that they were not sufficiently orthodox.

Samson Raphael Hirsch's first work was *The Nineteen Letters of Ben Uziel,* which was published in 1836. Written in the form of an exchange of letters between a young rabbi named Naphtali and his friend Benjamin, a young student who had become estranged from Judaism, *The Nineteen Letters* is a forceful statement of Hirsch's philosophy of Judaism; it is a beautiful piece of literature which won Hirsch the respect of even those who opposed his views.

To Hirsch the Jewish people was not a nation like all the other nations but a "religious nation," a nation founded upon the basis of religion, and not dependent for existence upon any one territory. It was to demonstrate this truth that the Torah was given to Israel not in Palestine but in the no man's land of the wilderness. Hence, when the Jews lost their political independence and went into exile, Judaism did not cease to exist. Instead, the Jews were to view exile as an opportunity to spread their ideals throughout the world. Eventually, in God's own time, the Messiah would come and return the people of Israel to their ancient homeland, and all the world would come to recognize and worship the Lord as the One Supreme Ruler of the Universe.

Man, Hirsch explained, had been endowed by God with the ability to choose between right and wrong, and it was the task of men to live and behave in accordance with the will of God so that His Name might eventually be recognized and acknowledged throughout the world. But because no one individual could be expected to be strong enough to fight alone against evil, there had to be introduced among men a model community which, standing apart from the rest of mankind, would show the world the proper way to God. To preserve its separate identity and character, this community would have to abide by certain special laws and would have to regard the fulfillment of God's will as its *raison d'être*. This is the role that was handed to the Jewish people, and the laws that set Israel apart from the rest of mankind were contained in the Torah and in the Oral Tradition set down in the Talmud. Since, then, the very existence of the people of Israel has been dependent upon its fulfillment of God's will by observing His Torah any Jew who either did not believe in the Torah at all or who attempted to introduce changes in the Jewish religion automatically placed himself outside the pale of Judaism.

Hirsch further expounded this philosophy in a series of essays entitled *Horeb,* and in the periodical *Yeshurun,* which he inaugurated in 1854.

In 1876 Hirsch obtained governmental recognition of his Orthodox congregation and school as a separate Jewish organization, independent in every respect from the rest of the Jewish community of Frankfort. Many other Orthodox congregations in Germany and elsewhere followed the example of Frankfort, so that many large cities actually had two Jewish communities, each recognized by the secular authorities as representative of its followers, the "greater" Jewish community on the one hand and the "independent" or "secessionist" Orthodox community on the other. However, there were many Orthodox rabbis who disagreed with this policy. They felt that it was unwise for Orthodoxy to secede from the existing Jewish communities and permitted their congregations to work together with the other elements in the Jewish community for purposes of common welfare.

During the last twelve years of his life, Hirsch wrote commentaries to the Pentateuch, the Book of Psalms and the *Ethics of the Fathers* which are considered classic, particularly by Western European Jewry. His notes to the Jewish prayer book were published after his death.

Hirsch died in Frankfort-on-the-Main in 1888 at the age of eighty. His views were perpetuated by other Orthodox leaders, particularly his grandson Isaac Breuer (1883-1946).

On the opposite end of the Jewish spectrum in Germany we find the extreme of assimilation which dissociated itself entirely from Judaism and whose adherents often resorted to baptism to make the final break with the religion of their fathers. Many of the members of the Jewish intelligentsia in Western Europe took pride in maintaining close associations with gentiles. They clustered around the salons or "drawing rooms" of Jewish social leaders such as Henriette Hertz, Dorothea Mendelssohn and Rachel Levin, where they had the opportunity of meeting the elite of gentile society. These close associations often led to intermarriage and, in many cases, to the baptism of Jewish individuals who had become alienated from their own tradition and had been searching for a way of ridding themselves of what was to them an irksome burden. Among the Jewish intellectuals who took this final step were Ludwig Börne, the essayist, Heinrich Heine, the poet, and Karl Marx, the father of modern socialism. Marx had been baptized by his father as a child.

Ludwig Börne, the noted satirist and essayist, was born in Frankfort-on-the-Main in 1786, of Orthodox parents. His father, who was well versed in Jewish law, saw to it that his son received a thorough Jewish education; he first taught him himself and later sent him away to a Yeshiva. Thereafter young Börne studied medicine and jurisprudence. In 1811 his father managed to secure for him a position with the municipal government of Frankfort. In 1815, however, the young man moved to Berlin, where he was drawn into the circle that gathered with regularity in the drawing room of Henriette Hertz. He quickly came under the spell of the spirit that prevailed in these assimilationist quarters and, in 1818, he underwent baptism. It was an act which Börne was to repent for the rest of his days and which he himself referred to as "an act of folly." He was never accepted as a full-fledged German by the gentile friends whom he had sought to impress. In 1830 he left Germany for good and settled in Paris, where he wrote sharp, acrimonious letters filled with harsh criticism of Germans. He often touched upon the Jewish problem in his writings and defended his erstwhile coreligionists, but he himself never returned to the fold of Judaism. He died in Paris in 1837.

Heinrich Heine, the second of this group of apostates, was born in Düsseldorf in 1799. Unlike Börne, Heine had received little Jewish education and completed his secular studies in a gymnasium run by a Christian order. During his frequent visits to Hamburg, where he had many relatives, Heine first came to know something of the conflict between Orthodox Judaism and the new Reform movement. Though Heine himself could hardly have been called an observant Jew, he had little liking for Reform Judaism which he viewed as nothing more than a feeble attempt on the part of the Jews to imitate Christianity. He found that he could much more readily respect the old-fashioned type of Jew, even though that way of life, too, was completely foreign to him. On a trip to Posen, Heine for the first time met one such Jew. Of this encounter he wrote to a friend that the old-fashioned Eastern European Jew, with all his outlandish garb and strange ideas appealed to him much more than the frock-coated, top-hatted Western Jew with his muddled-up thinking.

Heine called the Reform Jews "people who had been trained by actors, who seek to redecorate the old firm of Judaism with new, foreign trimmings by turning it into an abridged form of Protestantism behind a Jewish signboard. But an enterprise such as this will not last long. The bills of exchange which they will draw upon their philosophy will be irredeemable and it all will end in bankruptcy."

Heine studied law in Göttingen but found that he could not teach jurisprudence or even practice law unless he underwent the formality of baptism. He found, too, that he could never get far even in the field of literature as a Jew. In the end, with a heavy heart, he went to a clergyman and officially adopted Christianity. But he never could become reconciled to the decision which he had forced himself to make after so great a struggle within his soul.

Shortly after his baptism, Heine wrote to a friend, "If it were legal to steal silver spoons, I would never have let myself be baptized." Unfortunately, baptism did not bring Heine the professional advancement for which he had hoped, and he continued to live in dire want. But he did gain great popularity as a poet and many even compared him to the great Goethe, Germany's favorite poet.

During the latter years of his life Heine's remorse over his act of apostasy deepened. But though he felt a genuine sympathy for the Jewish people, he attempted neither to find an answer to the Jewish problem nor to become better acquainted with the culture and tradition of Judaism.

He died in Paris in the year 1856.

Karl Marx, the third of this group, who could trace his descent directly to Rashi, the author of the famous commentary on the Pentateuch, was born in 1818 in the city of Trier, Germany. His father, a lawyer, had had himself baptized and also put his entire family through this formality. Young Marx studied philosophy at the University of Bonn and planned to become a professor. Soon, however, he was diverted from his original plan by his increasing interest in the problems of capital and labor. He went down in history as the founder of modern socialism.

Marx was at best indifferent to Judaism. In two articles entitled *Zu der Judenfrage* ("On the Jewish Problem") which were published in a Cologne newspaper he expressed a dislike for Jews, and he actually went so far as to state in another article in a German-French annual that "the God of the Jews is money."

In view of what we have just read, we can hardly apply the term "Jewish thinker" to any of these three apostates. Yet it is important that they be mentioned here, since their lives will help the student to gain a better understanding of the period in Jewish history that produced them.

25. The Three Great Philosophers of Jewish Ethics

The Doctrine of Hermann Cohen, and His Books on the Ethics of Judaism—Franz Rosenzweig and His New Teaching About Judaism—Henri Bergson, Who Had Praise for Christianity but Proudly Wore the Yellow Badge During the Nazi Regime

The nineteenth century was a period of much fruitful activity in Jewish thought and learning. In previous chapters we have discussed the new trends in Jewish religious philosophy and studied, in brief, the views of those who sought to reinterpret Judaism as a religion in terms of the present day. In addition to the expounders of Reform, Conservatism and Neo-orthodoxy, there were also those thinkers who belonged to none of these categories but instead sought to give Judaism an interpretation of their own that was a blend of Jewish nationalism and mysticism. We shall now talk of three such philosophers, each of whom regarded Judaism from the moral and ethical standpoint, rather than from the strictly religious point of view. These were Hermann Cohen and Franz Rosenzweig, who both lived in Germany, and Henri Bergson, who was French. All three regarded Judaism first and foremost as an ethical teaching.

Hermann Cohen was born in 1842 in the town of Coswig, Germany. After being graduated from the gymnasium at Dessau, he studied at the Jewish Theological Seminary in Breslau and at the university in that city, in Berlin and in Halle. In 1873 he became an instructor at the University of Marburg where he eventually attained the rank of full professor. He retired from that position only in 1912, six years before his death. For some years prior to his resignation from the chair at Marburg, he served as a part-time lecturer at the Institute for the Science of Judaism in Berlin.

Hermann Cohen is regarded as the father of what is known as the "Neo-Kantian" philosophy. However, his views of the world are the same as those of Immanuel Kant; when it came to morals and ethics, he replaced the doctrine of Kant with the great teachings set forth by the prophets of Judaism.

Cohen wrote three major works, *Logik der Reinen Erkenntnis* (*The Logic of Pure Perception*), *Ethik des Reinen Willens* (*The Ethics of the Pure Will*), and *Aesthetik des Reinen Gefuehles* (*The Esthetics of Pure Emotion*), in which he expounded his philosophy. As regards purely Jewish thought, he

476

published *Ein Bekenntnis in der Judenfrage* (*A Confession of the Jewish Problem*) (1880); *Die Naechsten-Liebe in Talmud* (*Love for One's Fellow Men in the Talmud*) (1888) and a considerable number of articles.

As we have already said, all of Cohen's philosophy is founded on that of the German thinker Immanuel Kant which, basically speaking, is a system of theological ethics. It is the ethical teachings which Kant set forth in *Kritik der Reinen Vernunft* (*Critique of Pure Reason*) that Cohen regards as the most important part of the entire structure of Kantian philosophy and at this point he brings in Judaism. He stresses the words of the prophets who preached the lofty ideals of righteousness and humanity and gave the Jew a hope for a better world, an era of universal peace and justice. Cohen understood this yearning for a messianic age of world-wide peace and righteousness to be rooted in the Jewish concept of God as an eternally righteous judge who is the final resort of appeal wherever victims of human injustice put forth their claim for a fair hearing. Cohen has a much deeper understanding of the Messianic concept than had either the reformers or the conservatives of his day; he regards it as a symbol of the hope for the entire Jewish people for a time when justice will reign supreme. And he sees the ideal of eternal righteousness as the great mysterious force which pervades the Jewish people and has sustained it during all the ages of exile.

This trend of thought led Cohen to regard Judaism as the world's greatest and most powerful moral force for the good, and he came to feel closer to Judaism than he had ever felt before. He became a fervent believer in Judaism which he now viewed as the word of God Himself to mankind.

Judaism, however, could have been given only to a people chosen by God for this purpose, for to Cohen no ordinary people could have been capable of creating such lofty ideals as those held by the nation of Israel. Thus Cohen viewed the Jewish people as a nation with its own character and nature, a separate national entity which had been chosen to act as the bearer of the ideals of Judaism.

Cohen died in Berlin in 1918, at the age of seventy-six.

Franz Rosenzweig, a disciple of Cohen's, was born in 1886 in Cassel, Germany, the son of a wealthy, assimilated family. He spent years of study, first at the gymnasium and then at various universities, but his parents never attempted to give him a Jewish education. In fact, at a certain period of his youth, Rosenzweig was ready to give up Judaism and embrace Christianity. Since he was a thinker by nature, he felt that before leaving Judaism he should at least make a careful study of what it was that he was about to give up. When he looked more deeply into his Jewish heritage, he realized that it was pervaded with lofty ideals of justice and righteousness that were worthy of further study. Hence he traveled to Berlin to listen to the lectures of

Hermann Cohen at the Institute for the Science of Judaism. Soon teacher and pupil became close friends.

When the First World War broke out, Rosenzweig was drafted into the German army and sent to the Balkan battlefront. There, while crouched in the trenches, he began to write his great work entitled *Der Stern der Erloesung* (*The Star of Redemption*). He wrote his draft on army postal cards, which he sent home to his wife with instructions to save them until the time of his return. After his discharge from the army at the end of the war, Rosenzweig began a campaign for the Jewish training of the young. Together with like-minded friends, he set up the Freie Juedische Lehrhaus (The Free Jewish House of Study), where young people from assimilated homes might receive the Jewish training they had missed in their childhood. Rosenzweig had a profound influence upon the younger generation of German Jewry.

In 1922, when he was only thirty-six years of age, Rosenzweig noticed the first symptoms of the disease that was to kill him seven years later. It was a progressive paralysis which, toward the end of his life, left him without the power of speech and entirely motionless. Yet even during the years of his terrible illness he was able to do a great deal of writing, and collaborated with Professor Martin Buber on a new German translation of the Bible. His devoted wife Edith served as his secretary. When Rosenzweig was no longer able to speak, she devised an ingenious method by which he could communicate his thoughts to her, letter by letter, without either motion or speech. It was tedious, heartbreaking labor. After his death in 1929 his wife, with the help of some faithful friends, published the works which Rosenzweig had written during the last years of his life.

In his *Star of Redemption* Rosenzweig developed his own thoughts on Judaism, which are very much akin to "existentialism," the theory that was then the vogue in many European countries and proposed a new interpretation of the concepts of God, the world, and man. The ancient philosophers had said that the world had given rise to man and man in turn had created for himself the concept of God. The theologians and mystics of a later period ascribed both the world and man to God's creation, while the modern school of philosophy attributed both the world and God Himself to the genius of man. Rosenzweig could agree with none of these three views.

Rosenzweig felt that it was not important to determine what had originally given rise to what. What was important was that which existed now, at present. Thus the part of Judaism as such was not the most important element in the life of the Jew; it was mainly the form of Jewish life that was significant to present-day Jewry.

Rosenzweig considered as particularly significant the fact that the Jewish people had managed to survive through the ages without the attributes of political independence. He pointed out that, actually, Israel did not become a nation in its homeland of Canaan, but in Egypt and in the wilderness. Moreover, it was obvious that even during the centuries of their political independence in Palestine, the Jews had never been overly attached to their homeland; there had been a good deal of emigration even during the days of the Temple. Searching for an answer to what it was that kept the Jewish people alive through the ages, Rosenzweig came to attribute the survival of Israel to its nearness to God, which it never forfeited. In fact, the Jews had always regarded even the features of political autonomy, such as land and language, differently from the way they were viewed by other nations. To the Jews, their country had always been a "holy land" and their language the "holy tongue," and hence the Jews had always thought of themselves as a "holy nation" under special obligation to lead a life of holiness in accordance with the will of God. For this reason no other country could take the place of Palestine in the heart of the Jew, and no language could replace Hebrew as the sacred tongue of Israel. Thus Israel was an eternal nation. Rosenzweig did not consider it necessary for a Messiah or a Messianic era to arrive before the Jews could return to their ancient homeland; rather, it was his fervent hope that some time soon the Jewish people would go back to their own holy land, restore the holy tongue as the vehicle of every-day communication, and thus return to their roots as a holy nation which would endure forever.

Henri Bergson, the third and last of the three moral thinkers, was born in Paris in 1859 of a well known family which had originally come from Warsaw. Bergson was educated in France and received his degree from the University of Paris. When he was still quite young, he was appointed lecturer at the College de France where he later became a full professor and taught until 1921. He was the recipient of numerous academic honors, including membership in the French Academy.

When he was only thirty years old, Bergson published his first famous work, in his mother tongue, entitled *Time and Free Will*. In another book, *Creative Evolution,* he attempted to prove that time was the basic element of reality since man's existence was a constant process of evolution and change, and hence free will could not be regarded as a definite concept.

According to Bergson, reason alone cannot help man find his place in the world. For this purpose man requires, and does have, a mysterious force which Bergson calls *élan vital,* the impulse of life that acts as a "compass" to help man get his bearings and do the right thing as he plots his course through life. Thus Bergson entered into the realm of mysticism. He actually stated that man must use every possible means, including metaphysics and mysticism, to arrive at the absolute truth for which he has searched through the ages.

In *Two Sources of Morals and Religion* (published in French in 1933) Bergson goes one step further. Here he actually rates mysticism as more important than pure reasoning, and asserts that mysticism is the guide of the philosopher in his search for truth. There are two different moral teachings, one "hidden" and one "revealed," and two different concepts of religion, one "static" and one "dynamic." The hidden moral teaching serves as a guide, exerting much the same influence on the human soul as does magnetism on the physical world. The revealed ethical teaching, on the other hand, is derived from the doctrine and activities of a great genius. Placing the hidden moral teachings above the revealed doctrine, and associating Christianity with the former, Bergson comes to place Christianity above Judaism. In the end, however, Bergson acknowledges that the high ethical values contained in Christianity, a faith combining elements of paganism and Judaism, were all derived from the Jewish elements that had been taken over into Christian ideology. Thus, in the final analysis, Bergson is compelled to admit that it was Judaism that had first preached the lofty moral ideals which he had associated with Christianity.

Throughout the years Bergson never became a traitor to his people. When the Nazis marched into Paris, Bergson, who was then past eighty and quite ill, went to the German authorities and told them that he was a Jew. Even though the Nazis were willing to make an exception in his case, he insisted upon wearing the yellow badge which all the other Jews of Nazi-occupied France had to put on.

Bergson died in Paris in 1941. The immediate cause of death was pneumonia. He was buried in a Jewish cemetery.

Cohen, Rosenzweig, and Bergson, though poles apart as regards details, all essentially regarded Judaism from the same point of view. The looked upon it as a great ethical teaching rather than as a religion in the limited sense of the word. Moreover, the thinking of all three carries an undercurrent of Jewish nationalism, the hope that the Jewish people would return to Palestine within the foreseeable future and resume a wholesome, fruitful life in their own homeland.

26. Moses Hess and His "Rome and Jerusalem"

Hess's New Ideas About Labor—Hess and Karl Marx—Hess's Ideas About the Jews as a Nation—A New Jewish Philosophy

From the midst of all the intellectual and ideological torment that was rife among nineteenth century German Jewry, there now came a new voice, really two in one: one spoke solely to the Jewish people, and the other to every victim of oppression regardless of religion, particularly to the workingman who was then totally at the mercy of his employer. The voice was that of Moses Hess, the tenth of the outstanding Jewish thinkers of recent times.

Moses Hess was not content to spend his days searching into the history of his people or writing on the philosophy of Judaism. If he did study Israel's past, it was solely for the purpose of deriving from it important lessons for the future. His views on the Jewish future were quite clear. He felt that there was only one way in which Judaism and the Jewish people could survive in the modern age, now that the physical walls of the ghetto had tumbled down. The people of Israel had to be a nation like other nations, if it was to endure, and the only manner in which this could be done was for the Jewish people to return to its ancient homeland in Palestine and to resume their existence as a nation with a country of its own.

At the same time Hess was also keenly interested in the lot of all the other groups that suffered from oppression. What concerned him most was the situation of the workingman, whose sole means of salvation, he felt, was to begin an active fight against the employers who sought to exploit him. Thus Moses Hess became one of the pioneers not only of modern Jewish nationalism, but of modern socialism as well.

Moses Hess was born in the city of Bonn, Germany, in 1812. His father, a wealthy industrialist, named him Moritz, but in later years young Moritz Judaized his name to demonstrate his love for his people. (In fact, in his later writings, Hess expressed regret that his first name had not been one that was more popular among the masses of the proud Jewish communities of Eastern Europe.) When he was nine years old, Moses was sent to live with his grandfather, who, though he did not actively engage in the rabbinate, was a man of profound Jewish learning and was to have no little influence on the future of his young grandson.

At the age of eighteen, Hess enrolled at the University of **Bonn**, but he was never graduated because his interests lay elsewhere. For quite some time he had been aware of the appalling situation of the workingman as compared to the inordinate wealth of the manufacturer. It was obvious to him that the laborer, who had so important a share in the production of the world's wealth, certainly deserved a greater share of the profits than he had hitherto been given. In order to become better acquainted with the everyday life of the plain workingman, Hess went to England, where he lived among the working people for some time. In 1840 he moved to Paris. His father had often sent him letters requesting that he come home and assume his place in the family business, but Hess refused. He felt that his father was no better than all the other manufacturers who lived in plenty from the sweat of the workman's brow, and therefore refused to have any part of his father's offer. He was then busily engaged in literary endeavors, but this brought him little in the way of financial compensation. His father then told him that he had no intention of supporting a son whom he believed was dodging his responsibilities. His mother, however, secretly sent him a small amount of money each month so that he would not have to look for employment.

One time, however, his mother was ill and could not sent him the monthly allowance on which he was completely dependent. Hess had no food for two days and desolately wandered through the streets of Paris. As he aimlessly ambled through the city, he was accosted by a prostitute; he told her that he had no money and, in fact, had gone hungry for two days. Surprised, the woman invited him to her home and gave him bread, butter, cheese, and milk. While Hess was eagerly devouring the simple food she had set before him, his hostess told him something of her own life story. It turned out that she had come from a good home, the daughter of wealthy parents, whom she had left because they had been frantically religious.

When Hess was about to leave, the woman, whose name was Sybil Fritsch, pressed her own last two francs into his hand, and though he protested, she insisted that he take the money and promise her that he would return whenever he was in need of food or funds.

Hess was greatly impressed by the generosity of the young woman. Soon he had fallen in love with her and took on work as a plain laborer so that he might be able to marry Sybil and provide for her. This marriage was a most happy one, and endured until Sybil's death.

When his parents heard of their son's marriage, they cut him off without a penny and refused to have anything to do with him.

Moses Hess was not just a philosopher, or a thinker; he was a man of vision who foresaw the emergence of both socialism and Zionism long before either movement actually came into being. He was the teacher of Karl Marx, who was to perfect the structure of modern socialism. At the same time, he was the first to proclaim that the Jews and Judaism could survive only if the Jews would rebuild their ancient homeland in Palestine and make it the spiritual center of all Jewry as it had been in days long ago. In this he was the spiritual guide for such men of vision as Leon Pinsker and Theodor Herzl.

Hess's first book was entitled *Die Heilige Geschichte der Menschheit von Einem Jungen Spinozist* (*The Holy History of Mankind by a Youthful Adherent of Spinoza*). Actually, Hess had been influenced not so much by Baruch Spinoza as by Hegel, the thinker upon whose philosophy the Communists and other totalitarian movements based their ideologies. At that time, Hess was rather active in some of the radical movements that had formed in Paris. He met Friedrich Engels and Karl Marx and made a profound impression upon both of them. Later, he collaborated with Marx on a book entitled *Die Deutsche Ideologie* (*The German Ideology*), which was published in 1845. By this time, Hess was no longer a laborer, but was earning his living as the Paris correspondent of the *Rheinische Zeitung,* a well known German newspaper. He frequently visited Germany, attempting to spread the ideals of socialism there. After the revolution of 1848, however, a reaction set in in Germany and Hess was sentenced to death *in absentia* for having attempted to sow the seeds of radicalism in that country. Thus Hess had to avoid Germany. He traveled extensively throughout Europe, but finally returned to Paris, where he made his permanent home with his devoted wife.

Hess was now frequently asked to participate in meetings held by workingmen and intellectual circles. At one such meeting, when asked about the importance of philosophy to mankind, Hess replied simply:

"Any philosophy has value only to the extent that it brings happiness to mankind. Everyone in this world must be given the opportunity to achieve that end. The means for attaining universal happiness are brotherhood, freedom, and equality. The wealth of society must belong to the state, which means that it will then belong to all in equal measure, and everyone must have a share in controlling it." Here, of course, Hess meant that the power of control should be in the hands of the state.

Actually, it was Hess's intense concern for the welfare of the laboring classes that first led him to take an interest in the lot of his own oppressed people.

The solution to assimilation as offered by the Reform movement did not appeal to him. "Those bourgeois Jewish types seek equal rights only for themselves and for this they are ready to give up all of their great Jewish heritage. They are nothing but base egotists and I cannot tolerate them," he wrote in his famous book, *Rome and Jerusalem*.

But when he first witnessed a gathering of Hassidim praying to God with great fervor and ecstasy, he reported:

"These Jews are the real Jews; they have developed a commune of their own, a way of living together, and undaunted by persecution, they steadfastly carry the message of Judaism in their hearts. It is they who are the true bearers of the splendid Jewish heritage. This Hassidic type of Jew is a product of Poland and Russia. The German Jew is ready to disown all his Judaism because of the Jew-hatred that surrounds him, but this does not solve his problem. What the German Jew does not seem to understand is that the Germans do not hate his religion as such. What they hate is the Jews themselves. Reform, emancipation, or even baptism are not the cure. . . . The Germans will hate the Jew even after he has accepted baptism."

Less than a century later, the truth of this statement was more than amply and tragically proved by the rabid racial anti-Semitism of Hitler and his Nazi hordes.

In *Rome and Jerusalem,* published in 1862, Hess proposed a solution for the Jewish problem in these words:

"The Jews must retain their national characteristics. They have no cause whatever to be ashamed of them. Rather, they have every reason to take pride in them, for it was from the ideals of Judaism that the entire present-day humanitarian philosophy has sprung. There is not one concept either in Christian ethics or in modern philosophy that does not have its roots in Judaism. It is to Judaism that we owe all of our present civilization. Even as nature produces many species of plants and animals, so she also produced an infinite variety of men and nations, but of all these, the crown of nature is, and has ever been, none other but the Jewish people.

"It happened twice in our history that the Jewish people almost perished. But each time Israel was saved by a miracle. When the children of Israel were enslaved in Egypt, God sent them Moses to set them free. Later, when the Jews were in exile in Babylonia after the fall of the First Temple, and there was a real danger that they could have mingled with the idolators and gradually become like them, God sent them Ezekiel and the other prophets. And today, when the Jewish people are once again in danger, the Lord will send them a prophet once more to save them so that the Jewish people may rise again as a nation.

"True, at the present moment the Jewish people cannot reconquer Palestine, but it is important that the hope of the Jewish masses for a political rebirth be constantly kept alive. Thus, if at some later date, world conditions will permit practical work toward the establishment of a Jewish State, we shall be prepared. And when that time will come the Jewish people will also produce the right man for this task."

It was not until some thirty-five years later that Theodor Herzl convened the first Zionist Congress and another fifty-one years were to pass before the State of Israel was solemnly proclaimed in Tel Aviv. And one marvels at the foresight and vision of the thinker who saw and foretold the coming of these momentous events in Jewish history long before anyone else even dreamed that they could come to pass.

During the last years of his life, Moses Hess took an active interest in the resettlement of the land of Israel. It was Hess who managed to procure a substantial amount of money from Carl Netter, the founder of the famed "Alliance Israelite Universelle" for the establishment of "Mikveh Israel," the pioneer agricultural school of modern Palestine. He also made plans for the settlement of several hundreds of Jews from Poland and Roumania in Palestine so that they might help work the soil of the ancient homeland.

Hess died in Paris in 1875. He asked in his will that he be buried next to his grandfather who had had so a profound an influence upon the course of his life. His personal confession of faith which he left to posterity was brief. He had said, "Judaism is not a passive religion, but an active dynamic concept which is organically linked with that of Jewish nationhood in the Jewish homeland."

Hess's influence spread eastward from Paris to Russia where many small groups had already been active in behalf of the resettlement of Palestine. In Russia, there lived the great Ahad Ha-Am, the new philosopher of Jewish nationalism, of whom we shall learn more in the next chapter.

27. Ahad Ha-Am and His Contribution to Jewish Thought

Criticism of the Efforts at Colonization of Palestine—His Spiritual Zionism—A New View of Jewish Ethics—His Original Opposition to Herzl's "Jewish State"

The thesis of Moses Hess, advanced in *Rome and Jerusalem,* that Judaism could survive and grow only if the Jews were to rebuild their ancient homeland in Palestine had a powerful impact upon Jews throughout the Western world. Rabbi Hirsch Zvi Kalisher, a famous spiritual leader, warmly espoused the new proposal and founded a society in Frankfort-on-the-Main for this purpose, which he named "Yishuv Eretz Israel" (Society for the Settlement of the Land of Israel). Peretz Smolenskin, a Hebrew writer, preached Hess's ideas in *Ha-Shahar* (*The Dawn*), a Hebrew monthly journal. In 1876, the Englishwoman who wrote under the pseudonym of George Eliot, published her classic novel *Daniel Deronda,* which pictured the fulfillment of the dream of the rebuilding of Israel's ancient homeland. Finally, a new movement came to life. This movement, which called itself "Hibbat Zion" ("Love of Zion") spread the message of modern Jewish nationalism and soon had branches all over Europe.

In 1881, Dr. Leon Pinsker published a brochure which he called "Auto-Emancipation." In it he asserted the thought that, instead of waiting for the nations of the world to grant them emancipation, the Jews should emancipate themselves, placing themselves upon an equal footing with all the other nations by establishing for themselves a homeland of their own in Palestine. Soon the new thought gained a strong foothold among the youth of Russian Jewry, particularly among the students. In 1882, a number of young Jews from various colleges actually left Russia to go to Palestine and establish colonies there. They adopted for their group the name of "Bilu," (an acrostic formed from the initial letters of the Biblical quotation, "Beth Yaakov Lekhu Ve-Nelkha" (O House of Jacob, Let Us Go Forth).

It was then that Ahad Ha-Am (Asher Ginzberg) first became known among Russian Jewry as a writer and thinker. In the beginning, this young man had taken an active part in the "Hibbat Zion" movement of Odessa, which had been led by Leon Pinsker himself. Eventually, however, Ginzberg came to disagree with several aspects of the practical work of the movement. He expressed his critique of "Hibbat Zion" in his first published article, written in Hebrew and entitled "This Is Not the Way." This article he signed with the pen name by which he is best known today—"Ahad Ha-Am," which means "One of the People." But his greatest contribution to Jewish thought lay in his studies on Jewish ethics which we shall discuss elsewhere in this chapter.

Ahad Ha-Am was born in 1856 in the town of Skwira in the Russian province of Kiev. His parents both came from well known Jewish families and his father had distinguished himself as a very Orthodox Jew and a Talmudic scholar. Young Asher was afforded the same education that was then customarily given to all Jewish boys. First he studied at the elementary Heder and then at a rabbinical college. He was considered something of a child prodigy in his quick grasp of Talmudic literature. He would spend his evenings at Hassidic meeting places and listen to the tales for which the Hassidic sect had alway been famous. The pious Jews of Russia then looked askance at secular studies and thus Ginzberg had no worldly education until a later age. When he was only twelve, his family moved to a village where his father, Isaiah Ginzberg, had bought an estate. Asher was then taught by a private tutor until he reached the age of sixteen, when he was married to the daughter of the famous Rabbi of Zhitomir. Once he had established his own home and hence was free of parental control, Ginzberg began to study the works of the medieval Jewish philosophers. Later he moved to Odessa where he embarked on a most ambitious program of secular education. Within a very short time the youth who had never studied anything but Hebrew was ready to enter the university. He then proceeded to Austria where he intended to enroll at the University of Vienna. On the way there, in the city of Brody, he came upon a band of Jews who had escaped from the pogroms in Russia and were going to Palestine under the supervision of the "Alliance Israelite Universelle" which helped immigrant Jews settle in the Holy Land. Ginzberg traveled on the same train with them until they reached Vienna, where their ways parted.

Ginzberg could not forget the plight of these refugees from persecution. He enrolled at the university but could not adjust himself to the atmosphere that prevailed there. Eventually he returned home. But there, too, he could find no rest and once more he went abroad. He first went to Berlin and then proceeded to Breslau where he studied for two years. There he heard the news that the pogroms in Russia were becoming more widespread and violent, and he realized that hundreds of Jews would now be faced with the necessity of finding new homes abroad. He returned to Odessa and joined the group called "Hovevei Zion" (Friends of Zion) where he collaborated with such noted personalities as Dr. Leon Pinsker, Mordecai ben Hillel Ha-Cohen, Moses Leib Lilienblum, Mendele Mocher-Sforim and others, in the endeavor to make possible the creation of new agricultural settlements in Palestine. Eventually, however, Ginzberg came to the conclusion that little could be achieved by the mere founding of colonies in Palestine. Instead, Palestine should be a spiritual center to which Jews the world over could look for guidance and inspiration and which could have a beneficial influence upon all the Jews of the Diaspora. Ahad Ha-Am then stated his views in a series of essays that were widely read. But the major literary work for which he is best remembered is *Al Shtei Ha-S'ifim* in which he advanced a new theory on Jewish nationalism and thus pioneered a new era in Jewish thinking, a change as far-reaching as that brought about by Mendelssohn a century before. However, before we go on to discuss his ideas, we might state here that Ahad Ha-Am was not a religious philosopher in the accepted sense of the word. He did not concern himself with the nature of God, with freedom of will, with the problems of reward and punishment or with any of the other issues on which the Jewish philosophers of another day spent so much thought and discussion. We might call him, instead, a thinker who gave thought to certain practical issues in the realm of philosophy. He could be compared to Ralph Waldo Emerson and the other famous essayists of that generation. Yet the writings of Ahad Ha-Am did not deal with the problems of human life in general, but with immediate issues that were of direct concern to his contemporaries. Thus he became a pioneer who served as a guide for the younger generation of Jews of his day.

The literary works of Ahad Ha-Am consist of serious, thoughtful articles which he wrote in Hebrew, and which were published in various newspapers and periodicals. His style was unique, and each article had a forceful impact upon the Jewish world. All his works were later collected and published in a four-volume book entitled *Al Parashat D'rachim* (*At the Parting of the Ways*). After his death, his letters were published in Jerusalem in a six-volume collection.

The works of Ahad Ha-Am might be divided into two categories, namely: negative, that is, criticisms of various views and ways with which he disagreed, and positive, which were constructive suggestions for improvement where he felt it was needed.

As we have mentioned before, the maiden effort of Ahad Ha-Am's literary career was an article entitled "This Is Not the Way," which was published in 1889 in the Hebrew periodical *Ha-Melitz* (*The Advocate*). There he explained that a return to Zion could not be accomplished simply by setting up agricultural settlements in Palestine, one after another. He believed that Palestine could become the Jewish homeland only as a spiritual center for Jews the world over. Thus he preached "spiritual Zionism" as against "political Zionism" which was later expounded by Dr. Theodor Herzl in his *Judenstaat* (*The Jewish State*).

Ahad Ha-Am did not hesitate to attack in the sharpest terms those who were willing to discard their Jewish values in return for equality with their non-Jewish neighbors. Such civic liberties, obtained at the cost of one's own Jewish heritage, he declared, constituted no emancipation at all but only "slavery in the midst of freedom."

On the other hand, Ahad Ha-Am did not believe that religion, as expressed in the observance of the laws contained in the "Shulhan Arukh," (Code of Jewish Law) should be the standard by which to determine whether or not a person was a Jew, and here begins his positive constribution to Jewish thought. He was the first to dissociate Jewish ethics from the Jewish religion. The force which kept the Jewish nation living and united through the centuries, said Ahad Ha-Am, was not the bond of common religious observance, but one much stronger than that—a sense of brotherhood which united every Jew in spirit with all his fellow Jews wherever they might have been scattered. It was a sense of responsibility and obligation which compelled Jews to help each other in distress and to come to the aid of those Jewish communities that had become the victims of persecution. This was a much stronger cohesive force than religion, which had become considerably weakened, particularly within the recent past. In view of the foregoing, Ahad Ha-Am felt justified in saying that Jewish ethics was not part of the religion of Judaism but, instead, constituted the dominant force of Jewish nationalism. Therefore, Ahad Ha-Am concluded, a Jew who was not religious and felt that he could not possibly accept the tenets of religious observance as laid down in the "Shulhan Arukh" had no cause to believe that he therefore could not be a Jew in the full sense of the word. A Jew who was a freethinker by conviction could be just as good a Jew as one who was pious and Orthodox. Ahad Ha-Am did not deny that the Jewish religion contained nationalistic overtones, but he maintained that religion in Judaism was a private and personal matter. The ethics and morals of Judaism, then, were not inherent in the Jewish religion, but in the Jew himself, and he was the bearer of the higher Jewish ethics. It was the individual Jew who applied these principles to his own daily life, and if he did so, then he was a good Jew even if he did not observe the strictly religious tenets of Judaism.

This new doctrine had a profound influence upon great numbers of young Jews who were no longer religious. Formerly some of the most worthwhile young people had abandoned Judaism entirely because they felt that since they could not observe its religion they could no longer regard themselves as Jews. Reading the words of Ahad Ha-Am, many young Jews who would otherwise have cut all religious ties with Judaism decided that they could be good Jews even if they were not religious and they remained loyal to their people.

As we said before, during his younger days, when there seemed to be no chance that any practical work could be done toward the reestablishment of a Jewish state, Ahad Ha-Am emphasized the spiritual aspects of a Jewish homeland, and preached the importance of the creation in Palestine of a "spiritual center" to serve as a lighthouse for the Jews of the Diaspora. However, in 1917, when Lord Balfour, the Foreign Minister of Great Britain, wrote his famous letter to Lord Rothschild (which is known today as the "Balfour Declaration") in which he, Balfour, assured Rothschild that the

British government was willing to aid the establishment of a Jewish home-land in Palestine, Ahad Ha-Am realized that political Zionism, too, had been able to make a most important contribution to the welfare of the Jewish people. He then settled in Palestine, making his home in Tel Aviv on a street which was named for him. There the early expounder of "spiritual Zionism" died in 1927 after a long illness, and was buried next to Max Nordau, the pioneer philosopher of political Zionism.

28. Theodor Herzl and His "Jewish State"

Herzl, the Right Man at the Right Time—How Herzl first Became Interested in the Jewish Problem in Europe—"The Jewish State" as the Answer to the Jewish Problem—"Altneuland"—Palestine as the Only Site for a Jewish Homeland

A Jewish sage once said that even as fruits must ripen on their trees before they can be eaten by man, so ideas must first mature before they can be applied in practice and transformed into deeds. If fruit falls from the tree before it is entirely ripe, it perishes without having been of use to anyone on earth. But if the fruit is allowed to ripen on its branch, the proper reaper will come at the proper time to pluck it so that it may serve as food and nourishment. Much the same is true of ideas. An idea advanced before its time dies a premature death. It is only when it comes at the right time that it has the chance of living. So it was with political Zionism. When Dr. Theodor Herzl first proposed the establishment of a modern, independent state to serve as a homeland for the Jewish people, the masses of the people were ready for it. This was because the way had been paved for it by the writings of such men as Moses Hess and Leon Pinsker, by the outstanding men of the "Hovevie Zion" and the other groups that had sought ways and means of rebuilding Palestine as a Jewish land. Thus Theodor Herzl was the man who appeared on the scene of Jewish history at the right time. He brought about a consummation of these early efforts in his own concept of a Jewish homeland with all the attributes of a modern state. The age-old dream of the Jewish people, Herzl declared, could and would become a reality. "If only you will it," he wrote, "it shall be no dream."

Originally Theodor Herzl had not been a philosopher, nor had he given thought to the philosophy of Judaism. And yet he was to attempt to give his answer both to the Jewish problem and to the question of the nature of Judaism when he was inspired to write the *Jewish State,* the little booklet which became the Bible of modern Zionism.

Theodor Herzl was born in Budapest, Hungary, in 1860, the only son of Jacob and Jeanette Diamant Herzl. He received his early education at an elementary school maintained by the Jewish community of Budapest and then at a technical school. His Jewish education, however, was not much more extensive than the minimal Jewish training program that is afforded

491

today by some Sunday schools. In 1876 Herzl left the technical school and entered the gymnasium. From then on, literature became his major interest.

When the Herzl family left Budapest and moved to Vienna, Theodor enrolled at the University of Vienna, where he studied law, and received his doctorate in jurisprudence in 1884. He began to practice as an attorney, but most of his time was devoted to literary endeavors rather than to work at courts of justice. Eventually he joined the staff of the *Berliner Tageblatt* to which he sent articles each week from Vienna. In 1887 he was appointed *feuilleton* editor of the *Wiener Allgemeine Zeitung,* a Viennese newspaper. At the same time he also wrote plays, some of which were performed. Later he became a staff member of the *Neue Freie Presse* of Vienna, and was appointed its Paris correspondent. It was during his stay in Paris that Herzl first became interested in the problem of anti-Semitism and the Jewish problem in general. It was then, too, that he first heard from his friend, Oswald Boxer, about plans to set up Jewish colonies in Brazil where Jews could live as farmers. One day the *Neue Freie Presse* featured an article about the agricultural settlements which Baron Maurice de Hirsch had established in Argentina for Jews who had to escape persecution and were willing to work. The same paper also printed a report on the projected venture of one Paul Friedmann, a baptized Jew living in Berlin, to found a Jewish colony on the northwestern coast of Arabia. Soon Herzl himself came to contemplate the establishment of a Jewish homeland, perhaps in Palestine. But at that time he came to the conclusion, in an article in the *Neue Freie Presse*, that "the historic homeland of the Jews has no more meaning for them."

But the problem of anti-Semitism left Herzl no peace. He was particularly shocked at the treatment given the innocent Captain Alfred Dreyfus, the French Army officer who was convicted of espionage in 1894, and at the new volleys of Jew-baiting that his arrest had launched throughout the country. It was then that Herzl first truly realized that assimilation and baptism were no solution to the Jewish problem. At that time Herzl wrote a play entitled *The New Ghetto* from which it was clearly evident that by now the author, who had formerly looked upon Judaism with the detachment of an interested outsider, had become personally and closely identified with his people. Later, in 1896, Herzl wrote his famous work *Der Judenstaat (The Jewish State)*, where he explained in great detail an idea which had been quite new—the establishment of a Jewish state where every Jew could live a Jewish life freely and without fear of persecution.

In *The Jewish State* Herzl first asserted that the Jewish problem must be regarded as one of world-wide political significance and that, as such, it should be made the concern of all the nations of the world. Since the Jews will never disappear from the earth, and successful assimilation is possible only for those Jews who are in the highest echelons of the society in which they live, the world will not be able to rid itself of Jews. Persecution and anti-Semitic legislation have only served to make the Jews cling all the more tenaciously to their own teachings and to retreat even further into their isolation from their gentile neighbors. The Jewish people, said Herzl, is still possessed of enough vitality to fight against any force that might seek to destroy it. The present economic situation of the world, he continued, has made for the rise of a Jewish middle class which is undesirable competition to the corresponding strata in gentile society. At the same time the Jews are persecuted also by the non-Jewish proletariat. The laws promising equal rights to Jews in most countries are not forceful enough to guarantee the Jew freedom from anti-Semitic outbreaks on the part of the populace. Thus the only way to solve the Jewish problem and to rid Europe from the scourge of anti-Semitism is the emigration of all Jews to a homeland of their own where they can live in peace as an independent nation.

To carry out this plan, Herzl envisioned the founding of a "Society of Jews" which would be the legal representative of the Jewish people, and a "Jewish Company," which would take care of the economic aspects of the new Jewish state. It would be the task of the Society of Jews to enter upon negotiations with the heads of the nations of the world to secure their interest and support for the Jewish homeland.

What was more, Herzl felt that a Jewish state would not only provide a solution to the problem of anti-Semitism, but also answer the age-old need of the Jewish people for the freedom to develop and grow, and to be Jews in the full sense of the word, which they could not ever be while they were in exile.

This thought is brought home to the reader even more forcefully in Herzl's book *Altneuland (Old-New Land)* which he wrote in 1898 after his first visit to the Holy Land. This is an almost prophetic description of the Jewish state as Herzl thought it would be established by 1923. Herzl's Jewish Palestine of 1923 is a fertile land, with great cities and prosperous farms. The country is quite advanced in technology as well, and the minerals and chemicals of the Dead Sea are transported to the Mediterranean through a channel linking the two bodies of water, and then sent across the Mediterranean to Europe. There is a detailed portrayal, too, of the new nation's cultural and spiritual achievements, and of the development of a new and better Jewish life. Judaism, said Herzl, can be meaningful only if its spiritual center is in a Jewish state where it can grow and unfold to become a "light for the nations."

Though Herzl's visions of a Jewish state centered about Palestine, he would have been ready in practice, if necessary, to accept any other territory that the nations might have been willing to assign to the Jewish people. Thus Herzl would have been ready to agree to the proposal that the British territory of Uganda, in Africa, should serve as the site of the new Jewish home-land. It was only when Zionists the world over convinced Herzl that to the Jewish masses the idea of a "return" to independent nationhood was insepar-ably linked with Palestine and Jerusalem, that Herzl changed his views. Nor had Herzl originally thought of Hebrew as the language of the modern Jewish state.

It was indeed fortunate that Herzl was blessed not only with imagination and vision, but also with the talents and qualities that are needed to trans-late dreams into realities. Had this not been so, and had he not found enthusiastic and capable co-workers in behalf of the cause to which he dedicated the rest of his life, Herzl's "Old-New Land" might have remained a dream. But what happened during the next half century is part of world history. Herzl died in 1904, at only forty-four years of age, but by that time he had already won for his cause the hearts and minds of his people, and his vision became a reality in 1948 in the form of the little country that is known today as *the State of Israel*.

29. Other Creations of the Second Part of the Era of the Philosophers

❦ FURTHER DEVELOPMENT OF THE CABALA

From the eighth to the tenth century A.D., the study of the Cabala centered in Babylonia, from whence it was transplanted to Spain. It held sway in Spain, where it was cultivated as philosophical research, especially in the fourteenth and fifteenth centuries. The next epoch in the development of the Cabala began after the expulsion of the Jews from Spain and continued almost until the end of the nineteenth century. During this last epoch we find a parting of the ways in the study of the Cabala in three different schools, in three countries; that is, in Palestine, Italy, and Poland. We will discuss now each of these schools of Cabala and their place in the history of Jewish thought.

The Safed School

At the end of the fifteenth century, the ancient town of Safed in Palestine first attracted notice as a center of Cabalism. Rabbi Isaac Luria Ashkenazi had moved there with his disciples who devoted all their time and energy to the study of mystic lore. Ashkenazi's approach to Cabala was elucidated in detail by his favorite disciple, Rabbi Haim Vital, in his book entitled *Etz Chaim* (*The Tree of Life*). This group of Cabalists was the first to compose mystic songs, partly in Aramaic and partly in Hebrew. Many of these songs and prayers have been incorporated in to the Jewish prayer book, and some of these have become part of the *Zemiroth*, (*Table Hymns*) which pious Jewish families still sing on Sabbaths during the festive Sabbath dinner.

In addition to Isaac Luria Ashkenazi and Haim Vital, the following poet-scholars comprised the Safed School: Rabbi David ibn Abi Simra, Eliezer Askari, Abraham Maimon, Israel Nagara, Moses Alshich, Haim Ha-Cohen, Menahem di Loncano, Joseph Yedidiah Carmi, and Aaron Berachiah de Modena.

David ibn Abi Simra was born in Spain in 1479. When he was only thirteen, his family was expelled from Spain together with all the other Jews and he was brought by his parents to the town of Safed. There he studied with the noted Rabbi Joseph Saragossa. Later on David became a rabbi, practicing the rabbinate in Cairo and finally becoming chief rabbi of all of Egypt, an office which he held for forty years. The Rabbinical college which he established produced such famous scholars as Rabbi Bezalel Ashkenazi and Rabbi Isaac Luria, the founder of the Safed Group of Cabalists. When he was ninety years of age, David moved to Jerusalem where he became a member of the rabbinate under the leadership of Rabbi Joseph Caro, the author of the classic code *Shulchan Aruch*. He died at the patriarchal age of one hundred and ten.

Eliezer Askari, a friend of Rabbi Joseph Caro, founded the brotherhood "Succath Shalom" ("Tabernacle of Peace"). He is the author of a work entitled *Succath Hareidim* (*Tabernacle of the God-Fearing*).

Abraham Maimon lived in Safed during the second half of the sixteenth century and was a disciple of Rabbi Moses Cordovura.

Israel Nagara was born in Damascus and died at the end of the sixteenth century in Gaza where he had been a rabbi. Some of his songs in Hebrew and Aramaic were translated into Persian, Turkish, and Arabic; he was a prominent cantor and many of the melodies he composed are still used today in Sephardic synagogues. Nagara was the author of a two-volume compendium of hymns entitled *Zmiroth Israel* (*The Hymns of Israel*). Isaac Luria, the leader, said of Nagara's songs that "his hymns are very well thought of in heaven."

Moses Alschich, a student of Rabbi Joseph Caro and the teacher of Rabbi Haim Vital, practiced the rabbinate in Safed during the second half of the sixteenth century. He is the author of a well known commentary to the Pentateuch.

Haim Ha-Cohen of Aleppo, a disciple of Rabbi Haim Vital, was the compiler of the *Siddur Ha-Ari,* the prayer book which is employed by some Jewish communities in Eastern Europe, especially the Hassidic groups.

Menahem ben Judah de Loncano was a man of many talents. He was not only a noted Talmudist, but was also known as a lexicographer, bibliographer, grammarian, and printer. He published one work, entitled *Shitei Yadoth*. He died in Jerusalem in the year 1608.

Joseph Yedidiah ben Yekuthiel Carmi was born in Italy. He was a cantor of note and a fervent adherent of Rabbi Isaac Luria and the Cabala. He died during the first half of the seventeenth century.

Aaron Berachiah ben Moses of Modena was also a cantor. Both he and Carmi, who was his brother-in-law, wrote liturgical poems and composed hymns with mystic themes.

The Italian School

The "Italian School" of Cabalists was comprised largely of poets who lived in Italy during the seventeenth century, such as Moses Zaccuto, Daniel

Olmo, Israel Benjamin Bassani, Eliezer ben Gershon Chafetz, Moses Haim Luzzatto, Ephraim Luzzatto, and Samuel David Luzzatto.

Unlike the Safed School, the Italian School was not one of Talmudists and Rabbis. Most of the Italian Cabalists were poets and men of broad secular education, very much under the influence of the Renaissance. Naturally their approach to Cabala and mysticism as such was quite different from that of the scholars of the Safed School whose learning had been confined to purely Jewish studies.

Moses ben Mordechai Zaccuto was born in Amsterdam, Holland, in 1625, of an old family that had originally come from Spain. A friend of Baruch Spinoza, Moses had received a thorough training both in Jewish law and secular studies. When he decided to delve into the mysteries of the Cabala, he fasted for a period of forty days in an endeavor to forget the Latin he had learned, and then engaged in diligent study with Rabbi Benjamin Ha-Levi, a former disciple of Haim Vital. Moses Zaccuto practiced the rabbinate in Venice and Mantua, and wrote a number of learned treatises. For some time he was an adherent of Sabbatai Zvi, the false Messiah.

Daniel ben Abraham Olmo, a professor at the Rabbinical Seminary in Ferrara, had also been an adherent of Sabbatai Zvi. He wrote a book entitled *Eden Aruch* (*The Prepared Eden*).

Benjamin ben Isaiah Bassana, who served as a rabbi in the town of Reggio, was a friend of Moses Haim Luzzatto, and, like Olmo, had also been a member of the movement that rallied around Sabbatai Zvi.

Moses Haim Luzzatto, the author of many learned books, achieved prominence as a poet and moralist. Many believe that he, too, had been among the supporters of Sabbatai Zvi.

Ephraim Luzzatto studied medicine in Italy and later moved to London, where he practiced at the hospital maintained by the Portuguese Jewish community there. A talented poet with a strong tendency to mysticism, he published an anthology of the songs he had composed. In his Hebrew song entitled "Aidei al Pishia" ("I Confess My Transgressions"), he expressed his remorse at the sins of his youth. This song is typical of his views on ethics and morals.

Samuel David Luzzatto (1800-1865) is an important figure in the history of Jewish thought. A professor at the Rabbinical College of Padua, Luzzatto was one of the outstanding Jewish scholars of his day and one of the first expounders of modern Jewish studies. He showed a marked tendency to mysticism and was the author of several cabalistic songs.

Eliezer ben Gershon Chefetz wrote many philosophical works employing cabalistic terminology. He composed a hymn "How Great Is Thy Power, O Almighty," which extols the human soul, and a song entitled "At the Day of Birth."

All these members of the Italian school were men of broad learning in secular subjects. Their achievements are strongly reminiscent of those of the Golden Age of Spanish Jewry.

The Polish School

The Polish School of Cabalists, which is actually part and parcel of the mystic sect of Hassidism, had its beginnings during the days of the "Baal Shem Tov" (the second half of the eighteenth century) and extended through the era of the founding of the noted Hassidic dynasties of wandering rabbis.

The basic teaching of the Baal Shem Tov which formed the basis for the approach of the Polish School was mainly this: Man is to serve God with rejoicing and regard life as a joyous experience, rather than a vale of tears. This idea was the theme of the many songs and melodies of joy and longing for which Hassidism has been known through the years.

Among the leaders of this new movement were Rabbi Jacob Joseph Polnoher, Rabbi Pinhas Koretzer, Rabbi Aaron Karliner, Rabbi Shneur Zalman of Liadi (the father of the dynasty of Lubavitcher rabbis), Rabbi Levi Isaac Berditchever, and Rabbi Nachman Bratzlaver. Then there were the famous dynasties of Polish and Galician rabbis such as Rabbi Elimelech of Lizensk, Galicia, who was one of the pillars of Hassidism. Among the prominent Hassidic rabbis in Poland were the Seer of Lublin, Rabbi Bunim of Pzischa, the Rabbi of Kotzk, Mendele, the dynasty of rabbis known as the Gerer, and many others.

❦ THE "MUSAR" MOVEMENT AND ITS LITERATURE

A most important place in Jewish religious literature is occupied by the many books on ethics and morality which have been written to remonstrate with sinners and also with those who waste their lives on trivia and neglect the study of the Bible and Talmud. They are popularly called "Musar-Seforim" ("books on morals and ethics"). Such books have appeared from time to time beginning with the early days of the history of the Jewish people. At present there are some twenty major works dealing with that theme and dating from various periods of Jewish history up to and including modern themes.

One such work, by Rabbi Elijah ben Rabbi Moses of Vedage, is entitled *Reishith Chachmah (The Beginning of Wisdom)*; another, *Sheret Mussor (The Rod of Remonstrance)*, was written by Rabbi Elijah ben Moses Ha-Cohen, a judge in the religious community of Smyrna; another is *Kav Hayosher (The Right Path)* by Zvi Hirsch Keidanovei; Moses Haim Luzzatto, the Italian Cabalist, was the author of the work entitled *Missilath Yeshorim* (*The Road of the Righteous*); and a later scholar, Mendel Levin, wrote *Cheshban Hanefesh* (*The Accounting for the Soul*).

There were morality books written specifically for women such as the famous *Ze 'na U-r'eenah* (*Go Forth and Behold*) by Rabbi Jacob ben Rabbi Isaac Ashgenazi of Prague, which is actually a commentary on the Pentateuch in the Yiddish language. Anothed morality book, entitled *Menorath Hameor* (*The Lamp of Light*) by Rabbi Isaac Aboab was translated from the original Hebrew into Yiddish and enjoyed wide popularity among the Jewish women up to a few generations ago.

In the year 1842, however, an active "Musar" movement came into being which proposed the deliberate practice of what was preached in the morality books. Rabbi Israel Salanter, the founder of the movement, declared that mere reading and study of such writings was not enough. He therefore organized brotherhoods which made it their task not only to use this literature as a guide in their efforts to improve their own characters, but also to preach ethics and morality to the broad masses. This new movement, which eventually become known as "Musar" ("Morality"), had its beginnings in Vilna and Kovno, Lithuania, and young rabbinical students by the hundreds eagerly embraced the idea. As the movement grew in strength, many rabbinical colleges made the reading and practical application of Musar literature a compulsory part of their course of study. One of the guiding spirits of Musar was Rabbi Isaac Blaser, a student of Rabbi Salanter. With the help of a wealthy Jew named Lachman, who gave him the sum of ten thousand rubles for this purpose, Rabbi Blaser founded a Yeshiva at Slobodka which made the teaching and practice of Musar its cornerstone. This institution survived until the coming of the Second World War.

Other leaders of the Musar movement were Rabbi Samuel Lubetzer of Vilna, Rabbi Alexander Moses Lapidus of Rozin, Rabbi Jacob Joseph (later chief rabbi of New York), Rabbi Naftali Amsterdam of Slobodka, and Rabbi Zissel of Kelem.

In the beginning, the Musar movement had to fight against the opposition of some of the greatest rabbinical authorities, such as the famous Isaac Elhanan Spector of Kovno. Gradually, however, the idea spread throughout eastern Jewry so that even today there are some Yeshivas of this kind including one in New York and another in the State of Israel. The adherents of Musar do not content themselves simply with broadcasting their views to students and others willing to listen to them. They diligently and quietly work upon themselves as well, endeavoring to cultivate wholesome habits of mind and body. They seek to acquire a sane attitude toward life, the habit of following a regular orderly schedule in daily living, the virtues of patience, personal cleanliness, modesty, thrift, a passion for justice and righteousness, a zest for study and for doing good deeds, silence when silence is wise, and they believe in speaking the truth at all times. The Musarites actually are supposed to carry with them notebooks in which they have recorded all these virtues and regularly render an accounting to themselves of their progress in attaining them.

Summary

✤ 1. JUDAISM—STATIC OR DYNAMIC?

What, actually, is the nature of Judaism? This question has occupied the minds of thinking Jews throughout all the ages of the history of the people of Israel. Is Judaism a fixed structure, a mass of laws which the Jew must observe regardless of whether or not he believes in them or understands their significance? Or is Judaism a way of living, a dynamic force which should and must have meaning to every Jew in every aspect of his life, both as a member of a larger community and as an individual? Is Judaism a stagnant body of water, confined in space, or is it a stream of living waters, giving life and strength as it surges onward? The answer to this question can be found in the most ancient documents of Israel, in the Bible, the Midrash and the Talmud. Here we are told that Judaism is a dynamic force indeed, a wellspring of life. It is a teaching which is meant to be compatible at all times with the needs and demands of practical living.

Judaism, if properly practiced, should give the Jew three things: first, it gives his life a higher standard; second, it teaches him how best to live with himself; and finally, it teaches him the best way in which to live at peace with his fellow men.

Judaism teaches us the love of God. It holds not only that God is unique and all the terms which are applied to humans cannot be attributed to Him; it posits that He is the Creator of all things in the universe and none of His own creations, not even man, is capable of grasping His infinite greatness.

As for man's duty to himself, the laws of Israel always have a prefatory or subsequent remark such as, "and you shall guard your souls," "you shall choose life," or "that it may be well with you and with your children after you."

As to the third aspect: Jewish law is an excellent guide for human relations, giving as it does a wealth of commandments designed to teach the Jew both how to live with his fellow men as an individual, and how to behave as a member of a community. The entire Bible is filled with laws to this end, the demand such as "Justice, justice shall you pursue," "Love the stranger in your midst" and the prohibitions against "double standards" in any aspect of life, and against usury; and the classic commands such as "you shall not bear false witness against your neighbor" and "you shall not covet that which is your neighbor's." Finally there are the ceremonial laws which deal with religious observance, celebration of holidays.

Such is the philosophy of Judaism. Unlike the philosophy of many other civilizations, Judaism is a philosophy of life and not of idle speculation. Perhaps this is the reason why the Jews were able to produce the inspired poets and singers who gave to the world such treasures as the Book of Psalms.

And so it came about that Judaism, rather than any other ancient creed, has become the mother of all other civilized religions.

❦ 2. WHAT JUDAISM HAS GIVEN THE WORLD

Much has been written about the contribution of Judaism to the culture of the world. First and foremost, of course, the Jews have given to mankind that basic constitution upon which Western civilization rests—the Ten Commandments which were given by God to Moses on Mount Sinai, not only for the children of Israel but for all of mankind, for every nation that desires to call itself civilized. Without the Ten Commandments the world would be rent asunder by anarchy and immersed in chaos. Only that society can survive which accepts these divine laws as its fundamental guide to living.

The Ten Commandments are part of the Torah, the Law of God which was also given to the Jewish people, so that Israel, by its own example, might communicate it to the rest of the world. The Torah is a way of life, a teaching to aid us in our endeavor to live at peace with our fellow men. It is truly everyman's Bible.

The prophets regarded themselves as God's messengers, not only to the Jewish people, but to all mankind, for they knew well that the divine ideals of justice and righteousness which they preached could survive and prevail only if the entire world, and not just the people of Israel, would subscribe to them.

The Holy Writings, too, have become sacred to all men, regardless of religion. To give only a few examples, the Book of Psalms is filled with praises to God that all men can sing, if only they believe in Him. The Book of Job symbolizes the tragic element in human life, and the Proverbs are wise sayings that can serve as moral and ethical advice to people of all creeds.

Christianity and Mohammedanism, the two other great religions of our present-day civilization, are based on the same sacred ideals as is Judaism.

One of the outstanding Christian clergymen of our time, the Reverend Dr. John Haynes Holmes, in a brochure entitled "Christianity's Debt to Judaism; Why Not Acknowledge It?" spoke quite frankly of the debt which Christianity owes to Judaism. He wrote:

"Let me begin what I have to say this morning with Jesus, who is the center and soul of Christian faith. There are three things to be made plain about this man.

"In the first place, I would remind you that Jesus' parents were Jews. Whether his father, Joseph, was of 'the stem of Jesse,' and thus of the royal house of David, as the Bible states, is altogether unknown and quite improbable. The genealogies to this effect in the New Testament are valueless. As a matter of fact, we know very little about Joseph—only that he lived in Nazareth in Galilee, that he was a carpenter by trade, and that he died, in all probability, before Jesus came to manhood. . . . But amid all this obscurity, there remains the indubitable truth that these two persons, who are so venerated by the Christian church, were both of them Jews.

"The second fact is of course that Jesus, as the oldest child of these parents, was thus himself a Jew. Two attempts have been made to break down and destroy this simple fact. The first is theological, and is to be found in the dogma of the Virgin Birth, which represents Jesus as born not of Joseph and Mary, but of a divine conception of God upon Mary. But this leads to the fascinating and impressive conclusion, seldom mentioned in doctrinal discussion, that out of all the tribes of earth, God chose a Jewish maiden for the incarnation of his dearly beloved and only begotten son. . . .

"The third thing to be said about the Jewishness of Jesus is that he was reared and trained in the Jewish faith. His parents were pious Jews; they went up each year to Jerusalem to keep the feast of the Passover! They taught Jesus, by precept and example, to attend the synagogue, where he became acquainted with the Bible of his race. In his early manhood, it was his custom to go to the synagogue on the Sabbath day, which is more than a good many Jews do today; and he began his public ministry, so the record tells us, by standing up in the synagogue in Nazareth and reading from the Prophet Isaiah. In spirit as well as in blood, this Nazarene was a son of Israel.

"It is from these three points of view—his parents, his birth, and his religious training—that we must agree that Jesus was a Jew. It is to the Jews that the Christians owe this peerless leader and founder of their faith. I would go so far as to say that we cannot understand Jesus unless we acknowledge that his rightful place in history is that of the last and greatest of the Jewish prophets. It is to me as incredible that the Jews do not recognize this fact as it is discreditable that the Christians do not recognize it. . . ."

And he concludes:

"We are beginning now, perhaps, to understand how stupendous is the debt which Christians owe to Jews. Not only Jesus himself, but the Bible, the church, and Sunday all come from Jewish sources. But not yet have we gotten to the heart of the matter. What about the teachings of Christianity —those great truths of the moral and spiritual life which constitutes the essence of the Gospel? The things which Jesus taught—were these original with him, or did they spring from the Judaism in which Jesus was born and reared? . . .

"If any statement of Jesus is commonly cited as the complete and perfect summary of his religion, it is the dual commandment, Thou shalt love the Lord thy God, with all thy heart, and with all thy soul, and with all thy strength, and with all thy mind; and thy neighbor as thyself. Where does this come from? First of all from the New Testament story of the lawyer who tempted Jesus, saying, What shall I do to inherit eternal life? But originally from the Old Testament, in two famous passages. The first is from Deuteronomy 6:4— Hear O Israel, the Lord thy God, is one Lord; and thou shalt love the Lord thy God with all thy heart, and with all thy soul, and with all thy might. The second is from Leviticus 19:18: Thou shall not take vengeance, nor bear any grudge . . . but thou shalt love thy neighbor as thyself.

"If anything is original with Jesus, it would seem to be his non-resistance —his injunction in the Sermon on the Mount to "resist not evil." This received its supreme expression in Jesus' commandment that we should love our enemies. This is very obviously a protest against and correction of the Jewish law of retaliation—"an eye for an eye, and a tooth for a tooth." This law, without any question, appears in the Old Testament. Jesus was mindful of it, and would get rid of it. But he was not the first to take this stand. Long since the Jewish prophets had laid hold upon the doctrine of love and forgiveness, even of enemies. But in one brief passage of the Old Testament we have an anticipation of this positive aspect of non-resistance which is breath-taking.

"If I were asked to name the most beautiful expression of Jesus' teaching on this point, I would turn to St. Paul's great Epistle to the Romans, and read the closing verses of the twelfth chapter—If thine enemy hunger, feed him; if he thirst, give him drink; for in so doing thou shalt heap coals of fire upon his head. Be not overcome of evil, but overcome evil with good. If there is anything original in Christianity, this would certainly seem to be it. Yet turn to the twenty-fifth chapter of the book of Proverbs, the twenty-first verse, and what do you find? If thine enemy be hungry, give him bread to eat; and if he be thirsty, give him water to drink; for thou wilt heap coals of fire upon his head. Even in his teaching of love, for enemies as well as friends, Jesus was only faithful to the noblest precepts of the Jews!

"All this shows what Jesus was really doing in his ministry. Not preaching a new religion, but reviving the pure and undefiled religion of Israel! . . ."

Mohammedanism, too, is very obviously a daughter of Judaism. Most of the Koran, the Bible of Islam, is either taken directly from the Pentateuch and the works of the prophets, or else is a somewhat garbled version of these sacred writings of the people of Israel. Mohammed, the author of the Koran and founder of Islam, included in his work a good many legends which originated in the Talmud and which he had learned from his many Jewish friends and particularly from his two Jewish scribes who wrote down the

Koran at his dictation (because Mohammed himself could neither read nor write). It was from Jewish law that Mohammed took the regulations which he gave his followers concerning prayer, with the difference that, while the Jews are commanded to pray only three times each day, Mohammedans must turn to Allah in daily prayer five times. Mohammedan males, even as boys in Israel, must undergo circumcision, though not in early infancy but at the age of thirteen, and the faithful followers of Islam, again like the Jews, are forbidden to eat pork. Originally, hoping that the entire Jewish people would adopt his new creed, Mohammed ordained that his followers must fast on the Day of Atonement and that they must recite their prayers facing in the direction of Jerusalem, the Holy City. However, when it became obvious to him that he would never be able to effect such a mass conversion of Jews, he deliberately changed these laws so that, today, Mohammedans fast not on the Jewish Yom Kippur but during the month of Ramadan and, when they pray, they turn not to Jerusalem, the spiritual center of Judaism, but to Mecca, which has become the sacred shrine of Islam. All this was printed in detail in a work entitled *What Has Mohammedanism Taken from Judaism* by the well known scholar, Abraham Geiger (Bonn, 1883). In this work, Geiger points out the full extent to which Mohammedanism was rooted in the teachings of Judaism.

Now that the Jewish people have a spiritual center once more in the Holy Land, a new, great era has begun, not only in the history of the Jews, but in that of all the rest of the world as well. The world, devastated and stunned by the blood-bath that has engulfed it twice during this century, is in need of new spiritual guidance to fill the vacuum from which it now suffers so acutely. Thousands of years ago, when both Israel and mankind were still young, the Jewish people gave to the world the Bible, the eternal law which is the basis of all justice, righteousness, and peace. Today the people of Israel, now old and sorely tried by centuries of exile and oppression, have gained new life and vigor and are rebuilding their old-new homeland. The Jewish people, thus strengthened and rejuvenated, may yet bring forth a new teaching from its ancient spiritual home for the world. The nations of the world in their relations with the Jewish people have not always behaved as grateful disciples should to their teacher, but this will not deter the people of Israel, the ancient teacher of mankind, from continuing to spread the message of peace and justice among men, even as the prophet said long ago: "For from Zion shall go forth the Law and the Word of the Lord from Jerusalem."

Bibliography

❧ THE BIBLICAL ERA

BEWER, JULIUS A., The Literature of the Old Testament, 1912.
BONSIVVEN, J., Le Judaïsme palestinien au temps du Jésus Christ.
———, Sa Théologie, 2 vols., 1935.
———, Exégèse rabbinique et exégèse paulinienne, 1938.
BREHIER, E., Les Idées philosophiques et religieuses de Philon d'Alexandries, 2éme ed., 1925.
BRIGG, C. A., General Introduction to the Study of the Holy Scriptures, 1899.
BROWNE, LEWIS, The Graphic Bible, 1928.
CHEYNE, THOMAS K., Introduction to the Book of Isaiah, 1895.
CORNILL, C. H., Der Israelitische Prophetismus, 1896.
DELITSCH, F., The Hebrew Language, 1883.
DRIVER, SAMUEL R., Introduction to the Literature of the Old Testament, 6th ed., 1897.
DUHN, B., Kommentator über Jesaiah, 1902.
FINKELSTEIN, L., The Pharisees: The Sociological Background of Their Faith, 1938.
FOWLER, H. T., A History of the Literature of Ancient Israel, 1912.
FREUDENTHAL, L., Hellenistische Studien I, II, 1874-75.
GRANT, ELIHU, The Haverford Symposium on Archaeology and the Bible, 1938.
GRAY, G. B., A Critical Introduction to the Literature of the Old Testament, 1913.
HEINEMANN, J., Philons griechische und jüdische Bildung, 1932.
HEINISCH, P., Griechische Philosophie im Alten Testament, 1913-1914.
HOELSCHER, G., Geschichte der israelitischen und jüdischen Religion, 1922.
HUHN, E., Die Messianischen Weissagungen des Israelitisch-Jüdischen Volkes, 1899.
JOEL, M., Blicke in die Religionsgeschichte zu Anfang des zweiten christlichen Jahrhunderts, I, II, 1880, 1883.
KAMINKA, A., Le Prophète Isaïe, 1915.
KAPLAN, J. H., Psychology of Prophecy, 1908.
KITTEL, RUDOLPH, Geschichte des Volkes Israel, 1888, 1892.
KLAUSNER, J., The Prophets, 1954.
LEISEGANG, H., Der heilige Geist, das Wesen und Werden der mystischintuitiven Erkenntnis in der Philosophie der Griechen, 1919.
LEVY, H., ED., Philo Judaeus: Philosophical Writings of Philo, Selection, 1946.
MARGOLIS, MAX L., The Hebrew Scriptures in the Making, 1922.
PEAKE, ARTHUR S., A Commentary of the Bible, 1919.
RYLE, H. E., Canon of the Old Testament, 1892.

SAKHEIM, A., Das Jüdische Element in der Welt-Literatur, 1924.
STEINNAGEL, C., Einleitung in des Alte Testament, 1912.
WELLHAUSEN, JULIUS, Israelitische und Jüdische Geschichte, 1914.
WUNSCHE, AUGUST, Die Schönheit der Bibel, 1906.

❧ THE TALMUDIC ERA I AND II

BACHEM, WILHELM, Die Agada der Tannaiten, 2 vols., 1884-90.
——, Die Agada der Palästinensischen Amoräer, 3 vols., 1892-99.
——, Die Agada der Babylonischen Amoräer, 1878.
——, Tradition und Tradenten, 1914.
COHEN, ABRAHAM, Everyman's Talmud, 1932.
DALMAN, GUSTAF, Arbeit und Sitte in Palästina, 4 vols., 1928-35.
FRANKEL, ZACHARIAS, Introduction to the Mishnah, 1923.
GRAETZ, HEINRICH, Geschichte der Juden, 11 vols., 1853-75.
GÜDEMANN, MORITZ, Das Judentum in seinen Grundzügen und nach seinen geschichtlichen Grundlagen dargestellt, 1902.
HOFFMANN, DAVID, Zur Einleitung in die Halachischen Midraschim, Berlin, 1888.
JOSEPHUS, FLAVIUS, Against Apion
——, The Antiquities of the Jews
——, History of the Jewish War
JOST, ISAAC MARCUS, Geschichte des Judentums und seiner Sekten, 3 vols., 1857-59.
KAPLAN, JULIUS, The Redaction of the Talmud, 1933.
KASSOVSKY, HAYIM JOSHUA, Otzor Leshon Hamishnah, A Concordance of the Mishnah, 1927.
KRAUSS, SAMUEL, Die Mishnah, 1914.
——, Talmudische Archäologie, 3 vols., 1919-1912.
LEVIN, B. M., Rabbanan Sabboraim Vetalmidon, 1937.
MIELZINER, MOSES, Introduction to the Talmud, 3rd ed., 1925.
MOORE, GEORGE FOOT, Judaism in the First Centuries of the Christian Era, 3 vols., 1927-30.
SCHEFTELOWITZ, ISIDOR, Die Alt-Persische Religion und das Judentum, 1920.
SCHÜRER, E. A., History of the Jewish People in the Time of Jesus Christ, 5 vols., 1890-1900.
STRACK, HERMAN, Einleitung in Talmud und Midrasch, 4 vols., 1928-35.
WEBER, MAX, Gasammelte Aufsätze zur Religionssoziologie, 1921.
WEISS, ABRAHAM, Hatalmud Hababli lehithhavuth Hasifruth, 2 vols., 1937, 1939.
——, The Babylonian Talmud as a Literary Unit, 1943.

❧ THE ERA OF THE PHILOSOPHERS I AND II

ALTMAN, A., Saadya's Theory of Revelation: Its Origin and Background, Saadya Studies, 1943.
BACHER, W., Die Bibelexegese der jüdischen Religionsphilosophie des Mittelalters vor Maimuni, 1892.

BACK, J., Josef Albos Bedeutung in der Geschichte der jüdischen Religionsphilosophie, 1869.

BAMBERGER, F., Das System des Maimonides: Eine Analyse des More Nebuchim vom Gottesbegriffe aus, 1935.

——, Die geistige Gestalt Mendelssohns, 1929.

BANETH, E., "Jehuda Halewi and Gazali," Korrespondenzblatt der Akademie für die Wissenschaft des Judentums, 1923-24.

BERGER, E., Das Problem des Erkenntnis in der Religionsphilosophie Jehuda Halewis, 1916.

BLOCH, P., Die Willensfreiheit von Chasdai Kreskas, 1879.

——, Die Geschichte der Entwicklung der Kabbala und der jüdischen Religionsphilosophie, 1895.

COHEN, H., Ethik des reinen Willens, 1907.

——, Der Begriff der Religion im System der Philosophie, 1915.

——, Religion der Vernunft aus den Quellen des Judentums, 1929.

——, Jüdische Schriften, hrsg. von B. Strauss, mit Einleitung von Franz Rosenzweig, 1924.

DE BOER, T., "Maimonides en Spinoza," Meddeelingen der Koninglijke Akademie van Wetenschappen, 1927.

DIESENDRUCK, Z., Saadya's Formulation of the Time Argument for Creation. Jewish Studies in Memory of G. A. Kohut, 1935.

DREYER, K., Die religiöse Gedankenwelt des Salomo ibn Gabirol, 1929.

EISLER, M., Vorlesungen über jüdische Philosophie des Mittelalters, 3 Teile, 1870-1884.

FISCHER, K., Spinozas Leben, Lehre und Werke, 1909.

FORMSTECHER, S., Die Religion des Geistes, 1841.

FRANKL, P. F., Ein mu'tazilitischer Kalam aus dem 10. Jahrhundert, 1872.

FREUDENTHAL, J., Spinoza, Leben und Lehre, hrsg. von C. Gebhardt, 1927.

FREUND, Else, Die Existenzphilosophie Franz Rosenzweigs, 1933.

GEBHARDT, C., Spinoza und der Platonismus. Chronicon Spinozanum I, 1921.

GEIGER, A., Josef Salomo del Medigo, 1840, 1876.

GOLDBERG, D., Maimonides' Kritik einer Glaubenslehre, 1935.

GUTTMANN, JACOB, Die Scholastik des 13. Jahrhunderts in ihren Beziehungen zum Judentum und jüdischer Literatur, 1902.

——, Die Religionsphilosophie des Saadia, 1882.

——, Die Religionsphilosophie des Abraham Ibn Daud, 1879.

——, Die religionsphilosophischen Lehren des Isaak Abrabanel, 1916.

——, Die Philosophie des Salomon ibn Gabirol, 1889.

GUTTMANN, JULIUS, Religion und Wissenschaft im mittelalterlichen und modernen Denken. Festrede zum 50 jährigen Bestehen der Hochschule fürdie Wissenschaft des Judentum in Berlin, 1922.

——, Die Philosophie des Judentums, 1933.

——, Die Philosophie des Salomo ibn Gabirol, 1889.

——, Das Verhältnis von Religion und Philosophie bei Jehuda Halevi, 1911.

——, Die Religiösen Motive in der Philosophie des Maimonides: Entwicklungsstufen der jüdischen Religion, 1927.

——, Mendelssohns Jerusalem und Spinozas theologisch-politischer Traktat.

HEINEMANN, I., Die Lehre von der Zweckbestimmung des Menschen im griechisch-römischen Altertum und im jüdischen Mittelalter, 1926.

HIRSCH, S., Das System der religiösen Anschauung der Juden und sein Verhältnis zum Judentum, Christentum und zur absoluten Philosophie. Erster Band: Die Religionsphilosophie der Juden, 1842.

HOROWITZ, S., Die Psychologie der jüdischen Religionsphilosophie des Mittelalters von Saadia bis Maimuni, 4 Teile, 1898-1912.

——, Die Bekanntschaft Saadias mit der griechischen Skepsis. Judaica, Festschrift zu Hermann Cohns 70. Geburtstag, 1912.

HUSIK, I., History of Mediaeval Jewish Philosophy, 1930.

JOEL, M., Spinozas theologisch-politischer Traktat, 1870.

——, Zur Genesis der Lehre Spinozas, 1871.

KAUFMANN, D., Die Theologie des Bachia ibn Pakuda, 1874.

——, Geschichte der Attributenlehre in der jüdischen Religionsphilosophie von Saadia bis Maimuni, 1877.

——, Die Sinne: Beiträge zur Geschichte der Psychologie im Mittelalter, 1884.

——, Studien über Salomon ibn Gabirol, 1899.

——, Die Theologie des Bachja ibn Pakuda, 1874.

KINKEL, WALTER, Hermann Cohen, 1924.

KLATZKIN, J., Hermann Cohen, 1926.

LANDAU, J. L., Nachman Krochmal, ein Hegelianer, 1904.

LAZARUS, M., Die Ethik des Judentums, 1898, 1911.

LEVY, L. G., Maimonides, 1911.

LOEWITH, K., "Martin Heidegger and Franz Rosenzweig, or Temporality and Eternity," Philosophy and Phenomenological Research, No. 3, 1942.

MALTER, H., Saadia Gaon: His Life and Works, 1921.

MARMORSTEIN, H., The Doctrine of Redemption in Saadya's Theological System, Saadya Studies, 1943.

MENDELSSOHN, M., Gesammelte Schriften, hrsg. von G. B. Mendelssohn, VII Bde., 1843-45.

MIESES, J., "Spinoza und die Kabbala," Zts. für exacte Philosophie, VIII, 1869.

MUNK, S., Mélanges de philosophie juive et arabe, 1859.

NEUBURGER, C., Das Wesen des Gesetzes in der Philosophie des Maimonides, 1933.

NEUMARK, D., Geschichte der jüdischen Philosophie des Mittelalters nach Problemen dargestellt. I, II, 1; II 2. 1907-28.

——, Jehuda Halevi's Philosophy in Its Principles, 1908. Essays in Jewish Philosophy, 1929.

RAWIDOWICZ, S., Saadya's Purification of the Idea of God. Saadya Studies, 1943.

RENAN, E., Les Écrivains juifs français du XIV siècle, 1893.

——, and NEUBAUER, A., Les Rabbins français du commencement du quatorzième siècle, 1877.

ROHNER, A., Das Schöpfungsproblem bei Moses Maimonides, Albertus Magnus und Thomas von Aquin, 1913.

ROSENBLATT, S., The High Ways to Perfection of Abraham Maimonides, 1927, 1938.

ROSENZWEIG, F., Der Stern der Erlösung, 1921.

ROSIN, D., Die Ethik des Maimonides, 1876.

ROTH, L., Spinoza, Descartes, Maimonides, 1924.

SARACHEK, I., Faith and Reason: The Conflict over the Rationalism of Maimonides, 1935.

SCHECHTER, S., Some Aspects of Rabbinic Theology, 1909.

SCHEYER, S. B., Das psychologische System des Maimonides, 1945.

SCHOLEM, G., Major Trends in Jewish Mysticism, 1946.

SCHREINER, M., Der "Kalam" in Jüdischer Literatur, 1895.

SELLIN, E., Moses und seine Bedeutung für die Israelitisch-Jüdischen Religions-Geschichte, 1922.

SMIEDL, A., Studien über Jüdische, Insbesonders Jüdisch-Arabische Religions-Philosophie, 1869.

STEINHEIM, L., Die Offenbarung nach dem Lehrbegriff der Synagoge, 1835-1865.

STEINSCHNEIDER, M., Die hebräischen Übersetzungen des Mittelalters, 1893.

——, Die arabische Literatur der Juden, 1902.

STRAUSS, L., Philosophie und Gesetz, 1935.

——, The Literary Character of the Guide for the Perplexed, Essay on Maimonides, 1941.

——, Die Religionskritik Spinozas als Grundlage seiner Bibelwissenschaft, 1930.

——, "On Abrabanel's Philosophical Tendency and Political Teaching," Isaak Abrabanel, ed. Freud and Loewe, 1937.

TAENZER, A., Die Religions-Philosophie Josef Albo's nach seinem Werk "Ikkarim," systematisch dargestellt und erläutert, 1896.

UCKO, S., Der Gottesbegriff in der Philosophie Hermann Cohens, 1929.

WAXMAN, M., The Philosophy of Don Hasdai Creskas, 1920.

WEBER, M., Gesammelte Aufsätze zur Religionssoziologie, III: Das antike Judentum, 1921.

WITTMAN, M., Zur Stellung Avicebros (ibn Gabirols) in der Entwicklung der Arabischen Philosophie, 1905.

WOLFSON, H. A., Philo: Foundations of Religious Philosophy in Judaism, Christianity and Islam, 1947.

——, Crescas Critique of Aristotle, 1929.

——, The Kalam Arguments for Creation in Saadia, Averroes, Maimonides and St. Thomas. American Academy for Jewish Research, Vol. II, 1943.

——, The Philosophy of Spinoza, 1934.

ZELLER, E., Die Philosophie der Griechen, III, 1903.

Index

Index